Shifting Horizons of Public International Law

J.L. Kaul · Anupam Jha
Editors

Shifting Horizons of Public International Law

A South Asian Perspective

Springer

Editors
J.L. Kaul
Campus Law Centre, Faculty of Law
University of Delhi
New Delhi
India

Anupam Jha
Law Centre-II, Faculty of Law
University of Delhi, University Enclave
New Delhi
India

ISBN 978-81-322-3722-8 ISBN 978-81-322-3724-2 (eBook)
https://doi.org/10.1007/978-81-322-3724-2

Library of Congress Control Number: 2017936889

Printed on acid-free paper

This Springer imprint is published by Springer Nature
The registered company is Springer (India) Pvt. Ltd.
The registered company address is: 7th Floor, Vijaya Building, 17 Barakhamba Road, New Delhi 110 001, India

Dedicated to Siddheswari Daadi

Foreword I

In an era of exponential expansion of public international law marked by fragmentation and specialization where lex specialis prevails and iex generalis seems to be all but over,[1] this excellent work by Vice Chancellor J.L. Kaul, Dr. Anupam Jha, and the learned contributors tells us a special story. The unusual story is about how the SAARC region may have contributed to the progressive development of late post-Westphalian international legal development.

The work is focussed on 'peripheral' nations. This is a precious focus as contributions of such nations to the making and unmaking of international law have gone largely unrecognized. The term 'peripheral' has some wholesome meanings.[2] Kaul and Jha write (in the Introduction) that the SAARC contributions to international 'negotiations' regarding international law were rarely considered. A 'newer grouping of nations' is itself an important development, enhanced when perceived as a 'challenge to status quo in international affairs' and the fact that 'nations of South Asia have asserted their collective will which is, at times, at variance with the common will of other nations'. The work in your hands speaks about the 'greater involvement of these nations, which … have greatly influenced outcomes of international law making'. And yet the sad fact is that the contributions made by the SAARC region 'are yet to be' fully explored or even acknowledged in the burgeoning literature on international law.

A part of this neglect can be laid at the doorstep of Eurocentrism that still persists. Eurocentrism is a state of social consciousness as well as a state of social

---

[1] Andreas Fischer-Lescano & Gunther Teubner, 'Regime-Collision: The Vain Search for Legal Unity in the Fragmentation of Global Law', 25 *Mich. J. Int'l L.* 999 (2004). See also, 'Comment Commentary to Andreas Fischer Lescano & Gunther Teubner The Legitimacy of International Law and The Role of the State', https://antoniovaronmejia.files.wordpress.com/2010/04/fisher

[2] I was alerted to the less pejorative and more benign uses of the term by Prof. David Armitage when he termed the contributions of the Polish school of international law as' peripheral'. See, David Armitage and Jennifer Pitts, *C. H. Alexandrowicz, The Law of Nations in Global History* (Oxford: Oxford University Press, forthcoming, 2017). See also, Arnulf Becker Lorca, *Mestizo International Law* (Cambridge, Cambridge University Press, 2014).

organization of the empire. An ascendant imperialism was marked by an aggressive (and regressive) Eurocentrism—in which Charles de Gaulle can talk of Afghanistan as the 'dust of the empire',[3] King Leopold II of Belgium can claim the whole Congo and Rwanda as a 'piece of this magnificent cake',[4] Sir Winston Churchill may describe M.K. Gandhi as a 'half naked fakir',[5]and a Margaret Thatcher could name Nelson Mandela (without a later apology) as belonging to a 'terrorist' organization.[6] Self-determination and sovereign equality of nations now forbid official derogation of state and its leaders, explicit in new norms of interstate political correctness.

Subtle Eurocentrism persists in various forms. For example, very little work has been done on Radhabinod Pal (whose dissent in Tokyo trials should be better known)[7] and Justice Weeranmantry (who, among other things, delivered a learned dissent in the nuclear weapons case).[8] What has been named 'colonization without colonies'[9] is insidious as the experience of coloniality. And this work illustrates the perils of such colonialism as well as the promise of a genuine post-colonialism. I say genuine because I regard achievement of a true post-colonial condition as a reflexive task, rather than as merely a process of historical passage.[10]

I do not mean here to exhaustively deal with 'eurocentrism', which remains a protean term. Rather, I wish to indicate the value of studying this work which highlights some advantages of liberation from its iron cage.

The learned authors make a valuable contribution towards an understanding of chosen areas and themes. These include the promotion and protection of human

---

[3]Karl F. Meyer, The Dust of Empire: *The Race for Mastery in The Asian Heartland* (Century Foundation Book, 2004).

[4]See, generally, Thomas Pakenham, *The Scramble for Africa*: White Man's Conquest of the Dark Continent from 1876 to 1912 (Avon Books, 1992).

[5]Peter Gonsalves, 'Half-Naked Fakir': 'The Story of Gandhi's Personal Search For Sartorial Integrity' Gandhi Marg, 31:1, 5–30. (Gandhi Peace Foundation, New Delhi, 2019).

[6]See, James Hanning, 'The 'Terrorist' and the Tories: What did Nelson Mandela really think of Margaret Thatcher?', *The Independent*, Sunday 8 December 2013.

[7]Adil Khan, 'International Lawyers in the Aftermath of Disasters: Inheriting from Radhabinod Pal and Upendra Baxi', *Third World Quarterly*, 37:11, 2061–2079 (2016).

[8]See, Siddarth Mallavarpu, *Banning the Bomb*: The Politics of Norm Creation (Delhi, Person/Longman, 2007).

[9]The expression refers to the invisible processes of globalization rather than to the visible agents, See, Upendra Baxi, The Future of Human Rights (Delhi, Oxford University Press, 2013: 3rd edition, Chapters 8 & 9).

[10]It is my belief that many a Third World society, state, and people moved from colonialism to neocolonialism, which Kwame Nkrumah described as systems of 'power without accountability' and 'exploitation without redress': see Kwame Nkrumah, in his 'Introduction' to *Neocolonialism, The Last Stage of Imperialism*, (London, Thomas Nelson & Sons, Ltd. 1965; International Publishers Co., Inc. (1966; transcribed by Dominic Tweedie). He also said:' A state in the grip of neocolonialism is not a master of its destiny. It is this factor which makes neocolonialism such a serious threat to world peace.' What Nkrumah describes as neocolonialism appears in the times of hyper-globalization, neoliberalism, and austerity in face of 'debt' (and development) crises as illiberal governance and unconstitutional authoritarianism.

rights; use of force across internationally recognized borders and boundaries; humanitarian law, regional international law, and jurisprudence (as well as the process of International Criminal Court); law relative to diplomatic immunity; international trade; principles of law regarding state responsibility; maritime affairs; environmental protection; law of the sea; and indigenous peoples.

A main concern of this book, and one of its many notable successes, is to avoid the mistake of presenting the concept and histories of South Asia as homogenous. National differences, and regional diversities, stand fully recognized. If some of these differences persist because of geopolitical security considerations, others arise out of contemporary history. The principles of decolonization, self-determination, and sovereign equality of states have ushered in a fierce insistence to any emergence of a SAARC hegemon and even a global one. This work pursues remarkably well the ways in which the international legal framework of public international law has brought a modicum of universality within regional diversity in the difficult quest for a just cooperation in the world orderings. The book conveys a precious message: gains of learning from each other far outstrip the mere arrogance of power.

The canvas is rather vast as each of the arenas warrants a whole book by itself, and yet this work adroitly deals with commonalties as well as divergences of state values and practice in each domain of enquiry. Rather than engaging the vertiginous heights of state practice and diplomatic conduct, these areas have been analysed as resisting the 'legalized hegemony' of the 'Great Powers' in relation to their non-Euro Other (the enemy or the outlaw).[11]

I place this valuable work in your hands with 'great expectations'.

New Delhi
March 2017

Upendra Baxi
Emeritus Professor of Law
University of Warwick and Delhi

[11]See generally Antony Anghie, Imperialism, Sovereignty, and The Making of International Law 196–244 (2007); Gerry Simpson, Great Powers, and Outlaw States: Unequal Sovereigns in the International Legal Order (2004); Upendra Baxi, 'New Approaches to the History of International Law', Leiden J. Int'l L. 19:555 (2006). The term opens many an interpretation: see, particularly, Saskia Sassen, Territory, Authority, Rights: From Medieval to Global Assemblages (2006); Josè Medina, The Epistemology of Resistance: Gender and Racial Epistemic Injustice, and the Social Imagination (2013); Bonaventura de Sousa Santos, Epistemologies of the South. Justice against Epistemicide, (Boulder/London: Paradigm Publishers (2014).

Foreword II

I must confess that I am not a legal expert and was surprised when Dr. Anupam Jha asked me to write the foreword to this book. My experience of international law comes as a diplomat. Although a diplomat is involved in the process of creating and operating international law, the experience is slightly different from that of an academic or even legal practitioners. Unlike domestic law, which is *legislated*, international law is *negotiated*. A diplomat is intrinsic to the process of negotiation—which involves 'both the act of discussion aimed at reaching an agreement as well as the action or process of transferring legal ownership of the agreement thus reached'. Diplomats are usually the first point of contact and develop the lexicon and structure of exchange and transaction. They are involved with the formalization or drafting of the agreements and treaties, and thereafter, in implementation of the agreed law. The diplomat's task, however, does not end there, as they are also concerned with, especially in democratic societies, justifying the agreement to domestic and international opinion by creating an environment where it finds wider acceptability.

In the past few years, the forces of economic and cultural globalization have ushered in a focus on universally applicable normative legal instruments. In parallel, there has been a renewed interest in international law led by scholars working from a liberal institutionalist perspective which regards law not as a set of normative aspirations or mutual obligations but 'rather as a reflection of efforts to create self-enforcing equilibria in the international environment'.

International law flows from treaties and agreements, both freely concluded and imposed, or from widely accepted customary practice. It is not limited to legal obligations or restraints, but also establishes the normative aspiration of international behaviour. Every treaty or agreement reflects the relative power of the parties.

This hierarchy of International Agreements and Treaties is most visible in the use of 'exceptionalism' by Great Powers. The belief in exceptionalism is rooted in the notion that a particular State has, through its own genius or manifest destiny, developed a set of practices and rules, which are better than any other and should thus become the normative for the others to follow. It also flows from the exceptionalist argument that because of its internal inherent qualities, the said power is not, or should not be, subject to other international covenants and agreements. A sober examination reveals that there is no universal consensus on how countries are to be judged. It is all relative to the one who chooses the assessment criteria. Yet the belief in exceptionalism continues to persist.[12]

International law is at best a synthesis of national and regional exceptionalisms. There have been, and continue to exist, differences in the perception and narrative of how international law is created and operated. The underlying process of international law formation, and its application, thus, appears *relative* rather than *normative*.

A Euro-centric world vision often results in the flawed assertion that currently *en vogue* legal traditions, law formulation process, and institutions, which on closer examination are revealed to be Anglo-Saxon traditions, are the 'normative' and modern edifice of international law. These 'norms' were first imposed on most Europeans following sustained violence and then dressed as '*Westphalian*', and they piggy-backed on the European colonial expansions and became the implanted *but* dominant view in colonized lands often obscuring earlier legal traditions.

India's ancient civilization was a veritable source of rules on interstate conduct, from the laws of war, the law of treaties, the right of asylum, the treatment of aliens and foreign nationals, the modes of acquiring territory, and rules on navigation and interstate trade.[13] The *Mahabharata* reflects a well-developed and sophisticated tradition of diplomatic and interstate practices and rules of engagement. The Mauryan Empire was sending and receiving embassies[14] at a time when Western Europe and Britain were being 'discovered' by the Greeks.[15] Indian States had a well-developed code of maritime laws dealing with freedom of the seas, the rules of flag state jurisdiction on the seas, superior coastal state jurisdiction over all ships while near the coast, prohibition of piracy, the rules of charter party, customs and tolls, permits of entry and departure, and even some rules relating to contraband,[16] much before the English had a fortuitous escape from the Spanish Armada.

The post-colonial development of international law in India (and South Asia) is an example of the 'myriad ideological strands, historical origins and significant contributions to contemporary international law doctrines' formative and

[12]Robert Schlesinger, 'Obama has mentioned Exceptionalism more than Bush'. US News and World Report, 31 Jan. 2011

[13]RP Anand, Development of Modern International Law and India, (Nomos Verlagsgesellschaft, Baden-Baden, Germany 2005) 1–5, 29–30, 39–40, 54–55, 108–109, 121–130.

[14]Biswanath Sen, A Diplomat's Handbook of International Law and Practice, Springer, 06-Dec-2012, p. 04

[15]Robert Henry, The History of Great Britain: From the First Invasion of it by the Romans under Julius Caesar, Volumes 1–2, Cadell and Davies, 1814, Great Britain, p-207 (accessed via Google Books)

[16]Peter Fitzpatrick, 'Terminal Legality: Imperialism and the (de)composition of Law' in Diane Kirkby and Catharine Coleborne, Law, History, Colonialism: The Reach of Empire (Manchester University Press, United Kingdom, 2001).

qualification process—towards identifying, locating, and applying South Asian values and philosophical traditions.[17] The complexities of the emerging international law system have necessitated that the South Asian discourse on international law has focused on areas that create 'the most urgent development consequences: trade, investment and the international economic order; the Law of the Sea and the environment; international humanitarian law, self-determination, social, economic and cultural human rights'.[18]

Since the end of colonial rule, India and other states that emerged in the decolonization of South Asia have developed and enunciated their own perspective on international issues, even as they have continued to collaborate with the existing global legal framework. India led the way by rejecting the Euro-American monopoly on norm creation and insisted that under the new approach to positivist international law, the formulation and operation of the law had to be 'a broader process of development conjoined with the new realities and contingencies of international life'.[19]

In the domain of international security, the concept of Panch-Sheel, initially articulated in a 1954 treaty with China, would resonate across time to many of South and Southeast Asia's regional instruments on international law, most especially the 1976 Treaty of Amity and Cooperation of Southeast Asia that laid the foundation for the Association of Southeast Asian Nation (ASEAN) and the 1985 Charter of the South Asian Association for Regional Cooperation (SAARC).[20] India was a leading advocate of the decolonization process under United Nations, culminating with the General Assembly's landmark 1960 Declaration on the Granting of Independence to Colonial Countries and Peoples.[21] The concept of *non-alignment* was an innovation in international relations that allowed India to carve political space and create a mechanism independent of the Cold War.

In recent years, South Asia has seen remarkable progress in defining its own narrative of international law in several domains such as distribution of shared natural resources (Indus Water Treaty), maritime boundaries (India–Bangladesh maritime agreement), settlement of land boundary (India–Bangladesh land boundary Accord), issues of indigenous people (all Indians are indigenous),[22] war crimes, regional trade (SAFTA), counterterrorism, cross-border movement of

---

[17]Diane A Desierto, 'Postcolonial International Law Discourses on Regional Developments in South and Southeast Asia', International Journal of Legal Information: Vol. 36: Iss. 3, Article 4. (2008).

[18]SK Agrawala (tr), TS Rama Rao and JN Saxena, New Horizons of International Law and Developing Countries (N.M. Tripathia Private Limited, 1983); Sienho Yee, 'The Role of Law in the Formation of Regional Perspectives in Human Rights and Regional Systems for the Protection of Human Rights: The European and Asian Models as Illustrations' (2004) 8 SYBIL, p. 157–164.

[19]Desierto, op cit, p. 402

[20]ibid.

[21]UNGA Res 1514 (XV) (14 December 1960).

[22]Many other Asian States take a similar stand, for example, Bangladesh, China, Indonesia, and Laos, see Kingbury, 1998.

citizens (India–Nepal Friendship Treaty), ensuring sustainable development practices and technology transfers, space exploration, nuclear disarmament and fundamental international environmental law principles such as the prohibition against transboundary harms, the precautionary principle, common but differentiated responsibilities, intergenerational equity, and sustainable development.

India (along with other South Asian States) has been a major contributor to international peacekeeping operations under the United Nations flag, has engaged with our partners in shaping the Sustainable Development Goals (SDGs) agenda, and continues to work with like-minded countries to make the global financial and trade systems more equitable and transparent. India took the lead at the COP 21 at Paris to forge an international consensus and has become one of the strongest advocates of clean energy, particularly solar energy and energy innovation.

In instances where India has not become a party to the existing international system, uniquely local practices have been developed to resolve problems such as on treatment of refugees, where the Indian track record, arguably, is better than many European nations that are state parties to the UN Refugee Convention.[23]

Resistance from the existing power structures to India's demand for a seat on all global decision-making bodies is seen as undemocratic and unethical. It was articulated by the Vice President of India who proclaimed that '*as one sixth of the humanity and in keeping with the growing capacities and aspirations of our people, India has a much larger role to play in charting a more equitable and sustainable future for our world. For this reason we believe that any global forum which does not include India has limited relevance*'.[24] This has also led, at times, to India circumventing unfair multilateral international regimes by concluding bilateral agreements and seeking waivers in its own form of 'Indian exceptionalism' as in the case of India–US Civil Nuclear Agreement.

South Asia's multidirectional engagement of, and contributions to the development of, modern international law has, naturally, inspired concomitant proposals for teaching methodologies and curricular content of international law in South Asian law schools.[25] The answer to all parts of the not so rhetorical question posed by Prof. B. S. Chimni, 'Is there (a South) Asian approach to international law?', is an unequivocal yes.

Bringing together views by legal experts from India, Bangladesh, Nepal, and Sri Lanka, the present volume is a veritable *tour de* force of the emerging contours of the South Asian narrative on international law in its many manifest forms. This book, with contributions from emerging South Asian scholars in the field, presents a cross section of views on the dominant international law issues rooted in the South Asian perspective on these issues and their resolution. This volume also gives

---

[23]Lakshman, Sriram. 'We can learn from India on refugee crisis', The Hindu, September 12, 2016

[24]Keynote Address by Shri M. Hamid Ansari, Honourable Vice President of India at the Tunisian Institute of Strategic Studies, Carthage, Tunisia on 03 June 2016.

[25]Desierto, op cit, p. 412.

the readers an insight into the trajectory of international law study and teaching in South Asia.

The stated objective of this volume is to present to the reader a reference source on the recent developments in international law with South Asian perspective. The editors are to be congratulated as the book successfully achieves this aim. It covers a wide set of issues ranging from South Asian perspective on UN Security Council to social and economic reforms and from accountability in conflict and human right violations to combating terrorism. Other topics include a South Asian look at the International Criminal Court.

These, and other chapters, provide an insight into the complex issues that confront the modern global citizen and the approach taken by South Asian States to international problem-solving. It should be of interest not only to lawyers, academics, and diplomats, but also to students of law, international relations, and other sociopolitical disciplines as well as general readers who are looking to develop an understanding of international legal issues, particularly in the South Asian context.

Knowledge of international law is essential for the work of any lawyer today. There are few areas of legal practice that are not affected in some way by international law, whether transacted or litigated at a national, regional, or international level. International dimension of law impacts commercial and competition matters, as much as it does matrimonial matters. Awareness of treaty obligations is required for dealing with interstate trade disputes, as well as for computing personal income tax. Knowledge of the legal responsibilities and immunities of government is as vital for concluding a commercial contract as for reporting a human rights violation.

International law is increasingly providing us with a common framework where governments, institutions, corporates, and even individuals can interact on a more equitable plane. The world has never before had a standing International Criminal Court or a functioning World Trade Organization. We never had such an elaborate international human rights system. In a rapidly digitizing environment, issues such as intellectual property rights, privacy, identity and information ownership, virtual resources, cybercrime, and bioethics are likely to continue challenging the established norm and narrative in international legal system. Those dealing with the rapidly developing system would need to be nimble and well informed to cope.

New Delhi
January 2017

Anshuman Gaur*

*(*Anshuman Gaur is an IFS Officer. The views expressed here are personal and not those of the Government of India.)*

Acknowledgements

Although it is impossible to acknowledge the help, guidance, and inspiration received from many well-wishers and friends, we would begin with the students of University of Delhi. These students have always been a constant source of inspiration for us as they have prodded to write something for their use. Students of Faculty of Law, University of Delhi, felt a vacuum after the retirement of many stalwart Professors in the recent times. We took up the responsibility to fill the void created by these faculty members by producing an edited volume on International Law for their help and perhaps for other students of South Asian region.

Secondly, we would like to acknowledge the hard work of contributing authors to this book. These authors from India, Bangladesh, Nepal, and Sri Lanka stood their ground by reiterating their long commitment to produce the work of this magnitude. They promised to stand by us through thick and thin in the prolonged process of editing work of this book. Some of us have not seen each other, yet the only bond which kept us united together was the objective of producing a high-quality introductory book on public international law. Perhaps the students, practitioners, and policy makers would find this work useful.

We would like to extend our sincere gratitude to the vibrant atmosphere provided by the libraries of University of Delhi, University of Kansas (USA), Indian Society of International Law, and National Law University (Delhi) without which this work would not have been possible to accomplish. Freedom to use all the available software in these libraries both inside and through remote access proved to be of utmost trustworthy companion. Our heartfelt gratitude also goes to the Research and Development Grant (R&D) of University of Delhi, which provided financial help to buy essential reading and research materials from the market.

We would also like to thank all our friends and colleagues who directly or indirectly provided positive feedback to ensure the quality of this work. Without such intellectual reviews and inspirations, the production of this book would have lacked complete insights on many aspects. Each of the aspiring scholars and researchers has been really supportive in disseminating new dimensions to the completion of the current work.

Last but not the least, the publishers of this book deserve heartfelt gratitude from our side. The production team of Springer (India) has excellently done their best to design the work and has shown great perseverance in getting the high-quality manuscript from us. Their unflinching support has encouraged the South Asian scholars and researchers to join their hands together in accomplishing this difficult task.

Contents

Editors and Contributors

About the Editors

Prof. J.L. Kaul had been the Vice Chancellors of H.N.B. Garhwal University, and Vikram University. He is the Professor of Law at Campus Law Centre, Faculty of Law, University of Delhi for several years. He was a Fellow of Maastricht University, the Netherlands, and lectured at St. Thomas School of Law, Minneapolis (USA). He has published widely in international and national journals. His areas of interest are constitutional law, human rights, and international trade law.

Dr. Anupam Jha has been teaching international law at the University of Delhi for more than a decade. He has received prestigious fellowships to pursue his research interests at the University of Kansas (USA), University of Leeds (UK), and the University of Mauritius. His work has been published in reputed international journals. He specializes in international criminal law, human trafficking, human rights, and energy law.

Contributors

Madhu Bhatti Faculty of Law, University of Delhi, New Delhi, India

Raju Prasad Chapagai Program Department, Supreme Court Bar Association, Kathmandu, Nepal

Anupam Jha Law Centre-II, Faculty of Law, University of Delhi, New Delhi, India

Stellina Jolly Faculty of Legal Studies, South Asian University, New Delhi, India

Pankaj Kumar Karn Program Department, Supreme Court Bar Association, Kathmandu, Nepal

Divesh Kaul Gaeddu College of Business Studies, Gedu, Bhutan

J.L. Kaul Campus Law Centre, Faculty of Law, University of Delhi, New Delhi, India

Bipin Kumar National Law University, Jodhpur, Rajasthan, India

Shashi Kumar Department of Human Rights, School for Legal Studies, Babasaheb Bhimrao Ambedkar (Central) University, Lucknow, India

Leena Kumari School of Law, Guru Gobind Singh Indraprastha University, Delhi, India

Muthukuda A. Dona Shiroma Jeeva S. Niriella Department of Public and International Law, Faculty of Law, University of Colombo, Colombo, Sri Lanka

Ujjwala Sakhalkar New Law College, Bharati Vidyapeeth Deemed University, Pune, Maharashtra, India

Vivek Sehrawat School of Law, University of Kansas, Lawrence, KS, USA

Uday Shankar Rajiv Gandhi School of Intellectual Property Law, Indian Institute of Technology, Kharagpur, India

Brijesh Kumar Singh Faculty of Law, University of Delhi, Delhi, India

Vinai Kumar Singh Indian Society of International Law, New Delhi, India

M. Zahurul Haque Department of Law, Eastern University, Dhaka, Bangladesh

Abbreviations

AALCO	Asian African Legal Consultative Organization
ASEAN	Association of South East Asian Nations
BIMSTEC	Bangladesh, India, Myanmar, Sri Lanka, Thailand Economic Cooperation
CESCR	Committee on Economic, Social and Cultural Rights
CPA	Comprehensive Peace Accord
DPSP	Directive Principles of State Policy
DRDO	Defence Research and Development Organization
ERW	Explosive Remnants of War
FATA	Federally Administered Tribal Areas
GA	General Assembly
GATT	General Agreement on Trade and Tariff
ICC	International Criminal Court
ICJ	International Court of Justice
ICRC	International Committee of the Red Cross
ICT	International Crimes Tribunal (Bangladesh)
ICTR	International Criminal Tribunal for Rwanda
ICTY	International Criminal Tribunal for the Former Yugoslavia
IED	Improvised Explosive Devices
IGN	Intergovernmental Negotiation
IHL	International Humanitarian Law
ILC	International Law Commission
ILM	International Legal Materials
ILO	International Labour Organization
ITLOS	International Tribunal for the Law of the Sea
LTTE	Liberation Tigers of Tamil Eelam
MFN	Most Favoured Nation
NAM	Non-Aligned Movement
NGO	Non-Governmental Organization
NIEO	New International Economic Order

NNWS	Non-Nuclear-Weapon State
NWS	Nuclear-Weapon State
P5	5 Permanent Members of Security Council
PATA	Provincially Administered Tribal Areas
PCIJ	Permanent Court of International Justice
PKO	Peacekeeping Operations
PSO	Public Security Ordinance
RTA	Regional Trade Agreement
SAFTA	South Asian Free Trade Area
SC	Security Council
SLOS	Sri Lanka Overseas Service
TPP	Trans-Pacific Partnership
TRC	Truth and Reconciliation Commission
UAV	Unmanned Aerial Vehicles
UDHR	Universal Declaration of Human Rights
UN	United Nations
UNCIP	UN Commission for India and Pakistan
UNCLOS	UN Convention on the Law of the Sea
UNCTAD	UN Conference on Trade and Development
UNDRIP	UN Declaration on the Rights of Indigenous People

Chapter 1
Changing Horizons of International Law: A South Asian Perspective

J.L. Kaul and Anupam Jha

1 Introduction

International law has received a renewed attention after the end of the Cold War. This branch of law has not only expanded horizontally to bring within its fold new States which have been established since the end of the Second World War but also extended its scope of protections in vertical ways to individuals, groups, and international organizations, both private and public (Shaw 2008). Conceptually, it has also tried to proclaim legal regulations covering new fields, such as international trade, problems of environmental protection, human rights, law of the sea, international criminal law, State responsibility, indigenous law, and regulation of modern weaponry. Traditional subjects, such as States, and international organizations are still relevant, but new entities have not only been recognized; they have been given a new role (Brownlie 2008). Regional organizations are growing and taking a firm foothold in the international affairs and even providing newer directions for a robust and fulfilling international order. Non-governmental international organizations and individuals have become the new focus of international law in the present century.

South Asia, consisting of Afghanistan, Bangladesh, Bhutan, India, Maldives, Nepal, Pakistan, and Sri Lanka, is home of 1.7 billion people (in 2013) and of a quarter of the world's population. In South Asia and in the Third World, traditional Euro-centric international law has been questioned at times, paving way for either redefining existing doctrines of international law, or focusing on creation of new legal regimes. Professor Upendra Baxi noted, 'with the passing of colonialism,

J.L. Kaul
Campus Law Centre, Faculty of Law, University of Delhi, New Delhi 110007, India

A. Jha (✉)
Law Centre-II, Faculty of Law, University of Delhi, 38/12, Probyn Road, New Delhi 110007, India
e-mail: ajha@law.du.ac.in

J.L. Kaul and A. Jha (eds.), *Shifting Horizons of Public International Law*,
https://doi.org/10.1007/978-81-322-3724-2_1

Euro-centrism in thinking about international law has become anachronistic' (Anand 1972). He added that in its most acute form, Euro-centrism had led to needless denigration of indigenous traditions of the colonized nations. In its milder form, he observed further, it had led to a continuing indifference to these traditions even in the scholarly discourses. Lastly, he added that whatever be the causes of Euro-centrism, its cure was imperative. This book is an attempt to cure this anachronism by focusing upon the regional scholarship as well as regional themes, such as free trade in the region, protection of indigenous population, institutions of diplomacy.

International negotiations and engagements have involved newer grouping of nations, which is perceived as a challenge to *status quo* in international affairs. The nations of South Asia have asserted their collective will which is, at times, at variance with the common will of other nations. Consequently, greater involvement of these nations, which were at best 'peripheral' in international negotiations, has greatly influenced outcomes of international law making. The latest examples in this regard are the *Bali Summit* (2013) where India's chief concern of food security was not given due consideration resulting in the failure of the summit, *Paris Agreement on Climate Change* (2015) where India and other South Asian nations took a definite stand to prevent climate change and the summit was successful.

Toward institution making at international level, South Asia has played an important role in the past and in the current times. India was invited to participate in the San Francisco Conference in 1945 for drafting of the UN Charter, though still a British colony comprising India, Pakistan, Bangladesh. After India's independence in 1947, it advocated for universal membership of the UN and helped overcome the veto of Big Powers on the membership issue of newly independent countries (Anand 2006a, b). Prime Minister Nehru persuaded the Soviet leaders, on their trip to India in 1955, to refrain from exercising veto for admission of new members and that broke the ice and numerous newly independent States from Asia and Africa were admitted in the UN (Anand 2006a, b). Since the issue of Security Council reform and expansion of its membership was initiated in the UN General Assembly in the early 1970s, India has been supporting the principle of 'equitable representation on and increase in the membership of the Security Council.' The system of casting 'veto' has also been opposed by India. According to India's Permanent Representative to the UN, since the creation of Security Council in 1946 till today, 317 vetoes were cast, and as a result, in total, 230 draft resolutions or parts thereof have been vetoed, many of them pertaining to membership of the UN (Akbaruddin 2016). Other South Asian nations have also supported this principle of equitable representation.

India was among the very few select countries who were members of the former Commission of Human Rights throughout over 60 years of its existence. The formation of Human Rights Council in 2006 was hailed in the region. While presenting its candidature to the Human Rights Council for a 3-year term in December 2006, India made several voluntary pledges and commitments (OHCHR 2008). It extended a standing invitation to Special Procedures Mandate Holders during the 18th session of HRC in September 2011, in keeping with our Voluntary

Pledges and Commitments made to the HRC in May 2011 (OHCHR 2002). The Human Rights Council has a total strength of 47 members. India and Bangladesh have been its members from South Asian region during 2015–17. Pakistan (2006–2008, 2008–2011, 2012–2015), Sri Lanka (2006–2008), and Maldives (2010–2013, 2013–2016) have already been the members of the Council. This Council had also passed a resolution in the matter of large-scale violation of human rights of Tamils in Sri Lanka during the last years of civil war (1983–2009).

It is heartening that in this emerging international legal horizon, South Asian nations have played an important role. South Asian consciousness has been growing not only among the people of region but also in the Diasporas. South Asian culture, art, language, and history are taught in world-renowned Universities, increasingly Institutes of South Asian studies are coming up the world over, South Asian food and film festivals, trade fairs are taking place in a regular fashion. The concept of South Asia is having a global appeal today. Scholars argue that the destiny has already been proclaimed for Asia and South Asia will be the fulcrum for its growth in the coming decades (Delinic and Pandey 2015).

It is in this context that the editors of the present volume have conceptualized the publication of this book. The editors also note that there is no dearth of literature on international law; however, this edition is particularly of relevance and importance from a South Asian perspective. The world leaders look at South Asian continent in new context and importance; therefore, the need for such a work has been felt for a long time. As this book covers diverse topics related to public international law with a special focus on South Asian traditions, State practice, the editors hope that this volume would evoke strong interest among the readers of international law in the region. The readers would find the discussions and analysis presented in the book as very useful at the national, regional, and international level.

2 Rationale

According to Professor R.P. Anand, the doyen of international law in the South Asian region, the debate between universalism and regionalism has its own merits and demerits (Anand 1972). Supporters of regionalism argue that in a diverse and unwieldy world, global unity based upon a common way of life and common values was still a distant possibility. Regional arrangements and agencies afforded a directness of association which could not be attained through universal institutions. On the other hand, it was argued by the advocates of universalism that neighboring nations were not necessarily and always logical or actual cooperators, while distant nations often were. Physical proximity was no guarantee for friendly relations and more often tended to result in controversy. South Asian regionalism, however, is a combination of physical proximity as well as directness of association. This regionalism has influenced the international politics as well with the creation of the South Asian Association for Regional Co-operation (SAARC), European Union

(EU), African Union (AU), Asian African Legal Consultative Organization (AALCO), and Association of South East Asian Nations (ASEAN).

From Iran to Afghanistan and from Kashmir to Kosovo, international politics has been changing from universalism to regionalism. South Asia has become a theater of conflicts, smaller or bigger. The use of force during civil strife, insurgency, acts of terrorism, massive human rights violations of citizens, problems related to State responsibility, trade disputes, environmental degradation, maritime disputes, disputes related to access to water, etc., have equally raised new but distressing universal as well as regional issues in the international arena. A whole lot of work has been done by the International Law Commission on State responsibility (1949–2004), international crimes (1981–1995), individual criminal responsibility (1981–1995), effect of armed conflict on the law of treaties, protection of the environment in relation to armed conflicts (2013), the Most Favored Nations Clause (2006 onwards), immunity of State officials from foreign criminal jurisdiction (2006 onwards), protection of the atmosphere (2013).[1] Judicial pronouncements made by International Court of Justice, Permanent Court of Arbitration, and Supreme Courts of South Asia, for instance, *United States Diplomatic and Consular Staff in Tehran* (1980), *Interpretation of Case Concerning Avena and other Mexican Nationals* (2008), *Questions relating to the Obligation to Prosecute or Extradite* (2009), *Interpretation of Case Concerning Temple of Preah Vihear* (2011), *Obligation to Negotiate Access to Pacific Ocean* (2013), *The Indus Waters Kishenganga Arbitration* (2014), *The Enrica Lexie Incident* (2015), *Obligations Concerning Negotiations Relating to Cessation of the Nuclear Arms Race and to Nuclear Disarmament* (2016), are yet to be examined in its South Asian context.[2]

Supreme Courts and other prominent tribunals of South Asia have also enriched the regional jurisprudence. One of the outstanding examples of this contribution is from the International Crimes Tribunal of Bangladesh established to try the perpetrators of war crimes and crimes against humanity during the 1971 Liberation War. In South Asia, this tribunal applied the concept and law on war crimes and crimes against humanity for the first time. Nepal, a tiny Himalayan nation, has also constituted a five-member Truth and Conciliation Commission in accordance with the Enforced Disappearances Enquiry, Truth and Reconciliation Commission Act, 2014. One of the main objectives of the Commission is to find out and publish the incident of the grave violation of human rights committed in the course of the armed conflict between the State Party and the then Communist Party of Nepal (Maoist) from February 13, 1996, to November 21, 2006, and of the persons involved in those incidents upon realizing the essence and spirit of the Interim Constitution of Nepal, 2007 and the comprehensive peace accord. Similarly, the Courts in India have laid down a remarkable corpus of jurisprudence in the field of

---

[1]See, International Law Commission Web site at http://www.un.org/law/ilc/ (last visited on December 3, 2013).

[2]For the judgments of International Court of Justice, see http://www.icj-cij.org/docket/index.php?p1=3&p2=3 (last visited on December 3, 2013).

protecting human rights of its citizens. With a view to attain the objective of Constitutional philosophy of socioeconomic equality and freedom to all, the Supreme Court and various High Courts have implemented various international obligations undertaken by India, such as *Enrica Lexie* (2015) case relating to maritime disputes between India and Italy.

Maritime disputes in the South Asian region are also increasing in the present twenty-first century. It was not so in the distant past. From the first century A.D., regular maritime commercial relations were established between Rome and several States in India and the Indian Ocean region, and they continued for nearly 300 years (Rawlinson 1926; Warmington 1974). On the eve of European penetration into the Indian Ocean by the end of fifteenth century, the freedom of the seas and trade was well recognized in customary law of South Asia. When the Portuguese arrived in India by the end of fifteenth century, they found no maritime powers, no warships, and no arms in the sea (Anand 2006a, b). South Asians were essentially land powers. From fifteenth century to late twentieth century, South Asians remained under colonial domination and exploitation. After getting independence, these nations have grown in maritime power and international influence. India has a coastline of 7,516 km, its territorial waters extend to 155,889 km^2, and exclusive economic zone extends to 2,013,410 km^2. It has a strong fleet of offshore patrol vessels (Samarth, Samar, Vikram, Sankalp, Viswast), fast patrol vessels (Priyadarshini, Sarojini Naidu, Rani Abakka, Rajshree, Aadesh), pollution control, and air cushion vehicles to protect its coast. Pakistan's coast spreads to 1,050 km, which is protected by its strong fleet of fast patrol vessels, lethal interceptor boats, and other utility boats with latest equipment on board. South Asian nations are also parties to the UN Convention on the Law of the Sea (UNCLOS), 1982. Once maritime belt is secured, the trade routes through the sea become attractive to the international traders.

Trade and intellectual property disputes need new orientation, as the Bali Round and the earlier Doha Round have been not so successful. Nations are looking forward to regional free trade Agreements, regional common markets, such as South Asian Free Trade Agreement (SAFTA) launched in 2006, and Trans-Pacific Partnership (TPP) signed in early 2016. In terms of economic strength, South Asia accounted for around 2% of the world's gross national income at current U.S. dollars and 6% at purchasing power parity-corrected exchange rates. SAFTA was launched to reduce tariffs for intra-regional trade among SAARC countries. Member States have agreed to reduce their tariffs on each other's goods not on sensitive lists as long as those goods have been produced in accordance with the Agreement's Rules of Origin provisions. The Agreement also includes provisions related to customs cooperation, dispute settlement, trade facilitation, safeguards against inquiry to industry, and eligibility for technical assistance. The ultimate aim of SAFTA is to put into place a fully fledged South Asian Economic Union similar to the European Union. This will take a long time. Currently, SAFTA only covers trade in goods. However, the formation of this free trade group is considered a good start for further economic cooperation in the region.

The reasons behind rapid proliferation of the regional trade Agreements, need of Security Council reforms, sharing of trans-boundary rivers, appropriate selection of forum to resolve maritime disputes, growth of law on State responsibility, diplomatic immunities, etc., need a serious scholarly enquiry. Editors of this volume note that these are some of the pressing issues, which needs an exhaustive treatment by scholars of international law, particularly from South Asia. The editors also have in mind that the purpose of this book is to give ample space to specialist distinguished authors to examine these subjects in finer details and legal analysis. Indeed, we also note that such a study and analysis would prove most crucial to understand the changing horizons of international law. Consequentially, such an approach may supplement the increasing role of international law in current times.

3 Objectives of the Book

The book is intended to be a reference book on the recent developments in international law with South Asian perspective. South Asia has always remained desirous to promote peace, stability, amity, and progress in the region through strict adherence to the principles of the United Nations Charter and Non-Alignment, particularly respect for the principles of sovereign equality, territorial integrity, national independence, non-use of force, and non-interference in the internal affairs of other States and peaceful settlement of all disputes (SAARC Charter 1985). In an increasingly interdependent world, the objectives of peace, freedom, social justice, and economic prosperity are best achieved in the South Asian region by fostering mutual understanding, good neighborly relations, and meaningful cooperation among the Member States which are, in many instances, integrated by family ties and culture.

Keeping in view the above objectives of South Asian integration, this book involves many subject experts who are either the mid-level eminent scholars in the region or are emerging scholars in the field. Joint efforts of the contributors on the theme of the book have paved the way to incorporate the latest scholarship on the subject. This book has the potential to prove to be an important resource book for the five hundred plus Universities of India, 15 Universities of Sri Lanka, twenty plus Universities of Pakistan, four Universities of Nepal, fifteen plus Universities of Bangladesh, apart from other world universities dealing with international law and South Asian studies in a comparative outlook. Ten themes identified for the book are as follows:

(i) Protection of Human Rights and International Law;
(ii) Use of Force and Its Limitations;
(iii) International Humanitarian Law, International Criminal Court and National Tribunals;
(iv) Diplomatic and Consular Immunity;

(v) Trade and International Law;
(vi) State Responsibility;
(vii) International Law and Marine Affairs;
(viii) International Watercourses Law and Protection of Environment;
(ix) Law of the Sea;
(x) Indigenous People.

4 The Contributors' Perspectives and Topics

The chapter 'UN Security Council: South Asian Perspective and Challenges Ahead' is jointly authored by Ms. Ujjwala Sakhalkar from Pune and Mr. Brijesh Kumar Singh from Delhi. This chapter analyzes the functions and powers of the Security Council of the UN in light of the new dynamics of international power relations wherein the emerging powers of the world, including India from South Asia, assert their claim to a permanent seat. This claim has been also supported by France and UK, which also favors the inclusion of Brazil, Japan, and Germany. Many other countries, such as the U.S., also support this claim but with a rider that the veto would not be given to any new permanent member (Sreenivasan, T.P., Reform Eludes UN Security Council, The Hindu, September 17, 2015). The chapter also deals with the peacekeeping powers of the Security Council to which the South Asian nations have contributed wholeheartedly. India, Pakistan, and Bangladesh have spontaneously, without any reservation, participated in peacekeeping operations over the years, and it is a clear demonstration of the region's commitment to the objectives set out in the UN Charter. Finally, the chapter investigates Security Council' s role in resolving South Asian disputes, such as Kashmir, Sri Lankan civil war, Afghanistan occupation, and Bangladesh liberation. These disputes have tested the utility of Security Council in promoting international peace and security in the region.

In the chapter on 'Socio-Economic Rights in South Asia,' Dr. Uday Shankar from Indian Institute of Technology, Kharagpur, highlights the implementation of the obligations contained in the International Covenant on Economic, Social, and Cultural Rights (ICESCR) in the form of Constitutional values and goals. He examines the role played by the respective Constitutional norms of India, Bhutan, Sri Lanka, Bangladesh, and Nepal in achieving the universalization of this second generation of human rights. He further discusses the enforcement of these rights by the judicial system of these countries. Regarding India, he has discussed leading cases, such as *Keshavanad Bharati* (1973), *Minerva Mills* (1980). The reporting mechanism established by the ICESCR provisions has been also thoughtfully discussed by him. Another institution investigated by him to implement the socioeconomic rights in this region is called 'National Human Rights Commission' or simply 'Human Rights Committee.' He finds out that every South Asian nation is uniformly committed to dignified and economically independent life of every citizen with clear direction to the State agencies to achieve the same.

In another chapter titled 'Indigenous Peoples in South Asia and International Law,' Dr. Shashi Kumar from Central University of Lucknow investigates the legal protection available to the indigenous people in South Asia under international law. In the wake of United Nations Declaration on Indigenous Peoples, 2007, and the International Labor Organization Convention No. 169 on Indigenous and Tribal Peoples, the author discusses their rights to self-determination, protection of their traditional knowledge, and sociocultural value systems in the given international and domestic legal frameworks. Indigenous peoples in the region share the historical legacy of colonialism and their exclusion from the mainstream political, social, economic, and cultural life. The author has examined the domestic legal framework of South Asian nations to make the reader understand how these nations have incorporated the international legal framework in their respective legal systems. Dr. Kumar argues that the international commitments undertaken by these South Asian nations can only be effective when they effectively apply and implement those commitments through their domestic laws and policy.

Another chapter on 'Regional Trade in South Asia: An International Legal Analysis' is written by Mr. Bipin Kumar from National Law School, Jodhpur. His perspective on regional trade in South Asia is a balanced one as he analyzes the role of Regional Trade Agreements (RTAs) and its impact on regional and international trade. In doing so, he discusses various theories on multilateralism and regionalism and finds out that each theory has its own merits and demerits. He cites the latest WTO report to assert the point that substantial portion of the global trade takes place through the regional trading groups. Moving further, he examines the various RTAs entered into by India which is quite complex due to its overlapping jurisdictions. However, he thinks that the rapid proliferation of RTAs has certainly deepened the crisis of Rules of Origin and has led to trade diversion and distortion. Mr. Bipin then goes on to evaluate the formation and utility of South Asian Free Trade Agreement (SAFTA) which has a tremendous potential for the regional growth. As South Asian nations exhibit symmetric economic activities, the promotion and effective working of SAFTA should prove to be a game-changer at an international level. At the same time, Mr. Bipin submits that multilateral trade regime should not be dismantled.

Another trade-related chapter titled 'The Conundrums Of Trade Barriers in Preferential Trading: Prospects From SAARC' is authored by Mr. Divesh Kaul, S.J.D. candidate at Tulane University Law School, USA. He argues that multilaterism still remains an important stimulant in addressing contemporary challenges, such as reducing trade barriers as a means to stem mercantilist tendencies. He laments that South Asia remains one of the least-integrated regions of the world. In this chapter, Divesh examines the possibility of eliminating trade barriers in South Asian milieu. He compares SAPTA and SAFTA in this connection with FTAs agreed to by the small countries of South Asia. He lays down a blueprint of future SAARC trade liberalization in view of the current global trends.

The chapter on 'Access to Water and Sharing of Trans-boundary Rivers in South Asia,' written by Dr. Stellina Jolly from South Asian University, New Delhi, focuses on human rights aspect of the sharing of trans-boundary rivers and access to water.

She examined the issues of accessibility, sharing, and the application of public trust doctrine in the region by the establishment of Constitutional norms, judicial verdicts, and legislative initiatives. Her analysis reveals that most of the South Asian countries have carved out the right to a clean environment through the expansionist interpretation of Right to Life. In the context of water management, the doctrine of public trust confers on the Government ultimate control and ownership to water but directs it to hold water in its capacity as a trustee for the whole of public. She finds that the doctrine is firmly entrenched as part of jurisprudential development in the region. Apart from the domestic efforts, the author explores the UN Watercourse Convention and its importance in this region. As most of the nations of South Asia have not ratified it, the application of its norms depends on the State practice. She highlights the problem-solving capacity of international institutions such as Permanent Court of Arbitration (PCA) to resolve the water disputes between South Asian nations by giving an example of *Kishenganga* case. The author suggests that a comprehensive human rights declaration is needed for the SAARC region. She further suggests that an institutional mechanism to treat trans-boundary water issues from human rights perspective should be established for the region.

The chapter 'UNCLOS Dispute Settlement System and India,' written by Mr. Vinai Kumar Singh from New Delhi, explores the different forums envisaged for dispute settlement under the UN Convention on the Law of the Sea. One group advocated for compulsory jurisdiction of the ICJ, whereas the developing countries resisted such moves. Another group advocated for the creation of a new tribunal to resolve maritime disputes, as the ICJ lacked jurisdiction over international organizations, trans-national corporations, and individuals. Due to the potential rigidity of these forums, the third group advocated for flexible mechanisms, such as arbitration to resolve such disputes. To ensure universal adoption, the Convention incorporated the views of all the groups in its Article 287. India ratified the Convention on June 29, 1995, and made a declaration, inter alia, by which it reserved the right to make a proper choice as to appropriate forum to resolve such disputes. Mr. Vinai has successfully examined the advantages and disadvantages of each and every forum available under the UNCLOS with the cases law and State practice on these matters. Although he has focused on the State practice of India, his investigations are wider than India's position. As a result, he examines the interesting case of South China Sea (*The Republic of the Philippines* v. *The People's Republic of China*, 2016) and concludes that even if a State excludes jurisdiction while making a declaration under Article 298 of UNCLOS, the Convention provisions would apply with respect to those matters which are not excluded, such as a feature which meets the definition of an island and rock under Article 121(1) & (3). He suggests that India should not exclude 'all' disputes relating to maritime delimitation from compulsory procedure as laid down in Article 298(1)(a). South Asia has an important lesson to learn from the approach taken by India.

In a separate chapter 'Accountability for Conflict-Era Human Rights Violations in Nepal,' Mr. Raju Prasad Chapagai and Mr. Pankaj Kumar Karna from Kathmandu investigate the difficult progress of Nepal's tryst with justice for human rights violations during the civil war from 1996 to 2006. They have examined the role of Supreme Court of Nepal in relation to the issues concerning truth and reconciliation, commission of inquiry into disappeared people, amnesty and reconciliation, criminal investigation, and prosecution of serious crimes. The perspective of victim's right to effective remedy has been used to analyze the strengths and weaknesses of Supreme Court of Nepal. As Nepal is a party to various international human rights and humanitarian law instruments, such as ICCPR, CRC, CEDAW, CAT, and Geneva Conventions, the Supreme Court too has attempted to enforce the treaty obligations undertaken by Nepal at international level by the application of the provisions of the Constitution and the Nepal Treaty Act, 1990. Moreover, the scope of strategic litigation (public interest litigation) has been enlarged by the Constitution and by the Supreme Court of Nepal. The authors have cited a number of cases to establish that cases pertaining to arbitrary withdrawal of criminal prosecutions, enforced disappearance, and torture, relief, and reparation to the victims, accountability of the Government to set up a system of vetting, outlawing amnesty for serious crimes, promotion of independence, and impartiality of transitional justice mechanisms have altogether contributed to establish credibility in transitional justice processes and institutions established by Nepal in recent times.

In another chapter titled 'Contribution to Peace and Security (Combating Terrorism): Sri Lankan Perspective,' Ms. Jeeva Niriella from University of Colombo has investigated Sri Lankan perspective to combat terrorism within the nation. She views terrorism as a serious threat to the peace and security of the local people and ultimately for the whole world. She has extensively examined the counter-terrorism law of Sri Lanka in light of the relevant international standards adopted by United Nations treaties. Her main focus in the chapter has been to prove that the efficacy of counter-terrorism law does not lie in sending people behind bars or to punish them, but in upholding the human rights of accused persons in the process of their prosecution. Underlining the importance of counter-terrorism laws in upholding peace and security in the country, she suggests incorporation of certain safeguards against misuse of these laws by law enforcement agencies to increase their efficiency. As security personnel are given immunity by the counter-terrorism laws from prosecution, it remains a challenge for Sri Lanka to maintain a fine balance between the obligations undertaken by it at the international level to protect and promote human rights of its own citizens and to counter-terrorist activities inside its territory. This chapter is thus an important contribution of Ms. Niriella to understand Sri Lankan perspective to maintain international peace and security.

In one chapter titled 'International Crimes Tribunal (Bangladesh): The Issues of Fairness and Transparency,' Dr. Zahurul Haque of Eastern University, Bangladesh, has beautifully tried to locate the contribution of Bangladesh in the evolution of regional jurisprudence in international criminal law relating to war crimes, crimes against humanity, and genocide. Tracing the gross human rights violations committed by the Pakistan Armed Forces and the local collaborators during 1971 War of Liberation, he explains the reasons behind the establishment of International Crimes Tribunal (ICT) in 2010, a domestic mechanism, to try those collaborators who committed war crimes and genocide during that war. Once the Tribunal commenced its work, however, various aspects of its functioning have been criticized by the scholars and commentators. In light of those views and comments, the author analyzes the historic war crimes trial on the premise of fairness and transparency enshrined in its Statute, Rules of Evidence and Procedure. He finds that the Tribunal, its Statute, and Rules of Evidence and Procedure would not withstand strict legal scrutiny according to the established international standards of fairness and transparency. This chapter is an important piece of scholarly work on this Tribunal which has aroused a lot of international interest in its successful working and delivering justice to the victims after four decades of pain and suffering.

The chapter on 'Law of State Responsibility And South Asia' is written by Ms. Madhu Bhatti from Delhi, who has attempted to make the readers understand the law on State responsibility in an easy way. Important themes, such as the rules on attribution of responsibility, reparations, and defenses allowed by The Draft Rules on State Responsibility, 2001, are re-examined, and the efforts of the International Law Commission (ILC) have been discussed by her in this chapter. Major cases decided on the issues related to State responsibility by the International Court of Justice (ICJ), such as *The Military and Para Military Activities In and Against Nicaragua* (Nicaragua v. U.S.), *Avena and Other Mexican Nationals* (Mexico v. U.S.), *La Grand Case* (Germany v. U.S.), *The Barcelona Traction, Light and Power Limited case,* are also discussed by her. After re-examining the draft code rules and ICJ decisions, she discusses the position of South Asian scholars on the issue of State responsibility. As India has contributed significantly to the drafting of the Code, the views of P. Sreenivasa Rao and S.P. Jagota, who served the ILC, become relevant in such discussion. Pakistan's and Sri Lankan's position have also been discussed by her while discussing the cases of *Appeal Relating to the Jurisdiction of the ICAO Council* (India v. Pakistan), *Asian Agricultural Products Limited v. Republic of Sri Lanka.*

Another chapter of significance 'International Criminal Court: Baby Steps in South Asia' is written by Dr. Anupam Jha from University of Delhi. He has explored the establishment of the International Criminal Court at the international level in an extremely insightful manner. The role played by the United Nations in the drafting of draft code of offences against mankind is highlighted by him. Nations across the world united together very quickly to adopt the Rome Statute to establish International Criminal Court. Dr. Jha has also analyzed the voting pattern of the nations, powers, and functions of Assembly of States Parties, subject-matter jurisdiction, temporal jurisdiction, territorial jurisdiction, personal jurisdiction, doctrine of individual criminal responsibility, the concept of complementarity, and trigger mechanisms in a lucid fashion. The crimes of committing genocide, war crimes, and crimes against humanity are explained by him in good detail. He has also provided a survey of Kampala Conference of 2010 to amend the provisions on the crime of aggression in the Rome Statute. While discussing the position of South Asian nations, Dr. Jha endorses the stand taken by India, Sri Lanka, and Pakistan in not signing the Rome Statute and welcomes the baby steps of International Criminal Court in Maldives, Afghanistan, and Bangladesh. He has also discussed the major situations referred to the International Criminal Court, such as *The Prosecutor* v. *Katanga*, *The Prosecutor* v. *Jean Pierre Bemba Gombo*, *The Prosecutor* v. *Ahmed*

Harun, The Prosecutor v. *Ahmad Al-Bashir, The Prosecutor* v. *Saif Gaddafi*. However, he laments about the situation that most of the cases referred to the Court are from the continent of Africa.

In the chapter on 'Diplomatic and Consular Immunity: South Asian Perspective,' Dr. Anupam Jha and Leena Kumari have examined the international law on diplomatic and consular immunity with a South Asian perspective. They have explored the rich tradition of South Asia to give high regard to the diplomatic envoys. In doing so, they have discussed the actual practices during the ancient, medieval, and modern times to evaluate the position of diplomats. Moving ahead, they have re-examined the various theories on diplomatic and consular immunity and the development of modern international law on diplomatic and consular immunity after the adoption of Vienna Convention on Diplomatic Relations, 1961, and the Vienna Convention on Consular Relations, 1963. Almost all of the South Asian nations have adopted both these Conventions into their national legal systems. A brief overview of the law on internationally protected persons, such as the Head of a State, a Head of Government, or a Minister for Foreign Affairs, as well as members of his family who accompany him or any representative or official of a State or any official or other agent of an international organization of an intergovernmental character, is also done. They finally discuss the leading cases decided by the ICJ as well as the national Courts on diplomatic and consular immunity. The *Case Concerning U.S. Diplomatic and Consular Staff in Tehran, U.S.* v. *Khobragade, Abdulaziz* v. *Metropolitan Dade County*, Raymond Davis, etc., are discussed by them in a precise way. The authors conclude that the South Asian States have shown enough maturity not to prosecute the diplomats who are charged with the commission of crimes. These States have tried to accord full protection to the diplomatic and consular personnel despite the absence of matching action taken by the Big Powers of the world.

South Asia has witnessed a huge pileup of weapons, both conventional and modern. In another chapter titled 'Changing Horizons of Modern Weaponry in South Asia: A Legal Survey,' Vivek Sehrawat, a doctoral candidate at University of Kansas, U.S., has examined the available international legal regime to regulate the use of these weapons, ranging from conventional weapons, booby traps, incendiaries, anti-personnel land mines, explosive remnants of war, ballistic missiles, laser weapons, cluster munitions, chemical and biological weapons, drones and nuclear weapons. He underlines the existing weapons race between India and Pakistan and as a preventive step; he argues that the establishment of arms control process would partially resolve the risk of weapons race between these two countries. He has kept in mind the possibility of these weapons to be acquired by the terrorists' network operating in the region, such as Al-Qaeda. In view of such possibilities, he has discussed the International Committee of the Red Cross (ICRC) basic rules on the use of these weapons as contained in the Geneva Conventions and its Additional Protocols. He has tested these rules vis-à-vis the use of new and conventional weapons.

References

Akbaruddin S (2016) Statement by Ambassador Syed Akbaruddin at the Informal Plenary Meeting of the Intergovernmental Negotiations on 'Question of Equitable Representation on an Increase in the Membership of the Security Council and Other Matters Related to the Security Council': the Question of Veto, New York, 9 Mar 2016

Anand RP (ed) (1972) Asian states and the development of universal international law. Vikas Publications

Anand RP (2006a) Law of the sea in historical perspective. Martinus Nijhoff

Anand RP (2006b) Changing dimensions of international law: an Asian perspective. Martinus Nijhoff

Brownlie I (2008) Principles of public international law, 7th edn. Oxford University Press, Oxford

Delinic T, Pandey N (2015) SAARC: towards meaningful co-operation

OHCHR (2008) National report submitted in accordance with paragraph 15(a) of the Annex to Human Rights Council Resolution 5/1, 6 March 2008

OHCHR (2012) National report submitted in accordance with paragraph 5 of the Annex to Human Rights Council Resolution 16/21, 8 March 2012

Rawlinson HG (1926) Intercourse between India and the Western World from the Earliest Times to the Fall of Rome

Shaw M (2008) International law, 6th edn. Cambridge University Press, Cambridge

Warmington EH (1974) The commerce between the Roman Empire and India

Authors Biography

Professor J.L. Kaul had been the Vice Chancellors of H.N.B. Garhwal University, and Vikram University. He has more than 30 years of teaching and research experience, half of which he served the Faculty of Law, University of Delhi. His areas of specialization are: Public International Law, International Trade Law, Constitutional Law, and Human Rights. He was awarded Hague External Program Fellowship of ISIL in 1990. He was awarded fellowship by the International Institute of Public Law and International Law, Greece in 1990. He was a Visiting Fellow of School of Law, St. Thomas Law School, Minneapolis, USA. He has published several articles and books, the latest of which includes **Human Rights and Good Governance**, Satyam Publishers.

Dr. Anupam Jha is Assistant Professor (Senior) at the Faculty of Law, University of Delhi. He has been engaged in teaching and research for more than 14 years. He is recipient of several prestigious fellowships and nominations, such as Raman Fellowship (U.S.A.), Commonwealth Fellowship (U.K.), UGC-TEC Nomination (Mauritius). He has also been awarded the most active participant from India by UNHCR. His current areas of teaching and research are: public international law, international environmental law, international trade law, and jurisprudence. His latest publications include the following: "The Law on Trafficking in Persons: The Quest For an Effective Model", First Published Online in ***Asian Journal of International Law (Cambridge University Press)***, 27 October 2016, ISSN No. 2044-2521 (online).

Chapter 2
UN Security Council: South Asian Perspective and Challenges Ahead

Anupam Jha, Ujjwala Sakhalkar and Brijesh Kumar Singh

1 Introduction

The Security Council is one of the principal organs of the United Nations with the avowed objective to carry out decisive decisions concerning the maintenance of international peace and security and its implementation. It was created after the Second World War in the year 1945 by the victorious Allied Powers (U.S., Britain, France, and U.S.S.R.). It has 15 members, and each member has one vote. However, decisions on matters other than procedural shall be made by an affirmative vote of nine members including the concurring votes of the permanent members. Permanent membership is a special status granted to those countries which played key roles in the establishment of the United Nations. Since the inception of Security Council, it has five permanent members, namely Britain, France, U.S., U.S.S.R. (now Russian Federation), and China. The composition of the Security Council has been a contentious matter, particularly since the end of the Cold War. Critics have argued that the Security Council and its five permanent members do not reflect the new dynamics of global power structure. This chapter explores the possibilities of expanding the membership of the Council by way of analysis of South Asian States' recommendations, organizational and academic recommendations, etc.

A. Jha · B.K. Singh
Law Centre-II, Faculty of Law, University of Delhi, 38/12, Probyn Road,
New Delhi 110007, India
e-mail: ajha@law.du.ac.in

B.K. Singh
e-mail: brijeshclc@gmail.com

U. Sakhalkar (✉)
New Law College, Bharati Vidyapeeth Deemed University,
Building No. 2, Flat No. 4, Swarmayee Society, Bhakti Marg,
Opposite Law College Road, Pune, Maharashtra 411004, India
e-mail: ujjwalasakhalkar@yahoo.co.in

J.L. Kaul and A. Jha (eds.), *Shifting Horizons of Public International Law*,
https://doi.org/10.1007/978-81-322-3724-2_2

The UN Charter gives the Security Council primary responsibility for the maintenance of international peace and security. The Security Council in the first instance attempts to resolve disputes and disagreements through peaceful means alternatively it has authority to impose sanction and to use force for compliance. The terms 'peacekeeping', 'peacemaking', 'peace enforcement', and 'peace building' are used to denote the various responsibilities to fulfil the mandate to maintain international peace and security. Under Article 25 of the Charter, all members of the United Nations agree to accept and carry out the decisions of the Security Council. While other organs of the United Nations make recommendations to member States, only the Security Council has the power to make decisions that member States are then obligated to implement under the Charter. The resolutions passed by the Security Council pertaining to the maintenance of international peace and security are binding on members of the United Nations. In South Asia too, the Security Council has played an important role to defuse the conflict and to send peacekeepers to the region. In response, the South Asian nations have also contributed to the peacekeeping missions deployed by the UN Security Council. This chapter investigates the role of Security Council in the major conflicts occurring in the region. It also discusses the role played by the South Asian nations to contribute to this mission and the problems faced by them.

2 Veto Power and Permanent Membership: Need for Reforms

The composition of Security Council is provided for in Article 23 of the UN Charter. According to this provision, the Security Council consists of 15 members of the UN. The Republic of China, France, the Union of Soviet Socialist Republics (the Russian Federation), the United Kingdom of Great Britain and Northern Ireland, and the United States of America are permanent members of the Security Council. The General Assembly elects 10 other members of the UN to be non-permanent members of the Security Council, due regard being specially paid, in the first instance to the contribution of members of the UN to the maintenance of international peace and security and to the other purposes of the organization, and also to equitable geographical distribution. The non-permanent members of the Security Council are elected for a term of 2 years.

Of the 15-member Security Council, the five permanent members (also called P5) enjoy special voting power known as the 'right to veto' under Article 27 of the UN Charter, as adopted in San Francisco on 26 June 1945. The voting procedures of the Security Council were agreed upon at the tripartite Yalta Conference between Roosevelt, Churchill, and Stalin from 3 to 11 February 1945. At the time of establishment of the Security Council, the non-permanent members were only six in number. In 1963, the position changed when the General Assembly decided to enlarge the non-permanent seats from 6 to 10. From Asia, two seats were allotted, whereas from African States, three seats were given. Five non-permanent members are elected each year by the General Assembly for a term of two years. It means that election for getting a non-permanent seat of the Security Council takes place every year for five seats. Moreover, none are allowed to serve consecutive terms. The addition of four non-permanent members in 1963 was the last major reform made to the Security Council.

From South Asia, India was offered a permanent seat in the Security Council by the U.S., which it refused. The historical controversy of India's right to a permanent seat on the Security Council has, in the post-Nehru era, centred on the culpability of independent India's first Prime Minister, Jawaharlal Nehru, in not seizing the opportunity provided by the U.S. in 1950 and by the U.S.S.R. in the 1955 (Harder 2015; The Hindu 2005). Since then, India's leadership has made all efforts to get a permanent seat in the Security Council and to reform it. Hon'ble Pranab Mukherjee, the present President of India, speaking in the 50th session of the UN General Assembly in 1995, advocated that the new permanent member should be chosen not arbitrarily but objectively and it was his firm belief that on the basis of any such criteria, India would qualify to be a permanent member.

In his first address to the UN General Assembly after being elected as India's Prime Minister, Narendra Modi urged all member nations to deliver on the commitment of UN reform. He said institutions which reflect the compulsions of the twentieth century risk irrelevance (Modi 2014). However, all efforts of India and other aspiring nations for Security Council membership have been defeated by the veto power of the existing permanent members and the differences among the developing nations.

According to the UN website, it was agreed by the drafters that if any one of the five permanent members casts a negative vote in the 15-member Security Council, the resolution or decision would not be approved (UN 2016). All five permanent members have exercised the right of veto at one time or another. Even though the right of veto of the permanent members was expressed under Article 27 of the Charter, in subsequent practice, abstention by one or more permanent members did not defeat a Council decision, provided it was supported by seven members. After 1963, the position changed and if a permanent member did not fully agree with a proposed resolution but wished to cast a vote, it may choose to abstain, thus allowing the resolution to be adopted if it obtained the required number of nine favourable votes (UN 2016). If the data compiled by the UN on veto power used by the permanent members is analysed, it becomes clear that till 2004, Russian Federation (erstwhile U.S.S.R.) used the veto power 103 out of 193 times, whereas U.S. used it 79 times, UK 29 times, France used 16 times, and China 9 times (UN 2016).

Giving an elaborate historical perspective on the use of the veto in the 70-year history of the UN in March 2016, India's Permanent Representative to the UN, Syed Akbaruddin, stated in New York that from the time Security Council was created in 1946 till February 2016, 317 vetoes have been cast, and as a result, 230 draft resolutions or parts thereof have been vetoed in total. In effect, 10% of the 2271 resolutions adopted till February 2016 have been vetoed (First Post 2016). He further underscored that apart from the use of the veto within the Security Council, there have been expansion of the veto to the Council's subsidiary bodies such as Sanctions Committees. He said in these bodies, the veto has been extended to all 15 members of the Committees who can block, or object or place on hold any request of a member State, thereby in effect killing the proposal on grounds that consensus is required (First Post 2016).

Observing the history of the use of veto, it is not surprising that a significant number of member States call for the abolition of the veto or to limit and curtail its use to the extent possible. Several other member States also support voluntary restrictions on the use of veto in situations such as genocide, war crimes, ethnic cleansing, and gross human rights violations. For instance, France proposed a new code of conduct that would impose conditions on using the veto in the case of mass atrocities (Swart and Pace 2015). While some member States belong to the school of thought that restrictions should be placed on the use of veto, there are others who want no restrictions on its use (First Post 2016).

In view of the changing global geopolitical realities of the twenty-first century and the demands of new aspiring countries to get permanent membership, the need to reform Security Council on matters related to permanent membership and veto power was felt at the level of UN around three decades back. Formal discussion about reforming the UN Security Council began with the establishment by the General Assembly of the Open-ended Working Group on the 'Question of Equitable Representation on and Increase in the Membership of the Security Council and Related Matters' in 1993 (GA Res. 48/26). The Open-ended Working Group which worked from March 1 to September 1994 considered all aspects of this question and reported that:

> Although the debate was substantive and constructive, clarifying position of member States, no conclusion was drawn. While there was convergence of views that the membership of the Security Council should be enlarged, there was also agreement that the scope and nature of such enlargement required further discussion on the matter related to the Security Council.

Discord among the participants hampered the Working Group from making any concrete proposals. Although there was general agreement that reform should be undertaken and new members be added, there were significant disagreements over whether new permanent members should also be granted veto power (Kelly 2000). Even after more than 20 years of this Group, very little success has been achieved to respond to the demand of expansion of Security Council and reforming veto powers. The first phase of the effort culminated in the World Summit of 2005, when the high hopes of reaching a decision on reforming the Council were shattered mainly due to the divergence of interests among developing countries. Brazil, Germany, India, and Japan (also called G4) have voiced their strong aspirations to become permanent members. However, the G4 efforts are often opposed by 'Uniting for Consensus (UfC)' movement (also called 'Coffee Club') led by Italy. It calls for consensus before any decision is reached on the form and size of the Security Council. While India belongs to G4, its immediate neighbour Pakistan belongs to Uniting for Consensus (UfC). Bangladesh has also come up recently to support India's candidature for the permanent membership of Security Council (Thaindian 2010). Nepal has also backed India's bid for this seat (IANS 2014). Maldives and the African Union as a whole support India's candidature for the permanent seat. However, the position of P5 is also not clear. In public, the P5 claim that they are open to expansion with new permanent seats, but they disagree on which countries to support. Behind the scenes, China, Russia, and the U.S. have effectively prevented progress. China is even active in the UfC grouping (Swart and Pace 2015).

Another important grouping formed for the lasting and comprehensive reform of the Security Council is called L.69. It is an alliance of 42 developing countries from Africa, Latin America and the Caribbean, Asia and the Pacific. The group aims to expand the numbers of both permanent and non-permanent seats of the Security Council. It wants to achieve a more accountable, representative, transparent, and, more importantly, a 'relevant' Security Council. India describes the L.69 group as 'the friends of Security Council reform' (Chaudhury 2012).

Under India's leadership, the L.69 group put forward a proposal towards the end of the 61st session of the General Assembly in 2007. The main contents of this proposal were as follows: (a) expansion in both permanent and non-permanent categories, (b) greater representation of developing countries, including island and small States, (c) representation of developed countries and those with transition economies reflective of the contemporary world realities, (d) comprehensive improvement in the working methods of the Security Council, (e) equitable geographical distribution, and (f) provision for a review. According to Indian representative, the main purpose behind the L.69 proposal was to generate 'some momentum' to an otherwise painfully slow process. The proposal met with a strong reaction and generated acrimonious exchanges among members. As a result, the L.69 proposal of 2007 was withdrawn without being put to a vote (Choedon 2015).

A new phase of the initiative for expanding the Council was started by the President of General Assembly in 2007 through the establishment of a new mechanism of Intergovernmental Negotiation (IGN) on Security Council reform. After intense discussions, the IGN came out with a framework text which could be the basis of negotiations to reform the Security Council. This text was introduced in the General Assembly by its President Sam Kutesa on 1 August 2015. However, the prospect of fruitful negotiation and positive outcome in the 70th anniversary of the UN received a shocking blow when the U.S., China, and Russia came out against it (Choedon 2015).

A change in the structure of the Security Council would only come into effect after two-thirds of the UN member States (128 out of 193) in the General Assembly have approved the outcome by being present and voting according to Article 108 of the Charter. Moreover, all five permanent members need to ratify, providing each of them with a virtual veto. This seems very difficult given the financial superiority enjoyed by the P5 and the resisting positions of U.S., China, and Russian Federation. U.S. enjoys the most superior financial position in the UN as it provides around 22% of UN budget (UN 2014). UK, China, and France contribute very less as compared to the U.S. (only around 5%). Russian Federation has slid down in its contribution (only around 2%). While some of the aspiring nations for permanent membership (Germany and Japan) have relied mainly on their financial contributions to the UN, others have relied, though not exclusively, on the size of population and on their representative character (Blum 2005). For instance, India and Brazil contribute 0.737 and 3.823%, respectively, to the regular budget of the UN.

India has advanced a number of arguments to justify its demand for a permanent seat. It has the world's second largest population and is the world's largest liberal democracy. It is also the world's sixth largest economy and third largest in terms of Purchasing Power Parity (PPP). India is the third largest contributor of troops to UN peacekeeping missions. India has been elected 7 times to the UN Security Council as non-permanent member, most recently India from 2011 to 2012 after receiving 188 of the 190 votes. It is one of the few countries which is consistent in paying regularly its dues to the UN budget.

India is the foremost among the non-nuclear powers to expose the dangers of nuclear testing, and Nehru was the first head of the government to propose a test ban (Faridi 2014). India's efforts considerably reinforced the world wide campaign to ban nuclear tests and led to the signing of the Partial Test Ban Treaty in 1962. It also signed and ratified the Chemical Weapons Convention, but it refused to sign the NPT and CTBT because of their discriminatory nature. With the decline of colonialism by the 1960s, India played a leading role in bringing the newly independent States of Africa and Asia together and organized them into the Non-Alignment Movement (NAM). One of its significant achievements in the 1960s was the creation of the UN Conference on Trade and Development (UNCTAD). By the mid-1970s, it succeeded in getting a resolution adopted in the UN General Assembly asking for the creation of a New International Economic Order (NIEO). It played an important role in the reformation of G15 which aims at bringing greater coordination among the developing countries in the Third World (Faridi 2014). In the field of human rights, racial discrimination, and colonialism, India was the first country to raise the question of discrimination against the people of Indian origin in South Africa in the UN General Assembly in 1946 (Kumar 1992).

Taking the above arguments forward, Professor David P. Fidler and Sumit Ganguly of Indiana University argue that the Indo-US civilian nuclear cooperation accord struck in 2007 illustrated India's new strategic importance because this deal not only recognized the legitimacy of India's status as a nuclear weapons State, but also demonstrated the American need to improve security and political ties with India as a hedge against the relative decline in U.S. power as Chinese power and multi-polarity looms on the global horizon. According to them, India also has new stature in other political arenas, including multilateral actions to stabilize Afghanistan and prevent Pakistan from imploding, negotiations within the World Trade Organization, and diplomatic efforts to address the threat of climate change. India's relations with Iran also factor into strategies being contemplated in the U.S., Europe, and the UN concerning how to handle Iran's feared acquisition of the capability to make nuclear weapons. India's positions on controversial countries (e.g. Myanmar) and global policy initiatives (e.g. advocacy for the principle of the responsibility to protect) cannot be ignored. Although they concede that serious reform of the UN Security Council is unlikely to occur, yet they accept India's argument that it should become a new permanent member of the Council as the argument has not only political plausibility but also country's increasing significance across the range of pressing issues characterizing contemporary international relations (Fidler and Ganguly 2010).

However, Professor Michael Reisman from Yale Law School is of the view that the leading developing countries, such as India and Brazil, propose themselves as new 'Third World' permanent members of the Council. According to him, there is little assurance that, if they or others were elevated as representatives of this constituency, they would perform that mandate (Reisman 1993). He further adds that the Council's effectiveness might suffer due to the expansion of permanent members (Reisman 1994). Speaking about the difficult process of amending the UN Charter at American Society of International Law in 1994, Professor Reisman said:

> No reality- based discussion of Charter revision can ignore Article 108, which allows for amendments by two-thirds of the General Assembly members but requires ratification by all the Security Council permanent members in order for those amendments to come into force. This does not mean that reform is unattainable, but rather that international constitutional amendment, in its conventional understanding, is the least likely to succeed and to be satisfactory (Reisman 1994).

3 Security Council and Peacekeeping

According to Alan James, peacekeeping is different from collective security. Collective security relies ultimately on the mandatory use of force, while peacekeeping eschews force, except in self-defence, and requires the consent of host State for the admission of UN personnel (James 1969). Peacekeeping operations ('PKO'), in no way, have been enforcement actions against any specific State or States in 'the coercive and punitive sense' understood in Chapter VII of the UN Charter (Lal 1973). The primary objective of a UNPKO which at times may be called Preventive Diplomacy as well—if the essence of such an operation is to prevent involvement of the major powers in a specific dispute or in a given situation —is to prevent the deterioration of a situation lest there may arise the need for collective security operation (Lal 1973). Nevertheless, both collective security operations and PKO resemble each other in the sense that both are techniques for the maintenance of international peace and security (Lal 1973).

According to Whiteman, there has been a tacit transition from the concept of collective security, as set out in Chapter VII of the UN, to a more realistic idea of peacekeeping (Whiteman and Hackworth 1963). Peacekeeping operations are operations of a military, paramilitary, or non-military character which are to be conducted by the UN for the maintenance of international peace and security with the exception of enforcement action under Chapter VII (Raja and Murthy 1986). Following are the different forms which these operations could take:

(a) Observation of conditions on one side or on both sides of a frontier
(b) Fact-finding and observation in regard to alleged interference from outside in the domestic affairs of a member State
(c) Observation of supervision of a ceasefire line
(d) Missions of mediation and conciliation
(e) Assistance rendered to a country for the maintenance of law and order when requested by that country and in such conditions in which there was a likelihood of disturbance of international peace and security.

The term ‘peacekeeping’ was not precisely contemplated by the authors of the Charter. The drafters of the Charter had contemplated of ‘collective security measures’, and as a result, they had incorporated Chapter VII on ‘Action with Respect to Threats to the Peace, Breaches of the Peace, and Acts of Aggression’ (Articles 39–51). Collective security measures are also called ‘peacemaking’ and ‘peace enforcement’ measures. Collective security measures are authorized by the Security Council of the UN under Chapter VII, which defines in considerable detail what particular measures the Council may take, how to take them. However, the experiences of the exercise of veto power (Article 27), advent of Cold War, Korean War (1950–1953), non-implementation of Article 43 (Creation of UN Armed Force) during major crises, such as Kashmir (1947–1948) and Suez Canal (1956), forced the international community to think about peacekeeping operations and about the creation of peacekeeping forces.

Under Article 24 of the UN Charter, the General Assembly cannot discuss and make recommendations on peace and security matters which are at that time being discussed by the Security Council. However, if the Security Council is not able to act because of the obstructive tactics of a permanent member, the Charter does not leave the UN impotent. The obligation of all members to take action to maintain or restore peace does not disappear because of a veto. The Charter in Articles 10, 11, and 14 also vests in the General Assembly authority and responsibility for matters affecting international peace. The General Assembly can and should organize itself to discharge its responsibility promptly and decisively if the Security Council is prevented from acting (Acheson 1950).

The Uniting for Peace Resolution (‘UPR’) passed by the General Assembly in 1950 undertook to implement this philosophy (Nathanson 1965). In accordance with this resolution, if the Security Council fails to act, owing to the negative vote of a permanent member, then the General Assembly may act. This would happen in the case where there appears to be a threat to the peace, breach of the peace, or act of aggression. The General Assembly can consider the matter for collective measures to maintain or restore international peace and security. The resolution also provided for the calling of an emergency special session of the General Assembly, if it was not then in session. The resolution established a Peace Observer Commission composed of 14 members. This resolution was invoked only once in

UN peacekeeping history, when in 1956 the General Assembly established the First UN Emergency Force (UNEF I) in the Middle East.

Drawing partly on the early experiences of the UN intervention in Greece, Indonesia, Kashmir, and Palestine, Lester B. Pearson from Canada formulated the idea of setting up of a UNEF. He was the then Foreign Minister of Canada and who became Prime Minister of Canada later. He was also awarded the Nobel Peace Prize for this innovation in 1957. The credit for the further development of this idea into the concept of UN Peacekeeping Operations (UNPKO) goes to the political ingenuity and international Statesmanship of Dag Hammarskjold, the second Secretary General of the UN (Lal 1973). This distinctive and more realistic approach to international peacekeeping was further perfected during the UN Operations in the Congo (ONUC). It led to institutionalization of basic rules and principles governing various aspects of peacekeeping (Bowett 1964).

However, the legality of 'peacekeeping' has been questioned since its beginning. The Soviet Union argued that the Charter of the UN did not provide for such operations under the auspices of General Assembly. It said: 'Under Article 39 of the Charter, it is specifically the Security Council which "shall determine the existence of any threat to the peace, breach of peace or act of aggression"'. In other words, the Soviet Union took the position that General Assembly lacked the authority to take enforcement action (UN Doc 1964). On the other hand, the Government of the U.S. categorically denied the contention of Soviet Union on the basis that Article 24 of the Charter gave the Security Council 'primary responsibility' for the maintenance of international peace and security, primary but not exclusive authority. The contention was that Article 10 of the UN Charter authorized the General Assembly to discuss and make recommendations on any question or matters within the scope of the Charter and Article 11 authorized the General Assembly to discuss and make recommendations on any question relating to the maintenance of international peace and security. Article 14 authorizes the General Assembly to recommend measures for the peaceful adjustment of any situation likely to impair friendly relations among nations. Article 35 makes provision for bringing to the attention of Security Council or General Assembly any dispute or situation which might lead to international friction or give rise to a dispute (U.S. 1964).

Questions of legality of the UN peacekeepers were put to rest by the Advisory Opinion of International Court of Justice in *Certain Expenses of the UN* in 1962. The Court upheld the legality of UNPKO and observed that the Security Council did not have the sole authority under Chapter VII to make binding decisions, obligatory and compulsory on all Members for coercive or enforcement action, but that did not mean that the General Assembly could not make recommendations (as opposed to binding decisions) as to the preservation of the peace. The Court further clarified that the PKO could not be termed as 'enforcement action' which fell within the domain of the Security Council. The Court referred to Articles 11, 14, and 22 of the Charter as specific provisions on which peacekeeping operations organized by the General Assembly could be based (White 1996).

The impetus behind India's tacit support to UN peacekeeping came from India's first Prime Minister Jawaharlal Nehru. Nehru was eager to project India as 'great country' by articulating a vision of peace and harmonious coexistence. To him, peacekeeping was a crucial element in the broader effort to demonstrate India's vision (Banerjee 2013). After Nehru, the legacy continued and India's Representative stated at the Fourth Meeting of the Special Committee on Peacekeeping established by the General Assembly (UN Doc 1965a, b):

> The duties of the Security Council and the General Assembly were specific and well defined under the Charter and were intended to be complimentary.... the dispatch of armed personnel otherwise than for the purpose of observation or investigation should be within the exclusive power of the Security Council...a Convention might then be established that where the parties primarily concerned concurred, the Great Powers might agree, save in exceptional circumstances or for special reasons, not to vote against a proposal involving the dispatch of armed personnel...

The Indian representative cited the case of Cyprus in support of his contention wherein UN Peacekeeping Force in Cyprus (UNFICYP) was established by a Security Council resolution in 1964. The Indian stand was mostly on the lines of Soviet thinking (Raja and Murthy 1986).

Pakistan emphasized the relation of peacekeeping to the peaceful settlement of disputes under Articles 33 and 34 of the Charter. Its representative stated (UN Doc 1965a, b):

> The problem would be greatly simplified if the Security Council called upon the parties to a dispute, not merely to negotiate, but to settle the dispute by other peaceful means, such as inquiry, mediation, arbitration and judicial settlement which were mentioned in Article 33, and if the Council carried out the investigative functions laid down in Article 34 of the Charter. It was the disuse of those provisions of the Charter which had necessitated the employment of the palliatives known since 1956 as 'peacekeeping operations (PKO)'- a rather loose term which might have caused some confusion. It leads one to overlook the fact that those operations were different from the dispatch of a military force with a coercive mission and that UN intervention in a situation likely to lead to a breach of the peace might constitute nothing more than either the employment of the peaceful means envisaged in Article 33, at the parties own choice, or the taking of measures for the peaceful adjustment of the situation in accordance with recommendations under Article 14. It had been repeatedly pointed out that the scope of those operations was strictly limited because of their peaceful and voluntary nature; they were undertaken at the request or with the consent of the country involved; the use of force was barred except in self defence; and they placed no obligation on Member States to contribute to them in either personnel or material.

Despite initial reservations, Pakistan has since then contributed to UN peacekeeping with conviction. Pakistan deployed its first-ever contingent in UN Operation in Congo (ONUC). It has sent its peacekeepers to more than 40 UN peacekeeping missions in two dozen countries. According to the data available at UN in July 2016, Pakistan is the third largest contributor to peacekeeping after Ethiopia and India. Due to quantum and sincerity of contribution for its noble cause, Pakistan has one of the highest sacrifices ratios among the troops contributing countries (Khan 2014).

3.1 Principles of UN Peacekeeping

There are three basic principles that continue to set UN peacekeeping operations apart as a tool for maintaining international peace and security.

These three principles are interrelated and mutually reinforcing.

3.1.1 Consent of the Parties

UN peacekeeping operations are deployed with the consent of the main parties to the conflict. This requires a commitment by the parties to a political process. Their acceptance of a peacekeeping operation provides the UN with the necessary freedom of action, both political and physical, to carry out its mandated tasks.

The fact that the main parties have given their consent to the deployment of a United Nations peacekeeping operation does not necessarily imply or guarantee that there will also be consent at the local level, particularly if the main parties are internally divided or have weak command and control systems. Universality of consent becomes even less probable in volatile settings, characterized by the presence of armed groups not under the control of any of the parties, or by the presence of other groups.

3.1.2 Impartiality

Impartiality is crucial to maintaining the consent and cooperation of the main parties, but should not be confused with neutrality or inactivity. United Nations peacekeepers should be impartial in their dealings with the parties to the conflict, but not neutral in the execution of their mandate. Just as a good referee is impartial, but will penalize infractions, so a peacekeeping operation should not condone actions by the parties that violate the undertakings of the peace process or the international norms and principles that a United Nations peacekeeping operation upholds.

Notwithstanding the need to establish and maintain good relations with the parties, a peacekeeping operation must scrupulously avoid activities that might compromise its image of impartiality. A mission should not shy away from a rigorous application of the principle of impartiality for fear of misinterpretation or retaliation. Failure to do so may undermine the peacekeeping operation's credibility and legitimacy, and may lead to a withdrawal of consent for its presence by one or more of the parties.

3.1.3 Non-use of Force Except in Self-defence and Defence of the Mandate

UN peacekeeping operations are not an enforcement tool. However, they may use force at the tactical level, with the authorization of the Security Council, if acting in self-defence and defence of the mandate. In certain volatile situations, the Security Council has given UN peacekeeping operations 'robust' mandates authorizing them to 'use all necessary means' to deter forceful attempts to disrupt the political process, protect civilians under imminent threat of physical attack, and/or assist the national authorities in maintaining law and order. The UN has also the duty to implement its 'responsibility to protect' in the situations of crimes against humanity, war crimes, and genocide (SC Res. 2006a, b; GA Res. 2009).

3.2 Financing Peacekeeping

While decisions about establishing, maintaining, or expanding a peacekeeping operation are taken by the Security Council, the financing of UN peacekeeping operations is the collective responsibility of all UN member States. Every member State is legally obligated to pay their respective share towards peacekeeping. This is in accordance with the provisions of Article 17 of the Charter of the United Nations.

The General Assembly apportions peacekeeping expenses based on a special scale of assessments under a complex formula that member States themselves have established. This formula takes into account, among other things, the relative economic wealth of member States, with the five permanent members of the Security Council required to pay a larger share because of their special responsibility for the maintenance of international peace and security.

3.3 Views on Security Council Peacekeeping Operations

According to the South Asian countries participating in the UN peacekeeping operations, peacekeeping consumes more resources, employs more people, and occupies a greater share of the Security Council's time than any other single issue, and no other Council instrument has had a greater impact on the origin and application of international law and international humanitarian law than its peacekeeping mandates. Peacekeeping has also generated a reputation of impartiality and fairness for the United Nations. As experienced actors in peacekeeping, South Asian countries have witnessed the changing character of UN peacekeeping with both a keen interest and to maintain caution.

Gradually, South Asian countries have become the backbone of UN peace operations. Military personnel of three major South Asian countries, namely Bangladesh, India, and Pakistan, are relentlessly working with the Security Council.

South Asian countries look at their contribution to peace operations as a symbol of international recognition of their experience in handling delicate situations of internal unrest and their capacity to provide a positive difference in world politics. The African Union aptly describes India as an exemplary reference point in the area of peacekeeping.

South Asian countries have also sought to play a role in policy making and at deliberative forums. In an action that carried forward the South Asian tradition at the Security Council of the past decade, India organized a special meeting to discuss the future of peace operations during its presidency of the Security Council in August 2011, where other South Asian troops and police contributing countries made their positions known. Bangladesh and Pakistan also utilized their presidential rights to organize special discussions during their turn as non-permanent members at the Council in 2001 and 2004, respectively. While South Asian countries have wholeheartedly contributed to the UN peacekeeping, there have been disagreements between the host government and the UN over the command, control, and employment of peacekeeping troops (Krishnasamy 2007).

4 Security Council and Management of Interstate Conflicts in South Asia

Stated simply, conflict is a clash between two opposing groups, external or internal to the country. There are two types of internal conflict. The first is conflict against the State by the people of the country itself or civil war. Examples of these conflicts are terrorism, which is an extreme manifestation of conflict and reflects a certain degree of organization of conflict. It is carried out by a relatively organized group of non-state actors, and directed against the State. The second category includes those conflicts which are inflicted by other countries, either directly or by using the people if the attacked territory.

Some of the major disputes of the South Asian region include the following:

4.1 Kashmir Dispute

The territorial conflict between India and Pakistan over the region of Kashmir has served as the major obstacle to relations between the two States and to regional security in South Asia. Since the two States achieved independence from Great Britain, India and Pakistan have occupied different segments of the region and fought four wars, in which Kashmir's legal status was either the main inciting factor or close to the existence of armed conflict.

As per the provisions of Indian Independence Act, 1947, any Indian State could merge in the either dominion (India or Pakistan) by executing an instrument of accession or can remain independent. Maharaja Hari Singh, head of princely State of Jammu and Kashmir, decided to remain independent. On 22 October 1947, tribesmen of Pakistan supported by Pakistani government invaded Jammu and Kashmir. Maharaja Hari Singh sought help from India. India promised help to Maharaja Hari Singh on only one condition that Jammu and Kashmir would have to merge with Indian territory. On 26th October, Maharaja Hari Singh signed instrument of accession with Union of India with certain conditions. Article 370 was included in the India's Constitution to provide special status to Jammu and Kashmir. The national army of India helped Hari Singh's forces to repel the tribesmen invasion. To solve the Jammu and Kashmir dispute, Jawaharlal Nehru brought Kashmir issue in the Security Council of United Nations. He referred the matter to the Council on the advice of Lord Mountbatten, the then Governor General of India (Lowe et al. 2008). In January 1948, the Security Council established the United Nations Commission for India and Pakistan (UNCIP) to investigate and mediate the dispute (SC Res. 1948a, b). In April 1948, the Council decided to enlarge the membership of UNCIP and to recommend various measures including the use of observers to stop the fighting (SC Res. 1948a, b). At the recommendation of UNCIP, the Secretary General appointed the military adviser to support the Commission on military aspects and for a group of military observers to assist him. On 5 January 1949, UNCIP recommended a bilateral demilitarization, a truce agreement for the future, and an implementation of a free and fair plebiscite. The first team of unarmed military observers, which eventually formed the nucleus of the United Nations Military Observer Group in India and Pakistan (UNMOGIP), arrived in January 1949 to supervise the ceasefire between India and Pakistan and to assist the military adviser to UNCIP.

Both countries failed to arrive at any peace resolution. Pakistan demanded plebiscite to be held in Jammu and Kashmir to decide the choice of people of Kashmir. In 1951, free and democratic election was held in Jammu and Kashmir and Sheikh Abdullah became chief minister there. Lawyer and author A.G. Noorani says, 'the right of the people of Kashmir to a plebiscite is an inherent right and came even before UN resolutions. It was a pledge Pandit Jawaharlal Nehru made in a telegram to Pakistan's Liaqat Ali Khan' (Noorani 2014). He further argues that the people of India and the non-Muslim people of Jammu and Kashmir had no right to interfere in deciding fate of the Jammu and Kashmir's Muslims (Teng 2013).

UN stressed the need of plebiscite but India, in her defence, argued that people of Jammu and Kashmir by exercising their right to vote gave consent to be part of India and there was no need of plebiscite. Plebiscite is based on the principle of self-determination according to Article 1 of the UN Charter. It has binding force of international law in context of colonial State, and Kashmir is not colony of any country. As per the instrument of accession, Jammu and Kashmir is part and parcel of India. This position of Jammu and Kashmir is duly recognized by the Constitution of India. Not only has the Constitution given Jammu & Kashmir a status of full-fledged State but also a special category State enjoying more autonomy under Article 370. The instrument of accession cannot be termed as illegal.

After a valid merger, and proper system of democratic governance in place, the demand for plebiscite is unjustified.

4.2 Indo-Pak War 1965

Pakistan tried to destabilize India after the death of Jawaharlal Nehru. On the issue of a disputed area in Rann of Kutch and Kashmir, the war escalated from Pakistani infiltration to Indian response across the Ceasefire Line (CFL) to Pakistani offensive and the Indian counter offensive. The world started exerting pressure to bring about a quick end to the war. On September 6, the Security Council passed a unanimous resolution requesting cessation of hostilities and return to the 1949 CFL. It also called for the withdrawal of all armed personnel to the positions held by them before 5 August 1965. Both India and Pakistan ignored the resolution and continued fighting. On Security Council's passing another resolution, both India and Pakistan agreed to stop fighting as on September 23.

4.3 Pakistan's Intrusion in Kargil Area of Kashmir (April–May 1999)

Pakistan not only sent armed extremists or militants across the Line of Control (LoC) on the Indian side but Pakistan's regular army provided them strong support from behind. As regards legal position, Pakistan's violation of Line of Control (LoC) was a flagrant violation of the rules of international law. India resorted to use of force only to defend herself. This was the reason that world community criticized Pakistan's action and supported India's use of force in self-defence (Kapoor 2001).

A retired Pakistani General who was heading the analysis wing of Inter Services Intelligence (ISI) in 1999 Kargil conflict says only regular troops of Pakistan army took part in Kargil conflict with India and not Mujahideen fighters as claimed by Pakistan (Pubby 2013). However, no resolutions were passed by the Security Council regarding this important conflict during the time.

4.4 Terrorists Attack on Indian Parliament (13 December 2001)

Pakistani terrorists attacked Indian Parliament on 13 December 2001. This attack infringed Article 2(4) of the United Nation's Charter. It is now crystal clear that the persons who attacked Indian Parliament belonged to Lashkar-e-Taiba and Jaish-e-Mohammed, and they had support of ISI of Pakistani army. Therefore,

Pakistan is guilty of intervention against the sovereignty and political independence of India. Similar to the attack on twin towers of World Trade Centre (WTC) of America on 11 September 2001, the attack on 13 December 2001 was an armed attack against India and gave India the right of self-defence according to Article 51 of the United Nation's Charter. This right of self-defence permitted India to go across the borders and take necessary action against the terrorist group over there.

However, Security Council of the UN did not pass any resolution regarding the matter.

4.5 *Mumbai Attack, 2008*

The 26 November 2008 terrorist attack in Mumbai, which killed at least 172 people, has been referred to as 'India's 9/11'. Lashkar-e-Taiba's (LeT) role in the attack raised the issue of Pakistan's involvement. It is not known for sure whether LeT carried out this operation without the knowledge or approval of Pakistan's army or intelligence services, or whether the attack was instigated or encouraged by sectors of the Pakistani military or intelligence service to change the course of Pakistan's own government (Rabasa et al. 2009).

LeT is Pakistan-based terrorist group. If Pakistan does not take action against these terrorists, India has right in international law to use force to defend its territory. The Security Council attempted to play a role in the mediation at the inception of the conflict. However, its recommendations and attempts at mediation failed to bring about permanent resolution. The Security Council has remained silent since 1965 when it last articulated recommendations and has all but abandoned its mediatory role. In the meantime, attempts at resolution have been left largely to India and Pakistan.

4.6 *Uri Attack, 2016*

A group of heavily armed terrorists attacked security forces in the Line of Control ('LoC') border town of Uri on 18 September 2016. Police sources said that fidayeen militants stormed an army camp around 4 a.m. and killed 18 soldiers. Four militants were also killed in the encounter. Later, LeT accepted this responsibility of carrying out the attack. The UN Security Council members condemned the attack in Uri. Of the five permanent members, Russia and France outright named Pakistan or Pakistan-based organizations. Other permanent members, such as the U.S., and UK, came down strongly in India's favour, even as they stopped short of directly mentioning Pakistan.

India took retaliatory action against this attack and executed surgical strikes in the night of 29th September through its Special Forces. The Special Forces attacked the launch pads of the militants base in Pakistan occupied Kashmir ('PoK'). Two units of the elite 2 Paras comprising 18–20 soldiers flew across the LoC in the Uri sector in military helicopters and carried out operation that killed 20 suspected terrorists across three terror camps in PoK.

According to Professor Bharat H. Desai of Jawaharlal Nehru University, the counter attack by India has heralded a new era of assertive Indian posture in the region (Desai 2016). He defends India's surgical strikes as it took place in PoK. According to him, India has consistently claimed PoK under belligerent occupation by Pakistan. He gives the example of *Corfu Channel case* (1949) in which States like Pakistan was held responsible even if its pleaded that action of terrorist outfits take place without their knowledge. He gave the example of Article 2(4) of the UN Charter which prohibits threat or use of force as a peremptory norm. Right of self-defence has emerged as an exception to this general prohibition of force under Article 51. He further justifies India's strikes on the basis of UN Security Council resolution 1373 (2001b) which mandates all the States to regard acts of terrorism as 'a threat to international peace and security'. According to him, a State is responsible if it provides support 'to entities or persons involved in terrorist acts' or provides 'safe haven' or does not prevent 'those who finance, plan, facilitate, or commit terrorist acts from using their respective territories' (Nicaragua case 1986).

4.7 Liberation of Bangladesh

Pakistan had used force against East Pakistan in 1971. The Awami League, led by Sheikh Mujibur Rahman, won a landslide victory in the national elections in 1971 and demanded autonomy for East Pakistan. The party won 160 seats and a majority in the national assembly. This victory also gave it the right to form a government, but Zulfikar Ali Bhutto, the Chairman of the Pakistan People's Party, refused to let the Sheikh become the Prime Minister of Pakistan. This initiated the war. Pakistani army started killing, torture, rape, and other atrocities on East Pakistani citizens. This situation produced millions of refugees which caused refugee problem to India. 'Voluntary repatriation' was suggested by the world community as the best method. But it was not possible unless a safe and secure environment is developed in East Pakistan. Such conditions could have been created only after the political settlement of the problem between the East Pakistani leaders and the government of Pakistan that culminated in cessation of use of force by Pakistan on East Pakistan (Singh 1984).

The Government of Pakistan charged India with blocking of refugees from returning to East Pakistan. India wanted repatriation of the refugees. But she was not ready for repatriation unless a peace and secure atmosphere is created in East Pakistan. India had a legitimate claim in asking Pakistan to stop further influx of the refugees and to create condition for voluntary repatriation of refugees who were on the Indian soil. Under the UN Charter, the States have obligation of pacific settlement. The situation which arose had full potential to endanger international peace and security. Under these circumstances, India used force against Pakistani army on the ground of self-help to solve the refugee problem. But India never said that the use of force by it was directed against Pakistan to solve the refugee problem (Singh 1984). On 16 December 1971, Lt. General A.A. Niazi of Pakistan Armed forces surrendered to lieutenant general Jagjit Singh Aurora, General Officer Commanding in Chief of Indian and Bangladesh forces.

4.8 *Afghanistan Issue and Security Council*

The September 11 attacks (also referred to as September 11, September 11th, or 9/11) were a series of four coordinated terrorist attacks by the Islamic terrorist group al-Qaeda on the United States on the morning of Tuesday, 11 September 2001. The attacks consisted of suicide attacks used to target symbolic U.S. landmarks. In late 2001, the Security Council authorized the United States to overthrow the Taliban government.

These attacks were followed by war in Afghanistan led by USA wherein U.S. continuously invaded Afghanistan with the aim to dismantle al-Qaeda and to deny it a safe base of operations in Afghanistan by removing the Taliban from power. The main question was 'whether the USA invasions were legally justified by the 9/11 attacks?'

After 9/11, U.S. had four legal justifications to use of force against Afghanistan. These are (a) Chapter VII of the UN Charter, (b) intervention by invitation, (c) humanitarian intervention, and (d) self-defence. U.S. relied on self-defence as this area is very contentious and difficult to analyse (Byers 2002). In response to the '9/11' attacks, the Security Council recognized the U.S. right to self-defence against Afghanistan (SC Res. 2001a, b).

Since the founding of the United Nations in 1945, international law with regard to war has been defined by the UN Charter. Measured by this standard, the U.S.-led war in Afghanistan has been illegal from the outset. The main argument was that disputes are to be brought to the UN Security Council, which alone may authorize the use of force. Without this authorization, any military activity against another country is illegal.

4.9 *Role in Sri Lanka*

Force has been used by Liberation Tigers of Tamil Eelam (LTTE) and Sri Lankan State machinery against each other for more than three decades in Sri Lanka. Sri Lankan Civil War was started in 1983 for creating independent Tamil State and which ended in 2009. Method of use of force by LTTE was largely suicide terrorism against Sri Lankan State machinery. Suicide terrorism is characterized by the willingness of physically and psychologically war-trained individuals to die in the course of destroying or attempting to annihilate enemy targets in furtherance of certain political or social objectives (Schweitzer 2002; Whittaker 2002). LTTE raised a huge army to fight with regular forces of Sri Lanka. The LTTE was the only militant group to assassinate two world leaders: former Indian Prime Minister Rajiv Gandhi in 1991 and Sri Lankan President Ranasinghe Premdasa in 1993.

There have been a number of attempts to broker peace in Sri Lanka. Norway took part in the effort and mediated a Ceasefire Agreement (CFA) in 2002. Norway led six further rounds of talks, but the process broke down in April 2003. Additionally, Norway hosted another round of peace talks in Geneva in February 2006, but by April, both sides were engaging in 'major military operations'. By August, there was 'full-scale war'. In January 2008, the Sri Lankan government officially withdrew from the CFA. In March 2009, both sides reported a 'bloody escalation in the fighting in the country's north-east'. Even as the fighting entered April, and the LTTE continued to suffer defeats, they refused to surrender. On 15 May 2009, the Sri Lankan President Rajapaksa declared the war to be in its final stage, with the final offensive sure to end within 48 hours, declaring the following day that the LTTE had been defeated. This claim was substantiated when, on 17 May, the Tigers announced that the battle had 'reached its bitter end' (Crisis in Sri Lanka 2016).

The war in Sri Lanka which killed thousands of civilians tested the ability of UN Security Council to take collective measures or send peacekeepers. However, the 2009 massacre of Sri Lankan Tamils could not push Security Council to action and it remained silent due to the differing opinions of China and Russia on the one hand and the U.S., UK, and France on the other. Sri Lanka is an important ally of China and Russia, and it is believed in the last phase of Sri Lankan Civil War in 2009 that many Sri Lankan Tamils were killed by the Sri Lankan army and the forces of LTTE. China and Russia managed well to keep that issue and an inquiry or a possible resolution on the crimes of the Sri Lankan army off the agenda of the Security Council (Okhovat 2011). A search through press statements and meeting records of the Council shows that issue was not adequately discussed in the Council, and apart from issuing a press statement about the situation of Sri Lanka in May 2009, the UNSC did not take any other actions (Okhovat 2011). In a press statement issued on 13 May 2009, the members of the Security Council expressed 'grave concern over the worsening humanitarian crisis' in Sri Lanka and called for 'urgent action by all parties to ensure the safety of civilians'. The members condemned Sri Lankan army's use of heavy calibre weapons in the areas with high population of civilians and asked the government to fulfil its commitment in that regard. Although the content of this press statement might sound powerful, it was the only action that the Council took. This inactivity of the Council is more unacceptable if the scale of that massacre is taken into consideration (UN Report 2011).

5 Conclusion

The Security Council of the UN has been vested with executive powers to maintain international peace and security. For South Asian region, the Security Council has proved to be a useful institution to resolve the bilateral disputes. In view of regional regard for the Charter of the UN, the South Asian nations have contributed significantly in UN peacekeeping operations all over the world by providing well-equipped troops at the disposal of UN. The conflicts occurring in the region have the potential to extinguish whole human civilization as the nations of the region possess nuclear capability. However, all the conflicts have been resolved, either bilaterally or with the help of UN and the threat to peace or the actual breach of peace has been averted.

Nevertheless, there are areas of concern for South Asians vis-à-vis Security Council. First, the contributing nations for peacekeeping should be given greater role in policy making and in decision making. Second, the Security Council has remained symbolic of an institution representing twenty-first century international relations as it has not expanded its permanent membership and has used the power of veto to suit its immediate needs. Third, the Security Council has not acted uniformly in different disputes among South Asians. There is a need to follow a uniform set of rules in future to intervene in the territory of others. These challenges before the Security Council need to be addressed on a priority basis to revive the trust of newly independent nations in it.

References

Acheson (1950) UN General Assembly 5th Session Plenary 279 (A/PV.279)

'Assessment of Member States' Advances to the Working Capital Fund for the Biennium 2016–17 and Contributions to the United Nations Regular Budget for 2016. Available at http://goo.gl.4N4IVo

'Assessment of Member States' Contributions to the United Nations Regular Budget for the Year 2015 UN Secretariat, December 29, 2014. Available at http://goo.gl/TORImJ

Banerjee D (2013) India. In: Bellamy AI, Williams PD (eds) Providing peacekeepers. Oxford University Press, Oxford

Blum YZ (2005) Proposals for UN security council reform. Am J Int Law 99:632

Bowett DW (1964) United Nations forces. London, pp 183 and 233–236

Byers M (2002) Terrorism, the use of force and international law after 11 September. Int Comp Law Q 51:401–414

Chaudhury DR (2012) India changes tack to secure UN Security Council Seat, Global policy forum. Available at http://goo.gl/FyKSnn

Choedon Y (2015) A setback for the prospect of UN Security Council reform! IDSA comments. Available at http://goo.gl/nuLa3u

Desai B (2016) To be armed with law. The Tribune Daily, 11 October 2016, p 9

Faridi MH (2014) India's role in the UN in the post cold war era. Thesis submitted to Aligarh Muslim University, India. Available at Shodhganga: A Reservoir of Indian Thesis. http://goo.gl/gMuszc

Fidler DP, Ganguly S (2010) India and Eastphalia. Ind J Glob Legal Stud 17:147

First Post (2016) New permanent members in reformed UN Security Council must get veto: India. Available at http://goo.gl/uiDFxf
General Assembly Resolution A/RES/63/308 (2009)
Harder A (2015) Not at the cost of China: new evidence regarding U.S. proposals to Nehru for joining the United Nations Security Council, Wilson Centre, USA. Available at http://goo.gl/P3ir6H
International Coalition for the Responsibility to Protect (2016) Crisis in Sri Lanka. Available at http://goo.gl/3JOXom
James A (1969) The politics of peace-keeping. London, pp 1–12
Kapoor SK (2001) International law & human rights, central law agency, 18th edn. pp 1001–1002
Khan EM (2014) The role of Pakistan towards international peace and stability. Hilal: The Pakistan Armed Forces' Magazine. Available at http://goo.gl./4RYhAO
Krishnasamy K (2007) 'Recognition' for third world peacekeepers: India and Pakistan. Int Peacekeeping 8:4
Kelly M (2000) UN Security Council Permanent Membership: a new proposal for a twenty-first century council. Steton Hall Law Rev 31:319–399
Kumar S (1992) Towards a stronger and more democratic UN: India's role, New Delhi. Int Stud 30(2):173–188
Lal N (1973) Peace-keeping functions of the United Nations: a study of India's contribution with reference to United Nations Emergency Force. Thesis Submitted to Jawaharlal Nehru University. Available at http://goo.gl/0TY9ut
Lowe V, Roberts A, Welsh J, Zaum D (eds) (2008) The United Nations Security Council and war: the evolution of thought and practice since 1945. Oxford University Press, London
Modi N (2014) P.M. at UN. Press Information Bureau, Government of India, 27 September 2014. Available at http://pib.nic.in/newsite/mbErel.aspx?relid=1100
Nathanson NL (1965) Constitutional crisis at the United Nations: the price of peace-keeping. Univ Chicago Law Rev (32)4. Available at http://goo.gl/ICTtyi
'Nepal Prime Minister Backs India's Bid for Permanent Security Council Seat'. The Hindu, IANS, September 27, 2014. Available at http://goo.gl/Y88L2z
Noorani AG (2014) The Kashmir dispute 1947–2012. Oxford University Press, Karachi
Okhovat S (2011) The United Nations Security Council: its veto power and its reform. CPACS Working Paper, University of Sydney. Available at http://goo.gl/VBtreS
Pubby M (2013) No Mujahidin, only soldiers in Kargil: Pak general. The Sunday Express, Delhi
Rabasa A, Blackwill RD et al (2009) The lessons of Mumbai. Available at http://goo.gl/p7s6le
Raja CKN, Murthy HRS (1986) United Nations and peace-keeping. In: Saxena JN, Singh G, Koul AK (eds) United Nations for a better world. Lancers Books, Delhi, pp 39–41
Reisman WM (1993) The constitutional crisis in the United Nations, Yale Law School Legal Scholarship Repository. Available at http://goo.gl/QI75yT
Reisman WM (1994) Amending the UN charter, symposium on reforming the United Nations. Am Soc Int Law Proc 88:105
Report of the UN Secretary-General's Panel of Experts on Accountability in Sri Lanka. Available at http://goo.gl/synrC
Schweitzer Y (2002) Suicide terrorism: development and main characteristics. In: International Policy Institute for Counter-Terrorism (ed) Countering suicide terrorism. New York, pp 77–88
Security Council Resolution 39 (1948a)
Security Council Resolution 47 (1948b)
Security Council Resolution 1368 (2001a)
Security Council Resolution 1373 (2001b)
Security Council Resolution 1674 (2006a)
Security Council Resolution 1706 (2006b)
Security Council Veto List, Dag Hammarskjold Library, UN. Available at http://goo.gl/zOzBQQ
Singh JN (1984) Use of force under international law. Harnam Publication, New Delhi, pp 92–93
Swart L, Pace C (2015) Changing the composition of the security council: is there a viable solution? Available at http://goo.gl/qRtVMi

Thaindian (2010) Bangladesh supports permanent membership in UN Security Council for India. Available at http://goo.gl/8KopF4
The Hindu (September 28, 2005) This day that age. Available at http://goo.gl/P3ir6H
Teng MK (2013) A critique of A G Noorani's 'Kashmir Dispute 1947-2012'. Available at http://goo.gl/ykJtzD
UN Doc. No. A/5729 (1964) Soviet Memorandum
UN Doc (1965a) No. A/AC.121/SR7
UN Doc (1965b) No. A/AC.121/SR6
UN General Assembly Resolution 48/26 (1993) Question of equitable representation on and increase in the membership of the Security Council. Available at http://goo.gl/kvhe90
UN Report (2011) Report of the secretary-general's panel of experts on accountability in Sri Lanka
U.S. Letter (October 8, 1964) by Permanent Representative to UN Addressed to Secretary General A/5739
White ND (1996) The UN charter and peacekeeping forces: constitutional issues. Int Peacekeeping 3:4
Whiteman MM, Hackworth GH (1963) Digest of international law, vol 2. U.S. Department of State, Washington
Whittaker DJ (2002) Terrorism: understanding the global threat. Routledge, London

Author Biographies

Dr. Anupam Jha is Assistant Professor (Senior) at the Faculty of Law, University of Delhi. He has been engaged in teaching and research for more than 14 years. He is recipient of several prestigious fellowships and nominations, such as Raman Fellowship (U.S.A.), Commonwealth Fellowship (U.K.), UGC-TEC Nomination (Mauritius). He has also been awarded the most active participant from India by UNHCR. His current areas of teaching and research are: public international law, international environmental law, international trade law, and jurisprudence. His latest publications include the following: "The Law on Trafficking in Persons: The Quest For an Effective Model", First Published Online in ***Asian Journal of International Law (Cambridge University Press)***, 27 October 2016, ISSN No. 2044-2521 (online).

Ms. Ujjwala Sakhalkar is Assistant Professor, New Law College Pune and is pursuing her Ph.D from Bharati Vidyapeeth Deemed University, Pune. She has several articles, books and Distance learning material published to her credit. She is receipient of several Scholarships, grants and financial assistance by foreign universities to attend summer courses and training programmes. Her areas of research and interests include issues relating to human rights, International Law, international relations and access to justice. She has organized and participated in several international and national conferences/workshops/training programmes.

Mr. Brijesh Kumar Singh is a doctoral candidate in the Faculty of Law, University of Delhi. He also obtained his LL.M. degree from Faculty of Law and LL.B. from Campus Law Centre, University of Delhi. He was awarded Junior and Senior Research Fellowship by the University Grants Commission, New Delhi to pursue his doctoral research.

Chapter 3
Socio-Economic Rights in South Asia

Uday Shankar

1 Introduction

Socio-economic rights are founded on human dignity as civil and political rights. The cause of human dignity legitimizes constitutionalization of rights in foundational document of every country across the world. Rights are embedded in Constitution to limit the power of the Government and to confer primacy to dignity over other interests. Rights stemming out of value of dignity are divided into categories based on the obligation of state. Rights warrant immediate obligation of the state identified as civil and political rights whereas progressive realization of rights acknowledged as socio-economic rights. Constitutionalization across the world has seen asymmetrical arrangement of these rights. Former set of rights is ingrained as 'claimable interest' whereas the latter set of rights is embedded as 'aspirational values'. The distinct characteristic of the former has been judicial enforceable feature in contrast with the latter requires adequate policy formulation or enactment of law and non-enforceable in the Court of law.

In socio-economic rights, the elements of well-being such as access to food, cloth, water, housing, healthcare and education, a level of minimum income are recognized as inalienable entitlement. These entitlements are to be conferred the same character and status as the civil and political rights. Socio-economic rights have struggled for recognition and realization as human rights in the modern world. The current constitutional or legal position of the social rights in different parts of the world is also connected with the political and economic history of societies in those parts (Singh 2007a, b, p. 1). With the constitutionalization of socio-economic rights, the doubtful status of right to these groups of claims has been adequately addressed.

U. Shankar (✉)
Rajiv Gandhi School of Intellectual Property Law,
Indian Institute of Technology, Kharagpur 721302, India
e-mail: uday@rgsoipl.iitkgp.ernet.in

J.L. Kaul and A. Jha (eds.), *Shifting Horizons of Public International Law*,
https://doi.org/10.1007/978-81-322-3724-2_3

Contemporary human rights jurisprudence suggests parity between the two groups of rights and describes them as 'universal, indivisible and interdependent and interrelated'. Despite this progress in the landscape of human rights, there remains deep and often debilitating disagreement over the proper status of socio-economic rights and the nature of States' obligations towards their fulfilment.

The study on position of socio-economic rights in the Constitutions of South Asian countries would unfold the emerging debate on the constitutionalization of the rights and their enforcement. In this part of the globe, the oldest entry in the league of written Constitution is middle of the last century and the youngest entrant is September 2015. The structuring of the socio-economic rights in every country of the region reflects similarity in enforcement mechanism. This chapter, therefore, concludes with the observation that closer interaction between realization process, either through judicial process or legislative process, should be adopted in these countries which would go a long way in translating 'aspirations' into 'rights'.

2 Implementation Mechanism of Social and Economic Rights in International Arena

Human rights, traditionally, a subject matter of domestic concern and application, have been acquiring importance in the international field. Human rights have to be implemented first and foremost at national levels. The primary responsibility of States to realize human rights is towards the persons who live under the jurisdiction of these States. The compliance mechanism at the regional and international arena is not a substitute to the mechanism available to enforce the rights in the domestic jurisdictions. The international and regional implementation mechanisms are no substitute for national ways and means for implementing human rights, and they do have an important subsidiary role to play. Human rights are foundational theme of regional and international agreement or treaties. The world has witnessed formulation of human rights instruments, in addition to international instruments, to protect and promote human dignity of individual. The Universal Declaration of Human Rights ('UDHR') along with its two international Covenants can be said to be the originating source of other regional agreement on human rights. International Covenants provide for elaborative mechanisms of evaluating the performance of members States towards the rights incorporated in the Covenants. The compliance procedures vary from 'complaint' to 'reporting' mechanism under the framework of the Covenants. Generally, the 'complaint' method is associated with civil and political rights and 'reporting' method is with social and economic rights. In this section, the author, purposefully, deals with the implementation framework available under the International Labour Organization ('ILO') and ICESCR as they primarily deal with socio-economic rights.

2.1 International Labour Organization

A pioneering role in devising mechanism to control human rights obligation was laid down in the ILO, much before the acceptance of UDHR and other regional agreement. The ILO provides for two types of procedures: one entailing the obligation of States to report periodically on the application of international labour conventions and the other envisaging the examination by inquiry commissions of complaints submitted by a state or by the governing body of the ILO. In the first procedure, States, which are parties to international labour conventions, are under an obligation to report periodically on the application of the international standards they have accepted. Reports are prepared and supplied by the governments, but national organizations of employers and workers are entitled to make written observations which together with the reports of the governments are examined by the Committee of Experts on the Applications of Conventions and Recommendations. In the second method, any member state may file a complaint against another member state concerning the non-observance of a convention ratified by both. Also the governing body of the ILO, either on its own initiative or upon receipt of a complaint from a delegate to the International Labour Conference, may initiate this procedure.

2.2 International Covenant on Economic, Social and Cultural Rights

Articles 16 and 17 of the ICESCR require that the State Parties shall submit reports, at intervals to be defined by ECOSOC, on the measures they have adopted and the progress made in achieving observance of the rights in the Covenant. The reports are to be sent to the UN Secretary General who is required to transmit them to ECOSOC for consideration. ECOSOC may, in turn, transmit the state reports to the Commission on Human Rights for study and general recommendations or for information. It may invite the UN specialized agencies to report to it on the progress made in achieving observance of the rights. Finally, ECOSOC may from time to time submit reports and recommendations of a general nature to the General Assembly and may bring to the attention of other UN organs and specialized agencies any matters that may assist such bodies in deciding on the advisability of international measures likely to contribute to the effective progressive implementation of the Covenant.

The mentioned procedure failed to invite the desired attention in the implementation of social and economic rights. It is apparent that the system envisaged in Part IV of the CESCR does not clearly identify which body has central responsibility for supervision, nor does it stipulate the precise content of the reports to be submitted by State Parties or the nature of the scrutiny to be undertaken by the UN bodies mentioned.

Since 1987, the consideration of the reports has been entrusted to the Committee on Economic, Social and Cultural Rights, established by the UN Economic and Social Council. Now, the principal instrument for the protection of economic, social and cultural rights within the UN human rights system is the CESCR. The international monitoring of the CESCR rests completely on a reporting procedure, established by Article 16 of the Covenant. Previously, a nine-year reporting cycle of separate reports at three-year intervals on three categories of the CESCR provisions was applied, but the periodicity of State Party reports has been changed to comprehensive periodic reports every 5 years.

In practice, the reporting procedure under CESCR is based on dialogue between the State Party and the Committee on Economic, Social and Cultural Rights. This is achieved through a list of questions prepared by Committee members, on the basis of written report and public hearings, for discussion between the Committee and a Government delegation. The discussion between the Committee and the State Party is called as 'constructive dialogue'.

Following the oral hearing, the Committee on Economic, Social and Cultural Rights adopts its concluding observations in relation to a specific report. In addition to the country-specific observations, the Committee also uses general comments and general discussions reaching a better understanding of the contents of the treaty obligations.

In the Committee, NGOs are allowed to submit written statements and to participate in the day of general discussion. In May 1993, the Committee adopted a new procedure in relation to NGO participation in its work. NGOs now have certain possibilities to make not only written, but also oral presentations before the Committee.

The reporting system primarily depends upon the cooperation of the State Parties not only in terms of submission of the report but also in participation in constructive dialogue. However, the Committee has graduated its role from review committee to the supervisory committee. It has been adopting innovative method of sending fact-finding team to the State Party or seeking report from the State Party on the information received by NGOs. Hence, the Committee is performing quasi-judicial function in order to ensure compliance of the Covenant. The Committee has been doing remarkable work in the form of producing general comments, in which it attempts to outline its understanding of both substantive and procedural aspects of the Covenant. General comments are not merely providing tool for evaluation but also assisting States in the promotion and implementation of the rights. Thus far, it also helps in developing the normative content of individual right of the Covenant.

The effort of the Committee to have similar enforcement mechanism as available for civil and political rights under ICCPR bore fruit with adoption of Optional Protocol in the year 2008. The requisite number of ratification has brought the Protocol into force on 5 May 2013. It provides, inter alia, receipt of both individual and group communications, adoption of interim measures of protection and specific recommendation to the State Party to take specific measures to remedy the violation and prevent its recurrence. A long-standing demand of civil society has been met, and it is a vital addition to the international human rights protection system that is rooted in the UDHR, 1948. In the words of the UN High Commissioner for Human Rights, the Optional Protocol closed 'a historic gap in human rights protection under the international system'.

3 India's Position

The genesis of the vision, need, recognition, protection and enforcement of human rights which lies in the freedom struggle of Indians for more than a century culminated in the form of Fundamental Rights and Directive Principles of State Policy on which the mammoth structure of Indian Republic stands today (Dadwal 2003, p. 225). Conceived during the time of framing of Universal Declaration of Human Rights, the Indian Constitution indicates the effect of international development on its product. Though the Indian Constitution is not adoption of International Bill of Rights in *toto*, it reflects the incorporation of dichotomy in the form of implementation procedure. On the one hand, Fundamental Rights guaranteed enforceable rights to individual against the state, but on the other hand, Directive Principles obligate state machineries to legislate or to formulate policies and programme in order to fulfil social and economic rights of individual. Fundamental Rights are rights guaranteed to individual as an individual whereas Directive Principles guarantee right to individual as a member of society.

The Karachi Resolution of Indian National Congress on Fundamental Rights and Duties is said to have played 'a vital share in shaping India's future Constitution, and the provisions did in fact become the spiritual and in some cases the direct antecedents of the Directive Principles of State Policy (Austin 1966, p. 56)'. It did not draw any difference between the positive or the social rights on the one hand and the negative or civil and political rights on the other. It is only in 1945 that the Sapru Committee Report classified the rights into justiciable and non-justiciable rights which was later maintained by the Fundamental Rights Committee of the Constituent Assembly and finally led to the division between the Fundamental Rights (FRs) and the Directive Principles of State Policy (DPs) in the Constitution making the latter non-justiciable (Shiva Rao 1967, p. 294). Rights guaranteeing individual freedom have been made justiciable whereas rights ensuring freedom worth enjoying have been made non-enforceable due to administrative and practical difficulties in enforcing the latter.

3.1 Socio-Economic Rights in the Constitution of India

Though traditionally the Directive Principles of State Policy enlisted in the Part IV of the Constitution elaborate socio-economic rights, such enlisting defies the categorization of rights into two parts because some of the socio-economic rights are placed in the chapter of Fundamental Rights such as the right to form association and unions, the right to carry on any occupation, trade or business, the right to education and cultural and educational rights. Hence, it can be conveniently asserted that the allocation of rights under Part III and Part IV of the Indian Constitution has not been based upon internationally designed categorization of rights prescribed under two Covenants on Civil and Political, and Social, Economic and Cultural Rights. Fundamental Rights under Part III of the Constitution include primarily civil and political rights. And, individual enjoys right to move the Court to enforce these rights. Besides these rights, which may be found in any Constitution, it also provides for special rights in the context of Indian society such as prohibition of discrimination on grounds of race, religion, caste, sex, place of birth, etc., which were traditionally used or were capable of use for discrimination; abolition of untouchability—an evil practiced in Indian society; provision for special arrangements for women, children, SCs, STs and backward classes; subjection of religious freedom of Hindus to open entry to its religious places to all sections of Hindus. Some provisions expressly, but quite a few impliedly, have horizontal application and bind private citizens as much as they bind the state (Singh 2007a, b, p. 181).

Part IV of the Constitution encompasses wide range of directives, including socio-economic rights. It is interesting to note that all social and economic rights are not clothed in the language of ‘rights’ in the Constitution. They are formulated in the form of guidelines or objectives to be followed by the state. It is required to chart out the rights which are coloured as rights by the framers of the Constitution. Article 39(a) States that ‘the citizens, men and women, equally have the right to adequate means of livelihood’. Article 41 provides ‘The State shall, within the limits of its economic capacity and development, make effective provision for securing the right to work, to education and to public assistance in cases of unemployment, old age, sickness and disablement, and in other cases of undeserved want’. The only provision in the Part IV referred to implementation of rights subject to the economic development of the State. The realization of rights to work, education and social security has been qualified to the economic condition.

Apart from these rights, other social and economic rights are imposed as duty upon the state to give effect to them. Rights such as equal pay for equal work, protection from exploitation of youth and children, just and humane conditions of work, conditions of work ensuring decent standard of life and full enjoyment of leisure, free and compulsory primary education, and raising level of nutrition and the standard of living and the improvement of public health are not framed in the language of rights. Mere non-assertion of such essentials of life in the language of rights does not dilute their significance and importance. It is pertinent to note that Article 47 which speaks about ‘raising of the level of nutrition and the standard of living… and improvement of public health’ is formulated in the nature of duties for the State. The duty corresponds to rights of an individual. It is a guaranteed right of every individual to expect reasonable efforts from the Government in order to protect and promote rights.

3.2 Enforcement of Socio-Economic Rights in India

The Constitution of India categorizes civil and political rights and socio-economic rights on the ground of justiciability. Article 37 of the Constitution advises the Court of law to not to enforce the Directives, including socio-economic rights, and made them fundamental in governance of the country. However, the Supreme Court carved out a role for itself in the matter of socio-economic rights by introducing integrated approach between 'right to life' under Article 21 and socio-economic rights in the Part IV of the Constitution.

In the first two decades after independence, the Supreme Court adopted a conservative approach by treating Directive Principles inferior to the judicially enforceable Fundamental Rights (*Champakam Case* 1951). The reluctance of the apex Court to grant equal status to socio-economic rights as Fundamental Rights got diluted with the assertion made by a Bench of 13, the Court said that '…what was fundamental in the governance of the country could be no less significant than that which was fundamental in the life of an individual and therefore Fundamental Rights and DPSP were complementary (*Kesavananda Case* 1973)'. Justice Krishna Iyer has eloquently described the jurisprudential development of integrated reading of Fundamental Rights and Directive Principles by observing that '*Kesavananda Bharati* has clinched the issue of primacy as between Part III and Part IV of the Constitution. The unanimous ruling there is that the Court must wisely read the collective Directive Principles of State Policy mentioned in Part IV into individual Fundamental Rights of Part III, neither Part being superior to the other! Since the days of *Dorairajan*, judicial opinion has hesitatingly tilted in favour of Part III, but in *Kesavananda Bharati*, the supplementary theory, treating both parts as fundamental, gained supremacy (*Thomas Case* 1976)'. Justice Bhagwati observed that 'it is not possible to fit Fundamental Rights and Directive Principles into distinct and defined categories, but the reality is that Fundamental Rights represent civil and political rights while Directive Principles embody social and economic rights. Both are clearly part of the broad spectrum of human rights… It is, therefore, not correct to say that the Fundamental Rights alone are based on human rights while Directive Principles fall in some categories other than human rights. The socio-economic rights embodied in the Directive Principles are as much a part of human rights as the Fundamental Rights (*Minerva Mills Case* 1980)'.

The Indian judiciary has been playing constructive role in infusing dynamic content to Fundamental Rights with the help of social and economic charter enumerated in the Part IV of the Constitution. The non-justiciable character of Directive Principles could not refrain the judiciary for a very long time to employ social and economic values for ensuring dignified existence to individuals. The Court aptly started drawing support from the 'directives' to regulate the state action towards Fundamental Rights. The responsibility of state towards the realization of rights got impetus with integral approach between Fundamental Rights and Directive Principles. Since the early 1980s, India's Supreme Court has progressively interpreted the basic socio-economic needs of relatively disempowered groups as integral to the fundamental 'right to life' under Article 21 of the Constitution (Ruparelia 2012).

It has clearly made considerable advances in the realm of social and economic rights, despite the fact that the Indian Constitution incorporates them solely as 'Directive Principles' rather than as explicitly enforceable rights in Courts of law. 'This represents a compromise approach to enforceability that can be taken by State, behind which lies the implication that "justiciability" is a fluid notion, and that legal enforcement is not the only way human rights standards can be set and attained' (Wiles 2006, p. 58). The judicial pronouncements compel the policy and law-makers to attend the cause of socio-economic rights (Muralidhar 2004, p. 31). The judicial contribution to the synthesis and to the integration of the Fundamental Rights and the Directive Principles has been immense. The Indian judiciary has been helping millions of deprived and denied, in realizing their dreams through public interest litigations. On the other hand, the intervention by the Court on wide range of issues involving socio-economic rights has generated a debate about the competence and legitimacy of the judiciary in entering areas which have for long been perceived as belonging properly within the domain of the other organs of the State.

The absence of power to enforce social and economic rights is not to offend the prime role of protector and guardian of the Constitution. The realization of the Directive Principles, including social and economic rights, involves factors of budget, human resources, infrastructure and the like. It is arising out of this fact that the nature of rights enlisted in the Directive Principles requires different mechanisms and institutions for their enforcement. The judiciary has been kept away to arbiter on the matters where the state seeks to formulate policies for the society as a whole in respect of social and economic matters (Shankar and Tyagi 2009).

3.3 Submission Under ICESCR

India ratified the Covenant in the year 1979. The Government has not been very punctual in submission of reports as mandated under the Covenant. It has submitted five reports in two different phases. The latest submission is a combination of second, third, fourth and fifth periodic reports made in the year 2006. The Committee acknowledges the steps undertaken by the Government in the form of legislative and policy formulations for effective implementation of socio-economic rights. However, it rued about the approach of progressive nature of the realization of the rights. Though the apex Court has made remarkable progress in reducing the gap between the two sets of rights, the Committee expressed displeasure about non-committal attitude of the Government towards orders of the Court. The Committee has voiced the concern about the absence of effective mechanisms to coordinate and ensure, at both the federal and state levels, administrative and policy measures relating to economic, social and cultural rights, which constitutes a major impediment to the equal and effective implementation of the Covenant.

3.4 National Human Rights Commission, India

The National Human Rights Commission (NHRC) is anchored in the Protection of Human Rights Act, 1993. The Commission's mandate extends to protecting four categories of human rights: the rights to life, liberty, equality and dignity that are guaranteed by the Constitution or embodied in the International Covenants and which are enforceable by the Courts in India. This mandate takes away the cause of social and economic rights from the realm of National Human Rights Commission. The powers and functions of the NHRC speak about its role in inquiring, inter alia, violation or abetment of human rights, negligence by public officer to prevent such violation of human rights. The Commission can review and recommend changes in legislation concerning safeguarding of human rights. It can involve in research and promotion of human rights. The Commission is empowered to recommend to the Government the grant of 'immediate interim relief' to the victim or the members of her family. The Commission has been regularly passing direction to pay compensation to the victim or her family members. Until now, the record of complying with the order of the Commission is remarkable. The NHRC has been earning respect as competent institution to protect and promote human rights. However, performance assessments indicate that the Commission has been addressing violation of civil and political rights, custodial violence or police atrocities in particular. Though, it has been vehemently debated on the need to expand the role of the National Human Rights Commission for better compliance of social and economic rights.

4 Bhutan's Position

Bhutan, however little known to the outside world, is an ancient country that has remained independent throughout its history, and this determination for sovereignty is so strong that until 1958 the country deliberately followed a policy of isolation as a means to protect independence. Bhutan is a landlocked, least developed country situated in the Eastern Himalayas. It is bordered on the east, south and west by India and on the north by China. Bhutan was unified under one rule in the seventeenth century by Zhabdrung Ngawang Namgyel (first theocratic ruler of Bhutan), who promulgated the dual system of governance whereby authority was shared between a secular and a religious leader. In 1907, Bhutan became a monarchy with the election of Ugyen Wangchuck as the first hereditary King of Bhutan. Bhutan made a peaceful transition to a democratic constitutional monarchy in 2008.

In 2008, after many centuries of theocratic rule and a century of monarchy, Bhutan peacefully transited to a parliamentary democratic system of Government. Parliamentary elections were held in 2007 and 2008, and an elected Government was installed in April 2008. For the first time in its history, Bhutan adopted a written Constitution on 18 July 2009 which established a democratic constitutional monarchy.

4.1 Socio-Economic Rights in the Constitution of Bhutan

The Constitution of the Kingdom of Bhutan was adopted by the first session of the first Parliament on 18 July 2008. With this, Bhutan formally became a democratic constitutional monarchy. The Constitution of Bhutan has 35 Articles with several unique features. These include the retirement age of the King (65 years) and requiring the Government to maintain a minimum of 60% of total land area under forest cover at all times. The process began in the year 2001 and got culminated in the year 2008. Socio-economic rights are scripted under Principles of State Policy.

On traditional lines of differentiating between Fundamental Rights and the Policy, Article 7 provides for 23 Subclauses enlisting different rights and Article 9 provides 24 Subclauses enlisting the Principles of State Policy. The Constitution also has elaborative list, eleven in number, of fundamental duties. Civil and political rights are scripted in the chapter of Fundamental Rights. Interestingly, the right to equal pay for work of equal value is included under the heading of the Rights. Along with general guidelines, the Principles encapsulate different socio-economic rights.

The Principles of State Policy impose an obligation on the State to undertake necessary measures which relates with the accomplishment of socio-economic entitlements viz. to ensure a good quality of life, to protect human rights and dignity, to develop and execute policies to minimize inequalities of income and concentration of wealth, to promote equitable distribution of public facilities among individuals and people living in different parts of the Kingdom, to secure an adequate livelihood, right to work, vocational guidance and training and just and favourable conditions of work, to ensure the right to rest and leisure, including reasonable limitation of working hours and periodic holidays with pay, to ensure the right to fair and reasonable remuneration for one's work, to provide education for the purpose of improving and increasing knowledge, values and skills of the entire population with education being directed towards the full development of the human personality, free education to all children of school going age up to tenth standard and ensure that technical and professional education is made generally available and that higher education is equally accessible to all on the basis of merit, to provide free access to basic public health services in both modern and traditional medicines, to provide security in the event of sickness and disability or lack of adequate means of livelihood for reasons beyond one's control and encourage free participation in the cultural life of the community, to promote arts and sciences and to foster technological innovation.

4.2 Enforcement of Socio-Economic Rights in Bhutan

Section 23 of Article 7 says that all persons in Bhutan shall have the right to initiate appropriate proceedings in the Supreme Court or High Court for the enforcement of the rights conferred by this Article, subject to Section 22 of this Article and procedures prescribed by law. Article 21(10) empowers the Supreme Court and High Court to issue such declarations, orders, directions or writs as may be appropriate in the circumstances of each case. All the persons, i.e., citizens and persons staying in Bhutan, shall have the right to move the Supreme Court and the High Court for the enforcement of Fundamental Rights. The Constitution is silent about the enforceability of the Principles enunciated in the Constitution. The use of the word 'endeavour' in various sections of Article 9 indicates that the State shall undertake necessary measures for the fulfilment of the Principles and they are not to be brought before the Court for enforcement. Article 21(18) confers right in favour of every person to approach the Courts in matters arising out of the Constitution or other laws subject to Section 23 of Article 7. Liberal reading of this section allows the Supreme Court or High Court to examine the legislative or executive approach of the State towards socio-economic rights laid down in the Principles. The Court may also issue necessary directions to the State in the cases of unreasonable approach of the legislature or the executive in fulfilment of socio-economic rights by invoking Section 10 of Article 21.

Article 9(20) commands the State to create a condition to establish good and compassionate society which is inherently associated with the realization of socio-economic rights and the Court may review action or omission of the other two branches of the State that whether it is attaining the goal laid down in the Principles or not. Moreover, the principles of human rights are embodied in the four pillars of Gross National Happiness (GNH). On the economic front, the first pillar aspires towards sustainable and equitable socio-economic development and ensures that the present development does not compromise the right to development of future generations. Secondly, it ensures that socio-economic development is sustainable and that every person in the country benefits from development activities.

The second pillar is a commitment to the preservation and promotion of cultural and spiritual heritage of the people. This reflects the protection of cultural rights and the non-discriminatory approach of the country. The conservation of the environment as the third pillar reflects the state's commitment beyond the economic realm of development. Good governance as the final pillar gives responsibility to the state in acting as an efficient, transparent and ethical dispenser of public services. This also requires accountability on the part of political leaders and demands transparency in all Government and political institutions. The people, of course, now hold the power of the ballot to decide how each Government is living up to the high standards built into the GNH.

4.3 Submission Under ICESCR

Bhutan has not yet signed and ratified the Covenant.

4.4 Human Rights Committee, Bhutan

Bhutan has not established Human Rights Commission. However, the National Assembly has constituted a Human Rights Committee, which is one among the 10 standing committees constituted by the Assembly. In the year 2008, the Assembly has passed an Act to govern different committees. The Human Rights Committee may have members ranging from five to eleven. The Terms of Reference (TORs) of the Committee shall be (a) review and recommend amendments of the existing laws and policies relating to Human Rights and also propose new legislations; (b) the Committee may consider any questions falling within its TORs and its competence, whether they are submitted by the Government or proposed by one of its members, either of their own volition or on behalf of an aggrieved party; and (c) the Committee shall as and when directed by the House visit the prison cells/detention/lock-up to check any incidences of Human Rights violations and gather information from the victims. The Committee presents its report before the National Assembly. The perusal of the report indicates that the Committee suggests necessary measures in relation to employment and education of youth.

5 Sri Lanka's Position

The present Constitution of Sri Lanka has been adopted in the year 1978 which embraces democratic, socialist and republic values. The First Constitution, the Soulbury Constitution of 1947, held sway till 1972 and largely portrayed the features of a Westminster model of Government. The 1972 First Republican Constitution was considered the first Sri Lankan Constitution, as it severed the tie between the Crown and Sri Lanka. The foundation for the 1978 Constitution under which Sri Lanka is presently governed sprang from then Prime Minister J.R. Jayewardene's resurgent belief that the answer to an effective system of governance does not lie in a Westminster model but in the establishment of an executive presidency. The Constitution charts out a separate chapter on Directive Principles on State Policy and Fundamental Duties, in the Chapter VI, along with a dedicated chapter on Fundamental Rights.

5.1 Socio-Economic Rights in the Constitution of Sri Lanka

Socio-economic rights are generally placed under the chapter of Directive Principles of State Policy which should guide the functionaries of the State, Parliament, President and Cabinet Ministers while enacting laws under Article 27 (1). Article 27(2)(c) & (h) imposes an obligation on the functionaries to undertake necessary steps for the realization of an adequate standard of living for themselves and their families, including adequate food, clothing and housing, the continuous improvement of living conditions and the full enjoyment of leisure and social and cultural opportunities and the complete eradication of illiteracy and the assurance to all persons of the right to universal and equal access to education at all levels respectively. The Constitution of Sri Lanka does not recognize the right to health. Neither is there any reference to the right to health in the Directive Principles of State Policy. However, Article 27(2)(c) of the Directive Principles acknowledges the State's commitment to environmental health which includes 'the continuous improvement of living conditions' which may be regarded as an aspect of the broader concept of the right to health. Article 27(9) mandates the State to ensure social security and welfare of citizen. Article 29 States that the Directives are not in the nature of legal rights and also are made non-enforceable in the Court of law or tribunal. Article 17 of the Constitution distinguishes between civil and political rights, enumerated in the chapter on Fundamental Rights, and socio-economic rights, enlisted in the chapter on the Directives, by making former enforceable in the Court of law whereas the latter has been made non-enforceable. Various welfare goals indicated in the Chapter VI could facilitate the enjoyment of socio-economic rights.

5.2 Enforcement of Socio-Economic Rights in Sri Lanka

Article 17 of the Constitution entitles every person to apply to the Supreme Court for alleged violation or imminent infringement of the rights conferred under the heading of Fundamental Rights. Article 126 distinguishes the mechanism of enforcement of Fundamental Rights enumerated in the Chapter III from rights provided under Chapter VI, Directive Principles of State Policy and Fundamental Duties. Hence, the legislature's duty to incorporate the DPSP into the laws that are enacted is by no way removed by the Constitution. However, the question of justiciability is later addressed in Article 29 of the Constitution. The Article declares 'The provisions of this Chapter do not confer or impose legal rights or obligations, and are not enforceable in any Court or tribunal. No question of inconsistency with such provisions shall be raised in any Court or tribunal'. Article 125 empowers the higher judiciary to interpret the Constitution and to safeguard the implementation of its provisions. Thus, no case purely alleging a violation of any directive principle may be presented to the Courts for adjudication. Article 27 can be construed to mean that the legislature and the executive are formally expected to have regard to, and formulate, the laws in accordance with the Directive. The word 'shall' used in Article 27 plays an important function according to the theories of statutory interpretation as it adds the sense that it is a must for the legislature and the executive to integrate the Directive in the legislative enactments. Thus, even though the Directive may not be enforced by a Court of law or tribunal as of right, it is possible to state that an individual can raise the argument that the legislature or the executive has disregarded the provisions of Directive when formulating a particular legislative enactment. Articles 27(2)(d) & (e) suggest the way for the realization of socio-economic need by guiding the machineries of the State to ensure 'the rapid development of the whole country by means of public and private economic activity' and 'the equitable distribution among all citizens of the material resources of the community and the social product, so as best to subserve the common good'. While interpreting laws, the Court may give effect to socio-economic entitlements provided under the Chapter VI through 'non-discrimination' clause or by examining 'reasonableness' of the policies of the Government in furtherance of the Directive.

5.3 Submission Under ICESCR

Sri Lanka has ratified ICESCR in the year 1980. The Government of Sri Lanka delays the submission of the periodical report. It has submitted five reports; the latest one is in the year 2015. The Government in its five reports submitted in detail the effort undertaken for the implementation of socio-economic rights. For the first report, the Committee has empathized with the Government on difficulty to focus on the realization of the rights due to civil conflict prevailing in the country in the year 1998. The combined second to fourth report invited criticism from the Committee on the commitment of the Government towards these rights. The Committee expressed displeasure about the non-responsive attitude of the Government towards certain issues raised by the Committee.

5.4 National Human Rights Commission, Sri Lanka

The Human Rights Commission of Sri Lanka is a statutory body, which came into existence in 1996. The Commission comprises of five members from among persons 'having knowledge of or experience in matters relating to human rights' with one member nominated as chairman. The Commission commits to the vision of human rights for all and promotes and protects the rule of law. The Commission is empowered to investigate violation of Fundamental Rights and to resolute through conciliation or mediation. The Commission may advise the machineries of the Government to formulate guidelines and suggest for legislative framework required for the cause of Fundamental Rights. As the functions of the Commission confine only to matters relating to Fundamental Rights, socio-economic rights enshrined in the non-enforceable 'Directives' remain outside the realm of the Commission.

6 Nepal's Position

Nepal has abandoned monarchical system and started journey towards constitutional democracy with enactment of the Constitution in the month of September 2015. Nepal has witnessed transition from monarch to democracy through different phases of constitutional development. In 2007, the Interim Constitution of Nepal was adopted, replacing the 1990 Constitution of the Kingdom of Nepal. It created an interim Legislature Parliament, a transitional Government reflecting the goals of the 2006 People's Movement—the mandate of which was for peace, change, stability, establishment of the competitive multiparty democratic system of governance, rule of law, promotion and protection of human rights, full press freedom and independence of judiciary based on democratic values and norms.

6.1 Socio-Economic Rights in the Constitution of Nepal

Socio-economic rights in the Constitution of Nepal have been transformed from aspirational values to justiciable rights within less than two decades. Enumerated as the policy guidelines for the Government in the 1990 Constitution, socio-economic entitlements are converted into judicially enforceable rights in the 2007 Interim Constitution. In September 2015, the Constituent Assembly finalized a new progressive Constitution and continued the legacy of the Interim Constitution in the matter of socio-economic rights. Needless to mention that the Nepalese Constitution has become the youngest Constitution in the world which has strengthened the position of socio-economic rights by according the same status with civil and political rights.

The 2007 Interim Constitution has set up a very bold framework of enforceable rights that incorporates many socio-economic rights. Part III of the Constitution houses wide range of second-generation rights along with first-generation rights. The rights relating autonomy and well-being under the same chapter fortify integrated and interdependent nature of two generation of rights. The new Constitution establishes edifice of rights on the entrenched value of human dignity. Though the fundamental governing document provides for the Directive Principles of State Policy, it encapsulates socio-economic rights along with civil and political rights under Part 3, Fundamental Rights and Duties, of the Constitution. The very first right under this part guarantees right to live with dignity which reflects the commitment of the makers of the Constitution to ensure decent and worthy life to every individual.

Standing up to the expectation of the Constitution of twenty-first century, individuals are guaranteed clean environment with a right to get compensated by pollutant. Right to education up to secondary level has been assured to every citizen, and financially poor physically impaired citizen shall demand higher education under the new Constitution. Citizens are also guaranteed right to employment including unemployed allowance to be determined by federal law. State is obligated towards basic health services and equal access to health services. Clean water and hygiene is also a fundamental right. Right to food has been broadly recognized in different provisions viz. right to food for every citizen, right to be protected against food scarcity that may cause threat to life, every citizen has right to food sovereignty as provided by law and right to social justice—includes provision on food. Every citizen will have a right to shelter as determined by law. Social justice is accorded the status of right, and marginalized sections of the society enjoy constitutionally guaranteed inclusiveness. Interestingly, peasant has been given right to access to land. Social security to distress and deprived has been bestowed an eminence of right. Person as a consumer shall have a right to quality foodstuff and services. Individual enjoys right to get constitutional remedy in the cases of violation of rights. Part 3 elaborately and generously scripted many socio-economic rights as justiciable rights which are either institutionalized as aspirational values or recognized through innovative interpretative tool of the judiciary in many Constitutions of the world. By giving status of right to information, it will be encouraging to observe the employability of this right in complete realization of socio-economic rights. The makers of the Constitution decided, rightly so, on the time frame for the implementation of various socio-economic entitlements by commanding the State to make necessary legal provisions required within three years of the commencement of the Constitution. The implementation of socio-economic rights through legislative design also makes the case of same status of these rights doubtful. Therefore, the legislative enactment for the realization of these rights will be important for converting rhetoric into reality. Directive Principles, Policies and Responsibilities of State elaborately suggest determinative steps to be followed for making the country prosperous, inclusive and egalitarian.

6.2 *Enforcement of Socio-Economic Rights in Nepal*

The Constitution constitutes layered structure of judiciary with Supreme Court at the top, High Court at the mid-level and District Court at the bottom. There are enough provisions to make the judiciary independent and impartial in discharging the responsibilities entrusted by the Constitution. Along with appellate power, the Supreme Court and High Courts are entrusted with the responsibility to issue necessary directions for violation of rights guaranteed under the Constitution. Both these Courts are endowed with sweeping power to adequately address the infringement of the rights, including socio-economic rights. The existence of alternative remedy will not restrict the Supreme Court from passing suitable remedy in the cases of infringement of rights, if such remedy is found to be inadequate to redress the grievance of victim of right violation. The Court is allowed to be innovative in designing appropriate remedy, including prerogative writs, in the cases of infraction of constitutionally guaranteed rights. The framers of the Constitution reflected their visionary approach by entrusting the power to High Courts to enforce Fundamental Rights. High Courts have got a right to issue necessary and appropriate orders in the name of governments, office-bearers, institutions or individuals within its provincial jurisdiction. This provision makes individual as much responsible as the State would be for the realization of socio-economic rights.

Historically, the judiciary in Nepal has played an important role concerning the second-generation rights. The Court has instructed the executive and legislative bodies of the state to formulate laws and policies; constitute committees to study and report on these matters; and in appropriate cases, has issued orders on the basis of such reports and recommendations. The judiciary has been implementing a five-year strategic plan to strengthen stakeholder communication, improve access justice and public trust, and ensure the execution of judgments. Now with direct entrustment of power to enforce socio-economic rights, the higher judiciary in Nepal will prove to be a torchbearer for developing countries in the matter of judicial adjudication of these rights.

6.3 Submission Under ICESCR

The Government of Nepal (GoN) acceded to the ICESCR in 1991, submitted its initial report in 1998, 6 years later than it was due, and presented the second periodic report in 2006. Subsequent to the second periodic report, the Government of Nepal submitted the third periodic report to the CESCR on the measures taken to give the effect to the ICESCR in June 2011. The report outlines the progress made during the period since the second periodic report submitted in June 2006 and subsequently concluding observations made by the CESCR.

The second periodic report of the Government was submitted amidst historic changes in Nepal in June 2006. The second report yielded interesting remarks and recommendations in the concluding observations by the CESCR. The concluding comments made on 16 May 2007, for example, provide specific remarks on the positive aspects of the GoN report, raise several concerns and offer recommendations to the State Party. The latest report was submitted in the year 2013. The Committee expressed its satisfaction for the submission of the report in timely manner and replies to the Committee's questions. The Committee, however, also regretted that the information provided was, in some cases, not sufficiently detailed to advance its understanding of the level of enjoyment of the rights provided for in the Covenant.

The Committee commends the State Party for third periodic report, which was frank, informative and straightforward and complies with the Committee's guidelines for the preparation of reports. The Committee commends the State Party for its high-level delegation, headed by the Minister of State for Women, Children and Social Welfare, and appreciates the fact that the delegation included the Chairperson of the National Commission on Women, a woman member of the Human Rights Commission, a woman member of the National Dalit Commission and representatives of different ministries with responsibility for the implementation of the convention. It expresses appreciation to the State Party for the written responses to the issues and questions posed by the Committee's pre-sessional working group and the frank oral presentation made by the delegation. The Committee notes with satisfaction that the National Plan of Action on Gender Equality and Women's Empowerment covers the 12 critical areas of concern identified in the Beijing Platform for Action.

It is appreciable to see that the effective representation before the Committee has also been made by the non-state actors. Human Rights Treaty Monitoring Coordination Centre (HRTMCC) is a coalition of 63 human rights organizations, functioning as a joint forum for all human rights NGOs in Nepal. It monitors and disseminates information on the status of state obligations to the UN human rights treaties in the form of parallel reports as well as other publications. HRTMCC is also active in domestic lobbying for the protection and promotion of human rights.

6.4 National Human Rights Commission of Nepal

Pursuant to Article 83 of the Interim Constitution of Nepal, the legislature has enacted a law to establish the National Human Rights Commission in the year 2012. The new Constitution of Nepal, in the year 2015, continues to accord constitutional status of the Commission under Article 248 of the Constitution. The Commission has been conferred with the power to investigate and monitor prisons for the protection of the human rights. The Commission shall render assistance to the judiciary in the cases of human rights violations. The provision enables the Government to seek necessary opinion from the Commission before the submission of the report under international obligation. This provision will have constructive impact on the improvement of human rights record at the domestic level as the Commission may prevail upon the Government to do the needful in accordance with the international human rights regime. The Commission is allowed to entertain complaint from individual and may adopt redressal of 'naming' or 'shaming' of the violators.

The NHRC, a five-member body, comprises of one chairperson who must be a retired Chief Justice or judge of the SC or a reputed person and four persons having rendered an outstanding contribution to the protection and promotion of human rights or the field of social service. One must hold a bachelor's degree from a recognized university and be of high moral character in order to be eligible for the appointment to the office of commissioner of the NHRC. The President appoints them for six-year term, on the recommendation of the Constitutional Council.

In the appointments of the commissioners of the NHRC, diversity and inclusion of women have to be maintained. Their appointment gets confirmed only after the parliamentary hearing to be held by the parliamentary hearing special committee of the Legislature Parliament. The process of appointment of commissioners of NHRC is, thus, transparent. There is no direct role of Government officials in their appointment process at all.

In view of the conflict situation prevalent until 2006, the NHRC has focused its work on violations of civil and political rights (mainly related to abduction, disappearance, killings and torture) and only recently paid more attention to social, economic and cultural rights. The overarching approach of the new Constitution to incorporate social and economic rights under the chapter of Fundamental Rights enables the Commission to undertake necessary measures to respect, protect and promote human rights. The Constitution empowers the Commission to take up requisite steps to implement these rights. As the expression used under Article 248 is human rights, it would be interesting to observe the approach of the Commission to draw the meaning and content of the rights from the chapter of Fundamental Rights under the Constitution. The diversified composition of the Commission could play path-breaking role in designing means for the implementation of socio-economic rights.

7 Bangladesh's Position

Bangladesh emerged on the world map as a sovereign state on 26 March 1971, after fighting a nine-month war of liberation. The Constitution of Bangladesh as a supreme law declares Bangladesh as a secular democratic republic where sovereignty belongs to the people and lays down the framework defining fundamental political principles of the state and spells out the Fundamental Rights of citizens. It has been passed by the Constituent Assembly of Bangladesh on 4 November 1972, and it has come into effect from 16 December 1972.

The Constitution creates a dichotomy between civil and political rights on the one hand, and economic, social and cultural rights on the other by making the former enforceable by the Court and the latter non-enforceable. Economic, social and cultural rights which includes the provision of basic necessities of life including food, clothing, shelter, education and medical care, etc. are provided under Part II under the head 'Fundamental Principles of State Policy' whereas the Fundamental Rights, justiciable in nature, are provided in Part III.

7.1 Socio-Economic Rights in the Constitution of Bangladesh

Socio-economic rights form the part of the 'Fundamental Principles of State Policy' under Part II of the Constitution of Bangladesh. The Principles do not confer any right or create no legal remedies. They are in nature of general recommendations to authorities to aim for socio-economic goals in building the nation. The Principles act as a fundamental guide to the policy making, be it social, economic and administrative, governance of the country, making of the law and interpreting the Constitution and laws. Articles 8 to 25 house the range of socio-economic rights. Dignity of an individual has been explicitly mentioned in this Part as a cherished value in democracy. The State shall be obligated to provide for standard living by ensuring basic necessities of life, including food, clothing, shelter, education and medical care. The Principle refers to the right to work and reasonable wage in the chapter of the Principle. Right to social security and right to reasonable rest, recreation and leisure are identified as important rights under fundamental principles for fulfilling socio-economic need of individual. Though these socio-economic rights are placed in non-enforceable chapter of the Principles, they are clothed in the language of rights. The language indicates that the recognition of these rights as right is not disputable, and however, the machinery to enforce these rights could be different from traditional judiciary. The State has been duty-bound to adopt effective measures for the purpose of establishing a uniform, mass-oriented and universal system of education and extending free and compulsory education to all children. The implementation of the right to education is designed through legislative enactment. Identified as primary duties of the State to improve public health and to raise the level of nutrition, right to health has been conferred in favour of individual. Integrating the value of right and duty in the sphere of the realization of socio-economic rights, the Constitution treats work as a right and duty both and guarantees remuneration on the basis of the principle 'from each according to his abilities to each according to his work'.

7.2 Enforcement of Socio-Economic Rights in Bangladesh

Article 44(1) provides that the right to move the Supreme Court for enforcement of any of the Fundamental Rights is itself a fundamental right. Article 44(2) enables parliament to confer the jurisdiction to enforce Fundamental rights on any other Court, but such conferment cannot be in derogation of the power of the Supreme Court under Article 102(1) which means that such other Court may be given concurrent, but not exclusive, power of enforcement of Fundamental Rights. The Court must always have the power of enforcement of Fundamental Rights.

The Constitution has also expressly made these rights non-justiciable as Article 8 (2) clearly bars judicial enforceability of any principle under Part II of the

Constitution. In view of the express bar in Article 8(2) of the Constitution of Bangladesh, any argument for judicial enforcement of socio-economic rights must be premised on some sound, logical and legitimate grounds. If Article 8(2) bar against judicial enforcement is to be read as merely restricting positive enforcement, while implicitly allowing negative enforcement, such alternative reading of this constitutional provision has to be justified with reference to cogent constitutional necessities and reasons. Article 7(2) of the Constitution proclaims that as Constitution being the supreme law of the country provides that any other law being inconsistent with the Constitution shall be void to the inconsistency. As Fundamental Principles of the State Policy and socio-economic rights as part of them, and both taken together, while definitely forming part of the text of the Constitution, it would be interesting to see that they enjoy the same supremacy as Fundamental Rights.

The judicial enthusiasm to enforce socio-economic rights is encouraging sign for the advocates of the second-generation rights. The socio-economic rights are made enforceable by employing two pronged strategies, i.e. the first strategy is in asserting socio-economic rights under the umbrella of prominent Fundamental Rights such as right to life and liberty, freedom of association, expression and opinion, right to information, equality and non-discrimination and the second strategy is to emphasize the domestic application of ICESCR to enforce socio-economic rights.

7.3 Submission Under ICESCR

Bangladesh has ratified ICESCR in 1998 along with some other instruments in recognition of its constitutional commitment to human rights. The Government has not submitted any report to the Committee till date. However, the National Human Rights Commission has prepared a detailed report on the compliance of ICESCR in the year 2012. In the report, the Commission has highlighted the effort of the Government to comply with obligations under the Covenant and also underlined the shortcomings in the commitment.

7.4 National Human Rights Commission, Bangladesh

National Human Rights Commission came into existence through ordinance in the year 2008, and later, the enactment of law conferred statutory status to the Commission in the year 2009. The Commission is committed to the accomplishment of human rights in a broader sense, including dignity, worth and freedom of every human being, as enshrined in the Constitution of the People's Republic of Bangladesh and different international human rights conventions and treaties to which Bangladesh is a signatory. The Bangladesh NHRC is consisted of a chairman and six other members having proven expertise, interest in human rights and diverse backgrounds in accordance with the 'Paris Principles 1991'.

In accordance with its official mandate, the NHRC will serve as the major national human rights watchdog, monitoring the implementation of state obligations to respect, protect and fulfil the rights of every single member of society, addressing specific human rights complaints through investigation, mediation and conciliation, and where necessary, through constitutional litigation, and more broadly through raising public awareness. It is expected to play a strong role in ensuring consistency of laws and policies with international standards. The sweeping mandate to protect and promote human rights fails which may be utilized for the implementation of socio-economic rights.

8 Conclusion

Thorough survey of provisions on socio-economic rights in the Constitutions of South Asian countries uniformly presents the commitment towards dignified and worthy life of individuals in this subcontinent. Socio-economic entitlements are generally in the nature of policy guidelines for the State. The actors of the State—the legislature and the executive—are generally entrusted with the responsibility to implement the rights through law-making or policy formulations. As entrenched under the Indian Constitution, first one to be drafted and adopted, it appears that the traditional arrangement of branching of civil and political rights and socio-economic rights with separate mechanism of enforcement between these two rights has influenced the construction of the provisions in majority of the countries of South Asia. South Asian countries share commonality at various counts such as time of independence, similarity of cultural and milieu of life of individuals, and therefore, they may enrich themselves jurisprudentially on the accomplishment of socio-economic rights. The youngest Constitution, Nepalese Constitution, of the region is very progressive and historical for the development of socio-economic rights. It would be stimulating to observe the approach of the Nepalese Government towards these rights and may prove to be instrumental in guiding nations of this region.

References

Austin G (1966) The Indian constitution. Oxford University Press, Oxford
Constitution of Bangladesh (1972)
Constitution of Bhutan (2008)
Constitution of India (1950)
Constitution of Nepal (2015)
Constitution of Sri Lanka (1978)

Dadwal L (2003) Position of human rights: an Indian profile. Civ Mil L J 39:221–225
Jashim Ali Chowdhury M (2011, 2012) Claiming a 'fundamental right to basic necessities of life': problems and prospects of adjudication in Bangladesh. Indian J Const Law 5:184
Kesavananda Bharati v. State of Kerala (1973) 4 SCC 225
Minerva Mills v. Union of India, AIR 1980 SC 1789
Muralidhar S (2004) Economic, social and cultural rights: an Indian response to the justiciability debate. In: Ghai Y, Cotrell J (eds) Economic, social and cultural rights in practice
Ruparelia S (2012) Enacting socioeconomic rights: lessons from India. Addressing Inequalities—The Heart of the Post-2015 Development Agenda and the Future We Want for All Global Thematic Consultation
Shankar U, Tyagi D (2009) Socio-economic rights in India: democracy taking roots. Law Polit Africa Asia Latin Am 527–551
Shiva Rao B (ed) (1967) The framing of India's constitution, vol 2. IIPA, New Delhi
Singh MP (2007a) A theory of human rights for India. Indian Jurid Rev 4:1
Singh MP (2007b) Protection of human rights against state and non-state action. In: Oliver D, Fedtke J (eds) Human rights and the private sphere, 179
State of Kerala v N M Thomas, AIR 1976 SC 490
State of Madras v. Champakam Dorairajan, AIR 1951 SC 226
Wiles E (2006) Aspirational principles or enforceable rights? The future for socio-economic rights in national law. Am U Int Rev 22(1):35–58

Author Biography

Dr. Uday Shankar is Assistant Professor at Rajiv Gandhi School of Intellectual Property Law, Indian Institute of Technology, Kharagpur. He was awarded fellowship from prestigious Max-Planck Institute of Comparative Public Law and International Law, Heidelberg in the year 2008. He has participated in Law Teaching and Legal research Program at Cardiff University, U.K. He led a delegation of students for educational summit to George Washington University Law School, USA. He is a member of the International Association of Constitutional Law, South Africa. He has been awarded Ph.D. degree for his thesis on "Social and Economic Rights in India" by University of Delhi.

Chapter 4
Indigenous People in South Asia and International Law

Shashi Kumar

> *Indigenous peoples are not victims, but critical asset to the diversity of global humanity.*
> [Statement by H.E. Shekha Haya Rashid AL Khalifa, The President of the United Nations General Assembly at the adoption of the Declaration on the Rights of Indigenous Peoples, UN Headquarters, New York, 13 September 2007.]

1 Introduction

Indigenous people have suffered discrimination and subjugation across all parts of the world from centuries together. In view of their unique parochial cultural lifestyle, traditional social system, and normative value structure, the indigenous communities are different from the dominant society (Rehman and Hoffler 2009).

Even today in twenty-first century, the indigenous people are suffering from socioeconomic and political discrimination by the dominant society and the nation-states. In most parts of the world, the indigenous people are not politically recognized and have not been granted legal protection of their basic fundamental rights. Consequently, a number of indigenous people's movements have emerged in different parts of the world for recognition and protection of their distinct social and cultural rights.

Asia is a home to large number of indigenous peoples having multiple forms of social, cultural norms, and value systems. Within South Asia, indigenous peoples, who constitute a significant proportion in the Asian subcontinent, have been confronting with the problems of subjugation, exclusion, and deprivation. Many of the indigenous communities in South Asia are struggling for protection of rights to self-determination and have led social and political movements for autonomy,

S. Kumar (✉)
Department of Human Rights, School for Legal Studies, Babasaheb Bhimrao Ambedkar (Central) University, Lucknow 226025, India
e-mail: shashibbau@gmail.com

J.L. Kaul and A. Jha (eds.), *Shifting Horizons of Public International Law*,
https://doi.org/10.1007/978-81-322-3724-2_4

against economic and social exploitation, for preserving their social–cultural value system, for protection of their right over ancestral lands.

Though some of the national governments of South Asian countries have provided special provisions for safeguarding the sociocultural rights of indigenous people under their respective domestic legal framework, and have also depicted its concern and commitment for protection of indigenous peoples' right by signing or ratifying international human rights instruments related to protection of rights of the indigenous peoples, yet the situation of indigenous people in South Asia is deplorable and pathetic. In this chapter, the author examines the status of indigenous people and the availability of their rights within the domestic legal framework of the country.

This chapter is divided into four main parts. The first part addresses the complex issue of defining indigenous peoples. Part 2 examines the status of indigenous people in international law and United Nations Human Rights framework. The status of indigenous people and availability of their legal protection under the national legal framework of different countries of the South Asia are discussed in Part 3 of this chapter. The last part concludes the chapter with author's findings.

2 Indigenous People: Meaning and Definitional Debates

Defining the concept of 'indigenous' and interpreting who are indigenous people often seem to be a difficult task. There is no proper consensus on conceptualization of term 'indigenous' and its applicability in recognizing who are considered to be indigenous people in a given territory. In fact, 'indigenous' is a sociological term which has meaning like 'aboriginal' and 'organic' social identity. Indigenous is a relative concept that relates mainly with the 'land of origin of social group.' The aboriginal or organic identity is considered as a salient feature of indigenous people who reside in a particular region since pre-historic and pre-colonial era.

The process of colonization from western imperialists and non-western countries in many parts of Latin-American, Afro-Asian countries is also considered as significant factor in determining the status of indigenous people and recognizing the rights of indigenous peoples in different countries. However, this led to controversial debate over defining the term 'indigenous peoples' and the application of 'indigenousness' in context of certain ethnic groups in some countries.

The controversy about the meaning and application of indigenous people as an international concept is mainly based on norms applicable to indigenous peoples and their relationship within the state and the individuals. Prof. Bendict Kingsbury, a leading academician of international law, specialized in indigenous people studies has viewed that 'controversy arises in particular from the implementation that distinctive rights of indigenous people are justified by the destruction of their previous territorial entitlements and political autonomy wrought by historic circumstances of invasion and colonization' (Kingsbury 1998).

The differences on defining the term 'indigenous people' particularly evident during the discussion took place on the Draft UN Declaration on Rights of Indigenous Peoples.[1] Some states argued that 'Indigenous peoples applies only to certain regions, specially former European colonies in the Americas and Oceania and, therefore, does not apply universally' (UN Working Group Report 2001/85). Whereas the indigenous peoples and several states supported the 'principle of self-identification,' it was left to the group itself to decide whether or not it is indigenous. This was opposed by some states as it would lead to wide range of claims for certain rights related to 'self-determination.' The 'historical and ethnic complexity involved' in identifying indigenous people has made it difficult to devise a universal definition of indigenous people. The International Labour Organisation ('ILO') was the only international body which attempted to define the indigenous people under the international legal framework. Under its Convention, ILO defined the indigenous people in the independent countries who are regarded as indigenous because of their descent from the populations that inhabited the country, or a geographical region to which the country belongs to the time of conquest or colonization, or the establishment of present state boundaries and who, irrespective of their legal status, retain some or all of their own social, economic, cultural, or political institutions (Convention Concerning Indigenous and Tribal Peoples in Independent Countries, ILO No. 169, adopted 27 June 1989).

Later, the UN Special Rapporteur of the Sub-Commission on Prevention of Discrimination and Protection of Minorities, Jose R. Martinez Cobo, provided the definition of indigenous peoples that included continuous linkage of indigenous peoples with a pre-colonial or invasive society, and possession of distinct political, social, and cultural institutions. In defining the indigenous people, he also considered some factors such as indigenous people have important link with ancestral territories, are distinct from the rest of the population, having non-dominated status, and want to preserve their distinct identity (Cobo 1986).

In the South Asian context, the term 'indigenous' is perhaps the most difficult to define, not least of which because of its relative nature of application to the relevant groups and communities. For example, the *Veddas* of Sri Lanka and the *Adivasis* of India and Bangladesh were colonized well before the European imperialist powers created the Commonwealth (Rehman 1998). A similar situation arises in the case of *Sindhis, Baluchis,* or *Pakhtuns* of modern day Pakistan and Afghanistan. Colonization led to the destruction of many indigenous peoples, whereas the survivors were conquered or subjugated. The relative usage of concept of 'indigenous' in the South Asian context meant that in the transformation of the colonial world

[1]United Nation Human Right Commission had established the Working Group on Indigenous Population in 1982 to review events relating to the promotion and protection of human rights and fundamental freedom of indigenous peoples. It received and analyzed the oral and written information presented by many indigenous organizations, government bodies, and specialized agencies in its consultation sessions and produced its reports time to time. Subsequently, these reports helped in conclusion of drafting of Universal Declaration of Rights of Indigenous People in 2007. See http://www.iwgia.org/. Accessed on 25 December 2015.

into a world of new nation-states, the term 'indigenous' was primarily equated with those wanted independence from the western imperialists rulers or to say it is based on 'pigmentational' or 'racial' sovereignty (Mazuri Ali 1963). According to Russell Barsh, a leading exponent of indigenous peoples studies, argued, 'Bangladesh, Indonesia, the former Soviet China, and India have maintained that there are no indigenous peoples in Asia, only minorities.' It is viewed that 'indigenous situations only arises in the Americas and Australasia where there are imported populations' of Europeans (Barsh 1986). Thus, the states of South Asia have maintained that the concept of 'indigenous' cannot be applied to their populations. The official argument of the respective governments of the countries is that all peoples in their territorial boundaries are indigenous and, therefore, no distinctions could, on indigenousness, be made. It is on this ground that Afghanistan, Pakistan, India, or Bangladesh had not ratified the ILO Convention (No. 169; 1989) concerning Indigenous and Tribal peoples in independent countries. Even the same assumptions were also prevalent during the drafting stages of the UN Declaration on the Rights of Indigenous Peoples. Most of the South Asian countries had objection over the definition of 'indigenous people' and application of 'right to self-determination' in their respective countries at the time of voting in Human Rights Council for adoption of Declaration of Rights of Indigenous People in United General Assembly.[2]

However, the usage of term 'indigenousness' and recognition of 'indigenous people' in the international law has been significantly provided by United Nations. The United Nations had accepted the working definition of indigenous people as given in the report of UN Special Rapporteur Cobo (1986). He defines indigenous people as under:

> Indigenous communities, peoples and nations are those which, having a historical continuity with pre-invasion and pre-colonial societies that developed on their territories, consider themselves distinct from other sector of the societies now prevailing in those

[2]Some country representatives at United Nation had made different opinion and concerns of their respective country while having deliberation of drafting of UNDRIP, which show the contrasting views on understanding the concept and rights of indigenous peoples. For instance, the Pakistan representative at UN, Bilal Hayee, argued that 'his country had voted in favor of the Declaration both in the Human Rights Council and in the Assembly. Although the Declaration did not define indigenous peoples, he hoped that its adoption would fulfill the aims of the International Decade for the rights of indigenous peoples and enable them to maintain their cultural identity, with full respect for their values and traditions.' Whereas, Mr. Ajai Malhotra, the representative from India in United Nations said, 'while the Declaration did not define what constituted indigenous peoples, the issue of indigenous rights pertained to peoples in independent countries who were regarded as indigenous on account of their descent from the populations which inhabited the country, or a geographical region which the country belonged, at the time of conquest or colonization or the establishment of present State boundaries and who, irrespective of their legal status, retained some or all of their socioeconomic, cultural, and political institutions.' See Bilal Hayee and Mr. Ajai Malhotra, 'General Assembly Declaration on the Rights of Indigenous peoples; "Major Step Forward" towards Human Rights for all says President' 107th and 108th UN General Assembly Meetings. September 2007, 13 at, http://www.un.org/press/en/2007/ga10612.doc.htm. Accessed on 25 December 2015.

> territories, or parts of them. They form at present non-dominant sectors of society and are determined to preserve, develop and transmit to future generations their ancestral territories, and their ethnic identity, as the basis of their continued existence as peoples, in accordance with their own cultural patterns, social institutions and legal systems.[3]

The historical neglect and subjugation of indigenous people have led to various social and political movements of indigenous people in different parts of the world for recognizing rights of indigenous people. The prolonged struggle of indigenous people at the global level has provided them legal recognition in international law, and their basic rights are enumerated under the aegis of United Nations.

3 Indigenous People and International Law

The existence of indigenous people's movement at the global level is a major factor in recognizing the rights of indigenous people as an international legal concept. The people who were participating in the movement had mainly focused on elements of commonality that helped the movement to establish indigenous people's relation with their ancestral lands and territory, aspiration for autonomy and self-determination, renewed interest in distinct cultural and languages, the historic experience of incursion by other groups, continuing consequences of dispossession and subordination, concern over health and education, and relative disadvantage in child welfare, morality nutrition, and income levels (Stamatopoulou 1994).

For long period, the indigenous peoples did not have adequate recognition in the international legal framework. The only international agency, the ILO has been working on the issue of indigenous people since 1920s, and it had contributed significantly in addressing the problems of indigenous and tribal peoples at global level. It has adopted important conventions related to indigenous people, i.e., The ILO Convention on Indigenous and Tribal Population, 1957 (No. 107) and later, this convention was replaced by another convention, i.e., The ILO Convention on Indigenous and Tribal Peoples (No. 169). It was the emergence of indigenous people's movement at global level which began in the 1970s and accelerated during the 1980s, that drew the global attention toward the problems of indigenous and tribal communities (Anaya 2004). Various projects were undertaken for investigating the widespread discrimination of indigenous peoples in different countries. Subsequently, United Nations established a Working Group on the Indigenous Populations in 1982.[4] The mandate of the Working Group included the development of standard—setting instruments that led to the first draft of the United Nations Declaration Rights of Indigenous Peoples in 1994. The Declaration was important in understanding the problems of indigenous people and recognizing the

---

[3]Ibid.

[4]The Working Group on Indigenous Populations was established by Economic and Social Council resolution 1982/34 of 7 May 1982 (ESCOR Res. 1982/34 (1982)). Also See, Burger (1998).

rights of indigenous people. It provided the recognition of rights of indigenous people within legal and normative international order. It brought together all pre-existing rights relevant to indigenous peoples into one coherent document. The United Nations took the historic step in adopting a Declaration on the Rights of Indigenous Peoples (UNDRIP) on September 13, 2007.[5]

The UN Declaration on the Rights of Indigenous Peoples is formulated from a number of sources including the Universal Declaration of Human Rights, the Convention on the Rights of the Child, the Convention on the Elimination of Discrimination against Women, the Convention on the Elimination of All Forms of Racial Discrimination, the Genocide Convention, the ILO Convention (No. 169), and other human rights treaties. The important feature of the Declaration is that it recognizes the collective rights of indigenous people under the international law. It was debated during the formulation of the Declaration whether specific regime of human rights is needed for indigenous people. On one hand, it was argued that specific regime was not necessary for indigenous people due to rights enshrined in the general human rights law in UDHR, ICCPR, ICCESR; on the other, it was argued that due to unique collective rights that indigenous people have, a specific regime is absolutely necessary to allow full realization of the rights subsumed in international human rights law (Gilbert 2007).

The unique feature of the Declaration is that it synthesizes the individual and collective rights between the state and the individual people (Montes and Cisneros 2009). The Preamble of the Declaration says, ‘Indigenous people are entitled without discrimination to all human rights recognized within international law, and that Indigenous Peoples possess collective rights which are indispensable for their existence, well-being, and integral development as peoples.’ The UNDRIP is aimed to serve as ‘a standard of achievement to be pursued in a spirit of partnership and mutual respect’ between states and indigenous peoples, providing ‘the minimum standards for the survival, dignity, and well-being of the indigenous peoples of the world.’[6]

The Declaration contains several kinds of rights of indigenous people related to political, social, economic, and cultural aspects under its forty-six articles.[7] These rights include rights against any form of discrimination (Article 1), right to self-determination (Article 5), right to maintain and strengthen distinct cultural identity of indigenous people (Article 5), and right to practice and develop their spiritual, religious traditional customs and rituals (Articles 10–12). The indigenous peoples are not be forcefully assimilated in other culture (Article 8).

---

[5]The United Nations Declaration on the Rights of Indigenous Peoples (UNDRIP) was adopted by the General Assembly on Thursday, 13 September 2007, by a majority of 144 states in favor, 4 votes against (Australia, Canada, New Zealand, and the United States) and 11 abstentions (Azerbaijan, Bangladesh, Bhutan, Burundi, Colombia, Georgia, Kenya, Nigeria, Russian Federation, Samoa, and Ukraine) For details see www.ohchr.org/english.issues/indigenous/declration.htm. Accessed on 25 December 2015.

[6]See www.ohchr.org/english.issues/indigenous/declration.htm. Accessed on 25 December 2015, Article 43, Declaration on the Rights of Indigenous People.

[7]See www.ohchr.org/english.issues/indigenous/declration.htm. Accessed on 25 December 2015.

To protect the economic independence and livelihood rights of indigenous people, the Declaration holds that indigenous peoples shall not be forcefully removed from their traditionally owned lands or territories (Article 26). No relocation of indigenous peoples shall take place without their free, prior, and informed consent and agreement on just and fair compensation (Articles 10, 28). They have other economic rights such as freedom from economic exploitation (Article 17), right to maintain, control, protect and develop their cultural heritage, traditional knowledge and traditional cultural expression (Article 31), and right to conservation and practice of the environment (Article 29). The state shall not store or dispose of hazardous materials in the indigenous peoples' lands (Article 30).

Indigenous peoples also have right to participate in the decision-making process through political representation in political institution of governance (Articles 18, 19). They can also develop their own political, economic, and social systems or institutions (Article 20). Notably, the Declaration also says that the state in consultation and cooperation with indigenous peoples takes appropriate measures to achieve the ends of it.

4 Situation of Indigenous Peoples in South Asia

Asia is one of the most culturally and ethnically diverse regions of the world. The vast population of indigenous peoples resides in the countries of the Asian region (Gray 1995). The United Nations Special Rapporteur on the rights of indigenous peoples has noted that these indigenous peoples are particular groups that distinguish themselves from the broader populations of the country and fall within the scope of the international concern of the indigenous peoples as it has developed throughout the United Nations system.[8] These indigenous peoples are known as of different names such as 'tribal peoples,' 'hill tribes,' 'scheduled tribes,' '*Adivasis*,' or '*Janajatis*,' among others.

In Asia, the region of South Asia constitutes a subcontinent, which has a distinct social–cultural and ethnic pollution. Seven countries consists in South Asia include Afghanistan, Bangladesh, Bhutan, Nepal, India, Maldives, Pakistan, and Sri Lanka which are having more than 2,000 ethnic groups with populations ranging from hundreds of millions of indigenous and tribal communities. South Asia had been invaded and settled by many ethnic groups over the centuries—including various Dravidian, Indo-Iranian, Tibeto-Burman, and Austro-Asiatic groups. These invasions and settlements have brought different culture to the land of South Asia that transformed into composite culture and established a pluralistic society in different

---

[8]Report of the Special Rapporteur on the Rights of Indigenous Peoples, James Anaya, Consultation on the Situation of Indigenous Peoples in Asia. United Nations, Human Rights Council, July 31, 2013.

countries. For long period, the countries of South Asia remained under the European and British colonial rules.

The indigenous peoples in the South Asia have some commonalities which include common historical legacy of colonialism and experience of subjugation and exploitation by the foreign invaders and rulers. There exist similarities in their problems as well, for example, most of the indigenous and tribal communities suffer discrimination, exclusion, and exploitation from the dominant majority communities in their countries. Many indigenous and ethnic groups are not yet politically recognized in the countries and thus not granted legal protection of their rights in domestic legal framework.

Under the following section, an attempt has been made to examine the status of indigenous people in domestic framework of the countries. It's necessary to find out whether the indigenous communities have any special protection under the domestic legal policy and institutional framework of the nation. Here, I briefly analyze the position of indigenous people in the South Asian countries like Afghanistan, Bangladesh, Nepal, India, Pakistan, and Sri Lanka. However, as the indigenous population is either insignificant or non-existent, in Bhutan and Maldives, these countries are not included in the study.

4.1 Afghanistan

Afghanistan is primarily the country of tribal and ethnic people who are categorized into several subtribes and clans.[9] It has also the political obligation to create a 'prosperous and progressive society' and to 'maintain equality among all peoples and tribes,' and 'balance development of all areas of the country.'[10] In Afghanistan, Uzbeks and Turkmen are considered as vulnerable tribal ethnic groups, living in the northern parts of the country. They were farmers and largely economically independent till the advent of terrorist activities inflicted by Talibans in their territory in 1998. Since then, they have been subjugated and suffered impact of internal conflicts. Similarly, another small tribal group, Kuchis have suffered displacement and lead the nomadic life.[11] Afghanistan has not rectified any ILO Convention on Indigenous and Tribal peoples, however, it has supported the UNDRIP which render its commitment to protect the rights of its indigenous and tribal communities and work for their economic development.

[9]Article 4—The nation of Afghanistan shall be comprised of Pashtun, Turkman, Baluch, Pachaia, Nuristani, Aymg, Arab, Qirghizi, Qizilbast, Gujur, Brahwui, and other tribes. See *The Constitution of the Republic of Afghanistan.*

[10]Article 6—The State shall be obligated to create a prosperous and progressive society based on social justice, preservation of human dignity, protection of human rights, realization of democracy, attainment of national unity as well as equality between all peoples and tribes, and balance development of all areas of the country. See *The Constitution of the Republic of Afghanistan.*

[11]For further details see www.refworld.org. Accessed on 25 December 2015.

4.2 Bangladesh

In Bangladesh, around 3 million indigenous people (known as *Adivasis and Jumma*), reside and they include 45 different ethnic groups, who speak over 30 different languages. They are predominantly inhabited in the north and southeastern parts of the country, with the majority settled in the Chittagong Hill Tracts (CHT), where eleven distinct groups of indigenous peoples reside (Kapaeeng Foundation 2015).

Like other parts in South Asia, in Bangladesh also the condition of indigenous peoples is more vulnerable, and their status has become problematic because of various reasons. *Adivasi* have lost their ancestral lands, and their rights over natural resource have been denied. Many indigenous people were displaced because of economic development activities. Their local self-governance systems were also eroded. They have been suffering social and economic discrimination through the dominant communities.[12]

Adivasi of Chittagong Hill Tract (CHT) faces a problem of dispossession of their ancestral lands on which they have been living for long period.[13] The encroachment of lands of these indigenous communities, 'land grabbing' is done by dominant rich communities called 'Bengalis' (Salam and Aktar 2014). During the period of British colonial rule, in undivided India, in the wake of tribal revolt against encroachment of the government officials and exploitation by moneylenders in the tribal areas, the British administration had enacted regulation called Bangladesh CHT regulation 1900 for protecting their lands from outsiders.[14]

There has been continuous insurgency in Chittagong hill regions over land disputes between Adivasi and other Bengalis. For resolving this conflict and protecting the land rights to Adivasi, a peace accord was signed between the government of Bangladesh and Parbatya Chattagram Jana Sagati Samiti (PCJSS) in 1997 (Rashiduzzaman 1998). The accord provided for greater autonomy and special status to indigenous communities. It also created a central ministry of tribal affairs and an elected regional council for CHT. A Land Dispute Commission was set up to deal with land-related dispute. The Commission was intended to resolve the land dispute of Adivasi by taking into account the local customs and usage regarding land rights and claims. However, despite the Peace Accord, the indigenous communities of CHT continue to suffer from violence, discrimination, and exclusion. In November 2005, a British High Commission mission to Bangladesh

[12]See http://www.ilo.org/indigenous/Achtivitiesbyregion/Asia/Southasia/Bangladesh. Accessed on 25 December 2015.

[13]For details of Indigenous peoples protest movement in Chittagong Hill see https://www.culturalsurvival.org/. Accessed on 25 December 2015.

[14]http://www.ilo.org/indigenous/Achtivitiesbyregion/Asia/Southasia/Bangladesh. Accessed on 25 December 2015.

visited the region and observed that the Land Disputes Resolution Commission set up to facilitate the effective implementation of the Peace Accord was failed in its objective.[15]

The instability and internal conflict in the CHT for long period have hindered the sustainable development of the region and jeopardized the life of indigenous peoples who live there. The Peace Accord of 1997 provides the framework for the development of the region, and the CHT has been recognized as a semi-autonomous tribal region governed through an institutional framework based on traditional indigenous institutions of chiefs, headmen, known as *karbaris*, who settle the disputes. In comparison with indigenous peoples living in hill areas, the indigenous and tribal peoples of plain regions have very little representation in mid-to-high levels of government bodies, and there is no central ministry or regional development authority to deal with the issues of indigenous peoples living in plains. Moreover, the status of indigenous women from both CHT and plains regions in respect of their socioeconomic condition and political participation in government bodies is very critical (Haque 2011).

While studying the constitutional framework of Bangladesh, it is viewed that the Bangladesh government has shown its commitment for upholding the values of democracy and human rights in the country by protecting the rights and human dignity of each persons.[16] It is mentioned in the Constitution of Bangladesh that 'all citizens are equal before the law and entitled to equal protection of law'[17] and 'the state shall not discriminate any citizen on the grounds only of religion, race, caste, sex, or place of birth.'[18]

However, as far as the protecting the rights of indigenous people are concerned, the government of Bangladesh had depicted very ambivalent approach. Bangladesh had only ratified the ILO's Indigenous and Tribal population Convention, 1957 (No. 107) in 1972. During the adoption of UNDRIP in 2007, Bangladesh remained absent from voting which indicated her inconclusive approach toward indigenous people in her country.

---

[15]For further details, see Javaid Rehman (2007), World Directories of Minorities: Bangladesh (MRG, London). http://www.minorityrights.org/5636/bangladesh/adivasis.html. Accessed on 25 December 2015.

[16]In the Constitution of Bangladesh, Part II—Fundamental Principles of State Policy under Article 11(Democracy and Human Rights) reads that 'The Republic shall be democracy in which fundamental human rights and freedoms and respect for dignity and worth of the human person shall be guaranteed and in which effective participation by the people through their elected representative in administration at all levels shall be ensured.'

[17]Article 27 in the Constitution of Bangladesh. http://bdlaws.minlaw.gov.bd/. Accessed on 25 December 2015.

[18]Article 28 in the Constitution of Bangladesh. http://bdlaws.minlaw.gov.bd/. Accessed on 25 December 2015.

4.3 Nepal

Nepal is a small Hindu Kingdom nation, situated in Himalaya mountain range. Around 59 officially recognized indigenous communities (known as *Adivasi Janajati*) exist in Nepal.[19] The National Foundation for Development of Indigenous Nationalities ('NFDIN') Act of 2002 has defined the *Adivasi Janajati* as indigenous peoples or nationalities, and they are those ethnic groups or communities which 'have their own mother tongue and traditional customs, distinct cultural identity, distinct social structure, and written or oral history of their own.' They have distinct cultures, languages, and belief system. As per the 2001 government census, indigenous people constitute 37.19% of total population of Nepal. Indigenous peoples reside across the country, in the mountains, hills, and plains areas (*terai* regions). The largest concentration of indigenous people is found in the eastern region. The indigenous peoples of Nepal extent from small hunter–gatherer communities to those with an advanced urban culture, but they are predominately inhabited in remote rural areas and mainly depend on subsistence farming for their survival. Among the indigenous peoples, the Magar, Tharu, Tamang, Newar, Rai, Gurung, and Limbu are the largest groups.

Adivasi Janajati differ from the other majority Hindi- and Nepali-speaking communities in a various ways, like differences in their social structures, having own languages (approximately 103 dialects), distinct cultural and religious traditional ways of life. Indigenous people of Nepal mainly have been suffering from social discrimination and economic exploitation since a long period, which is a major cause of internal social conflict and political instability in the country.

A large population of indigenous communities in Nepal have suffered with poverty, and they have mainly experienced the political, economic, and social discrimination. Many of them have affected by inequalities in income, education, health, jobs, and political representation. At different levels, most indigenous peoples in the country have faced situations of social and political marginalization, lack of cultural recognition, and economic disadvantage.[20]

---

[19]The official list of indigenous peoples is contested, and the United Nations Committee on Economic, Social and Cultural Rights expressed concern in 2008 about the 'lack of clarification about the criteria used by' NFDIN, the government indigenous development agency to recognize indigenous peoples and the implications of this recognition (E/C.12/NPL/CO/2, para 28). The special rapporteur found indications that there are several groups that share in the history, characteristics, and common human rights problems of the *Adivasi Janajati* and Indigenous peoples elsewhere, but that is not on the official list. These include the *Kulung*, *Bahing*, and *Yamphu*, which are among the most marginalized in the country. In a welcome development, a 'List Renewal Task Force' composed of nine indigenous representatives is currently being established by the government for the purpose of re-examining the official list with the participation of the main indigenous organizations.

[20]For details of human rights situation of indigenous people in Nepal, see IWGIA Yearbook, Indigenous World, 2016. Available at www.iwgia.org. Accessed on 10 October 2016.

Over long period, the indigenous communities in Nepal have led the social and political movement against their discrimination, for inclusion in the social and political life of the country and for recognition and protection of their basic human rights. In 2002, Nepal government had passed the National Foundation for the Development of Indigenous Nationalities Act, and later in 2007, the indigenous communities were recognized in the Interim Constitution.[21] In consequence of sustained lobbying and struggle undertaken by various indigenous groups and activists, the government of Nepal has ratified ILO Convention No 169 in September 2007. In 2015, the Constituent Assembly of Nepal drafted a new Constitution of Nepal, which has been rejected by the indigenous peoples leaders and groups as it has not incorporated the rights of indigenous peoples, Madhesis, Muslims, Dalits, women, and other minority groups in accordance with the interim constitution.[22]

It is viewed that the indigenous peoples' movement in Nepal mainly aimed at the issues of governance and political representation. According to the report published by Nepal's Department for International Development (DFID), the indigenous peoples seek greater equality in linguistic rights and guarantees of access to common property and resources.[23] In a significant report 'Unequal Citizens,' the DFID highlighted the indigenous peoples' struggle for political recognition and political representation in the mainstream society, urging for the need of constitutional reform—to remove current discriminatory provisions and make new provisions for equitable representation.[24]

In the present context of state's political transformation in the aftermath of over a decade of conflict in the country, the indigenous peoples' movement in Nepal have been lobbying for a secular, federal state system, in which their rights to self-determination, ethnic and linguistic autonomy are ensured, and also for affirmative action and proportionate representation.

4.4 Pakistan

Pakistan is predominately a Muslim country. The number of all the non-muslim minorities is estimated at 4.9 million out of a population of 143 million. Around

---

[21]Interim Constitution of Nepal 2007, under its Part IV, Obligation, Directive Principles and Politics of the State, 33(d) the provision is 'To have participation of *Madhesi*, *Dalit*, indigenous peoples, women, labors, farmers, disabled, backward classes, and regions in all organs of the State structure on the basis of proportional inclusion' available at http://www.wipo.int/wipolex/en/text.jsp?file_id=189180. Accessed at 15 September 2016.

[22]For details on rejection of new Constitution of Nepal by the indigenous peoples, see http://www.indigenousvoice.com/en/why-indigenous-peoples-reject-new-constitution-of-nepal-2015.html. Accessed on 10 October 2016.

[23]See for details https://www.gov.uk/government/world/organisations/dfid-nepal. Accessed on 25 December 2015.

[24]Unequal Citizens: Gender, Caste and Ethnic Exclusion in Nepal (DFID and World Bank publication, 2006).

15% of the total population is indigenous or tribal people who are primarily concentrated in northern region. The most numerous tribal populations of the country are the Pashtun (13.8%), the Sindhis (7.7%), and the Baluchs (4.3%).[25] Among these tribes, the Pashtun tribal groups enjoy special status under Federally Administered Tribal Areas (FATA), while all of these groups are afforded special status in national development plans. There are smaller indigenous and tribal people who live in Pakistan, such as Kihals and Mors, indigenous peoples of the Indus, the Buzdar from the Suleiman Mountains, and the Kailasha people in Chitral. These smaller groups, many of whom are semi nomadic boat people or pastoralists, are often not accounted for in national census figures.

Though the government of Pakistan does not recognize indigenous peoples officially, however some ethnic groups reside in some regions are refered as tribes. The national population of Pakistan comprises several ethnic groups including Punjabis, Pakhtuns, Sindhis, Seraikis, Muhajirs, Balochis, and others. Tribes are included in 'others' category along with the Jhabels, Kihals, Mores, and Kutanas. The main groups of tribal peoples in the country are the tribal fishing peoples, the pastoral groups of the Middle Indus Valley, the Baloch tribes, fisher folk of coastal areas, tribal peoples of Sindh, tribal peoples of Gilgit-Baltistan, tribal peoples of Chitral Valley, tribal peoples of Pothohar Region, and the tribal peoples of North-West Frontier Province (NWFP) and Federally Administered Tribal Areas (FATA).

Indigenous and tribal peoples in Pakistan are among the most marginalized and excluded groups in society, although considerable diversity exists between the different groups. Though the Pakistan government does not have any national policy on indigenous and tribal peoples, but under special administrative arrangement of Federally Administered Tribal Areas (FATA) and Provincially Administered Tribal Areas (PATA), the government has been running the affairs of some tribal areas through regulations or laws enacted during the British rule. These include the Frontier Crimes Regulations, 1901 (Regulation III of 1901), providing for the suppression of crime in certain frontier districts.

Some administrative reform measures have been taken for governance of tribal areas. On August 13, 2009, President Asif Ali Zardari announced political, judicial, and administrative reforms for the tribal areas, which include changes in century-old Frontier Crimes Regulations (FCRs) and an extension of the Political Parties Order 2002 to the tribal areas.[26] These reforms include setting up an appellate tribunal curtailing arbitrary powers of political agents, giving people the right to appeal and bail, and excluding women and children from the territorial responsibility clause (Shah 2012).

There are, however, some national policies made which have adversely affected the life of tribal peoples in various parts of the country. For example, the national forest policies and practices have been a matter of serious concern for the forest

[25]These figures are available on the regional report of International Labour Organisation related to Indigenous and tribal peoples. See www.ilo.org, Accessed on 25 December 2015.

[26]See for details. http://new-pakistan.com/2009/08/page/3/. Accessed on 25 December 2015.

people of the country.[27] The forest peoples, however, have rejected these policies as against their rights. Indigenous and tribal people have struggled for a long time for forest royalties and against the illegal felling of forests by private contractors.

The indigenous and tribal people in Pakistan have been suffering exploitation and discrimination for long period. Moreover, in many cases, their vulnerability is further exacerbated by mainstream development processes. Though the government of Pakistan has shown some concern in relation to indigenous people for their protection of rights and development issues by ratifying international instruments on the subject, the situation of indigenous and tribal communities in the country is still pathetic. Pakistan has ratified the ILO Convention No 107 on Indigenous and Tribal Populations in 1960.[28] It has so far not signed the ILO Convention No. 169 on indigenous and tribal peoples. In 2007, the country voted for the adoption of the United Nations Declaration on the Rights of Indigenous Peoples in the UN General Assembly.

Notably, the visibility of indigenous and tribal peoples' issues in state and national policies has been ambivalent. This ambivalence is due to the fact that some tribes are ruled under legislations like FATA and PATA but still there are some tribes which are not legally recognized and their conditions are more vulnerable.

4.5 India

India being a pluralistic democratic country has the largest indigenous and tribal population in Asia (8.43 million), which is primarily concentrated in two different regions. One concentration of tribes lives along the Himalayas stretch ranging from the hills of northwest region to northeastern regions of the country.[29] In the northeastern states of the country, about 90% of the population is tribal. Another concentration of indigenous population exists in central peninsular regions of the country.[30] Most of the indigenous people reside in the hills and forest regions and largely depend upon the forest and agricultural farming for their livelihood (von Furer-Haimendorf 1982; Elwin 1959; Xaxa 2008).

[27]Several National Forest Policies have been made since 1950s after independence of Pakistan. The country's first forest policy was announced in 1955, followed by the forest policies of 1962, 1975, 1980, 1988, 1991, 2001, 2005, and 2010. For details, see Babar et al. (2006), see http://www.lead.org.pk/. Accessed on 25 December 2015.

[28]http://www.ilo.org/indigenous/Achtivitiesbyregion/Asia/Southasia/Pakistan. Accessed on 25 December 2015.

[29]Tribal density is scantly persist in the states of Jammu and Kashmir, Himachal Pradesh, and Uttaranchal in the North India and heavy density in the northeast states such as Assam, Meghalaya, Tripura, Arunachal Pradesh, Mizoram, Manipur, and Nagaland. Ministry of Tribal Affairs, government of India. Available at http://tribal.nic.in/index. Accessed on 25 December 2015.

[30]Andhra Pradesh, Jharkhand, Chhattisgarh, Madhya Pradesh, Odisha. *ibid.*

Though India has not officially accepted the presence of 'indigenous peoples' within its territory, however, the indigenous or tribal communities, popularly known as *Adivasis* (meaning original inhabitants) in the country, are legally recognized as 'Schedule Tribes' in the Constitution of India.[31] There are 630 federally recognized Scheduled Tribes communities, speaking a plethora of different languages within the country.[32] Keeping view of their distinct social and cultural attributes and ethnic identity, the Scheduled Tribes have been provided a 'special protection' apart from other general constitutional rights, i.e., 'fundamental rights' as a citizen under the Constitution of India. Under the Part III of the Indian Constitution, Scheduled Tribes are provided all fundamental rights similar to other citizens of the country, such as the right to equality, freedom from exploitation, right to religion, and other civil and democratic rights.[33] Besides this, the Indian state has the political obligation to take special measures to promote the educationally and economic interests of the Scheduled Tribes.[34] Moreover, certain percentage of seats are reserved in the Union Parliament and legislative assemblies for providing political participation in the decision-making process to indigenous and tribal communities.[35]

In order to protect the indigenous and tribal communities against exploitation and intrusion from outsiders and to protect their distinct cultural identity and social system, the Indian state has created 'Scheduled Areas' which are predominantly inhabited by indigenous communities. In these 'Scheduled Areas,' the non-tribal communities are prohibited to settle or acquire property.[36] Under the Fifth

[31]Article 342 provides for specification of tribes or tribal communities or parts of or groups within tribes or tribal communities which are deemed to be for the purposes of the Constitution the Scheduled Tribes in relation to that State or Union Territory. The essential characteristics first lay down by the Lokur Committee, for a community to be identified as Scheduled Tribes are—(a) indications of primitive traits; (b) distinctive culture; (c) shyness of contact with the community at large; (d) geographical isolation; and (e) backwardness. See The Constitution of India, 1950 and Xaxa (1999).

[32]There are other nomadic and primitive tribes which are also known as denotified tribes, which are not legally recognized as 'Schedule Tribe'. See, Ministry of Tribal Affairs, government of India. Available at http://tribal.nic.in/index. Accessed on 25 December 2015.

[33]The Constitution of India, 1950, Part-III Fundamental Rights (Articles-14–32).

[34]Article 46 'the state shall promote, with special care, the educational and economic interests of the weaker sections of the people, and in particular, of the Scheduled Caste and the Scheduled Tribes, and shall protect them from social injustice and all forms of exploitation.' The Constitution of India, 1950.

[35]The Constitution of India, 1950, Articles 330, 332 and 334.

[36]The definition of Scheduled Areas (under the fifth scheduled of the constitution) is 'such areas as the President may by order declare to be Scheduled Areas.' The criterion for declaration of an area as Scheduled Area was identified by the first Scheduled Areas and Scheduled Tribes Commission (Dhebar Commission). The features of such area were as follows: the preponderance of tribal population; compactness and reasonable size of the area, underdeveloped nature of the area, and marked disparity in the economic standard of the people. See The Constitution of India, 1950.

Schedule[37] and Sixth Schedule[38] of the Constitution of India, special administrative arrangements have been made for 'Scheduled Areas' for safeguarding the fundamental rights and development of tribal communities. These two schedules have distinct mechanisms for governing schedule tribes under their respective jurisdiction. The Fifth Schedule permits the state government to extend its executive power to the Scheduled Areas[39] and the Governor of the state has the authority to 'make regulations for the peace and good government of any area Scheduled Area.'[40] The Governor could also preclude the application of any federal or state law in the 'Scheduled Area.' Moreover, the Governor of each state having Scheduled Areas shall, annually or whenever required by the President of India, submit a report regarding the administration of the Scheduled Areas[41].

The Fifth Schedule also creates Tribes Advisory Council (TAC) in each state having 'Scheduled Areas.'[42] The duty of the TAC is to advise the Governor on the matter related to the 'welfare and advancement' of the Scheduled Tribes.[43] These councils could make law for management of land, forest, shifting cultivation, appointment or succession of chiefs or headpersons, inheritance of property, marriage and divorce, social customs, and any matter relating to village or town administration.[44]

The Sixth Schedule which contains the administrative mechanism for tribes of northeastern regions of the country seems to have provided considerable autonomy to indigenous communities for self-governance. It has created several 'autonomous' regions, each allocated to a particular tribe.[45] The Scheduled Areas

---

[37]Under the Vth Schedule, the 'Scheduled Areas' are marked in was initially made applicable only to the states of Madras, Bombay, West Bengal, Bihar, Central Provinces and Bihar, United Provinces and Orissa.

[38]In the VIth schedule, in tribal areas in the states of Assam, Meghalaya, and Mizoram, Autonomous District Councils and Regional Councils were constituted. See The Constitution of India, 1950.

[39]Under the Fifth Schedule of the Indian Constitution states include Andhra Pradesh, Jharkhand, Chhattisgarh, Himachal Pradesh, Madhya Pradesh, Gujarat, Maharashtra, Odisha, and Rajasthan, The Constitution of India, 1950.

[40]The Constitution of India, 1950, Vth Schedule, Section 2; These provision are subjected to only two restrictions: (i) that the Governor would consult a Tribal Advisory Council (TAC) 'before making any regulation,' and (ii) that all regulations would receive statutory assent from the President of India before taking effect.

[41]The Constitution of India, 1950, Vth Schedule, Section 2.

[42]TAC can be created in the States having Scheduled Tribes but not Scheduled Areas. TAC consists of twenty members of which three-fourth must be representatives of Scheduled Tribes in the Legislative Assembly of that State. See The Constitution of India, 1950.

[43]The Constitution of India, 1950, Vth Schedule [Articles 244(1) 4(2)].

[44]The Constitution of India, 1950, VIth Schedule [Articles 244(1) 4(3)].

[45]Autonomy means the tribes are given right to self-determination in exercising some sort of executive, legislative, and judicial power in their governance, The Constitution of India, 1950, VIth Schedule [Articles 244(2) and 275(1) Section 1]; The Sixth Scheduled provides for Administration of tribal areas in the States of Assam, Meghalaya, Tripura, and Mizoram.

of northeastern states are governed through Autonomous District Council (ADC) and Regional Council (RC) endowed with legislative, judicial, and executive powers.[46]

Apart from the constitutional protection to Scheduled Tribes, there are several legislative measures taken at federal and state levels for protection of rights of scheduled tribes. There are three major laws which are specific to the protection of constitutional rights of the scheduled tribes and their welfare. These are as follows: the Scheduled Caste and Schedule Tribes (Prevention of Atrocities) Act 1989 (SC/ST Act) protecting the scheduled tribes from any kind of socioeconomic discrimination and against any criminal offense; Panchayat (Extension to Scheduled Areas) Act, 1999 for decentralizing the administrative control of Scheduled Areas under the Fifth Schedule and providing for protecting tribal self-governance and providing right to participation in decisions-making bodies.[47] Lastly, the Scheduled Tribes and Other Traditional Forest Dwellers (Recognition of Forest Rights) Act was passed in 2006 for the protection of forest rights of indigenous communities.[48] This act is instrumental in providing legal entitlement over forest land to tribes and compensation in case of diversion of forest for any development proposes.

In spite of several legislative and administrative measures taken up by the Indian state for protection of rights of tribal communities and for their welfare, indigenous communities continue to suffer the discrimination, subjugation, and deprivation even after six decades of India's independence (Walter 2008). In fact, the development programs for tribe have not been effectively implemented because of various loopholes in government administration.[49]

Noticeably, India has shown its concern on the issue of indigenous people and tribal at global forums. Indian government has ratified the ILO Convention on Indigenous and Tribal Populations, 1957 (No. 107); however, it has yet to ratify the ILO Convention on Indigenous and Tribal Populations, 1989 (No. 169). Importantly, India is also a signatory to UNDRIP which indicates its concern toward the preservation of indigenous people. However, in spite of all these welfare

[46]The Constitution of India, 1950, VIth Schedule [Articles 244(2) and 275(1) Section 1].

[47]The PESA mandates the State government to devolve certain political, administrative, and fiscal powers to local governments elected by the tribal communities in the Scheduled Areas. See Panchayat (Extension to Scheduled Areas) Act, 1999 at http://tribal.nic.in/index. Accessed on 25 December 2015.

[48]Scheduled Tribes and Other Traditional Forest Dwellers (Recognition of Forest Rights) Act, 2006 provides several kinds of rights to tribes that hitherto restricted by earlier legislation enacted in relation to forest and environment protection. These include the right to live in the forest, the right to cultivate for their livelihood, the right to collect minor forest produce, the right to graze cattle, the right to convert lease or grants (*pattas*) to titles, the right to convert forest village into revenue village, the right to settlement in the old habitations and un-surveyed villages, the right to access and community right over intellectual property and traditional knowledge related to forest biodiversity and cultural diversity, the right to manage the community forest resources, and right to enjoy any customary traditional except hunting. See Saravanan (2009).

[49]Ibid.

measures and legislative protection safeguards, the situation of indigenous people is not much better, and they are still struggling for protection of their human rights.[50]

4.6 Sri Lanka

In Sri Lanka, a small population of indigenous communities known as *Veddas*, also called *Wanniyala-Aetto*, live in isolated parts of the island. At present, they predominantly inhabited in Sinhalese areas.[51] *Veddas* were originally hunter–gatherers communities. In the 1950s, their territory was opened up for Sinhalese settlers, and the tribe's forests and hunting grounds were bulldozed and flooded.

Veddas suffer social and political discrimination. They are struggling for survival and possession of their ancestral lands. Between 1977 and 1983 under the various governmental development projects, approximately 51,468 ha lands were turned into a gigantic hydroelectric-cum-irrigation project (Spittel 1950). Later on in 1983, their last remaining forest refuge was turned into the Maduru Oya National Park. The *Wanniyala-Aetto* were moved to government villages and banned from entering the park without permits. They were also forbidden to hunt in the park. They are still losing their land to outsiders who continue to be resettled in the area.[52]

The loss of forests lands and the creation of the National Park have robbed the *Wanniyala-Aetto* of their means of subsistence. They also suffer from health problems due to addiction of alcoholism and to mental illness. Many of them are harassed, exploited, and discriminated by the forest guards and outside settlers.

Some observers note that *Veddas* are disappearing and their distinct culture is declining.[53] Land acquisition for mass irrigation projects, government's forest reserve restrictions, and the civil war have disrupted the traditional life pattern of *Veddas*.[54] In 1985, the *Vedda* Chief Thissahamy and his delegation were obstructed from attending the United Nations Working Group on Indigenous Population.[55] In 1996, Warige Wanniya, Chief of *Vedda* indigenous peoples group had addressed the United Nations Working Group on Indigenous Population and decribed the pathetic condition of indigeious communities in Sri Lanks.[56]

---

[50]The Committee on the Convention on the Elimination of Racial Discrimination in its state report on India (2007) revealed Indian government's failure to protect indigenous peoples. See India, 05/05/2007, CERD/C/IND/CO/19, at paras 19–26.

[51]For further details, see Seligmann and Seligmann (1911); also http://www.encyclopedia.com/topic/Vedda.aspx. Accessed on 25 December 2015.

[52]See http://www.survivalinternational.org/tribes/wanniyala. Accessed on 25 December 2015.

[53]http://vedda.org/wanniyalaeto.htm. Accessed on 25 December 2015.

[54]Ibid.

[55]Idid.

[56]For details, see Address of Warige Wanniya to the UN, at United Nations Working Group on Indigenous People (UNWGIP) 14th session held in Geneva, 1996, see http://vedda.org/wanniyalaeto.htm. Accessed on 25 December 2015.

According to the provisions in the Constitution of Sri Lanka, right to equality has been granted to all its citizens. It is mentioned under Article 12(2) relating to the Fundamental Right: 'No citizen shall be discriminated against on the grounds of race, religion, language, caste, sex, political opinion, place of birth, or any one of such grounds.'[57] Moreover, the government of Sri Lanka also has political obligation under the Directive Principles of State policy and Fundamental Duties for protection of basic fundamental rights of all its citizens.[58] Inspite of these constitutional provisions, the indigenous communities in Sri Lanka are not equality treated and their basic human rights are not protected.

Today, the situation of *Vedda* communities is more vulnerable. They are socially and economically exploited and discriminated. The *Vedda* women are sexually exploited through trafficking and prostitution trade.[59]

5 Conclusion

It is discerned from the above discussion that the concept of 'indigenous' is not only problematic in its interpretation, but also it has become more complex in its application for identifying the indigenous people in different countries particularly in South Asia. Indigenous people have distinct social and cultural identity, which separates them from majority of general population. Due to their parochial social system and traditional practices, they are treated indifferently and so they continue to suffer discrimination and exclusion of the dominant society. They also suffer political discrimination in the sense that many of the indigenous people are not yet politically recognized, and they have been denied right to self-determination. However, because of various social and political struggles of indigenous peoples, the identity of indigenous people got recognition under the international law, and their various distinct collective rights are enumerated under international conventions and UN Declaration.

In South Asia, a large number of indigenous and tribal communities inhabit. They havc commonalities in their historical legacy of colonial rule and experienced similar kind of exploitation from foreign invaders and non-tribal outsiders that had destroyed their traditional systems and encroached their land.

---

[57]The Constitution of the Democratic, Socialist Republic of Sri Lanka. See https://en.wikipedia.org/wiki/Constitution_of_Sri_Lanka. Accessed on 25 December 2015.

[58]Directive Principles of State policy and Fundamental Duties Article 27(2). The state is pledged to establish in Sri Lanka a democratic socialist society, the objectives of which include—the realization by all citizens of an adequate standard of living for themselves and their families, including adequate food, clothing, and housing, the continuous improvement of living conditions, and the full enjoyment of leisure and social and cultural opportunities. See The Constitution of the Democratic, Socialist Republic of Sri Lanka. See https://en.wikipedia.org/wiki/Constitution_of_Sri_Lanka. Accessed on 25 December 2015.

[59]See http://vedda.org/wanniyalaeto.htm. Accessed on 25 December 2015.

The earlier discussion on the situation of indigenous people in South Asia makes us understand that indigenous and tribal communities have been confronted with lots of socio-economic and political problems. The right to self-determination of indigenous communities is not protected in many parts of South Asia. The indigenous communities like Pakhtun and Baluch in Pakistan and Afghanistan, the Adivasi of CHT in Bangladesh, and some tribal communities in India are asserting their claims for protecting their right to self-determination through political and social movements for autonomy and self-governance which have generated many internal conflicts in South Asia.

The political discrimination in the form of not providing political status to indigenous communities in the domestic legal framework and denial of political rights is another problem being faced by indigenous people in South Asia. For instance, some tribal groups in Pakistan and Afghanistan have been denied the right to vote in the national election. Similarly, the primitive and nomadic tribes in India and Bangladesh are not yet legally recognized. In Nepal, the indigenous people are struggling for getting their political and legal recognition under the Constitution of Nepal.

Like in other parts of the world, the indigenous people of South Asia also suffer with economic exploitation and discrimination. The dispossession of ancestral lands, denial of rights over forest and its products, exploitation of natural resources available on their land, and misappropriation of traditional knowledge are such problems which currently the indigenous people face mostly. In the name of economic development, the land of indigenous people are being acquired and their rights over forest are denied, which is the only means of their survival. In the wake of globalization and economic liberalization, the socioeconomic condition of indigenous communities has become more vulnerable. The rapid industrialization and development process have caused the problem of displacement and migration of indigenous peoples. Millions of indigenous people are displaced from their ancestral lands and migrated to other regions leading the life of destitute in different parts of the South Asia. Moreover, the indigenous people are also economically exploited by the many foreign pharmaceutical companies as they are misappropriating the traditional medicinal knowledge of indigenous people for manufacturing drugs and ripping huge profits.

In order to examine the situation of indigenous peoples in Asia, the UN had conducted a study through, James Anaya, the Special Rapporteur on the rights of indigenous peoples, who visited and had consulted with the indigenous peoples representatives in different parts of South Asia during March 18, 2013 to March 19, 2013 (OHCHR 2013). In his report submitted to Human Rights Council in UN General Assembly, James Anaya has provided an overview of various problems being faced by indigenous people in Asia which were mainly related to denial of land and resources rights, economic exploitation through extraction of minerals, and misappropriation of natural resources by setting up development projects in indigenous peoples inhabited regions. The report also highlighted the dismal socioeconomic and political status of indigenous peoples in some Asian countries. Significantly, the report also recommended the need of taking up effective governmental policies by the national governments for ameliorating the condition of indigenous people in South Asia, which includes social and economic development plans for their welfare and protection of their human rights enshrined in UNDRIP.

Nevertheless, the national governments of South Asian countries have shown its concern for protection of rights of indigenous people in their respective countries by signing or ratifying the international instruments related to indigenous peoples, yet the human rights of indigenous peoples are being violated either due to political apathy or non-implementation of governmental policies. India, Bangladesh, Nepal, and Pakistan have signed ILO Convention 107, but they have not yet ratified the important legally binding ILO Convention 169 related to indigenous and tribal people. Nepal is the only country till date which has ratified ILO Convention 169. Except Bangladesh, all South Asian countries have voted in favor for adoption of UN Declaration of Rights of Indigenous People in 2007. But as the UNDRIP is not a legal binding instrument, so it does not obligate the signatory states to protect the rights of indigenous people, which is one of its shortcomings. For this reason, the struggle for indigenous peoples at the domestic and global level seems to be not ended yet. Lastly, the status of indigenous peoples in South Asia can only be improved and their due human rights would be recognized if the respective national governments of the states implement the UNDRIP provisions through their domestic laws and policy with political willingness and national obligation.

References

Anaya J (2004) Indigenous peoples under international law, 2nd edn. Oxford University Press, Oxford

Barsh RL (1986) Indigenous peoples: an emerging object of international law. Am J Int Law 80:372–385

Babar S, Tanvir A, Qaiyum SA (2006) A critical analysis of forest policies of Pakistan: implication for sustainable livelihoods, mitigation and adaptation strategies for global change. Springer, Berlin

Béteille A (1998) The idea of indigenous people. Commentary. Curr Anthropol 39(2)

Burger J (1998) Indigenous peoples and the United Nations. In: Price Cohen C (ed) Human Rights of Indigenous Peoples. Transnational Pub., New York

Burman BKR (2003) Indigenous and tribal peoples in world system perspective. Stud Tribes Tribals 1(1)

Cobo JM (1986) Study of the problem of discrimination against indigenous population. UN Doc. E/CN.4/Sub.2/1986/7/Add. 4: 379–380

Cohen CP (ed) (1998) The human rights of indigenous peoples. Transnational Publishers, Ardlsey

Elwin V (1959) India's north-east frontier in the nineteenth century. Oxford University Press, London

Gilbert J (2007) Indigenous rights in the making: the United Nations declaration on the rights of indigenous peoples. Int J Minor Group Rights 14:210–212

Gray A (1995) The indigenous movement in Asia. In Barnes RH, Gray A, Kingsbury B (eds) Indigenous peoples of Asia. Association for Asian Studies, Inc. Monograph and Occasional Paper Series, vol 48. Ann Arbor, MI

Haque T (2011) Militarization and the fate of women's body: a case study of CHT. In: Mohsin A (ed) Women and militarization in South Asia complexities. The University Press limited, Dhaka

International Labour Organisation, Convention on Indigenous and Tribal Peoples (1989). Convention no 169. See http://www.ilo.org

Kapaeeng Foundation (2015) Human rights situation report of indigenous peoples in Bangladesh. Dhaka

Kingsbury B (1998) "Indigenous peoples" in international law: a constructivist approach to the Asian controversy. Am J Int Law 92:414–457

Mazuri Ali A (1963) Consent, colonialism, and sovereignty. Polit Stud 11:36–55

Montes AR, Torres Cisneros G (2009) The United Nations declaration on the rights of indigenous people: the foundation of a new relationship between indigenous peoples, states and societies. In: Charters C, Stavenhagen R (eds) Making the declaration work. The United Nations declaration on the rights of indigenous peoples. IWGIA Document No. 127. International Work Group for Indigenous Affairs, Copenhagen

Rashiduzzaman M (1998) Bangladesh's Chittagong Hill Tracts peace accord: institutional features and strategic concerns. Asian Surv 38(7):653–670

Rehman J (1998) Indigenous peoples at risk: a survey of indigenous peoples of South Asia. In: Roy Burman BK, Verghese BG (eds) Aspiring to be: the tribal, indigenous condition. Konark Publishers, Delhi, pp 72–121

Rehman J, Hoffler H (2009) Indigenous peoples: an introduction to the socio legal framework with a special focus on the declaration on the rights of indigenous people and South-Asia. Eur Yearb Minor Issues 8:211–245 (Leiden: Brill Academic Publishers)

Richardson BJ, Imai S, McNeil K (eds) (2009) Indigenous peoples and the law: comparative and critical perspectives. Hart, Oxford

Salam F, Aktar H (2014) Ethnic problems in Bangladesh: a study of Chittagong Hill tracts. SUST J Soc Sci 22(2):53–63

Saravanan (2009) Political Economy of the Recognition of Forest Rights Act, 2006: conflict between environment and tribal development. South Asia Res 29(3):199–221

Shah SWA (2012) Political reforms in the federally administered tribal areas of Pakistan (FATA): will it end the current militancy? Heidelberg Papers in South Asia and Comparative Politics. See http://hpsacp.uni.hd.de/WorkingPaperNo.64. Accessed on 25 Dec 2015

Spittel R (1950) Vanished trails: the last of the Veddas. Oxford University Press

Stamatopoulou E (1994) Indigenous peoples and the United Nations: human rights as a developing dynamic. Hum Rights Q 16(1):58–81

Seligmann C, Seligmann B (1911) The Veddas. Cambridge University Press

von Furer-Haimendorf C (1982) Tribes of India: the struggle for survival. University of California Press, Berkeley

UN Working Group Report 2001/85, for details see http://www.iwgia.org/human-rights/un-mechanisms-and-processes/working-group-on-indigenous-populations/sessions-of-the-working-group-on-indigenous-populations

Walter F (2008) Sixty years of development—induced displacement in India: impacts and the search for alternatives. In: Mathur HM (ed) India social development report, 2008: development and displacement. Centre for Social Development and Oxford University Press, New Delhi, pp 89–102

Xaxa V (1999) Tribes as indigenous peoples of India. Econ Polit Wkly 34(51), 18 Dec 1999

Xaxa V (2008) The concept of indigenous peoples in India. In: Erni C (ed) The concept of indigenous peoples in Asia. A resource book. IWGIA Document No. 123. Copenhagen/Chiang Mai: International Work Group for Indigenous Affairs and Asia Indigenous Peoples' Pact Foundation

Author Biography

Dr. Shashi Kumar is Associate Professor in the Department of Human Rights, Babasaheb Bhimrao Ambedkar University, Lucknow. He has received Fellowship from International Institute of Human Rights, Strasbourg, France in 2009. He was also awarded Raman Post-doctoral fellowship in 2014-2015 to pursue research in the U.S. by the University Grants Commission, New Delhi. His scholarship is in the areas of human rights, indigenous peoples' rights, and Ambedkar's political philosophy. He has been engaged in teaching and research for the last 15 years and has supervised many dissertation work of students in the area of human rights.

Chapter 5
Regional Trade in South Asia: An International Legal Analysis

Bipin Kumar

1 Introduction

Long before the advent of the World Trade Organization or even the General Agreement on Tariff and Trade (GATT) its predecessor, trade agreements existed between nations within the same geographical location in the form of bilateral or regional agreements. A regional trade agreement is an agreement undertaken by countries located within a defined geographical area whereby the participating countries align themselves with each other for the purpose of achieving a predetermined form of economic integration (WTO Secretariat 2016). These groupings of countries are mainly formed with the main objective of reducing barriers to trade between member countries. Contrary to what the name suggests, these groupings or unions may be concluded between countries not necessarily belonging to the same geographical region. According to Krueger (1995), a preferential trade agreement (as most RTAs are referred to) is any trading arrangement that permits the import of goods from countries signatory to the preference at lower rates of duty than those imposed on imports from third countries.

The first wave of regionalism, led by the western European customs union which followed the 1957 Treaty of Rome, was analyzed within the framework of Vinerian customs union theory. The second wave, which was characterized by agreements in the 1980s going beyond preferential tariff reduction toward deeper integration, was considered to be a "new regionalism" requiring new tools. The third wave of bilateral agreements in the early 2000s continues many of the trends toward deeper integration, although it is in some respects hardly even regionalism (Pomfert 1997).

B. Kumar (✉)
National Law University, Nagour Road, NH-65, Mandore,
Jodhpur, Rajasthan 342304, India
e-mail: bipin.bk@gmail.com

J.L. Kaul and A. Jha (eds.), *Shifting Horizons of Public International Law*,
https://doi.org/10.1007/978-81-322-3724-2_5

Complete regional formations in the form of customs union had long received exemption from the MFN principle in bilateral arrangements, and there was a debate whether or not this exception should be allowed into the GATT. There was also a controversy on whether future preferences should be encouraged or discouraged and if permitted whether they should be subject to voting pre-approval by the organization. In the final analysis, a case was made for the retention of the exceptions given to customs unions and free trade areas under previous agreements subject to some conditions (Jackson 1969).

There has been a rapid growth in the number of Regional Trade Agreements (RTAs) in recent years. In Europe, these are mainly centered on the European Union, spreading to the Central and Eastern European countries, the Baltic States, the Mediterranean, and beyond. In the Americas, two agreements—NAFTA and MERCOSUR—have had a significant impact. In Asia, SAFTA and ASEAN are the major RTAs. There has also been an increase in the extent to which RTAs overlap, although there are significant variations in the product coverage and the rules of origin (Inama 2011).

On the whole, the newer agreements tend to have deeper coverage, extending into areas of domestic disciplines beyond the exchange of tariff concessions, and a number of agreements now also cover the services sector. The scope and geographical reach of RTAs have expanded significantly in the recent years. Apart from merely removing tariffs on intra-bloc trade in goods, the newer agreements tend to have deeper coverage. The new generation of RTAs, especially those comprising developed countries, includes more regional rules on investment, competition, and standards, as well as provisions on environment and labor. Most of these new agreements also include preferential regulatory frameworks for mutual services trade.

Developments in recent years suggest that RTAs have become an important trade policy instrument for WTO Members. RTA's scope and configuration are, respectively, far-reaching and innovative in terms of design and choice of RTA partners. Besides their own dynamics, the appeal for RTAs carries systemic implications for the Multilateral Trading System (MTS), noticeably by increasing discrimination and complexity in trade relations and by undermining the transparency and predictability of the system and by extension the standing of the WTO with regard to these principles. The challenge for the latter will be to ensure the effectiveness of its RTA surveillance mechanism as an interface between preferential and Most Favored Nation (MFN) trade relations (Fiorentino 2006).

The preference for FTAs is a reflection of the defining characteristics of the current RTA race; the key attributes of this race appear to be speed, flexibility, and selectivity; and the FTA is, in most cases, the configuration that best meets these needs. Although negotiation of an FTA may take years to conclude, evidence suggests that the timing from the launching of the negotiations to their conclusion has been shrinking in recent years, especially for agreements among like-minded countries. FTAs afford their parties ample flexibility in terms of the desired trade policy scope and choice of partners.

2 Regional Trade Agreements Across the Globe

According to the latest WTO Annual Report, currently substantial proportion of the global trade now takes place through the regional trading groups. The 2010 Annual Report of the WTO indicated that out of 153 (now the number is 163) WTO Members only Mongolia is outside the preview of the RTAs. As per the present data available at the WTO Web site, there is not a single country which is not a member of the one RTA or the other. Some of the WTO Members are the party to as many as more than a dozen RTAs.

In the recent years, there has been a surge in the number of RTAs that have been formed among countries. The surge in RTAs has continued unabated since the early 1990s. In 2009, 37 new notifications were received by the WTO. This is the largest number of RTA notifications in any single year since the WTO's establishment in 1995. Under WTO rules, the goods and services aspects of RTAs have to be notified separately, so they are counted separately.

The scope and geographical reach of regional trade agreements have expanded significantly in the recent years. Apart from merely removing tariffs on intra-bloc trade in goods, the newer agreements tend to have deeper coverage. The new generation of RTAs, especially those comprising developed countries, includes more regional rules on investment, competition, and standards, as well as provisions on environment and labor. Most of these new agreements also include preferential regulatory frameworks for mutual services trade.

WTO statistics tend to exaggerate the total number of RTAs since they are based on notification requirements which do not reflect the physical number of RTAs. On the other hand, the available information confronts us with non-exhaustive and inaccurate figures since it is practically impossible to verify the data for the many RTAs that either have not yet been notified or are at different phases of implementation.

At the multilateral level, the protracted Uruguay Round (1986–1994) had prompted several countries to pursue preferential deals as an insurance against an eventual failure of the multilateral trade negotiations. At the regional level, the fragmentation of the former Soviet Union and the disbandment of the Council for Mutual Economic Assistance (COMECON) had generated a new cluster of RTAs between transition economies and the European Union and the EFTA States as well as among transition economies themselves.

Europe is the region with the largest number of RTAs, accounting for almost half of the agreements notified to the WTO and in force. The main regional groupings are the European Union (EU) and the EFTA. Beyond its immediate neighborhood, the EU has focused on furthering already commenced RTA negotiations; these include FTAs with MERCOSUR, the GCC, and the six Economic Partnership Agreements (EPAs) with subgroupings of the African Caribbean and Pacific (ACP) countries.

In the Americas, Latin American countries share a tradition of regional integration which is quite different from the recent and more market-oriented RTAs being pursued by Canada and the United States. The latter and Brazil are the vocal representatives of these differences in the troubled negotiations for the Free Trade Area of the Americas (FTAA) which aims at a continent-wide FTA. RTA developments in Latin America suggest increasing efforts toward consolidation and deepening of the network of RTAs among South and Central American countries. MERCOSUR members are working toward the objective of a full-fledged customs union and have concluded a framework agreement with three members of the Andean Community, which aims to the gradual establishment of an FTA. On the initiative of the United States, the Trans-Pacific Partnership Agreement comes to the fore in the form of mega-regional trade agreement which according to some authors is having the potential to threaten the very existence of the WTO itself. The Trans-Pacific Partnership (TPP) negotiations have been of interest and intrigue to economists, lawyers, and policy makers alike.

In South Asia, India has been the main focus of RTA activities. With its SAARC counterparts, it has signed the South Asian Free Trade Agreement (SAFTA), designed to revamp the SAPTA, and a framework agreement under the name BIMSTEC (Bangladesh, India, Myanmar, Sri Lanka, Thailand—Economic Cooperation); it is also engaged in FTA negotiations with ASEAN and Thailand, having signed framework agreements with both, and is negotiating a Comprehensive Economic Cooperation Agreement (CECA) with Singapore. Further, India has signed a partial scope agreement with MERCOSUR, as a preliminary step to an FTA, and is considering FTAs with Chile as well.

3 Role of RTAs in the Multilateral Trading System

The big debate in the current international trade literature is about whether regionalism can help or hinder the multilateral trading system. There are opposing views among economists about the role of regionalism in the current global trade system. While some hold the view that regionalism acts as a compliment to multilateralism (i.e., acts as a building block), others hold the view that RTAs are a "stumbling block" to the multilateral trade negotiations.

3.1 RTAs as Stumbling Blocks

The dominant view among mainstream economists suggests that regionalism is harmful to the multilateral trading system (Parthapratim 2004). The main proponents of this view are Bhagwati, Krueger, and Panagariya. The arguments in favor of the proposition that RTAs are harmful to the multilateral trading system can be found in the writings of Jagdish Bhagwati who initiated literature in this area. The views of this school of thought can be seen in the expositions by

Bhagwati and Krueger (1995) in their essays "The Dangerous Drift to Preferential Trade Agreements."

3.1.1 RTA Violation of MFN

The preliminary attack on RTAs under this school of thought is that they undermine the basic "Most Favored Nation" (MFN) principle which forms the core of WTO. While it is conceded that the architects of the WTO/General Agreement on Tariffs and Trade exempted free trade areas from the MFN rule, it is argued that proliferation of agreements would fragment the trading system. Given the number of RTAs and the way they are proliferating, the result would be a "spaghetti bowl" of rules, arbitrary definitions of which product comes from where and a multiplicity of tariffs depending on the source (Bhagwati and Panagariya 2007).

Unabated proliferation of RTAs has started creating a maze of different regulatory regimes that undermine the principles of transparency and predictability in trade relations.

3.1.2 Domination of Smaller Nations by Bigger Partners

According to Bhagwati and Krueger (2007), increased regionalism is dangerous because it leads to inter-block trade wars and domination of small countries by bigger partners in the regional blocks. Bhagwati illustrates the latter point regarding the dominance of small countries by big partners by taking the example of Mexico's entry to NAFTA. NAFTA's passage was made subject to Mexico's acceptance of supplemental agreements on environmental and labor standards. He argues that these agreements are completely unrelated to trade and could not have been forced upon Mexico under the multilateral trade regime. However, under the RTA regime, these conditions were made preconditions to freer trade. To put it crisply in his words:

> So, free trade agreements become a process by which a hegemonic power seeks (and often manages) to satisfy its multiple trade unrelated demands on other, weaker trading nations more easily than through multilateralism….And if this analysis has an element of truth to it, then free trade arrangements seriously damage the multilateral trade liberalization process by facilitating the capture of it by extraneous demands that aim, not to reduce barriers, but to increase them (Bhagwati 1995).

3.1.3 Indirect Impact on Multilateral Negotiations

The above point highlighted by Prof. Bhagwati, apart from showing how bigger nations can dominate smaller nations, also indicates how issues (such as labor and environment standards) which would never be part of multilateral trading agreements under the WTO auspices would be forced upon smaller nations, thereby depriving them of the comparative advantage. Further, once these requirements have been forced upon the countries, they are indirectly forced to accede to them in the multilateral negotiations too.

This has been articulated better by some economists (Bhagwati and Panagariya 2007) when they say that, by pushing aggressive trade treaties on a bilateral basis, developed countries are weakening the bargaining power of developing countries in multilateral trade negotiation. They attribute this to the fact that developing countries are forced to agree to issues in the multilateral framework that they have acceded to on a bilateral basis (Bartels and Ortino 2010). Another example illustrating the point is the protection of intellectual property by the U.S. (Bhagwati and Panagariya 2007). The U.S. has used both inducements and punishments to secure its interests. During negotiations over the North America Free Trade Agreement, Mexico was told that the price of a deal was acceptance of intellectual property protection provisions. It was a price Mexico was prepared to pay. But the U.S. has also demanded that other countries accept similar provisions or face retaliatory tariffs. Subsequently, during the Uruguay Round of trade liberalization, the U.S. was able to insert the Trade-Related Intellectual Property Regime (TRIPs) into the WTO, even though no intellectual case had ever been made that TRIPs, which is about royalty collection and not trade, should be included.

3.1.4 Formation of Trade Blocs

Another important argument is that RTAs will push the world toward trading blocs leading to inter-block trade wars (Krueger 1995). This argument has its basis on the "trade-diverting" aspects of FTAs. Krueger also illustrates this by using the example of administered protection by the USA. To elaborate, if Mexican exports of a particular item should increase rapidly in competition with products from, say, Taiwan, the American response after an FTA with Mexico might be to use the administered protection remedies of antidumping or countervailing duty relief against non-partner countries, in this case Taiwan (Krueger 1995). As a result, a trade bloc is created wherein the USA encourages imports from Mexico and discourages Taiwanese imports after the creation of the RTA.

Krueger also says that creation of FTAs will weaken the support of those otherwise favoring the open multilateral system, while simultaneously creating interest groups opposing multilateral liberalization. Insofar as trade diversion does take place under FTAs, new interests will oppose further liberalization (Krueger 1995).

3.1.5 Diversion of Attention and Energy from Multilateral Trade

These authors also express strong concerns about the negative effects of growing regionalism, and they worry that RTAs divert attention from the multilateral trading system (Bhagwati and Krueger 1995). This is a fallout of the formation of trade bloc-like phenomenon explained above, which in turn is a result of trade diversion. To put it in the words of Krueger (1995):

> …The attention of policy makers is distracted from the multilateral system when FTAs are under discussion or negotiation. When attention should center on the formation and strengthening of WTO, it is instead diverted to proposals for a more powerful Asia-Pacific Economic Cooperation and for new members in NAFTA…

3.1.6 Bhagwati's Exceptions

Prof. Bhagwati, however, makes an exception and permit PTAs (Preferential Trade Agreements—his term for RTAs) in two cases. First, he would permit an RTA when a group of countries wants to develop a common market with full factor mobility, a common external tariff, and even political integration. In a common market, not just trade but also investment and migration barriers are eventually eliminated just as in a federal state, and the full advantages of such economic and political integration flow. Second, he would permit a PTA where it represents the *only feasible* way to achieve multilateral free trade among nations because the Multilateral Trade Negotiation (MTN) process made available by the GATT/WTO is stalled (Bhagwati et al. 1999).

The threat posed by the proliferation of RTAs to the WTO mechanism is summarized in a speech by Dr. Supachai Panitchpakdi, the former WTO Director General, he observed on November 26, 2002:

> Regionalism can be a powerful complement to the multilateral system, but it cannot be a substitute. The multilateral trading system was created after the Second World War precisely to prevent the dominance of rival trading blocks. The resurgence of regionalism today risks signaling a failure of global economic cooperation and a weakening of support for multilateralism. It threatens the primacy of the WTO, and foreshadows a world of greater fragmentation, conflict, and marginalization, particularly of the weakest and poorest countries.

3.2 RTAs as Helping the Multilateral Trade Regime

Another bunch of economists propagate the other school of thought and are of the opinion that regional trade blocs are welfare oriented in nature and are unlikely to have any negative impact on the multilateral trade system. This school is mainly propagated by the likes of Summers (1991) and Krugman (1991) apart from other noted economists which are discussed below.

3.2.1 The View Taken by Lary Summers

According to Summers (1991), if the world is divided into a small number of trade blocs, multilateral negotiation will be easier as it will remove the free riders from the system. The view taken by Summers is well explained by his famous quote in the World Bank Conference in 1992, where he said: "I like all the 'isms', unilateralism, regionalism and multilateralism (Baldwin 2016)."

Summers dismisses the arguments of the Bhagwatian school of thought on the following grounds. He says that there is no evidence to show that regionalism has side-tracked multilateralism. RTAs were present even in the 1980s and 1990s, but they did not thwart the Uruguay Round of negotiations then. Further, most of the important multilateralists such as the USA, the UK, and Canada have been regionalists and have been so since World War II. The nations that steered this multilateral liberalization—the U.S., the UK, the EEC6, the Nordics, and Canada—are the same ones that drove regional liberalization since the 1958 Treaty of Rome, the 1960 Stockholm Convention, and the 1965 Canada–U.S. Auto Pact.

The propounders of this school also argue that regional integration efforts promoted multilateral liberalization via "competitive liberalization." To elaborate, using an example, most scholars believe that formation of the EEC induced the U.S. to push for multilateral tariff cutting via the Kennedy Round. They say that, first, the phase-in of EEC preferences harmed U.S. exporters. Second, redressing the issue of discrimination required multilateral liberalization (the direct way to offset it, joining the EEC, was unthinkable). In this roundabout way, European regionalism created a burst of free trade multilateralism among U.S. exporters, and the U.S. government followed suit (Ferd Bergsten in Bergsten 1996).

3.2.2 Baldwin's Juggernaut Theory

Baldwin (1997) proposed a Juggernaut theory of liberalization and explained how RTAs can further the process of multilateral liberalization. The Juggernaut theory asserts that liberalization begets liberalization, so once the liberalization ball starts rolling, it is difficult or impossible to stop.

Briefly put, this theory states that initially tariffs started at levels that were politically optimal. Import-competing firms (firms within the domestic country which would be affected by competition from foreign firms in case import duties are cut) opposed the idea of reducing the protection. However, on the basis of the principle of reciprocity between nations, some multi-tariff cutting takes place. As a result of this, export trade increases (because the reciprocating nation reduces its import tariffs), while at the same time the business of import-competing sectors falls (because of competition from foreign firms). This means that the export sectors in all nations have expanded while all of the import-competing sectors have shrunk. Exporters, who have become anti-protectionist or pro-liberalization because they have benefited from the multi-tariff cutting, will have a more influential say than import-competing sectors (who are pro-tariff) as their numbers are up.

This is because a sector with lots of workers, lots of capital, and lots of profit will have more influence. This exporter's lobby will in turn affect the nation's policy, and it will be willing to promote the case of tariff reduction at every round of multilateral trade negotiation. Therefore, any sector which is included in the reciprocal trade talks of a nation will eventually get liberalized.

Refuting the point made by Krueger and Bhagwati that regional agreements will increase anti-liberalization forces, Baldwin (1997) says, because trade is "already quite free in major trading nations, few regional liberalizations are capable of creating anti-liberalization forces." Therefore, he concludes that most regional trade agreements will weaken the opponents of trade liberalization while simultaneously strengthening its key proponents (exporters) and hence will promote and foster multilateral trade liberalization.

After having explained how reciprocal tariff cutting will lead eventually to complete liberalization, Baldwin says that the logic of the juggernaut theory of liberalization by reciprocity also applies to regional trade agreements. He takes the example of how RTAs have helped foster liberalization without affecting the WTO by taking examples of Mexico, the USA, and EU.

To illustrate his point, let us take the example of Mexico that he dealt in detail: Mexico followed a classic import-substitution policy till 1990. This policy explicitly aimed at preventing US industry from crushing nascent Mexican industry. Mexican tariffs were high, and Mexico stayed out of the GATT until 1986. The Mexico–U.S. free trade agreement (NAFTA) changed all this. Since the FTA was announced under the GATT's Article XXIV, Mexican tariffs had to go to zero on substantially all trade in about 10 years. Once NAFTA had been implemented, Mexico had zero tariffs on three-quarters of all of its imports. Moreover, because the U.S. and Canada have very low MFN tariffs on their non-food, non-clothing imports, free trade with NAFTA is not much different than free trade with the world (with a few spectacular, but low-volume exceptions like steel). Or, more to the point, Mexico's regional liberalization forced out or downsized all the import-competing industries that would have otherwise resisted multilateral liberalization. Basically, the NAFTA-launched juggernaut crushed in 10 years the sort of protectionist forces that took the GATT 40 years to crush in the U.S. and Canada.

Throughout this process, Mexico's stance in WTO was never affected. Having realized the importance of liberalizing trade through the NAFTA route, Mexico sought FTAs with the EU and Japan. Additional, Mexico signed free trade agreements with its poor and economically small neighbors, including Honduras, Costa Rica, Columbia, Venezuela. Mexican exports have quadrupled since 1990 with all of the growth accounted for by its non-oil exports. It has also doubled its inflow of foreign direct investment, and although it suffered a macro-shock in 2001, its foreign debt has come down steadily and is now less than a third of what it was in 1990.

3.2.3 Exceptions to the Baldwin Juggernaut Theory

Baldwin (1997) himself acknowledges that his Juggernaut theory of liberalization will not be applicable in two cases of regional trade agreements, namely South–South RTAs (RTAs between developing countries) and RTAs like the EU's Common Agriculture Policy which leads to the creation of strong anti-liberalization forces.

Explaining the case of EU's Common Agriculture Policy, Baldwin admits that the early EU, say up to 1981, was a classic example of how regionalism can be a stumbling block, at least when it came to one small sector—agriculture. Since the EU had extremely high external protection, the customs union created brand new opponents to multilateral liberalization. For instance, British farmers had been largely weaned away from tariff protection by the time Britain joined in 1973. But once Britain was in, British farmers acquired a vested interest in maintaining the Common Agriculture Policy. Or, to put it in supply terms, the high levels of external protection lead to a *ceteris paribus* expansion of EU farm output that reinforced opposition to multilateral liberalization.

FTA among developing nations may lead to an anti-juggernaut effect. That is, they may strengthen rather than weakening the political power of anti-liberalization forces. That is, because developing nations often have high tariffs, South–South FTAs may hinder multilateral liberalization by creating or supporting uncompetitive, import-substituting industries. This point is especially true of South–South FTAs announced under the Enabling Clause. The Enabling Clause disables all the GATT disciplines that tend to foster domino and juggernaut effects because as per the Enabling Clause developing nations do not have to make tariff concessions in order to gain better market access (Baldwin 1997).

3.2.4 Other Proponents of This School

Other proponents of the proposition that RTAs benefit the multilateral trading system include Ethier and Lawrence. Lawrence (1996) has a similar opinion as Baldwin in that he also concludes that most RTAs will weaken the opponents of trade liberalization and hence will promote and foster multilateral trade liberalization. Ethier (1998) argues that "The new regionalism is in good part a direct result of the success of multilateral liberalization, as well as being the means by which new countries trying to enter the multilateral system compete among themselves for direct investment." In his estimation, the current wave of regionalism does not in any way threaten multilateral liberalism and in fact is a direct consequence of multilateralism. To him, countries use regionalism as a stepping-stone for entering the multilateral trading system.

Apart from the above, The International Chamber of Commerce (2004) in their report on "Regional Trade Agreements and The Multilateral Trading System" also opine that RTAs can act as an important building block for future multilateral liberalization given that "they enable parties to conclude levels of liberalization beyond the multilateral consensus and are able to address specific issues that do not register on the multilateral menu."

4 Overview of Regional Trade Agreements Entered into by India

India has always stood for an open, equitable, predictable, non-discriminatory, and rule-based international trading system. India gives primacy to engagements in multilateral negotiations at the WTO. However, recognizing the fact that the RTAs would continue to feature for a long time in the world trade, India engaged with its trading partners with the intention of expanding its export markets. Recent times have witnessed an increasing emphasis on India's economic partnership arrangements with various countries and regions, some of which are in the immediate neighborhood and some are in the inter-regional framework of economic cooperation. The interactions have ranged from bilateralism to subregionalism to regionalism. At the same time, India stands committed to the multilateral process of trade and trade-related rules like under the aegis of the WTO.

For a long time, India refused to jump on the bandwagon of RTA's as it wanted to show a committed stand toward multilateralism. However, now India has entered into several RTAs and is beginning to build a base. India has shown greater openness in recent years toward negotiating free trade or other preferential trading arrangements either bilaterally or in a regional framework. With the economy performing well and industry shower greater competitiveness, India is feeling more confident in exploring this parallel track of trade liberalization with select trading partners. This is keeping with the worldwide trend which has swept with even the countries such as Japan and Mongolia which were long desisted from entering into RTAs.

The Government of India is taking a very positive stance toward innovative bilateral/regional trade arrangements. Serious talks are going on to forge stronger economic ties with the EU that may eventually lead to a Comprehensive Economic Cooperation Agreement (CECA). Despite the fact that there are several issues to be ironed out, both trading partners are aiming to conclude the FTA talks soon. The 27-member EU had been insisting on including non-trade issues such as child labor and environment in the trade pact, which was strongly opposed by India. Besides this, the other issues of concern between both the parties are government procurement-, pharmaceutical-, and automobiles-related issues.

India had entered into comprehensive economic cooperation with Japan and South Korea. These agreements cover a strong bilateral tie-up in goods, services, and investment. The agreement with Japan is another historic landmark since it is India's first North–South trade agreement. Both Japan and Korea are major economies in Asia with whom India is seeking to develop closer ties as part of its

"Look East Policy." In the case of EU, with which India had begun yearly summit meetings and strategic partnership there is already an urge to take bilateral relationship to a higher level.

A North–South RTA by its very nature however is different in terms of the issues and concerns India has to navigate through. The average tariff levels in developed economies are generally low. Some of them also offer Generalized System of Preferences (GSP) tariff concessions for developing countries. There is therefore not much to gain when the tariff barriers come down or get eliminated as part of RTA commitments. But many developed economies, including EU and Japan, do have tariff peaks and tariff escalation for a small percentage of tariff lines that is of export interest to developing countries. These often relate to labor-intensive items such as textiles and apparel, leather goods, and marine products. Clearly, the focus will be to see how far there can be market access gains in these areas and toward ensuring that these products did not get included in the sensitive or negative lists of the developed partners. Most important, however, will be removal of non-tariff barriers and to address the various regulatory measures relating to health and other standards. These aspects would need to be resolved with suitable mutual recognitions wherever necessary, preferably before the signing of the agreement and not to be left for endless discussion later.

India has moved in a phased manner in concluding RTAs with some select trading partners. India's approach to RTAs was quite reserved till the late 1990s, when trade was closely regulated by a regime of imported licenses, high tariffs, and prevalence of quantitative restrictions. Following a slow and cautious start with an FTA in goods with Sri Lanka and Thailand, India concluded Comprehensive Economic Cooperation Agreement with Singapore encompassing trade in goods, services, and provision on investment protection and a double taxation treaty, economic cooperation in science and technology, air transport services, and intellectual property. This model is to be followed in most of India's future trade agreements. On the regional front, SAFTA and BIMSTEC are less comprehensive in content, but include emphasis on greater collaboration in trade facilitation (Roy 2006).

India's PTAs and FTAs with other developing countries have taken into account the comfort level of its partners. India has not insisted on a certain model FTA or pronounced very ambitious scope in such cases. India is, thus, looking beyond WTO and multilateralism to meet its strategic needs for market access worldwide. Since India is not a member of any RTA that has a strong influence on world trade, India will stand to lose because of trade-diverting effects of any RTAs and the new formations where it is not involved. The Indian textile sector, for instance, has been badly affected because the U.S. gives preferential treatment and duty-free access to textile products from Mexico under NAFTA.

Even as India progresses on expanding its RTA portfolio it would need to reflect on the effect, the rapid surge in RTAs worldwide would have on the multilateral trading system. Are they a creeping threat to WTO or can they exist in parallel, even as RTAs are rising in number on the one hand and Doha Round completion is proving elusive on the other?

The question of what should be India's general stand on RTAs is difficult to arrive at. For this, India will have to look at whether or not RTAs promote global welfare; i.e., it has to analyze the extent of trade diversion due to RTAs and its impact on Indian exports. However, India's present agreements with the regional partners have opened the markets for Indian goods in the countries concerned. All these agreements constitute unilateral tariff reduction except India–Sri Lanka FTA. India's overall trade balance with SAFTA is positive. The share of India's exports in South Asian countries has increased from 2.73 to 6.2% over the period 1990–2006. Hence, its existing and recent initiatives in regional/bilateral trade liberalization may help to divert some trade of the countries concerned from their other trading partners in favor of India given their supply capabilities and therefore may be beneficial to India (Nataraj 2007).

India is a member of the SAARC which has the free trade agreement (SAFTA) with Bangladesh, Bhutan, Maldives, Nepal, and Pakistan which came into full effect in 2006. India is also a part of Bangladesh, India, Myanmar, Sri Lanka, Thailand Economic Cooperation (BIMST-EC), with the other member countries being Bangladesh, Myanmar, Sri Lanka, and Thailand. India also entered into a bilateral free trade agreement with Sri Lanka in 2000 and more recently with Thailand in 2004.

Even as India has proceeded with negotiations on some RTAs, a number of Asian countries have also made similar deals with most of them concluded after the year 2000 only. There are several instances where two and more countries may be a party to more than one RTA raising a question as to which RTA will apply to trade between these countries. In the case of India and Sri Lanka, for example, apart from the bilateral FTA, both are also members of SAFTA and APTA. As BIMSTEC gets to have a free trade dimension, this would be yet another overlapping arrangement with its own rules of origin and timetable of tariff reductions. While the traders in the two countries will no doubt seek to use the rules that will be most favorable for their business, trade analysis and economists have pointed to the confusion that such different sets of applicable rules can create among trade administrators.

Expressing concern over the rise of recent mega-RTAs, the Indian government needs to gear up to meet the challenges that would emerge from these pacts. The major concern that these agreements have imposed is with respect to the erosion of already existing preference for Indian products in traditional markets. In order to tackle these situations, India has shown various steps. For instance, various sectoral strategies have been set up to monitor, examine, and adopt the evolving standards and regulations (Seshadri 2013), and there is an improvement in making already existing aware about our commitments with respect to the FTAs signed with them.

There appears to be a range of powerful responses that India has taken to address the challenges put forth by these mega-RTAs. First, India's internal market follows the principle of a Single Internal Market which involves a competitive pressure on India's internal economy which would rival the competitive benefits that members of mega-RTAs will receive from those agreements (Ciuriak 2015). Second, India like China has improved in unilateral trade and investment-related initiatives. Like it has involved itself in acquisition of technology and has initiated a number of trade and investment negotiations with these mega-regions itself, including India–EU FTA, India–Canada FTA, and the India–U.S. agreement. Further, there is a strong view that India is on its way to quickly conclude its already pending Broad-based Trade and Investment Agreement (BTIA) with EU.

Finally, India has also entered into trade- and investment-related initiatives with RCEP, which is its key instrument in neutralizing preference erosion, form the mega-regionals. It has also shown concern over South–South Cooperation on Capacity for Standards Conformance to meet higher standards not only being developed internally, but also emanating from the mega-regionals. India is also showing concern to improve its IP enforcement trends with Anti-Counterfeiting Trade Agreement (ACTA) and Trans-Pacific Partnership Agreement (TPPA).

India's RTAs have been examined for WTO compatibility by some analysts. On the one hand, most of the Indian RTAs will get covered by the "Enabling Clause"; on the other, there is substantial flexibility for developing countries to enter into RTAs with other developing countries. Shadan Farasat has commented that there could however be compatibility questions about the CECA with Singapore, which is not regarded as a developing country. This RTA has been notified by India for the goods sector, under Article XXIV of GATT, 1994, which requires tighter conditions to be fulfilled. The items that have been excluded from tariff liberalization in CECA constituted less than 25% of Singapore export to India. Exclusion of so many tariff items and some major sectors of trade raised serious questions about CECA satisfying the "substantial all" coverage under GATT Article XXIV. Again in respect of the services component of the CECA that has been notified under Article V of the GATS, certain aspect such as selective permission by India to only three Singaporean banks could be hit on the grounds of violation of the non-discriminatory requirement of Article V: 1(b) of GATS, particularly if the interpretation in the Canada-Auto Case by the Dispute Settlement Body of the WTO be taken into account (Farasat 2008).

5 Understanding the South Asia Free Trade Agreement—SAFTA—Mechanism

The wheel of India's economic liberalization that started rolling in the year 1991 is traveling across the rutted road of the international trade development successfully and has covered many landmarks by far in its journey. This is an ongoing journey of making the economy more market-oriented through measures such as reduction in tariffs, quotas deregulation of markets, reduction in taxes, and escalation in the role of private and foreign investment. Nations modulate their trade policies as per the changing economic, political, geographical, social, and other requirements, not only of their own nations but also that of the globe at large. The economic liberalization programs and policies form the heart of any nation as they help the nations not only to survive but "grow." "Trade" forms the nucleus of the phenomenon of economic liberalization, and in essence, "economic liberalization" is "trade liberalization" or "free trade."

5.1 Formation of SAARC

In December 1985, seven South Asian Nations came together and pledged to dedicate themselves to regional political and economic cooperation in South Asia in order to achieve economic, technological, social, and cultural development emphasizing collective self-reliance. With this objective, the governments of these seven nations, namely Bangladesh, Bhutan, India, Maldives, Nepal, Pakistan, and Sri Lanka, formally adopted a charter, i.e., The South Asian Association for Regional Co-operation (SAARC) to promote:

- Welfare economics,
- collective self-reliance among the countries of South Asia,
- Sociocultural development in the region, and
- Friendship and cooperation with other developing countries.

Afghanistan became its eighth member in 2007.

The combined economy of SAARC is the third largest in the world in the terms of GDP (PPP) after the United States and China and the eighth largest in the terms of nominal GDP. SAARC nations comprise 3% of the world's area and in contrast having 21% (around 1.7 billion) of the world's total population. India makes up over 70% of the area and population among these eight nations. The broad economic objectives of the SAARC are listed below:

- Welfare of the people of South Asia and improvement in their quality of life.
- Granting all individuals the opportunity to live in dignity and realize their full potential, thereby accelerating the economic growth in the region.
- Promoting and strengthening collective self-reliance among the countries of South Asia.
- Establishing mutual trust, and understanding and appreciating one another's problems.
- Activating collaboration and mutual assistance in the economic as well as social, cultural, technical, and scientific field.
- Facilitating and strengthening cooperation with other developing countries.
- Strengthening cooperation among themselves in international forums on matters of common interest.
- Cooperating with international and regional organization dedicated to similar aims and purposes.

SAARC is an economic and geopolitical regional organization. Its domain of influence is the largest of any regional organization in terms of combined population of its member states. The Sixth SAARC Summit at Colombo in 1991 started implementing the concept of free trading arrangement among the SAARC countries. In this early step to promote economic integration, an Inter-Governmental Group was set up to prepare an agreement to establish a South Asian Preferential Trade Arrangement (SAPTA) with the aims of promoting and sustaining mutual trade and economic cooperation through exchange of concession and reducing tariffs for intra-regional trade among the SAARC members.

5.2 Formation of SAPTA

The agreement on SAPTA was signed at the ministerial meeting during the seventh Dhaka Summit in 1993 and came into operation in December 1995.

SAPTA envisaged the following broad objectives:

- Greater specialization,
- Cost reduction,
- Substantial trade creation,
- Significant tariff reductions,
- Removal of other Non-Tariff Barriers,
- Complementarities in resource endowment, technical know-how, and expanding production capability.

SAPTA acted as the catalyst of the process of economic cooperation and integration among the SAARC countries. It was the initial step toward the creation of a trade bloc in the South Asian Region. Under the SAPTA mechanism, around 226 items for exchange on tariff concessions were identified ranging from 10 to 100%. India extended tariff concessions on around 106 items, and 62 items were for the Least Developed Countries (LDC) in the SAARC. Thus, there was a difference of treatment recognized between the LDCs and developing nations. Furthermore, the regulatory modifications with respect to Non-Tariff Barriers were not discussed.

Following were the shortcomings of SAPTA:

- Not much significant tariff cuts.
- Most concessions related to the products that were not relevant to the trade interest of other member countries.
- Benefit in the form of tariff concessions failed to create any significant gains in the intra-SAARC trade.
- The rules of origin prescribed under SAPTA were stringent that also contributed to its failure.
- Destination/port restrictions.
- Restrictive product coverage.

According to the SAARC Secretariat Report 2004, nevertheless, SAPTA managed to provide the economy of the SAARC nations "satisfactory progress."

5.3 Formation of SAFTA

Agreements on Preferential Trade Arrangements (PTA) are considered as the "first stage" of economic integration (Dalimov RT Modelling 2008). An agreement for PTA generally has an eventual aim of getting converted into a Free Trade Agreement. On the same lines, SAPTA was seen as the first step toward South Asian Free Trade Area (SAFTA) and it did pave the way for the agreement to form an FTA among SAARC nations. The SAFTA agreement came into force on July 1, 2006, and was conceptualized to develop common market in the region with the implementation of SAPTA. It involves agreement on tariff concessions such as national duties concession and non-tariff concession. The agreement aims to establish a tariff-free market in the region, bringing down customs duties of all traded goods to zero with an eventual aim of the creation of a South Asian Economic Union (Kemal 2005).

5.4 Working of SAFTA

The SAFTA emphasizes to work according to the following broad principles:

- Trade liberalization for the expansion of trade;
- Enhancing mutual trade and economic collaboration;
- Promoting free movement of goods, commercial services, income-generating programs;
- Establishing direct connectivity among the member countries;
- Promoting healthy competitive market among SAARC nation staking into account their respective levels and pattern of economic development;
- Sharing of equal trade benefits among all SAARC nations and maintaining overall reciprocity so as to benefit equitably;
- Gradual tariff reform negotiations, through periodic reviews;
- Inclusion of all products, manufactures, and commodities in their raw, semi-processed, and processed forms;
- Public and private sector cooperation, particularly joint ventures;
- Harmonization of standards;
- Simplification of customs procedures;
- Cooperation among the central banks;
- Effective administrative operation;
- Joint resolution of disputes and its effective implementation.

The execution of the above-mentioned principles of SAFTA is done by way of following mechanisms:

5.4.1 Trade Liberalization Program

- Reduction in existing tariff to 30% tariff by the Least Developing Countries and 20% reduction by the other countries.
- Sensitive list, i.e., which does not include tariff concession, be negotiated among the contracting countries for common agreement and then to be traded. The list has to be reviewed by the SAFTA Ministerial Council every four years in an attempt to reduce the list.

5.4.2 Rules of Origin

As mentioned in the earlier sections of this paper:

- Minimum extent of local material inputs prescribed has to be fulfilled in order to receive preferential treatment.
- Local transformations adding value to the goods must be there for making any product or service eligible for concessions.

5.4.3 Non-Tariff Barriers Comprises of

- Infrastructure barriers,
- Procedural barriers,
- Barrier of standardization,
- Para-tariff barriers: Para tariffs refer to duties and taxes that are over and above the "border tariffs." Normally, these include domestic taxes charged either by the Central Government or the State Government. These could, for instance, be the countervailing duty.

5.4.4 Institutional Arrangements

Ensuring Inter-Regional Cooperation, the SAARC nations have dedicated themselves to develop mutually beneficial links between SAARC and the following:

- Other regional organizations,
- International organizations,
- International bodies and entities,
- States outside the region, interested in SAARC activities.

5.4.5 Consultations and Dispute Settlement Procedures

- Predictable,
- Flexible,
- Joint participation,
- Mutually agreed solution.

5.4.6 Safeguard Measures

As mentioned earlier in this paper following are the few measures:

- Principle of De Minimis,
- *Regional Value Content*,
- *Tariff Shift*.

5.5 Shortcomings of SAFTA

- Long sensitive lists of commodities, i.e., not covered for preferential treatment; however, it is intended that over time, the sensitive list of commodities will be reduced and, meanwhile, members retain the MFN tariff rates which are also often quite significant.
- Services trade is excluded.
- No substantial provision for escalating investment when investment is always important in strengthening the regional economy, not so effective implementation due to political hurdles.
- The SAFTA Members also party to several other PTAs, which make the system of trade concessions complicated.
- Destination/port restriction—Though done in order to curb illegal flow, South Asian countries specify the port of entry. Sometimes, this reflects potential inadequate administrative capacity. The port-specific restrictions have increased transactions costs of trading across border and sometimes led to a virtual blockage of imports.

Moreover, according to few economists, Regional Trade Agreements (RTAs) can be welfare reducing when it results in substantial trade diversion, and given the relatively high levels of protection in the region, most analysts predicted that trade diversion would be a dominant effect of SAFTA. Nonetheless, there is constant effort being made for strengthening such agreements probable reason being the rise of PTAs across the globe because of its effective functioning. Furthermore, the member countries have almost identical pattern of comparative advantage that too in a narrow range of products, and hence, few economists hold the view that the low level of intra-regional trade seems inevitable as trade complementarily are dismal (Banik et al. 2006).

Thus, apprehensions abound as to how effectively the schedules of the SAFTA agreement would actually be implemented. Though the effective enforcement of the agreement is full of challenges due to various political and a technical reason, it cannot be denied that Intra-SAARC trade has all the potential of flourishing:

- Owing to its geographical proximity, rising income, and falling tariffs;
- Through efficient use of capital and labor as well as distribution of goods and services across borders;
- By way of greater regional integration through increased flow of FDI;
- Strategically when the South Asian countries negotiate as a unified group in a multilateral set up;
- By developing regionally integrated approach toward provision of regional public goods such as environment, water conservation, and other natural resources including the regional ecosystem and related biodiversity as they are best addressed in a cooperative framework.

More importantly, South Asian countries exhibit symmetric economic activity. There is evidence of long-term co-movement in supply-side components of output in the SAARC region, meaning thereby that an economic boom in one of these nations is likely to echo throughout the region. In fact, this aforementioned economic characteristic of South Asian countries will enable them to go beyond the FTA framework and work for deeper economic integration, such as forming a common market and economic union which in fact is the eventual goal of SAFTA.

6 Conclusion and Suggestions

The present chapter has analyzed in detail the reasons for the proliferation of RTAs and its impact on the multilateral trade regime. RTAs act as an important source of access to foreign markets and foreign trade for several countries, which the multilateral regime has failed in providing. However, we have also seen that freeing up trade may not be the only reason why countries forge such alliances. In certain cases, RTAs have been the detriment of smaller countries which form part of the alliance.

The survey of scholarly work on the impact of the RTAs on the multilateral trade regime and the future of WTO has brought to light the debate concerning the desirability of RTAs. We have seen two schools of thought, one which says that proliferation of RTAs is side-tracking the attention of countries from WTO and gradually leading to trade bloc formation with perpetuating trade preferences which will ultimately fail the objective of freeing up trade. The other school of thought says that RTAs are a stepping-stone rather than a stumbling block to the multilateral trade regime. This school proposes that RTAs act as an important source of trade liberalization and, with the growth of pro-liberalization forces, ultimately, the objective of reducing tariffs and freeing up trade will be achieved.

Whatever are the arguments for RTAs, there can be no denying of the fact that the rapid proliferation of RTAs has certainly deepened the crisis of rules of origin and has lead to trade diversion and distortion. Several South–South RTAs have led not to tariff reduction, but have been motivated by political reasons. RTAs have also brought, rather forced, into the ambit of international trade, factors which are not part of the WTO. The attitude of countries has also become cynical with countries treating RTAs as a fallback option to get what they want. This is especially relevant when developing countries are forced to accede to things which they would not ordinarily accept in multilateral negotiations. Evidence of this is the statement credited to a negotiator in Geneva who said "if we do not get what we want in the negotiating agenda, why should we worry? We have our own RTA, that's where the action is (Crawford and Laird 2000)." Such an attitude undermines the very existence of WTO and relegates its status to mere bystander.

Under such circumstances, it is strongly felt that something has to be done so that the multilateral trade regime is not dismantled. Further, leaving apart the effect of RTAs on the multilateral regime, it is also important to note that issues concerning ROOs and harmful trade diversion also need thorough examination.

Dismantling the whole system of RTAs is not a tenable idea because RTAs have proliferated to such an extent that the whole system is irreversible. Also, in spite of the harmful effects that RTAs can have on the multilateral trade regime, it is also true that RTAs have given a breather for several economies such as Mexico and Chile and have opened up trade opportunities for such countries, thereby promoting their development.

Understanding the impact that RTAs are having on the multilateral regime, two plausible solutions emerged from the discussions at the WTO level. The first solution proposed by Prof. Bhagwati is for countries to put efforts toward concluding the Doha Round so that confidence in the effectiveness of WTO is restored among members. The other solution called for something to be done beyond Doha. Basically, Baldwin, the propagator of this solution, says that Doha has failed, and even if it were to be actively pursued no convergence on a workable solution to the problem of RTA, spaghetti bowls can be reached in the near future. So he calls for a creative approach toward the problem. Given the state of affairs in the ministerial conferences, it is certainly felt that a creative solution which goes beyond the ambit of interpretation of RTA favoring clauses is needed if the multilateral trade regime is to be protected from getting fragmented.

For India, these RTAs can go a long way. These RTAs can be a useful policy tool in further developing India's external economic relations, particularly in relation to the development of cooperation among the countries. It allows India to experiment with bolder economic trade liberalization even if it is restricted within few countries. There are chances of India to get some good reciprocal benefits in this process. Domestic stakeholders can be greatly benefitted from these regional trade agreements. RTAs liberalization will assist in easing domestic acceptance to Doha Round commitments as and when they will get finalized. Creating an RTA is also a valuable experience in the services sector with respect to putting together MRAs. These negotiating experiences can also be useful in the WTO negotiations since these are relatively newer areas where the options for liberalization are many and some of the RTA solutions can serve as models.

Notwithstanding the shortcomings of the SAFTA Agreement, there is immense potential for expanding trade within the region. South Asia, with a population of 1.4 billion, is expected to be the biggest free trade area of the world. The region has been experiencing a GDP growth rate of six to seven percent in the last five years. It has an increasing middle class of 400 million people. All these indicators point to the immense potential for these countries to expand their intra-regional trade, as the path toward the goal of a free trade area and the preconditions under the SAFTA Treaty have been defined. However, given the fact that there are several shortcomings in the Treaty, the need of the hour is to identify them and rectify them to make the SAFTA a success.

References

Baldwin RE (1997) The causes of regionalism. World Econ 20(7):865–888

Baldwin RE (2016) Stepping stones or building blocks: regional and multilateral integration. http://citeseerx.ist.psu.edu/viewdoc/download?doi=10.1.1.463.3203&rep=rep1&type=pdf. Last accessed on 5 June 2016

Banik N, Biswas B, Saunders P (2006) An optimum currency area in South Asia: is it plausible? J World Trade 40:387–405

Bartels L, Ortino F (eds) (2010) Regional trade agreements and the WTO legal system. Oxford University Press, Oxford

Bhagwati J (1995) U.S. trade policy: the infatuation with the free trade areas. In: Bhagwati J, Krueger A (eds) The dangerous drift to preferential trade agreements. American Enterprise Institute, Washington

Bhagwati J, Krueger A (1995) The dangerous drift to preferential trade agreements. American Enterprise Institute, Washington

Bhagwati J, Panagariya A (2007) Bilateral trade treaties are a Sham

Bhagwati J, Krishna P, Panagariya A (eds) (1999) Trading blocs-alternative approaches to analyzing preferential trade agreements. MIT Press, London

Ciuriak D (2015) India's response to the challenge of the mega-regionals, changing global economic scenario: implications for India's trade policy and make in india programme conference

Crawford J, Laird S (2000) Regional trade agreement and the WTO. CREDIT Research Paper No. 00/3. http://www.nottingham.ac.uk/economics/credit/research/papers/cp.00.3.pdf. Last accessed on May 2016

Dalimov RT Modelling (2008) International economic integration: an oscillation theory approach. http://www.pearsonschool.com/index.cfm?locator=PSZ13f. Last accessed on 5 May 2016

Ethier WJ (1998) Regionalism in a multilateral world. J Polit Econ 106(6)

Farasat S (2008) India's quest for regional trade agreements: challenges ahead. J World Trade 42(3):433–460

Ferd Bergsten in Bergsten F (1996) Competitive liberalization and global free trade: a vision for the early 21st century. Institute for International Economics, Washington, DC

Fiorentino RV, Verdeja L, Toqueboeuf C (2006) The changing landscape of regional trade agreements: 2006 Update. http://www.wto.org/english/res_e/booksp_/discussion_papers12a_e.pdf. Last accessed on 5 June 2016

Inama S (2011) Rules of origin in international trade. Cambridge University Press, Cambridge

Jackson JH (1969) World trade and the law of GATT—a legal analysis of the general agreement on tariffs and trade, pp 575–623

Kemal AR (2005) SAFTA and Economic Cooperation. http://www.southasianmedia.net/conference/Regional_Conference/safta.htm. Last accessed on 2016

Krueger AO (1995) NAFTA: strengthening or weakening the international trade system. In: Bhagwati J, Krueger A (eds) The dangerous drift of preferential trade agreements. American Enterprise Institute, Washington

Krugman P (1991) Is bilateralism bad? In: Helpman E, Razin A (eds) International trade and trade policy. MIT Press, Cambridge

Lawrence RZ (1996) Regionalism, multilateralism and deeper integration. Brookings Institution, Washington, DC

Nataraj G (2007) Regional trade agreements in the Doha Round: good for India? http://www.adb.org/sites/default/files/publication/156705/adbi-dp67.pdf. Last accessed on 5 May 2016

Pal P (2004) Regional trade agreements in a multilateral trade regime: an overview. http://www.networkideas.org/feathm/may2004/survey_paper_RTA.pdf. Last accessed on 5 June 2016

Pomfret R (1997) The economics of regional trade agreements. Oxford University Press, New York

Roy J (2006) Why isn't India a major global player? The Political Economy of Trade Liberalization. http://cadmus.eui.eu/bitstream/handle/1814/28917/RSCAS_2013_84.pdf?sequence=1. Last accessed on 5 May 2016

Seshadri VS (2013) Transatlantic trade and investment partnership, research and information system for developing countries

Summers L (1991) Regionalism and the world trading system—policy implications of trade and currency zones wyoming. Federal Reserve Bank of Kansas City

Understanding the WTO (2016) WTO Secretariat Publications, Information and External Division. http://www.wto.org/english/tratop_e/region_e/region_e.htm. Accessed 6 June 2016

Author Biography

Mr. Bipin Kumar is Assistant Professor at National Law University, Jodhpur in Rajasthan for the last 12 years. He holds an LL.B. and LL.M. from University of Delhi. He recently submitted his Doctoral Thesis "Legal Framework of Regional Trade Agreement in WTO: A Case Study of India's RTAs" to National Law University, Jodhpur. Mr. Kumar had also worked with Centre for WTO Studies of Indian Institute of Foreign Trade, New Delhi. He holds the specialization of International Trade Law/WTO and Commercial Transactions. He regularly writes and delivers lectures on International Trade and WTO matters and is Executive Director of Centre for WTO Law and Policy, Member of Institute of BRICS Laws and Faculty-in-Charge of Journal of Trade, Law and Development.

Chapter 6
The Conundrums of Trade Barriers in Preferential Trading: Prospects from SAARC

Divesh Kaul

1 Introduction

The South Asian Association for Regional Cooperation (SAARC) is a regional intergovernmental association of eight least developed countries (LDCs) and non-least developed countries (non-LDCs) of South Asia. SAARC's LDCs are Afghanistan, Bangladesh, Bhutan, the Maldives, and Nepal (classification of LDCs is same as the LDCs designated by the United Nations except the Maldives, which SAARC continued to classify as LDC despite being graduated from being a LDC in 2011 as per the United Nations guidelines). SAARC's non-LDCs are India, Pakistan, and Sri Lanka (Articles 1 & 12—SAFTA; United Nations, 2017). These countries share cultural, historical, and family ties and face similar socioeconomic and development challenges. Over the years, SAARC has initiated various programs in the areas of agriculture, rural development, education, energy, environment, poverty alleviation, biotechnology, and finance for the collective welfare of the people of South Asia. Preferential trade agreements (PTAs) have emerged as one of the means to further regional and collective progress and strengthen intra-regional association. They offer a model of self-contained trade regimes, distinguishable from the General Agreement on Tariffs and Trade (GATT)/World Trade Organization (WTO) regime.

Preferential trade agreements remain an indispensable vehicle of trade liberalization, and examining the reduction of trade barriers at regional and bilateral levels becomes an important chapter in the study of global trade liberalization. In this examination, various discourses on the scope and benefits of removal and elimination of tariff and non-tariff trade barriers require consideration. Removal of tariff barriers is important for trade liberalization, but is it the only way? The role of other "non-tariff" barriers and their importance in trade liberalization demand evaluation.

D. Kaul (✉)
Gaeddu College of Business Studies, Gedu, Bhutan

J.L. Kaul and A. Jha (eds.), *Shifting Horizons of Public International Law*,
https://doi.org/10.1007/978-81-322-3724-2_6

Through these spectrums, the performance of SAARC's trade liberalization agenda will be explored. This chapter examines the hallmarks of other regional trade agreements and assesses how SAARC can beat the forefront of ambitious regional trading endeavors in the twenty-first century. This chapter evaluates the reduction of trade barriers with respect to SAARC's regional trade agreements over the course of five Parts.

Part I introduces the topic and the scheme of the chapter. Part II lays the background of trade liberalization in international trade regime. This Part discusses the GATT/WTO regime on trade liberalization. This Part concludes with evaluating the ambit of trade liberalization through preferential PTAs in light of GATT/WTO provisions on preferential trading.

Part III examines SAARC's trade liberalization regime, the journey that began with Bangladesh's 1980 proposal for regional cooperation. Part III also discusses SAARC's mandate for, and implementation of, trade liberalization in goods and services through three trade instruments: the South Asian Preferential Trading Agreement (SAPTA), the Agreement on South Asian Free Trade Area (SAFTA), and the SAARC Agreement on Trade in Services (SATIS). It concludes with enumerating the challenges faced in regional integration in South Asian region.

Part IV assesses SAARC's accomplishments through the trends of "regional" global governance and reduction of trade barriers achieved in other regions, including Latin America, Southeast Asia, North America, and the European Union. Part IV explores ways to further global trade governance though preferential trade agreements. This Part also considers the hurdles in liberalizing trade at regional level and proposes various ways to address the gaps in trade integration and liberalization with respect to SAARC's trade mechanisms.

Part V concludes the chapter by noting that, despite the existence of many novel and cutting-edge preferential trade models, FTAs do not replace the WTO; they complement it. Like the WTO, FTAs are also premised on promoting trade as a mean of attaining peace and prosperity. Lastly, the chapter highlights the peculiarity of the South Asian region, which houses more than 40% of the world's poor, and is afflicted by several non-tariff hurdles, including corruption. However, the South Asian region posits an aspiration to raise the living standards of its people with the help of collective efforts under the auspices of SAARC to promote peace and welfare and to reduce trade barriers.

2 Perspective on Trade and Liberalization

2.1 Free Trade and Tariffs Interconnection

The international economic order bases upon the market economy, promotion of global welfare and to some extent, the prevention of economic warfare. International trade focuses on the stipulations of "comparative advantage," (i.e., promoting individual cross-border exchanges, specialization, and global welfare). The international trade regime, coupled with the pillars of National Treatment (NT) and Most Favored Nation (MFN) standards, seeks to eliminate cross-border impediments, to free global market connectivity from hindrances and to liberalize trade (Qureshi and Ziegler 2011: 1; Bhala 2015).

Sovereign nations have long used "tariffs" (also known as "custom duties") to give a price advantage to locally produced goods over similar imports, to shield domestic industries from foreign competition, and to raise revenue by imposing border taxes on incoming foreign commodities (WTO Secretariat 2016; Lester and Mercurio 2010). There are three types of tariffs: First, an "*ad valorem*" tariff is based on a fixed percentage of the imported commodity's value; second, a "specific" tariff is a flat tax per imported item; and third, a "mixed" tariff is a hybrid of both *ad valorem* and specific tariffs. Two of the most important goals of the international trade regime are reducing and binding tariffs, both of which are achieved by including them in Schedules of Concession annexed to the GATT Agreement (Matsushita 2006; Hoda 2001; WTO Secretariat 2016).

In the Schedules of Concession, every WTO Member is required to document a ceiling (also called a bound tariff), or maximum rates, that may apply to a particular commodity. Once the tariffs are bound, Member States make tariff concessions to their counterparts on the basis of reciprocity. The "tariff list" or "tariff schedule" consolidates an item-by-item list of product categories run by the World Customs Organization (WCO). A Member State may apply tariff rates lower than the bound tariff fixed in the Schedules of Concession, but in no case, can a State impose a tariff exceeding that amount. GATT Article II expounds the commitment of WTO Members to bind their tariff rates in the Schedules of Concession and mandates the Members accord tariffs no less favorable than those in the appropriate Schedule. The tariff concessions bound in the Schedule extend to other Members on a MFN basis (Koul 2013; WTO Secretariat 2016; Bhala 2015: 1).

Reducing tariffs has been an essential element of GATT/WTO negotiations. The result of the Uruguay Round (1986–1994) included the States' commitments to cut tariffs (achieving average tariff reduction from 5 to 0% on weighted average) as well as to bind their customs duty rates to levels that were difficult to raise. In the initial tariff rounds (those implemented before Kennedy Round), tariff reduction materialized on item-by-item basis, and the latter rounds implemented a linear cut approach (WTO Secretariat 2016; Koul 2013).

There has been a 15% reduction in average tariffs applied by WTO Members between 1996 and 2013. Simultaneously, global trade in goods nearly quadrupled, from US$ 5 trillion (in 1996) to US$ 19 trillion in 2013. Tariff reduction is an essential element in boosting global trade, and in the past two decades, WTO Members consistently reduced their tariffs despite negotiating high ceilings at the time of joining the WTO (WTO Secretariat 2016).

2.2 Preferential Trade Agreements and Trade Liberalization

Several nations have been keen to enter preferential trade agreements (PTAs). As of September 1, 2016, as many as 267 regional trade agreements (RTAs) are in operation worldwide, and WTO Member States have made 424 notifications for goods, services, and accessions. Of these RTAs, free trade agreements (FTAs) account for almost 90% and customs unions (CUs) for the remaining 10% (WTO Secretariat 2016).

Article XXIV of the GATT and Article V of the GATS provide a mandate for PTAs within the global trade regime. These provisions validate the coexistence of PTAs with the WTO framework, whether in the form of an FTA or a customs union (CU). WTO texts elucidate PTAs' intended use that "the purpose of these should be to facilitate trade between the constituent territories and not to raise barriers to the trade of other contracting parties with such territories." The regional trading blocs have always evoked controversies, since in essence they oppose the vital principle of international trade, the MFN clause (Gupta 2002). However, the aim of WTO in allowing the FTA regimes is to expedite the process of dismantling trade-distorting barriers, both tariff and non-tariff (WTO Secretariat 2016).

Professor Bhagwati (2008) noted that very few contemplated that the Article XXIV exception would be used except in rare circumstances. It was envisioned that progress toward free trade and extending it to nearly all commodities would discourage States from resorting to Article XXIV exception. Professor Bhala (2015: 2) advocated a three-tier process for "competitive liberalization" by moving as aggressively as possible toward the end of global free trade by simultaneously pursuing trade liberalization at multilateral, regional, and bilateral levels. Professor Bhala denoted this strategy using other terms such as "complimentary liberalization" and "parallel liberalization." Indeed, joining an FTA may lead to some multifaceted benefits, including domestic policy reforms, increased multilateral bargaining power, strategic linkages, more political stake in multilateral negotiations, and enhanced national security (Whalley 1996; Bhagwati 2008).

PTAs create preferential tariffs among trading partners that may be discriminatory or incongruous with the multilateral trading system. Scholars express apprehensions regarding States' over-indulgence with FTAs and the potential to create an erosion of the global economic order through: forum shopping for dispute settlement, trade diversion from cost-efficient non-Member States to less efficient Member States, and a chaotic crisscrossing of multiple PTAs with varying tariff trajectories, sometimes called the "spaghetti bowl" concern. At the same time, not all PTAs are created equal, and their impact on different Member States may vary and yield uneven benefits. The domestic-level reform strategies may also differ from State to State, thus, there is no single yardstick or panacea (Bhagwati 2008; Bhala 2015: 2; Krueger 1999).

3 SAARC's Path to Increasing Trade and Reducing Barriers

3.1 SAARC's Institutional Mechanisms on Trade Liberalization and Cooperation in Trade

3.1.1 South Asian Preferential Trading Arrangement (SAPTA)

The Sixth Summit held in Colombo, Sri Lanka, in December 1991, first highlighted Member States' commitment to trade liberalization "in such a manner as will ensure that the countries in the region can share the benefits of trade expansion equitably" (Kumar 2005). The Heads of State underscored "the need for vigorously promoting South–South economic cooperation to offset the negative consequences of international economic developments." They recognized "the importance of securing less restrictive trading and marketing opportunities for their products, more extensive technology and resource transfers to South Asia, debt relief and access on favorable and on more concessional terms to resources from multilateral financial institutions." The Summit approved the establishment of an intergovernmental group to formulate an agreement to establish preferential trading agreement, initially proposed by Sri Lanka (Declaration of the Sixth SAARC Summit).

With the Seventh Summit Declaration, SAARC deliberated pressing international economic issues and recognized the importance of a strengthened and liberalized international trading system. SAARC viewed the ongoing negotiations of the Uruguay Round under the WTO with optimism and reckoned that its success would translate into further economic growth, aided by doing away with protectionist policies and gradual removal of trade barriers. The WTO negotiations encouraged SAARC members to carry out a similar venture among themselves (Seventh SAARC Declaration).

SAPTA Agreement projected the collective desire of the Member States to promote and sustain mutual trade and economic cooperation within South Asia through the exchange of concessions based on the following principles: "overall reciprocity and mutuality of advantages"; "negotiating gradual tariff reforms with periodic reviews"; "recognizing the special needs of the LDC States and granting them concrete preferential measures"; and "including all products, manufactures, and commodities in their raw, semi-processed, and processed forms" (SAARC Secretariat 2016).

SAPTA provided a platform for SAARC Member States to negotiate tariff concessions and subsequently agrees to a gradual removal of both tariff and non-tariff barriers. The Agreement provided a stimulus to intra-regional trade while covering around 5000 commodities over four rounds of trade negotiations (SAARC Web site 2016). SAPTA negotiations helped produce the offer of tariff concessions for a total of 226 products in the First Round. The Association's relatively more developed countries (India, Pakistan, and Sri Lanka) offered hundreds of products on concessional tariff (special treatment) to their least developed SAARC counterparts (Bangladesh, Bhutan, Maldives, and Nepal) without any reciprocity requirement. The Second Round of negotiations offered 213 products for concessional tariff, while 764 products were designated for SAARC's LDCs (Ranjit Kumar 2005).

Incidentally, SAARC countries never thought seriously about securing adequate and reciprocal market access from each other, despite their shared regional location. At the time of endorsing SAPTA, SAARC Members carried out only 3% of trade among themselves. After SAPTA, the number rose to 5%. These are very inconspicuous numbers for an intra-regional bloc of eight countries, in which one-fifth of the world population resides (Kumar 2005).

3.1.2 Agreement on South Asian Free Trade Area (SAFTA)

SAPTA was envisioned as the first step toward the adoption of various instruments of trade liberalization on a preferential basis, the progression toward the FTAs leading subsequently toward a customs union, a common market, and an economic union. SAFTA was signed during the 12th SAARC Summit held in Islamabad, Pakistan, in January 2004, and entered into force in January 2006. Although the path to economic integration culminated nineteen years after the establishment of SAARC, this step gathered momentum toward broadening economic cooperation to ensure equitable distribution of trade benefits (SAARC Secretariat 2016). Article 3 of the SAFTA Agreement laid down various objectives and principles on: eliminating trade barriers; facilitating cross-border movement of goods; promoting conditions of fair competition; ensuring equitable benefits; and further cooperation including joint administration for the resolution of disputes.

Furthermore, the SAFTA Agreement under Article 8 *inter alia* recommended additional measures, such as: the "harmonization of standards, reciprocal recognition of tests and accreditation of testing laboratories of Contracting States and certification of products"; "simplification and harmonization of customs clearance procedure"; "removal of barriers to intra-SAARC investment"; "harmonization of national customs classification"; "transit facilities for efficient intra-SAARC trade"; "simplification of banking procedures for import financing"; and "simplification of procedures for business visas."

SAFTA Agreement pledged a governance model for its FTA based on the "existing rights and obligations" of the Member States with respect to one another under the GATT/WTO regime. It acknowledged reciprocity, entailed adopting trade facilitation and progressive harmonizing Contracting States' legislations in relevant areas, and adopted "concrete preferential measures" for LDCs on a non-reciprocal basis.

The Trade Liberalization Program (TLP) under the aegis of SAFTA authorized Contracting States to a "Schedule of Tariff Reductions." The following are features of the tariff reductions schedule.

First, non-LDC States had to reduce existing tariff rates by 20%, preferably in equal annual installments, within two years from the agreement's entrance into force. In the event of actual tariff at less than 20%, annual reduction would materialize on a margin of preference basis of 10% on actual tariff rates for each of the two years. Second, LDC States had to reduce 30% from existing tariff rates within two years from the Agreement's entrance into force. In these States, should an actual tariff be less than 30%, annual reduction would materialize on a margin of preference basis of 5% on actual tariff rates for each of the two years. Third, non-LDC States were obligated to a subsequent tariff reduction from 20% or below to 0–5% within a second time frame of five years, beginning from the third year from the date of the Agreement's entry into force. Sri Lanka, as a special case, was given six years to comply with the requirement. Contracting States could adopt reductions in equal annual installments, so long as reductions were not less than 15% annually. Last, LDC States had to do a subsequent tariff reduction from 30% or below to 0–5% within the second time frame of eight years, beginning three years from the date of the Agreement's entry into force. The LDC States could adopt reductions in equal annual installments but not reductions of less than 10% annually (SAFTA Agreement—SAARC).

Despite a tardy commencement, SAFTA's tariff reduction agenda was encouraging, particularly the special attention given to the demands of the LDCs in the Association. Moreover, SAARC implemented a framework of annual review by the Committee of Experts of all the Contracting States' notifications "para-tariff" and "non-tariff measures" (SAARC Secretariat 2016). The Agreement required the Contracting States to eliminate all quantitative restrictions, except those restrictions otherwise permitted under GATT 1994 with respect to commodities included in SAFTA's Trade Liberalization Program (TLP). Under the provisions specifying Special and Differential Treatment for the LDC States, the Agreement, *inter alia*, stressed the need for the Contracting States to establish an appropriate mechanism to compensate the LDC States for their loss of customs revenue until alternative domestic arrangements were formulated to address this situation. An anomaly to SAFTA's trade expansion agenda is the non-application of TLP to the tariff lines included in the "Sensitive Lists" as negotiated by the Contracting States. The Sensitive List is to be reviewed at least every four years, and the number of products in the List is subject to a mutually acceptable maximum ceiling, with built-in flexibility to LDC States to seek derogation, with respect to the products of their export interest (SAFTA Agreement—SAARC).

3.1.3 SAARC Agreement on Trade in Services (SATIS)

To further expand the horizons of intra-SAARC trade both in goods and services, the SAARC Agreement on Trade in Services was signed at the 16th SAARC Summit held in Thimphu, Bhutan, in April 2010 and ratified two years later in November 2012. The objectives of the SATIS Agreement included: promoting trade in services among SAARC Members; liberalizing and promoting trade in services, with broad-based and deeper coverage of majority of services sectors; and negotiating specific commitments for progressive liberalizing based on "request-and-offer" approach.

The SATIS Agreement (Article 3) specified non-applicability to particular categories of government procurement or services, supplied in the exercise of governmental authority and transportation (and non-transportation) air services. This includes domestic and international services other than aircraft repair and maintenance services, and the marketing and sale of air transport services and computerized reservation system services.

SATIS (Article 21) seeks cooperation to expand trade in services through the following four mechanisms. The first initiative is to develop regulatory capacity through the exchange of experiences and best practices among the Contracting States' regulatory bodies. Second, SATIS incorporates working groups for specific sectors of interest comprising the relevant national authorities and stakeholders. Third, it encourages cooperating and coordinating with WTO/GATS negotiations. Fourth, it seeks to constitute a working group under the Heads of SAARC Statistical Organisations (SAARCSTAT) to collect and exchange statistics and regulations to improve collection of trade statistics in services.

The Association, by way of the SATIS Agreement (Preamble), acknowledged the importance of services sector and stressed its increasing role in the Member States' trade economics, as well as its immense potential to strengthen intra-regional trade in services in a mutually beneficial way. The provisions on market access amplify TLP's approval by ensuring that no measures, unless otherwise specified in the "Schedule of Specific Commitments," (Article 8—SATIS Agreement) shall:

- be maintained or adopted which limit the number of service suppliers through quotas or monopolies;
- put a bar in the form of numerical quotas on the total value of service transactions or assets;
- enforce a quota on the total number of service operations or on the total quantity of service;
- restrict the total number of natural persons that the service supplier may employ; and
- limit the participation of foreign capital in terms of maximum percentage limit on foreign shareholding or the total value of individual or aggregate foreign investment (Article 6—SATIS Agreement).

Transparency is paramount in any robust institutional mechanism. The SAARC ensures through SATIS (Article 19) that each Contracting State promptly publishes all relevant measures of general application pertaining to the Agreement (unless there is an emergency) at least fourteen days prior to their entry into force.

3.2 Challenges in South Asian Regional Integration

Home to over one and a half billion people and economic growth of 7.1% over the last decade, Asia is increasingly recognized as one of the world's most dynamic regions (World Bank 2016). However, maintaining this growth requires a free flow of goods, services, and capital across borders. Although South Asia has great potential for integrating trade, investment, and production space, it remains one of the least-integrated areas in the world. Even the economic integration under the auspices of SAARC was visualized as late as the 1990s. Historically, Asia has substantially relied on access to large markets in Europe and the USA for its commodities and to stimulate growth in production. Even so, the rise of Asia ought to coincide with an endeavor among the Asian countries to cooperate and integrate as a collective market of their own (Moinuddin 2013).

The World Bank (2010) acknowledges some of the factors limiting intra-regional trade, such as limited transport connectivity, onerous logistics, and regulatory impediments. Incidentally, in 1948, right after the British exit from the Indian Subcontinent, intra-regional trade in the South Asian region (broadly between the current territories of Kabul, Afghanistan and Chittagong, Bangladesh) was as high as 19%. This double-digit figure declined to a mere 2% by 1967. The factors responsible for this decline include high tariff and non-tariff import barriers successive governments' adoption of inward-looking and import-substituting policies (Kumar and Singh 2009). In recent years, intra-regional trade has risen but remains far from reaching a double-digit figure. Indeed, historical political tensions and mistrust among South Asian nations, cross-border conflicts, terrorism, and other security conflicts have tempered the attempts to normalize trade relationships in the region. These factors impact trade more within South Asia than between South Asia and the other regions across the world. Intra-regional trade within South Asia is minuscule, even in comparison to neighboring Southeast Asia. Moreover, intra-regional investment is less than 1% of overall investment (World Bank 2016).

Acclaimed author, former United Nations diplomat, and federal Indian minister, Dr. Shashi Tharoor, pointed out that before India sets itself on a path of liberalization and sturdy integration into the global economic system in the 1990s, under the leadership of former Prime Minister, P.V. Narasimha Rao and his then Finance Minister Dr. Manmohan Singh, the country (between the year of independence, 1947, and the late 1980s) reeled under enormous protectionism, industrial inefficiency, and economic stagnation resulting from stern central planning, a state-controlled economy, burgeoning bureaucracy, and the "License Raj" (Dr. Tharoor (2012) shares a former Indian diplomat's anecdotal corroboration from the 1970s, likening Indian diplomatic machinery to the "love-making of an elephant, conducted at a very high level, accompanied by much bellowing, and the results of which are not known for two years").

Protectionism, propelled by an ideal of self-sufficiency and nationalism, resulted in distrust of foreign investment and extremely high tariffs, as high as 350% duty for certain commodities, and in 1991, a top rate of 300%. The near five decades of economic stifle since India's independence, however, is the result of historical causes. Bitter experiences of colonial oppression engendered skepticism toward foreign companies and foreigners drawn to India by investment interests. Tharoor remarked, "Nehru like many Third World nationalists, saw the imperialism that had subjugated his people as the logical extension of international capitalism, for which he therefore felt a deep mistrust." Thus, self-sufficiency and non-alignment were the ideals that provided an appropriate platform for nationalistic sentiments. Nehru's socialism and adherence to principles of self-reliance and distributive justice, to the detriment of economic growth, drove India for the better part of the near half a century following independence to trail "an economic policy of subsidizing non-productivity, regulating stagnation, and distributive poverty." Unsurprisingly, the annual growth rate of exported manufactured goods was 0.1% until 1985 (Tharoor 2003, 2012).

Nonetheless, India and South Asia demonstrate impressive growth since the 1990s. The economic growth of constituent countries particularly India, which accounts for more than three-quarters of the region's gross domestic product, makes a decisive impact on the region's overall growth. Other countries, including Bangladesh and Pakistan, have also advanced economically. Scholars observe that first-generation policy reforms such as greater global integration, economic deregulation, and reducing trade restrictions like import tariffs, triggered this growth in South Asia. Yet, despite making remarkable gains in integrating with the global economy, South Asian intra-regional integration has been limited (Ahmed and Ghani 2007).

SAARC's regional integration and the prospects of sustainable growth in the region need policy reforms to address the high cost of doing business, weak institutions, weak knowledge economy, and weak infrastructure. These reforms should focus on increasing transparency, developing better governance with stronger checks and balances, expanding market-based allocation of resources, and enhancing public–private partnerships in the provision of infrastructural services (Ahmed and Ghani 2007).

As the biggest economy in the region, India enjoys nearly 80% of South Asia's gross domestic product (GDP). In comparison, the other two sizeable economies in the region, Pakistan and Bangladesh, account for 10 and 7% of the region's GDP, respectively (The World Bank 2010). Quite naturally, some perceive rising trade as a result of increasing dominance of India and other countries' dependence on her. The sense of distrust among these regional neighbors appears in various instances. For example, Nepal and Bangladesh import certain commodities from suppliers outside SAARC's region despite higher costs, showing reluctance to accept Indian investments. Another example of distrust is Sri Lanka's import of railway coaches from Romania, despite that neighboring India offers better-quality coaches at a much cheaper price (Kher 2012).

South Asia is a dynamic region boasting the fastest economic growth in the world. South Asia's growth figure of 6.9% in 2014 was projected to accelerate to 7.1% in 2015. Yet, poverty is widespread; roughly 400 million people in the region, amounting to 40% of the world's poor, live on less than $1.25 a day. Among other factors, rapid urbanization and uneven development have relegated 200 million people in this region to slums and shanties and have rendered half a billion people without electricity (World Bank 2016).

Regional integration provides a window to shared prosperity through accelerated economic activities and collective focus on economic growth and poverty alleviation. Regional integration plays a crucial role in the South Asian region as it may help strengthen the region's economic gains against vulnerabilities caused by global economic crises, create more decent jobs by promoting manufacturing sector, aid individual countries to enhance their specific business capacities to gain comparative advantage, boost smaller countries and LDCs' responsiveness in the regional market, and contribute long-term peace and stability by ensuring more jobs and sustained growth (Dhungana 2016).

4 A South Asian Case of Ambitious PTAs?

4.1 Discourses on "Regional" Global Governance and Reduction of Trade Barriers

4.1.1 Global Trade Governance—Elements and Factors to Consider

Considering the trading system's changed nature, it is imperative to account for the additional changing nature of trade barriers. Although, being the traditional mode of trade barrier, tariffs' general decline pursuant to a series of trade rounds did not stop the emergence of various non-tariff barriers. The rules pertaining to "valuation," "customs clearance," "product standards," and "country of origin" are anachronistic, and therefore, they continually pose trade hurdles under contemporary trade practices (Cho and Kelly 2012).

A multilayered trade governance model is essential to cater to the changing realities of global trade. Lester and Mercurio (2010) laid out the important elements of the third era of global trade governance: non-discrimination; reducing non-discriminatory trade barriers; harmonization of national laws or mutual recognition; good governance; efficient, effective and reasonable law making; free movement of labor; promotion of competitive markets; free movement of capital through foreign investment; intellectual property protection; labor rights and environmental protection; and multilateralism or anti-unilateralism.

These elements overlap and influence one other. For example, harmonization of laws can prevent regulations from being used as disguised protection, and coupled with good governance (Unescap.org, 2016), this harmonization can help prevent non-discriminatory trade barriers and limit protectionism. Given that efforts to combat protectionism and discrimination foster economic efficiency, other interventions such as introducing anti-trust/anti-competition norms and free market policies go a long way (Lester and Mercurio 2010).

International trade law is, by and large, the product of state-centered and top-down treaty making. The treaty-making process is a consensus-building exercise that involves an enormous amount of diplomatic and political effort and enthusing credibility to liberalization commitments among sovereign states. In certain areas of law such as financial regulation, exercising "soft" laws in addition to "hard" treaty law is both more frequent and better-promoted. The "top-down" and "state-centered" approach of the treaty-making process is perhaps insufficient in certain areas of international trade law, specifically in areas necessitating intricate and technical rules, for example, the customs guidelines (Cho and Kelly 2012; USlegal.com). Haidempergher (2015) cited this issue in the governance model of *Mercado Común del Sur* (MERCOSUR or the Common Market of the South), a model that bases the integration process on a top-down, rather than a bottom-up, scheme and displays a resulting dissociation between the speeds of legal and commercial integration. Cho and Kelly (2012) opined that like financial regulators, domestic legislators and trade regulators had apprehensions in committing to complex rules ex ante in an uncertain world, and soft law commitments allow regulators and innovators to overcome their initial apprehension to develop rules. They suggested that the global trade regime needs an innovative bottom-up approach, as the top-down model was becoming increasingly ill-suited for many of the trade regime's new challenges.

Rolland (2014) sheds light on another aspect of trade liberalization, stating that the WTO's approach to trade liberalization is producer-oriented, as it prioritizes ensuring that goods and services can be offered across borders with minimal discrimination and administrative barriers; however, consumers as a legal category are virtually absent from WTO agreements. Consumers undoubtedly benefit from trade liberalization as they have access to a greater variety of goods and services at a cheaper price, but such benefits do not address the full spectrum of consumer interests. Consumer interests include more than just the quantity, quality, and price of goods, but also include protection from harmful or defective products or services, privacy protection, preservation of legal interests (e.g., bans or restrictions on unfair credit or contract terms), and regulations of deceptive and unfair practices in commerce.

The WTO regime, considering its theoretical foundation in "classical liberal economics," has not done much to respond to these matters. Although the WTO regime has the MFN and NT principles in place to address "unfavorable discrimination" (between comparable products/services from differing nations) and "less favorable treatment" (toward imported goods/services in contrast to like nationally sourced commodities), it does not limit producers or sellers from discriminating between domestic and foreign consumers to obtain greater earnings. For example, in India, museums levy higher entry fee on most foreign nationals than on domestic consumers. Rolland (2014) noted, "although these consumer issues are typically not articulated as trade concerns, they are, in fact, consumer-oriented trade barriers that the producer-oriented regime does not capture." She further stated, "the state may have other policy reasons for allowing or implementing the differential pricing, which trump trade-liberalizing concerns."

Global trade governance is not a static phenomenon and certainly is not limited to MFN and NT principles and reducing tariff barriers. As discussed above, addressing contemporary challenges, such as by reducing non-tariff trade barriers, helps stem the mercantilist tendency and furthers the cause of global trade governance. In doing so, multilateralism remains as an important stimulant.

4.1.2 Furthering Global Trade Governance Through PTAs

Freund and Ornelas (2010) noted, "the formation of regional trade agreements has been, by far, the most popular form of reciprocal trade liberalization in the past 15 years." The average WTO Member now has agreements with more than fifteen countries and therefore reflects the trend of growing regionalism. The PTAs are flourishing in a gap left between the global trading system and States' action. Iqbal (2012) analogized FTAs to "flying geese that made cooperative efforts to reach a desirable destination." With the growing onus on preferential trading scheme, the regional governance level forms an important link in the chain of global trade governance. This section attempts to approach the governance patterns through a variety of factors that enable PTAs to play an important role.

First, the Rules of Origin (ROO) are an important element to "preserve the mercantilist bargain of managed trade." There are two types of rules: first, "non-preferential" rules that apply in the ordinary course where there is no claim of special treatment under a regional trade agreement; and second, "preferential" that apply when there is a claim for special treatment under a regional trade agreement. Cho and Kelly (2012) observe that non-preferential rules of origin intend to protect bargain trading among GATT members. On the other hand, preferential rules of origin allow States to favor certain countries by according better market access, such as zero tariffs, to imports. This discriminatory mechanism is crucial to administering an RTA and sustainable only when members can screen out goods from Member States that are eligible for duty-free treatment in favor of securing goods from non-Member States still subject to tariffs.

ROOs in most preferential arrangements have been termed as manipulative and messy because they have "deprived many developing countries of their comparative advantage stemming from their natural endowments (such as good quality raw materials) and cheap labor." The present complicated and unintelligible regime of ROO is an anomaly due to its multi-locational manufacturing based on global supply chains. For instance, as per the "yarn-forward" rule, Mexican producers did not qualify for duty-free access to the US market under NAFTA because they procured Indian yarns in their manufacturing rather than using yarns sourced from NAFTA countries. Such a rule hampers the spirit of free trade as it strips Mexican textile producers, Indian yarn producers, and US textile consumers of considerable economic welfare (Cho and Kelly 2012).

Critics characterize ROO systems as outdated largely because they "stem from a fundamental conception of trade that simply no longer holds true, i.e., the single-country production model." Incidentally, because every country is entitled to MFN status, the non-preferential rules no longer serve that purpose in any meaningful way (Cho and Kelly 2012). Therefore, the negotiators and policy makers must revisit this ROO framework as much in the PTAs, to simplify it and ensure its consistency with contemporary multi-locational trading system. Even the countries negotiating the Trans-Pacific Partnership (TPP) Agreement by and large support more liberal ROOs, oppose product- or country-specific ROOs, and are pushing instead for region-wide rules instead (Barfield 2011).

Former WTO Director General Pascal Lamy, in his 2010 speech before the French Senate, stated:

> [T]he concept of country of origin for manufactured goods has gradually become obsolete as the various operations, from the design of the product to the manufacture of the components, assembly and marketing have spread across the world, creating international production chains. Nowadays, more and more products are "Made in the World" rather than "Made in the UK" or "Made in France." …
>
> What we call "Made in China" is indeed assembled in China, but what makes up the commercial value of the product comes from the numerous countries that preceded its assembly in China in the global value chain, from its design to the manufacture of the different components and the organization of the logistical support to the chain as a whole. In other words, the production of goods and services can no longer be considered "mono-located," but rather, "multi-located." …
>
> [T]ime has come to explore new channels so that accounting and statistical systems can take account of the new geography of international trade in an economy which, in the words of the American Tom Friedman, has flattened under the influence of globalization and internationalization of production relations. In today's world, the old mercantilist notion of "us" against "them," of "resident" against "rest of world," has lost much of its meaning (WTO Secretariat 2016).

Pascal Lamy proposed a way forward in ROOs with his idea of "Made in the World" as a method of evaluating trade based on its value, rather than by its country of origin. The WTO has since begun to push the concept by launching a Web site and forum and facilitating a dialogue based on the idea of "Made in the World."

Second, the global and regional trade regimes need the bottom-up approach running alongside the top-down model. Although agreements regulate trade, the market drives trade. Scholars propose an agenda to modernize global trading rules with the help of "trade networks" as a bottom-up approach. A trade network may allude to an amalgam of "public and private networks composed of customs officials on one hand, and private lawyers, academics, and transnational businesses on the other." Such diversity in stakeholders includes both public (regulators) and private (regulatees) players' voices in trade matters, sharing their knowledge and concerns on particular technical issues and potentially generating certain soft law in the form of guidelines and recommendations (Cho and Kelly 2012).

Third, consumer interests require due consideration in the multilateral trading regime as, after all, they are the ultimate beneficiaries of the whole trade arrangement. Rolland (2014) cites the instance of the European Union's (EU) trade liberalization and integration model since the 1970s and observes that the EU had alternative approaches to allocating the burdens and benefits of trade liberalization between producers, consumers, and workers. Within the EU, free movement of persons has been a key component of liberalization and a means of efficiently allocating labor and capital. For example, EU universities cannot charge higher tuition to nationals of other EU countries than they charge their domestic students, and museums cannot charge higher entrance fee to other EU visitors than they charge locals. Another instance relating consumer interests and trade liberalization is the EU directive on distributorship, which allows distributors a geographic allocation of markets, given that distributors allow consumers to potentially buy cheaper goods in other EU markets. EU trade integration is an illustration of both consumer and producer interests furthering the cause for trade liberalization. To implement such rules, multilateral international cooperation is imperative.

Fourth, free movement of capital is an important element of encouraging deeper trade integration, as well as an important dimension of world trade law, that the WTO fails to emphasize (Schwartz 2013). Two methods of trading commodities overseas are suggested: first, "produc[ing] them in your home country and then ship them overseas"; and second, "set[ting] up operations abroad to make the products there." Bilateral Investment Treaties (BITs) are the primary tool for protecting foreign investment. Securing capital and investment is becoming pivotal for international trade, and there have been attempts to incorporate relevant rules into trade agreements. For example, Chap. 11 of NAFTA on investment lays the framework for non-discriminatory treatment, fair and equitable treatment, and compensation for expropriation. NAFTA sets the benchmark for preferential trading regimes around the world to encompass investment protection alongside trade agreements.

Fifth, labor rights and environmental protection are thorny reform areas; they remain important pillars of the third era of global governance. Traditionally, these two have been antagonistic to trade. For example, laws promulgated to protect the environment or labor rights may be considered violations of trade rules. The quest to increase trade prompts arguments concerning a race to the bottom, causing countries to disregard the environment and offer minimal labor protection (Lester 2011). Nonetheless, NAFTA was the first PTA to address these concerns and more recent ones such as the Dominican Republic—Central America FTA (CAFTA-DR), which lays guidelines to ensure labor standards.

The CAFTA-DR Agreement lays some guidelines (Chap. 17) with respect to the environment, but they are not as strong as those for labor protection. Yet, the agreement provides for voluntary mechanisms to enhance environmental performance and establishes the Environmental Affairs Council, opportunities for public participation, and collaborative environmental consultations.

Professor Alberto do Amaral Júnior (2015) noted that the multi-level global trade governance displays a gradual increase in complexity as it evolves. He noted three outright layers of global trade governance. First, despite the WTO's status as the major guardian of economic liberalization rules, its strength has been progressively undermined since the 1990s, and its legacy rendered obsolete as a result of the gulf formed between the plethora of regulatory demands from developed and developing countries and the WTO's capacity to respond. Second, he notes the so-called "mega-agreements," which gathered developed and developing countries and concentrated the most relevant share of the world economy. He describes the third layers as the multitude of preferential trade agreements of a lesser scale, which have varying sizes and degrees of normative depth. He notes that while the WTO became the venue of low-intensity regulation, PTAs and mega-agreements enacted high-intensity regulation. Nevertheless, centralization and de-centralization coexist and complement one another.

Deeper integration is easier at the regional level than at the multilateral level, as regional negotiations tend to be faster than multilateral. Professor of international economic law, Rafael Leal-Arcas (2011) noted the helplessness of the WTO member States in advancing forward the multilateral trade agenda. Liang (2014) opines that, considering the role of PTAs in trade liberalization since the Uruguay Round, WTO Member States have yet to readily accept that trade liberalization is increasingly performed through the "plurilateral" approach of PTAs, and not multilaterally at the WTO. She suggests a possible solution to "multi-lateralize" regionalism in order to provide greater coherence between PTAs and the WTO. According to Liang (2014), another approach is to "identify new trading rules (e.g., investment and competition policy) and technical standards commonly found among PTAs, and co-opt them into the WTO system." The preferential trading arrangements have furthered the multilateral liberalization process, but there are many non-tariff trade barriers (Bhala 2014) that require a full implementation of the multi-level global trade governance, a simplified and efficient "third" era of trade governance.

4.2 SAARC's Milestones and Challenges in Expanding Trade Through PTA and Liberalization

Thanks to the TLP, exports under SAFTA are increasing. By September 20, 2013, the overall FOB, or free-on-board, value of exports by Contracting States reached US$ 3 billion since July 2006, at TLP's launch (SAARC Secretariat 2016). Yet some consider that SAFTA has had remarkable, but partial, achievements (Kumar 2005). The Asian Development Bank data (South Asia's intra-region trade *vis-à-vis* its global trade rose from 4.55% in 2010 to 5.58% in 2015) shows that the figure of South Asian intra-region trade has risen from 2% from 1967, but it remains below 6%. In contrast, the Association of Southeast Asian Nations (ASEAN) boasts an impressive intra-regional trade figure of approximately 24% (between 24.64% in 2010 and 23.56% in 2015) of its total trade with the rest of the world (Asian Development Bank 2016).

Comparing the trade volume of regional trading blocs in other parts of the world such as NAFTA (total trade rising from US$ 1348.9 billion in 2000 to US$

2399.9 billion in 2014), MERCOSUR (total trade rising from US$ 42.3 billion in 2000 to 108.0 billion in 2014), EU (total trade rising from US$ 3347.6 billion in 2000 to US$ 7800.2 billion in 2014), and ASEAN (total trade rising from US$ 185.2 billion in 2000 to US$ 608.4 billion in 2014) displays that South Asia (total trade rising from US$ 6.3 billion in 2000 to US$ 51.3 billion in 2014) remains an underperformer (WTO Statistics 2016; Asian Development Bank Statistics 2016). Despite the comparatively lower trade volume within South Asia, trade volume within the region saw an increase by eightfold between 2000 and 2014. Nonetheless, coupled with the unilateral trade policy liberalization in the individual countries, regional collaboration has redirected trade discourses on a more optimistic path since the 1990s (Kumar and Singh 2009).

Bhala (2015: 2) summarizes four important variables to determine an FTA's ambition. First, the larger the number of parties, the more ambitious the FTA may become. Second, comprehensiveness revolves around the number of tariff lines the FTA covers and, at the same time, how many sensitive product categories it exempts. Regarding services, this assessment refers to the number of covered sectors and sub-sectors, the modes of service supply, and number of commitments made. The FTA is more ambitious if the number of commitments is high, the number of modes covered by those commitments is greater, and if it uses a "Negative List." Third, the timing is crucial, in terms of the duration that the FTA takes to bring down tariffs and non-tariff barriers. The sooner these barriers are eliminated, the better it is. Fourth, the FTA ought to be composed of novel mechanisms, to cover not only the tariff barriers, but also the behind the border, non-obvious, and inconspicuous measures such as Sanitary and Phyto-sanitary (SPS) and Technical Barriers to Trade (TBT).

For an agenda to be executed efficiently, a streamlined schedule or timetable is important. This timing part, although very crucial for an ambitious FTA, has been overlooked. Like SAFTA, the implementation part of SATIS has also been slow. Member States notified their ratification two and a half years (November 2012) after the agreement came into effect. This instance is cited as a typical characteristic of the slow movement of South Asia's economic integration agenda (Daily Mirror 2014). Under SAARC, the first round of concessions occurred when SAPTA became operational in 1995. Between 1995 and 1999, two more rounds of tariff reductions were completed. Nevertheless, these three rounds of tariff concessions barely influenced trade integration within South Asia.

SAPTA had many inherent flaws. Many important trade sectors were ignored due to slow, tedious, commodity-by-commodity negotiations and an avoidance of even an agenda of removal of non-tariff barriers. There were occasions of unthoughtful tariff concessions. For instance, Sri Lanka was accorded ample concessions to export snow plows, although, unluckily the production of snow plows did not occur in the country (out of this situation, a new term, "snow plow syndrome" was coined). Indeed, SAPTA's tardy progress prompted many Member States to engage a "fast-track" trade liberalization by way of bilateral trade agreements, such as "India-Bhutan FTA," "India-Sri Lanka FTA," and "Pakistan-Sri Lanka FTA" (Prema-chandra Athukorala 2013; Rodrigo 2004).

Article 7 of SAFTA lays a two-stage tariff reduction program to achieve a tariff regime of below 5% for India, Pakistan, and Sri Lanka by 2015, and for the remaining Member States by 2018. Effectuating these stipulated tariff reduction programs has hitherto made inadequate progress. Also, there have been reservations that free trade may not be attained even when the proposed tariff reduction program is fully implemented. This incredulity ascribes to all the Contracting States retaining a long list of sensitive products in efforts to shield their specific economic sectors from SAFTA's duty exemption. As of 2013, approximately 53% of intra-SAARC imports are restricted under the Sensitive List. Moreover, some countries imposed various para-tariffs, which virtually counter-balance the Contracting States' limited tariff concessions offered to SAFTA (Athukorala 2013).

The protection afforded to every Member State's sensitive commodities through sustaining the "Sensitive/Negative" lists is another proviso of SAFTA's TLP influence on trade. In addition to the top-down mechanism of tariff reduction with different scheduled concessions for developing and least developing States, the Sensitive Lists cover roughly 20% of the tariff lines. This percentage implies that the Sensitive Lists blanket a substantial trade proportion not bound by tariff reductions. If the number of items on the Sensitive Lists is not downsized, SAFTA's trade agenda may not yield optimal effectiveness (Kardar 2011).

Another concern for SAARC's LDC Members regards SAFTA not fetching them a good bargain with respect to an FTA. Nepal and India, as neighbors, share trading relations that precede SAARC. They also have bilateral agreements. Nepalese scholars observe that Nepal has benefitted regardless from "basic customs duty-free market access to the Indian market in almost all products, subject to ROO." SAFTA, having the same ROO as Nepal-India Trade Treaty, is therefore just as burdensome and does not offer Nepal additional market access in the Indian market, the biggest in the region. In contrast, as a result of an FTA with India, Bhutan (another LDC in the region) enjoys duty-free access without quantitative restrictions or ROO in the Indian market (Adhikari and Kharel 2011). Therefore, SAARC has yet to address the anomalies between bilateral and multilateral trade in the region, which may restrict the yields of its FTAs.

Although promotion of investment is a central component in many regional trade agreements, SAFTA fails to deal with the liberalization of investment, except by enumerating it as an "Additional Measure" under Article 8. Nonetheless, SAARC set up a Group of Eminent Persons (GEP) in 1997 that recommended the creation of a Common Investment Area. Many proposals to streamline intra-regional investment emerged and India even drafted an investment agreement; however, as of 2013, no progress was registered (Athukorala 2013).

SAFTA's features on TLP, technical assistance for LDCs, and non-tariff barriers are encouraging. SAFTA has been ambitious in honoring the schedule of tariff reduction, which included tariff reduction by developing States to 20% and tariff reduction by LDCs to 30% by 2008 (SAARC 2016). Empirical studies conducted on the net impact of SAFTA show its benefit. Although LDCs' gains were modest in the first phase of liberalization, it is suggested that the benefits would be significant in the second phase, with the proviso that there is total liberalization (Asian Development Bank and UNCTAD 2008).

4.3 Future Path of SAARC's Trade Liberalization with Respect to Global Trends

Regional trade agreements are an important part of today's international trade regime as they are the actors that handle more than 50% of actual international trade. Thus, trade is a critical element in regional integration. Yet, it is interrelated with many other dimensions that also warrant due attention. SAARC's progress in terms of liberalization and the elimination of barriers exhibits that greater milestones need to be realized to prove SAFTA and SATIS as ambitious free trade endeavors. The Lead Economist in the World Bank's South Asia Regional Cooperation and Integration Unit, Kathuria (2013), surmises that "regional integration is a long and incremental process" and regional agreements "suffer from a gap between intentions and implementation." In addition to timely implementation of the tariff reduction schedule (although the allocated time frame is long, and its concessions may be outsmarted earlier by way of South Asian bilateral agreements), or elimination, there are several ways to address these gaps with respect to SAARC.

First, a credible institutional mechanism, preferably at SAARC Secretariat, is necessary to oversee conformity and corollaries. In addition to significant perseverance, institutional development, strengthened monitoring, and stronger political resoluteness are desirable to improve regional outcomes by increased trade volumes. Second, the role of trade facilitation is vital to broadening and deepening South Asian economic integration. The stagnation of intra-regional trade in South Asia suggests that trade impulses from mutual tariff reduction have exhausted. In other words, tariff reduction or elimination may not completely liberalize regional trade. Further, unilateral liberalization performed by several South Asian countries seems to have implicitly undermined SAFTA's trade liberalization benefits (Kumar and Singh 2009). Therefore, there is a need to identify the non-tariff barriers and address the non-tariff barriers to improve the trade facilitation process (Asian Development Bank 2009).

Gilbert and Banik (2008) note that shortfall in trade facilitation and deficiencies in physical infrastructure accessibility increase trade cost. High logistics costs, slow application of SPS measures and technical standards, inadequate infrastructure, requirements of endless documentation, cumbersome transit process, and bribes are all impediments to cross-border trade. Each of these hindrances prevails at varying degrees across South Asia. The Federation of Indian Chambers of Commerce and Industry (FICCI) also gives valuable suggestions, such as: easy visa regulations; linkage of physical infrastructure (roads, railways, shipping, and air links); harmonization of customs, banking, insurance, quality standards, and arbitration procedures for easy conduct of trade throughout the region; and proposal of a SAARC Agreement on Investment Promotion and Protection (Kumar 2005). The decision to establish the SAARC Standards Coordination Board is positive. The Board is stipulated to function as a precursor to the SAARC Regional Standards Body (to achieve uniform quality standardization within South Asia).

Third, downsizing the size of Sensitive Lists is necessary to increase the volume of regional trade efforts. Some steps have been taken in this direction. The Working Group on Reduction in the Sensitive Lists attempted to narrow down SAFTA's Sensitive Lists by 20%. The Maldives made a reduction of 78% (bringing tariff lines down from 681 to 152), and India reduced its Sensitive List for LDC States by 95% (by reducing tariff lines from 480 to 25). The implementation of Phase-II Revision began in 2012 with a stipulated time frame to implement the phase out for the tariff lines. The non-LDC countries have a time frame of 3 years (except Sri Lanka, which has a six-year time frame), and the LDC States have eight years to do the same. Also in 2012, negotiations began for further reduction of the Sensitive Lists (SAARC 2016). Reducing tariff lines is a very promising step, provided the reductions are realized in the stipulated time frame.

A fourth component is to expand focus from trade in goods to trade in other significant areas. One of the fundamental hindrances restricting the intra-Asian RTAs' efficacy is that such integration selectively centers on liberalization concerning market access for goods and ignores or undermines other trade sectors, namely non-tariff barriers, services, investment, intellectual property, government procurement, and competition policy (Mercurio 2011). All these areas are growing increasingly important and cannot be ignored for long. Cross-border investments have surfaced as a major feature of globalization and catalyst for trade in both goods and services. Foreign direct investment (FDI) has been a pivotal vehicle of external financing and development for developing countries. With the right policies, FDIs may leave long-lasting benefits on a country's manufacturing potential and infrastructure, create new jobs, and provide additional tax revenue (Bhala 2015). Therefore, it is time for SAARC to incorporate a South Asian investment regime that not only focuses on intra-regional investment and capital flows but also includes other factors that influence investment. Such strategies include developing strong, regional financial and banking institutions, determining and mitigating barriers to capital movement, encouraging macroeconomic stability, as well as establishing general or investor-state dispute settlement, minimum standards of protection, and rules for compensation and expropriation.

Fifth, there is a need to concentrate on trade creation and avoid diluting the fruits of trade liberalization by indulging in trade diversion. Iqbal (2012) noted that, apart from increasing overall quality of goods to global standards, development of infrastructure is required on a priority basis to link countries and facilitate the easy flow of goods, making South Asia as transit point between the East and the West.

Sixth, whether in Latin America or South Asia, non-tariff trade barriers have evolved into an area of serious concern. Eventually, they will pose obstacles to the overall framework of regional and global trade governance. Efficient reduction and elimination of non-trade tariff barriers will translate into stronger regional global trade governance through PTAs.

Seventh, SAARC must make timely and consistent progress to meet the milestones of an FTA, a customs union, a common market, and a common economic and monetary union to envisage the South Asian Economic Union (SAEU). Trade liberalization is sought as a stepping stone for greater cooperation and a step toward setting up a SAEU along the lines of the EU.

Last, the process requires patience, yet countries must also be ambitious. Given the challenges and circumstances of South Asia, SAARC's performance as a trading bloc is not quite so disheartening. Steady implementation of the time frame is indispensable to attaining the milestones mandated by the SAARC agenda. Lack of ambition is characterized as one of the foremost impediments to intra-Asian RTAs that have the result that "liberalization commitments are often not deep enough to be meaningful or are otherwise stymied by the presence of significant exclusions and non-tariff barriers which reduce the impact of the RTA." In order to improve low sectoral coverage and the high number of exceptions and exclusions, SAPTA calls for stronger efforts (Mercurio 2011). RTAs across the world keep up with new challenges by streamlining trade mechanisms and eliminating non-tariff barriers. For example, the majority of the ASEAN countries set up Trade Information Portals (TIP) or Single Window systems, which improve trade facilitation and bring down transactional expenses and thus contribute to intra-ASEAN trade growth. The TIPs are an efficient medium for traders to electronically access all the documents required for government approval. The Single Window mechanism facilitates electronic compliance of regulatory documents from a single location. With the 2002 Residence Agreement, MERCOSUR eased the mobility of workers (nationals of Member States) to obtain residence and work permit for other Member States for a period of two years, after which the temporary permit could be converted into a permanent one. The Common Market for Eastern and Southern Africa (COMESA), East African Community (EAC), and Southern African Development Community (SADC), as a conglomerate, sought economic integration and a common market for its Member States, and in the process, implemented an active web-based procedure to identify, monitor, and eliminate non-tariff barriers (Kathuria 2013; Acosta 2016). NAFTA came into effect in 1994, creating one of the largest free trade zones. NAFTA added many laurels to RTA success stories from across the world through several innovations: establishing an efficient dispute settlement system, liberalizing FDI and side agreement on labor and environment, removing barriers to investment, and providing protection to all forms of investments, such as contracts, debts, and intellectual property rights, among others (NAFTA 2016). Notwithstanding the US withdrawal from the TPP, the Agreement's leaked provisions show several revolutionary elements including strategies for improved transparency and risk management techniques (Kaul 2017). SAARC may benefit from evaluating these best practices of other RTAs and help introduce them in South Asia.

5 Conclusion

The EU and other experiments in regional trade show that the RTAs are not a substitute for the WTO but a complement it. In a way, the RTAs encourage the WTO's trade liberalization agenda by exploring mechanisms to reduce and gradually eliminate trade barriers regionally. One of the premises on which the WTO rests is to promote trade as a mean of attaining peace and prosperity. In a region which houses more than 40% of the world's poor, SAARC supplements this effort to enhance prospects of poverty reduction and shared growth by way of regional economic integration.

Thanks to SAARC's preferential arrangements, trade liberalization received a stimulus through SAPTA and proceeded to SAFTA and SATIS. Removal of trade barriers is an essential feature of the international trade regime. Like GATT/WTO regime, SAARC also pursues trade liberalization to boost cross-border trade in the Subcontinent. Although tariff eventually burden the end consumer, they generally are viewed as a double-edged sword. For example, lowering tariffs on rice imports after the 2010 earthquake in Haiti proved disastrous for local population, 50–60% of whom relied on subsistence agriculture (O'Connor 2013; Haiti Grassroots Watch 2013).

Despite a modest beginning, SAFTA successfully sets a path of tariff reduction for its LDC and non-LDC Member States with varied time frames for implementation. Given the historical hostilities in the Subcontinent, asymmetrical economies, and several other challenges, SAARC has faced many obstacles, and intra-regional integration is limited.

TLP is a step in the right direction. Yet, intra-regional trade remains below 6%. The tariff reduction agenda must be followed in a time-bound manner. I submit in this chapter that FTAs entail complex rules of origin. Although integration at customs level in SAARC currently appears a distant milestone, a certain harmonization in common external tariffs may mitigate these complexities of rules of origin.

I have argued that the removal of tariff barriers is not the single way out to liberalize trade in South Asia. There is a great need to work as much to ease the cross-border trade in the region. All the benefits of liberalized tariffs will not make any impact on trade if a commodity is stuck at the border, delayed in customs clearance, SPS, or other TBT lapses. These procedural delays, sometimes lasting months, may lead to a commodity's expiration or render it unsuitable for consumption. RTAs in other regions have taken several steps to eliminate non-tariff barriers.

Therefore, the need of the hour is not only to liberalize but also to be effective, transparent, consistent, and predictable. These features have slowly emerged as international best practices. There is an additional need to set up a credible institutional mechanism and harmonize SAARC-level standards to enjoy tariff reduction benefits.

SAARC's free trade agreements do not have to embrace the international best practices exclusively or follow the mandated time frame strictly. To effectively harness the fruits of trade liberalization, the "parallel" waves of liberalization caused by unilateral, bilateral, and multilateral removal of trade barriers must be regulated under the auspices of SAARC. Critics of preferential trading arrangements cite Jagdish Bhagwati's term "spaghetti bowl" to convey the web of varying tariffs and rules that may be carved out by various RTAs. South Asia faces its share of challenges, but one hopes that SAARC efficiently and consistently tackles these challenges and emerges as one of the institutional leaders of the twenty-first century.

References

Acosta D (2016) Free movement in South America: the emergence of an alternative model? *Migration Policy Institute*, 23 Aug 2016. Retrieved from http://www.migrationpolicy.org/article/free-movement-south-america-emergence-alternative-model

ADB and UNCTAD (2008) Quantification of benefits from economic cooperation in South Asia. Retrieved from http://www.gsid.nagoya-u.ac.jp/sotsubo/SouthAsian-Quantification-Benefits.pdf

Adhikari R, Kharel P (2011) Nepal and SAFTA: issue, prospects and Challenges. *SAWTEE*. Retrieved from http://www.sawtee.org/Research_Reports/R2011-05.pdf

Ahmed S, Ghani E (2007) South Asia's growth and regional integration: an overview. South Asia: growth and regional integration, World Bank. Retrieved from http://pendientedemigracion.ucm.es/info/eid/cursodcd/IMG/pdf_SouthAsiaGrowthandRegionalIntegration.pdf

Amaral Júnior A (2015) Is trade governance changing? Braz J Int Law 12:371–382

Asian Development Bank (2009) Development partnership for South Asia: study on interregional trade and investment in South Asia. Philippines: Asian Development Bank. Retrieved from https://www.adb.org/sites/default/files/publication/28658/intraregional-trade-investment.pdf

Asian Development Bank website. Retrieved from https://aric.adb.org

Athukorala P-C (2013) Intra-regional FDI and economic integration in South Asia: trends, patterns and prospects. UNCTAD background paper no. rvc 7, 2013. Retrieved from http://unctad.org/en/PublicationsLibrary/ecidc2013misc1_bp7.pdf

Banik N, Gilbert J (2008) Regional integration and trade costs in South Asia. ADB Institute working paper no. 127. Available at https://www.researchgate.net/publication/254144239_Regional_Integration_and_Trade_Costs_in_South_Asia

Barfield C (2011) The TPP: a model for 21st century trade agreements? East Asia Forum, 25 July 2011. Retrieved from http://www.eastasiaforum.org/2011/07/25/the-tpp-a-model-for-21st-century-trade-agreements/

Bhagwati J (2008) Termites in the trading system: how preferential agreements undermine free trade. Oxford University Press, Oxford

Bhala R (2014) Trans-Pacific partnership or trampling poor partners: a tentative critical review. Manchester J Int'l Econ L 11:2

Bhala R (2015) International Trade Law: An Interdisciplinary, Non-Western Textbook, vols 1 and 2 (4th edn). Carolina Academic Press

Cho S, Kelly C (2012) Are world trading rules Passé? Virginia J Int Law 53 (20 June 2012)

Daily Mirror Business (2014) SAARC agreement on trade in services: tardy progress, 24 Nov 2014. Retrieved from http://www.dailymirror.lk/57189/saarc-agreement-on-trade-in-services-tardy-progress

Dominican Republic-Central America-United States Free Trade Agreement. Retrieved from http://www.sice.oas.org/Trade/CAFTA/CAFTADR_e/chapter13_22.asp#Chapter16. Last visited 27 Oct 2016

Dhungana S (2016) One south Asia. *My República*, 18 June 2016. Retrieved from http://www.myrepublica.com/news/382

Freund C, Ornelas E (2010) Regional trade agreements. Annu Rev Econ 2(1):139–166

Gupta A (2002) SAARC: SAPTA to SAFTA. Shipra Publications, Delhi

Haidempergher LL (2015) An introduction to Mercosur. Int Law News 44(31):34. Retrieved from http://www.bomchil2.com.ar/Uploads/Documents/14-5-15%20-%20LLH%20An%20Introduction%20to%20Mercosur_20150514104041.pdf

Haiti Grassroots Watch (2013) Haiti: aid or trade? The nefarious effects of U.S. policies. Centre for Research on Globalization, 6 Nov 2013. Retrieved from http://www.globalresearch.ca/haiti-aid-or-trade-the-nefarious-effects-of-u-s-policies/5357204

Hoda A (2001) Tariff negotiations and renegotiations under the GATT and the WTO: procedures and practices. Cambridge University Press, Cambridge, New York

Iqbal BA (2012) Is SAFTA a myth or reality? J World Investment Trade 13(1):103–124

Kardar S (2011) South Asia—intraregional cooperation: the way forward. ADB working paper. Retrieved from https://www.adb.org/sites/default/files/linked-documents/rcs-south-asia-2011-2015-oth-02.pdf

Kathuria S (2013) Lessons on regional integration. World Economic Forum, 23 July 2013. Retrieved from https://www.weforum.org/agenda/2015/07/5-lessons-on-regional-integration/

Kaul D (2017) Trans Pacific Partnership Trump (ed). The Citizen, 06 Mar 2017. Retrieved from http://www.thecitizen.in/index.php/NewsDetail/index/4/10090/Trans-Pacific-Partnership-Trumped; republished in http://dailykashmirimages.com/Details/133207/trans-pacific-partnership-trumped

Kher P (2012) Political economy of regional integration in South Asia. UNCTAD background paper no. rvc 5. Retrieved from http://unctad.org/en/PublicationsLibrary/ecidc2013misc1_bp5.pdf

Koul AK (2013) Guide to the WTO and GATT: economics, law and politics, 4th edn. Satyam Law International, New Delhi

Krueger AO (1999) Are preferential trading arrangements trade-liberalizing or protectionist? J Econ Perspect 13(4):105–124

Kumar R (2005) South Asian Union: problems, possibilities and prospects. Manas Publications, New Delhi

Kumar R, Singh M (2009) India's role in South Asia trade and investment integration. Asian Development Bank working series on regional economic integration, no. 32. Retrieved from https://www.adb.org/sites/default/files/publication/28506/wp32-india-role-south-asia-trade.pdf

Lamy P (2010) Pascal Lamy's speech to the French Senate in Paris on October 15, 2010. Retrieved from https://www.wto.org/english/news_e/sppl_e/sppl174_e.htm;see also the flyer for Made in the World initiative, https://www.wto.org/english/res_e/statis_e/miwi_e/flyer_miwi_e.pdf. Last visited 25 Oct 2016

Leal-Arcas R (2011) Proliferation of regional trade agreements: complementing or supplanting multilateralism? Chicago J Int Law 11(2):597

Lester S (2011) The role of the international trade regime in global governance. UCLA J Int'l L Foreign Aff 16:209

Lester S, Mercurio B (2010) World trade law: text, materials and commentary. Hart Publishing

Liang M (2014) The international trading system post-bali: the need for a new paradigm. Asian J WTO Int'l Health L Pol'y 9:351

Matsushita M et al (2006) The world trade organization: law, practice, and policy, 2nd edn. Oxford University Press, Oxford

Mercurio B (2011) Trade liberalisation in Asia: why intra-asian free trade agreements are not utilised by the business community. Asian J WTO Int'l Health L Pol'y 6:109

Moinuddin M (2013) Economic integration and trade liberalization in South Asia. Asia Pathways: a blog of the Asian Development Bank Institute, 27 Aug 2013. Retrieved from http://www.asiapathways-adbi.org/2013/08/economic-integration-and-trade-liberalization-in-south-asia/

NAFTA Agreement (2016) Text retrieved from https://www.nafta-sec-alena.org/Home/Legal-Texts/North-American-Free-Trade-Agreement?mvid=1&secid=539c50ef-51c1-489b-808b-9e20c9872d25. Last visited 25 Oct 2016

NAFTA website. Retrieved from www.naftanow.org

O'Connor MR (2013). Subsidizing Starvation: How American Tax Dollars are Keeping Arkansas Rice Growers Fat on the Farm and Starving Millions of Haitians. Foreign Policy, 11 Jan 2013. Retrieved from http://foreignpolicy.com/2013/01/11/subsidizing-starvation/

Qureshi Asif H, Ziegler Andreas R (2011) International economic law, 3rd edn. Sweet & Maxwell, London

Rodrigo N (2004) SAARC as an institutional framework for cooperation in South Asia. In: Thakur R, Oddny W (eds) South Asia in the World: problem solving perspectives on security, sustainable development, and good governance

Rolland SE (2014) Are consumer-oriented rules the new frontier of trade liberalization. Harv Int'l L J 55:361

SAARC website. Retrieved from www.saarc-sec.org

SAARC Secretariat (2016) Article 3, SAPTA Agreement-SAARC. Retrieved from http://saarc-sec.org/digital_library/detail_menu/agreement-on-saarc-preferential-trading-arrangement-sapta

Schwartz B (2013) Reinvigorating the World Trade System. Asper Rev Int'l Bus Trade L 13, 1

Tharoor S (2012) Pax Indica: India and the world of the 21st century. Penguin Books, Allen Lane

Tharoor S (2003) Nehru: the invention of India. Arcade Publishing

The Economic Times (2014) SAARC to have "Meaningful Engagements" with 9 Observer States, 24 Nov 2014. Retrieved from http://articles.economictimes.indiatimes.com/2014-11-24/news/56420745_1_observer-member-states-foreign-affairs (Last visited July 16, 2016)

The World Bank (2010) World Bank South Asia economic update: moving up, looking east. Retrieved from http://siteresources.worldbank.org/SOUTHASIAEXT/Resources/223546-1269620455636/6907265-1275784425763/SAREconomicUpdate7June2010.pdf

United Nations Website. Retrieved from www.un.org

Whalley J (1996) Why do countries seek regional trade agreements? National Bureau of Economic Research. Working Paper 5552, Cambridge

World Bank (2016) Retrieved from http://www.worldbank.org/en/programs/south-asia-regional-integration

World Bank website. Retrieved from www.worldbank.org

World Trade Organization website. Retrieved from www.wto.org; https://stat.wto.org

Chapter 7
A Legal Analysis of Linking Human Right Approach to Access to Water and Sharing of Trans-Boundary Rivers in South Asia

Stellina Jolly

1 Introduction

Water is the fundamental economic and social good without which life in any form is impossible. Unfortunately, access to clean and safe water is a gripping struggle for billions of population, and a sizeable populace spends their entire life deprived of an adequate amount of clean water (Curry 2010). The gravity of the situation is clear from the reports highlighting the loss of millions of death as a result of lack of water (UNICEF–WHO 2000). However, it is not easy to determine whether water is a scarce commodity (Hecht 2004). Although 70 percent of the surface area of earth is water-centric, 97.5% of the available water is saltwater, leaving only a minuscule percentage of freshwater (Ally 2014). In terms of available freshwater, there exists an amount of scarcity which has been exacerbated especially in the wake of growing population, industrialization and climate change. (Reid 2006).

It is reported that 1 in 10 people lack access to safe water (WHO/UNICEF 2015). This water scarcity is linked to both surface as well as groundwater as 97% of the freshwater supply comes from groundwater sources (Murad 2005). India, Pakistan, and Bangladesh are among the largest users of groundwater in the world (Soeb 2016). Annual average groundwater extraction in India is a valued 200 billion cubic meters per year. The agrarian base economy, expanding industrialization, and the huge population contribute to this situation make India the highest groundwater extractor in the world (Jha 2016; Ananda 2009; Aguilar 2011). Increasing industrialization and rampant use of pesticides severely threatens the quality of groundwater (Gun 2013). The regional trend of groundwater contamination pattern shows domination of arsenic and fluoride resulting from both natural and anthropogenic factors. Arsenic and fluoride are the major contaminants in

S. Jolly (✉)
Faculty of Legal Studies, South Asian University,
Akbar Bhawan, Chanakyapuri, New Delhi 110021, India
e-mail: stellinajolly@sau.ac.in

J.L. Kaul and A. Jha (eds.), *Shifting Horizons of Public International Law*,
https://doi.org/10.1007/978-81-322-3724-2_7

Bangladesh, Nepal, and Pakistan. Fluoride is the primary identified contaminant for arid and semiarid regions in India (Sangam Shrestha 2016).

At the same time the water scarcity in the region cannot be looked at merely from the perspective of assuring an adequate amount of domestic water supply, the situation also makes a strong case for bringing up an equitable and justiciable mechanism for sharing of water between nations. This requirement of sharing can be justified on two grounds. Firstly, a human right interpretation about water could be advanced. Secondly, water can be interpreted as a public trust and common heritage of humanity, (Kemal 1997) which needs to be shared and cannot be under the private expropriation. Additionally, the relations of States are governed not only by treaty mechanism but also by the customary international law. The practice of States, which forms the basis of customary international law, clearly depicts a strong support to share the trans-boundary waters in an equitable and reasonable manner (Thompson 2011).

2 The Human Right to Water

Among the domestic legal systems, South Africa is the sole jurisdiction, which proclaims right to sufficient water as an explicit fundamental right (Bird et al. 2009). A look at the general international law documents and human right conventions shows a lack of explicit acceptance of right to access to water. UN Charter (1945), which contains the basic principle of governance, is silent as far as the right to water is concerned. In the absence of explicit provisions governing right to water, guidance could be sought from implicit interpretation of right to life under human right documents. Article 25 of the Universal Declaration on Human Rights, 1948, declares a basic right to life for one self and family, where one could be assured of certain basic standard of living (Universal Declaration of Human Rights 1948). It is argued that appreciating and implementing the assured human rights under the Declaration will not be possible without assured of an adequate quantity and quality of water. Article 6(1) of International Covenant on Civil and Political Rights 1966 (ICCPR) could also be resorted for the argument. Article 6 guarantees a basic right to life which cannot be deprived of arbitrarily. In terms of access to water, the term arbitrary deprivation could be interpreted as any action of government where it fails to provide for basic conditions with out which, existence of a dignified life will not be possible. Many other conventions could be interpreted to include access to water (Convention on the Rights of the Child 1980; Convention on the Elimination of All Forms of Discrimination against Women 1979; International Covenant on Economic, Social and Cultural Rights 1966 (ICESCR)). Arguments for access to water, as an implicit human right is simple, life and water go together and there can be no right to life without water (Hardberger 2005). The integral and conjoined relations between access to water and enjoyment of other declared human rights have been noted as a pre condition for the successful implementation of declared human rights in human right reports (ECOSOC 2005).

Many writers were not satisfied with this implicit approach and have constantly advocated for recognizing water as an autonomous human right. They point to several advantages, which could flow out of an explicit declaration of right to water. From a legal and social perspective, acceptance of right to water as a self-standing right would lead to better enforcement and accountability for the enforcement of the right (Scanlon et al. 2004). Since access to water is related to all other basic rights, recognition of a right to water may lead to enhanced implementation of other rights. For instance, water is a primary requirement of sanitation and an assured water supply will greatly enhance the provision and implementation of sanitation programs.

General Comment No. 15 on the right to water provides for an all-encompassing articulation of the substantive legal framework of human right to water (General Comment 2002). The document can be categorized as soft law hence non-binding in nature (Riedel 2006). The Comment contains a firm affirmation of the right to water as a human right. Further, the Comment elaborates on the content and component of the right as including "sufficient, safe, acceptable, physically accessible, and affordable water for everyone's personal and domestic uses." The Comment confines the recognition to right to water only for personal and domestic uses. The Comment recognizes the right to water not just from an economical perspective but also from a broader social political and environmental milieu (General Comment 15 Right to Water 2002). The Comment also acknowledges the role of integration and provides guidelines for integrating the access to water as part of the implementation of other human rights. The Comment specifically points out Article 11 (the right to an adequate standard of living) and Article 12 (the right to health) of the International Covenant on Economic, Social and Cultural Rights as closely interrelated with the enjoyment to water (Winkler 2014). It emphasizes on three aspects of right to water

(1) Availability;
(2) Quality; and
(3) Accessibility (General Comment 15 Right to Water 2002).

The first dimension tries to guarantee a sufficient quantity of available water to individuals (Hardberger 2005). This aspect points to the need to have an equitable sharing of trans-boundary waters without which jurisdictions cannot envisage to provide for adequate quantity of water. The second aspect highlights that it is not enough to have an assured supply of water, but the maintenance of adequate quality is necessary (Riedel 2006). The last component covers economic, social, and political elements of water supply and accessibility (Riedel 2006). For a human rights perspective, the accessibility dimension enables the governments to undertake extensive legislative and policy reforms at the substantive and procedural level to provide accessibility to water at an affordable price and implement legislative initiatives to completely end social and economic discriminatory practices as highlighted by the

UN (Special Rapporteur on the human right to safe drinking water and sanitation 2012). This aspect holds significance for South Asia as the region still suffers from practices of discrimination and inequality on the basis of caste and poverty (Bueren 2010).

Environmental concerns made an entry in the region with the Stockholm Declaration (1972). The Declaration was followed by a flurry of legislations. Indian parliament led the initiative in South Asia and the Water (Prevention and Control of Pollution) Act (1974) was passed in order to comply with country's international commitments. Through a constitutional amendment in 1976, Articles 48-A and 51-A(g) were incorporated as directive principles of State policy and as a fundamental duty in the Constitution of India, respectively (Constitution of India 1950). Article 48-A provides for the protection and safeguards of the environment, forests, and wildlife (Constitution of India 1950). Article 51-A(g) imposes solemn duty on individuals to protect and improve the natural environment. It specifically lists forests, lakes, rivers, and wild life, which needs to be protected. Article added a moral dimension to the provision by requiring compassion for living creatures (Constitution of India 1950). However, unlike fundamental rights which are directly enforced directive principles of State policy and fundamental duties are not justiciable rights.

The Supreme Court of India adopted the protective approach for environment through a host of procedural and substantive modifications (Jolly 2014). Procedurally, the *locus standi* rule was modified and the concept of public interest litigation was brought into operation (Shukla 2008). This gave an impetus to environmental movement in the country (Shukla 2008). Substantially an expansionist interpretation was given to Article 21 which incorporates right to life (Shukla 2008). Through the expanded notion of Article 21, right to life was interpreted to include a healthy and clean environment (T. Damodar Rao v. The Special Officer, Municipal Cooperation of Hyderabad 1987). The court emphatically ruled atmospheric pollution as infringing the sacrosanct right proclaimed under Article 21 of the Constitution. Supreme Court also utilized this expansion to adopt and apply the recognized international environmental principles[1] (Rural Litigation and Entitlement Kendera v. State of U.P. 1988; Himachal Pradesh v. Ganesh Wood Products 1996). In *Subhash Kumar v. State of Bihar* (1991), the Supreme Court of India categorically Stated the purpose of Article 32 as the protection of fundamental rights. The court also declared right to water as forming an essential ingredient of right to life under Article 21. In this case, the court protected the right to water as a negative right in the environmental sense of having an unpolluted source of water. Social and economic aspect of water has not been highlighted. In *A.P. Pollution Control Board* Case, the court seems to have recognized the social and political aspects of access to drinking water; however, detailed discussion on the components and modalities of the same is missing

[1]Supreme Court of India through a catena of decisions adopted principles of sustainable development, precautionary principles and intergenerational equity, etc.

(Kothari 2006). An attempt to pronounce on positive rights, which imposes obligation on the States to take positive actions, was taken in the context of right to food in *Peoples Union for Civil Liberties (PUCL) v. Union of India & Ors* (Kothari 2006). Kothari argues that enjoyment of positive right to food is inherently linked to a positive access to water (Kothari 2006). In *M C. Mehta v. Union of India* (2004), the groundwater was acknowledged as a social asset. The court also recognized the unbridled use of air and water under Article 21 of the Constitution. However, the judgment seems to merely suggest that water and air are social assets, beyond private appropriation. The judgment does not talk about right to water in a broader sociopolitical context. In 2014, the question before the Mumbai High Court was concerning the lack of access to water for illegal slum dwellers. Right to water was held to be an integral part of the right to life under Article 21 of the Indian Constitution (Historical judgement on the Right to Water in India 2015). The evolutionary landscape of Indian judicial decisions has thus clearly elevated right to water as a constitutionally protected fundamental right to its people.

Indian judiciary provided the momentum for other South Asian jurisdictions in enunciating an environmental jurisprudence (Jolly 2014). Among all the South Asian countries, only Nepal has incorporated right to environment as a fundamental right. Article 30 of the Nepalese Constitution guarantees an explicit right to life in a healthy and clean environment (Constitution of Nepal 2015). A progressive aspect of the Article is its explicit recognition to provide for compensation to the victim of environmental pollution and degradation (Constitution of Nepal 2015). Even before the introduction of the new Constitution in Nepal, in *Suray Prasad Sharma Dhungel v. Godavari Marble Industries and others*, the court through a positive interpretation has linked right to environment as part of right to life under the Article 12(1) of the Constitution of the Kingdom of Nepal 1990 (United Nations Environment Programme 2005). Gellers points that the explicit recognition of right to clean environment in Nepal was greatly influenced by the peoples movement and the deeper understanding of a continuous environmental degradation (Gellers 2015).

Constitution of Bhutan has elaborate provisions for the protection of the environment. Article 5 of the Constitution reads the following:

> Every Bhutanese is a trustee of the Kingdom's natural resources and environment for the benefit of the present and future generations and it is the fundamental duty of every citizen to contribute to the protection of the natural environment, conservation of the rich biodiversity of Bhutan and prevention of all forms of ecological degradation including noise, visual and physical pollution through the adoption and support of environment friendly practices and policies (The Constitution of the Kingdom of Bhutan 2008).

The above provision elaborates the holistic and innovative approach adopted for the protection of the environment. A comprehensive understanding was provided to the concept of environment as including noise visual and sound pollution. Unlike the right centric approach, the major focus of the Article seems to be on the individual and overall responsibility of individual for the protection of environment. The provision recognizes the equity between generations (A guide to the Constitution of Kingdom of Bhutan 2008).

If the emphasis of Article 5 was on the duty of individuals, Article 5(2) focuses on the governmental responsibility. It envisages governmental steps to protect and safeguard environment and biodiversity and measures to control pollution and environmental destruction. It declares sustainable development as a goal to be achieved in a condition, which promotes economic and social development goal (The Constitution of the kingdom of Bhutan 2008). Bhutan is the only Constitution in South Asia which has attainment of sustainable development as a declared constitutional goal. The protection of environment and natural resources is a high priority for the society that there is a constitutional mandate under Article 5(3) to earmark and preserve a minimum of sixty percentage of Bhutan's total land under forest cover for all time (The Constitution of the Kingdom of Bhutan 2008). It is interesting to analyze, in spite of the heavy reliance and emphasis placed on the protection of environment under Constitution of Bhutan, the protection and preservation of environment have not been elevated to the position of fundamental rights. One explanation could be the reliance of Bhutanese society on the duty of individuals rather than on rights to protection of environment.

Article 15 of Afghanistan Constitution envisages measures for the protection of forests and living environment (The Constitution of the Islamic Republic of Afghanistan 2004). The reason for qualifying the term environment has not been substantiated. This provision is in line with Indian and other South Asian jurisdictions where protection of environment has not been explicitly elevated to the level of fundamental rights. Unlike other South Asian jurisdictions, there is no judicial statement, which has come from Afghanistan on the interrelationship between right to life and right to clean environment.

Sri Lanka is one of the rare Constitutions (the Constitution of 1978), which has not incorporated a right to life. In the absence of an explicit right to life, Constitution is silent on the right to have clean environment (Attapattu 2001). However, in the chapter on directive principles, there is a specific reference to environmental protection (Attapattu 2001). The Draft Constitution, 2000, which is under consideration, has proposed to incorporate right to life, but fell short of incorporating right to clean environment. In *Wattegedera Wijebanda v. Conservator General of Forest and Eight Others*, they gave an innovative interpretation. In the absence of explicit environmental rights, the court traced the right to have a clean environment as inherently part of the equal protection provisions contained in Article 12(1) of the Constitution[2] (Karunaratne 2009). Unlike other South Asian jurisdictions, where the right to clean environment has been carved out of right to life, in Sri Lanka the same has been done through the invocation of right to equality. Gellers observes that the primary focus on stability and modernization is the reason for the absence of environmental rights in the Constitution (Gellers 2015).

[2]Article 12 (1) guarantees equality and equal protection clause and (2) prohibits any kind of discrimination on account of race, religion, language, caste, sex, political opinion, etc. The right to equality is provided for all, whereas the right against discrimination is available only for citizens.

In the case of *Shehla Zia v. WAPDA* 1994, public interest litigation was filed against construction of grid station in Islamabad. The court, invoked Article 14 of the Constitution, which guarantees the dignity of man and inviolable right to privacy and Article 9 which guarantees right to "life" (Shehla Zia v. WAPDA 1994). The court created an interlinkage between both these rights and held that dignity of a person cannot be guaranteed in the absence of an adequate and assured access to "food, clothing, shelter education, health care, clean atmosphere, and unpolluted environment" (Shehla Zia v. WAPDA 1994). The court cited with approval Indian cases on environmental pollution, recognizing that relief could be granted if there was potential violation of the right to life (Hassan 2005).

The court gave a broader interpretation to right to life and held that the right to life does not mean mere subsistence. The court further linked the right to life with right to dignity guaranteed under Article 14 of the Constitution. The court emphatically held that dignity of a man would be violated if he were deprived of the basic necessities of life including food clothing, water and unpolluted environment.

In the *General Secretary, W.P. Salt Mines Labour Union v. Director, Industries and Mineral Development* (1994), "right to clean and unpolluted drinking water" was held to be a fundamental right under Article 9 of the Constitution. The court barred mining in the area, as it will lead to water contamination and violate right to life (Ahmad, Chief Justice Pakistan).

Article 18(1) of the Constitution of the People's Republic of Bangladesh (1971) considers environmental protection as forming non-justiciable principles. The scope of the Article is comprehensive and lists out different categories of environment and biodiversity including "wetlands, forests, and wild life." Article aims to protect and preserve these resources for "the present and future citizens." Instead of recognizing the rights of present and future generations, Article has narrowly focused on the right of citizens. In terms of trans-boundary sharing of water, these provisions become problematic as it gives primacy to citizens rights over others. The case of *M. Farooque v. Bangladesh and Others* (1997) brought a new paradigm in environmental jurisprudence in Bangladesh. Firstly, the court incorporated right to have a clean environment as an integral part of right to life. Secondly, the rules on *locus standi* were expanded to include socially spirited individuals or organizations to file cases on behalf of people who are deprived of access to justice[3] (M. Farooque v. Bangladesh and Others 1997).

Constitutional provisions and judicial statements from South Asia have unambiguously recognized the right to a clean environment. This has been mainly achieved through a dynamic elucidation of right to life (Karunaratne 2009). Indian legal and judicial landscape has clearly elevated right to water as fundamental human right. Pakistan has interpreted the right to water as negative rights: the right

---

[3]*M. Farooque v. Bangladesh and Others* (1997) 49 DLR (AD) 1 Articles 31 and 32 of the Constitution was relied on by the Court. Article 32 guarantees right to life in classical sense of non deprivation with out law. Article 31 guarantees protection to preserve life, liberty, property, and reputation. Court applied the doctrine of integration and held that right to life includes the right to a healthy environment.

not to have water polluted. Judicial statements are missing in this context from other jurisdictions. In the case of Nepal, the right to water could be interpreted as part of an explicit right to clean environment.

Going by the evolution and current position of legal jurisprudence, right to water has not acquired an independent self-standing status of substantive human rights. Looking at the issue from a human right perspective will lead to obvious enactment of laws, a sense of participation and inclusiveness on the part of public, and an increased accountability (Birnie 2009). The absence of an explicit recognition to a substantive human right to water has encouraged multilateral environmental to incorporate procedural aspects of human rights. The inclusion of procedural human right under multilateral environmental convention has been dominated by recognition of public access to information, participation, and access to justice in environmental governance (Birnie 2009). In *Orissa Mining Corp v. MoEF & Ors* (2013), Supreme Court of India handed down a landmark decision and ordered that mining in the region cannot proceed without consultation with the inhabitances of the area. While reiterating the principles of natural justice, Supreme Court was adopting the current international trend of environmental governance heralded through Rio Declaration (Rio 1992). Principle 10 of Rio Declaration directs that basic principle of good governance is promoted when decision making, pertaining to environment and natural resources proceeds on the basis of inclusive participation (Rio 1992). The judgment is an indication that a human right-based approach brings element of democratic principles and promotes rule of law.

One of the prominent criticisms, which have been raised in the context of international environmental governance, is the weak and ambivalent legislations and ineffective implementation, a human right dimension operates as a safety net mechanism which will reduce the weakening of environmental legislations (Boyd 2012) and promote fairness, a fundamental concept of rule of law (Jolly and Jaswal 2010). The courts have articulated that the human right principle, based on the right to a healthy environment, represents a reference point, and not the ultimate object to be achieved. It represents a bare minimum baseline from which improvements can be created but not weakened as far as the current environmental policies and principles are concerned (Boyd 2012). Another critical dimension, which will be in prominence with the explicit declaration of right to environment and water, relates to information sharing. At the political level, right to information is gathering a lot of attention and acceptance across jurisdictions and is considered the basis of good governance. Human rights approach will highlight the need to ensure transparency, accountability, and information at the level of access to water (Riedel 2006).

At the same time, we should be aware of the inherent challenges involved in the process of elevating right to water as a human right (Salman and McInerney-Lankford 2004). Salman, who analyzes the issue of right to water points that the classical understanding of human right, imposes a binding obligation on the State to initiative legal and policy measures to positively realize the recognized human right for its own citizens. It becomes problematic, as right to water is intrinsically connected to economic and political capacity of States (Salman and McInerney-Lankford 2004). In this scenario, a successful realization of the human rights to water will require State responsibility to manage the water governance through the Public Trust Doctrine.

3 Water as Public Trust

Public Trust Doctrine as the name suggests places certain resources under the trusteeship of State authorities. In the initial times, Public Trust Doctrine concept was initialized by the decisions of US courts primarily pertaining to navigational rights and related aspects (Feris 2012). The doctrine made its official jurisprudential acceptance at the legal lexicon in the US in 1821 (Blumn and Wood 2015). The subject matter of the case related to water management and specifically addressed the rights of riparian owners (Blumn and Wood 2015). The court in a path breaking judgment opined and ruled that tidal waters, including the riverbed, were common property (Feris 2012). The content and scope of the doctrine were explained, revived, and expanded with the celebrated work of Joseph Sax. His article titled The *Public Trust Doctrine in Natural Resource law: Effective Judicial InterventionT* (Sax 1970) developed the legal contours of the application of doctrine.

He explains the focus of the doctrine and the basic responsibilities of States in the following terms.

- "Public purpose" is the defining point of Public Trust Doctrine. Trust property should be used and held for public purpose.
- The property may not be sold.
- It should be maintained for particular types of uses (quoted in Mbote 2007).

Over the years, there has been an expansion of the contours and application of the doctrine to new areas and is adopted in a multitude of settings in different jurisdictions (Kanner 2005). In *National Audubon Society*, the California Supreme Court, while applying Public Trust Doctrine, restrained the City of Los Angele right to divert water from Mono Lake basin to its service area (Watson 1998). The court through a landmark decision held that the Public Trust Doctrine applies in the context of water rights and that the City's water rights were not "vested" but were subject to continuing State regulation and control (Watson 1998). In the context of water management, Doctrine of Public Trust confers on the government ultimate control and ownership to water but directs it to hold water in its capacity as a trustee for the whole of public.

The case of *M.C. Mehta v. Kamal Nath* (1997) is credited with bringing the doctrine to Indian environmental jurisprudence. The issue in contention was the restraint order passed against a private company from encroaching upon the declared forest land. The court eloquently wrote on the significance of the doctrine. "The Public Trust Doctrine is premised on the belief that certain resources are infinite and have great utility for the society". These resources include air, sea, waters, and the forests. The court further held that taking into account the significance of these resources, these resources have to be operated under public domain. Privatization and Public Trust Doctrine are antithesis to each other (M.C. Mehta v. Kamal Nath 1997).

The court further traced the origin and purpose of the doctrine to the law of nature, where natural resources belong to common humanity, the concept of Public Trust defines a common ownership where sovereign States own all natural resources which are on the land and beneath the land for the benefit of the public (M.C. Mehta v. Kamal Nath 1997).

The court applied a dynamic interpretation and pointed out that Public Trust Doctrine was always part of the country's jurisprudence. The justification was drawn from the common law origin of Indian legal system. Considering the opinions raised by Joseph Sax, the court held that contours of Public Trust Doctrine demand natural resources to be held in trust by State and used for absolute public purposes only (M.C. Mehta v. Kamal Nath 1997).

Several cases followed this dictum and expanded the scope of the doctrine further to other subject matter (M.I. Builders v. Radhey Shyam Sahu 1999). In *Intellectuals Forum, Tirupathi v. State Of A.P. & Ors* 2006, the court expounded and traced the origin and foundational principles of the doctrine in India to right to equality and right to life under the Constitution. The court also identified basic articles dealing with environment protection as significant for environmental governance in the country. While adopting the test of integration, the court highlighted the need to have a harmonious interpretation which will take into account environmental provisions contained under directive principles of State policy and fundamental duty to elucidate the scope and normative content of Articles 14, 19, and 21 of the Constitution of India (Intellectuals Forum, Tirupathi v. State of A.P. & Ors 2006).

A single-judge-bench decision of Kerala High Court attempted to apply the doctrine in the context of groundwater (Perumatty Grama Panchayat v. State of Kerala Perumatty Grama Panchayat 2004). The court emphasized on the public use of groundwater and highlighted the positive obligation of States to prevent over exploitation and extraction of groundwater by private bodies (Perumatty Grama Panchayat v. State of Kerala Perumatty Grama Panchayat 2004). However, division bench of the same court overruled the decision (Hindustan Coco-Cola beverages v. Perumatty Grama Panchayat 2005).

The Doctrine of Public Trust Doctrine was invoked for the first time in the case of *Bulankula v. Secretary, Ministry of Industrial Development* (2000). Case related to the continuous phosphate mining in Eppawala causing major environmental hazards in the area. Contention of the petitioners was based on the violation of their fundamental rights. The court gave an innovative interpretation, even though Public Trust Doctrine vests the trusteeship of resources on the State, "shared responsibility" is the philosophical basis of the Public Trust Doctrine. J. Amaresinghe observed "The idea of shared responsibility is significant because it imposes responsibility upon all the organs of the government to protect the environment as well as responsibility is vested upon all the people to protect the environment" (Bulankulame v. Secretary Ministry of Industrial Development 2000).

In a progressive interpretation, J. Amaresinghe traced the origin of doctrine to principles of democracy and sovereignty as found under Article 3 of the Constitution (Constitution of the Democratic Socialist Republic of Sri Lanka 1978). The Sri Lankan Constitution recognizes sovereignty as inalienable and is vested in the people. Constitution of Sri Lanka operationalizes the sovereignty through free and fair franchise (Samararatne 2010). In 2003, the Supreme Court of Sri Lanka was confronted with the legality of water resources bill, which attempted to privatize the water resources in the country. In this case, court broadened the doctrine of Public Trust Doctrine and held that water resources are natural and common heritage of people. By implication, these natural resources cannot be granted for private proprietorship. The court held that any deviation from this core principle of public trust and policy of privatization of those resources required special majority in the parliament and approval of the people at a referendum (Siriwardana 2015). Article 85(1) of the Sri Lankan Constitution deals with referendum and States that "The President shall submit to the People by Referendum every Bill or any provision in any Bill which the Cabinet of Ministers has certified as being intended to be submitted to the People by Referendum, or which the Supreme Court has determined as requiring the approval of the People at a Referendum if the number of votes cast in favour of such Bill amounts to not less than two-thirds of the whole number of Members (including those not present)" (Constitution of the Democratic Socialist Republic of Sri Lanka 1978).

As far as the position of Bhutan is concerned, the Constitution of Bhutan explicitly provides that "every Bhutanese is a trustee and environment for the benefit of the present and future generations" (The Constitution of the Kingdom of Bhutan 2008). Recently, a climate litigation suit was filed in Pakistan for the delay and lack of implementation of the 2012 National Climate Policy and Framework (Vents 2015). Climate change was acknowledged as a serious threat to the nation and society. While ordering quick action from the government, the court relied on constitutional principles of right to life, human dignity, drew inspiration from the core political social and economic principles including democracy, equality, social, economic, and political justice. Apart from the domestic principles, reliance was placed on "the international principles of sustainable development, precautionary principle, environmental impact assessment, inter- and intra-generational equity, and Public Trust Doctrine" (Vents 2015).

In *Yogi Narahari Nath and other v. Honourable Prime Minister Girija* (1955), the Supreme Court of Nepal through an innovative approach not only implicitly declared right to environment but also invoked the Doctrine of Public Trust to be an integral part of constitutional principles. The court ordered an injunction against the governmental decision to lease out the Devghat area, which is considered to be sacred by people of the area (May and Daly 2014; United Nations Environment Programme 2005). The court declared that protection of environment is a primary responsibility of government (United Nations Environment Programme 2005).

Various statutes operating in relation to water management attempt to incorporate the Public Trust Doctrine in South Asia. The Planning Commission Model Bill for the conservation, protection, and regulation of groundwater in India (Planning Commission of India 2011) recognizes "groundwater is the common heritage of the people of India held in trust, for the use of all, subject to reasonable restrictions to protect all water and associated ecosystems. In its natural State, it is not amenable to ownership by the State, communities, or persons" (Planning Commission of India 2011). Bill imposing obligations on the appropriate authority that it "must ensure that water is protected, used, developed, conserved, managed, and regulated in a sustainable and equitable manner, for the benefit of all persons and ecosystems" (Planning Commission of India 2011). Bangladesh Water Act (2013) provides that all rights over all water including groundwater within the State territory shall be, on the behalf of people, vested in the State. Section 3 of Water Resources Act (WRA) 2049 (1992) of Nepal grants the proprietorship of the water resources in the State (Bradlow and Salman 2006).

Analysis of the judicial decisions in South Asian jurisdictions reveals that the Public Trust Doctrine is firmly entrenched as part of jurisprudential development. Except Bhutan where the doctrine is an explicit constitutional mandate, in all other jurisdictions, the doctrine is a judicial innovation founded on the overarching principles of Constitution dealing with right to equality, right to life, democracy, and sovereignty of people. Treating "water as a public trust" is legally desirable and is in harmony with human right approach. The concept of government, been assigned trusteeship over water resources for the absolute benefit of public, will prompt the State to accord primary priority to ensure that accessible, available, and quality water for personal and domestic needs. The aggrieved citizens who are denied adequate access to water will have a legitimate opportunity to urge that the nation has failed to meet its trust responsibilities (Scanlon et al. 2004). More importantly, the application of Public Trust Doctrine will expand the traditional notion of human right concept being confined to one's own citizens. It will impose obligations on the States to guarantee that their human right obligations are not aimed at mere progressive realization of the water accessibility and availability to its own citizens but extend to taking ant steps, which may negatively affect the enjoyment of the right to water in other States (McCaffrey 1992). The extraterritorial application of human right will be highly relevant and contested in the context of trans-boundary water sharing and management. Mclntyre considers that General Comment 15, which contains the most comprehensive enunciation of the right to water, appears to recognize the possibility of extraterritorial implication of the human right to water in paras 31 and 34–35 (Mclntyre 2013). It enjoins the States to look at the sharing of water resources with a spirit of cooperation and respect for human rights (Mclntyre 2013).

4 Sharing of Trans-Boundary Water Sources in South Asia from a Human Right Perspective

This part of the chapter explores the possibility of a human right approach to the sharing of trans-boundary water sources. At an international level, sharing of water resources has always remained contentions due to the conflicting interests of upperstream and downstream nations. Four main principles govern the rights and obligations of riparian States over international rivers: absolute territorial sovereignty, absolute territorial integrity, limited territorial sovereignty, and limited territorial integrity (Wouters 1997).

Years of effort and negotiations finally culminated in the conclusion of 1997 UN Convention on the Law of the Non-navigational Uses of International Watercourses (Watercourses Convention 1997). It is a framework convention, and it provides a basic foundational structure of principles and procedural formalities that may be applied to ensure equitable sharing of water resources. The convention lays down the widely accepted principle of equitable and reasonable utilization as well as participation as its touchstone foundation (Watercourses Convention 1997). To encourage participation, various cooperative mechanisms are envisaged (Clarke 2005). The convention is the result of years of codification attempts made by International Law Commission (ILC) and is representative of the customary principles of international law (Helal 2007). By laying down obligations on the States, it represents an important contribution to the strengthening of the rule of law and progressive development of international law in the field.

Reception to the UN convention was not very encouraging in South Asia. India and Pakistan abstained; Bhutan absented itself, and only Bangladesh and Nepal voted in favor of the convention. The question arises in the absence of ratification by most of the States what is the status of application of international law to the States concerned in the region. The basic premise of international law is that States will carry out international obligation in good faith. However, whether international law becomes binding on States immediately after ratification of a treaty or it requires a specific act of incorporation in domestic law has been left to the States concerned (Agarwal). As far as the relationship between municipal law and international law is concerned, most of the South Asian Nations follow the Dualist Approach. Dualist School emphasizes the distinct and independent character of international law and municipal legal systems (Crawford 2012). According to Dualist School, municipal law can apply international law only through the act of incorporation (Crawford 2012). The act of incorporation can be through a legislative function, executive action, or adopted by the courts (Crawford 2012). In legal terms, provisions of the conventions do not become binding on the States unless ratified by the concerned States. In the case of *Jolly Jeorge v. Bank of Cochin* (1980), the court stated that a Dualist Approach is followed in India as far as the incorporation of international law is concerned. The Division Bench of the Rajasthan High Court in *Birma v. State* (Birma v. State 1951) was analyzed a question as to whether a treaty, which was not given effect to by means of legislative enactment, could be regarded as part of the domestic law. Observation of the court is relevant:

> …Treaties *which are part of the international law do not form part of the law of the land unless expressly made so by the legislative authority*. In the present case the treaty remained a treaty only and no action was taken to incorporate it into a law. That treaty cannot therefore be regarded as part of the Municipal Law of the then Dholapur State and the *practice of surrendering fugitive criminals, which was being followed by the former Dholapur State cannot be deemed to be a law that could be continued under Article 372 of the Constitution of India……* (Birma v. State 1951; Halashetti 2011).

The observation of the court clearly points to the adoption of a Dualist Approach as far as the position of international law is concerned.

Similar legal points are articulated in the context of Sri Lanka, without an enabling legislation at domestic level, courts in Sri Lanka are not authorized to invoke international law whether in the form of treaty provisions or customary international law. The case of *Srilanka Singarasa v. Attorney General* (2006), specifically identifies the dualist approach, the court categorically ruled that Sri Lankans could not rely on the recognized rights under ICCPR, as mere accession to the convention does not guarantee any additional rights to its people at domestic level.

Afghanistan's position with regard to application of international law is far from clear. No judicial statement has come from Afghanistan laying down the criteria and fundamental principles in this regard. Different interpretations have been ascribed to various provisions of the Constitution (Afghanistan Legal Education Project 2015). The Preamble of Afghan Constitution emphasizes on observing the United Nations Charter as well as the Universal Declaration of Human Rights as binding obligations to the people of Afghanistan. But across the world, the courts and academics have always debated on the legality of preamble to interpreting the Constitutions and varied interpretations followed (Jolly 2007; Kesavanada Bharati v. State of Kerala 1973).

Article 7 of Afghan Constitution declares "State shall abide by the UN charter, international treaties, international conventions that Afghanistan has signed, and the Universal Declaration of Human Rights" (Constitution of Afghanistan 2004). Article 94 lays down that "law shall be what both houses of the National Assembly approve and the President endorses, unless this Constitution States otherwise" (Constitution of Afghanistan 2004). The term "unless this Constitution States otherwise" signifies that apart from the laws passed by national assembly and endorsed by president, the definition of law would include stated Constitutional provisions. Article 7, which enjoins the State to abide by international law, could be interpreted as constituting an exception to the definition of law under Article 94 (Afghanistan Legal Education Project 2015). As for customary international law and agreements are concerned, Constitution does not contain any mention of custom, general rules of international law (Afghanistan Legal Education Project 2015).

Principle of equitable and reasonable utilization under Watercourses Convention has not remained merely a legal provision; it has acquired the status of customary international Law as articulated by the International Court of Justice (Case Concerning the Gabcikovo-Nagymaros Project Hungary v. Slovakia 1997). In India, the rules of International customary laws are part of the Municipal Law provided that they are not inconsistent with any legislative enactment or the provision of the Constitution. Indian courts will apply customary international law, if they are not overridden by the clear rules of the domestic law (Basu 1956).

An analysis of trans-boundary arrangements in the region will reveal the extent of application of the customary principle of equitable sharing and mutilation principle in the South Asian context. Regarding the water sharing, India and Pakistan have concluded Indus Water Treaty of 1960 (Sarfraz 2013). It was the first major trans-boundary river agreement in South Asia (Sidhu 2013).

The *Kishenganga* case marks the first instance of arbitration relating to sharing of water in South Asia. The dispute was related to India's construction of the Kishenganga Hydro-Electric Project ("KHEP"), and the diversion of water, from the dam site to another river of the Indus system (Sidhu 2013). The final award gave an approval for Indian project; however, it instructed "India shall release a minimum flow of 9 cumecs into the Kishenganga/Neelum River below the KHEP at all times" (Indus Waters Final Award 2013). The verdict has not resolved the problem. Pakistan claims that India has impounded water at the dam and reduced flow in its tributaries (Kishanganga Project: Victory claims cloud final arbitration award 2013).

Water sharing of rivers between Nepal and India has strained the relationship between both the nations (Earle et al. 2015). Nepalese feel that they have not been treated equitably under the water resource agreement with India including kosi and sarada (Earle et al. 2015). Mahakali Treaty was signed in 1996 (Gyawali 1999). It came up as a solution to the disagreement between India and Nepal; however, the treaty has not silenced the critics (Earle et al. 2015). The conflict regarding the sharing of trans-boundary river water between India and Bangladesh, having 54 such rivers, is a legacy of partition for India and succession for Bangladesh (Khan 1996). In 1972, an Indo-Bangladesh Joint Rivers Commission (JRC) was set up, but its mandate excluded the sharing of river waters (Khan 1996). Finally, in 1996, the two countries signed the 30 years of Ganges Water Treaty (Khan 1996). The treaty recognized Bangladesh's lower riparian rights. However, the Treaty has not been very successful in amicably resolving issues (Siwakoti 2011). The Indian project, which is under consideration to interlink the peninsular rivers with Himalayan Rivers, has become a contentious issue between both the countries who have not been able to sort out their riparian differences in an amicable manner (Siwakoti 2011; Adhikari 2014).

A bitter political dispute exists between Pakistan and Afghanistan over Indus–Kabul basin. Construction of dams is believed to be the solution to all of Afghan issues. In the words of former irrigation minister, "Once we have water, no one will grow poppies, no one will fight, no one will leave Afghanistan [for work] … water will resolve all problems in Afghanistan" (quoted in Thomas 2014).

None of these bilateral treaties operating in the region explicitly contains provisions detailing the application of equitable sharing and utilization. One of the possible arguments could be that these treaties were signed before the UN Watercourses convention was signed and it could not have foreseen the development of the principle of equitable utilization. However, the Mahakali Treaty between India and Nepal and Ganges Water Treaty between India and Bangladesh were concluded when the negotiations were at a much advanced stage for the UN Watercourses Convention and there was acceptability of the principle as a customary international law articulated by ICJ (Case Concerning the Gabcikovo-Nagymaros Project Hungary v. Slovakia, 1997). No steps were ever taken to amend the treaties to incorporate the equitable utilization principles to share its trans-boundary rivers. This is not to argue that in the absence of an explicit treaty provision with regard to equitable utilization and sharing of trans-boundary waters, the principle is inapplicable. Customary international law binds States in their international relations.

The incorporation of equitable sharing and utilization of water is also significant from the perspective of attainment of sustainable development. The interrelationship between sustainable development and equitable sharing of resources has been clearly enunciated by International Court of Justice in Pulp Miils case (Argentina v. Uruguay 2006). Countries in South Asia are struggling to achieve sustainable development and their pursuit becomes complicated with its regional imbalances in power among the countries, mutual hostility, and suspicion. Sharing of trans-boundary water resources in an equitable manner can create a scenario of cooperation assisting them in a path of sustainable development.

In the current context, some of the experts argue for human rights-based approach, which they believe will advance effective enactment of substantive and procedural laws, State-to-State cooperation, and individual participation in a more coordinated manner. Such an approach brings an element of extra territoriality as it will not only ensure the accessibility and availability of water to its own citizens but also avoid infringing on the enjoyment of the right to water in other States (McCaffrey 1992).

If one analyzes the logical corollary of the expansionist interpretation of right to life, the formulation and pronouncement of a self-standing human right to a healthy environment and right to water seems to be the natural progression. However, an analysis of international legal developments does not point to the automatic acceptance of a right to environment. Juristic opinions are clearly divided on the topic. Ramcharan argues, "There is strict duty imposed on the States and community as a whole to take effective measures to prevent and to safeguard against the occurrence of environmental hazards which threaten the lives of human beings" (Ramcharan 1985; quoted in Sancin 2012; quoted in Turner 2013). However, the above view is representative of the African Charter position which provides that all peoples "shall have the right to a general satisfactory environment favorable to their development" (African Charter on Human and Peoples Right 1988). In other regional context, right to clean environment has not been expressed as separate right, it has been considered as a necessary corollary to right to life. Even if we argue that a brand new right to clean environment has emerged at the international level, whether it incorporates right to water remains to be seen. The real implication of linking equitable utilization/sharing of waters and human rights, Dinah Shelton argues, might lead to a potentially vast expansion of the territorial scope of States obligation, States action will be assessed not just in terms of its effect vis a vis its own citizens but also with a trans-boundary impact analysis. In the context of water sharing, it becomes problematic given the mammoth economical costs and the human emotions and sentiments attached to the issue (Shelton 2008). Under the traditional approach, States are bound to ensure human right protections to its citizens within their boundaries. Extending the human right approach to equitable sharing of water resources will expand the State human right obligation beyond its borders. Extraterritorial application of human right in trans-boundary water sharing context will force the States to move beyond State centric approach and see the protection of human beings beyond territory from the perspective of Individuals (Mclntyre 2013).

Further, there are inherent difficulties involved in implementing the contents of right to water as articulated in South African case in *Manqele v. Durban Transitional Metropolitan Council in South Africa* (2002). Water supply to the petitioner had been disconnected as a result of the non-payment. The South African Water Services Act 108 (1997) assures the right to a basic water supply and fixes first six kiloliters of water per month free (Water Services Act 1997). In the present case, the amount has already been consumed by the appellant (Challenges in claiming the Right to water in South Africa 2012). The court held that in the absence of regulations, it has no power to interpret the contents of the Act (Challenges in claiming the Right to water in South Africa 2012).

In spite of these challenges, there is a great merit in arguing for a human right interpretation in terms of access to water and sharing of water resources. In the context of access to water at domestic level, some amount of right-based approach has been adopted by most of the South Asian Nations through their expansionist interpretation of right to life. However, in the context of water sharing, a human right approach is missing. The UN Watercourses Convention nowhere talks about the individual right of access to water and grievances of the affected people. Revisiting the convention from a human right perspective will encourage transparency and accountability in the implementation of convention. One of the problems witnessed in the sharing of trans-boundary water sources in South Asia is the lack of participation, transparency, and information sharing. In spite of the establishment and conclusion of numerous bilateral treaties, agreements, and joint-commissions regulating the use and management of shared rivers between Bangladesh, India, Nepal, and Pakistan, information on these agreements is notoriously hard to access (Dutt 2008). Generally, negotiations have been conducted in secrecy leading to mistrust and exploitation of real stakeholders and a complete absence of grievance mechanism of the affected parties (Dutt 2008). It is understandable that a human right approach can provide for a grievance mechanism for the effected parties. World Bank projects have adopted this human right approach and have in built public grievance facilities. An inclusive human right mechanism can help in ensuring the rights of affected parties and improving trans-boundary water governance. On the lines of individual complaints procedure under ICESCR, UN water convention could be modified where effected people can voice their grievances and incorporate provisions for individual information access and participation.

The basic aim and objective of the SAARC was to promote regional cooperation in a spirit of understanding, transcending economic, social, technical, cultural, and scientific fields (Jolly and Mahajana 2014). SAARC could play a significant role in bringing human rights consciousness including right to water (Harshe 1999). The initiative in the direction is to come up with a comprehensive human rights declaration in South Asia, which will encourage addressing issues of water from a more regional, and human right point of view (Kumar and Goyal 2016). On the lines of Individual complaints under International Covenant on Economic Social and Cultural rights (ICESCR), a complaint mechanism can be established where effected people can voice their grievances (Boer 2015). SAARC could also explore the possibility of establishing trans-boundary water management institutions to foster a human right-based approach (Bourquain 2008). He points that "the mounting water scarcity will not be solved through unilateral action and there is an urgent need to develop cooperative mechanisms on a permanent scale" (Bourquain 2008). Trans-boundary water management institutions based on human right approach are much better suited to respond to the regional needs of water management (Bourquain 2008). Human right approach can promote cooperation and avoid conflict to build a better future for the people of South Asia (Jolly and Mahajana 2014). This may have the advantage of looking at the issue of water from a more regional, realistic, and human rights point of view. Looking at the looming water crisis in the region and the experience gathered from the failed diplomatic and political negotiations of access to water in the domestic and trans-boundary context, it is imperative that the issue of water is viewed from a new human rights perspective.

5 Conclusion

South Asian Nations have acknowledged the necessity and existence of a right to water as a human right under the expansionist interpretation of right to life. However, this interpretation covers only access to water in the domestic context. With regard to trans-boundary water sharing, the principle of equitable sharing is accepted as the foundational principle under UN Watercourses Convention as well as a declared a customary international law. The convention fails to incorporate substantive human right dimension and individual access to water. In the context of South Asia, countries have yet to evolve an equitable mechanism wherein sharing of water proceeds on rightful basis. In this context, it is recommended countries in the region address the accessibility and availability of water not only from its own perspective and from the perspective of regional comity of nations, but also from a human right perspective. A country has the obligation to protect not only the rights of its own citizens, but also the duty not to interfere and violate the rights of the citizens of other States. Clear-cut co-relations between water and human rights have been evidenced by the judicial and legislative pronouncements in the region as water constitutes a significant factor in the enjoyment of basic human rights. Another dimension of this interrelatedness is the potential and existing interstate rivalries contributing to human rights violations. UN has already pointed the possibilities of water wars in South Asia (Chellane 2013). An explicit recognition of right to water at domestic, regional, and international level will encourage better enactment and effective implementation of laws. For the SAARC region, a comprehensive human right declaration and an institutional mechanism to treat trans-boundary water issues form the perspective of human right needs to be established, and individual complaints procedure in the matters of access to water should be recognized by the regional agreements. The complicated issues of access to water and sharing of trans-boundary water resources may not be completely addressed through human rights law mechanisms. However, a human rights perspective will ensure much needed legal and moral urgency and assist in the progressive development of international law.

References

A Guide to the Constitution of Kingdom of Bhutan (2008). http://www.judiciary.gov.bt/html/education/high%20court%20book.pdf. Accessed 13 June 2016

Adhikari KN (2014) Conflict and cooperation on South Asian water resources. IPRI J XIV(2): 45–62

Afghanistan Legal Education Project S.L. (2015) An introduction to international law for Afghanistan. https://www-cdn.law.stanford.edu/wp-content/uploads/2015/12/Intro-to-International-Law-for-Afg.pdf. Accessed 10 May 2016

Agarwal SK (n.d.) Implementation of international law in India: role of judiciary. Working paper, Dean Maxwell and Isle Cohen Doctoral seminar in international law. http://oppenheimer.mcgill.ca/IMG/pdf/SK_Agarwal.pdf. Accessed 6 June 2016

Aguilar D (2011) Groundwater reform in India: an equity and sustainability dilemma. Tex Int Law J 46:623

Ahmad JS (n.d.) Legal and institutional framework for the protection of environment in Pakistan. http://www.unep.org/delc/Portals/119/publications/Speeches/PAKISTAN.pdf. Accessed 8 June 2016

Ally RM (2014, February) Impending water wars in South Asia. The Express Tribune. http://tribune.com.pk/story/674611/impending-water-wars-in-south-asia. Accessed 10 Feb 2016

Ananda J (2009) Water institutions in India: an institutional design perspective. In: Lin Crase VP (ed) Reforming institutions in water resource management: policy and performance for sustainable policy development. p 106

Attapattu S (2001) Sustainable development myth or reality, sustainable development under international law and Srilankan law, a survey. Georget Int Environ Law Rev 14:265

Bangladesh Water Act (2013) Act No. 14 of 2013

Barton H, Thompson J (2011) Water as a public commodity. Marquette Law Rev 95:17

Basu DD (1956) Commentary on the constitution of India. LexisNexis Butterworths Wadhwa, Nagpur

Bird J, Arriens WL, Von Custodio D (2009) Water rights and water allocation issues and challenges for Asia. Asian Development Bank, Mandaluyong

Birma v. State, AIR Raj 127 (High Court 1951)

Birnie PA (2009) International law and the environment, 3rd edn. Oxford University Press, Oxford

Blumn MC, Wood MC (2015) Public trust doctrine in environmental and natural resources law. Carolina Academic Press, Durham

Boer B (2015) Environmental law dimensions of human rights. Oxford University Press, Oxford

Bourquain K (2008) Freshwater access from a human rights perspective: a challenge to international water and human rights law. Brill Publishers, Leiden

Boyd DR (2012, July–August) The constitutional right to a healthy environment. http://www.environmentmagazine.org/Archives/Back%20Issues/2012/July-August%202012/constitutional-rights-full.html. Accessed 3 May 2016

Bradlow D, Salman MA (2006) Regulatory framework for water resources management. World Bank, Washington

Bulankulame v. Secretary Ministry of Industrial Development, SRi.L.R, 3 (2000)

Bueren VG (2010) Freedom from poverty as a human right: law's duty to the poor. UNESCO, London

Case Concerning the Gabcikovo-Nagymaros Project Hungary v. Slovakia, ICJ 7 (International Court of Justice Feb 5, 1997)
Case Concerning Pulp Mills on the River Uruguay (Argentina v. Uruguay) (2006) ICJ Rep 113
Challenges in Claiming the Right to water in South Africa (2012) The rights to water and sanitation. http://www.righttowater.info/rights-in-practice/legal-approach-case-studies/challenges-in-claiming-the-right-to-water-south-africa/. Accessed 8 May 2016
Charter of the United Nations (1945)
Chellane B (2013) Water: Asia's new battleground. Georgetown University Press, Washington
Clark AR (2005) International law and sustainable development. IWA Publishing, London
Constitution of Afghanistan (2004)
Constitution of India (1950)
Constitution of Nepal (2015)
Constitution of the Democratic Socialist Republic of Sri Lanka (1978). http://www.wipo.int/edocs/lexdocs/laws/en/lk/lk007en.pdf. Accessed 8 May 2016
Constitution of the Peoples Republic of Bangladesh (1971)
Convention on the Elimination of All Forms of Discrimination against Women (1979)
Convention on the Rights of the Child (1980)
Crawford J (2012) Brownlie's principles of public international law. Oxford University Press, Oxford
Curry E (2010) Water scarcity and the recognition of the human right to safe freshwater. Nw J Int'l Hum Rts 9:103
Dutt KL, Wasson RJ (2008) Water first: issues and challenges for nations and communities in South Asia. Sage Publishers, New Delhi
Earle A, Cascao AE et al (2015) Transboundary water management and the climate change debate. Routledge Publishers, Abington
Eckstein G, Sindico F (2014) The law of transboundary aquifers: many ways of going forward, but only one way of standing still. Rev Eur Community Int Environ Law 3(1):32
ECOSOC (2005) Relationship between the enjoyment of economic, social, and cultural rights and the promotion of the realization of the right to drinking water supply and sanitation. Preliminary report of the special rapporteur El Hadji Guissi, ECOSOC Sub-Comm'n on the Promotion and Protection of Human Rights. http://www.ohchr.org/Documents/Issues/Water/Sub_Com_Guisse_guidelines.pdf. Accessed 3 June 2016
Feris L (2012) The public trust doctrine and liability for historic water pollution in South Africa. Law Environ Dev J 8(1):195
Gellers JC (2015) Environmental constitutionalism in South Asia: analyzing the experiences of Nepal and Sri Lanka. Transnatl Environ Law 4:395–423
General Comment 15 Right to Water (2002) Committee on Economic, Social and Cultural Rights, General Comment 15, The right to water (Twenty-ninth session, 2003), U.N. Doc. E/C.12/2002/11 (2002), reprinted in Compilation of General Comments and General Recommendations Adopted by Human Rights Treaty Bodies, U.N. Doc. HRI/GEN/1/Rev.6 at 105 (2003). http://hrlibrary.umn.edu/gencomm/escgencom15.htm. Accessed 18 May 2016
General Secretary, W.P. Salt Mines Labour Union v. Director, Industries and Mineral Development, SCMR 2061 (Supreme Court 1994)
Gun JM (2013) Groundwater around the world: a geographic synopsis, 149
Gyawali D (1999, February 27) Mahakali impasse and Indo-Nepal water conflict. Econ Polit Wkly, 553–564
Halashetti JS (2011, May 8) The status of international law under the constitution of India. http://www.legalindia.com/the-status-of-international-law-under-the-constitution-of-india. Accessed 11 June 2016
Hardberger A (2005) Life, liberty, and the pursuit of water: evaluating water as a human right and the duties and obligations it creates. N W U J Int Hum Rts 4:331–359
Harshe R (1999, May 8) South Asian regional co-operation, problems and prospects. Econ Polit Wkly, 100–1105
Hassan P (2005) Shehla Zia vs. WAPDA: Ten years later, PLD J 48

Helal MS (2007) Sharing blue gold: the 1997 UN convention of the law of the non-navigational uses of international watercourses ten years. Colo J Int Environ Law Policy 18:338
Hecht DA (2004) Meeting the global water challenge, water and sustainable development: opportunities for the chemical sciences. In: Wood-Black F, Norling P (eds) A workshop report to the chemical sciences roundtable. National Research Council, National Academic Press, Washington, pp 13–25
Himachal Pradesh v. Ganesh Wood Products, AIR SC 149 (Supreme Court 1996)
Hindustan Coco-Cola beverages v. Perumatty Grama Panchayat, (2) Kerla law Times, 554 (2005)
Historical Judgement on the Right to Water in India (2015, January) The right to water and sanitation. http://www.righttowater.info/historical-judgement-on-the-right-to-water-in-india/. Accessed 1 July 2016
Indus Waters, Kishenganga (Pakistan v. India) Final Award 20 December 2013. https://www.pcacases.com/sendAttach/48. Accessed 4 May 2016
Indus Water Treaty (1960)
Intellectuals Forum, Tirupathi v. State of A.P. & Ors, 3 SCC 549 (2006)
International Covenant on Civil and Political Rights (1966)
International Covenant on Economic, Social and Cultural Rights (1966)
Jha B (2009) Towards better management of groundwater resources in India. Retrieved June 3, 2016, from cgwb.gov.in/documents/papers/incidpapers/Paper%201-B.M.Jha.pdf
Jolly Jeorge v. Bank of Cochin, AIR SC 470 (Supreme Court 1980)
Jolly S (2007) Ninth schedule, basic structure, and constitutionalism. Panj Univ Law Rev 48: 51–62
Jolly S, Jaswal P (2010) Fairness and rule of law in climate change discource: a critical analysis. J Indian Law Inst 52(1):3–15
Jolly S (2014) Application of solar energy in South Asia: promoting intergenerational equity in climate law and policy. Int J Priv Law 7(1):20–39
Jolly S, Mahajana S (2014) Climate change and security: forging cooperative mechanism in South Asia. Int J Public Policy 10(6):315–332
Kanner A (2005) The public trust doctrine; parens patriae, and the attorney general as the guardian of the state's natural resources. Duke Environ Law Policy J 16(1):62
Karunaratne W (2009) Some significant environmental judgments in Sri lanka, United Nations Environment Programme. Environmental Foundation Limited, Colombo
Kemal B (1997) The concept of the common heritage of mankind in international law. Kluwer Law International, Hague
Kesavanada Bharati v. State of Kerala, 4 SCC 225 (Supreme Court 1973)
Khan T (1996) Management and sharing of the Ganges. Nat Resour J 36:456
Kishanganga Project: Victory claims cloud final arbitration award (2013, December). http://tribune.com.pk/story/648986/kishanganga-project-victory-claims-cloud-final-arbitration-award/. Accessed 10 May 2016
Kothari J (2006) Right to water: constitutional perspective. http://www.ielrc.org/activities/workshop_0612/content/d0607.pdf. Accessed 15 June 2016
Kumar R, Goyal O (2016) Thirty years of SAARC: society, culture and development. Sage Publishers, Thousand Oaks
M.C. Mehta v. Union of India, (12) SCC 118 (2004)
M. Farooque v. Bangladesh and Others, 49 DLR (AD) (1997)
M.C. Mehta v. Kamal Nath, SCC(1) 388 (1997)
M.I. Builders v. Radhey Shyam Sahu, SCC 464 (1999)
Manqele v. Durban Transitional Metropolitan Council in South Africa, (6) SA 423 (Durban High Court 2002)
May JR, Daly E (2014) Global environmental constitutionalism. Cambridge University Press, Cambridge
Mbote PK (2007) The use of the public trust doctrine in environmental law. Law Environ Dev J 3(2):195. http://www.lead-journal.org/content/07195.pdf

McCaffrey S (1992) A human right to water: domestic and international complications. Georget Int Environ Law Rev 5(1):3
McIntyre OM (2013) Reconciling the UN water course convention with developments in customary international law. In: Rieu-Clarke A, Loures FR (eds) The UN water course convention in force: strengthening international law for transboundary management. Routledge, London
Murad FD (2005) A new legal framework for managing the world's shared groundwaters: a case study from the middle east. IWA Publishing, London
Orissa Mining Corpn. v. MoEF & Ors. SCR 6 (2013)
Perumatty Grama Panchayat v. State of Kerala (2004) Perumatty Grama Panchayat. Kerala Law Times 31(1)
Planning Commission of India (2011) Planning commission model bill for the conservation, protection and regulation of groundwater. Delhi. ielrc.org/content/e1118.pdf. Accessed 3 June 2016
Ramcharan BG (1985) The concept and dimensions of the right to life. In: Ramcharan BG (ed) The right to life in international law. Martinus Nijoff Publishers, Leiden, pp 1–33
Reid J (2006, February 28) Water wars: climate change may spark conflict. (independent, producer) global policy forum. https://www.globalpolicy.org/component/content/article/198/40372.html. Accessed 10 Feb 2016
Riedel EH (2006) The human right to water. BMV Berliner Wissenschafts, Berlin
RIO Declaration on Environment and Development (1992) UN Doc. A/CONF.151/26/Rev. 1
Rural Litigation and Entitlement Kendera v. State of U.P, AIR SC 2187 (Supreme Court 1988)
Salman MA, McInerney-Lankford S (2004) The human right to water: legal and policy dimensions. World Bank, Washington
Samararatne D (2010) Public trust doctrine the Srilankan version. International Center for Ethnic Studies, Colombo
Sancin V (2012) International environmental law: contemporary concerns and challenges. Ljubljana
Sangam Shrestha VP (2016) Groundwater environment in Asian cities: concepts, methods and case studies. Butterworth-Heinemann, Oxford
Sarfraz H (2013) Revisiting the 1960 Indus waters treaty. Routledge, London (Water International)
Sax J (1970) The public trust doctrine in natural resource law: effective judicial intervention. Mich Law Rev 68:471
Scanlon J, Cassar A, Nemes M (2004) Water as a human right? World Conserv Union Environ Policy Law 51:13–25
Sidhu BK (2013) The Kishenganga arbitration—transboundary water resources governance. Environ Policy Law 43(3):147
Siwakoti G (2011) Trans-boundary river basins in South Asia: options for conflict resolution. Chintan
Stockholm Declaration of the Human Environment (1972, June 16) Report of the United Nations conference on the human environment. UNEPOR, UN.Doc.A/CONF.48/14/Rev.1, 1973
Shehla Zia v. WAPDA, SC 693 (Supreme Court 1994)
Shelton D (2008) Human rights and the environment, what specific environmental rights have been recognised? Denver J Int Law Policy 35(1). http://djilp.org/wp-content/uploads/2011/08/Human-Rights-Environment-What-Specific-Environmental-Rights-Been-Recognized-Dinah-Shelton.pdf. Accessed 12 May 2016
Shukla V (2008) Constitution of India. Eastern Book Company, Lucknow
Siriwardana G (2015) The application of public trust doctrine as a mechanism to ensure environmental protection by means of law: a comparative analysis between Sri Lankan and Indian legal context. In: Proceedings of 8th international research conference. KDU. http://www.kdu.ac.lk/proceedings/irc2015/2015/law-023.pdf. Accessed 3 May 2016
Soeb ZR (2016, June 17) South Asia creates regional water forum. The thirdpole.net understanding Asian water crisis. https://www.thethirdpole.net/2016/06/17/south-asia-creates-regional-groundwater-forum/. Accessed 3 June 2016

Special Rapporteur on the Human Right to Safe Drinking Water and Sanitation (2012) Stigma and the realization of the human rights to water and sanitation. UN General Assembly, Human Rights Council

Srilanka Singarasa v. Attorney General, 138 ILR 469 (2006)

Subhash Kumar v. State of Bihar, SC 420 (Supreme Court 1991)

T. Damodar Rao v. The Special Officer, Municipal Cooperation of Hyderabad, AIR AP 171 (High Court 1987)

The Constitution of the Islamic Republic of Afghanistan (2004). https://www.constituteproject.org/constitution/Afghanistan_2004.pdf?lang=en. Accessed 10 May 2016

The Constitution of the Kingdom of Bhutan (2008)

Thomas V (2014) Afghanistan and Pakistan: a decade of unproductive interactions over the Kabul–Indus basin. Retrieved April 4, 2016, from The thirdpole.net, understanding Asian water crisis. https://www.thethirdpole.net/2014/07/07/afghanistan-and-pakistan-a-decade-of-unproductive-interactions-over-the-kabul-indus-basin/

Turner SJ (2013) A global environmental governance. Routledge, London

UNICEF-WHO (2000) Global water supply and sanitation assessment report. WHO–UNICEF joint monitoring program for water supply and sanitation. UNICEF

Universal Declaration of Human Rights (1948)

United Nations Watercourses Convention (1997), 36 ILM

United Nations Environment Programme (2005) Compendium of summaries of judicial decisions in environment related cases. UNEP, Nairobi

Vents J (2015, September 26) Lahore Court orders Pakistan to act on climate change. http://blogs.law.columbia.edu/climatechange/2015/09/26/lahore-high-court-orders-pakistan-to-act-on-climate-change/. Accessed 4 May 2016

Water (Prevention and Control of Pollution) Act, India (1974)

Water Issues in South Asia (n.d.). file:///Users/apple/Desktop/Anupam%202/Water%20Issues%20in%20South%20Asia%20__%20South%20Asian%20Water%20Conflicts.html. Accessed 4 May 2016

Water Services Act (1997) South Africa. https://www.dwa.gov.za/io/Docs/a108–97.pdf. Accessed 11 May 2016

Watson RE (1998) The public trust doctrine in the water rights context. Nat Resour J 29:587

Winkler I (2014) The human right to water: significance, legal status and implications for water allocation. Oxford and Portland, Oregon, Hart Publishing

Wouters P (1997) International water law—selected writings of Professor Charles B. Bourne. Kluwer Law International, London

WHO/UNICEF (2015) 25 years progress on sanitation and drinking water: 2015 update and MDG assessment. UNICEF/WHO, New York

Yogi Narahari Nath and other v. Hon Prime Minister Girija Prasad Koirala and other (Supreme Court of Nepal 1955)

Author Biography

Dr. Stellina Jolly is currently Assistant Professor at South Asian University (SAU), New Delhi, a collaborative effort by SAARC countries. She started her professional career with NLU Jodhpur in 2004 after which she served in Symbiosis Law College and in University Institute of Legal Studies, Chandigarh. She received her Ph.D. degree from Punjab University, Chandigarh in 2009. Her teaching interests include International Environmental Law, Conflict of Laws, and Bio-Ethics. She has published articles in European Asian Journal of Law and Governance, UNESCO Journal of Bio-Ethics, International Journal of Public Law and Policy etc.

Chapter 8
UNCLOS Dispute Settlement System and India

Vinai Kumar Singh

1 Introduction

Part XV of UNCLOS 1982 contains the dispute settlement clauses. Section 1 of Part XV, entitled "General Provisions", essentially requires States to settle disputes through diplomatic channels prior to referring the matter to the compulsory procedures prescribed in Section 2 of Part XV. Part XV describes that some subject matters (freedom of navigations, overflight and laying of submarine cables and pipelines; protection and preservation of marine environment; fishing; marine scientific research; maritime delimitation; and finally military activities) are essentially required to be settled through the forum prescribed by the UNCLOS, i.e. third-party dispute settlement (Section 2 of Part XV). This part further allows the States to exclude some subject matters from the jurisdiction of forums prescribed by the UNCLOS (Section 3 of Part XV).

Accordingly, Part XV has been divided into three sections. Section 1 prescribes some general obligations for States to seek mutual and voluntary dispute settlement. Section 2 provides for compulsory dispute settlement mechanisms that result into binding decisions (UN Doc 1976) and Section 3 exempts some subject matters from the applicability of Section 2 known as optional exclusions. Thus after the exhaustion of the measures prescribed for the voluntarily settlement of the disputes under Section 1 and subject to the exceptions carved out under Section 3, the disputes related to the interpretation or application of this Convention have to be compulsorily settled as per the mechanisms prescribed under Section 2. It is also important to underline the essence that after the exhaustion of the measures prescribed for the voluntary settlement of disputes under Section 1 and subject to the exceptions carved out under Section 3, the disputes related to the interpretation or

V.K. Singh (✉)
Indian Society of International Law, 9, V.K. Krishna Menon Bhawan,
Bhagwan Das Road, New Delhi 110001, India
e-mail: vinaikumarsingh@gmail.com

J.L. Kaul and A. Jha (eds.), *Shifting Horizons of Public International Law*,
https://doi.org/10.1007/978-81-322-3724-2_8

application of this Convention have to be compulsorily settled as per the mechanisms prescribed under Section 2.

2 Background and Forums of Dispute Settlement under the UNCLOS

Section 2 (Articles 286–296) of Part XV of the UNCLOS seeks compulsory settlement of disputes that result in binding decisions, but the State parties have leverage to choose one or more forums or give preference among forums identified under the UNCLOS. Article 287 prescribes four mechanisms that could be used by member States to settle their disputes. These mechanisms are as follows:

- The International Tribunal for the Law of the Sea established in accordance with Annex. VI of the UNCLOS.
- The International Court of Justice.
- An arbitral tribunal constituted in accordance with Annex. VII.
- A special arbitral tribunal constituted in accordance with Annex. VIII for one or more of the categories of disputes specified therein. These categories are as follows: (1) fisheries, (2) protection and preservation of the marine environment, (3) marine scientific research and (4) navigation, including pollution from vessels and by dumping (Article 1, Annex. VIII).

Thus, State Parties are required under Article 287(3) and (5) to declare their choice or choices among these options at the time of either signature, ratification or afterwards. However, if the disputing parties fail to agree on a forum for dispute settlement by either virtue of their declaration or mutually after the rise of dispute, such disputes will automatically be submitted to the arbitral tribunal constituted under Annex. VII. Thus, arbitration under Annex. VII will always be a default mechanism to settle the disputes in any case of discord as to the respective forums. The declaration made under Article 287(1) in respect of forums, however, can be withdrawn after three months of the deposition of the notice of revocation to the UN Secretary General (Article 287(6)).

It is also important to note here that any declaration under Article 287(1) does not affect the obligation of a State Party to accept the jurisdiction of the Sea-Bed Disputes Chamber under Part XI, Section 5. Thus, the jurisdiction of the Sea Bed Dispute Chamber neither affects nor would be affected by any such declaration. The declaration under Article 287(1) only relates to the declaration of the appropriate forum for the compulsory settlement of disputes resulting in binding decisions.

The basic purpose for providing these options is to assuage the concerns of many States in respect of some existing forums of dispute settlement. For instance, Cuba expressly stated that it does not accept the jurisdiction of the ICJ under Article 287. States were having different opinions during the negotiation of UNCLOS III as to the exact forum for the compulsory settlement of disputes. It seems essential to understand the basic aspirations and fears of States during negotiations that caused the inclusion of the provisions for four different forums for the compulsory settlement of disputes. It will help in evaluating those concerns in the current state of affairs before making any declaration.

There were mainly four groups advocating different forums for the compulsory settlement of disputes (Rosenne and Sohn 1989). The first group was advocating for the conferment of jurisdiction to the International Court of Justice (ICJ) over the disputes related to the law of the sea (Netherlands and Switzerland). This group pointed out the contribution of ICJ's decisions in the development of law of the sea (Rosenne and Sohn 1989). They emphasised the need for the uniformity of international jurisprudence and underlined the fear of conflicting decisions if other body would be entrusted with the powers of compulsory settlement of disputes. The similar concerns were also raised by some scholars of international law (Oda 1995).

However, this advocacy for ICJ has been challenged mostly by developing countries. Their fear of pro-Western bias of the ICJ that was specially formed by the 1963 judgement of the Court in *Northern Cameroons case* (*Cameroon v. UK*) and the 1966 *South West Africa cases* (*Ethiopia v. South Africa*; *Liberia v. South Africa*) has been the prominent reasons for most of the Third World states to negate the ICJ as a forum for the compulsory settlement of the disputes (Kwiatkowska 1996). Moreover, even the academic concerns in respect of fragmentation of international law were also well responded by international legal scholars (Charney 1996).

The second group was of the view that the "new" law could be more efficiently handled by a new tribunal. They argued the need for the special law of the sea tribunal that would be less rigid, more democratic and representative, and have better understanding of the new law of the sea. They also pointed out that the ICJ is only open to the States, but in some law of the sea matters, it would be important to allow international organisations, corporations and individuals the task that could not be fulfilled by the International Court of Justice. In this context, it is important to note that the International Tribunal for the Law of Sea (ITLOS) statute under Article 20(2), Annex. VI provides standing for the suitable entities in proceedings before it.

The third group pointed towards the rigidness of the standing courts or tribunals and thus advocated for the more flexible arbitration (France and Madagascar). They were of the view that the standing courts or tribunals are too rigid because the parties could not choose the judges and are abide by the previously determined rules and procedures that are generally lengthy and tardy. The supporters of this view also argued that parties can also design an expeditious arbitration procedure that would result in the prompt decisions of their disputes. There was another group of States that considered that most of the provisions of the UNCLOS involved many technical issues and thus advocated for the functional approach that should take care of the technical necessities involved in any dispute (France, German Democratic Republic, Japan, Bulgaria, Poland, Trinidad and Tobago).

By providing four different forums, it ensured wider acceptance of the Convention and also allowed States to manoeuvre their choices of forums for the compulsory dispute settlement (Merrills 2005). So any declaration by a State Party must take care of its own interest and its chances of comfort in getting prompt and judicious result that should reflect its legitimate aspirations from the Convention. Thus, the assessment of pros and cons of the available options becomes necessary before any such declaration.

However, initially at the Third Conference on the Law of the Sea, it was noted "States are reluctant to give up their control over diplomatic and political options for resolving disputes and are more comfortable seeking political legitimization, rather than declarations of legal validity, for their actions" (Noyes 1989). In other words, during the Third Conference, dispute resolution through negotiations received "overwhelming support". Though, recently, availability of a third-party process is considered a deterrent for unilateral interpretation of the terms of the Convention (for example, US and China are continuously making unilateral interpretations of the provisions of the UNCLOS). A further justification for the third-party process is the perception that it could be a way of protecting less powerful States when dealing with the new subject matter area or less developed jurisprudence on the subject (for instance continental shelf) in international law.

On the other hand, there is a provision in the UNCLOS which prevents any misuse of the provisions of third-party process. For instance, provision regarding safeguards against abuse of legal process under the UNCLOS has recently been used as a tool to deter the States from unnecessary suits and also to protect coastal States against harassment. In the present circumstances, to a certain extent, the need for compulsory dispute settlement is certainly justified. In brief, recourse to international process provides a check on powers granted to States as well as provide a means to protect those powers.

India made a declaration upon ratification of the UNCLOS on 29 June 1995:

(a) The Government of the Republic of India reserves the right to make at the appropriate time the declarations provided for in Articles 287 and 298, concerning the settlement of disputes;
(b) The Government of the Republic of India understands that the provisions of the Convention do not authorise other States to carry out in the exclusive economic zone and on the Continental Shelf military exercises or manoeuvres, in particular those involving the use of weapons or explosives without the consent of the coastal state.

The question arises whether the present India's declaration is sufficient to protect the India's interest or requires a comprehensive declaration on the choice of forums which may declare specific subjects to be covered and not to be covered by these choices of forums.

3 Analysis of Advantages and Disadvantages of Forums Prescribed under the UNCLOS and State Practice

3.1 Option 1: Arbitration Under Annex. VII

Advantages and Disadvantages: The reasons identified may be advantageous, and at the same time, it may be counterproductive in similar circumstances. In other words, the reasons identified for advantages for one or other forums in some instances/circumstances can become disadvantageous in other circumstances because the reasons advanced for in support or against may not impact the subject in similar manner in all circumstances. The advantages and disadvantages of any proceedings depend on the facts of each case. For instances, third-party interventions in proceeding may in some cases be useful for the disputant party or sometime be adverse to the interest of State. However, this study attempts to highlight in general sense the reasons advanced for and against the forums stipulated in Article 287 of the UNCLOS.

1. *Expenses*: As party to the UN Charter and the UNCLOS, India is already contributing its share towards the functioning of ICJ and ITLOS. If India opts for arbitration, there must be some concrete justification to further incur additional expenditure in the arbitration proceeding constituted under Annex. VII. Thus, as per the provisions of Annex. VII, the arbitral tribunal consists of five persons. Each disputing party appoints one member under to the tribunal and the rest three are appointed jointly by the disputing parties (Article 3(b), (c) and (d), Annex. VII, UNCLOS 1982). For these appointments, States have to incur extra expenditures for their services. In brief, Arbitration tribunals involve high costs and high fees paid to arbitrators and court registrars, together with rental expenses of premises in which proceedings are carried on, secretarial and interpreting services, are well known for the adverse effect they have on public opinion. To the contrary, costs of the ICJ are borne by the UN (Kariotis 1997).
2. *No Substantial Reasons*: Also scholars and legal advisers throughout raise the concern that it may be difficult to justify regular financial contribution to the expenses of the ITLOS and ICJ without using them as a forum for dispute resolution. Arbitration will always demand the constitution of tribunal and each time state has to take extra steps in the constitution of the tribunal and thus to incur additional expenses, while at the same time paying towards maintenance of the ICJ and ITLOS.
3. Arbitration is more flexible than the procedure followed by the ICJ. Statute and Rules of which are defined in advance and are applied in the same manner to all cases brought before it. In the case of arbitration, particularly if a case is brought before the arbitral court on the basis of a special agreement, the parties have more freedom of movement and option, e.g., for a non-public procedure

regarding court proceedings, which in fact is excluded from the framework of the Court of Hague.

4. *Confidentiality, Control on the Proceedings and Expediting the Process*: As mentioned above, there are both pros and cons for arbitration proceedings. Arbitration proceedings are mostly confidential and remain completely in the hands of the disputing parties. This may sometimes be useful in the case, especially in maritime boundary disputes where, if the parties to such a dispute still have outstanding differences with other States over their maritime boundaries, they may well not want that the arguments that they use in the dispute settlement proceedings to be made public lest this may disadvantage their position in negotiations over their other outstanding unresolved maritime boundaries (Freestone et al. 2006). From appointment of the arbitrators to the decision about procedures and rules of arbitration are remained under the control of the disputing parties.
   However, in the extreme condition of discord between the disputing parties as to the appointment of three other members, the President of the ITLOS is authorised to appoint these members (Article 3(e), Annex. VII, UNCLOS 1982).
   These three members constitute the majority; thus, the basic logic that the disputing parties have some control in the constitution of the arbitral tribunal stands little bit compromised. However, it also acts as impetus for the disputing parties to promptly agree on the remaining three members.
5. *Delay the Process*: However, it is possible that one party may use this process to delay the appointment of above-mentioned three arbitrators and get them appointed by the President of the ITLOS or other senior most judge of the tribunal in case the President belongs to the nationality of one of the disputing parties (Article 3(e), Annex. VII, UNCLOS 1982). This arbitration procedure, being default in the situation of discord as to the choice of respective forum under Article 287(1), can be invoked by any State party in diversified circumstances. In some circumstances, this option for the appointment by the President of ITLOS may be exploited with some ulterior motives.
6. *Third-Party Intervention*: Arbitration does not permit third-party intervention in any dispute as it may be done in proceedings before any standing courts and tribunals. This gives the disputing parties latitude to calibrate their arguments in different circumstances. Thus, if any State invokes some arguments against another State then a third state cannot intervene in this proceeding to take benefit without the wishes of the disputing parties. Hence, it provides flexibility and space to manoeuvre to States to settle their dispute. It also gives chances that similar kinds of disputes can be settled using different principles with different States. Thus, it may in some cases be advantageous and may also result into disadvantages.
7. *Time Bound*: The arbitration proceedings under Annex. VII are time bound, and the traditional excuses of delays are not available under this process.
8. *Default Mechanism*: Apart from this, the option of arbitration under Annex. VII, if invoked in default, prevents or does not give opportunity to the States to

assess the advantages of use of other forums stipulated in Article 287(1). Some scholars believe that except the fact that arbitration remains confidential, immuned from third-party intervention and facilitates the disputing parties to use it as an ad hoc measure to solve the disputes, the resolution of the disputes by the arbitral tribunal under Annex. VII seems not to offer any other prominent benefit to the disputing parties.

9. *Lack of Institutional Commitment with the UNCLOS*: Annex. VII arbitration tribunal is unlikely to have the same degree of institutional commitment to the UNCLOS as a standing tribunal like the ITLOS. For instance, it is almost impossible to imagine the ITLOS downplaying the compulsory element in the dispute settlement under the UNCLOS in the way that the Annex. VII arbitration tribunal did in the *Southern Bluefin Tuna* Case (Freestone et al. 2006).
10. Last but not least, any government may find it difficult to justify before public opinion the implementation of an unfavourable ruling issued by an arbitration court, which lacks the prestige of the ICJ. In other words, at last, whether win or lose the case, any government has to make extra effort to convince the public by interpreting the judgment/award or highlight the positive effect of the judgement/award of the tribunal, if any.

State Practice: It must be noted that the drafting history of the UNCLOS does not provide encouragement for default mechanism under Annex. VII, as the proposal made by the President of the Third United Nations Conference of the Law of the Sea in the Informal Single Negotiating Text (ISNT) on dispute settlement that the ITLOS should be default forum was emphatically rejected (Freestone et al. 2006). However, it must be noted that recently many States are choosing and giving preference to ITLOS under the Annex. VI over the Annex. VII arbitration.

Apart from the above-mentioned concerns, the indicative list (attached as Table 1) of the respective declarations made by State parties also indicates the larger rejection of the arbitration under Annex. VII. In recent cases under the auspices of Annex. VII Tribunal, its jurisdiction to hear the cases was contested vigorously by each of the defendant States concerned. While proceedings in *Saiga and Swordfish* maritime boundary delimitation cases have remained confidential so that it was not possible to know whether challenges to the jurisdiction of the Annex. VII arbitration hearing have been made. And subsequently these two cases were transferred by means of agreement between the parties to the ITLOS (*Southern Bluefin Tuna* 2000). In other words, the default jurisdiction vested to Annex. VII arbitration is also not easily accepted by the States to resolve the law of the sea disputes. Most of the countries, except erstwhile Soviet Block, Canada and Egypt, do not prefer arbitration under Annex. VII and declare their choice of either ITLOS or ICJ. Interestingly, Bangladesh has also declared ITLOS as its choice with respect to its disputes with India and Myanmar in the Bay of Bengal. Thus generally speaking, recent trends are in favour of choosing ITLOS as the forum to settle disputes. There are views that the declaration should be made indicating either of these two choices to avoid the default invocation of arbitration proceeding under Annex. VII (Freestone et al. 2006).

Table 1 Indicative list of the preferences declared by State Parties

Algeria	Not considered ICJ (specifically exclude ICJ)
Angola	
Argentina	In order of preferences: (1) ITLOS (2) An arbitral tribunal constituted in accordance with Annex. VIII for questions relating to fisheries, protection and preservation of the marine environment, marine scientific research and navigation, in accordance with Annex. VIII, Article 1
Australia	Without specifying any order of preference: (1) ITLOS (2) ICJ
Austria	In the following order: (1) ITLOS (2) Special Tribunal under Annex. VIII (3) ICJ
Bangladesh	With respect to India and Myanmar for purposes of respective delimitation of the maritime boundary with them in the Bay of Bengal: – ITLOS
Belarus	In respect of interpretation or application of the Convention: – Arbitral Tribunal under Annex. VII In respect of disputes concerning fisheries, protection and preservation of the marine environment, marine scientific research or navigation, including pollution from vessels and by dumping: – Special arbitral tribunal under Annex. VIII In respect of the prompt release of detained vessels or their crews, as envisaged in Article 292 of the Convention: – ITLOS
Belgium	
Bolivia	No mention
Brazil	No mention
Canada	Without any order of preference: (1) ITLOS (2) Arbitral Tribunal under Annex. VII
Cabo Verde	In order of preference: (1) ITLOS (2) ICJ
Chile	In order of preference: (1) ITLOS (2) A special arbitral tribunal under Annex. VIII, in respect of fisheries, protection and preservation of the marine environment, and marine scientific research and navigation, including pollution from vessels and by dumping
China	No mention
Costa Rica	No mention

(continued)

Table 1 (continued)

Croatia	In order of preference (1) ITLOS (2) ICJ
Cuba	Specifically exclude the jurisdiction of the ICJ in any kind of disputes
Czech Republic	No mention
Denmark	– ICJ Further, she also excludes any jurisdiction of the arbitral tribunal under Annex. VII for the settlement of disputes pursuant to Article 298
Ecuador	Without mentioning anything about preference: (1) ITLOS (2) ICJ (3) A special tribunal under Annex. VIII, for—dispute related to fisheries, protection and preservation of the marine environment, marine scientific research and navigation, including pollution from vessels and by dumping
Egypt	Arbitration under Annex. VII
Equatorial Guinea	No mention
Estonia	Without mentioning anything about preference: (1) ITLOS (2) ICJ
European Community	No mention
Fiji	ITLOS
Finland	Without mentioning anything about preference: (1) ICJ (2) ITLOS Also for Part XI disputes
France	No mention
Gabon	No mention
Germany	In the following order (1) ITLOS (2) Arbitral Tribunal under Annex. VII (3) ICJ
Ghana	No mention
Greece	ITLOS
Guatemala	No mention
Guinea	No mention
Guinea-Bissau	Specifically excludes the jurisdiction of ICJ
Honduras	Chooses ICJ but also reserves its right for considering any other means of peaceful settlement, including the International Tribunal for the Law of the Sea, as agreed on a case-by-case basis
Hungary	In the following order: (1) ITLOS (2) ICJ (3) A special tribunal constructed in accordance with Annex. VIII for all the categories of disputes specified therein

(continued)

Table 1 (continued)

Iceland	No mention
India	No mention
Iran	No mention
Iraq	No mention
Ireland	No mention
Italy	Without any order of preference: (1) ITLOS (2) ICJ
Kiribati	No mention
Latvia	Without mentioning anything about preference (1) ITLOS (2) ICJ
Luxembourg	No mention
Kuwait	No mention
Lithuania	Without mentioning anything about preference (1) ITLOS (2) ICJ
Madagascar	ITLOS
Malaysia	No mention
Mali	No mention
Malta	No mention
Mexico	No order of preference: (1) ITLOS (2) ICJ (3) A special arbitral tribunal constituted in accordance with Annex. VIII for one or more of the categories of disputes specified therein
Moldova	No mention
Montenegro	In order of preference: (1) ITLOS (2) ICJ
Morocco	No mention
Netherlands	ICJ in respect of those state Parties that have also accepted ICJ
Nicaragua	No mention
Norway	ICJ
Oman	Without mentioning anything about preference (1) ITLOS (2) ICJ
Pakistan	No mention
Panama	No mention
Philippines	No mention
Portugal	Mentions all the four dispute settlement mechanism provided in Article 287 of the Convention. However, specifically prefers for the arbitral tribunal under Annex. VIII for disputes involving issues related to fisheries, protection and preservation of living marine resources and marine environment, scientific research, navigation and marine pollution are concerned

(continued)

Table 1 (continued)

Qatar	No mention
Republic of Korea	No mention
Republic of Palau	No mention
Romania	No mention
Russian Federation	Arbitration under Annex. VII Arbitration under Annex. VIII in respect of issues fisheries, the protection and preservation of the marine environment, marine scientific research, and navigation, including pollution from vessels and dumping
Saint Vincent and the Grenadines	ITLOS as the means of settlement of disputes concerning the arrest or detention of its vessels
Sao Tome and Principe	No mention
Saudi Arabia	No mention
Serbia and Montenegro	No mention
Slovenia	Arbitral Tribunal under Annex. VII
South Africa	No mention
Spain	Without mentioning anything about preference (1) ITLOS (2) ICJ
Sudan	No mention
Sweden	ICJ
Switzerland	ITLOS
Thailand	No mention
Timor-Leste	Mentions all four options
Trinidad and Tobago	In order of priority (1) ITLOS (2) ICJ
Tunisia	In order of priority (1) ITLOS (2) Arbitral Tribunal under Annex. VII
Ukraine	(1) Arbitral Tribunal under Annex. VII (2) Arbitral Tribunal under Annex. VIII for fisheries, etc.
United Kingdom of Great Britain and the Northern Ireland	ICJ But also agree to ITLOS on case-by-case basis
United Republic of Tanzania	ITLOS
Uruguay	ITLOS
Vietnam	No mention
Yemen	No mention

Above reasons advanced may require assessment of India's position in the context of its role/maritime aspirations. For instances, India with a large maritime boundary is a coastal State eager to protect and enforce its right in its coastal zones. At the same time, India is also an aspiring maritime power that strives for its significant presence in international waters (freedom of navigation). This increases the possibility of disputes with varied circumstances, possibilities and legal issues. It is not advisable each time to invoke the arbitration proceedings under Annex. VII in which economic burden and uncertainty of composition always hinge on its legitimate aspirations.

3.2 Option 2: The International Court of Justice

Now the study weighs the suitability of ICJ. Though ICJ has produced the significant and almost coherent jurisprudence on the maritime issues, it is basically a body that deals with issues in general international law, including those related to the law of the sea. However, the view has been expressed that the setting up of chambers under the revised new Rules of the ICJ in 1978 lacks the continuity and cohesion of the Court's case law. The delicate balances attained within the plenary Court, in which the most important forms of civilisation are represented nowadays, cannot be realised in the case of setting up chambers consisting of 3, 5 or 7 members (*Gulf of Maine* 1982). Besides, for reasons of policy relating to States opting for the alternative of the chamber, certain judges might be favoured at the expenses of others, the latter remaining excluded (Schwebel 1987). However, preferences shown by States for Chambers stopped in the 1990s and more recent cases being referred to the Plenary Court. They are persons with high moral character and have eligibility to be appointed as highest judicial officer in their respective countries or a jurist of competence in international law. However, it is difficult to guarantee that all the fifteen judges have the deep knowledge of the legal niceties of the Law of the Sea.

The ICJ is also a very time consuming process. Its involvement with other categories of disputes generally may delay the legal process relating to the law of the sea disputes. It is not always possible to get prompt and effective remedy from the ICJ. Moreover, it is the general perception that the ICJ is a very politicised body, so there are probabilities that some extra legal concerns may infiltrate the legal language of the Court. The control over the selection procedure of its members by the General Assembly and Security Council also does not immune it from considering bare political realities through legal language.

Apart from this, the procedural jurisprudence established by the ICJ, like its judgement in *Monetary Gold (Preliminary Question)* that established the principle that where a third State's legal interests would not only be affected by a decision but form the very subject matter of the decision, proceedings may not be maintained in the absence of that third State. The invocation of this principle in politically charged and much criticised *East Timor* judgement of 1995 still evince the political colour of the court.

The ICJ by virtue of its jurisprudence also left open the chances for the third State to intervene as a non-party under Article 62 of the ICJ statute. In the 1990 judgement of the *Gulf of Fonseca (Intervention)*, the ICJ Chamber for the first time granted a State (Nicaragua) permission to intervene as a non-party under Article 62 of the ICJ Statute. Though subsequently the requests for the intervention have been dismissed in 1995, this chance of third-state non-party intervention will always loom large to the prospects of any dispute resolution through ICJ (Kwiatkowska 1996). Also there are instances when the Court has taken the view not to decide the case on merits that compromises its chances for providing prompt and effective dispute resolution of the law of the sea disputes.

Moreover, Article 290 of the UNCLOS discusses the provisions for the issuance of the provisional measures. According to this, a Court or tribunal if satisfied about its own jurisdiction in the dispute may issue provisional measures on the request of a disputing party (Article 290(1), UNCLOS 1982). To establish this link of jurisdiction is not always easy in case of the International Court of Justice. Moreover, as per the ICJ statute, any provisional measures prescribed by ICJ must also be reported to the Security Council (Article 41). This unnecessarily further politicises the issue.

Probably, these chances of politicisation of disputes through ICJ have prompted some States to categorically declare their rejection of the ICJ as a forum for compulsory settlement of disputes (see, attached Table 1, for Algeria and Cuba Declarations). Moreover, if one gives a cursory look to the respective declarations made by the Parties, it becomes quite clear that most of the developing countries have not preferred ICJ or have given it secondary priority. Thus, it seems that the probable political manoeuvring in ICJ and its non-efficacy in giving prompt and effective remedy for most of the developing States from declaring ICJ as a cherished forum for dispute settlement under UNCLOS (Kariotis 1997).

Importantly, the question of optional jurisdiction of the ICJ as one of the alternative forums to settle the disputes related to the law of the sea was discussed at the First Conference of the UNCLOS (Klein 2005). At the Conference, referral of law of the sea disputes to the ICJ due to its optional jurisdiction was considered inappropriate to accord it mandatory jurisdiction. However, India, by way of compromise, proposed that a proviso be added to the Article to the effect that the jurisdiction of the ICJ should be subject to Article 36 of the ICJ Statute (India Proposal, UN Doc. A/CONF.13/C.4/L.61). This discussion led the debate how far the declarations made by the States under optional jurisdiction of the ICJ could lead or prevent the subject matter for the jurisdiction of the ICJ.

Only 72 out of 193 United Nations member states, about 26%, have declarations of acceptance of ICJ jurisdiction under Article 36(2) of the ICJ Statute. Declarations have been made unconditionally or on condition of "reciprocity" on the part of several or certain States. Thus, for example, if Egypt has not accepted the compulsory jurisdiction, then even if Portugal has accepted it, the ICJ would not have jurisdiction over a dispute between Portugal and Egypt. States have frequently made reservations excluding disputes arising before a certain date or even if the disputes arises after such a date, if it arises out of facts or situations existing before that date (see the Belgian reservation), the disputes prior to that date or falling within specified situations would be out of the Court's jurisdiction. Declarations can be for a specified period of time, like Brazil's declaration was made to be in application for a certain period. Another example is condition of reciprocity for instance Norway Declaration. The UK declaration contains both these reservations (Collier and Lowe 1999). In brief, jurisdiction of ICJ will rest on the scope of declaration of each state. This would also indicate that ICJ forum may serve limited purpose at present.

Apart from this, the forum of ICJ always makes any dispute very high profile. Though there is no hierarchy in international law and even the judgements of the ICJ or ITLOS are binding only on parties to the dispute, the mere invocation of the ICJ puts the dispute on high pedestal. This may involve emotional involvement of citizenry of the disputing parties and thus may also become the issue in domestic politics. It will unnecessarily complicate the enforcement mechanism and further may compromise the prospect of peace.

Advantages: Through special agreement under Article 36(1) of the Statute to submit the dispute to the ICJ has the advantage of the dispute being concisely defined in the special agreement. In fact, contesting parties may agree through the special agreement and in advance on the exact extent and content of their dispute, avoiding thereby subsequent submission of preliminary exceptions by the defendant, as can happen and has often taken place in cases of unilateral applications. During negotiations for special agreement, both litigants may agree to refer only part of their dispute to the Court, leaving final settlement to their own discretion.

3.3 Option 3: The International Tribunal for the Law of the Sea (ITLOS)

1. *Expertise*: The ITLOS is a special tribunal for the law of the Sea and it consists of twenty-one members. These members must be the persons of high moral character and have recognised competence in the Law of the Sea. Thus, the recognised competence in the Law of the Sea is an essential condition for becoming the member of the tribunal. Article 289 of the UNCLOS encourages the use of scientific or technical experts who may sit with the judges but without a vote (Anderson 2008). This gives it more expertise in comparison with ICJ in the matters of the law of the sea.
2. *Representative in Nature*: The constitution of the ITLOS is also much representative in comparison with ICJ. There is no condition in ITLOS that judges of particular nationalities will always be there on the Bench as is the case with the ICJ in respect of the permanent members of the Security Council. The members of ITLOS are elected by the secret ballot by the member States. The constitutive Articles also guarantee the minimum number of members from each geographical region. According to the present scheme of affairs, there must not be less than three members from each of the following groups. These groups are as follows: (i) African States, (ii) Asian States, (iii) Eastern European States, (iv) Latin American and Caribbean States, (v) Western European States and (vi) other States.

3. *Avoidance of Multiplicity of Forum*: The composition of ITLOS is more democratic and represents the interests of State Parties in a better way than that of ICJ. The record of the ITLOS is also very persuasive in this respect. Moreover, in most of the cases of provisional measures and prompt release of vessels and crew, ITLOS almost has a compulsory jurisdiction. So there may always be a need to deliberate before ITLOS in respect of these measures. Thus, any preference of other forums may engage India in two different forums at two successive junctures. It unnecessarily increases the burden to be involved in two different forums for a similar dispute.
4. *Special Reason for Developing Countries*: Apart from this, ITLOS is a new specialised body of the UNCLOS. The selection of its members is governed totally by democratic processes that remain under the control of each and every member State in equal capacity. Probably these are the decisive concerns that made most of the developing countries to declare ITLOS as their choice for compulsory settlement of disputes (Noyes 1999).
5. *Autonomy*: ITLOS is a completely separate entity created by the Convention but not an organ of a larger organisation, such as the UN, the Council of Europe or the European Community. Such autonomy may bring the advantages of genuine independence. At the same time, autonomy increases the numbers of arrangements which have to be put in place at present. Autonomy may also mean that the ITLOS has only the periodic meetings of the State Parties from which to seek help should any unexpected problem arises (Anderson 2008).
6. *Access to the ITLOS*: The jurisdiction of the ITLOS is wide enough to cover non-State entities, such as the International Seabed Authority, mining consortia or the EC.
7. *Application of Other Rules of International Law and Local Remedies Rule*: Article 293 provides that courts and Tribunals with jurisdiction under the Convention are to apply both in terms "and other rules of international law not incompatible with" the Convention. One example of such other rules is provided by Article 295 which imports into the procedures the well-known "local remedies" rule, according to which an available local remedy has to be sought before the recourse is taken to an international body. Article 293 means, in practice, that the ITLOS will have to consider not only the law of the sea, including customary law on certain matters, but also a wide range of other legal issues. These include the law of treaties (for instance, the interpretation or application of the Convention as a treaty subject to the Vienna Convention on the Law of Treaties; or the effects of national declarations); the effects of previous judicial decisions (as in case decided by a Chamber of the ICJ about the *Gulf of Fonesca*); and the law of State responsibility, of which the local remedies rule forms part (Anderson 2008).
8. *Cost Effectiveness*: The idea of "cost effectiveness" has been taken from the Agreement of July 1994 on the Implementation of Part XI of the Convention. Section 1 of the Annex. to this Agreement requires all institutions constituted by the Convention to be cost-effective. This provision applies therefore to the ITLOS as well. In practice, the ITLOS is expected to adopt procedures which

avoid unnecessary expenses, both for the litigants and the State parties which fund the ITLOS.

9. *Compliance by the Disputant Parties with the Decision of the ITLOS*: Article 95 requires each party to a case to report to the ITLOS upon its compliance with any provisional measures prescribed under Article 290 of the UNCLOS.

As per the provisions of the Convention, if the disputing parties may not agree upon the similar mechanism for the dispute settlement, the arbitration under Annex. VII will be invoked automatically. Thus not to take risk of the arbitration procedure and to use the more democratic and specialised forum, the study finds it appropriate to declare ITLOS as a primary forum for the settlement of disputes. This will allay the uncertainty as to the forums because it fits with the declarations of the most of the States that also choose ITLOS.

3.4 Option 4: Special Arbitration Under Annex. VIII

In respect of disputes related to particular subject matters (disputes concerning fisheries, protection of marine environment, marine scientific research and navigation), the procedure of special arbitral tribunal under Annex. VIII seems, preferred by States. This method of settlement is known as "functional approach" to dispute settlement under the law of the Sea. A partial attempt was made in the third 1958 Geneva Conventions on the Law of the Sea, which provided for the appointment of experts to decide the disputes relating to fishing and conservation of living resources of the sea. When such a dispute arose, the procedure laid down by that Convention envisaged a special commission of five members established by agreement between the parties. The members were to be drawn "from among qualified persons being nationals of states not involved in the dispute and specialising in legal, administrative or scientific questions relating to fisheries, depending upon the nature of the dispute to be settled". The decisions of special commissions were to be made in accordance with scientific and technical criteria set out in the Convention and were binding on the States concerned. This functional approach to dispute settlement is taken considerably further in Annex. VIII of the UNCLOS 1982 concerning special arbitration (Merrills 2011).

The idea of "functional approach" was supported by some States in the Working Group of 1974 Caracas Session (the second session of the UNCLOS) which envisaged that certain law of the sea disputes will be more amenable to settlement by a panel of technical experts rather than by judges in courts or tribunals. Thus, the Working Group supported the "functional approach" to dispute settlement under the UNCLOS instead of "general approach". They also believed that not all law of the sea disputes are suitable for settlement exclusively through formal courts of law or tribunals. The question of relationship between these two approaches was addressed by the Working Group subsequently. In the course of the Working Group discussion, it was pointed out that the functional approach relied upon a rather rigid and artificial classification of disputes into categories which could be difficult to apply in certain real situations. An example was given where a foreign fishing vessel alleged to have violated certain fishing regulations under the UNCLOS is also alleged to have engaged in marine pollution and also interfered with the navigation use of the sea. In this situation, it is not certain whether the resulting dispute is to be classified as a fisheries dispute or marine pollution dispute or a navigation dispute. Thus, there would be problems in deciding first which of the functional procedures had jurisdiction over the dispute, or problems with litigation if it is decided that separate proceedings be conducted against the same vessel in each of the functional procedures concerning the respective alleged violations (Adede 1987).

Special arbitration is one of the binding methods of settlement and will normally be adjudicative. To assist States in setting up a tribunal, list of experts in each of the four fields are to be maintained by, respectively, the Food and Agriculture Organization, the UN Environmental Programme, the Inter-Governmental Oceanographic Commission and the International Maritime Organization. Each State party may nominate to each list two experts "whose competence in the legal, scientific or technical aspects" of the fields is established and "who enjoy the highest reputation for fairness and integrity" (Article 3). It seems that the arrangements for constituting a tribunal essentially follow the pattern of conciliation, rather than arbitration, in that each party selects two members, preferably from the appropriate list, and the President is chosen by agreement. Similarly, vacant places must be filled from the appropriate list by the Secretary General of the UN and not the President of the ITLOS.

Article 5 of Annex. VIII provides that in certain circumstances, its functions can be broadened to include fact-finding and conciliation. By agreement, the parties may set up a special arbitral tribunal to carry out an inquiry into the facts of any dispute of a type amenable to special arbitration. Such a tribunal's findings of fact are conclusive as between the parties. Thus, the clear advantage of machinery of special arbitration is its additional form of conciliation.

It is submitted that it is appropriate to leave questions involving the discretion of coastal State to a special tribunal in matters related to fishing, marine scientific research, and the prevention of pollution since consideration of equity rather than law is involved (Table 2).

4 Maritime Delimitation

As mentioned above, Article 298 of the UNLOS allows States Parties to exclude certain categories of disputes from compulsory procedures. States may declare when signing, ratifying or acceding to the Convention, or at any time thereafter, that they do not accept the procedures available under Section 2 for those disputes in Article 298. Declarations permitted under Article 298 relate, to maritime delimitation disputes in relation to the territorial sea, EEZ or continental shelf of States

Table 2 Differences between arbitration under Annex. VII and Annex. VIII

UNCLOS provisions	Annex. VII	Annex. VIII
Kinds of dispute	Wide variety of disputes	Disputes concerning fisheries, protection of marine environment, marine scientific research and navigation
Appointment of President	Parties to the dispute will appoint President of arbitration by agreement. In the absence of agreement, President of the arbitration tribunal will be appointed by the ITLOS	Parties to the dispute will appoint President of special arbitration by agreement. In the absence of any agreement, secretary general will make appointment of President of special arbitration to a dispute
Nature of decision	The arbitration will make an award with reasons and will be confined to the subject matter of the dispute	Special arbitration has to conduct fact-finding alone that is conclusive between the parties
Force of decision	The award shall be final and without appeal	The special arbitration may formulate recommendations which without having the force of a decision

with opposite of adjacent coasts as well as disputes involving historic bays or title. It will also apply to outer continental shelf by analogy. Importantly, the dispute-related provisions to special rights in EEZ (rights, jurisdiction and duties of coastal State set in Article 58 of UNCLOS) will be covered by Article 297(1) and not by Article 298(1) (a) (Rosenne and Sohn 1989). In addition, the scope of Article 298(1) (a) is limited that a State will only be obliged to submit dispute to Conciliation procedure which suggest that proposed agreement (on the basis of Conciliation Commission) does provide for a procedure entailing a binding decision only upon mutual consent. In other words, however, importantly, Conciliation Commission's recommendations cannot be subjected directly to judicial review (Suarez 2008). Still the UNCLOS allows States an option to exclude the subject covered under Section 298(1) (a). Importantly, need to also highlight that Article 298 title is not "Optional Exception" rather title is "Optional Exception to Applicability of Section 2".[1]

[1]The Socialist States indicated that "they would not accept any formula—nor indeed the whole convention—if it contained provisions on compulsory procedure entailing binding decisions relating to delimitation disputes". This problem became particularly acute when the decision was reached that no reservations could be made to the UNCLOS. The compromise reached was that maritime delimitation and historic title disputes would be included with the compulsory dispute settlement framework, but States could optionally exclude these disputes, subject to an obligation to refer the matter to conciliation if certain conditions were met. Interestingly, Section 2 of Part XV purports to require the use of the procedure entailing a binding decision; on the other hand, the whole purpose of the optional exception and the use of conciliation are to exclude resort to compulsory procedure.

4.1 UNCLOS and Continental Shelf

Article 76 of the UNCLOS refers to continental shelf not only as a geomorphologic but also as a special legal term that applies to area of the seabed, beyond the territorial sea under the sovereign rights of the coastal state for the purpose of exploring and exploiting its natural resources. As the continental shelf comprises—according to para 1 of the said Article—"the seabed and subsoil of the submarine areas" that extend "throughout the natural prolongation of its land territory", the outer limit may alternate: either 200 nautical miles measured from the territorial sea baselines, where the outer edge of the continental margin does not extend to that distance; or, where this extension exceed it, different criterion in accordance with Article 76, paras 4, 5 and 6 of the Convention. This indicates that continental shelf has been described as combining the "influences of geography, geology, geomorphology and jurisprudence, a *tour de force* of interdisciplinary cooperation" (Johnston 1988).

A group of several States whose natural prolongation into the sea exceeded 200 nautical miles from the coast, known as the "broad margin States", were not willing to relinquish their rights over their extended continental shelf and, therefore, supported a continental shelf definition that would attribute to them exclusive rights over the part of their continental shelf that extended beyond the 200 nautical-mile limit. These States (joint submission by Canada, Chile, Iceland, India, Indonesia, Mauritius, Mexico, New Zealand, and Norway) proposed a 200 nautical-mile limit for the continental shelf that could, however, be extended in case that the natural prolongation of the land territory extended beyond the limits (UN Doc 1974). On the other hand, a group consisting of States with a narrow continental shelf, and especially of land-locked and geographically disadvantaged States, insisted on the 200-nautical-mile continental shelf limit, hoping to place as much of the deep seabed as possible under the legal status of the area (Article 1(1) (a), UNCLOS), the mineral resources of which are regarded as the Common Heritage of Mankind (Article 136) and are to be administered by the International Seabed Authority (ISA) acting on behalf of mankind as a whole (Article 137(2); Statement of Austrian Delegate 1994).

In accordance with the distance criterion, a coastal State's continental shelf extends 200 nautical miles from the baselines from which the breadth of the territorial sea is measured "where the outer edge of the continental margin does not extend up to that distance". Thus, even in cases where a coastal State's continental shelf does not extend up to 200 nautical miles into the sea, the coastal State has sovereign rights over the seabed and its subsoil up to that distance.

In cases where the continental margin extends beyond the normal 200 nautical-mile limit, the outer edge of the continental shelf is generally to be established in accordance with the criteria of Articles 76(4) to (7) of the UNLOS. In any case, the continental shelf may legally not exceed a maximum of 350 nautical miles from the baselines from which the breadth of the territorial sea is measured or 100 nautical miles from the 2,500 m isobaths the line connecting the depths of

2,500 m (Article 76(5)). Despite the safeguards of Article 76 regarding the limits of outer continental shelf, it was considered necessary to establish a Commission on the Limits of the Continental Shelf (hereinafter, CLCS or Commission). It consists of twenty-one international experts from the fields of geology, geophysics and hydrography (Annexure II, Article 2(1)) to oversee the procedure and to ensure that States respect the regulations mentioned in Article 76 of UNCLOS.

Coastal States that claim continental shelves beyond 200 nautical miles are free to start a negotiated settlement, but this cannot be completed without the participation of the Commission on the Limits of Continental Shelf (CLCS). These states must go through the submission process and have their claims evaluated and affirmed by the Commission. A coastal state which disagree with the Commission's recommendation cannot avail of the dispute settlement mechanism offered under Article 287 but must make a new or revised submission (Rosenne and Sohn 1989).

4.2 *India and the Commission on the Limits of Continental Shelf*

On 11 May 2009, the Republic of India submitted to the Commission on the Limits of the Continental Shelf (CLCS), in accordance with Article 76, para 8, of the UNCLOS (the Convention came into force for India on 29 July 1995), information on the limits of the continental shelf beyond 200 nautical miles from the baselines from which the breadth of the territorial sea is measured, with the following statement:

> According to the submitting State, this is a partial submission and, as a coastal state in the Southern part of the Bay of Bengal, India reserves the right to make at a later date, notwithstanding the provisions regarding the ten-year period, a separate submission on the outer limits of its continental shelf, based on the provisions of the Statement of Understanding contained in Annex. II to the Final Act of the Third United Nations Conference on the Law of the Sea.

India has reserved the right to make a separate second partial submission of information and data to support the outer limits of continental shelf in accordance with the provisions of the Statement at a later date, notwithstanding the provisions regarding the ten-year period (Submission to the CLCS 2009).

India has established continental shelf beyond 200 nautical miles in the following regions: Eastern Offshore Region comprising the eastern offshore region of Mainland India in the Bay of Bengal and the Western Offshore Region of Andaman Islands; and Western Offshore Region of India in the Arabian Sea (Submission to the CLCS 2009).

India also mentions in its submission that, although India has entered into a series of agreements with its many neighbouring coastal States, but outer limits of continental shelf with Pakistan, Oman, Sri Lanka, Bangladesh and Myanmar are yet to be settled. It further states that this submission has been made without prejudice to the matters of delimitation with its neighbouring states (Submission to the CLCS 2009). Pakistan and Oman have also made submissions of similar pattern. This indicates that States generally make Submissions to the Commission without compromising with their right to delimit the continental shelf through peaceful means or compulsory binding procedures.

After India made its Submission to the Commission, Myanmar, Bangladesh and Oman objected to it and they requested the Commission to consider this submission without any prejudice to the continental shelf areas that these countries are entitled to (Communications received by CLCS 2009). India is yet to receive the recommendations from the Commission.

4.3 Conciliation Commission Under Annex. V of the UNCLOS and Overlapping Continental Shelf

Article 298 allows State to exclude the disputes concerning the interpretation or application of Articles 15, 74 (Delimitation of EEZ between States with opposite or adjacent coasts) and 83 (Delimitation of Continental Shelf between States with opposite or adjacent coasts). Article 298 does not make reference to Article 76 which gives definition of Continental Shelf. This allows some scholars to buy an argument that there is no provision for an exclusion of disputes related with outer limits of continental shelf from the judicial recourse to any of the compulsory procedure enumerated under Article 287 (Suarez 2008). However, Article 298 does refer to exclude disputes related to Article 83 where issues of overlapping continental shelf areas arise. This exclusion can be done by making a declaration in writing to this effect in accordance with Article 298(1)(a). In that case, Article 298 applies with its provision for compulsory recourse to conciliation under Annex. V. Once provision related to Conciliation triggered, States cannot refer the matter to compulsory procedures entailing a binding decision unless they so agree.

4.4 Maritime Delimitation and Choice of Forums: India

The question arises why should a State party approach to ITLOS instead of arbitration or approach ICJ, which is a well-established forum. For this reason, we have to discuss the advantages of ITLOS over these alternative remedies. It has the following advantages (ITLOS 2016).

Firstly, the fact that the tribunal is a specialised judicial body places it in a better position to decide cases that demand special expertise. Furthermore, the tribunal's jurisdiction is limited to decide on the interpretation and application of the UNCLOS means it has the advantage to decide a case expeditiously than the ICJ which may be requested to decide many cases related to other issues besides the one that has to do with law of the sea. There is a general perception about expeditious handling of cases by tribunals.

Secondly, the special composition of ITLOS might be the subject of considerations before a dispute is submitted to the Tribunal. In comparison with ICJ, the Tribunal is a much bigger body with respect to the strength of the bench. Moreover, the election of judges/members is completely independent from the United Nations unlike ICJ. Judges from Third World countries are in proportion more numerous at ITLOS than at the ICJ. Also, the permanent members of the Security Council do not enjoy the same position they (de facto) have in the election of the judges of the ICJ.

Thirdly, ITLOS has wider jurisdiction power and is different from other international judicial bodies in this respect. Unlike ICJ, ITLOS is open to cases involving "entities other than States". It can be concluded that the Tribunal my deal with cases involving a State, on the one hand, and a private commercial corporation, an intergovernmental organisation or a non-governmental organisation, on the other hand (Ehlers and Lagoni 2006).

Fourthly, the Convention recognises the exclusive jurisdiction of the Tribunal's Seabed Disputes Chamber to entertain both disputes arising out of interpretation or application of the provisions of the Convention concerning activities in the Area and requests for advisory opinions made by the Assembly or the Council of the Authority "on legal questions arising within the scope of their activities". Thus, the framers of the Convention granted preferential treatment to the Tribunal, since none of the other "means of dispute settlement" referred to in Article 287 of the Convention has jurisdiction to deal with such disputes or requests.

Fifthly, one major benefit apart from saving expenses is that it saves time. It would require much less time to put a panel in place than would be the case in selecting an arbitral tribunal. This would be so even if the parties to the agreement decide not to use the full bench of the 21 judges of ITLOS. As an alternative, the parties could select a chamber to deal with the dispute. The Statute of ITLOS provides for the establishment of chambers to deal with specific categories of disputes. Two such chambers have already been established, namely Chamber for Fisheries Disputes and Chamber for Marine Environment Disputes. An agreement conferring jurisdiction on the Tribunal could stipulate that disputes under the agreement should be submitted to one or other of these chambers, or to a special chamber established for those disputes. Moreover, the Statute of ITLOS requires ITLOS to form a special chamber for dealing with a particular dispute submitted to it, if the parties so request. The composition of such a chamber is to be determined by the Tribunal with the approval of the parties.

Accordingly, a dispute arising under an agreement conferring jurisdiction on ITLOS could be submitted to a special chamber if the Agreement so provides or if the parties in the particular dispute so require. Such an arrangement would give to the parties to the agreement, or the parties in a particular dispute, the ability to influence the composition of the chamber to sit on the case, in the same way as they would in choosing an arbitral tribunal.

Moreover, ITLOS is not confined only to the disputes related to the interpretation or application of UNCLOS. It is pertinent to note here that the Tribunal is competent to deal with any dispute submitted to it, if the dispute concerns an international agreement and if this agreement confers jurisdiction to the Tribunal. This means that ITLOS can exercise jurisdiction conferred on it by an agreement which is related to maritime and law of the sea matters (Mensah 2004).

Compared to arbitration, ITLOS presents a permanent platform especially in cases that require urgent judicial action. It would be unpragmatic, for example, to resort to arbitration in a case that involves provisional measures or prompt release. In fact the tribunal has managed to develop good jurisprudence in relation to prompt release and this, arguably, may place confidence on the tribunal by States.

While ITLOS has many advantages over other adjudicating bodies, there are quite a few advantages of Arbitration over ITLOS and ICJ.

To begin with ICJ as mentioned above, Third World States have criticised the jurisprudence and structure of the International Court of Justice (ICJ), and the lack of familiarity of many Third World States with formal adjudication also may have inhibited them from accepting formal mechanisms of international adjudication (David and Brierly 1985; Anand 1987). This has been contended by many scholars and States. Besides, this process is cumbersome and time consuming. Therefore, it would be wise to exclude the jurisdiction of the ICJ.

ITLOS in comparison with Arbitration is a complex process. It is not as flexible as Arbitration. States have the autonomy to choose arbitral panel under Annex. VII of the UNCLOS while they cannot do so for ITLOS or ICJ. Furthermore, ITLOS is cheaper as compared to Arbitration because India being a member already contributes while as in Arbitration it needs to bear half of the expenses.

Arbitration is offered as an alternative to adjudication. Some States preferred arbitration to adjudication because it allows for a more flexible procedure enabling disputes to be settled more expeditiously (Rosenne and Sohn 1989). The preference for arbitration is in accordance with an increasing trend to include arbitral clauses in treaties (Klein 2005). The appeal of arbitration may be found in the possibility of secrecy, party control over the composition of the tribunal and the questions addressed to the tribunal as well as the ability to avoid a third State's intervention in the proceedings (Klein 2005).

On 29 October 2015, an Arbitral Tribunal issued its award on the questions of jurisdiction and admissibility in the arbitration between the Republic of Philippines and the People's Republic of China concerning the South China Sea. In brief, the Tribunal found that it had jurisdiction to decide seven of the Philippines' fifteen substantive claims. As to the Philippines remaining claims, the Tribunal decided that the question of its jurisdiction is needed to be deferred for further consideration in conjunction with its hearing of the merits of the claims (Christopher 2016).

According to China's Position Paper, the dispute could be characterised in two ways, both of which excluded the Tribunal's jurisdiction (Christopher 2016). First, China characterised the dispute as concerning territorial sovereignty-related questions over features in the South China Sea. On that basis, China contended that the dispute did not concern the "interpretation and application of UNCLOS", being the threshold requirement for the Tribunal's jurisdiction under Article 288 of UNCLOS.

The Tribunal rejected this characterisation, finding that, while a dispute between the parties did exist concerning land sovereignty over certain features, the Philippines' claims did not require the Tribunal to make determinations on questions of sovereignty. The Tribunal found that each of the Philippines' claims concerned the interpretation and application of UNCLOS (Christopher 2016).

Secondly, China contended that the dispute was properly characterised as relating to maritime boundary delimitation which, for the reasons given below, was excluded from the Tribunal's jurisdiction by an exclusionary provision in the UNCLOS that China had activated in 2006 (Christopher 2016).

In rejecting this contention, the Tribunal distinguished between a dispute concerning the existence of an entitlement to maritime zones (the present matter), and a dispute concerning the delimitation of those zones where parties' entitlements overlap. The Tribunal also emphasised that, while it would determine the nature of particular maritime features in dispute, insofar as this resulted in overlapping entitlements between the parties the Tribunal's determination would not go so far as to delimit boundaries (Christopher 2016).

Relying on Articles 281 and 282 of UNCLOS, China contended that State parties had agreed on a peaceful dispute resolution mechanism of their own choice, precluding recourse to the compulsory dispute settlement procedures under UNCLOS. The articles essentially prevent a State from resorting to the compulsory procedures in the event that they have already agreed on another means of dispute resolution. In this regard, China pointed to a series of joint statements by State parties starting in the mid-1990s that referred to the resolution of their dispute by negotiation, as well as the *Treaty of Amity and Cooperation in South East Asia.* Having regard to these statements and instrument, the Tribunal concluded that they did not prevent the Philippines from resorting to arbitration under the compulsory dispute resolution provisions (Christopher 2016).

The Tribunal also found that the Philippines had satisfied the precondition for resorting to arbitration, namely that the parties had an "exchange of views" regarding settlement of the dispute (Article 283). In so finding, the Tribunal relied upon diplomatic communications by the Philippines to affected parties in which it proposed multilateral negotiations to resolve the dispute. China insisted on bilateral talks only and the parties ultimately failed to identify a mutually agreeable mode of settlement.

The Tribunal also noted that it was not deprived of jurisdiction by either China's non-participation in the arbitration to date or the absence of other States with claims to features in the South China Sea (such as Vietnam).

Therefore, it should be drawn from this case that even if a State excludes jurisdiction under Article 298 of UNCLOS, it will continue to apply between claimant States concerning the interpretation or application of the provisions of UNCLOS which are not within the exclusion in Article 298. They include:

1. A dispute on whether a feature meets the definition of an island under Article 121(1) because it is a naturally formed area of land, surrounded by water, which is above water at high tide.
2. A dispute on whether an island is a rock which cannot sustain human habitation or economic life of its own within Article 121(3) and is therefore not entitled to an EEZ or continental shelf of its own.
3. A dispute on whether a feature is a low-tide elevation pursuant to Article 13.
4. A dispute on whether the use of straight baselines by a State is consistent with Article 7.
5. A dispute on the interpretation or application of Article 6 on reefs (Beckman 2013).

Therefore, excluding jurisdiction would not be a wise decision. Furthermore, Article 298 para 1(a) provides for Compulsory Conciliation. Compulsory Conciliation puts equal political pressure and needs equal efforts as that of compulsory binding settlement procedures. Therefore, the option of excluding the jurisdiction under Article 298 should be ruled out. In support of third-party adjudication or judicial settlement of maritime disputes, Charney concludes that the delimitation of maritime zones has been subject to third-party dispute settlement in the past despite the highly discretionary nature of the applicable legal principles (Charney 1994). This history could indicate that the subject of the dispute would be conducive to settlement under the compulsory procedures in Part XV of the UNCLOS. Klein in her study clarified that this may well be another contributory factor as to why governments negotiating at the Third Law of the Sea Conference did not insist on the complete exclusion of maritime delimitation dispute from the compulsory dispute settlement regime (Klein 2005).

Another possible approach that could be, keeping in view India's economic, political and strategic sensitivity in surrounding oceans where the overlapping claims by neighbouring countries are possible, some of the areas (keeping in mind India's emotive considerations) may be excluded from third-party jurisdiction. This is legally justified as Article 298(1)(a)(i) makes impliedly that a State may exclude the sensitive dispute with one of its neighbours but does not want to offend its other neighbours by a broad gauged exclusion. Article 298(1)(a)(i) says that where disputes relating to sea boundary delimitations are separated by a disjunctive "or" from disputes involving historic bays or titles, thus enabling a State to select only one of these subcategories for an exclusion through its declaration (Rosenne and Sohn 1989).

Even if above-mentioned implied understanding is questioned, it can be argued, undoubtedly, that this is a grey area (gap in law) where UNCLOS has not made explicit rules and limited declaration of this nature may be best way to protect sensitive areas of India' seas. On this basis, India may exclude one or two maritime areas (and not all maritime areas with all of our neighbours).

5 Declarations of States Parties Relating to Settlement of Disputes in Accordance with Article 298 (Optional Exceptions to the Applicability of Part XV, Section II of the Convention)

See Table 3.

5.1 *State Practice*

From above-mentioned Table 3, there are 25 States out of 60 States which have made declarations under Article 298 and have excluded the disputes related to maritime delimitation from the compulsory procedure. Out of 25 States, there are 7 States who have not even made the choice of forums (China, France, Gabon,

Table 3 Declarations of states parties relating to settlement of disputes in accordance with Article 298 (optional exceptions to the applicability of Part XV, Section II of the Convention)

S. No.	States	Exclusion (delimitation)	Forum of choice
1.	Algeria	–	No choice of forums
2.	Angola	–	No choice of forums
3.	Argentina	Excluded	(a) The International Tribunal for the Law of the Sea; (b) an arbitral tribunal constituted in accordance with Annex. VIII for questions relating to fisheries, protection and preservation of the marine environment, marine scientific research and navigation, in accordance with Annex. VIII
4.	Australia	Excluded	(a) The International Tribunal for the Law of the Sea established in accordance with Annex. VI of the Convention; and (b) The International Court of Justice
5.	Austria	Not excluded	1. The International Tribunal for the Law of the Sea established in accordance with Annex. VI 2. A special arbitral tribunal constituted in accordance with Annex. VIII 3. The International Court of Justice
6.	Bangladesh	–	ITLOS (India) ITLOS (Myanmar)

(continued)

Table 3 (continued)

S. No.	States	Exclusion (delimitation)	Forum of choice
7.	Belarus	Excluded	An arbitral tribunal constituted in accordance with Annex. VII. Relating to fisheries, the protection and preservation of the marine environment, marine scientific research and navigation, including pollution from vessels and by dumping, the Byelorussian Soviet Socialist Republic chooses a special arbitral tribunal constituted in accordance with Annex. VIII
8.	Belgium	Not excluded	The International Tribunal for the Law of the Sea established in accordance with Annex. VI (Article 287.1(a)) or the International Court of Justice
9.	Brazil	–	No Choice of forums
10.	Canada	Excluded	(a) The International Tribunal for the Law of the Sea established in accordance with Annex. VI of the Convention; and (b) An arbitral tribunal constituted in accordance with Annex. VII of the Convention
11.	Cabo Verde	Not excluded	(a) The International Tribunal for the Law of the Sea (b) The International Court of Justice
12.	Chile	Excluded	(i) The International Tribunal for the Law of the Sea established in accordance with Annex. VI (ii) A special arbitral tribunal established in accordance with Annex. VIII, for the categories of disputes specified therein relating to fisheries, protection and preservation of the marine environment, and marine scientific research and navigation, including pollution from vessels and by dumping
13.	China	Excluded	No choice of forums
14.	Croatia	–	(i) The International Tribunal for the Law of the Sea established in accordance with Annex. VI (ii) The International Court of Justice
15.	Cuba	–	Does not accept jurisdiction of ICJ
15.	Czech Republic	–	–

(continued)

Table 3 (continued)

S. No.	States	Exclusion (delimitation)	Forum of choice
16.	Denmark	Excluded from Arbitration under Annex. VII	ICJ No arbitration under Annex. VII (with Article 298)
17.	Ecuador	Excluded	1. The International Tribunal for the Law of the Sea 2. The International Court of Justice 3. A special tribunal constituted in accordance with Annex. VIII, for one or more of the categories of disputes relating to fisheries, protection and preservation of the marine environment, marine scientific research and navigation, including pollution from vessels and by dumping
18.	Egypt	–	The arbitral procedure
19.	Equatorial Guinea	–	Rejected for any forums
20.	Estonia	–	The International Tribunal for the Law of the Sea established in accordance with Annex. VI and the International Court of Justice
21.	Fiji	–	The International Tribunal for the Law of the Sea established in accordance with Annex. VI
22.	Finland	–	The International Court of Justice and the International Tribunal for the Law of the Sea
23.	France	Excluded	No choice of forums
24.	Gabon	Excluded	No choice of forums
25.	Germany	–	1. The International Tribunal for the Law of the Sea established in accordance with Annex. VI 2. An arbitral tribunal constituted in accordance with Annex. VII 3. The International Court of Justice
26.	Greece	–	The International Tribunal for the Law of the Sea
27.	Guinea-Bissau	–	Does not accept the jurisdiction of ICJ
28.	Honduras	–	The International Court of Justice
29.	Hungary	–	1. The International Tribunal for the Law of the Sea 2. The International Court of Justice 3. A special tribunal constructed in accordance with Annex. VIII for all the categories of disputes specified therein
30.	India	–	No choice of forums

(continued)

Table 3 (continued)

S. No.	States	Exclusion (delimitation)	Forum of choice
31.	Iran (Islamic Republic of)	–	No choice of forums
32.	Italy	Excluded	The International Tribunal for the Law of the Sea or the International Court of Justice
33.	Latvia	–	(1) The International Tribunal for the Law of the Sea established in accordance with Annex. VI of the Convention (2) The International Court of Justice
34.	Lithuania	–	(a) The International Tribunal for the Law of the Sea established in accordance with Annex. VI; (b) The International Court of Justice
35.	Madagascar	–	The International Tribunal for the Law of the Sea
36.	Mexico	Excluded	1. The International Tribunal for the Law of the Sea established in accordance with Annex. VI 2. The International Court of Justice 3. A special arbitral tribunal constituted in accordance with Annex. VIII for one or more of the categories of disputes specified therein
37.	Montenegro	Excluded	(i) The International Tribunal for the Law of the Sea established in accordance with Annex. VI of the Convention and (ii) the International Court of Justice
38.	Netherlands	–	The International Court of Justice
39.	Nicaragua	Not excluded	The International Court of Justice
40.	Norway	Excluded Arbitration under Annex. VII	The International Court of Justice
41.	Oman	–	The International Tribunal for the Law of the Sea, as set forth in Annex. VI to the Convention, and the jurisdiction of the International Court of Justice
42.	Pakistan	–	No choice of forums
43.	Portugal	Excluded	(a) The International Tribunal for the Law of the Sea established in pursuance of Annex. VI (b) The International Court of Justice (c) An arbitral tribunal constituted in accordance with Annex. VII (d) A special arbitral tribunal constituted in accordance with Annex. VIII

(continued)

Table 3 (continued)

S. No.	States	Exclusion (delimitation)	Forum of choice
44.	Republic of Korea	Excluded	No choice of forums
45.	Republic of Palau	Excluded	No choice of forums
46.	Russian Federation	Excluded	An arbitral tribunal constituted in accordance with Annex. VII as the basic means for the settlement of disputes concerning the interpretation or application of the Convention. It opts for a special arbitral tribunal constituted in accordance with Annex. VIII for the consideration of matters relating to fisheries, the protection and preservation of the marine environment, marine scientific research and navigation, including pollution from vessels and dumping. It recognises the competence of the International Tribunal for the Law of the Sea, as provided for in Article 292, in matters relating to the prompt release of detained vessels and crews
47.	Saint Vincent and the Grenadines	–	The International Tribunal for the Law of the Sea established in accordance with Annex. VI
48.	Saudi Arabia	Excluded	No choice of forums
49.	Slovenia	Excluded	Arbitral tribunal constituted in accordance with Annex. VII
50.	Spain	Excluded	The International Tribunal for the Law of the Sea and the International Court of Justice
51.	Sweden	–	The International Court of Justice
52.	Switzerland	–	The Tribunal for the Law of the Sea
53.	Thailand	Excluded	No choice of forums
54.	Timor-Leste	–	(a) The International Tribunal for the Law of the Sea established in pursuance of Annex. VI (b) The International Court of Justice (c) An arbitral tribunal constituted in accordance with Annex. VII (d) A special arbitral tribunal constituted in accordance with Annex. VIII
55.	Trinidad and Tobago	Excluded	(a) The International Tribunal for the Law of the Sea established in accordance with Annex. VI (b) The International Court of Justice

(continued)

Table 3 (continued)

S. No.	States	Exclusion (delimitation)	Forum of choice
56.	Tunisia	Excluded	(a) The International Tribunal for the Law of the Sea (b) An arbitral tribunal established in accordance with Annex. VII
57.	Ukraine	Excluded	An arbitral tribunal constituted in accordance with Annex. VII For the consideration of questions relating to fisheries, protection and preservation of the marine environment, marine scientific research and navigation, including pollution from vessels and by dumping, the Ukrainian SSR chooses a special arbitral tribunal constituted in accordance with Annex. VIII The Ukrainian SSR recognises the competence, as stipulated in Article 292, of the International Tribunal for the Law of the Sea in respect of questions relating to the prompt release of detained vessels or their crews
58.	United Kingdom of Great Britain and Northern Ireland	Not excluded	The International Court of Justice
59.	United Republic of Tanzania	–	The International Tribunal for the Law of the Sea
60.	Uruguay	–	The International Tribunal for the Law of the Sea for the settlement of such disputes relating to the interpretation or application of the Convention as are not subject to other procedures, without prejudice to its recognition of the jurisdiction of the International Court of Justice

Republic of Korea, Republic of Palau, Saudi Arabia and Thailand). These statistics can be summarised as follows:

1. The expressions (over enthusiasm for exclusion) from these 7 States reflect their position in this connection either they believe that the compulsory procedure may be counterproductive or more political/sovereignty/security aspects are connected or as a precaution this measure is required or they have settled their disputes and do not want to open the subject once again for the settlement.

Out of 60 States, there are 5 States (Austria, Belgium, Cape Verde, Nicaragua and UK) who have not excluded the subject from compulsory procedure and also have given their choice of forums. These States have chosen forums either ITLOS or ICJ or both where majority of States have given preference to ITLOS as a forum.

Out of 60 States, there are 30 States that have not expressly made any declarations under Article 298 either of exclusion or non-exclusion. Among 30 States who have not made declarations under Article 298, 4 states have not even given choice of forums, i.e., there are 26 States out of 30 States who have given choice of forums but have not shown interest in making declarations. These 26 States can be considered as not against per se exclusion of maritime delimitation disputes. Need to note that Article 298 is declaration of exclusion; until a declaration is made excepting some disputes, these disputes remain within the jurisdiction of the appropriate tribunal designated in accordance with Article 287 of the Convention (Rosenne and Sohn 1989). In this situation, the absence of declaration would amount to non-exclusion of subject from compulsory procedure. Hence, 51 States can be understood who have not shown interest in excluding the subject (maritime delimitation) from compulsory procedure. Various reasons can be advanced for this position:

(i) Article 298(1)(a) scope is limited in a sense that a State will only be obliged to submit the dispute to conciliation proceeding and the proposed agreement by the Conciliation Commission will not be binding on States.
(ii) One of the legal reason for non-exclusion can be that the past dispute before the UNCLOS has been completely excluded from the scope of Article 298(1)(a).
(iii) It could be argued that this optional exclusion potentially denies a range of advantages otherwise accruing to States in dispute but is a realistic reflection of State preferences for political, rather than third-party adjudication when dealing with an important matter such as title. There is a strong belief that marine resources are very important for States and required optimal exploitation for its nation development. In their view, keeping it away from the scope of Article 298(1)(a) will not serve any purpose for States. The importance of international marketability illustrates why non-exclusion is an essential complement to maritime delimitation. Without legal resolution, a State may lose all capacity to harvest and market resources—or at best the questionable title will significantly diminish the value of the concession—and this is because it can no longer market exclusive rights to private fishing fleets or oil companies (Klein 2005).
(iv) Overlapping entitlements "the most dangerous disputes" as they lie "at the very heart of sovereignty" may not remain issues for these States (Klein 2005).

In Europe, except France, Denmark (excluded only from Arbitration under Annex. VII), Portugal, Italy and Norway, majority of west European States have not excluded the compulsory procedure of the UNCLOS. As history suggests these five States have grave pain in settlement of disputes related to maritime delimitation which essentially become emotive issues, also these States have in principle settled the issue by Court or through agreements, and they believe there is no need to re-agitate the dispute.

In brief, it can be suggested that India should not exclude the dispute related to maritime delimitation mentioned in Article 298(1)(a) of the UNCLOS.

However, there are States who have made declaration under Article 310 which may have intended to either strengthen their positions to either exclusion or non-exclusion of maritime delimitation disputes from the scope of Article 298(1)(a).

China

1. In accordance with the provisions of the United Nations Convention on the Law of the Sea, the People's Republic of China shall enjoy sovereign rights and jurisdiction over an exclusive economic zone of 200 nautical miles and the continental shelf.
2. The People's Republic of China will effect, through consultations, the delimitation of the boundary of the maritime jurisdiction with the States with coasts opposite or adjacent to China, respectively, on the basis of international law and in accordance with the principle of equitability.
3. The People's Republic of China reaffirms its sovereignty over all its archipelagos and islands as listed in Article 2 of the Law of the People's Republic of China on the territorial sea and the contiguous zone, which was promulgated on 25 February 1992.

Malaysia

7. The Malaysian Government interprets Articles 74 and 83 to the effect that in the absence of agreement on the delimitation of the exclusive economic zone or continental shelf or other maritime zones, for an equitable solution to be achieved, the boundary shall be the median line, namely a line every point of which is equidistant from the nearest points of the baselines from which the breadth of the territorial sea of Malaysia and of such other States is measured. Malaysia is also of the view that in accordance with the provisions of the Convention, namely Articles 56 and 76, if the maritime area is less [than] or to a distance of 200 nautical miles from the baselines, the boundary for the continental shelf and the exclusive economic zone shall be on the same line (identical).

Malta

The Government of Malta interprets Articles 74 and 83 to the effect that in the absence of agreement on the delimitation of the exclusive economic zone or the continental shelf or other maritime zones, for an equitable solution to be achieved, the boundary shall be the median line, namely a line every point of which is equidistant from the nearest points of the baselines from which the breadth of the territorial waters of Malta and of such other States is measured.

5.1.1 Baselines and Delimitation

A claim that the drawing of baselines or the delimitation of maritime zones is in accordance with the Convention will only be acceptable if such lines and zones have been established in accordance with the Convention.

Oman

Declaration No. 5, on the exclusive economic zone

1. The Sultanate of Oman determines that its exclusive economic zone, in accordance with Article 5 of Royal Decree No. 15/81 dated 10 February 1981, extends 200 nautical miles in a seaward direction, measured from the baselines from which the territorial sea is measured.
2. The Sultanate of Oman possesses sovereign rights over its economic zone and also exercises jurisdiction over that zone as provided for in the Convention. It further declares that, in exercising its rights and performing its duties under the Convention in the exclusive economic zone, it will have due regard to the rights and duties of other States and will act in a manner compatible with the provisions of the Convention.

Declaration No. 6, on the continental shelf

The Sultanate of Oman exercises over its continental shelf sovereign rights for the purpose of exploring it and exploiting its natural resources, as permitted by geographical conditions and in accordance with this Convention.

Philippines

8. The agreement of the Republic of the Philippines to the submission for peaceful resolution, under any of the procedures provided in the Convention, of disputes under Article 298 shall not be considered as a derogation of Philippines sovereignty.

6 Conclusion

An examination and assessment of the different forums available under Article 297 indicate that at present, ITLOS and Arbitration under Annex. VII have been used extensively by States. 33 States so far expressly have chosen ITLOS and 11 States have chosen expressly Arbitration under Annex. VII. However, 44 States in the Table 1 of this study have not shown their choice of forums, i.e., by default, the Arbitration under Annex. VII will be the forum for settlement of law of the sea disputes for these States. It means that 44 plus 11 states (total 55 States) are of the view that Arbitration under Annex. VII are their preferred mode of settlement of law of the sea disputes. In brief, ITLOS and Arbitration under Annex. VII are most preferred forums by States. There should not be any doubt on the advantages of these forums as discussed above on any given situation.

With regard to ICJ as a preferred mode for law of the sea disputes, views are at variance. Indeed, India has already made the declaration with regard to optional jurisdiction of ICJ under Article 36(2) of the ICJ Statute and excluded various aspects of maritime disputes including maritime delimitation. Similarly, many other states have also excluded maritime disputes from ICJ jurisdiction. Hence, ICJ may only remain a forum with mutual consent among parties for "application and interpretation of UNCLOS". Unless, India declares the jurisdiction of ICJ or gives preference under Article 287, jurisdiction of ICJ is of limited use to settle the maritime disputes.

Keeping in view different and varied positions of various States on the Coastal States' rights to enjoy residual rights in the exclusive economic zone and taking a lesson from South China Sea disputes, it can be suggested that India's earlier declaration submitted at the ratification of UNCLOS on this aspect is of limited use or there is a strong need to strengthen India's position on this issue by specific exclusion of the subject from compulsory procedure of the UNCLOS.

As discussed above, the importance of timing of submission of declaration is highly useful and of strategic importance. This study has advanced four propositions in this regard: (a) during the continuation of declaration, a State which has a declaration regarding the optional exception clause (Article 298(1)) cannot bring disputes falling within that category against any other State, even if that State has not made a similar declaration of exception (Article 298, para 3); (b) a State making such a declaration may at any time withdraw it, or agrees to submit a dispute so excluded. Thus, whenever need arises and if State (A) is interested to sue other States (B or C), a State party may agree in a particular case to submit to adjudication a dispute which is excluded from adjudication by its declaration of exemption/exclusion. This differs from general withdrawal of a declaration, as the declared exclusions remain applicable to other disputes under Article 238(2), even those with the State with which the special agreement was concluded, (c) according to Article 298(5), a new declaration or withdrawal of a declaration does not in any way affect proceedings pending before a court or tribunal unless the parties otherwise agree. In other words, declaration or withdrawal has no retroactive effect on the proceedings, and (d) interestingly, a State can withdraw the declaration and, at the same time, can file a new declaration which is either broader or narrower.

Importantly, three reasons are required to be highlighted related to declarations under Article 298:

(i) Article 299 contains two clauses in which first clause says that any dispute excluded under Article 297 or excepted under Article 298 from the dispute settlement procedures provided for in Section 2 cannot be submitted to such procedure by any party to a dispute through unilateral application. Any such action might be considered, pursuant to Article 294 of the Convention, "an abuse of legal process" or "prima facie unfounded".

(ii) The declaration made by States under Article 298 does not preclude from an agreement to submit the dispute to some other procedure outside the framework of Part XV of the UNCLOS.
(iii) Part XV is silent on the legality of declaration made under Article 298 by any forum envisaged under Article 287 so it is possible to make a comprehensive declaration of a nature which can deal with the grey areas of the UNCLOS, i.e., where there is no law or there is a gap in law. This may take care of issues of sensitive matters. It should be used optimally.

As discussed above, declaration under Article 298 requires a State to exclude the subjects covered under Article 298. In brief, declaration under Article 298 is declaration of exclusion. In other words, until a declaration is made excepting some disputes, these disputes remain within the jurisdiction of the appropriate tribunal designated in accordance with Article 287 of the Convention. In this situation, the absence of declaration would amount to non-exclusion of a subject from compulsory procedure. Hence, keeping in view of India's stand during the UNCLOS negotiations and India's strategies in Indian Ocean and specially Arabian Sea and its needs for development, India must ensure a comprehensive declaration under Article 298 on the sensitive matters including military activities.

This study finds that 51 States have not shown interest in excluding the subject (maritime delimitation) from compulsory procedure. In Europe, except France, Denmark (from Arbitration under Annex. VII), Portugal, Italy and Norway, majority of west European States have not excluded the compulsory procedure of the UNCLOS. As history suggests these five above-mentioned States have grave pains in settlement of disputes related to maritime delimitation which essentially become emotive issues, also these States have in principle settled the issue by Court or through agreements, and they believe there is no need to re-agitate the dispute. Keeping in view the study's finding, it can be suggested that India should not exclude the dispute related to maritime delimitation mentioned in Article 298(1)(a) of the UNCLOS. This position of non-exclusion of maritime delimitation can also get support from the view of Dr. P.S. Rao's concurring and dissenting opinion and separate opinion in the *Case of Bay of Bengal Maritime Boundary Arbitration between Bangladesh and India* (Bay of Bengal Maritime Boundary Arbitration between Bangladesh and India 2012). I agree with him that due to creation of this area, India could not get economically resourceful advantages in the Bay of Bengal. Excluding the maritime delimitation from compulsory procedure of the UNCLOS may hurt India's interest in long time. However, as mentioned above in Part III, India may adopt another alternative approach by excluding one or two maritime areas by making declaration under Article 298 (and not all maritime areas with all of India's neighbours).

References

Adede AO (1987) The system for settlement of disputes under the United Nations convention on the law of the sea. Martinus Nijhoff Publishers, The Netherlands, pp 27–28

Anand RP (1987) Attitude of the new Asian-African countries toward the international court of justice. In: Snyder FE, Sathirathai S (eds) Third world attitudes towards international law. Martinus Nijhoff, Boston, p 163

Anderson D (2008) Modern law of the sea. Martinus Nijhoff, Leiden, p 514

Bay of Bengal Maritime Boundary Arbitration between Bangladesh and India (2012) https://goo.gl/uWKOIr

Beckman R (2013, October 24–25) International conference of "the South China sea: UNCLOS and state practice. Organized by National Institute for South China Sea Studies Haikou

Charney JL (1994) Progress in international maritime boundary delimitation law. Am J Int Law 88:228

Charney JI (1996) The implications of expanding international dispute settlement systems: the 1982 convention on the law of the sea. Am J Int Law 90(1):69–75

Christopher L (2016) The South China sea ruling: Philippines v China. http://goo.gl/1JDgvQ

Collier J, Lowe V (1999) The settlement of disputes in international law: institutions and procedures. Oxford University Press, Oxford, p 41

Communications made by Myanmar, Bangladesh and Oman with respect to the Submission made by India to the Commission. http://goo.gl/ij8Avi

David R, Brierly J (1985) Major legal systems in the world today, 3rd ed. Stevens and Sons Ltd., p 28

Ehlers P, Lagoni R (2006) International maritime organisations and their contribution: towards a sustainable marine development. LIT Verlag Münster, p 311

Financial Assistance to the Parties to ITLOS. https://goo.gl/miba3H

Freestone D et al (2006) The law of the sea: progress and prospects. Oxford University Press, Oxford, p 396

ITLOS (2016) Available at https://www.itlos.org/index.php?id=139&L=0

Johnston DM (1988) The theory and history of ocean boundary making. McGill-Queen's University Press, Montreal, p 96

Kariotis TC (ed) (1997) Greece and the law of the sea. Kluwer Law International, The Hague, p 170

Klein N (2005) Dispute settlement in the UN convention on the law of the sea. Cambridge University Press, Cambridge, p 15

Kwiatkowska Barbara (1996) The international court of justice and the law of the sea-some reflections. Int J Mar Coast Law 11(4):499

Maritime Delimitation in the Area between Greenland and Jan Mayen (Denmark v. Norway), ICJ, Verbatim Record, pp 50–78

Mensah T (2004) The significance of the international tribunal for the law of the sea for the shipping industry. WMU J Marit Aff 2:111–121

Merrills JG (2005) International dispute settlement, 4th edn. Cambridge University Press, Cambridge, p 185

Merrills JG (2011) International dispute settlement, 5th edn. Cambridge University Press, Cambridge

Noyes JE (1989) Compulsory third party adjudication and the 1982 United Nations convention on the law of the sea. Conn J Int Law 4:675–678

Noyes JE (1999) The international tribunal for the law of the sea. Cornell Int Law J 32:109–119

Oda S (1995) Dispute settlement prospect in the law of the sea. Int Comp Law Q 44(4):864

Rosenne S, Sohn LB (1989) United Nations convention on the law of the sea 1982: a commentary, vol 5. Martinuus Nijhoff Publishers, Dordrecht, pp 41–42

Schwebel S (1987) Ad hoc chambers of the international court of justice. Am J Int Law 81:840

Southern Bluefin Tuna Case (Australia and New Zealand v. Japan) Award on Jurisdiction and Admissibility, 4 August 2000 (2000) 39 ILM 1359; *MOX Plant Case* (Irelan v. United Kingdom) Order no. 3 of 24 June 2003; *Cases concerning Land Reclamation by Singapore in and around the Straits of Johor* (Malaysia v. Singapore), Request for Provisional Measures, Order of 8 October 2003
Statement of the Austrian Delegate at the 16th Meeting of the Second Committee (2nd Session) in UN Document A/CONF.62/C.2/SR.16 (1994), para 4
Suarez SV (2008) The outer limits of the continental shelf: legal aspects of their establishment. Springer, Berlin, p 250
The binding and compulsory dispute settlement procedures were to be "the pivot upon which the delicate equilibrium of the compromise must be balanced" (Memorandum by the President of the Conference on doc. A/CONF.62/WP.9, UN Doc.A/CONF.62/WP.9/Add.1 (1976) reprinted in 5 Third United Nations Conference on the Law of the Sea: Official Records at p. 122)
The Indian Continental Shelf, Partial Submission to the Commission on the Limits of the Continental Shelf, pursuant to Article 76, paragraph 8 of the United Nations Convention on the Law of the Sea, Executive Summary, Part 1, 2009. http://goo.gl/ij8Avi
The question of composition of the Chambers was considered both from theoretical point of view as well as by the Court itself in 1982, *the US and Canada in the Gulf of Maine case*
UN Document A/CONF. 62/L.4 (1974), Article 19(2)

Author Biography

Mr Vinai Kumar Singh is Assistant Professor and Deputy Director of Indian Society of International Law (ISIL) in New Delhi. He is also the Assistant Editor of the Indian Journal of International Law and of the ISIL Yearbook of International Humanitarian & Refugee Law. He secured LL.M. from University of Delhi and M.Phil. from Centre for International Legal Studies, Jawaharlal Nehru University, New Delhi. His papers are published in reputed journals nationally and internationally.

Chapter 9
Accountability for Conflict-Era Human Rights Violations in Nepal: An Appraisal of Strategic Human Rights Litigation

Raju Prasad Chapagai and Pankaj Kumar Karn

1 Context and Background

Modern Nepal traces its origin to 1769, when the ruler of the small kingdom of Gorkha conquered and united the many kingdoms and principalities into a single State. The Shah dynasty ruled Nepal until 1846, when a member of the Rana aristocracy reduced the Shah King to a figurehead and assumed direct power founding a system of hereditary prime ministers (OHCHR, Nepal Conflict Report 2012). The aristocratic rule of Rana family that would prevail for over a century was overthrown by an emerging pro-democracy movement, and the Shah dynasty came into power in 1950. Though restored because of the democratic movement, the King sidelined the agenda of the election of a constituent assembly to draft a new Constitution (Constitution 1959). However, with the gradual expansion of pro-democratic space during the 1950s, the country's first Parliamentary election resulted in first elected Government in 1959. After short span of Parliamentary democracy, in 1960 King Mahindra dismissed the elected Government, banned all political parties, and established a party-less Panchayat system that ruled the country for the next 30 years (Constitution 1962). Popular pro-democracy movements launched by several political parties in early 1990s succeeded to put an end to the Panchayat system and restored multiparty democracy (Hachhethu 1990). Though three general and two local elections were held and multiple Governments were formed during the 1990s, the democratic system was criticized for its failure to keep the promises for democracy, economic development, good governance,

R.P. Chapagai (✉) · P.K. Karn
Program Department, Supreme Court Bar Association,
Mandwi, Kalikaasthan, Dillibajar, Kathmandu, Nepal
e-mail: rajuforjustice@gmail.com

J.L. Kaul and A. Jha (eds.), *Shifting Horizons of Public International Law*,
https://doi.org/10.1007/978-81-322-3724-2_9

security, and prosperity. Although some positive developments in the economy were observed in early 1990s, the living conditions of most people remained poor and the longstanding problems including exclusion, discrimination, and marginalization could not be unaddressed properly (OHCHR, Nepal Conflict Report 2012).

Drawing a rationale on the basis of popular dissatisfaction of different strata of Nepali people, Communist Party of Nepal (Maoist) ("CPN (Maoist)") began its armed conflict in February 1996 and continued until 2006 (Chapagai 2014). It caused wide range of violations of human rights and humanitarian laws including unlawful killings, enforced disappearances, torture and other cruel, inhuman or degrading treatment or punishment, arbitrary arrests, and sexual violence. As reported by Office of the High Commissioner for Human Rights, the armed conflict resulted in the death of about 16,729 persons, displacement of about 78,689 persons, disappearance of about 1,327 people, and severe damage to public infrastructures valued at approximately 5 billion rupees (OHCHR, Nepal Conflict Report 2012). On 21 November 2006, the conflict officially ended with the signing of a Comprehensive Peace Accord (CPA) that vowed not only for writing a new Constitution through an elected Constituent Assembly but also for dealing with the past human rights violations. Giving effect to the CPA, the Interim Constitution of Nepal 2007 also required addressing the conflict-era human rights violations including through adopting a credible transitional justice processes. However, the commitments for truth and justice were not generously implemented and the right of the victims of human rights violations to effective remedy was virtually denied. Such a situation triggered the strategic use of the jurisdiction of the Supreme Court for compelling the authorities take steps towards turning the right of the victims to truth, justice, and reparation into a reality (NJA Report 2016).

The judicial activism, especially under the extraordinary jurisdiction of the Supreme Court under Article 107 of the Interim Constitution of Nepal, 2007, appeared to have been a silver lining in terms of taking forward the transitional justice issues. The Supreme Court has so far positively entertained a number of issues including in relation to Truth and Reconciliation Commission and Commission of Inquiry into Disappeared People, amnesty and reconciliation, criminal investigation and prosecution of serious crimes, and vetting for those implicated in human rights violations and promotion of reparation measures. In this backdrop, this chapter aims to analyse the Supreme Court of Nepal's key decisions pertaining to promoting accountability for the past human rights violations and unpack the strengthens and weaknesses of judicial response in the light of the victims' right to effective remedy guaranteed under the international human rights treaties and jurisprudence. This chapter finally generates suggestions towards strengthening the transitional justice process in Nepal.

2 Commitments for Accountability

2.1 Comprehensive Peace Accord

The decade long armed conflict came to its end with the signing of the CPA. Through CPA, both parties to the conflict vowed to eliminate impunity by upholding the rule of law and maintaining an independent judiciary and good governance in compliance with universally accepted human rights standards (CPA Preamble). Similarly, the CPA contained an important provision that stands for "impartial investigation and action shall be carried out in accordance with law against the persons responsible for creating obstructions to exercise the rights stated in the Accord and ensure that impunity shall not be encouraged". It also promised for ensuring the rights of the victims of conflict including the family of disappeared persons to obtain relief (CPA Article 7.1.3). These provisions signify the clear intent of both parties to condemn impunity and call for investigations and other actions to bring perpetrators of serious human rights violations to justice. As a key of the methods to deal with the past, the CPA provided for the establishment of a high-level Truth and Reconciliation Commission (TRC) "in order to investigate truth about those who have seriously violated human rights and those who were involved in crimes against humanity in course of the armed conflict" (CPA Article 5.2.5). Through CPA, both sides also agreed to "make public within 60 days of the signing of the Accord and the whereabouts of the people who 'disappeared' or were killed during the conflict and convey such details to the family members" (CPA Article 5.1.4).

2.2 Interim Constitution

Many of the commitments made under the CPA were subsequently transformed into the Interim Constitution that guaranteed the right under Article 32 to a Constitutional remedy for those whose fundamental rights had been violated (Interim Constitution 2007). The Interim Constitution contained an imperative under Article 33© for the State to adopt a political system that is fully compliant with the universally accepted basic human rights and rule of law. Similarly, the political system should opt for "ending corruption and impunity..." (Interim Constitution 2007). As a verbatim recital of the CPA, the Interim Constitution of Nepal requires the Government under Article 33(s) to constitute a TRC to "investigate the facts regarding grave violation of human rights and crimes against humanity committed during the course of conflict". While the CPA did not explicitly mention the establishment of Disappearances Commission, the Interim Constitution of Nepal made it the responsibility of the State under Article 33(q) "to provide relief to the families of the victims, on the basis of the report of the Investigation Commission constituted to investigate the cases of disappearances made during the course of the conflict".

2.3 Prevailing Constitution

The *Interim* Constitution was adopted for the purpose of writing a new Constitution through a Constituent Assembly elected by Nepali people. Accordingly, the Constituent Assembly was first elected in 2008. However, after termination of its extended term, it came to its dissolution without completing the Constitution writing process. The Constituent Assembly reelected for its second term in November 2013 succeeded to deliver the Constitution of Nepal on 25 September 2015 that has repealed the Interim Constitution.

Unlike Interim Constitution, the new Constitution does not directly refer to accountability for human rights violations committed during the conflict. However, it contains a number of provisions that demand for State actions towards addressing the past violations. The preamble documents the State commitment to "....civil liberties, fundamental rights, human rights......independent, impartial and competent judiciary and concept of the rule of law..." As indicated in the preamble, the Constitution is aimed at fulfilling the aspirations including for "sustainable peace" and "good governance".

Most importantly, under Article 21, the Constitution guarantees the right of victim of crime to "get information about the investigation and proceedings of a case" and "the right to justice including social rehabilitation and compensation". Similarly, like 1990 Constitution and the Interim Constitution, under Article 46 of the Constitution, the victims of the violations of the fundamental rights guaranteed under the Constitution are entitled to the right to Constitutional remedies.

The "right to social justice clause" under the fundamental rights has a direct reference to the victims of the violations: "The families of the martyrs who have sacrificed their life, persons who were forced to disappear, and those who became disabled and injured in all people's movements, armed conflicts and revolutions that have been carried out for progressive democratic changes in Nepal, democracy fighters, conflict victims and displaced ones, persons with disabilities, the injured and victims shall have the right under Article 42(5) to get opportunities on a priority basis, with justice and due respect, in education, health, employment, housing and social security, in accordance with law (Constitution 2015)". As stipulated under the directive principles, the State is obliged under Article 51(b)(3) "to maintain rule of law by protecting and promoting human rights" and "to implement international treaties, agreements to which Nepal is a party". Similarly, the Constitution also directs the State under Article 126(1) to protect and promote fundamental rights and human rights. By empowering the courts to deliver justice "in accordance with this Constitution, other laws and the recognized principles of justice", the Constitution also opens up a room for bridging the gap in national law with the recognized principles enshrined in the international law and jurisprudence.

2.4 International Human Rights Law (IHRL)

Nepal is a party to many of the major international human rights treaties. It also ratified the four Geneva Conventions on 7 February 1964. However, Nepal has not ratified the Additional Protocols I and II to the Geneva Conventions. Nepal is also a party to Convention on the Prevention and Punishment of the Crime of Genocide (CPPCG). As a party to numerous treaties, the Government of Nepal is obligated to respect and ensure a wide range of human rights for individuals in its jurisdiction. During the period affected by the conflict, Nepal was party to six out of the nine core Human Rights instruments, including the International Covenant on Civil and Political Rights (ICCPR), the Convention on the Rights of the Child (CRC), the Convention on the Elimination of All Forms of Discrimination against Women (CEDAW), and the Convention Against Torture and Other Cruel, Inhuman or Degrading Treatment or Punishment (CAT). Under these treaties, a range of fundamental rights, such as Articles 6, 7, 9, 21 of ICCPR and Articles 2, 16 of CAT, were applicable during the conflict.

Notably, the right to an effective remedy underlies all human rights the Government is obligated to guarantee, including those provided by Nepal's Constitution and national laws that implement its international commitments. Effective remedies serve first as a means to repair injuries suffered by individuals whom the Government fails to protect and then as a deterrent to prevent future violations, which are more likely to occur in conditions of impunity (OHCHR 2011).

2.5 International Humanitarian Law (IHL)

As the conflict was between governmental forces and a non-governmental armed group, the provisions of IHL concerning non-international armed conflicts were also applicable (OHCHR, Nepal Conflict Report 2012). Nepal remained party to the four Geneva Conventions and is subject to their provisions, including Common Article 3 of the Geneva Conventions which provides minimum standards governing any non-international armed conflict. Notably, Common Article 3 requires that each party to the conflict protects persons taking no active part in the hostilities, including civilians and "*members of armed forces who have laid down their arms and those placed* hors de combat *by sickness, wounds, detention, or any other cause*". Other obligations incumbent on parties to a conflict are those under customary international law, including the obligation to distinguish at all times between civilians and combatants and target only the latter; to refrain from indiscriminate attacks; to forego any offensive where the incidental damage expected "*is excessive in relation to the concrete and direct military advantage anticipated*"; and to take all feasible precautions to minimize incidental loss of civilian life and injury to civilians. The Principles of Humanity require that civilians and those who are *hors de combat* must be treated humanely, meaning that abuses of such persons, such as killing, torture, rape, mutilation, beatings, and humiliation, are prohibited. Violations of these rules may constitute violations of the laws and customs of war and trigger individual criminal responsibility.

2.6 Duty to Investigate and Prosecute Serious Crimes

Certain violations of international law are deemed to constitute "international crimes" including crimes against humanity, war crimes, genocide, trafficking, piracy, slavery, torture, and enforced disappearance. Both IHL and IHRL obligate States to investigate allegations of any serious violations of their respective regimes, particularly when they amount to international crimes, and when appropriate, prosecute suspected perpetrators, and compensate the victims.

As Nepal is a party to a number of IHLR and IHL treaties, the Government of Nepal is obliged to promptly and impartially investigate credible allegations of international crimes including enforced disappearance, torture, and ill-treatment and to punish the perpetrators. Both IHRL and IHL prohibit acts of sexual violence as well in peace time and during conflict. IHL prohibits rape, sexual slavery, forced prostitution, forced pregnancy, enforced sterilization, and other forms of sexual violence of similar gravity, which can include assault, trafficking, and strip searches. Under IHRL, gender-based violence including sexual violence "is discrimination within the meaning of Article 1" of CEDAW.

2.7 Interface of National and International Law

The Interim Constitution under Article 33(n) in the past and the Constitution of Nepal 2072 under Article 51(b)(3) at present require the State to implement international treaties to which Nepal is a party. By virtue of this, Nepal is Constitutionally bound to take steps to ensure the right of the victim to an effective remedy as guaranteed under the ICCPR and the Convention Against Torture (CAT), to which Nepal is a party. Similarly, the Nepal Treaty Act 1990 remains as a specific legislation that deals with the matter of treaties. This Act provides a normative framework concerning the ratification process of treaties and specifies their effect in Nepal. A key provision is Article 9(1), which provides "In case the provision of a treaty to which the Kingdom of Nepal or HMG has become a party following its ratification, acceptance or approval by the Parliament conflict with the provisions of current laws, the latter shall be invalid to the extent of such conflict for the purpose of that treaty, and the provisions of the treaty shall be applicable in that connection as Nepal law". By virtue of this provision, if the provisions under ratified treaties conflict with those under Nepalese laws, the provision(s) of ratified treaties get primacy over the provisions of Nepalese law, meaning that the conflicted provisions of Nepalese deem invalid to the extent of such conflict.

The provisions of the human rights treaties including the ICCPR are applied as Nepalese law in such a context. Thus, these Constitutional and the Treaty Act provisions provide a strong basis to benefit from the international human rights and humanitarian treaties (Chapagai 2009).

2.8 Scope of the Strategic Litigation

Since the promulgation of 1990 Constitution, the Supreme Court of Nepal has been enjoying sweeping power under Article 88 to enforce judicial accountability against legislative and executive excesses violating human rights. As the key judicial institution designed to safeguard rights and freedoms guaranteed under the Constitution, the Supreme Court was empowered to exercise its independent check against legislative and executive excesses infringing on the exercise of fundamental rights and freedoms. Most importantly, the 1990 Constitution as well as subsequent 2007 Interim Constitution empowered the Supreme Court under Article 107(1) "to declare any law void, either *abinitio* or from the date of its decision if it appears that the law in question is inconsistent with the Constitution". Besides, the Supreme Court was entrusted under Article 107(2) with the original jurisdiction over "any Constitutional and legal question involved in any dispute of public interest and concern". The Supreme Court has extraordinary power to settle any such dispute of public interest and concern through issuing any appropriate order and writs including the writs of habeas corpus, mandamus, certiorari, and any other appropriate orders. The 2015 Constitution of Nepal adopted by the Constituent Assembly of Nepal not only widened the scope of rights but also paved the way for judicial remedy in case of their violations. While retaining the writ power of the Supreme Court under Article 133, the Constitution also entrusts the provincial high courts under Article 144(1) with the writ jurisdiction involving the power to entertain public interest litigation. Like previous Constitutions, the right to Constitutional remedy is guaranteed as a separate fundamental right, which can be invoked to directly access the Supreme Court and high courts. In addition, the Supreme Court of Nepal has been enjoying the final authority to interpret the Constitution under Article 128(2) of the 2015 Constitution. As stated under the present Constitution [Article 128(4)] as well as the past Constitutions [Article 116(2) of Interim Constitution], "any interpretation given to a law or any legal principle laid down by the Supreme Court in the course of the hearing of a law suit shall be binding on the Government of Nepal and all offices and courts". By virtue of these provisions, there has been wider scope for strategic use of litigation including for invalidating legislative and executive actions that pose barrier in ensuring accountability, securing effective implementation of affirmative legal provisions, accelerating reform of national laws in view of the Constitutional obligation and obligations under international human rights and humanitarian treaties, and filling in the gap of law through adopting progressive interpretation.

For over past 25 years, the Supreme Court has been able to adjudicate a significant number of human rights issues through utilizing its Constitutional review and public interest litigation jurisdiction. By virtue of the PIL jurisdiction, disadvantaged and marginalized groups including women, children, and other poor and vulnerable groups were represented by any public spirited organizations and individuals before the court. In the post-conflict scenario, public interest litigation has been strategically used to hold Government accountable for not taking measures towards addressing the past human rights violations. Transitional justice has been one of the vital areas in which the Supreme Court entertained a number of PIL cases including in relation to amnesty and reconciliation, criminal investigation and prosecution of serious crimes, and vetting for those implicated in human rights violations and promotion of reparation measures.

3 Review of the Supreme Court Jurisprudence Established Through Strategic Litigation

3.1 Preventing Arbitrary Withdrawal of Criminal Prosecutions

In the post-conflict scenario, the withdrawal of criminal prosecution has been frequently employed as a weapon to bypass criminal accountability (OHCHR 2011). Against this backdrop, the Supreme Court has played vital role in checking arbitrary withdrawal of criminal prosecution in response to cases initiated by aggrieved individuals as well as in the public interest. Interpreting the Constitutional as well as legal provisions dealing with withdrawal of cases, the Supreme Court has set numerous judicial precedents and principles to control unbridled practice of withdrawing the criminal prosecution under the State Cases Act, 1992. Even under the 1990 Constitution, the Supreme Court, in *Government of Nepal v. Dil Bahadur Lama and others*, had clarified that "Before permission is granted to the Government for the withdrawal of cases, the court should check whether the intention is for good cause or not". Confining the scope of withdrawal of criminal charges at the trail stage, the Supreme Court ruled out the possibility of withdrawing the criminal prosecution at the appellate level (Supreme Court 1994).

Responding to *Government of Nepal v. Devendra Mandal,* the Court found that the consent of the district court is necessary to proceed with case withdrawals, including in order for upholding victims' access to justice and the right to an effective remedy (Supreme Court 2007a, b, c). The reasoning of the Court reads; "As the decision of the Government to withdraw the case is an executive decision, the Court should make necessary and reasonable judgment regarding whether or not to withdraw the case balancing the reasonable cause to withdraw the case and right to justice of the victim". The Court emphasized that the judicial permission is not merely a "rubber stamp" and that case withdrawals must be weighed against potential denials of victims' access to justice and effective remedies (Supreme Court 2007a, b, c).

Responding to *Government of Nepal v. Gagandev Raya Yadhav*, the Supreme Court required the respective district court to give special scrutiny to the withdrawal of cases that involve violations of human rights and humanitarian law weighing such withdrawals against potential denials of justice (Law Reporter 2008). On 29 December 2008, another public interest litigation, *Madhav Basnet* et al. *v. Prime Minister Puspa Kamal Dahal* et al., was filed with the Supreme Court demanding, *inter alia*: the invalidation of the Council of Ministers' decision to have 349 criminal cases withdrawn; the setting and enforcement of judicial guidelines to govern future withdrawals of criminal charges until another appropriate legal arrangement is made; and an interim order staying the implementation of the respective Government decision (Petition 2012a, b, c, d). The petitioners based their demands on right to effective remedies guaranteed including under Article 2 of the ICCPR along with Constitutional provisions and relevant jurisprudence developed by the Supreme Court of Nepal. After initial hearing of the case, the Court issued an interim order on 1 January 2009 preventing the further implementation of the Council of Ministers' decision of 27 October 2008 recommending the withdrawal of 349 criminal charges.

The Court based its interim order on the fact that the Comprehensive Peace Agreement (CPA) provides only for the withdrawal of cases filed with political motives, while the list of cases recommended for withdrawal included numerous charges seemingly unrelated to political offences. Delivering its final decision on 23 February 2011, the Supreme Court maintained that any decision of the Government of Nepal recommending a withdrawal of criminal cases under the State Cases Act must be fair, reasonable, and just. At the same time, the Court stated that it is the competence of respective district courts to confirm the compliance of a specific case withdrawal with applicable law. However, the Supreme Court refused the petitioner's demand to issue a set of judicial guidelines to control arbitrary case withdrawals, stating the Policy Guidelines and Procedures in Relation to Withdrawal of Criminal Charges.

The Supreme Court of Nepal's activism towards checking ongoing practice of case withdrawal has gained momentum in *Sukdev Raya Yadhev v. Government of Nepal* (Petition 2009). The Supreme Court stressed the need of paying serious precaution to ensure that the case withdrawal is not misused to bypass criminal accountability and promote impunity. The Court, in view of the developing norms of international human rights and humanitarian law, established an exempted list of cases that cannot be subject to withdrawal. The verdict also warned the Government authorities that if withdrawal of prosecutions in the context of serious crimes including crime against humanity, genocide, war crime, organized crimes, crimes against women and children, and crimes against State and public interest is allowed, the State system will be shattered with impunity and anarchy.

Expressing serious concern about the criminalization of politics and politicization of crimes, the Court clarified that the Section 29 of the State Cases Act cannot be utilized to fulfil petty purpose of protecting partition leaders and activists from criminal accountability. Likewise, the Supreme Court, with a view to fill in the gaps of law and ensure uniformity in the application of the case withdrawal clause, issued a set of judicial guidelines aimed at strengthening the protection against arbitrary withdrawal of prosecution.

In addition to setting up the guidelines and criteria, the Supreme Court ordered the Government to factor the guidelines into the Procedures and Standards Relating to Withdrawal of Criminal Cases, 1998. Giving an effect to the judicial order, the Government, subsequently, revised the Policy Guidelines and Procedures in Relation to Withdrawal of Criminal Charges to exclude the serious crimes from the scope of the withdrawal and set further criteria to regulate the process of withdrawing case.

3.2 Securing Criminalization of Serious Human Rights Violation Including Disappearance and Torture

The lack of criminalization of serious human rights violations, such as genocide, crimes against humanity, torture, and enforced disappearance, in view of the international human rights and humanitarian treaties to which Nepal is a party remains a key barrier in ensuring accountability for human rights violations committed during the armed conflict. This has attracted numerous judicial interventions including in relation to securing necessary enactments criminalizing serious human rights violations including enforced disappearance and torture as specific criminal offences under Nepali law and remove barriers for prosecution of such offences (Bowcott 2015).

The *Rajaram Dhakal v. Office of the Prime Minister* and others were the first such litigation which raised the issue of criminalization (Petition 2002). The Supreme Court was called upon to order the Government for enacting necessary law to implement the Geneva Conventions to which Nepal is a party. Stressing the need of a specific legislation implementing the Conventions, the Supreme Court directed the Government to formulate a national legislation giving effect to the four Geneva Conventions. Similarly, in the *Rabindra Dhakal* case, the Supreme Court categorically directed the Government to criminalize enforced disappearance in accordance with the UN International Convention for the Protection of All Persons from Enforced Disappearance, and other international standards (Supreme Court 2007a, b, c). Through its interpretation, the Supreme Court also recognized that the legislation criminalizing enforced disappearance would have a retrospective effect so as to ensure that impunity would not be available to those involved in cases of enforced disappearance committed during the armed conflict.

The continued lack of a legislation criminalizing torture was also brought to the Supreme Court's scrutiny through *Rabindra Ghimire v. Office of the Prime Minister* (Petition 2005a, b). The Supreme Court, in this case, took the Government's inaction towards filling the gap in existing laws seriously and directed the

Government to criminalize torture in line with its obligations under the UN Convention Against Torture and Other Cruel, Inhuman or Degrading Treatment or Punishment (CAT). The Government has recently introduced in the Parliament a bill providing for criminalization of torture, which is under the process of committee deliberations in the Parliament. However, the bill has been criticized by Civil Society Organizations including for its failure to comply with the definition of torture under CAT, penal provisions, and statutory limitation clause not consistent with the gravity of crime (Ju-Ri Nepal & INSEC 2016).

Against the backdrop that the Government did not take genuine steps to enact the criminalization-related legislation as required by the stated Supreme Court decisions, *in Madhav Kumar Basnet and others for JuRI-Nepal v. Government of Nepal*, was called upon again to scrutinize the governmental lethargy towards enacting laws and issue necessary order to hold the Government accountable for not implementing its previous decisions (Petition 2012a, b, c, d). The Supreme Court once again ordered the Government to respect its previous decisions by enacting laws for implementation of the conventions including through criminalizing war crimes, enforced disappearance, and torture. The Supreme Court, in *Suman Adhikari and others v. Government of Nepal*, also expressed serious concern about the lack of the national legislation criminalizing serious violations including enforced disappearance and torture and directed the Government to enact necessary laws (Petition 2013a, b, c).

Similarly, in *Sapana Pardhan Malla for FWLD v. the Government of Nepal and Raju Prasad Chapagai and others for JuRI-Nepal v. Government of Nepal,* the Supreme Court stressed the need to revise the provision on 35-day statute of limitation concerning rape in view of the international human rights obligations (Petitions 2004, 2013a, b, c). Noting that the statutory limitation on rape served as a barrier to access effective remedy and reparations by victims, the Court directed the Government to fix flawed Section 11 of Chapter 14 of the *MulukiAin* (General Code) *2020* in the light of international human rights obligations of Nepal. Subsequently, while the Gender Equality Act amended the General Code provision to provide for 6-month statute of limitation, the statute of limitation proposed for rape cases in Section 225(2) under the Penal Code Bill is one year. Unless scraped the existing prescription and provided for non-application of statutory limitation to prosecute sexual offences committed during the armed conflict, statutory limitation would remain as a barrier in accessing justice.

3.3 *Ordering the Government to Make Arrangement for Interim Relief and Reparations for the Victims*

There are several instances where the Supreme Court has exercised its extraordinary jurisdiction to protect and promote the right of the victim of human rights violations to adequate reparations. Key of the judicial interventions in this regard relates to providing interim relief and compensation to the victims, and enacting law to require authorities provides compensation and restitution. For the first time in the post-conflict context, the Supreme Court, in *Bhim Prakash Oli vs. His Majesty Government of Nepal*, was called upon to consider the issue of compensation for the conflict victims. The petitioners had demanded for a clear judicial order to the Government for bringing relief and compensation schemes into the ambit of rule of law by setting legal standards and other necessary arrangements (Petition 2005a, b). In response to this case, the Supreme Court directed the Government to "formulate clear legislation and make appropriate arrangements provide services and facilities to conflict victims" respecting the right to equality and non-discrimination guaranteed under the 1990 Constitution.

Rabindra Dhakal v. Government of Nepal is another important verdict of the Supreme Court in terms of developing and shaping the right to interim relief and compensation. In this case, the Supreme Court not only ordered the Government to make necessary legal arrangement to provide adequate compensation and relief to the victims of enforced disappearance and their families, but also issued an order of mandamus to compel the Government for awarding compensation ranging from Rs. 100,000 to Rs. 200,000 to the families of Chakra Bahadur Katuwal, Rabindra Dhakal, Bipin Bhandari, Dil Bahadur Rai, and other disappeared persons who are the subject of Supreme Court cases.

Regarding the State obligation towards ensuring the right to compensation and reparations, the Supreme Court observed that "....the State has the obligation to provide immediate relief and adequate compensation to the victims of serious violations of human rights. On the grounds deliberated above, it is found that the persons stated in the petitions were disappeared during the time of the conflict and it has been established that the State has a special obligation to such persons. It is now appropriate to provide interim, immediate relief to the victims, in light of the physical and mental torture, as well as economic loss, that the families of the victims have suffered during their search and attempts to obtain justice". In coming to its conclusion, the Supreme Court not only referred to the Constitutional provisions of Nepal but also referred to the decisions of foreign courts and regional human rights courts, international instruments concerning human rights to which Nepal is a party, and documents and proposals issued by the United Nations and the international community.

Following its already established judicial stance, the Supreme Court in *Buddhi Bahadur Parja* and *Kale Tamang* also ordered the Government for enactment of a separate and comprehensive law to provide for compensation to the victims without further delay (Petitions 2006a, b). In a separate case, *Liladhar Bhandari and others v. Government of Nepal*, a group of displaced people brought a strategic litigation to the Supreme Court for an order of mandamus to obligate the Government to take immediate steps to ensure the return of their properties seized by the Maoist insurgents during the conflict. Similarly, the Court was called upon for payment of an appropriate compensation against damages incurred due to the deprivation to use such properties (Petition 2007a, b). Linking the right to life to various other economic, social, and cultural rights, the Supreme Court observed that in order to obtain respect for the life of a person it is important to protect the right to property, and the right to profession and occupation which are the basis of livelihood.

The Supreme Court not only upheld the State's mandatory obligation to protect individual property but also ordered the formation of a five-member committee for return of properties with the representation of the victim community, law enforcement agencies, and political activists at district level where the petitioner resides and in districts where there is a similar problem of seizure of property. The court also ordered the Government to ensure that the property be returned through the committee to the actual owners within three months of the receipt of this order, the loss, depreciation, and loss of income from the property thus seized be assessed and the compensation be awarded to them as demanded. The Government was also ordered to set up a fund for providing compensation and relief to those who have become victims due to damage caused by seizure of the property (Petition 2007a, b).

3.4 Holding Government of Nepal Accountable to Develop a System of Vetting

In view of the promotion of security officials implicated in human rights violations at the absence of a transparent selection process and a fair vetting mechanism, the Supreme Court of Nepal recognized vetting as one of the measures of transitional justice in a number of cases including *Rajendra Dhakal v. the Government of Nepal, Liladhar Bhandari v. the Government of Nepal* and *Sunil Ranjan Singh v. the Government of Nepal.*

In order to secure institutional reform, the Supreme Court focused on the need of a new legislation as well as certain temporary guidelines. The promotion of police officer Kuber Singh Rana, one of the suspects in the disappearance and extrajudicial killing of five students in Dhanusa district during the conflict, to the post of Assistant Inspector General (AIG) of Nepal Police was made in June 2011. A group of lawyers had brought a strategic litigation *Sunil Ranjan Singh & Ors. v. Government of Nepal & Ors,* in the Supreme Court of Nepal demanding for withdrawal of the Government decision to promote him and send him pending investigations into the allegations against him (Petition 2010). The Court refused to invalidate the Government decision to promote him stating that there was no reasonable legal ground to halt his promotion as Rana had already been promoted once despite allegations of human rights violations. However, the Supreme Court instructed the Government to formulate necessary law on vetting and adopt a temporary guideline for vetting public officials while considering new appointments, promotions, or transfers until that law is formulated.

The court observed that it would be appropriate to vet the individuals for position of authority involving public accountability in order to create an environment conducive to sustainable peace and justice. Recognizing the vetting as a measure to ensure non-repetition of human rights violation in future, the Court stated that the setting up a system is pertinent to test the eligibility of the candidates before deciding on their appointment, transfer, and promotion. Though the law to this effect has not been enacted yet, the law governing the establishment and mandate of Truth and Reconciliation Commission (TRC) and Commission on Investigation of Disappeared Persons (COID) contains a provision mandating the commissions to make recommendations for institutional reform.

On 25 April 2014, the Parliament of Nepal passed the Act on Commission on Investigation of Disappeared Persons, Truth and Reconciliation, 2071 (2014), to create two Commissions: the Truth and Reconciliation Commission and the Commission on Investigation of Disappeared Persons. On 21 May 2014, the Act was published in the Official Gazette.

3.5 *Outlawing Amnesty for Serious Crimes*

The "Commission on Investigation of Disappeared Person, Truth and Reconciliation Ordinance—2069 (2013)" (the Ordinance) was promulgated by the President of Nepal on 14 March 2013. The Ordinance not only elaborated the powers and function of the TRC but also provided for amnesty. Article 23(2) stated that "Notwithstanding anything contained in Subsection (1), serious crimes which lack sufficient reasons and grounds for granting amnesty following the investigation of the Commission, including rape, shall not be recommended for amnesty by the Commission". Two strategic litigation cases *JuRI-Nepal and others v. Government of Nepal and Ram Kumar Bhandari and Others v. Government of Nepal* were filed in the Supreme Court challenging the sated amnesty clause as well as other provisions dealing with reconciliation and prosecution (Petitions 2012a, b, c, d).

Responding to these cases, the Supreme Court handed down a landmark judgment embracing the evolving understanding of international law that stands against impunity for serious crimes including genocide, crime against humanity, war crime, torture, enforced disappearance, and some forms of sexual violence. The Supreme Court held that any measures of impunity including amnesty that eliminate accountability for those responsible for serious human rights violations are impermissible. The Court explicitly ruled out the idea of empowering the Truth and Reconciliation Commission to recommend amnesty for those responsible for serious crimes including enforced disappearance. The verdict also requires that when considering amnesty for other crimes, genuine consent of the victim be sought. Though Court did not strike down the Clause 23(2) of the Ordinance, it ordered the Government to amend the Ordinance to ensure impermissibility of amnesty for serious crimes.

The verdict also gives clear guidance on the consultative and participatory process of making transitional justice-related law by requiring the Government to form an expert team consisting of representatives from victim groups, petitioning organizations, and human rights law experts. Such a team was envisioned to offer expert opinion including in terms of setting standards in relation to amnesty.

In ordering the Government for enactment of transitional justice legislation consistent with international human rights standards and previous decision of the Supreme Court, the Court observed that "If amnesty is granted for the perpetrators involved in crimes of serious nature and grave violations of human rights having them forcibly linked with political conflicts, not only will impunity be promoted but the rule of law will also not be maintained. The Commission may not be conferred with uncontrolled powers of granting amnesty in all type of crimes depriving of the right of victims of serious crimes to get effective justice from independent and competent authority (Petition 2012a, b)".

Referring to its previous verdict (Supreme Court 2007a, b, c), the court stated that "the State cannot ignore its obligation of finding out the actual position of the disappeared persons and making their condition public; of taking actions against those officials found to be guilty and providing for appropriate relief to the victims and that no amnesty can be granted in cases of serious cases". Identifying the types of human rights violations that could not be subject to any amnesty under Nepali Constitution, the Court went on to say that "No amnesty or pardon may be granted against any fundamental right including the right to life, right to equality, right against torture…."

Pursuant to this verdict, the Government created an 11 Members Expert Task Force mandating to draft two separate bills. Accordingly, the Task Force submitted its report to the Government suggesting three different bills relating to TRC, Disappearance Commission, and criminalization of enforced disappearance in view of the Supreme Court verdict together with suggestions and views collected during the consultations (Report 2013). The TRC bill suggested by the Expert Task Force contains a provision that clearly excluded serious crimes including enforced disappearance, torture, extrajudicial killing, and rape from the ambit of amnesty. However, setting aside the Task Force's recommendations, the Government, based on the cross-parties negotiation, introduced a bill with a view to replace the Ordinance that contained an amnesty clause (Article 26(2)) closer to the provision under the Ordinance. Without fixing the flaws of the bill, the Legislature-Parliament enacted the Act on Commission on Investigation of Disappeared Persons, Truth and Reconciliation, 2071 (2014), to create two Commissions: the Truth and Reconciliation Commission and the Commission on Investigation of Disappeared Persons. Giving the TRC broad powers to recommend amnesties, Section 26(2) provided that "[notwithstanding whatsoever mentioned in Subsection (1), the Commission shall not recommend for amnesty to the perpetrators involved in rape and other crimes of serious nature in which the Commission follows the investigation and does not find sufficient reasons and grounds for amnesty". Similarly, Section 26(4) authorized the Commission to recommend amnesties for "gross violations of human rights committed during the course of armed conflict" where a perpetrator submits an application stating the acts committed, accepts repentance, agrees to apologize, and commits not to repeat such acts in future. Section 25(2) excluded taking legal action against perpetrators "who have reconciled with victims pursuant to Section 22" or "who are recommended for amnesty pursuant to Section 26".

A group of 234 victims of the conflict-era human rights violations came together and jointly filed a PIL, *Suman Adhikari and others v. Government of Nepal*, challenging the amnesty-related provisions of the Act again (Petition 2013a, b, c). The Supreme Court issued its verdict stating that amnesty cannot be granted for serious crimes including enforced disappearance. Based on the "doctrine of severability", a portion—"...in which the Commission follows the investigation and does not find sufficient reasons and grounds for amnesty"—of Subclause 2 of Clause 26 of the law was scraped by the Court to put serious crimes out of the scope of amnesty. By virtue of the judicial verdict, the Subclause 2 of the Section 26 has been ended up with the following language: "Notwithstanding whatsoever mentioned in Subsection (1), the Commission shall not recommend for amnesty to the perpetrators involved in rape and other crimes of serious nature".

Though the Supreme Court held impermissibility of amnesty for serious crimes, the court did not offer a list of such crimes. It is therefore necessary to go for the amendment of the Act to provide a clear list of the offences that cannot be amnestied. The TRC formed under the Act has also suggested for the amendment of the Act including for defining serious crimes (Interim Report 2015). However, there has not been any concrete step taken on behalf of the Government to address the concerns in relation to amnesty.

3.6 Recognizing the Complementary Between Criminal Justice System and Transitional Justice Mechanisms

There are a number of instances where the authorities referred to the Interim Constitution's provision aimed at the establishment of transitional justice mechanisms to bypass the duty to investigate and prosecute the human rights violations (OHCHR 2011). Against this backdrop, the Supreme Court considered the issues of interrelationship between the criminal trials and the transitional justice mechanism in a number of cases. One of the main messages emerging from recent jurisprudence is that the establishment of transitional justice mechanisms must not displace the role of the criminal justice system; rather, they should complement each other.

Ruling on a case involving one of the Maoists leaders, Agni Sapkota, the Supreme Court stated that the promise for establishing transitional justice mechanisms cannot be taken as a pretext to justify non-cooperation to criminal investigation into in the extrajudicial killing of Arjun Lama (Supreme Court 2011).

This position is reinforced by a number of other subsequent decisions of the Supreme Court. For instances, in *JuRI-Nepal v. Governemnt of Nepal*, the Supreme Court observed that the transitional justice mechanisms are not substitution of the criminal justice system. Most importantly, examining the power of the TRC under Section 13(2) of the TRC Act to inquire into cases under consideration in courts "*in consultation with the court*", examining the structure of Section 13(2), the Supreme Court in *Suman Adikari and others v. Govenment of Nepal*, clarified that this power cannot be read to mean that the courts are compelled to surrender the cases under consideration to the Commissions. The Court further elucidated that the Commission does not replace the jurisdiction of the Courts; rather, the Commission can only use the case files as a relevant source or reference during the course of its inquiry into the violations.

The Supreme Court also observed:

> ... the Commission formed under the Act cannot displace a judicial body, nor can it replace judicial functions or provide for an alternative to judicial functions. In fact, the Commission in itself merely provides assistance to the judicial process. The resultant cases of serious violation of human rights, filed on the basis of the truth and evidence unearthed by the Commission will ultimately be settled by the Courts and thus it is necessary to differentiate between a temporary body established to help the judicial process and the judiciary as a permanent organ of the State. Hence, it needs to be understood accordingly.

In another instance where the Attorney General instructed his subordinate Government Attorney to postpone investigation and prosecution of those involved in extrajudicial killing of a journalist, Dekendra Thapa, the Supreme Court invalidated the Attorney General's circular to the Government Attorney Office of Dailekh District and directed the Attorney General to let the investigation take its course smoothly. In issuing its ruling, the Court relied on the same logic that the transitional justice institutions can only complement the criminal justice system (Supreme Court 2014).

3.7 Holding Government Accountable for Investigation and Prosecution of Violations

Though the commitment for putting an end to culture of impunity was reflected in the CPA, there was a growing problem of refusing to register FIR and the reluctance for investigating into the FIR those registered. There has rarely been successful prosecution of a serious human rights violation committed during or after the conflict. There are several instances where the victims had to invoke the writ jurisdiction of the Supreme Court and Appellate Courts. In a number of cases, the Supreme Court and the Appellate Courts intervened positively to hold the authorities accountable for fulfilling the duty to investigate and prosecute the human rights violations.

For instances, in *Devi Sunuwar v. Government of Nepal,* the Supreme Court was called upon *to* issue a writ of Mandamus ordering the authorities to investigate FIR for murder of Maina Sunuwar, a 15-year-old girl who was allegedly tortured to death while in the custody of the Army in 2004 (Petition 2007a, b). Responding to the case, the Supreme Court issued *mandamus* requiring the investigating authorities to complete criminal investigation into the case within three months.

Also, the court ordered the registrar of the SC to provide the petitioner access to court-martial judgment and other documents in relation to court-martial proceedings undertaking. As required by the judicial order, in January 2008, the District Government Attorney's Office filed a charge sheet accusing four Nepalese Army officers of the intentional homicide of Maina Sunuwar. In reaching to the conclusion, the Court held that it is the duty of the Police Office to prosecute the case as per the laws after conducting investigation effectively. Highlighting the serious nature of the involvement of Army Officials in the killing of a minor girl, the Court held that the investigation of such matter should be conducted in a responsible manner as well as in a speedy manner. The Court also held that the killing of a civilian should be dealt with in an ordinary court and also implicitly rejected the double jeopardy argument put forward by the Government side referring to the court-martial proceeding initiated against those implicated in her killing.

In *Rabindra Dhakal Case*, the Supreme Court recognized the obligations of the Government under the Constitution and international law to investigate and prosecute such offences. Taking seriously the absence of investigation initiative, the Supreme Court established its own Detainees Investigation Task Force and employed it to probe into cases of disappearances raised in the case. Based on the report of the Task Force, the Court delivered a landmark judgment containing several orders including for requiring the police and prosecutors to initiate criminal investigation and prosecutions.

The issue of failure of the Attorney General's Office to guide the police in investigations was raised in the case of *Reena Rasaili*, who was allegedly raped and killed by security personnel in February 2004 (Supreme Court 2007a, b, c). The Supreme Court's December 2009 order requiring the authorities to proceed with investigations resulted in the arrest of one suspect (an army deserter) in September 2010. In another case of a 17-year-old *Subhadra Chaulagain* who was allegedly killed by a group of soldiers in February 2004, the Supreme Court ordered the police and the respective Office of the Government Attorney to conduct a prompt investigation (Supreme Court 2009). The Court found that the authorities had completely overlooked the investigation including by failing to give necessary direction to the police personnel. There are also several similar cases, where the Supreme Court ordered the authorities to conduct investigation and prosecution of violations as appropriate. Not only the Supreme Court, the Appellate Court also held the authorities accountable for bypassing the legal duty to investigate into crimes (NJA 2016).

3.8 Promoting Independence and Impartiality of Transitional Justice Mechanisms

The Supreme Court activism through strategic litigation not only checked the executive and legislative actions that go against the very idea of transitional justice but also concerned about how the transitional justice process is carried out, whether the credibility of transitional justice mechanisms is ensured.

In its 18 June 2007 decision responding to *Rabindra Dhakal case*, the Supreme Court for the first time alerted the Government that there should be an independent probe into disappearance cases (Supreme Court 2007a, b, c). The court pointed out the need of investigating cases of enforced disappearance by creating a separate commission of inquiry and stated that "it is necessary to adopt as guidelines the Criteria for Commissions on Enforced Disappearance, developed under the auspices of the United Nations Office of the High Commission for Human Rights". The court finally ordered the Government to enact a law establishing a commission of inquiry on disappearances, using as guidance the international standards summarized by OHCHR-Nepal in its Criteria for Commissions on Enforced Disappearance with sufficient powers to investigate conflict-related disappearances.

Referring to *Rabindra Dhakal decision,* the Supreme Court in *JuRI-Nepal v. Government of Nepal* also reinforced the importance of the independence and competence of the transitional justice mechanisms (Petition 2014). Furthermore, the Court prescribed a list of criterion to check the longstanding trend of defeating the *raison d'etre* of the commission by making arbitrary appointments. According to the judicial prescription, those who supported the armed rebellion or were involved in suppressing it and those who have negative track record of violating human rights are ineligible for the commission.

Concerning over the Act on Commission on Investigation of Disappeared Persons, Truth and Reconciliation, 2071 (2014), the issue of independence of the transitional justice commissions was also raised in the *Suman Adhikari and others v. Government of Nepal* (Petition 2015). However, the Supreme Court found that the provisions dealing with appointment of commissioners and terms and conditions of the commission under the Act at par with evolving standards and good practices concerning transitional justice. However, the Court also expressed its confidence that the commissioners appointed under the Act would not themselves act in such a way to jeopardize the independence and impartiality of the commissions.

4 Concluding Observations

Together with the national and international legal protection of a plethora of rights enforceable on Nepal, the judiciary of Nepal remains empowered to play a vital role in shaping and developing the domestic legal regime on human rights through interpretation of the law into line with relevant international human rights standards and principles.

The review of the Supreme Court decisions above illustrates that the strategic litigation has been instrumental in terms of guiding and shaping transitional justice process in Nepal. Most of the judicial responses to the issues taken up through strategic litigation have significantly contributed in taking forward post-conflict justice initiative into line with the international human rights standards and best practices. Based on the review of the decisions, it appears that key of the Supreme Court jurisprudence promoting accountability for serious human rights violations committed during the armed conflict basically includes the following:

- Amnesty is impermissible for those involved in committing serious crimes including enforced disappearance;
- Power to withdraw criminal charges cannot be exercised arbitrarily to protect those responsible for serious crimes;
- Transitional justice mechanisms do not replace or displace the criminal justice system; rather, the temporary mechanisms of transitional justice are supposed to complement the criminal justice system;
- Prompt and effective investigation of the violations of rights protected under the national Constitution and the international treaties to which Nepal is a party is enforceable duty of the authorities;
- Victims of the human rights violations have right to have claim interim relief and reparations;
- Criminalization of serious violations of the international human rights law and international humanitarian laws is not a choice of the State;
- System of vetting or institutional reform measures should be in place to ensure non-repetition of violations in future.

The Supreme Court of Nepal may also be credited including for adopting constructive and victims-sensitive approach, frequent reference to international treaty provisions and jurisprudence developed by international and foreign courts, and issuance of judicial guidelines to fill gaps in the law and recognizing the interconnectedness of the right to live with dignity and other human rights.

However, it does not mean that the judiciary has always acted positively. There also appears to be a lack of uniformity in terms of its understanding the transitional justice vis-a-vis criminal justice system. Similarly, the court failed to become innovative in terms of addressing the vetting-related issues simply referring to the gaps of law. It could have followed the approach of issuing judicial guidelines in order necessary to fill in the legal gaps.

The Attorney General of Nepal is also entrusted with the Constitutional mandate to monitor whether the case laws are complied with. However, the compliance of judicial decisions continues to remain challenging. The instances where the Supreme Court has made repeated interventions for compelling the Government to act towards enacting national laws criminalizing serious violations including enforced disappearance and torture illustrate the gravity of the problem of non-compliance. Even when noticing the obvious defiance of its orders, the Supreme Court did not take any proactive measures (e.g. contempt proceeding, continuous mandamus, or supervisory order) towards correcting such trend.

A recent study undertaken by National Judicial Academy in collaboration of International Commission of Jurists illustrates the poor implementation status of the court decisions in the context of transitional justice and accountability. The underlying causes for the lack of judicial compliance that the study has unpacked, among others, include the lack of political will, misinterpretation of the CPA clause providing for withdrawal of politically induced criminal prosecutions, politicization of transitional justice agenda, misconception about interface of criminal justice and transitional justice, ineffective role of civil societies, the victims communities and National Human Rights Commission, lack of clarity about implementing and monitoring agency, and lack of a provision of accountability against deliberate defiance of the decisions. If non-compliance with judicial decisions continues to remain, it not only hinders the transitional justice process but also risks diminishing the public trust towards justice system and thereby deterring the victims to seek justice within the country, rather opting for redressing avenues out of the country.

Having said that, I put forward the following suggestions towards ensuring that the transitional justice process is into line with the Supreme Court jurisprudence and the international standards and best practices:

- As ordained by the Supreme Court, serious attention should be paid towards enacting national laws criminalizing serious violations including enforced disappearance, torture, and other serious violations of international human rights and international humanitarian law and thereby secure national legal capacity to investigate and prosecute serious crimes prohibited under international law.
- Mindful of the supreme court decisions and the applicable international legal standards and practices amend exiting transitional justice legislation to fix its flaws in the context of definitions of serious crimes, amnesty, reconciliation, prosecution, and interface of transitional justice mechanisms and the criminal justice system.
- Promote awareness among the victims' groups and other stakeholders on the strategic use of judicial process to combat impunity and promote accountability as well as on the decisions handed down and jurisprudence developed by the Supreme Court and Appellate Courts.
- Consideration might be given to utilizing ongoing legislative reform initiative in the context of implementing the new Constitution as an opportunity to harmonize the national legal framework with the case laws as well as international human rights treaties.
- As the Truth and Reconciliation Commission and the Commission on the Disappeared Persons are already in operation, they not only should fully adhere the supreme court rulings that guide the transitional justice process but also play proactive role towards promoting compliance of the judicial decisions by others.
- Judiciary should also consider taking innovative approaches such as continuous mandamus and supervisory order in the context of the cases involving greater public interest and concern.
- Strategic use of lower court's jurisdiction should also be promoted so as to enable the victims of the conflict to get their grievances addressed at the district level.
- Consideration should be given towards promoting Parliamentary oversight system as well as the oversight of National Human Rights Commission over the transitional justice.

References

Bowcott O (2015) Nepalese Colonel Faces Torture Trial in UK, The Guardian. Available at http://goo.gl/Z5MkTv, (27 February 2015)
Chapagai RP (2009) National application of international human rights law: a Nepali perspective, NJA (National Judicial Academy). Law J vol 3, Kathmandu
Chapagai RP (2014) Review of the legislative framework and jurisprudence concerning the right to adequate food. Office of the Food and Agriculture of the United Nations, Rome. http://goo.gl/L9j22F
Constitution of the Kingdom of Nepal 2015 (1959 AD) was promulgated. http://goo.gl/uRYfqt
Hachhethu K (1990) Transition to democracy in Nepal negotiations behind constitution making. http://goo.gl/nmuQ8q
Law Reporter, Nepal 2065 (2008 AD) No. 9, p 1108
NJA (2016) A Study on Implementation Status of the Supreme Court and Appellate Court Decisions and Orders concerning Impunity, Transitional Justice and Accountability, documents 18 Appellate Court Orders requiring the authorities to file FIR or proceed criminal investigation as provided under the State Cases Act and the Regulation
OHCHR, Nepal Conflict Report (2012), pp 112, 117, 152, 180
Office of the High Commissioner for Human Rights (OHCHR) (2012) Nepal Conflict Report, pp 36–39. http://www.ohchr.org/Documents/Countries/NP/OHCHR_Nepal_Conflict_Report2012.pdf
OHCHR-Nepal (2011) Legal Opinion, 'The relationship between Transitional Justice mechanisms and the Criminal Justice system Can conflict-related human rights and humanitarian law violations and abuses be deferred or suspended on the basis of commitments to establish a Truth and Reconciliation Commission?', pp 1–3. Available at http://goo.gl/E2YUPb
OHCHR-Nepal's Legal Opinion on Remedies and Rights Revoked: Case withdrawal for serious crimes in Nepal, 2011. http://goo.gl/33hxhn
Petition, Writ (2002) No 2942 of the year 2059, decision dated 9 January 2004
Petition, Writ (2004) No 3393 of 2061(BS), decision dated 11 July 2008
Petition, Writ (2005a) No 3219 of the year 2062, decision dated 17 December 2007
Petition, Writ (2005b) No 3394 of the Year 2061, decision dated 10 February 2006
Petition, Writ (2006a) No 3348 of the Year 2063, decision dated 12 May 2008
Petition, Writ (2006b) No 3348 of the Year 2063, decision dated 12 May 2008
Petition, Writ (2007a) No 0863 of the year 2064, decision dated 7 December 2008
Petition, Writ (2007b) No 434 of the Year 2007, decision dated 18 September 2008
Petition, Writ (2009) No 1333 of the Year 2066, decision dated 2069-01-05
Petition, Writ (2010) No 067-wo-1198 of the year 2067, decision dated 13 August 2010
Petition, Writ (2012a) No 0057 of the year 2069 (BS), decision dated 2070-9-18(BS)
Petition, Writ (2012b) No 0057 of the year 2069(BS), decision dated 2 January 2014
Petition, Writ (2012c) No 069-WS-0057 & of the Year 2069(BS), decision dated decision dated 2 January 2014
Petition, Writ (2012d) No 069-WS-0058 & of the Year 2069(BS), decision dated 2 January 2014
Petition, Writ (2013a) No 0050 of the year 2070(BS), decision dated 26 February 2015
Petition, Writ (2013b) No 711 of the Year 2070 (B.S.), decision dated 10 June 2015
Petition, Writ (2013c) No 0050 of the year 2070(BS), decision dated 26 February 2015 Report, Interim (2015), Truth and Reconciliation Commission
Petition, Writ (2014) No 0057 of the year 2069(BS), decision dated 2 January 2014
Petition, Writ (2015) No 0050 of the year 2070(BS), decision dated 26 February 2015
Report (2013) Expert Task Force mandated to draft bills concerning Truth and Reconciliation Commission and Commission on Inquiry into Disappeared People submitted to the Ministry of Peace Reconstruction, dated 2070-12-20 (BS)
Submissions to the Parliament by Justice and Rights Institute (JuRI-Nepal) and Informal Sector Service Center (INSEC), April 2016

Supreme Court (1994) *Government of Nepal* v *Dil Bahadur Lama and others*, NKP 2051, vol 7, p 504; Criminal Appeal No. 4940 of the year 2051(BS), 18 August 1994

Supreme Court (2007a) *Government of Nepal* v *Devendra Mandal and others*, Criminal Appeal No. 0197 of the year 2064(BS), 3 September 2007

Supreme Court (2007b) *Rabindra Prasad Dhakal and Advocate Rajendra Prasad Dhakal and Ors v Nepal and Ors*, Decision on Petition for Habeas Corpus and Mandamus, Nepal Law Review 49(2), Decision No. 7817P, 169, ILDC 756 (NP 2007)

Supreme Court (2007c) *Rasaili* v. *Government of Nepal*, Supreme Court of Nepal, order of December 14, 2009 in Writ No. 0339/2064 (2007)

Supreme Court (2009) *Kedar Chaulagain v. Kavre District Police Office and District Attorney's Office*, Supreme Court of Nepal, Chief Justice Anupraj Sharma and Justice Ram Kumar Prasad Shah, Writ No. 064-WO-0339, 14 December 2009

Supreme Court (2011) *Sushil Pyakurel and Others* v. *Prime Minister Jhalanath Khanal and Others*, Writ No 1094 of the year 2068, decision dated 21 June 2011

Supreme Court (2014) *Govinda Sharma Bandi* v. *Attorney General Mr. Mukti Pradhan*, Office of the Attorney General, Writ petition no 04740 of the Year 2069, decision dated 2 April 2014

The Constitution of Nepal, 2019 (1962 AD)

Author Biographies

Mr. Raju Prasad Chapagai is a Constitutional and Human Rights lawyer based in Kathmandu (Nepal). He currently leads human rights NGO called JuRI-Nepal and is particularly engaged in litigating human rights and transitional justice issues. Previously, he served as Legal Advisor in UN-OHCHR office in Kathmandu during 2007–2012. He was nominated by the Government of Nepal in 2014 to serve as a Member of an Expert Task Force entrusted with the responsibility to advise on formulation of draft laws in relation to Truth & Reconciliation Commission (TRC) and Commission of Inquiry on Enforced Disappearance (COIED). He has also served as an Adjunct Professor in Kathmandu School of Law.

Mr. Pankaj Kumar Karn is Kathmandu based Constitutional and Human Rights lawyer and has successfully litigated a wide range of Constitutional and human rights issues in the Supreme Court of Nepal since the last 17 years. He also served USAID funded Nepal Government Citizen Partnership Project as Local Governance Advisor. He is General Secretary of Public Defender Society Nepal, JuRI- Nepal and Community Mediator Society Nepal. He has also served Pro-Public (Forum for Protection of Public Interest) as a Regional Director. He completed his Masters of Comparative Laws (M.C.L.) from University of Delhi.

Chapter 10
Contribution to Peace and Security in the World: Sri Lankan Perspective

Muthukuda A. Dona Shiroma Jeeva S. Niriella

1 Introduction

Terrorism is an unconventional crime which is a serious threat to the peace and security in the world. No one can deny the fact that people and their properties were destroyed at massive scale which finally extended to the severe devastation of the natural environment due to terrorism/terrorist attacks. Some examples for such attacks are as follows: on 11 September 2001, the disastrous events which happened in U.S. in New York city Arlington County, Virginia, and Shanksville resulting in the deaths of 3,000 people; on 23 November 2006, the brutal attack which involved a series of car bombs and mortar attacks targeting the Shiite Muslim slums in the city of Baghdad, where around 215 people were killed while 257 were wounded; on 11 July 2006, a series of seven bomb blasts which happened on the Suburban Railway in Mumbai, resuling in the death of 209 people and 714 other were wounding; on 6 March 2007, the attack which was committed against Shia Muslims, who were on their way to a pilgrim in Al Hillah and lives of nearly 200 people were lost; on 14 August 2007, four suicide bombs which exploded in the towns of Yazidi and Jazeera led to the death of 796 and 1562 people were injured. Therefore, each and every country has a prime (moral, ethical and legal) responsibility to take all necessary measures to address this issue and to combat this crime in order to ensure peace and security both nationally and internationally.

This chapter intends to critically evaluate the security laws in the field of criminal justice in the context of combating terrorism, and also to evaluate the contribution of those laws in ensuring peace and security in the country and in the world as a whole. This chapter first discusses the theoretical definitions of peace, security and terrorism, to suggest that terrorism is a crime which intimidates peace

M.A.D.S.J.S. Niriella (✉)
Department of Public and International Law, Faculty of Law,
University of Colombo, No. 433/1, Dalupotha, Negombo, Colombo, Sri Lanka
e-mail: jeevaniriella@gmail.com

J.L. Kaul and A. Jha (eds.), *Shifting Horizons of Public International Law*,
https://doi.org/10.1007/978-81-322-3724-2_10

and security and negative peace is a subdivision of positive peace. It further analyses Sri Lanka's contribution to international treaty law on peace and security to assess the responsibility of having strong security laws for combating terrorism. Next, this chapter appraises how the security laws in the criminal justice system in Sri Lanka efficiently facilitate to combat terrorism. Some specific laws such as the Prevention of Terrorism Act, Public Security Ordinance and Emergency Regulations, that are directly relevant to this topic are extensively examined, to argue that the term 'efficacy' does not stand for, sending people to jail/punishing people at large-scale, but the ability to combat this crime without violating the human/fundamental rights of accused persons and contain adequate safeguards against misuse of security laws.

2 Peace and Security Versus Terrorism: Theoretical Definitions Under International Treaty Law

2.1 Peace

'Peace' means a state of quiet or tranquility which is free from disturbance or agitation. In common usage, the term 'peace' is often associated with absence of violence/war or conflicts. Therefore, it may be claimed that violence-free or conflict/war-free situation reflects a peaceful situation in a society/country. Today, the meaning of the term 'peace' cannot be confined to the above said definition. It is embraced with different subtexts depending on the context in which this word is used. As Galtung says, peace could be identified theoretically under two categories, namely, negative peace and positive peace. According to him, negative peace means the absence of conflict/war or violence and positive peace refers to the presence of social, political, legal, environmental and economic justice (Galtung 1964, 1996). It is true in the present scenario that peace denotes a wider description than the absence of physical war, and it is not wrong to describe negative peace as an area which is located within positive peace. According to Kofi Annan, peace is necessarily connected to security (Annan 2001; Shy and Collier 2007). He further says that peace cannot be understood/existed/sustained without security. Though there is no actual war situation in a country, peace cannot be sustained and assured without guaranteeing security of that country.

2.2 Security

In common usage, security is the degree of resistance to, or protection from, harm. Security applies to any vulnerable and valuable asset, such as a person, organization, community, nation, immovable or movable property. Though the early societies defined security as war- or conflict-free situation, it has now been changed to encompass many areas in normal society. Therefore, security is understood today as the status of being safe including free from danger, risk, poverty, apprehension, fear and injustice. The term security has been extended to the term human security which is very much connected to peace.

The concept of 'human security' came into appear in the international forum in early 1990s, and it was first popularized by the United Nations Development Programme (UNDP). Under this programme, human security was described as freedom from want and fear as the goal of human security. It deeply concerns the protection of people while promoting peace and assuring sustainable development of society. Therefore, it may claim that human security means upholding the existence of social, political, legal, environmental and economic justice and guaranteeing the sustainable development of society. It is further clear in UNDP Human Development Report in 1994 which states that the scope of the human security should be expanded to include economic, food, health, environmental, personal, community and political security. According to Kofi Annan, former Secretary General of the United Nations, in the broader sense, human security embraces far more than the absence of war, conflict or violence and covers many aspect of day-to-day life of a human being such as access to education, health, democracy, human rights, protection from environmental degradation, poverty alleviation, freedom from starvation, violence, want, fear and injustice (Annan 2001). Though the 1994 report introduced a new concept of human security, still it could be argued that where there is war, conflict or violence, the above-mentioned aspect of day-to-day life of human being would be in jeopardy.

2.3 *Terrorism*

Committing violence/war or creating fear in the minds of ordinary people/government is not a new phenomenon, though the term terrorism started to be used in legal and political disciplines recently. As Valerie (2015) says, terrorism is a word which creates a great extent of fear just from its pronunciation. Terrorism is a threat against all civilizations and the whole of humanity in general. It is a serious threat to peace and security at both national and international levels (Kedar 2013). Generally, terrorism means exercising of aggression or in other words use of unlawful force/violence and threats to intimidate or coerce, especially for political purposes. In other words, terrorism means unofficial or unauthorized use of violence and intimidation in the pursuit of political aims. Many scholars describe the term 'terrorism' as actual exercise of violent acts or intimidation by use of violence in any form committed unlawfully to achieve political idea/purpose (Levitt 1986; Skubisseviski 1989; Walter 2003). Though it is difficult to define the term 'terrorism' accurately, what it is and how it is perceived, UN General Assembly Resolution 49/60 adopted on 9th December 1994 and UN Security Council Resolution 1566 in 2004 attempted to describe terrorism in more comprehensive manner. According to the above-mentioned two resolutions, terrorism is a crime committed by a group of persons with the objective of creating a state of grave fear in the general public/legally elected government to achieve an unjustifiable political purpose which is invoked to justify from their point of view.

Another praiseworthy attempt was taken to define terrorism in 2000, by proposing the treaty, the Comprehensive Convention on International Terrorism. This proposed treaty intends to criminalize all forms of international terrorism and denies terrorists, their financiers and supporters access to funds, arms and safe places. According to Article 2(1) of this proposed treaty, any person who commits murder, grievous hurt, severe damage to public or private property, including a place of public use, a State or government facility, a public transportation system, an infrastructure facility or the environment, resulting or likely to result in major economic loss and when the purpose of the conduct, by its nature or context, is to intimidate a population, or to compel a legally elected government or an international organization to do or refrain from doing an act, is considered as terrorist activities. And those unlawful acts should be committed with having the height status of guilty mind: wrongful intention.

It is significant to note that, as some scholars argue, this is a wide definition, which has been criticized for its lack of accuracy (Andreu Guzman 2003). As Guzman states under this definition, terrorism includes not only action causing death or serious bodily injury but also serious damage to public or private property and any damage that is likely to result in major economic loss. This is qualified by a requirement of intent either to intimidate a population or to compel a government or an international organization to do or abstain from doing any act. The threat of any such action, where it is credible or serious, is also an offence, and it is an offence to attempt terrorist action or to contribute to the commission of terrorist offences. Further, this article highlights the tension between security and human rights approaches (Further see Article 15 of ICCPR and Article 7 of ECHR).

In addition to the above-mentioned universal attempts, there are some international instruments that define nearly or almost fifty criminal offences as terrorist activities. Those international instruments are as follows: Convention on Offences and Certain Other Acts Committed on Board Aircraft in 1963 which is considered to be the first international treaty against terrorism which has been acceded by Sri Lanka on 30 May 1978 and started to take effect from 28 August 1978; Convention for the Suppression of Unlawful Seizure of Aircraft in 1970 which has been ratified by Sri Lanka in 1978; Convention for the Suppression of Unlawful Acts against the Safety of Civil Aviation in 1971 which has been ratified by Sri Lanka in 1978; Convention on the Prevention and Punishment of Crimes against Internationally Protected Persons, including Diplomatic Agents in 1973 which has been ratified by Sri Lanka in 1991; International Convention against the Taking of Hostages in 1979 which has been ratified by Sri Lanka in 2000; Convention on the Physical Protection of Nuclear Material in 1980 to which Sri Lanka is not a State Party; Convention for the Suppression of Unlawful Acts against the Safety of Maritime Navigation in 1988 which has been ratified by Sri Lanka in 2000; Protocol to the Convention for the Suppression of Unlawful Acts against the Safety of Fixed

Platforms Located on the Continental Shelf in 1988 to which Sri Lanka is not a member state and a Protocol for the Suppression of Unlawful Acts of Violence at Airports Serving International Civil Aviation in 1988, supplementary to the 1971 Convention for the Suppression of Unlawful Acts against the Safety of Civil Aviation which has been ratified by Sri Lanka in 1997; Convention on the Marking of Plastic Explosives for the Purpose of Detection in 1991 which has been ratified by Sri Lanka in 2001; International Convention for the Suppression of Terrorist Bombings in 1997 which has been ratified by Sri Lanka in 1999; International Convention for the Suppression of Financing of Terrorism in 1999 which has been ratified by Sri Lanka in 2000; International Convention for the Suppression of Acts of Nuclear Terrorism in 2005 which has been ratified by Sri Lanka in 2007. Amendment in 2005 to the Convention on the Physical Protection of Nuclear Material; Convention on the Suppression of Unlawful Acts Relating to International Civil Aviation in 2010; Protocol Supplementary to the Convention for the Suppression of Unlawful Seizure of Aircraft in 2010; and Protocol in 2014 to the Convention on Offences and Certain other Acts Committed on Board Aircraft. It is important to note that Sri Lanka is not a signatory to the last four international instruments mentioned above.

The above-mentioned discussion reveals that terrorism is a crime which causes harm to people, property, environment or anything in the world directly or indirectly and intimidates peace including both negative and positive peace and security. Further, terrorism is not merely a criminal conduct, and it violates the basic human rights too.

3 Sri Lanka as Member State to International Treaty Law on Peace, Security and Counterterrorism

The primary responsibility of the member states, which was expressed in the international treaty law against terrorism (which are briefly mentioned in the preceding part of this chapter) is to include the criminal offences/criminal activities/criminal behaviour described in the conventions to the domestic criminal law, and to bring the terrorists before the law to punish them according to the gravity of the crime committed by them. Further, international treaty law accepts the obligation of the member States either to extradite any suspect or to begin criminal proceedings against the suspects in the country where the suspect was arrested or the crime was committed and to protect the rights of suspected/accused/detained persons in due (criminal justice) process. The United Nation Organization urges all nations/countries to be a State party by ratifying the conventions that the UN adopts from time to time.

In December 1955, Sri Lanka became a member State to the UN. Since then, Sri Lanka is an active member of the international community through the UN. From 1976 to date, Sri Lanka has actively participated in all meetings of the General

Assembly, the UN's main forum for debate, and expressed the concerns of member countries on any issue including peace and security of human beings. Further, by ratifying many UN treaties, Sri Lanka has disclosed her willingness to accept the international standards declared by the UN from time to time.

In addition to the above-mentioned international instruments which set out legal standards against terrorism, Sri Lanka is also signatory to some other international conventions which affirm norms and principles of human rights. The Universal Declaration of Human Rights (UDHR-1948) and the International Covenant on Civil and Political Rights (ICCPR-1966) are the two most notable instruments. The norms accepted by those instruments are applicable to all on an equal footing and cannot be violated arbitrarily. Those norms are recognized as basic human rights of the people. Some of the rights which are related to this discussion are as follows: the right to life, right to liberty and security, right not to be subjected to torture or to cruel, inhuman or degrading treatment or punishment, right to be free from arbitrary arrest, detention or exile right to be presumed innocent until proved guilty according to law in a public trial, right to defence and right to freedom of opinion and expression. Therefore, the national laws of security and counterterrorism should be compatible with the above said international norms/right.

Two different theories, monism and dualism, are applied in relation to the implementation of the international treaty law (international conventions) in the national legal system. Sri Lanka follows the theory of dualism, which means, if there is a difference between domestic law and international law, a translation of such international law into the domestic law by explicit incorporation through enacting legislation or in other words enabling statute is required. Without translating into national law, international law does not exist as a law in Sri Lanka. This principle is acknowledged by Sri Lanka and took significant efforts to contribute to uphold the international norms and standards on peace and security and eradicate terrorism, by ratifying many conventions mentioned above and by enacting some enabling statutes having the specific intention of ensuring peace and security and eliminating terrorism.

4 National Laws for Peace, Security and Counterterrorism

The international human rights law encourages States to ensure the necessary protection to their citizens by establishing required safeguards. It includes a strong criminal justice system, which would be able to bring the criminals before the law and punish/rehabilitate them accordingly. In that sense, it may be argued that the international human rights framework does not prevent restrictions on certain human rights on the basis of necessity to ensure the security of people, protect people from crimes and criminals and maintain public order. Since terrorism is considered as a crime (international crime in international treaty law), each State has a duty to enact strong counterterrorism laws to prevent terrorist attacks as well as to investigate, prosecute and punish/rehabilitate them. This duty is derived from the general obligation to protect all citizens in the country from crimes and criminals and to ensure their security too. Therefore, like many other countries, Sri Lanka also enacted laws that specifically focus on preventing, investigating, prosecuting and punishing persons involved in committing this offence. Public Security Ordinance No. 25 of 1947 (PSO) as amended by Acts No. 22 of 1949, No. 34 of 1953, No. 8 of 1959, No. 6 of 1978, No. 22 of 1949, No. 34 of 1953, No. 8 of 1959 and No. 28 of 1988, Emergency Regulations, Prevention of Terrorism Act No. 48 of 1979 (PTA) as amended by Acts No. 10 of 1982 and No. 22 of 1988 and Convention on the Suppression of Terrorist Financing Act No. 25 of 2005 as amended No. of 2013 are the most significant legislations passed by the Sri Lankan Parliament for this purpose: fighting against terrorism and ensuring the peace and security in the country. Although some local modern legal experts in Sri Lanka criticize PSO as an attempt which was taken by the British rulers to suppress and control political dissent by locals against the arbitrary ruling of British and suggest to be repealed (Coomaraswamy and de los Reyes 2004), it is important to state this is the main legislative enactment passed by the State of Sri Lanka to control/prevent any rebellious activity committed unlawfully.

4.1 The Public Security Ordinance No. 25 of 1947

This ordinance contains three parts: Part I (General)—Sections 1–4, Part II (Emergency Regulations)—Sections 5–11 and Part III (Special Powers of the Head of the State)—Sections 12–24. According to the preamble of Public Security Ordinance, it is a statute to make available emergency regulations or the option of other procedures/steps/measures in the interest of public security and protection of public order or in other words, protection and maintenance of law and order. It is not wrong to say that the foundation of Sri Lanka's emergency regulations dates back to British rule as one of the final legislations enacted in the colonial era. Under this ordinance, State has the legal power to enact emergency regulations and take other actions/steps/measures to make sure the security of the people in the country when in need, including the circumstances which create any urgent or grave necessity.

There are some salient features that can be identified in this Ordinance. As set out in Section 2 of the Public Security Ordinance, the head of the State (the president of the country) has the absolute power to enact emergency regulations (ERs), when the head of the State is of opinion that there is an existence or proximity of a situation of public emergency that is necessary to take measures under the Ordinance (Section 2.1). According to the Ordinance (Sections 7 and 5), the regulations declared under the Ordinance may come into operation throughout Sri Lanka or in part/parts of Sri Lanka as may be specified in the proclamation/declaration according to the opinion/view and discretion of the head of the State. These regulations are considered as laws in the country. This is a special circumstance that the head of the State has power to issue a declaration of emergency and then to obtain the approval of the legislature. In other words, the head of the State has the absolute power of enacting emergency laws. *Prima facie*, this provision reveals the preparedness of the legislation in providing strong security laws to ensure security and order for the people and its function as a strong counterterrorism law, which may lead to violation of civil and political rights of the innocent people.

The second important feature is that the fact of the existence or imminence of a state of public emergency or regulations enacted under this Ordinance is excluded from judicial review. It is clear in Section 3 of the Ordinance. Further, Section 8 of the Ordinance states that no emergency regulation, and no order, rule or direction made or given there under shall be called in question in any court. Since judicial review ensures that the legal response is in accordance with principles of rule of law and strengthens the values of fairness, equality and justice, exclusion of judicial evaluation may lead to violation of principles of rule of law and taking no notice of the values of fairness, equality and justice. It may provide occasions for ineffective or arbitrary law enforcement in the (adversarial) criminal justice process too. The above-mentioned issues were discussed in *Diriwardene vs. Liyanage* (1983) 2 SLR 164; *Visualingam vs. Liyange* (1984) 2 SLR 123; *Adirisuriya vs. Navaratnam* (1985) 1 SLR 100; *Hidramani vs. Ratnavale* (1971) 75 NLR 67 and *Gunasekera vs. Ratnavale* (1972) 76 NLR 316.

The third important feature of the statute is the regulations which are enacted under this Ordinance have the legal effect of overriding, amending or suspending the operation of the provisions of any existing law in the country except the provisions of the Constitution. It is clear in the Public Security (Chapter XVIII) Article 155 of 1978 Constitution. The Article 155(1) of the Constitution states that the emergency regulations have the legal effect of overriding, amending or suspending the operation of the provisions of any law, except the provisions of the Constitution. It is significant to note that the Public Security Ordinance was amended as to a new law enacted by the Parliament immediately prior to the commencement of the 1978 Constitution. Therefore, one may say that the prevailing ordinary criminal justice process is superseded by the process followed under emergency situations/emergency regulations. Such situations provide both positive consequences such as ensuring public security and public order and negative consequences such as violation of certain civil rights of the people. However, it may be argued that, theoretically, Article 155(2) of the Constitution attempts to cover Chapter 3 of the Constitution (the fundamental rights chapter) which recognizes the civil, political and economic rights/human rights.

It is also significant to discuss the applicability of Article 15 of the Constitution which declares the provisions relating to the restriction on fundamental rights. Article 15(1) stipulates that the exercise and operation of the fundamental rights declared and recognized by Articles 13(5) and 13(6) may be subjected to restrictions as may be prescribed by law in the interests of national security. Further, it states that 'law' within the meaning of that paragraph includes regulations made under the law for the time being relating to public security. Further, Article 15(7) states that exercise and operation of all the fundamental rights declared and recognized by Articles 12, 13(1), 13(2) and 14 may be subjected to restrictions as may be prescribed by law in the interests of national security, public order, and the protection of public health or morality, and for the purpose of that specific provision the term 'law' covers regulations made under the law relating to public security (*Jayantha Finance and Investment Ltd vs. Liyanage* 1983 2 SLR 111; *Joseph Perera vs. The A.G* (1992) 1 SLR 199; *Thavaneethan vs. Dayananda Dissananyake* (2003) 1 SLR 74; *Neville Fernando vs. Liyanage* (1983) 2 SLR 214; *Malalgoda vs. The A.G.* (1982) 2 SLR 777). Therefore, it is correct to say that in the broad sense, the Constitution also recognizes the emergency regulation enacted under the authority of the Public Security Ordinance. The Constitution allows the President to validly restrict the function of certain fundamental rights in order to ensure the national security and public order.

Fourthly, the immunity protection is also guaranteed by the Constitution in respect of acts orders or direction done/given in good faith (*Hidramani vs. Ratnavale* (1971) 75 NLR 67; *Gunesekera vs. De Fonseka* (1972) 75 NLR 246; *Gunasekera vs. Ratnavale* (1972) 76 NLR 316; *Hevamanna vs. De Silva* (1983) 1 SLR 1; *Rathnasara Thero vs. Udugampala* (1983) *1 SLR 416; and Jayantha Finance and Investment Ltd vs. Liyanage* 1983 2 SLR 111 under any emergency regulation (Section 9) of the Public Security Ordinance).

4.2 Emergency Regulations

In this section, the main provisions of emergency laws which have been enacted under the Public Security Ordinance are critically evaluated. As said earlier, there are no contradictions between maintaining peace, security, public order and combating terrorism. However, at the same time, these laws should be compatible with the broader sense of upholding the rights of the people. Although nearly twenty-five regulations have been passed since independence (in the last seven decades from 1953 to date) in this discussion, Regulations No. 1 of 2005 (Emergency [Miscellaneous Provisions and Powers] Regulations) and Regulations No. 7 of 2006 (Emergency Regulations (Prevention and Prohibition of Terrorism and Specified Terrorist Activities)) will only be reviewed.

The 2005 emergency regulations were introduced under Section 5 of the Public Security Ordinance (*Joseph Perera vs. The A.G.* (1992) 1 SLR 199). Regulations No. 1 of 2005 mainly deals with the powers of arrest, detention, search, seizure, trial procedure, admissibility of confession, bail and immunity of prosecution.

Part 2 provides certain regulations for taking into possession of properties or forfeiture of the properties which were used in the course of the commission of any terrorist activity prescribed under any counterterrorism law. The Regulation 8(1) provides some remedies for the true owners of such properties who are not aware of the commissions of such offensive activities. According to Regulation No. 19(10), a remedy which is provided under Regulation 8(1) should not be called in question in any court on any ground. Therefore, it is clear that these remedies are also excluded from judicial review (*Visualingam* v. *Liyange* (1984) 2 SLR 123; *Adirisuriya* v. *Navaratnam* (1985) 1 SLR 100). However, these remedies are not that much effective as they are applicable subsequently to taking possession of the properties from them without any prior notice. This may create a violation of property rights of innocent people who do not commit any offence under any counterterrorism statute or public security statute.

Regulation 19(1) introduces rules on preventive detention (*Visualingam* v. *Liyange* (1984) 2 SLR 123; *Adirisuriya* v. *Navaratnam* (1985) 1 SLR 100). According to this provision, if the Secretary to the Ministry of Defence is of the view that a person acts in any manner detrimental to the national security, the Secretary can issue an order to any police officer, or member of the Sri Lanka Army, Navy or Air Force to take that person into custody (arrest) in order to prevent him/her engaging in that activity. Such person could be detained for the period of one year (maximum) if the Secretary is of the view that it is necessary. Due to this provision, the discretion of determining the detention period of a suspect has been transferred from judiciary to Secretary who is a part of the executive. In that sense, this emergency provision provides more power to the Secretary to determine the period of detention than a judicial officer/judge. This may be described as a defensive tool which any State/administrative authority can use to get hold of terrorist suspects in order to prevent a potential threat or danger of any terrorist activity taking place and a legitimate means of public security and public order. Conversely, since this regulation excludes judicial review (Regulation No. 19.10), one may argue that it leads to violation of certain fundamental rights (Article 13(1 & 2), 14.1, (h) of the Constitution) of the citizens in the country.

Certain regulations were promulgated with regard to search premises, arrest and detain suspects. By Regulation No. 20, powers were given to the officers of police or security forces to arrest any person, enter and search any premises, stop and search any individual or any vehicle, seize any document or thing without warrant or informing the reasons for such arrest (*Susila de Silva vs. Weerasinghe* (1987) 1 SLR 88).

According to Regulation 21(1), provisions of 36, 37 and 38 of the Code of Criminal Procedure Act No. 15 of 1979 are not applied for a suspect person who is arrested under Regulation 19. According to this regulation, any person who has been arrested under Regulation 19 should be produced before the magistrate within a reasonable time based on the circumstances of the case subject to the maximum period of thirty days. Magistrate cannot grant bail to the suspect without prior approval of the Attorney General (AG) (Proviso to Regulation 21.1). This provision has taken away the discretion of granting bail from the courts and granted to the AG who is part of the executive. The thirty day period may be extended up to the maximum period of ninety days with the discretion of the Inspector General of Police (IGP) (Regulation 21.2). Issuing permits to visit such detainees and the place where that detainee should be detained are decided by the IGP at his discretion. This situation restricts the power vested in the courts on detaining suspects and related matters, and shifts it to IGP who is part of the executive.

Regulation 22 stipulates that a person who is surrendered to any police officer or any member of security forces or any person authorized by the President by order in correlation with any offences under Explosive Act (Chapter 183), the Offensive Weapons Act (No. 18) of 1966, the Firearms Ordinance, the Prevention of Terrorism Act No. 48 of 1979, Chapter VI, VII and VIII of the Penal Code (Ordinance No. 2) of 1882, any emergency regulation or any person who is surrendered due to fear of terrorist activities should be surrendered to the officer in charge of the nearest police station within 24 hours and then should be produced before the magistrate to obtain an appropriate order. Under this provision, persons who have connection with terrorist activities and innocent people who are suspected of committing those activities are treated equally and could be sent to rehabilitation camps where they could be detained for up to two years of the period. This may lead to violation of the fundamental rights of the citizens who actually did not commit any offence but expect their protection from the State.

Regulation 23 gives the power to the officer-in-charge (OIC) of every police station to demand householder list at any time to prohibit providing accommodation to the people who are not the residents of the same area without prior information to the OIC.

Part 5 describes a range of offences that come under this regulation along with the penalties. Further, it removes the applicability of Section 306(2) of the Code of Criminal Procedure Act No. 15 of 1979 for persons who are convicted under emergency regulations (Regulation 45.3).

Wide powers are given to the police officers in relation to the investigation of offences under any emergency regulation. This is in addition to the powers given by any other law (Part 5 of the Emergency Regulations No. 1 of 2005). These additional powers cannot be derogated in the emergency situation. These extensive powers may also be exercised by any person authorized by the President (Regulation 52) or any commissioned or non-commissioned officer of security forces under the order of the Commander of any security force in the country (Regulation 52). Further, the applicability of the provisions in the Code of Criminal Procedure is completely removed with regard to the investigation conducted under emergency regulations (Regulation 64).

According to Regulation 63(1), the confession statement made by the suspect to the police officer whose rank is not below of Assistant Superintendent of Police (ASP) can be proved against him/her at the trial. As many legal experts argue, this is against the basic principles of the law of evidence. Since the provisions, namely, Sections 25, 26 and 30 of the Evidences Ordinance are not applied in the case of any offence under any emergency regulations (Regulation 63.4), the suspect can be indicted purely based on the involuntary confession made by the suspect under the circumstances of torture.

Although some regulations (Regulations 8, 12, 13, 14 and 15) in 2005 were repealed by 2010 regulations, 2006 emergency regulations still remain in force together with some other counterterrorism law (Prevention of Terrorism Act). Therefore, it may be argued that this revocation has zero effect on the excessive powers granted to the police and to the security forces in terms of investigation, arrest or detaining persons under Public Security Ordinance.

The 2006 Emergency Regulations were introduced in December 2006. Regulation No. 7 of 2006 mainly deals with criminalizing and defining terrorism by introducing new offences including engaging in transactions with a terrorist or terrorist group/s despite the wrongful knowledge and criminal intention; *mens rea*.

According to Regulation 5, the particular set of emergency regulations was promulgated in good faith of fulfilling the need of an efficacious attempt to cast the obligation of Sri Lanka towards the international instruments which declared standards for prevention of terrorism. Further, this particular set of emergency regulations is a special attempt taken by Sri Lanka to acknowledge the norms and standards adopted by the United Security Council Resolution No. 1373 (2001) under Chapter VII of the Untied Nations Charter and to take meaningful measures to prevent and suppress terrorism. Under this special regulation, a range of activities were prohibited by Regulations 6, 7, 8 and 9. Regulation 6 prohibits engaging in terrorism and committing specified terror activities described under the Prevention of Terrorism Act. Regulation 7 forbids participation (aiding and abetting) in the activities by person/s, group/s or organization/s that contravene Regulation 6. Engaging in any form of transaction with any person/s, group/s, or organization/s that violate Regulation 6 is illegal under Regulation 8. According to Regulation 9, providing information which is detrimental to national security to any person/s, group/s or organization/s that act in contravention of Regulation 6 is illegal. More importantly, Regulation 20 provides a definition of the term 'terrorism. It permits for the criminalization of a range of activities including offences under Section 3 of the Money Laundering Act No. 5 of 2006, an offence under Section 3 of the Convention of the Suppression of Terrorist Financing Act, No. 25 of 2005 and any offence committed under Sections of 114, 115, 116, 117, 121, 122, 128 and 129 of the Penal Code. This is in addition to the offences specified under the Prevention of Terrorism Act No. 48 of 1979 and any offence committed under the Public Security Ordinance (Chapter 40). Regulation No. 7 of 2006 recognizes the doctrine of strict liability and the accused could be indicted and convicted by proving only the *actus reus* of the offence (Regulations 10, 11 and 12).

Pessimistic effect of these provisions is that the innocent civilians, (liveing in the areas which are controlled by such groups acting in contravention of Regulation 6), who may have followed the orders given by such groups, are criminally liable. Since the mental element is irrelevant in proving these offences, these civilians are victimized by groups who act contravening Regulation 6 as well as the State actors (*Visualingam vs. Jayasekara* Supreme Court Case No. 32/2008). The blanket immunity granted to the public servants who take actions in terms of these regulations may lead to worsen the situation (Regulation 19).

4.3 Prevention of Terrorism Act No. 48 of 1979

The Prevention of Terrorism Act No. 48 of 1979 (PTA) is a special statute enacted to deal with the acts of terrorism. It is a law which provides the police and security forces with extensive powers to arrest and detain suspects, search premises and conduct the investigation in relation to the terrorist acts. It was initially passed by the Parliament as a temporary law in 1979, but was made permanent in 1982. PTA is enacted under Article 84 of the Constitution. According to Article 84, bills which are inconsistent with the Constitutional provisions also can be passed with the two-thirds majority of the members of the Parliament to comply with the necessity of public protection. Though many scholars criticize the statute (PTA) on the basis of its inconsistency with the provisions in the Constitution, in *Weeravansa vs. The AG* (2000 1 S.L.R. 387), the court held that PTA is a constitutionally valid law in the country.

As far as the offences described in PTA are concerned, a wide range of acts, which have been already criminalized by the Penal Code and certain other specific acts are criminalized under PTA (Sections 2–4) too. It also criminalizes the acts of violence or religious, racial or communal disharmony or feelings of ill will or hostility between different communities or racial or religious groups by the use of words, signs or any other visible representations. According to this Act, harbouring, concealing, hindering or interfering with the apprehension of a person, knowing or having reason to believe that such person has committed or attempted to commit offence under the Act and failure to report offences committed, and attempt to commit offences or any other known information relating to the offences under this Act is a criminal offence (Section 5). It maybe said that by criminalizing the above-mentioned acts, the legislature attempts to deprive people committing crimes for achieving political objectives, which is essential for peace and security of the country/nation.

Punishments envisaged for the offences under this Act are more severe than the punishments prescribed for the similar offences stipulated in other penal statutes including the Penal Code. Moreover, mandatory minimum sentencing rule is applicable in respect of all the offences committed under the Act (Sections 2–4). Imposition of harsh punishments is plausible explanation to increase the deterrence value of the PTA which leads to deter potential criminals/offenders who will attempt to achieve their political ideas through illegal manner. However, it is not understandable as to why a crime like murder which carries the death penalty under the Penal Code carries life imprisonment under PTA.

Part II and III set out provisions for investigation of offences, detention of arrestees and issuing restrictions orders. The provisions in these two parts of the statute provide extensive powers to the police in this regard. According to Section 6, any police officer not below the rank of Superintendent or any other police officer not below the rank of Sub-Inspector authorized in writing by Superintendent on his behalf may arrest any person, enter and search any premises, seize any document or thing and search any individual or any vehicle, vessel, train or aircraft without a warrant (Section 6.1). Obstruction caused to a police officer who is exercising the power conferred on him under this Act is a criminal offence (Section 6.2). Such arrestee may be kept in police custody for a period of 72 hours (Section 7) and such suspect could be detained in remand prison for a period up to eighteen months which is renewable by order of the magistrate every three months if the Minister of Defence has reasons to believe that the suspect person is connected with or concerned in any unlawful activity under this Act (Section 9.1). Further, the said Minister has the power to restrict the movement outside the place of residence, employment and travel within or outside Sri Lanka (Section 9.1).

According to Section 10, the orders given to arrest and detain any suspect person or seize any thing cannot be questioned or challenged in any court or tribunal in any manner. One may criticize this provision as a violation/breach of Article 13(3) of the Sri Lankan Constitution which is meant to guarantee a fair trial.

Section 15 has the effect of eliminating preliminary inquiry in relation to the crimes committed under this Act and permits trial on an indictment before the High Court without jury or before a High Court at Bar (Trial at Bar) by three judges. Further, the provisions of Sections 450 and 451 of the Code of Criminal Procedure Act, No. 15 of 1979, should *mutatis mutandis*, apply to the trial of offences under this Act by the High Court at Bar and to appeal from judgments, sentences and orders pronounced at any such trial held by the High Court at Bar.

Under this Act, constructive safeguards given to suspect/accused in the Evidence Ordinance No. 14 of 1895 with regard to the admissibility of confession have been removed by Section 16. Thus, a confession statement made to a police officer of or above the rank of Assistant Superintendent is admissible evidence against the accused who is charged under this Act. In some instances, the court convicted the accused solely on the basis of such confession made by suspect while the suspect was in police custody (*Nallaratnam vs. Singharasa*). The wide power given to the police officers under this provision may compel the suspects to make (involuntary) confession statements under threat/harassment/torture in police custody (*Tissanayagam Case*) HC 4425/08.

Bail is not allowed under the Act other than the exceptional circumstances determined by the Court of Appeal (Section 19). Blanket immunity is granted to the security personnel from prosecution for the actions taken under this Act, stating that no suit, prosecution or other proceeding, civil or criminal, should lie against any officer or person for any act or thing in good faith done or purported to be done in pursuance or supposed pursuance of any order made or direction given under this Act (Section 26). Superiority of the PTA over all other written law is the most significant feature of the Act which is stipulated in Section 28.

In addition to the above said counterterrorism laws, Sri Lanka has enacted the Convention on the Suppression of Terrorist Financing Act No. 25 of 2005 as amended No. of 2013, to give effect to the UN Convention on Suppression of Terrorist Financing adopted in 1999 as a signatory. According to Section 3, providing or collecting funds for terrorist activities is a criminal offence. Subsequent to the 2013 amendment, conspiring to provide material support or resources to any terrorist/s or (a) terrorist organization/s in any manner is also considered as a punishable offence under this Act.

The funds collected in contravention to the Act should be frozen or seized until the conclusion of the trial and be forfeited to the State at the time of the conviction of the perpetrator. Only the High Court of Sri Lanka in Colombo or the High Court established under Article 154P of the Constitution for the Western Province, in Colombo, is vested with jurisdiction to try the offences committed under this Act by a citizen of Sri Lanka, or by a national of another State which is a party to the main Convention, or by a stateless person who has his habitual residence in Sri Lanka.

5 Conclusion

There is no doubt that increasing insecurity of the people in a country due to war on terrorism is a threat to the global peace and security. Responsibility lies with all the nations to enact strong counterterrorism laws which would be able to criminalize terrorism. And put those laws into practice through a strong criminal justice system to bring the offenders before the law and punish them to protect the civil society from these criminals and criminal activities and to deter people committing crimes this nature. Therefore, it is vital, to implement the emergency regulations/provisions and separate anti-terrorism laws in combating terrorism/terrorist activities.

Sri Lanka is one of the countries in the world that utilizes separate laws to proscribe terrorism and considering it under emergency situation in protection of the security of the people and maintain the peace and order in the country. Categorically, such laws contribute to world peace and security. However, in the above discussion revealed that there was a pessimistic collision of the local security laws due to the misuse of them. This suggests the insertion of safeguards against misuse (or in other words abuse) of these laws in order to increase their efficiency.

References

Andreu Guzman F (2003) Terrorism and human rights no. 2—new challenges and old dangers. International Commission of Jurists Occasional Papers No. 3

Anna K (2001) Definitions of human security United Nations definitions Kofi Annan.www.nobelprize/humansecurity/sites

Coomaraswamy R, des los Reyes C (2004) Rule by emergency: Sri Lanka's postcolonial constitutional experience. Int J Const Law 2(2):272–295

Counter-terrorism training post-9/11 (2004) In: Gunaratna R (ed) The changing face of terrorism. Marshall Cavendish Academic, Singapore

Delimiting human security: a South Asian perspective. A paper presented at ISYP conference (2003) Advancing human security, Halifax, Nova Society, 15–17 July

Galtung J (1964) An editorial. J Peace Res 1(1):1–4

Galtung J (1996) Peace by peaceful means: peace and conflict, development and civilization. Sage, Norway

Human security: concept and measurement, occasional paper no. 19, August 2000, Kroc Institute; Arabinda Acharya and Amitav Acharya, Human security in Asia: conceptual ambiguities and common understandings. http://www.robarts.yorku.ca/pdf/acharya_delhi.pdf

Kedar M (2013) Middle East and terrorism: Islam in the United States. www.isrealagainstterror.blogspot.com/2013

Levitt G (1986) Is terrorism worth defining? Northern University Law Review, Ohio

Peace and security, human resources and their development (2010) Encyclopedia of life support system, vol II

Re-thinking 'preventive detention' from a comparative perspective: three frameworks for detaining terrorist suspects (2009) Yale Law school student scholarship paper, Yale law School, USA

Shy J, Collier TW (2007) Revolutionary war. In: Paret P (ed) Makers of modern strategy: from Machiavelli to the nuclear age. Princeton University Press, Princeton

Skubisseviski K (1989) Definition of terrorism, Israeli year book on human rights

Terrorism as a challenge for national and international law: security *vs*. liberty? (2003) Springer, Berlin

Towards a culture of peace. http://www.unesco.org/opi2/lettres/TextAnglais/AnnanE.html

Under Secretary (2003) Ministry of law, justice and parliamentary affairs, Nepal, at 9th Asia Crime Prevention Foundation (ACPF) World Conference edited by Minoru, Chairman, Board of Directors (ASPF), Asia Crime Prevention Foundation, Japan

U.S. response to terrorism: a strategic analysis of the Afghanistan Campaign (2010) J Strateg Secur

Valerie TM (2015) The complexity of combating terrorism and terrorist groups file:///F:/2015 Activities New Folder/papers to be submitted/human security/(1) Seminar Essay-2 Topic

Walter C (2003) Defining terrorism in national and international law. In: Walter C, Voneky S, Volker R, Schorkopf F (eds) Terrorism as a challenge for national and international law: security versus liberty? Springer, London

Author Biography

Ms. Muthukuda A. Dona Shiroma Jeeva S. Niriella the Head of the Department of Public International Law in the Faculty of Law, University of Colombo (Sri Lanka). She won the Professional and Career Women Award 2011/2012 (Legal Category), organized by Women in Management, Sri Lanka. The award was a mark of recognition of the services she rendered to the legal field through her contribution of knowledge to the legal academic arena. She was granted post graduate research scholarship in 2011 by the University of Colombo to pursue her doctoral research. She has been a prolific writer on the issues of international law and criminal law at national and international levels.

Chapter 11
International Crimes Tribunal (ICT) (Bangladesh): The Issues of Fairness and Transparency

M. Zahurul Haque

1 Introduction

War crimes, crimes against humanity, crimes against peace and genocide are crimes under both international and national laws specifically legislated to address these issues. During the war of 1971 between Bengali liberation forces and Pakistan Armed Forces, millions of people were subjected to these atrocious crimes. While there were allegations of violations on both sides, for instance, in some areas non-Bengali populations were subjected to massive brutality; defenseless Bengali civilians, including Hindu minorities were the main victims of attacks by their adversaries (Jurists 1972). This costly war—both in terms of human lives and property—ended with the intervention by India on humanitarian grounds.

In a post-liberation period when global communities remained disinclined on Bangladesh's proposals for international initiatives to investigate war atrocities and hold war crimes trials (MacDermot 1973), Bangladesh passed two separate pieces of legislation to try local collaborators and members of Pakistan Armed Forces in connection with the events of 1971. For many years, political considerations prevented the war crimes trial, but in 2010, trials resumed or started afresh when Bangladesh established International Crimes Tribunal (Tribunal).

Despite the fairly broad global support it received, the war crimes trial initiative raised a number of doubts and criticisms with regard to fairness and transparency (Knoops 2014), principally on dubious political motivations behind the trials and soundness of legal procedures—two potential threats to the traditional concept of justice. Labeled by some as 'real political vendetta' (Jalil 2010) or a 'wolf in sheep's clothing' (Key 2010) and demanded to be 'permanently scrapped' by those who categorically opposing—the trial continues to stir debate. This chapter assesses

M. Zahurul Haque (✉)
Department of Law, Eastern University,
House 26, Road 5, Dhanmondi R/A, Dhaka 1205, Bangladesh
e-mail: zahurul_haq@yahoo.com; zahurul_haq@easternuni.edu.bd

J.L. Kaul and A. Jha (eds.), *Shifting Horizons of Public International Law*,
https://doi.org/10.1007/978-81-322-3724-2_11

the strengths and weaknesses of the demand to abandon the trial permanently (BBC 2013; Jalil 2010) on account of its potential failure in ensuring 'justice' in its most traditional sense, and how this discourse fits in the existing political reality of Bangladesh. The author used 'justice' in the sense of legal justice to mean the general observance of fair rules avoiding any subjective distinctions among people to whom such rules apply or have effect on (Kearns and Sarat 1996).

The main aim of this chapter is to provide the readers with a broader overview of war crimes trial's jurisprudential dimension in the historic and cultural context of Bangladesh, focusing on the questions of 'fairness' and 'transparency' of the process. Therefore, an important objective of this chapter is to investigate the specific historical events responsible for the Bangladesh Liberation war, creation of Bangladesh, and the establishment of International Crimes Tribunal. This investigation also identifies the political dimensions of this war crimes trial and some major issues of 'fairness' and 'transparency' with regard to the Rule of Procedure and Evidence of the Tribunal.

The author adopts a sociolegal approach, that is, considering not only the legal texts and principles but also the specific 'contexts in which they are created, destroyed, used, abused, avoided, and so on' (Perry-Kessaris 2013) to address the specific objectives of this chapter. The author argues that the doubts and question as regards 'fairness' and 'transparency' surrounding war crimes trial must be read and understood in the relevant historic and cultural context. A number of past and contemporary social, cultural, and political factors have influenced the laws of war crimes in Bangladesh. This chapter examines how this interface works in changing political and social environment of Bangladesh.

In Order to understand the changing sociopolitical scenario where the laws of war crimes are created and implemented, this chapter begins with a brief historic account of the creation of Bangladesh. These facts will assist readers with the knowledge on how and why war crimes trial became relevant in this country, conceptions of doubts of fairness and transparency in the trial, and how they affect national perception of the jurisprudence of war crimes trial when held under a domestic mechanism. The author uses 'war crimes' in broad sense to include crimes against peace, crimes against humanity, genocide, and war crimes, as it was used by ICTY (International Criminal Tribunal for the former Yugoslavia) when it referred to 'serious violations of international humanitarian law.'

2 Historical Overview

Independence of Pakistan (and India) in 1947 from the British rule came through an enormous human and material cost of partition. Abul Kalam Azad, one of the most prominent leaders of the Indian independence movement, mentioned that the partition of India was a consequence of the political disagreements between leading pre-partition Indian political parties—All-India Muslim League and Indian National Congress (Azad 1959). Historians of both countries, on the other hand, contended that 'contradictions and structural peculiarities of Indian society and politics' are probably the main reasons why Pakistan was a necessity (Bose and Jalal 2004).

Declaration of partition, that is, the creation of Pakistan (divided into East and West) as a separate state for Indian Muslims, and India for Hindu majority erupted massive communal violence in some parts of the subcontinent. One of the key reasons behind this turmoil was attributable to parties' overstated demands with regard to sharing of land. Besides, there were pressing concerns as regards dividing the finances and armed forces, as well as demarcations of land boundaries and all had to be completed within weeks or months (Azad 1959).

Right after the independence, India and Pakistan fought a bitter war in 1947–1948 over Kashmir due to their competing claims over this land. In 1965, they met again in the battlefield over the same dispute. Although border conflict between these two neighbors is not new, one of the key elements of Kashmir crisis was Pakistani irredentism something India disavowed vigorously (Paul 2005). This issue continuingly abetted rivalry between two nations in the subsequent period. In 1971, world witnessed another encounter between them. While Pakistan called it a military intervention of India in the former's territory after a civil war broke out in East Pakistan, that is, 'an internal conflict,' India and Bangladesh, as a rebuttal to this point, argued that, this was only humanitarian intervention by India for the protection of civilians in 'Bangladesh liberation war.'

2.1 Emergence of Bangladesh

Two wings of Pakistan—West and East—separated by thousand miles were a rather peculiar creation of politics. People almost anonymous to each other in terms of language, culture, economy, and political traditions were brought under a single flag only because they shared a common religion. These huge differences in ways of life coupled with lack of power sharing made it near impossible for the people of the East to participate equally in economic and political life of united Pakistan. Eventually, deeply rooted suspicion of people in political institutions and mistrust among political leaders of both wings acted as catalyst for the events that led to political unrests in the East.

People and political leaders in East Pakistan believed the West Pakistan could not be trusted as they were always hesitant in sharing political power in a constitutional framework and thereby recognize the equal rights of the people of the East (Sisson and Rose 1991). These power struggles were fueled by both 'the constitutional crisis that developed during the existence of the first Constituent Assembly [which] strengthened the role of central institutions—the bureaucracy and army—at the expense of regional parties in the provinces' and the anti-democratic attitudes of the pro-military elites and military leaders of West Pakistan who always feared power sharing (Chadda 2009). The West on the other hand was somewhat doubtful about East paying homage toward Pakistani values. They believed East Pakistan never shared the same feeling for Kashmir as the people of the West did.

They recognized the Muslims of East 'converts' and not 'original' Muslims as the territory had been historically populated by Hindus, hence, more inclined toward their Indian neighbors (Sisson and Rose 1991).

Also, scholars often mentioned the post-colonial concept of Pakistan as politically unworkable due to the wings' physically secluded locations and social life fundamentally different from each other. They stressed that all these significant differences actually set the course of disintegration of Pakistan in the very beginning. The creation of Bangladesh was, therefore, inevitable. In contrast, this is also true that Bengali politicians were always willing to become part of united Pakistan's central politics and contribute to the development of Pakistan (Ahmed 2004). This variation in the facts makes it a little harder to come up with a simple explanation as to why East chose to become Bangladesh and why their attempt succeeded.

Historical evidence suggests that even after Pakistan had gained independence people of East Pakistan faced another colonial style administration during their partnership with the West. The people of the East were neglected in both civil and military services. Even with a much lower rate of literacy (Punjab 1971), the West wing held 90 and 95% of all positions in civil and military services of Pakistan, respectively. Then again, although the East wing earned 75% of the total foreign exchange of Pakistan, they received only 25% of total imports. That is, most of the earnings of the East from their agriculture sector would be invested in industrial development in West (Rao 1991).

While the 'internal colonialism' of the West is widely blamed for grossly unequal representation in the service sectors, economic disparities, and uneven development of the wings, many of these problems were actually inherited from the colonial era. Some statistics suggest that the partnership between two wings of Pakistan began with inequality in its core. East represented only 15% of the total area of Pakistan, although hosting 56% of its population (Rizvi 1988). Besides, thanks to heavy investment Punjab traditionally received from the British due to Punjabi soldiers' unshaken loyalty to colonial power during the Mutiny of 1857 (first war of independence to Indians), Punjab was one of the most fortunate regions of British India. Therefore, at the time of independence, West wing's province of West Punjab was economically much better off than East Bengal (later East Pakistan) (Maddison 1971).

When the East's disappointments in the area of economy, politics, civil, and military services reached a soaring height, the Government made a move to make Urdu as the only state language of Pakistan (D'Costa 2011). Ironically, however, a strong declaration in this regard came directly from Khawaja Nazimuddin, the second Prime Minister of Pakistan (1951–1953), a politician and statesman from the Dhaka Nawab Family, a Bengali.

If implemented, this would take away another cultural identity—mother tongue Bangla—from the people of East who already lost their historic name as 'Bengali' and became 'Pakistani.' This move annoyed the people of East quite heavily. Growing tension ignited a student revolt against the Government in 1952, which had a far-reaching impact (Rao 1991; D'Costa 2011). Later, this complex situation along with other crucial sociopolitical concerns became the basis of political mobilization in the East. Sheikh Mujibur Rahman declared his six-point program—Bengali nationalist movement—in 1966 asking decentralization of power and full provincial autonomy. This movement resulted in a massive uprising in 1969 and eventually led the struggle for liberation (Rao 1991; Sisson and Rose 1991).

In 1970, a general election was held in Pakistan and its result revealed the inner feeling of the people of East to West, for all the inequality and mistreatment they were subject to. Under the leadership of Sheikh Mujibur Rahman, Awami League won 167 out of 313 seats in the Pakistan national assembly. However, Sheikh Mujibur Rahman—the leader of Pakistan's majority party—would never be invited to form Government due to fierce opposition from Zulfikar Ali Bhutto—founding Chair of Pakistan People's Party and subsequently President of Pakistan in post-1971 period. Bhutto, in an extreme undemocratic move, denied any possibility of forming Government under the leadership of Mujib (Ahmed 2004).

On March 7, 1971, Sheikh Mujibur Rahman appeared before a huge public gathering in Dhaka and virtually declared the beginning of the struggle for independence. In the night of 25 March, thousands of Bengalis were brutally killed during an army crackdown in Dhaka city. Right after this incident, declaration of independence was signed. From this day, Bangladesh liberation war began and lasted until 16 December of the same year. During the war, the atrocities of Pakistan Armed Forces and their collaborators made international headlines (Quaderi 1972). Jamaat-e-Islami Pakistan's East wing, later Bangladesh Jamaat-e-Islami (Jamaat-e-Islami, Jamaat), fiercely opposed the independence of Bangladesh and actively supported Pakistan Armed Forces in the war. On the first week of December, Pakistan launched preemptive attack on India and their forces clashed on the Western front. Subsequently, India intervened militarily in their Eastern wing (Bangladesh) and achieved a decisive victory.

2.1.1 Would There Be Any Trials? Who Would Be Tried?

The war ended on December 16, 1971, when Pakistan's Eastern command surrendered in Dhaka to India–Bangladesh joint command with over 93,000 Pakistani (Prisoners of War) POW (Khanna 2007; Burke 1973). After the war, the question of whether Pakistani soldiers responsible for war crimes would be tried or not caused much debate. This apparently simple question required a significant amount of political processing. The war devastated Bangladesh lacked the adequate administrative and logistical preparedness to take charge of such a vast number of POW, as a result, they were eventually handed over to Indian custody. Besides, there were valid questions concerning bringing back around 30,000 Bengali soldiers and thousands of Bengali civilians detained forcibly in Pakistan (Khanna 2007) along with the question of political recognition of Bangladesh from Pakistan.

The future of thousands of POW and other detainees on both sides was not actually hanging in balance, but this issue, at least temporarily, created a political stalemate as all three parties decided to hold intractable positions. India refused to release Pakistani POW on the ground that they surrendered to a joint command and hence unable to make unilateral decisions. Bangladesh on the other hand would not give their consent to the release unless Pakistan politically recognizes Bangladesh something Pakistan viewed possible only if two historic rivals Mujib and Bhutto sat together. However, this proposed conference of two adversaries appeared politically remote since Mujib reaffirmed his strong commitment about the trials of Pakistani POW (Burke 1973).

After a series of negotiations, India and Pakistan signed the Simla Agreement in July 1972 with a promise to respect the line of control in Jammu and Kashmir resulting from the ceasefire of December 17, 1971. This agreement also created avenue for both parties to exchange POW, but the matter was further complicated when Mujib passed Bangladesh Collaborators (Special Tribunal) Order 1972 to prosecute Bangladeshi citizens for having collaborated with Pakistan Armed Forces during the war, and also vowed to try the Pakistani POW. Any person, who participated, aided, or abetted the Pakistan occupation army in their act of illegal occupation of Bangladesh, would be tried for such activities and other crimes linked to such activities, as Bangladesh declared.

At this stage, a repatriation process between India and Pakistan was underway with regard to POW captured on the Western front. Some scholars indicated that the repatriation stopped as India agreed upon the request of Bangladesh to hand over about ten thousand POW to Bangladesh captured in the Eastern front. This number finally reduced to only 195 to be charged for crimes of genocide (Bassiouni 1999) and not crimes against humanity or war crimes. This is interesting to see both India and Bangladesh somewhat supported the Pakistani view toward the events of 1971 as 'internal conflict' (Bassiouni 1999) since only alleged genocide was in focus for these proposed trials.

In 1973, Bangladesh enacted the International Crimes (Tribunals) Act (ICT Act) 'to provide for the detention, prosecution, and punishment of persons for genocide; crimes against humanity; war crimes and other crimes under international law, and for matters connected therewith.' This new piece of legislation gave the Government a better tool to try the crimes under international law committed in the territory of Bangladesh. This preparation caused Pakistan bringing action with the International Court of Justice against the Indian decision to handover POW to Bangladesh mainly on two grounds. First, if any incidents of genocide actually took place, it occurred at a time and within a territory universally regarded as of Pakistan, thus, only Pakistan had the jurisdiction. Second, holding such trial in Bangladesh would not fulfill the condition of 'Competent Tribunal' within the meaning of Article VI of the Genocide Convention as the situation in Bangladesh right after the war was 'emotionally charged' (Bassiouni 2011).

At the same time, Pakistan also made it clear through some of their initiatives that they were set to repatriate thousands of 'stranded East Pakistani' or Bengali civil and military officials and civilians only in exchange for Pakistani POW (Jahan 2013). In 1973, the matter came to an end as the parties agreed to accept a political solution and ICJ removed the case from its docket with the consent of both parties. Later, in 1974 an agreement had been reached following continuing negotiations between Bangladesh, India, and Pakistan. All 195 POW were eventually sent back home as Pakistan issued a statement condemning war crimes and promised to try those personnel in Pakistan; something never took place (Khanna 2007; Bassiouni 1999). Pakistan recognized the independence of Bangladesh afterward.

3 War Crimes Tribunal: Issues of Fairness and Transparency

After the Bangladesh Liberation War, the International Crimes (Tribunal) Act, 1973 (ICT Act), was enacted by the Parliament of Bangladesh to provide for the establishment, structure, and management of the International Crimes Tribunal (ICT) for the prosecution of persons alleged to have committed crimes against humanity, war crimes, genocide, or other crimes under international law. Although enacted in 1973, the first tribunal under this Act was finally established and came into operation on March 25, 2010, and another one on March 22, 2012. Based in capital Dhaka, Tribunals consist of three judges each—a chairman and two members. Any person who qualified to be a judge or has been a Judge of the Supreme Court of Bangladesh may be appointed as a chairman or member of a Tribunal. A Registry, an Investigation Agency and a Prosecution team headed by a chief prosecutor, assists the operation of the Tribunal. As regards its jurisdiction, Section 3 of the ICT Act provides that the:

> … [t]ribunal shall have the power to try and punish any individual or group of individuals, [or organisation,] or any member of any armed, defense or auxiliary forces, irrespective of his nationality, who commits or has committed, in the territory of Bangladesh, whether before or after the commencement of this Act …

The Tribunal has wide jurisdiction to try crimes mentioned above as well as violation of any humanitarian rules applicable in armed conflicts laid down in the Geneva Conventions of 1949. Authorized by Section 22 and 19 of the ICT Act, the Tribunal has formulated its own Rules of Procedure (RoP) and Rules of Evidence, respectively. Section 19 authorizes the Tribunal not to remain bound by 'technical rules of evidence' and to 'adopt and apply to the greatest possible extent expeditious and non-technical procedure, and may admit any evidence,' 'which it deems to have probative value.' Accordingly, Rule 44 of RoP lays down:

> The Tribunal shall be at liberty to admit any evidence oral or documentary, print or electronic including books, reports and photographs published in news papers, periodicals, and magazines, films and tape recording and other materials as may be tendered before it and it may exclude any evidence which does not inspire any confidence in it, and admission or non-admission of evidence by the Tribunal is final and cannot be challenged.

Originally intended to try Pakistani POW, the ICT Act is now the means to establish war crimes tribunal and complete the unfinished trials of local collaborators. Although Bangladesh Awami League's (Awami League) 2008 pre-election pledges included a solid promise to hold these trials which helped them win enormous public support and come into power, the initiatives with regard to the trials of alleged war criminals of 1971 raised several debates and doubts questioning the 'possibility' and 'legality' of holding any such trials.

Some of these issues and doubts were purely political and old, fueled debate over whether Bangladesh would ever be able to unite on the issue of holding a war crimes trial without risking a blow against national sovereignty (Khan 2008). Because a significant period has elapsed since the war and most of the alleged top war criminals are now affiliated with major political parties, any initiative to open the old wounds might divide the nation, create instability, and bring about anarchy. These issues often came into the public media after the restoration of democracy in 1991 and remained active in subsequent years. Other issues were fresh, legal in nature, and kept resurfacing as the discourse of trial evolved during the period of military backed interim Government between 2007 and 2008, and afterward when the Tribunal was finally established.

While there is no doubt whether war crimes were actually committed during the events of 1971, nevertheless, the questions about the actual scale of violence aroused debate. If one takes the example of civilian casualties only, literatures lead to erratic claims suggesting diverse figures (Khan 2008; Jurists 1972; Payne 1973; Trivedi 2008)—including nonexistent, and thus, untraceable 1981 UN Human Rights Commission report on Bangladesh genocide available in published literature in different formats, which give only a distorted view of the matter. In December 2015, BNP Chairperson and former Prime Minister of Bangladesh joined this debate when she raised doubt about the officially accepted number of liberation war martyrs, which is three million (Correspondent 2015, December 23), in a public meeting. Subsequently, BNP denied the allegation saying 'BNP chief mentioned the controversy on the exact number of martyrs as a reference' only (UNB 2015).

Other questions raised by many, including the political block allegedly opposing the trial initiatives, were why the trials have not been held as of this date (Ullah 2008)? Why now? Isn't it a settled matter? Is there any justification for the trials of crimes committed decades ago (Alam 2008; Jalil 2010; Reporter 2010)? These queries and doubts invite debate on the historical background of the trial initiatives and their relevance in the current context. Newly independent Bangladesh took number of specific initiatives for holding a war crimes trial, however, only either to be discarded or blocked due to a number of pressing political considerations. Another uncomfortable fact for Awami League is their failure to initiate any process of the war crimes trial when they were in power for the second time between 1996 and 2001 after winning the general election against BNP (Ullah 2008).

However, one of the most appealing questions or doubts national war crimes trial movement and subsequent initiatives frequently raised was whether it was at all 'possible' to try the alleged war criminals after so many years (Ullah 2008; Khan 2008). If yes, will it be considered as political vendetta (Jalil 2010)? Is it a conspiracy to divide the nation (Karzon 2008)?

Clearly, this doubt is aimed at the strength of domestic political 'will' to investigate into war crimes occurred almost four decades ago and set off a trial process, primarily, against persons now firmly established as known politicians in a democratic environment. These questions have already been answered since the trial had already begun. A discussion is still necessary to understand the nature of the challenge war crimes trial movement faced in the beginning and subsequently affected the discussion on fairness and transparency of the Tribunal.

As the question of applicable law came forth the Government had to decide which law should govern the trial—international law in international forum, or any of the previously passed domestic laws in a domestic forum (Rahman 2008; Ullah 2008)? Are there any statutory limitations (Islam 2008)? Here choice of law became relevant, as there had never been any assistance from the International Community; neither did Bangladesh have any prior experience to hold such trials. Then again, the question of statutory limitations came up when a Pakistani Envoy in Dhaka rejected any plan to try Pakistani nationals accused of murder, rape, and arson stating 'let bygones be bygones' (Dawn 2009).

A further doubt that remained alive for a long time, despite some campaigns offering truth to debunk the rumor, was the issue of general amnesty granted by Prime Minister Sheikh Mujibur Rahman. Days before the national celebration of victory day in 1973, a general amnesty was declared that is viewed by many as a process to absolve collaborators. Therefore, to many, the question of holding collaborators' trial after so many years is irrelevant and does not arise at all, as collaborators were granted clemency (Karzon 2008; Hosain 2008; Ullah 2008; Khan 2008).

The most recent addition to this ongoing debate was a statement made by the Minister of Home Affairs Asaduzzaman Khan Kamal (Bangladesh). He said, in reply to a query of a journalist in December 2015, that the Government would take initiative to bring the 195 members of the Pakistan Armed Forces and try them for war crimes in Bangladesh (Report 2015). This statement came following the reaction of the foreign ministry of Pakistan in response to the execution of Ali Ahsan Mohammad Mojaheed—Secretary General of Jamaat and Salauddin Quader Chowdhury—Member of the Standing Committee of BNP on November 22, 2015. In their official statement, Pakistan said 'We have noted with deep concern and anguish the unfortunate executions… Pakistan is deeply disturbed at this development.' Bangladesh sharply reacted at this statement by calling the Pakistani Envoy to the office of the Secretary of Foreign Affairs and lodging a formal protest (Karim and Bhattacharjee 2015). Some critics, including Pakistani authority claim that those officers of Pakistan Armed Forces, were forgiven by Sheikh Mujibir Rahman under a tripartite agreement signed between Bangladesh–India–Pakistan in 1974 (Jalil 2010; Syed 2015). Part of the Clause 15 of this agreement read:

> having regard to the appeal of the Prime Minister of Pakistan to the people of Bangladesh to forgive and forget the mistakes of the past, the Foreign Minister of Bangladesh stated that the Government of Bangladesh had decided not to proceed with the trials as an act of clemency. It was agreed that the 195 prisoners of war may be repatriated to Pakistan along with the other prisoners of war now in the process of repatriation under the Delhi Agreement (Sassoli et al. 1974).

The other dimension of the debate is jurisprudential. There had been concerns whether persons accused under the ICT Act would enjoy globally recognized fair trial rights. The Tribunal received substantial attention and support from international bodies, including the UN (McCormack 2011), that had conversely (and naturally) served to attract attention of many critics. Critics scrutinized the legislation and Court procedures and came up with several concerns they believe form serious drawbacks of the Tribunal. Most of these issues are apparently identified through a comparative analysis of standards currently maintained by the Tribunal with international standards of human rights applicable in the trial process.

With the first amendment of the Constitution of Bangladesh, Clause (3) to Article 47 and a new Article 47(A) were added. This amendment made it impossible to declare any law, created to try POW, crimes of genocide, war crimes, crimes against humanity, and other crimes under international law, unlawful, or void even if the said law is not in agreement with the Constitution [Article 47(3)]. Besides, Article 47(A) removes applicability of constitutional provisions on right to protection of law (Article 31), guarantee against the retrospective application of the criminal law (Clause 1, Article 35), right to a speedy and public trial (Clause 3, Article 35), and right to move the High Court Division for the enforcement of fundamental rights (Article 44) to any person to whom a law specified in Clause (3) of Article 47 applies. Often critics see this amendment as biased as it makes accused under the ICT Act 1973, if put in their language, 'second-class citizen,' (Cammegh 2011) since they are categorically deprived of certain constitutional rights, including the right to the protection of law.

On the basis of the evidence available, it seems fair for many to suggest that at least two of the judgments handed down so far—death sentences of Abdul Quader Mollah and Salauddin Quader Chowdhury—might have undermined the fundamental fairness and transparency of the trial process. Critics denounced the death sentence of Abdul Quader Mollah, Jamaat's Assistant Secretary General, arguing the trial was based on hearsay evidence (Jamaat-e-Islami 2013; Maslen 2014) and it had violated 'almost every fair trial guarantee,' although concurrently agreed that Bangladesh made substantial efforts to establish a transparent process (Maslen 2014). With regard to transparency of the trial process, some critics observed that there were notable limitations on defense. Specially, the number of witnesses allowed to be called by the defense and the hours allotted for presentation of defense cases raised questions. They argued that, while the prosecution had no limits placed on the number of witnesses they could call, the Tribunal restricted the defense witness to a fixed number (Bergman 2015a, b, c).

3.1 *The Controversies, Elaborated*

Like most of the events in the history of war crimes trials, war crimes trial in Bangladesh had been hardly free from criticisms. Although a UN-led international tribunal never investigated the alleged incidents of genocide or any other questions of war crimes during the war of 1971, which is often used to question the validity of alleged charges of genocide, whether genocide, war crimes and crimes against humanity actually took place during the war of 1971 in the land now called Bangladesh is actually a settled matter. Another apparently appealing question that aided lengthy discourse among the readers of the subject was about the actual scale of atrocities.

While the question concerning the exact number of victims generally should not be an important issue in the trial process, as this question cannot be answered scientifically at all, some research is necessary to understand the legitimacy of popular public demand of war crimes trials in Bangladesh. The most accepted claim among renowned scholars, journalists, think tanks, and members of the indefatigable civil society about the number of civilians killed (excluding victims of other crimes under international law) in the war was three million. Although there was no national or international investigation to ascertain the gravity of the violence, the number can be traced back in the writing of Payne (1973). In his book 'Massacre,' he quoted President Yahya Khan of Pakistan saying in a military conference in February 1971—'Kill three million of them and the rest will eat out of our hands.'

Parties who deny this number claim that the figure is nowhere near reality. The Pakistan Government commissioned and published 'Hamoodur Rahman Commission of Inquiry into the 1971 India–Pakistan War: Supplementary Report' suggesting the number of people killed in the war was barely 26 thousand. 'It is possible that even these figures may contain an element of exaggeration as the lower formations may have magnified their own achievements in quelling the rebellion' as the report goes. Does the phrase 'quelling the rebellion' mean the figure includes only the members of Bengali liberation forces and no civilians? The report does, however, indicate on the massive civilian casualties across East Pakistan and according to its estimation, around 100,000–500,000 civilians were killed. Nevertheless, the theory about the identity of these victims and the alleged perpetrators, as the Commission produced, could be greatly disappointing to many. According to this report, all the victims were helpless Biharis, West Pakistanis, or patriotic Bengalis killed at the hands of none but Awami League militants.

A legal study by the secretariat of the International Commission of Jurists in 1972 under the title 'The events in East Pakistan, 1971,' however, gave a balanced description of the violence. The study indicated that the main victims of the atrocious Army crackdown were helpless Bengalis, especially Hindu minorities. There were, however, several brutal attacks on non-Bengali communities, including Biharis and West Pakistanis in some areas. According to their estimation, the number of civil casualties during the war was about a million. An elaborate description of the events as covered by international media may be found in 'Bangladesh Genocide and World Press'—a painstaking work of Quaderi (1972).

If the whole question of 'figures' is laid aside, the simple fact is, in some places non-Bengalis were the victim of same hideous carnage as Bengalis. Yet, as this chapter goes to press, no charge has been filed against any person for having committed war crimes against non-Bengalis. In view of that, the war crimes trial runs the risk of being viewed as 'partial' because of the virtual silence on this issue. Migrated from India during partition, these Urdu-speaking Biharis had always demonstrated inclination toward Pakistan and many of them even actively collaborated with Pakistan Armed Forces in 1971. On the brink of war, they were targeted by mainstream Bengali people and were subjected to almost all forms of war crimes (D'Costa 2011). Anthony Mascarenhas, a Pakistani reporter, who published 'Genocide' in the UK's Sunday Times on June 13, 1971, revealing Pakistan Army's brutal campaign on Bengali civilians, received widespread admiration among the Bengalis; unfortunately, however, the stories of war crimes against non-Bengalis captured on the same article attracted little attention.

4 Trial Under the Bangladesh Collaborators (Special Tribunal) Order 1972

Does the delay alone invalidate current efforts to hold war crimes trial or automatically make it appear politically biased? Trials of collaborators who allegedly participated with, or aided, abetted, or rendered material assistance to Pakistan Armed Forces during the war of 1971 first began in 1972. Recruited from local community, they were primarily the members of Al Badr, Al Shams, and Razakars —armed auxiliary forces created under a legal framework by the Pakistan Government to assist Pakistan Armed Forces during the war of 1971 (Hiro 2015). After independence, some 37,471 alleged collaborators were brought for trial and 2848 trials were completed convicting 752 criminals in total with only one death sentence (Sharif et al. 1987).

As the trial process, continued Bangladesh Government felt it necessary to legally validate the violence of freedom fighters' armed resistance in fighting against enemies. The Government passed Bangladesh National Liberation Struggle (Indemnity) Order, 1973, in February, giving freedom fighters immunity from criminal accountability for acts committed during the liberation war. In 1973 when the wounds of the war were still pretty fresh, would it be socially acceptable for people to assess this incident 'one sided' and/or denote general amnesty for collaborators that came in November of the same year a context-sensitive balancing approach? Apparently, overwhelmed by mixed emotions of victory and memories of most unpleasant events of Bengali history, people had little, if any, doubt concerning whether all actions of their gallant freedom fighters were legitimate acts of warfare, and hence, if they would be entitled to indemnity 'all together.'

After the massacre of Sheikh Mujibur Rahman in 1975, a military Government under the leadership of General Ziaur Rahman came into power. He passed the Bangladesh Collaborators (Special Tribunal) (Repeal) Ordinance, 1975, and thereby put a legal end to the trial process. In post-Mujib period, there had been an uprising of religion-based politics in Bangladesh. General Ziaur Rahman amended the Constitution and substituted the words 'absolute trust and faith in Allah' for 'secularism.' He placed several persons involved in war crimes or anti-liberation activities in dominant positions in the Government. Many of them had their seized property restored and were employed in positions previously lost owing to their allegiance to Pakistan Government. These initiatives virtually paved way for political rehabilitation of the persons accused of various crimes under both pieces of legislation. At the same time, there was an attempt to align Bangladesh more with the Islamic world (Jaffrelot 2004).

The post-liberation political climate was truly uneasy for Awami League Government. The circumstances were so challenging that it would push them making controversial choices that would not only draw harsh criticism but also benefit their emerging political rivals. Awami League created Bangladesh Krishak Sramik Awami League (BAKSAL)—a single political platform in response to massive political and economic disorder the new country was facing. Despite the much needed administrative and economic reforms on its agenda, BAKSAL would be heavily criticized as a political vehicle to bring about a 'one-party state,' as it practically interdicted activities of any other political parties. In Order to quash the violent activities of the radical revolutionaries that engulfed the country, Prime Minister Sheikh Mujibur Rahman declared a state of emergency in 1974. Subsequently, in a desperate attempt to unite all political forces and find a stable political system, he pushed the fourth amendment of the Constitution in 1975 dissolving all political organizations and providing for a one-party presidential system in place of original parliamentary one (Molla 2004; Schottli et al. 2015).

Later, the military Government of General Ziaur Rahman promulgated Political Parties Regulation, 1976, as Martial Law Administrator and Political Parties Ordinance, 1978, after being elected as President. Promulgation of these laws reopened the gate for multiparty politics, offering simultaneously an opportunity for pro-Pakistani religion-based political elements to rehabilitate themselves. Several Islamist parties, including Jamaat-e-Islami, took this occasion to be politically reorganized as legitimate Bangladeshi political parties (Riaz 2014).

President Ziaur Rahman was assassinated in 1981 when second martial law period began under Lt General Hussain Muhammad Ershad. Ershad took over the power as Chief Martial Law Administrator (subsequently President) in 1982 following a bloodless military *coup*. He remained in power until democracy was finally restored in 1990 and BNP came into power through the general election of 1991.

Since Bangladesh is a country of Muslims majority, military rulers readily exploited this opportunity to gain rapid popular support and make quick friends in the Islamic world. Just as President Ziaur Rahman, Ershad too emphasized on institutionalization of religion in Order to win the heart, support, and vote of the Muslim population. He brought constitutional amendments to declare Islam as the state religion. This way he followed the path of his predecessor and in one way or another backed religion-based politics in Bangladesh. During the administration of Ershad, the questions of war crimes were practically dormant as the Government remained reluctant to bring the issues on the agenda.

After the regime of Ershad, latent war crimes trial issues received fresh momentum from a civil society movement when Jahanara Imam, a prolific writer, and several other sociopolitical activists mobilized civil society against the political rehabilitation process of alleged war criminals of 1971. She coordinated Ghatak-Dalal Nirmul Committee (Committee to exterminate Killers and

Collaborators) and set up Gono Adalat (people's Court), a mock trial, asking the people's verdict against social and political rehabilitation process of alleged collaborators. The Gono Adalat accused Ghulam Azam, the newly elected Jamaat-e-Islami Chief, as 'war criminal' and demanded his trial along with other alleged collaborators. This movement virtually sets off the national war crimes tribunal movement afresh (Debnath 2012; Schottli et al. 2015).

5 Trials Under the International Crimes (Tribunals) Act 1973

As indicated earlier, the ICT Act provides for the setting up of tribunals and prosecution and punishment of persons committed or otherwise responsible for war crimes, crimes against humanity, genocide, and other crimes under international law. In 2009 and 2013, some significant amendments were brought into ICT Act; for instance, new amendments enabled the Tribunal to charge and place on trial even organizations for crimes under this Act. Under this Act, the prosecutors investigate into alleged crimes and submit reports to chief prosecutor who examines the reports and files them as formal charges. After examination of all documents and giving the defense adequate opportunities to defend their interests, the Tribunal, if there is a *prima facie* case, frame charge(s) (Act 1973). The Tribunal is actually a domestic judicial arrangement to try crimes recognized internationally under various international legal instruments.

After a massive win in the general election of 2008 Awami League swept into power. During the rule of previous Government under BNP, Bangladesh witnessed the emergence of several Islamist movements. Most notably, Bangladesh Jamaat-e-Islami's becoming part of a coalition Government with BNP gave the former a long-awaited opportunity to get closer to the people through administrative apparatus and revalidate itself as an important Bangladeshi political party. Later, due to soaring corruption and resurfacing of a number of groups involved in radicalism, political image of BNP was on the wane.

Afterward, continuing clash between BNP and Awami League ultimately paved way for a military backed interim Government. When finally the election was declared, Awami League put the issue of war crimes trial on the top of their agenda. Therefore, the sweeping victory in the election once again gave them the long waited and needed mandate to start war crimes trials under the ICT Act 1973. As indicated earlier, trials under this Act never began as the Pakistani POW were sent back to Pakistan, and a separate law was passed to hold trials of local collaborators.

The argument about the virtual silence of Awami League during their tenure between 1996 and 2001 with regard to war crimes trial fits the current discussion quite well. When Bangladesh Awami League came into power in 1996, it was expected that the war crimes trial process would get a new force as Awami League gave their support to Ghatak-Dalal Nirmul Committee (Hashmi 2011).

Unfortunately, however, it did not happen. One important reason behind this political oversight was probably the gradual growth of Islamism in Bangladeshi politics that began in the era of General Ziaur Rahman. Apparently, Awami League had to wait to assess the political strength of the religion-based politics before taking any tangible steps toward war crimes trials.

Some researchers pointed that unlike Pakistan, Bangladesh was a land of secular beliefs, hence, the defeat of radicalism in the hand of homegrown secular forces was only a matter of time, and thus, when the time was right, war crimes trial would be an effective way to eliminate this radicalism. Nevertheless, some scholars strongly believed that any attempt to hold a war crimes trial could actually divide the nation and push the society for civil war (Prakash 2011).

This could be one of the most eminent factors why Awami League had to wait until the period when Jamaat would be viewed as part of a corrupt and inefficient power block. In fact, the election of 1996 when Jamaat won only 3 seats in the parliament compared to 18 in 1991 (EC Bangladesh 1996) and then 2 seats in the 2008 election compared to 17 in 2001 (EC Bangladesh 2008), virtually served this purpose, exposing the vital crack in Jamaat's politics. These election results perhaps suggest that the success of Jamaat's religion-based politics is heavily dependent on the success of BNP as an ally. Their religion-based politics that was so instrumental against military backed Government in the decade of the 1980s appeared weaker in the political arena of Bangladesh in 1996 and also in 2008 when Army-backed caretaker Government came into power (Islam 2015). Possibly this is one of the most confident explanations Awami League could provide to counter the blame that their inaction against alleged war criminals between 1996 and 2001 was due to a backdoor friendship with Jamaat.

'What form of tribunals should be established for the trial of persons accused of these crimes? Clearly, they may be tried under the domestic criminal law either before the normal criminal Courts or before special tribunals established for the purpose'—a question asked and then answered by the International Commission of Jurists immediately after the war, in 1972, is still highly relevant in the present context. The questions involving the most suited forum and choice of statute to govern the trial did not leave Bangladesh with many options in 1972 or in 2010, once again, due to the war's historical background, as the researchers argued (Rahman 2008; Ullah 2008; Khan 2008).

Some researchers pointed to the Cambodian hybrid tribunal as one option (Rahman 2008; Karzon 2008) but then warned instantly about its extremely high chance of failure because of the historical background of the war. Although the war of 1971 managed to draw attention of the world community in many ways, its violence, however, remained largely unnoticed by world community due to the active and direct anti-Bangladesh role of the USA and China as close allies of Pakistan. Therefore, it was highly improbable that Bangladesh would be able to create the level of universal consensus required to hold such trials in an international forum (Rahman 2008).

The other option was, of course, under domestic criminal law before the regular criminal Court, but this option had already been proved unworkable for the type of charges to be brought. In 2007, a former commander of freedom fighters, Muzaffar Ahmed, filed a case against specific Jamaat-e-Islami leaders for killing two members of the Bengali liberation force in 1971. On January 28, 2008, the officer-in-charge of police concerned submitted his report to the Court stating no evidence to support the allegations had been found (Ullah 2008), which was obvious after decades. In the same way, the charges brought in 1982 against Dr. Syed Sajjad Hussain—former Vice Chancellor of the University of Dhaka and a declared sympathizer of Pakistan—for collaboration with Pakistan Armed Forces, remained unsuccessful (Billah 2008). Hence, the most suitable alternative, since international community remained unwilling to initiate any process, for Bangladesh was to employing an easy, constitutionally valid, and speedy trial process offered by the ICT Act of 1973 (Hosain 2008; Karzon 2008).

Would Bangladesh be acting in conformity with international law if it assumed national jurisdiction for alleged war crimes? Although the issue of national jurisdiction in war crimes trial remained quiet for a long period, its relevance grew over time. Under the relevant Articles of Geneva Conventions of 1949 (Articles 49, 50, 129, and 146, respectively), states are actually obliged to bring persons accused of ‘grave breaches’ of these Conventions before its own Courts or hand them over to another High Contracting Party. From this standpoint, Rahman will not be alone in author’s view that as long as confronting the crimes of genocide is concerned, for a long period—1948–1993 (until the establishment of the ICTY)—when the world community remained sunk in the bottomless darkness of inertia, Bangladesh lit the only light of hope through the passing of the ICT Act in 1973 (Rahman 2008).

Above arguments provide some positive evidence that seeking international assistance would probably prove futile, and hence, the best option was to make use of the ICT Act initially passed to try members of Pakistan Armed Forces. This may, however, be noted here that the local collaborators were actually made part of Pakistan Armed Forces through the East Pakistan Razakar Ordinance promulgated on June 1, 1971 by Pakistan Government (Hiro 2015). Nevertheless, at the same time it would be, to some extent, morally unsound to assume that UN’s offer to assist Bangladesh in planning the current war crimes tribunal (McCormack 2011) was baseless. As it was indicated earlier, unlike International Military Tribunal at Nuremberg, which was composed of judges from victorious countries only, Bangladesh could have assessed the prospect of trying the alleged war criminals in international tribunal under the authority of the UN (Jurits 1972) or at least under the planning of the UN as gestures to satisfy international opinion.

More to the point, there had been a discussion about the applicability of limitations of law in war crimes trial. Islam (2008) stressed that such confusion is baseless as there is no such legal restriction. In international law, certain crimes, including war crimes and crimes against humanity, are not subject to statute of limitations. This means, perpetrators of certain crimes under international law can always be brought to justice, no matter how long it has been since the crimes had been committed (Schabas 2010), and gradually, this non-applicability of statutory limitations has become a norm of customary international law (Saulnier 2013).

With regard to the question of general amnesty, there is, apparently, obstinate refusal to accept the truth on the part of many observers including the political block that directly opposes the trials. On November 30, 1973, Sheikh Mujibur Rahman declared a general amnesty to grant clemency to persons convicted or accused of offenses under the Bangladesh Collaborators (Special Tribunal) Order, 1972. Under the general amnesty, persons convicted under this Order were released from jail and cases pending against persons were withdrawn. Some researchers labeled this as blanket amnesty (Cammegh 2011), wrongly.

They probably overlook para 2 of the declaration which says that the clemency granted under para 1 shall not extend to persons accused of specific serious crimes under the Penal Code, namely murder, rape, mischief by fire of explosive (Jahan 2013; Karzon 2008; Ullah 2008; Khan 2008). This selective reading and manifestation serve at least one purpose; they confer political validity to General Ziaur Rahman's amnesty to all collaborators irrespective of the gravity of the charges brought against. Therefore, the attempt to freeing persons accused of petty offenses or against whom no indictments were brought could be best described by categorizing this as an attempt to restore peace rather than seeking retribution. If Bangladesh carried out its intentions ignoring the political considerations prevailing at that time, it could have been devastating for the thousands of 'stranded Bengalis' in Pakistan awaiting repatriation.

Similarly, the claim that the clemency shown by Sheikh Mujibur Rahman's Government to the 195 POW under the 1974 tripartite agreement had diminished any chances of investigation and prosecution of their atrocities is probably an example of the lack of even basic insight into the whole matter under investigation. This agreement was only an instrument to ensure uninterrupted repatriation and subsequent trial procedure of the accused 195 POW. On May 11, 1973, Mr. J. G. Kharas, Ambassador of Pakistan to the Netherlands, submitted to the ICJ in the Case Concerning Trial of Pakistani Prisoners of War that:

> That Pakistan has an exclusive right to exercise jurisdiction over the one hundred and ninety-five Pakistani nationals or any other number, now in Indian custody, and accused of committing acts of genocide in Pakistani territory by virtue of the application of the Convention on the Prevention and Punishment of the crime of Genocide of 9 December 1948, and that no other Government or authority is competent to exercise such jurisdiction.

Accordingly, in the subsequent oral arguments presented in this case between June 4 and 26, 1973, as recorded by ICJ, Mr. Yahya Bakhtiar, Attorney General of Pakistan appearing as the Chief Counsel submitted that:

> the representative and democratic Government of Pakistan of today stands for the principle of accountability for any wrongs that may have been committed by Pakistani nationals in East Pakistan. In the absence—I request the Court to mark my submission—of an international penal tribunal agreed upon between the parties and functioning on neutral territory, the Government of Pakistan has made it clear that the principle of accountability will be upheld by us.

He further submitted that:

> In this connection I refer again to the statement of the Government of Pakistan issued on 20 April 1973, in which the Government policy has been clearly stated as follows: "The Government of Pakistan reiterates its readiness to constitute a Judicial Tribunal, of such character and composition as will inspire international confidence, to try persons charged with the alleged actions.

Interestingly, those who do not hesitate to criticize in strongest terms the substance and procedure of ICT Act—an Act of Parliament—remains mysteriously silent when it comes to questioning the legality of the general amnesty (to local collaborators) of Sheikh Mujibur Rahman, and the clemency shown to the 195 POW (charged with the crimes of genocide) under the tripartite agreement which had not been passed by any parliament. Observers argued that the said general amnesty was not reflective of the general popular opinion (Hosain 2008) and hence, entirely contradictory to the spirit of the Constitution of Bangladesh. Besides, war crimes are crimes under international law and thus granting clemency by any person or state could be presumed illegal, as Ullah argued (2008). In its observation in 2013 judgment in the case against Abdul Quader Mollah, the Tribunal said 'Amnesty shown to 195 listed war criminals are opposed to peremptory norms of international law.' The Tribunal further stated that 'any agreement and treaty amongst states in derogation of this principle stands void as per the provisions of international treaty law convention [Article 53 of the Vienna Convention on the Law of the Treaties, 1969],' and therefore, 'the [ICT] Act of 1973 still provides jurisdiction to bring them to the process of justice.'

Now the question is why the trial is labeled as political vendetta. Is it merely because Awami League is the initiator and most of the persons accused, at least in the initial stage, are known leaders of Jamaat-e-Islami? Is it a politically influenced judicial process to separate Jamaat-e-Islami from BNP and thereby weaken the latter (Hasan 2014), or a premeditated mechanism to settle old political vendetta against the remnants of former Jamaat-e-Islami Pakistan (Jalil 2010)?

Apparently, the current discourses of 'political vendetta' might have its ideological root in the political history of the subcontinent. Historically, Bangladesh Jamaat-e-Islami has its origin in Jamaat-e-Islami Pakistan—a party vigorously opposed the creation of Pakistan when they found out Pakistan would be a secular homeland for Indian Muslims not an Islamic State. That is, not a political system drawn from the principles of four Caliphs of Islam. Based on the same ideology, the East Pakistan wing of Jamaat-e-Islami Pakistan, later Bangladesh Jamaat-e-Islami, actively opposed the creation of Bangladesh fearing, under the leadership of secular Awami League (Rahman 2010), any chances of creating an Islamic State would perish. Is this ideological clash so acute that it would ultimately instigate political vendetta?

Historical accounts indicate that there had always been a workable relationship between these parties. In 1962, Jamaat-e-Islami was one of the political allies of Awami League in the movement against Ayub Khan's martial law administration. As a member of the National Democratic Front (NDF) Jamaat-e-Islami Pakistan struggled along with Awami League for restoration of parliamentary democracy in Pakistan (Ahmed 2004). Besides, in 1991 Awami League enjoined Jamaat parliamentary support for their presidential candidate (Hashmi 2011) when Jamaat was under the leadership of Ghulam Azam and then again made Jamaat their strategic political ally in 1994 in the struggle against BNP Government (Islam 2015). These examples probably indicate that ideological distance is forgotten when political proximity is necessary.

However, there is another theory that may help understand the alleged political vendetta from a different perspective. Jamaat's coalition with BNP always proved to be beneficial for BNP and almost the opposite for Awami League. After the 1991 general election, Jamaat with their 18 seats in the parliament supported BNP from outside to form Government, which ultimately pushed Awami League to the opposition. Then, in 2001, Jamaat once again won 17 seats in Parliament through an electoral alliance with BNP and became part of a coalition Government for the first time in history, pushing again Awami League out of power.

This historic tie benefitted both almost equally. On the one hand, BNP received immense support from Jamaat in most of their anti-government struggles, as well as vital coalition in winning election and forming a Government. On the other hand, Jamaat lived worry free when BNP was in power as the question of holding a war crimes trial implicating Jamaat was not even a remote possibility. Irrespective of the reasons why Jamaat remained attached to the BNP, the alliance gave them the vital insurance against probable perils, apparently coming from Awami League. No doubt, this alliance proved to be truly problematic for Awami League.

In the political field, Awami League would appear stronger if Jamaat struggles to establish their social acceptance as pro-Bangladeshi political party. Similarly, Awami League also benefits if BNP appears to be the ideological friend of convicted war criminals or the 'foes' its founder Ziaur Rahman—a renowned freedom fighter—fought against in 1971. Both of these targets would be achieved if Jamaat-e-Islami leaders could be brought to trial and convicted for war crimes. Undoubtedly, many would find this suggestion as good focus through which the war crimes trials in Bangladesh would clearly appear as 'political vendetta.'

Therefore, despite Jamaat's ambiguous stand in Bangladesh politics, they would always be viewed as rivals of Awami League at least owing to their political alliance with BNP. Historically Jamaat is the political ally of BNP and ideologically closer to each other as long as issues of war crimes trials, anti-Indian stance and closing the gaps with Pakistan are concerned (Ray 2007; Pant 2011; Mazumdar 2014). Besides, as of January 2016, when the Appellate Division of the Supreme Court upheld the death sentence of Motiur Rahman Nizami, Jamaat-e-Islami Ameer (Sarkar 2016), the Tribunal issued 21 verdicts since its inception in 2010 convicting 26 persons, most of whom were connected with the politics of Jamaat or BNP. Although, Jatiya Party leader Syed M Kawsar and expelled Awami League leader Mobarak Hossain were also among these 26 persons, as well as 24 persons now (as of January 2016) under trial in 14 cases are from local level with no known political connections (Roy 2015), the initial arrests, detentions, and prosecution of known leaders of Jamaat and BNP aroused doubt about Government's motive.

Therefore, any attempts against alleged war criminals, which would naturally be taken by Awami League at least for the time being, would always run the risk of being viewed as politically motivated.

5.1 Controversies with Regard to Trial Process Under ICT Act 1973

Because this chapter adopts a sociolegal approach—how did social and political organizations shape the laws of war crimes or how were these organizations shaped by those laws—the author spends most of his efforts analyzing the sociolegal context in which the Tribunal exits and operates. Accordingly, there is little scope, if any, to focus on legal research. Nevertheless, since the question of fairness and transparency is tied with the law and the procedure of the Tribunal, the author will discuss the outcome of some legal research initiatives about the war crimes trial in Bangladesh.

Benjamin M. Joyes conducted a thorough research on the ICT Act and the war crimes trial process in Bangladesh and concluded that the Tribunal failed to ensure a wide range of internationally recognized fair trial rights, especially for the accused and convicts. Joyes mentioned that rights of the persons involved in the investigation—witnesses and accused—are grossly denied, as there are no provisions allowing the right to freedom from coercion, duress, or threat. Most importantly, as Joyes identified, the statute does not require investigators to inform an accused the reasons for the interview or interrogation. An accused does not have the right to remain silent as articulated in the International Covenant on Civil and Political Rights (Joyes 2010).

Joyes further mentioned that the Rules of Evidence and Procedure allow the tribunal to enjoy unchecked liberty with regard to admissibility of evidence in the trial. Any decision of the tribunal is final in this regard. Joyes views this liberty as a violation of the Rome Statute, which prohibits, in general, the collection of evidence by means of a violation of the Statute. In brief, there is a potential risk of political biases since the Tribunal is authorized to take judicial knowledge of a wide range of Governmental and non-governmental documents. In addition, there is a lack of clarification on standard of proof and accused persons may not enjoy the protection offered by the presumption of innocence (2010).

Other major issues Joyes indicated as contrary to international standards are the issues relating to privileges of the defense Counsels, right to appeal of the accused, and death penalty. He mentioned that the ICT Act does not offer any protection to the Counsels, so that they could perform their duties without any fear of being persecuted, a privilege guaranteed in the Rome Statute. He also mentioned that accused under the ICT Act are deprived of certain fundamental rights guaranteed in the Constitution of Bangladesh (Joyes 2010). That is, accused persons are not entitled to any interlocutory appeal to the higher Courts, and other fundamental rights guaranteed in the Constitution as such rights are removed by Article 47(3) of the Constitution for those who are charged under the ICT Act (Cammegh 2011). With regard to judgment and sentence, the ICT Act does not provide any clear guidelines, but allows the Tribunal to award sentence it thinks 'just and proper.' The only sentence the ICT Act mentions is the sentence of death. Joyes argued that this might not allow Tribunals to conduct trials responsibly (Joyes 2010).

Joyes' arguments have merit, especially with regard to few specific incidents of 'harassment of defense Counsel' (Watch 2012) that took place at the initial stage when the Tribunal was established, as well as the case of 'interlocutory appeal' to the higher Courts, among others. However, his arguments with regard to 'fundamental rights' may not, at least in some cases, hold up under closer inspection. Allama Delwar Hossain Saydee's (Nayeb-e-Ameer, Jamaat) death sentence passed by the Tribunal was commuted to imprisonment for life (rest of his natural life) by majority of the judges in the appeal, and the question on whether persons sentenced under the ICT Act be allowed to file review petition with the Supreme Court was also resolved in favor of the defense.

Besides, the provisions of Clause 3 of Articles 47 and 47(A) which are considered, by some critics, to have rendered the constitutional rights inapplicable for persons accused under the ICT Act have the approval of both BNP and Jamaat. The main intention of the legislature behind introducing these changes to the Constitution was not to deprive an accused under the ICT or similar Act of the fair trial guarantees, but only to ensure speedy trial of most heinous crimes. Probably this is the reason why BNP, even when they formed coalition Government with Jamaat after 2001 general election, never amended these provisions despite more than two-thirds majority in the parliament.

Recently, the death sentences and executions of three top-raking Jamaat leaders and one Standing Committee member of BNP have fostered debate on the issues of fairness and transparency of the trial. Many for being one entirely based on hearsay evidence (Maslen 2014) criticize the judgment of Abdul Quader Mollah, Jamaat's Assistant Secretary General. Initially, the accused received life in prison, which ignited the biggest peaceful protest in Dhaka in two decades. Ultimately, an amendment was brought in ICT Act 1973 to allow the Government, complainants, or informants the right to appeal against any Order of acquittal or Order of sentence. Originally, only the convicted had this right (Paulussen et al. 2013). Since the Government's appeal was granted under retrospectively applied law, many argued that '[c]hanging the law and applying it retroactively after a trial offends basic notions of a fair trial under international law' (Human Rights Watch 2013).

In addition, there was a vibrant debate among the observers on legal grounds when Mollah's appeal petition against death sentence before the apex Court was rejected and the question of filing a review petition against this decision came forth (The Daily Star 2013a, b). This may be noted here that initially the law on this point remained unclear, as there was no settled legal principle in Bangladesh with regard to scope of filing a review petition in cases where the trial ran under special law like the ICT Act 1973. The petitioner filed a review petition under Article 105 of the Constitution of Bangladesh which says '[t]he Appellate Division shall have power, subject to the provisions of any Act of Parliament and of any rules made by that division to review any judgment pronounced or Order made by it.' However, it was held that due to the protective provisions in Article 47A(2), the provision mentioned in Article 105 could not be engaged for persons accused of crimes against humanity, the Court could pass an Order to correct mistakes in the judgment applying the doctrine of *ex-debito justitiae* (Abdul Quader Mollah v. The Chief Prosecutor 2013; Kamaruzzaman v. Bangladesh 2015).

Apparently Petitioner's claim rests on the assumption that the provisions on review confers a right to the litigants and the Supreme Court can always use its inherent power to review. The general practice is that the Supreme Court may review its judgment and Orders in civil proceedings. In a criminal proceeding, review may be done 'only on the ground of an error apparent on the face of the record' as stated in Order 26 and Rule 1 of the Supreme Court of Bangladesh (Appellate Division) Rules, 1988. In the criminal review petition of Muhammad Kamaruzzaman, the Supreme Court observed that:

> We unequivocally expressed that it is now well settled that a review of an earlier Order is not permissible unless the Court is satisfied that material error, manifest on the face of the Order, undermines it's soundness or results in miscarriage of justice. We observed that a review of judgment is a serious step and the Courts are reluctant to invoke their power except where a glaring omission or patent mistake or grave error have crept in earlier by judicial fallibility.

From this point of view, Mollah was allowed to file a review petition not based on Constitutional provisions or the Supreme Court Rules, but from the inherent power of the Supreme Court. Although there is Constitutional bar as mentioned earlier, it appears that the petition was allowed to keep a door open for review in case there is a material error in future in any judgment, although it was not allowed in the law. In 2015, three more criminal review petitions were filed against the decisions passed in Criminal Appeals in connection with the death sentences passed by the Tribunal against Muhammad Kamaruzzaman—Senior Assistant Secretary General of Jamaat, Ali Ahsan Mohammad Mojaheed—Secretary General of Jamaat and Salauddin Quader Chowdhury—Member of the Standing Committee of BNP.

The Tribunal's bar on the maximum number of defense witness to be heard, as it was observed in the cases of Abdul Alim (former BNP leader, jailed until death), Motiur Rahman Nizami, Kamaruzzaman, Abdul Quader Molla, and Chowdhury, has been a popular topic in the ongoing discourse on the transparency of war crimes trial in Bangladesh. In the view of some critics, putting restriction on maximum number of defense witnesses without any 'rationale' was 'gross inconsistency' as the decisions were made 'arbitrarily' (Bergman 2015a, b, c). Bergman (2015a, b, c) stated that:

> [t]he ICT's restriction on how many defense witnesses can be called has been common. In the case of Abdul Alim, the prosecution summoned 35 witnesses, but the defense was restricted to three witnesses to disprove 17 offences. Four witnesses were permitted in the case of Motiur Rahman Nizami's defense relating to 16 charges; five witnesses in the trial of Kamaruzzaman involving seven offences; and six in the case of Abdul Quader Molla in defense of six offences.

However, the debate over the issue of transparency in the trial and review petition of Salauddin Quader Chowdhury attracted greater attention of many. In the trial, Chowdhury was allowed to bring only five witnesses in relation to 23 offenses, where the prosecution was allowed to call 41 witnesses. After the testimony of the last prosecution witness, the prosecution applied with the Tribunal 'arguing for the cancellation of the whole defense witness list on the grounds that it did not provide the "details" of the charges on which these witnesses would give evidence, as required by the rules of procedure.' In its Order passed subsequently, the Tribunal mentioned that the defense was permitted to examine only five witnesses. The Tribunal, however, did not indicate anything with regard to the 'lack of details' as referred by the prosecution; but stated that 'the number of defense witnesses […] appears to be an attempt to delay the trial of the case which is not permitted by law.' Initially, the defense provided the Tribunal with a list of 1153 witnesses 'whom they hoped would later to testify as witnesses' (Bergman 2015a, b, c).

The question of transparency in connection with the trial of Chowdhury reappeared at the time of review petition from the judgment of the Appellate Division of the Supreme Court in his Criminal Appeal. The accused petitioner filed a petition before the Supreme Court requesting to record statements of eight alibi witnesses, including five Pakistanis, at the time of review. The prosecution labeled this move 'at this stage of legal proceedings … unprecedented' (Staff Correspondent 2015a, b). However, it would not be necessary to call these witnesses—whose names were initially listed on the 26 (6 foreign and 20 Bangladeshi witnesses) defense witness list but never had a chance to testify—at this stage if they were heard earlier (Bergman 2015a, b, c).

The evidence of these five Pakistani witnesses was crucial in that their evidence supports Chowdhury's alibi defense that, from April 1971 onward, when the offenses he was charged with took place, Chowdhury was actually in Pakistan pursuing his education in the University of Punjab. After filing of the review petition, he filed an application for issuing summons upon Mr. Muneeb Arjamand Khan, a social worker; Mr. Ishaq Khan Khakwani, ex-Rail Minister; Mr. Riaz Ahmed Noon, Mr. Mohammedmian Soomro, former Pakistani Prime Minister, and Amber Haroon Saigol, Chairman of the Dawn media group of Pakistan 'to testifying as defense witnesses on the ground that if those witnesses are examined, the defense plea of alibi could have been substantiated' (The Supreme Court of Bangladesh 2015a, b Criminal Appeal No 63). This application was rejected on November 2, 2015. As these alibi witnesses were never allowed to testify, therefore, it is difficult to say whether their evidence would bear up any level of scrutiny; the question remains, however, whether the defense was able to take the full advantage of the opportunity available.

In support of his alibi claim, Chowdhury presented a 'duplicate certificate allegedly issued by the University of Punjab certifying that the petitioner has obtained Bachelor of Arts with honors in political science in August, 1971' in the review. With regard to this certificate, the Court observed that 'this duplicate certificate was issued on May 22nd, 2012, and the same was attested by the alleged Vice Chancellor of the Punjab University and the Registrar on November 4 and 5,

2015, respectively.' Then, the Court (Appellate Division in review) stated that they failed to understand why Chowdhury did not submit that certificate before the Tribunal or during the appeal hearing although he had filed 'good number of documents which he procured in 2013' including 'a testimonial allegedly issued by a professor of the department of Political Science' of the same university. 'When this point was drawn to his attention, the learned Counsel [appearing on behalf of the petitioner] [found] it difficult to repel the doubt.' His attempt to offer 'an explanation to the effect that the petitioner applied for a duplicate copy earlier but he did not receive the same until November 2015' appeared to have 'no basis at all since the alleged certificate was issued in 2012,' as the Court stated (The Supreme Court of Bangladesh 2015, Criminal Appeal No 63).

Further doubt was cast by the Attorney General (AG) on the point that the academic session as mentioned in the certificate had been '1971' was true. The learned AG argued that the 'academic session ought to have been 1968–1971, inasmuch as, the honors course during that period was for three years.' The learned Counsel in response to this argument submitted that the petitioner studied at the University of Dhaka earlier and then he transferred his credit to the University of Punjab in 1971, however, he failed to produce any paper in his support. This claim, therefore, virtually urged the Court to accept the fact that 'in May, the petitioner admitted to Punjab University in honors and obtained graduation in August in political science' (in 4 months). The Court found this to be 'totally an absurd story to believe,' and therefore, the Court concluded that 'no reliance could at all be attached on this certificate—it is a forged document which is apparently created for confusing this Court' (The Supreme Court of Bangladesh 2015, Criminal Appeal No. 63).

In this case, prosecution relied on three vital witnesses and two reports, among others. The testimony of the prosecution witnesses—two freedom fighters—who narrated how they attacked the car of Chowdhury killing his driver and injuring him severely, was supported by another witness, a doctor, who was on duty at Chittagong Medical College Hospital, Chittagong, at late September 1971, when he saw Chowdhury 'receiving treatment for severe injury to his leg.' Prosecution's case that Chowdhury was very much present in Bangladesh also relied on two crucial reports. They submitted a report of the *Dainik Pakistan* [Daily Pakistan] of September 29, 1971, with the headline 'Son of Fazlul Quader wounded in bomb attack: driver shot dead,' as well as, 'a fortnightly report on the political situation for the second half of September 1971 from Special Branch [of Police], East Pakistan, Dacca, … prepared on October 2, 1971 by … deputy inspector general of police.' This second report, which was written at a time when the administration was under Pakistan Army's control, corroborated the news paper article stating that on the evening of September 20, 1971, rebels fired at the car of Salauddin Quader Chowdhury, son of Fazlul Quader Chowdhury—president, Pakistan Muslim League—at Chandrapara, Chittagong (Adhikary 2013; Farhad 2015).

In this case, the Court further observed that the 'authenticity of the certificate has not been certified by an authorized officer of the High Commission Office of Bangladesh stationed in Pakistan,' despite the fact that Section 19 of the ICT Act authorizes the Tribunal not to remain bound by 'technical rules of evidence.' The section also states that the Tribunal can 'adopt and apply to the greatest possible extent expeditious and non-technical procedure and may admit any evidence.' Therefore, the law 'makes clear that technical rules of evidence should be ignored —and the prosecution have taken great advantage of this in the past. So why not the defense,' Bergman argued (November 20, 2015).

Above legal issues offer only a brief synopsis of the vast array of legal discourses still dominating the thinking of many concerned with the war crimes tribunal of Bangladesh, and hence, no way exhaustive. A number of years have passed since the tribunal was established and now there are several judgments available for public examination and understanding of the effect, if any, of the alleged flaws in law and procedures on the judgments. All Orders and judgments of the Tribunals as well as the Appeal Court are available online on the respective websites, which anyone can get access. There are some vital amendments in the law and procedures of the Tribunal that were adopted at a later stage.

After the amendments of the Rules of the Tribunal, accused persons have the right to be presumed innocent and have the right to apply and be granted bail. Now, the prosecution bears the burden of proving a charge beyond any reasonable doubt and no person may be convicted twice for the same offense as the amendments suggest. The tribunal also assented to create a witness and victim protection system after some allegations of harassing a defense witness and Counsel. These amendments, among others, were introduced in the trial process mainly in response to international criticisms. Regardless, many still believe that the Tribunal does not meet international standards in its operations (Knoops 2014).

5.2 *Future of the ICT Bangladesh*

Undeniably, the above findings lend support to the claim that the ICT Act 1973 and the Tribunal probably will not withstand any rigorous legal scrutiny. Then, how does Bangladesh propose to deal with this alleged legally defective regime? Will the domestic political, social, and cultural considerations prevail and the trials proceed in the usual way? Alternatively, will it be discarded owing to the clearly visible legal 'imperfections' which have raised a few eyebrows among national and international observers together with fierce criticism from Jamaat? Or Bangladesh will adopt a more internationally accepted approach to remove the alleged impurities in the law and thereby take a constructive step to ensure 'justice' in its most traditional sense?

A quick revisit to the historical background of war crimes trial in Bangladesh will indicate that initially it was more legal rather than a political proceeding. At a later stage in 2008 when Awami League kept frequent mentioning of the war crimes trial in their pre-election speeches and eventually initiated the trial process after forming Government, the issue appeared fairly the opposite. Is the trial a political vendetta? If not, then why the Government is reluctant to rectify some of the notable procedural issues raised by the critics? Or, is it merely an honest attempt to implement campaign promise made to relieve the country of a long standing obligation to bring the alleged perpetrators of 1971 liberation war to trial? Therefore, it might be difficult to draw a conclusion on the real motivation behind the ongoing trials, and depending on which conclusion one supports, the analysis and understanding of the relevant laws and procedure may vary. Now, where could current Awami League Government position them in the risk-benefit balance?

If the trial continues in the usual way, the criticism with regard to inherent defects in the law and procedure will also prolong with every new verdict. Besides, there could be growing threat of backlash from Jamaat. However, so far, the Government has been able to handle this particular risk quite successfully. Government's achievement in successful execution of a number of top alleged war criminals through long open trial won unprecedented public support in its favor and brought them more applause than the condemnation for the alleged flaws in the trial process. Also, the initial demonstrations of violent backlash of Jamaat during *hortal* (general strike) are now virtually absent due to extremely poor public support and uneasy silence on behalf of BNP that never showed any reactions, official or otherwise, to any of the executions of the top leaders of their closest political ally.

On the contrary, if the trials are abandoned at this stage for reasons described earlier, this will be marked as a political victory for Jamaat-e-Islami but both political and moral defeat for Awami League. There is every chance that the young voters who turned against Jamaat and BNP in the 2008 election would be disappointed and Awami League would lose their political supports. Simultaneously, their credibility as pro-independence political party of Bangladesh could also be seriously diluted should Bangladesh fails to fulfill its obligations to bring person accused of 'grave breaches' of international law into justice.

However, the single most important example of legal battle win of Awami League regarding war crimes trial so far is, probably, the review petition of Ali Ahsan Mohammad Mojaheed. For charges 3, 5, 6, and 7 (abetting and facilitating the commission of offense of confinement of one Ranjit Nath; abetting and facilitating the commission of killing of freedom fighters Altaf Mahmud, Bodi, Rumi, Juel, and Azad; planning, abetting, conspiring, and facilitating the killings of intellectuals starting from December 10, 1971; and launching attack against the Hindu Community, respectively), he was sentenced to 5-year imprisonment, imprisonment for life and death sentence (for both charges no. 6 and 7), respectively. Nevertheless, in the review, his Counsel did not press grounds in respect of charges no 3, 5, and 7, that is, 'the petitioner left his grievance of awarding conviction and sentences in respect of those charges, thereby, accepted the verdict.' The learned Counsel appearing on behalf of the petitioner 'kept his submission confined in respect of the allegation mentioned in charge No. 6 only' (*Ali Ahsan Muhammad Mujahid* v. *The Government of Bangladesh* 2015). Therefore, with a top Jamaat leader accused of crimes against humanity accepting his sentences, continuation of the trials of rest of the persons appears more beneficial than abandoning it, since the Government seemed to be less worried about international criticism. How about choosing the third option and adopting more internationally accepted fair trial guarantees?

Even if it were possible to build the required international consensus founding an international mechanism (see Sect. 5 above), would it be of much help? If Bangladesh has learned anything from recent history, it is that choosing the third option will not be too different from choosing the second (abandonment of the trials), as long as political and cultural considerations are concerned. This might become extremely difficult or virtually impossible to prosecute anyone successfully after so many years if put through an internationally accepted approach under which alleged war criminals would enjoy a broader scope to defend their interests. Furthermore, this would not actually help much to deter ongoing criticism at home, at least initially. Jamaat-e-Islami emphatically denies even their slightest involvement in the alleged war crimes and constantly calls the trials politically motivated. Their points of argument are more political than legal. As the Government appears least worried about international reactions to the standard of fairness in the trial, hence, the main chunk of the quandary Bangladesh is apparently concerned about is actually homegrown and political in nature. How safely Bangladesh can ignore these matters.

Until now, the Government has been able to retain the enormous support of the general mass in their political struggle against anti-war crimes trial forces at home. Several judgments have been passed by the Tribunals to date convicting and sentencing a number of top-ranking Jamaat and BNP leaders including Motiur Rahman Nizami, the Ameer of Bangladesh Jamaat-e-Islami. Even three of the convicted high-ranking Jamaat leaders—Abdul Quader Mollah, Muhammad Kamaruzzaman, and Ali Ahsan Mohammad Mojaheed—and one top-ranking BNP leader Salauddin Quader Chowdhury were executed in Dhaka amid concerns of the international community, including the UN and EU. However, Jamaat's general strike and random destruction of life and property through violent demonstration (common practice for all major political parties in Bangladesh) across the country were of little help. With every pronouncement of death sentence, thousands of general people take the street and burst into cheers. Up till now this is the vital strength Government is being able to count on and continue the trials. Besides, the current Awami League Government could argue, whether rightly or wrongly, that history and general nature of war crimes trial appear to lend support in their favor.

While there is 'a certain tendency to see war crimes trials, somewhat romantically, as mechanisms for neutral, impartial justice' this is only half of the truth. In reality, this will remain a matter of huge debate whether the issue is 'justice' or 'political and strategic consideration' or a combination of both.

> 'This is so because war crimes justice is framed and carried on in a political context of sovereign states. War crimes are frequently committed to advance political agendas. The responses to them are necessarily political as well, whether expressed through a criminal trial or a negotiated pardon' (Moghalu 2006).

Besides, this is not new that accused war criminals may gain sympathy of some parts of the society and be viewed as victims of political vengeance. There is overwhelming evidence corroborating the notion that time often transforms 'criminals' of atrocities into 'victim' of injustice as they face trial. Simpson (1997) portrayed it well as he described how Eichmann—whose name was synonymous with war criminal—gained sympathy, and the Japanese General Yamashita the 'ultimate war criminal' and person responsible for 'literally indefensible atrocities' slowly transformed from a criminal to 'victim of American injustice' and continued to be considered innocent by many legal experts even decades after his hanging. Also, the prosecution and subsequent acquittal of John Demjanjuk in Israel and Ivan Polyukhovich in Australia along with the prosecution of Klaus Barbie in France, which resulted cultural turmoil and agitation Simpson (1997)—further supports this view.

If the trial is abandoned, Bangladesh achieves nothing, but, if continues, this will satisfy the demand for long-awaited justice millions of war crimes victims deserve. Hence, the most relevant question probably is, to what extent Bangladesh will compromise its obligation to observe international standards of fair trial with popular political demand to bring the alleged perpetrators of 1971 war crimes into justice anyway.

6 Conclusion

Although the initiatives of war crimes trial in Bangladesh received enormous international support and attention, it has attracted some harsh, constructive criticisms at the same time. The trial is heavily criticized for assumed doubtful political motivation and flawed legal procedures—two common issues often considered potential threats to customary notions of fairness and transparency. While critics have always used these two grounds to question the validity of most war crimes trials in recent history, it is obvious that war crimes trials are barely based only on the popular concept of justice—violations are rectified, wrongdoers get punished. Rather, such trials are purportedly used as vehicle to press forward political goals, since war crimes trials are designed and implemented in a political context (Moghalu 2006, p. 5).

Trials of atrocious crimes and the efforts to prevent their recurrence are part of the initiatives aimed at establishing the administration of justice nationally and worldwide. Therefore, irrespective of the time and place of occurrences of such offenses, both state and international society have the responsibility to bring offenders under trial. War crimes trials are often practically challenging because such attempts may seriously threaten the peace process or destabilize social Order in jurisdictions already in peace. In addition, maintenance of fairness and transparency becomes increasingly difficult as time passes by. These assumed impurities and the risk engraved in the process do not, however, invalidate its necessity, neither it authorizes bypassing 'general principles of law recognized by civilized nations' in its process, although, at times exactly this is what may appear to have been preferred.

References

Abdul Quader Mollah v. The Chief Prosecutor (2013) Criminal review petition nos. 17–18 of 2013, the Supreme Court of Bangladesh: Appellate Division. http://www.supremecourt.gov.bd/resources/documents/683352_CRIMINAL_Rev_Nos_17-18_of_2013_2.doc.pdf. Accessed 21 Nov 2015

Adhikary TS (2013) Amusing alibi plea. http://archive.thedailystar.net/beta2/news/amusing-alibi-plea/. Accessed 11 Dec 2015

Ahmed S (2004) Bangladesh: past and present. APH Publishing, New Delhi

Alam MS (2008) Trial of the perpetrators of genocide, crimes against humanity and war crimes of 1971. In: Rahman M (ed) Trials of the war criminals: a legal investigation. Polol Publisher, Dhaka, pp 9–15

Ali Ahsan Muhammad Mujahid v. The Government of Bangladesh (2015) Criminal review petition no 62 of 2015, the Supreme Court of Bangladesh: Appellate Division. http://www.supremecourt.gov.bd/resources/documents/868734_CrlRP_No_62_2015.pdf. Accessed 7 Jan 2016

Azad MAK (1959) India wins freedom. Orient Longman, Bombay

Bangladesh Jamaat-e-Islami (2013) Life sentence against Abdul Quader Mollah is on the basis of hearsay. http://Jamaat-e-Islami.org/en/newsdetails.php?nid=NjU0. Accessed 15 July 2015

Bassiouni MC (1999) Crimes against humanity in international criminal law, 2nd edn. Kluwer Law International, Hague

Bassiouni MC (2011) Crimes against humanity: historical evolution and contemporary application. Cambridge University Press, Cambridge

BBC (2013) Bangladesh strike over war crimes trials sparks clashes. http://www.bbc.com/news/world-asia-21271872. Accessed 11 July 2013

Bergman D (2015a) Bangladesh war crimes tribunal: was the court right to rule that Chowdhury's University certificate was a forgery? http://bangladeshwarcrimes.blogspot.com/2015/11/was-court-right-to-rule-that-chowdhurys.html. Accessed 11 Dec 2015

Bergman D (2015b) Salauddin Quader Chowdhury: explaining the 'missing' 26 witnesses, Bangladesh war crimes tribunal. http://bangladeshwarcrimes.blogspot.com/2015/10/salauddin-quader-chowdhury-explaining.html. Accesses 4 Dec 2015

Bergman D (2015c) Bangladesh's war crimes tribunal under fire from human rights group for "flawed" trials but government hits back, International Justice Tribune. https://www.justicetribune.com/articles/bangladeshs-war-crimes-tribunal-under-fire-human-rights-group-flawed-trials-government-hits. Accessed 3 Dec 2015

Billah M (2008) Accountability of Bangladesh in the trial of war crimes, crimes against peace and humanity. In: Rahman M (ed) Trials of the war criminals: a legal investigation. Polol Publisher, Dhaka, pp 55–63

Bose S, Jalal A (2004) Modern South Asia: history, culture, political economy. Routledge, London

Burke SM (1973) The postwar diplomacy of the Indo-Pakistani war of 1971. Asian Surv 13 (11):1036–1049

Cammegh J (2011) The Bangladesh war crimes tribunal: reconciliation or revenge? Crimes of war. http://www.crimesofwar.org/commentary/the-bangladesh-war-crimes-tribunal-reconciliation-or-revenge-2/. Accessed 15 July 2015

Chadda M (2009) Imagining alternative ethnic future for Pakistan. In: Sokolski HD (ed) Pakistan's nuclear future: reining in the risk. U.S. Army War College Strategic Studies Institute, Carlisle, pp 243–282

Dawn (2009, February 17) Pakistan urges Bangladesh to forgive war crimes. http://www.dawn.com/news/906161/pakistan-urges-bangladesh-to-forgive-war-crimes. Accessed 15 July 2015

D'Costa B (2011) Nationbuilding, gender and war crimes in South Asia. Routledge, Oxon

Debnath A (2012) The Bangladesh genocide: the plight of women. In: Totten S (ed) Plight and fate of women during and following genocide. Transaction Publishers, New Jersey, pp 46–66

Election Commission Bangladesh (1996) Statistical report, 7th Jatiya Shangshad Election. http://www.ec.org.bd/MenuExternalFilesEng/125.pdf. Accessed 12 July 2015

Election Commission Bangladesh (2008) Statistical report, 9th Jatiya Shangshad Election. http://www.ec.org.bd/MenuExternalFilesEng/304.pdf. Accessed 12 July 2015

Farhad SA (2015) SQC trial: why plea of alibi failed. http://www.thedailystar.net/op-ed/sqc-trial-why-plea-alibi-failed-175945. Accessed 11 Dec 2015

Hasan R (2014, January 19) BNP won't cut Jamaat link. In: The daily star. http://www.thedailystar.net/bnp-wont-cut-jamaat-link-7353. Accessed 15 July 2015

Hashmi T (2011) Islamism beyond the Islamic heartland. In: Ahmed I (ed) The politics of religion in South and Southeast Asia. Routledge, Oxon, pp 26–44

Hiro D (2015) The longest august: the unflinching rivalry between India and Pakistan. Nation Books, New York

Hosain AMD (2008) The trial procedure against collaborators in post liberation period: an analysis. Trial of the war criminals of Bangladesh and international law. In: Rahman M (ed) Trials of the war criminals: a legal investigation. Polol Publisher, Dhaka, pp 38–42

Human Rights Watch (2013, September 18) Bangladesh: death sentence violates fair trial standards. http://www.hrw.org/news/2013/09/18/bangladesh-death-sentence-violates-fair-trial-standards. Accessed 15 July 2015

ICJ (1973, May 11) Case concerning trial of Pakistani prisoners of war: Pakistan v. India. In: International Court of Justice. http://www.icj-cij.org/docket/files/60/9460.pdf. Accessed 30 Dec 2015

Islam R (2008) Trial of the war criminals of 71: a synopsis. In: Rahman M (ed) Trials of the war criminals: a legal investigation. Polol Publisher, Dhaka, pp 93–100

Islam M (2015) Limits of Islamism. Cambridge University Press, Delhi

Jaffrelot C (2004) A history of Pakistan and its origins. Anthem Press, London, New York

Jahan R (2013) Genocide in Bangladesh. In: Totten S, Parsons WS (eds) Centuries of genocide: essays and eyewitness accounts. Routledge, New York, pp 249–278

Jalil MA (2010) War crimes trial in Bangladesh: a real political vendetta. J Polit Law. doi:10.5539/jpl.v3n2p110

Joyes BM (2010) International Fair Trial Standards and the Bangladesh International Crimes (Tribunal) Act 1973 (as amended) at a Glance. International Criminal Law Bureau. http://www.internationallawbureau.com/blog/wp-content/uploads/2011/02/International_Fair_Trial_Standards_and_the__Bangladesh_International_Crimes_Tribunal_Act_1973_as_amended_at_a_Glance_B._M._Joyes_.pdf. Accessed 12 July 2015

Jurists IC (1972) The events in East Pakistan, 1971: a legal study. Retrieved from http://icj.wpengine.netdna-cdn.com/wp-content/uploads/1972/06/Bangladesh-events-East-Pakistan-1971-thematic-report-1972-eng.pdf. Accessed 14 July 2015

Karim R, Bhattacharjee PP (2015, November 23) Dhaka reacts sharply to Pak statement. In: The daily star. http://www.thedailystar.net/frontpage/dhaka-reacts-sharply-pak-statement-176635. Accessed 7 Jan 2016

Karzon SHR (2008) Trial of the war criminals of Bangladesh and international law. In: Rahman M (ed) Trials of the war criminals: a legal investigation. Polol Publisher, Dhaka, pp 24–37

Kay S (2010) Bangladesh war crimes tribunal: a wolf in sheep's clothing? The International Criminal Law Bureau. http://www.internationallawbureau.com/blog/wp-content/uploads/2010/11/Bangladesh-International-War-Crimes-Tribunal.pdf. Accessed 14 July 2015

Kearns TR, Sarat A (1996) Legal justice and injustice: toward a situated perspective. In: Sarat A, Kearns TR (eds) Justice and injustice in law and legal theory. University of Michigan Press, Michigan, pp 1–34

Khan SR (2008) Trial of the war criminals and collaborators of 71. In: Rahman M (ed) Trials of the war criminals: a legal investigation. Polol Publisher, Dhaka, pp 64–73

Khanna VN (2007) Foreign policy of India, 6th edn. Vikas Publishing House Pvt Ltd., New Delhi

Knoops GJ (2014) An introduction to the law of international criminal tribunals: a comparative study, 2nd edn. Brill Nijhoff, Leiden

MacDermot N (1973) Crimes against humanity in Bangladesh. Int Lawyer 7(2):476–484

Maddison A (1971) Class structure and economic growth: India and Pakistan since the Moghuls. Routledge, Oxon
Maslen SC (2014) The war report: armed conflict in 2013. Oxford University Press, Oxford
Mazumdar A (2014) Indian foreign policy in transition: relations with South Asia. Routledge, Oxon
McCormack T (2011) A guide to state practice in the field of international humanitarian law. In: Schmitt MN et al (eds) Yearbook of international humanitarian law—2010. T.M.C Asser Press, The Hague, pp 449–660
Moghalu KC (2006) Global justice: the politics of war crimes trials. Praeger, Westport
Molla SG (2004) The Bangladesh Awami League: from charismatic leadership to political party. In: Mitra SK, Enskat M, Spiess C (eds) Political parties in South Asia. Praeger Publishers, Westport, pp 216–235
Muhammad Kamaruzzaman v. the Government of Bangladesh (2015) Criminal review petition no 8 of 2015, the Supreme Court of Bangladesh: Appellate Division. http://www.supremecourt.gov.bd/web/documents/812267_8of15Kamaruzzaman.pdf. Accessed 15 July 2015
Pant HV (2011) India's relations with Bangladesh. In: Scott D (ed) Handbook of India's international relations. Routledge, London, pp 83–94
Paul TV (2005) The India–Pakistan conflict: an enduring rivalry. Cambridge University Press, Cambridge
Paulussen C, Dorsey J, Koulen SJ (2013) In: Gill TD et al (eds) Yearbook of international humanitarian law 2013. T.M.C. Asser Press, The Hague, pp 187–236 (Year in Review)
Payne R (1973) Massacre: The tragedy at Bangladesh and the phenomenon of mass slaughter throughout history. Macmillan, New York
Perry-Kessaris A (2013) Socio-legal approaches to international economic law: text, context, subtext. Routledge, Oxon
Prakash V (2011) Encyclopaedia of terrorism in the world, vol 2. Kalpaz Publications, Delhi
Quaderi FQ (1972) Bangladesh genocide and world press. Songha, Dhaka
Rahman M (2008) Genocide, crimes against humanity and trial. In: Rahman M (ed) Trials of the war criminals: a legal investigation. Polol Publisher, Dhaka, pp 16–23
Rahman S (2010) Historical dictionary of Bangladesh. Scarecrow Press, Maryland
Rao KVK (1991) Prepare or perish: a study of national security. Lancer Publishers, New Delhi
Ray JK (2007) Aspects of India's international relations, 1700 to 2000: South Asia and the World, vol 10. Pearson Education India, New Delhi
Report SO (2015) 195 Pak army men to be tried for war crimes: minister. In: The daily star. http://www.thedailystar.net/country/195-pak-army-men-be-tried-war-crimes-minister-188638. Accessed 9 Jan 2016
Riaz A (2014) Islamist politics, elections, and democracy in Bangladesh. In: Mecham Q, Hwang JC (eds) Islamist parties and political normalization in the Muslim World. University of Pennsylvania Press, Philadelphia, pp 156–174
Rizvi HA (1988) The military and politics in Pakistan: 1947–1986. Konark, New Delhi
Roy K. (2015) Trials of the crimes against humanity: 29 war crimes suspects still on trial. In: The daily star. http://en.prothom-alo.com/bangladesh/news/86875/29-war-criminals-still-on-trial. Accessed 5 Dec 2016
Sarkar A (2016) Death stays for death designer. In: The daily star. http://www.thedailystar.net/frontpage/death-stays-death-designer-198268. Accessed 7 Jan 2016
Sassoli M, Bouvier AA, Quintin A (1974) ICRC. How does law protect in war? Bangladesh–India–Pakistan: agreement on the repatriation of prisoners of war and civilian internees. https://www.icrc.org/casebook/doc/case-study/bangladesh-india-pakistan-1974-agreement-case-study.htm. Accessed 9 Dec 2016
Saulnier FB (2013) The practical guide to humanitarian law. Rowman and Littlefield Publishers, Maryland
Schabas W (2010) The international criminal court: a commentary on the Rome Statute. Oxford University Press, New York

Schottli J, Mitra SK, Wolf S (2015) A political and economic dictionary of South Asia. Routledge, Oxon
Sharif A, Nuruzzaman K, Kabir S (1987) Ekattorer Ghatok O Dalalera Ke Kothay. Muktijoddha Chetona Bikash Kendro, Dhaka
Simpson GJ (1997) War crimes: a critical introduction. In: MacCormack T, Simpso GJ (eds) The law of war crimes: national and international approaches. Kluwer Law International, The Hague, London, Boston, pp 1–30
Sisson R, Rose LE (1991) War and secession: Pakistan, India, and the creation of Bangladesh. University of California Press, California
Staff Correspondent (2015) Khaleda draws flak for martyrs remark. In: The daily star. http://www.thedailystar.net/frontpage/khaleda-remark-draws-flak-191164. Accessed 7 Jan 2016
Staff Correspondent (2015) SC review on death penalty: condemned war criminal SQ Chy petitions for Pakistani witnesses. http://www.thedailystar.net/frontpage/sq-chy-petitions-pak-witnesses-159823. Accessed 8 Dec 2015
Staff Reporter (2010) The government is staging war crimes trial on fabricated charges after failing to confront Jamaat politically. http://www.dailysangram.com/news_details.php?news_id=28318. Accessed 15 July 2015
Syed BS (2015) Reference to Mujib's promise offends Bangladesh. In: Dawn. http://www.dawn.com/news/1221842. Accessed 9 Jan 2016
The Daily Star (2013) Execution of Mollah: UN official calls for a stay. http://archive.thedailystar.net/beta2/news/eu-uk-worried-at-execution-move/. Accessed 15 July 2015
The Daily Star (2013) Mollah hanging, irate Erdogan. http://www.thedailystar.net/mollah-hanging-irate-erdogan-3008. Accessed 15 July 2015
The International Crimes (Tribunals) Act of 1973
The Supreme Court of Bangladesh (2015) Muhammad Kamaruzzaman v. the Government of Bangladesh. Criminal review petition no. 8 of 2015. http://www.supremecourt.gov.bd/web/documents/812267_8of15Kamaruzzaman.pdf. Accessed 15 July 205
The Supreme Court of Bangladesh (2015) Salauddin Quader Chowdhury v. The Chief Prosecutor. Criminal review petition no. 63 of 2015. http://www.supremecourt.gov.bd/resources/documents/833468_Criminal_Review_Petition_No_63_2015_2.pdf. Accessed 10 Dec 2015
Trivedi R (2008) India's relations with her neighbours. ISHA Books, Delhi
Ullah MR (2008) Trial of the war criminals: responsibility of the government. In: Rahman M (ed) Trials of the war criminals: a legal investigation. Polol Publisher, Dhaka, pp 43–54
UNB (2015) BNP defends Khaleda Zia's remarks on martyrs. In: The independent. http://www.theindependentbd.com/printversion/details/28513. Accessed 7 Jan 2016
University of Punjab (1971) Statistical profile of education in West Pakistan. Manager of Publications, Karachi
Watch HR (2009) Ignoring executions and torture: impunity for Bangladesh's security forces. In: Human Rights Watch. https://www.hrw.org/report/2009/05/18/ignoring-executions-and-torture/impunity-bangladeshs-security-forces. Accessed 11 Jan 2016
Watch HR (2012) Bangladesh: end harassment of war crimes defense counsel, armed raid on defense offices gross interference with trial process. https://www.hrw.org/news/2012/10/17/bangladesh-end-harassment-war-crimes-defense-counsel. Accessed 7 Jan 2016

Chapter 12
Rules of State Responsibility: A South Asian Perspective

Madhu Bhatti

1 Introduction

Theory on the rules of state responsibility could not be developed till the end of twentieth century in spite of various efforts made from time to time. The new scenario emerged with the adoption of a resolution by the General Assembly of UN (56/83) on the 'Draft Articles on the Responsibility of States for Internationally Wrongful Acts' in December 2001. The Draft Articles are not only structured form of rules of state responsibility, but also show progressive development of international community. These rules are having positive effect on states towards their international responsibilities and are therefore well received. Further, they have already found mention in the various decisions of the International Court of Justice. Notwithstanding that nature of these rules is universal, but certain cases are excluded from their operation. For example, the General Agreement on Tariffs and Trade (GATT) and the European Convention on Human Rights provide their own principles and mechanism of responsibility.

Earlier, the term 'state responsibility' alluded just with state responsibility for injuries to aliens. It included not only 'secondary' rules of attribution and remedies, but also the 'primary' rights and obligations of states, for example, the asserted international standard of treatment and the right of diplomatic protection. Previous attempts of League of Nations and other private bodies to codify the rules of 'state responsibility' primarily focused on responsibility for injuries to aliens. In 1930, the League held a conference in The Hague and codified rules only on 'secondary' issues of imputation, but not on substantive obligations of the treatment of aliens and their property.

M. Bhatti (✉)
Faculty of Law, University of Delhi, 38/12, Probyn Road, New Delhi 110007, India
e-mail: madhubhatti@rediffmail.com; madhubhatti.mb@gmail.com

J.L. Kaul and A. Jha (eds.), *Shifting Horizons of Public International Law*,
https://doi.org/10.1007/978-81-322-3724-2_12

2 Responsibility Defined in International Law

There is an English maxim 'the King can do no wrong'—this 'irresponsibility' of the State mirrored in the municipal laws of the States in the western Europe during the time of their emergence and consolidation. This concept could not be transported to the international territory. To some extent, it can be said to be the reflection of dual perception of 'sovereignty', in the domestic or international legal regime: at domestic level, sovereignty denotes the absolute and unrestricted authority of the State; and at international level, the sovereignty of the State is encountered with the similar sovereign powers of other States, and responsibility is the mandatory governing structure through which the confrontations are reconciled because the interests of particular State may not coincide with those of other.

Another famous formula, which found mention in the famous case decided by ICJ that for establishing 'an abandonment of its sovereignty', the probability of a state to invoke responsibility 'is an attribute of state sovereignty' (Wimbledon 1923). Similarly, the liability of an individual is the ramification of his/her liberty (Popecu 1966), it is therefore stated that the State is sovereign, and by virtue of this it synchronizes along with other bodies which are similarly situated, that the state can invoke its own responsibility and appeal to the responsibilities of other states: 'if it is the strength of sovereignty to demand protection of its interests, the corresponding obligation of the sovereign State is to fulfil its duties' (ILC Yearbook 1973). Despite the fact that there is hardly any distinction amongst the responsibility of individuals and of State, Grotius nevertheless conceded that from a damage occasioned 'there arises an obligation by the Law of Nature to make Reparation for the Damage, if any be done' (Grotius 1625).

This concept created the groundwork for developing the rules of international responsibility. To facilitate his way, Vattel correctly comprehended and constrained responsibility (this word he did not use) to the duty to bring about reparation (Jouannet 1998). This classic approach nevertheless was supported by some authors (Combacau 2009) and was explicitly mentioned by Anzilotti: 'the wrongful act, that is to say, ordinarily speaking, the breach of an international obligation, is associated with emergence of new juridical coalition between the State which is liable for the breach and the one which is oblige to bring about reparation, and the State towards which an unaccomplished duty subsist, which can call upon reparation' (Anzilotti 1929).

This conclusion is reflected in the popular *dictum* of the permanent court in *Chorzow Factory case* that responsibility is confined to a duty to bring about reparation: 'it is a norm of international law, and also a natural perception of law, that any violation of commitment is followed by a duty to bring about reparation' (PCIJ 1927). In this mechanism, other states may also have concerns that reparation should be brought for the injury and international juridical harmony is established, without having any entitlements to that effect (Anzilotti 1929). If a breach of international obligations resulted into injury, reparation had to be brought in. 'In the absence of any rule as to *mens rea*, the intention, in terms of the international obligation, it is only the action of the State is considered, irrespective of any intention' (Commentary to Article 2).

3 Codification of the Rules

Since the time of its origin, the United Nations ('UN') endeavoured to classify and summarize rules of state responsibility. International Law Commission spent almost 45 years after which it prepared more than thirty reports. Five special rapporteurs did excellently well in reaching an accord on the decisive content for the complete Draft Articles, with commentaries. Similarly, the customary law of state responsibility relating to the subjects of detention and physical ill-treatment of aliens and their right to a fair trial lost its importance with the advancement of international human rights law, which does not make distinction between individuals on the basis of their origin. The rules of state responsibility have replaced the customary framework of legal responsibility, which is a starting point of the civil law system and considerably alien to the common law tradition.

Since its inception in 1949, the International Law Commission ('ILC') started working on codification of the rules on state responsibility. The ILC mentioned the subject of 'state responsibility' for codification in 1953, and it was remarkably differentiated from the province of 'treatment of aliens', which echoed the increasing trend that state responsibility covers the violation of an international obligation. F.V. García Amador of Cuba, who was appointed as ILC's first special rapporteur on state responsibility in 1955, stated that 'It would be difficult to find a topic beset with greater confusion and uncertainty', García Amador's contribution highlighted the conventional importance of responsibility for injury to aliens. His task was taken forward by the ILC after his tenure concluded in 1961. The next special rapporteur Roberto Ago of Italy re-conceptualized the ILC's efforts to distinguish between primary and secondary rules and further set up the key organizational arrangement of future Draft Articles. Ago focused on general rules and tried to constitute a politically guarded atmosphere amidst which the ILC could complete its task and further abstain from complex issues of the times. Ago accomplished his task on Part One of the Draft Articles during his tenure till he was appointed to the ICJ in 1980, concentrating on the basis of state responsibility. The thirty-five articles conceived during his time find mentions in the final version of Draft Articles.

During 1980s and early 1990s, the development of the rest of the articles was comparatively slow. Willem Riphagen of the Netherlands, who was appointed as next special rapporteur till 1986, pointed out that 'a specific primary rule may specify the repercussions of its violation'—the concept which has included in the articles through the acknowledgement of *lex specialis*. Thereafter, Goetano Arangio-Ruiz, special rapporteur appointed in 1988, stressed on ramifications of violation of international obligations. The ILC finished its first reading of parts 2 and 3 during next eight years.

A resolution was adopted by the UN General Assembly in 1995, for the purposes of pressurizing the ILC to rapidly develop the rules on the state responsibility and subjects which were pending for long time. In 1997, 49th session of General Assembly was held; the ILC incorporated a working group on state responsibility to deal with the affairs of the second reading of the Draft Articles (52/156). In the same session, the Commission further named James Crawford of Australia, next special rapporteur, who decided to take a practical approach towards the subject. The ILC pushed swiftly towards second reading of the Draft Articles, acceding the articles consented upon, and leaving the remaining. And most important article was Article 19, which dealt with state crimes and provisions for dispute settlement.

3.1 Draft Articles on State Responsibility

The ILC accepted the definite content of the Draft Articles in August 2001, with one of the most enduring and complex task reached to its conclusion. The UN General Assembly passed a resolution accepting the articles on responsibility of state for internationally wrongful acts on 12 December 2001, (56/83); the content of articles was attached to the resolution and referred them to governments for future adoption as convention or other appropriate action. The General Assembly included an item entitled 'Responsibility of States for internationally wrongful acts' in the provisional agenda for Assembly's fifty-ninth session.

The General Assembly passed a resolution on 6 December 2010 (65/19), to the effect of considering the comments and observations of governments and proposed to discuss in the provisional agenda of its sixty-eighth session, which was held in 2013, the term 'responsibility of states for internationally wrongful acts', and to further explore the possibility of convention on responsibility of states for internationally wrongful acts or other appropriate action on the basis of the articles, within the framework of a working group of the sixth committee.

3.2 Framework of the Draft Articles

'The Draft Articles on the responsibility of states for internationally wrongful acts' are 59 in number and segregated into four parts. Part One 'The internationally wrongful act of the state' (Articles 1–27) further consists of five chapters namely—'General Principles' (Articles 1–3), 'Attribution of conduct to state' (Articles 4–11), 'Breach of an international obligation' (Articles 12–15), 'Responsibility of state in a connection with the act of another state' (Articles 16–19), and 'Circumstances precluding wrongfulness' (Articles 20–27). Part Two, titled 'Content of International Responsibility of state' (Articles 28–41) is divided into three chapters—'General Principles' (Articles 28–33), 'Reparation for injuries' (Articles 34–39), and 'Serious Breaches of obligations under Peremptory Norms of General international law' (Articles 40–41). Part Three, namely 'The implementation of the international responsibility of a State' (Articles 42–54) consists of two chapters—'Invocation of the responsibility of State' (Articles 42–48) and 'Countermeasures' (Articles 49–54). Lastly, Part Four (Articles 55–59) contains the final general provisions of the text.

3.3 Scope of 'Internationally Wrongful Acts'

In consonance with the Draft Articles (Article 2), an 'internationally wrongful act' has to be an act which must: '(a) be attributable to the state under international law and (b) constitute a breach of an international obligation of the state'. International crimes are different from 'internationally wrongful acts'. Earlier drafts of the 'International Law Commission's Articles, 1991' on the 'state responsibility' consisted a provision (Article 19), which recognized 'state crimes' and incorporated an Article as follows: '2. an internationally wrongful act which results from the breach by a State of an international obligation so essential for the protection of fundamental interests of the international community that its breach is recognized as a crime by that community as a whole constitutes an international crime' and '4. any internationally wrongful act which is not an international crime in accordance with para 2 constitutes an international delict'. This provision (Article 19) was not incorporated in the final 'Draft Articles on the responsibility of states for internationally wrongful acts', as accepted in 2001.

4 Theory of Attribution/Imputation

It is mandatory to determine an incidental link between the damage and an official act or omission attributable to the state, prior to fixing the responsibility of its action, purported to be in violation of its primary obligations. It is becoming more and more important in the contemporary scenario where non-state actors such as multinational corporations and non-governmental organizations have started playing international roles, and as governments privatize its various conventional tasks such as road maintenance, fleet operations and public works to education, and public health services.

The state is answerable for its every action performed through its officials and organs, despite the fact that the organ or official is conventionally autonomous and they are acting beyond the powers conferred on them. Other individuals and organizations not covered within the definition of state may still make the State responsible, if state otherwise delegates the governmental authority, and they function under that authority in a specific circumstance. Individuals and organizations executing public authority may also make the State responsible, if they are directed to actually perform certain functions of the state. If there is situation of rebellion and breakdown of governmental machinery, such as in so-called 'failed states', the functions of those acting as the 'ruler' in a *de facto* manner shall be taken to be acts of the state. The functions of an 'insurrectional or other movement' that later on usurp government authority and take the position of new government of that particular state or succeed in rebellion and form the government are also attributed to the state. Similar consequences follow where the state approves and accepts the actions of private individuals as its own.

In spite of the fact that Draft Rules are absolute, the criteria set in some of the rules have important perplexities, and their implementation shall usually require convincing fact-finding and judgment. Some of the rules on 'state responsibility' are related to individual acts which are already mentioned under primary rules. For example, environmental and human rights agreements call upon states to counter delinquency by private parties.

4.1 Notion of 'Imputation'

The act declared as unlawful according to primary obligations must be imputable to the State. The imputation is the consequence of a rational activity compulsory to link the disparity amongst the individual or group of individuals and the attribution of a breach of a primary obligation and responsibility towards the State (Starke 1938). Thus, imputability becomes a basic notion in the law of state responsibility and reference to it cannot be avoided. It is not to be confused with the State's obligation which may rest on 'fault' or 'risk' or 'strict liability', as the case may be in different situations, depending on the relevant international standard. Such considerations would be pertinent only in determining whether an act or omission in breach of international obligation has taken place. The notion of imputability becomes particularly important because conflict may come up, in a particular circumstance amongst domestic law and international law relating to the powers of State functionaries or officials. Such complications can only be resolved by a definite and clear conception of the nature imputability.

4.2 The Territorial Test

It is not everything that happens to a foreigner within the territorial jurisdiction of a State. The test of imputability is not whether the damage suffered by the alien can be said to have occurred on the territory of a particular State. The decision of the *Corfu Channel Case* shows clearly that it is not the test, even though that case dealt with injury to the assets of a foreign State and not of aliens. There it was held that the mere fact that mines had exploded in Albanian territorial waters and damaged British ships did not automatically entail the international responsibility of Albanian (ICJ Report 1949).

4.3 Private Individual's Responsibility Distinguished from Liability

It may also be said at the very outset that the State cannot be held liable for all the acts or omission of every individual present on its territory. Thus, normally it is not liable for the wrongful act of the private individuals.

The above conclusions, it must be noted, do not mean that a State can never be responsible for the act or omission of private individuals. For there may be circumstances where the State is responsible for the damage resulting from such act or omissions because it has occurred as a result of an omission by an entity and, in the circumstances, is imputable to the State. For instance, where the damage appears as a consequence of the negligent omission of a State police to prevent it, then the omission of the State become responsible for the damage (García 1955).

It is in this connexion that the distinction must be made between the liability of a State and its responsibility for a breach of international obligation. Where an individual commits an injury against an alien, the State does not become responsible for that injury by the very fact that the injury was committed by an individual on its territory, as has been pointed out. Nevertheless, it is possible that because of the nature of the injury, international law would require that the State take some action to punish the wrongdoer and even provide a proper remedy through its courts for the injured alien. Its failure to do either of these obligations entails international responsibility. The State is duty bound to punish the wrongdoer and provide a remedy for the alien. On the basis of this view, responsibility arises for this failure and not for the wrong originally committed by the individual. Liability, therefore, arises on the basis of a primary obligation with respect to acts of individuals. Responsibility would arise by failure of an organ or individual to discharge this liability which will be imputed to the State.

This liability is to be distinguished, firstly, from the duty that a State has in respect of the prevention of wrongs, which is a different kind of obligation imposed by the international law and for a breach of which a State would become responsible when an organ or individual whose acts are imputable to the State fails to perform act in discharge of that duty (the *USA vs. Panama*). Secondly, it must be distinguished from the situation where the State is responsible directly for a wrong committed by an individual or organ because the act constituting the wrong is imputable to the State under the rules of primary obligations (Anzilotti 1928).

4.4 Concept of Injury

The act or omission characterized as a violation of international law must cause injury to the alien (Finnish Ships Arbitration 1934). Causation of injury is essential. It is important that the injury to an alien which gives rise to state responsibility should comprise both material loss and moral injury resulting from the violation of international obligations. This is general principle of importance, although it is not as such discussed in the literature on the subject nor it is mentioned in draft conventions. The acceptance of material loss affords no problem, as there are numerous examples in international decision of such loss having been compensated (Whiteman 1937). But there is evidence in the jurisprudence of Claims Commissions that moral injury has also been compensated under the principle of international law.

4.5 Availability of 'Defences'

After the basic components for state responsibility are settled, the controversy arises as to whether the respondent state can raise any defences which may be available under the Draft Rules. Regarding the basic principles of wrongfulness, Chapter V of Part One provides for 'Circumstances precluding wrongfulness' which may also be called 'defences'. Defences available under the Draft Code are 'Consent' (Article 20), 'Self-Defence' (Article 21), 'Legitimate countermeasures' (Article 22), '*Force majeure*' (Article 23), Distress (Article 24), and 'Necessity' (Article 25).

5 Resulting Consequences of Breach

The violation of primary obligations by the state brings about two different legal consequences. Firstly, it gives rise to new obligations for the delinquent state, essentially, 'duties of cessation' and 'non-repetition' (Article 30), and a 'duty to make full reparation' (Article 31). Secondly, the articles build new entitlements for complainant states, essentially, 'the right to invoke responsibility' (Articles 42 and 48) and a 'limited right to take countermeasures' (Articles 49–53).

These entitlements in the form of rights revolve around state governments and are not equipped with implementation tools especially when it is a case of violation of individual or organization's rights. The basic component of this aspect in this area is Article 48, which states that some breaches of primary obligations by states can affect the whole international community, and in these matters, the state responsibility can be called upon to be implemented on behalf of even private individuals and organizations. This principle was even applied by the ICJ's in its famous decision in *Barcelona Traction, Light and Power Company, Limited* (1970) where the court suggested that 'some obligations are owed *erga omnes*, towards the international community as a whole'.

5.1 Form of Reparations

If violation of international obligation continues, the delinquent state has a 'duty to cease'. Not only this, but also the state in question has 'duty to make reparation', which may be in the form of 'restitution', 'compensation', or 'satisfaction'. These remedies are based upon the approach taken by the particular forum which has been approached by the injured state, such as the UN, International Court of Justice, World Trade Organisation, International Tribunal for the Law of the Sea, International Criminal Court, and the object of reparation.

6 Analysis of Important Judgements (ICJ)

*6.1 Avena and Other Mexican Nationals (*Mexico v. the USA*) 2003*

On 9 January 2003, Mexico made a claim against the USA in a controversy relating to alleged violations of Articles 5 and 36 of the Vienna Convention on Consular Relations of 24 April 1963. These violations pertained to the treatment of various Mexican nationals who were convicted and sentenced to death after conclusion of criminal proceedings in the USA. The main dispute concerned with 54 such individuals, but in a later reconciliation by Mexico, only 52 individual cases were pursued. In January 2003, Mexico requested the court to give interim directions to the effect of directing the USA that no Mexican national was executed during the pendency of the claim before the court. In February 2003, the court concurrently issued directions to the above-said effect, stating inter alia, that the 'United States of America shall take all measures necessary to ensure that Mr. César Roberto Fierro Reyna, Mr. Roberto Moreno Ramos, and Mr. Osvaldo Torres Aguilera … are not executed pending final judgment in these proceedings'.

The court then examined four objections of the USA to the court's jurisdiction and five to the admissibility of the claims of Mexico. It rejected those objections after first having rejected the objection of Mexico to the admissibility of the US objections.

Ruling on the merits of the case, the court first addressed the question of whether the 52 individuals had Mexican nationality only, or whether some of them were also US nationals, as claimed by that State. Concluding that the United States could not prove that claim, the court found that the United States did have obligations (to provide consular information) under Article 36, para 1(b), of the Vienna Convention towards the 52 Mexican nationals.

The court then examined the meaning of the expression 'without delay' used in para 1(b) of Article 36. It found that the duty to provide consular information existed once it is realized that the person is a foreign national, or once there are grounds to think so, but considered that, in the light *inter alia* of the convention's *travaux préparatoires* the term without delay is not necessarily to be interpreted as meaning 'immediately upon arrest'. The court then concluded that on the basis of this interpretation, the United States had nonetheless violated its obligation to provide consular notification in all of the cases except one.

The court then took note of the interrelated nature of the three subparagraphs (a), (b), and (c) of para 1 of Article 36 of the Vienna Convention and found, in 49 of the cases, that the United States had also violated its obligation under subparagraph (a) to enable Mexican consular officers to communicate with, have access to and visit their nationals; while, in 34 cases, it found that the United States, in addition, violated its obligation under subparagraph (c) to enable Mexican consular officers to arrange for legal representation of their nationals.

The court then turned to Mexico's submission in relation to para 2 of Article 36, whereby it claimed that the United States violated its obligations under that paragraph by failing to provide 'meaningful and effective review and reconsideration of convictions and sentences impaired by a violation of Article 36(1), *inter alia* as a result of the operation of the procedural default' rule. The court observed that the procedural default rule had not been revised since it drew attention in its judgment in the *La Grand* (*Germany v. the USA 2001*) case to the problems which its application could cause for defendants who sought to rely on violations of the Vienna Convention in appeal proceedings. The court found that in three cases, para 2 of Article 36 was violated by the United States, but the possibility of judicial re-examination was still open in 49 of the cases.

Turning to the legal consequences of the above-found breaches and to what legal remedies should be considered, the court noted that Mexico sought reparation in the form of restitution *in integrum*, i.e., partial or total annulment of conviction and sentence, as the necessary and sole remedy. The court, citing the decision of its predecessor, the Permanent Court of International Justice, in the *Chorzów Factory* (*Germany v. Poland 1928*) case, pointed out that what was required to make good the breach of an obligation under international law was 'reparation in an adequate form'. Following its judgment in the *La Grand case* (*Germany v. the USA* 2001), the court found that in the present case, adequate reparation for violations of Article 36 should be provided by review and reconsideration of the convictions and sentences of the Mexican nationals by US courts.

Finally, with regard to Mexico's request for the cessation of wrongful acts by the United States, the court found no evidence of a 'regular and continuing' pattern of breaches by the United States of Article 36 of the Vienna Convention. And as to its request for guarantees and assurances of non-repetition, the court recognized the US efforts to encourage implementation of its obligations under the Vienna Convention and considered that commitment by the United States met Mexico's request.

The court observed that it found in relation to the three persons concerned in the order (amongst others), that the United States committed breaches of its obligations under Article 36, para 1, of the Vienna Convention; and that moreover, in respect of those three persons alone, the United States also committed breaches of Article 36, para 2. The review and reconsideration of conviction and sentence required by Article 36, para 2, which was the appropriate remedy for breaches of Article 36, para 1, was not been carried out. The court considered that in these three cases, it was for the United States to find an appropriate remedy having the nature of review and reconsideration according to the criteria indicated in the judgment.

6.2 *The Military and Paramilitary Activities in and Against Nicaragua* (Nicaragua v. the USA) *1985*

In this case, it was claimed by Nicaragua that the U.S. engaged itself, since March 1981, in the use of force against Nicaragua through the instrumentality of a mercenary army ('contras') of more than 10,000 men recruited, paid, equipped, supplied, trained, and directed by the U.S. As a result, Nicaragua suffered grievous consequences consisting of huge loss of life and damage to property. Nicaragua argued that the U.S. violated the UN Charter and treaty obligations by recruiting, training, arming, equipping, financing, supplying and otherwise encouraging, supporting, aiding, and directing military and paramilitary actions in and against Nicaragua.

The degree of control which must be exercised by the State in order for the conduct to be attributable to it was a key issue in this case. The question was whether the conduct of the *contras* was attributable to the U.S. so as to hold the latter generally responsible for breaches of international humanitarian law committed by the *contras*. This was analyzed by the court in terms of the notion of 'control'. On the one hand, it held that the USA was responsible for the 'planning, direction, and support' given by the USA to Nicaraguan operatives, and on the other, it rejected the broader claim of Nicaragua that all the conduct of the *contras* was attributable to the USA by reason of its control over them.

Thus, while the USA was held responsible for its own support to the *contras*, only in certain individual instances were the acts of the *contras* themselves held attributable to it, based upon actual participation of and directions given by that State. The court confirmed that a general situation of dependence and support would be insufficient to justify attribution of the conduct to the State. The court called upon the USA to immediately cease and refrain from such activities and make reparation to Nicaragua for all injury caused to it. It was decided that the form and amount of such reparation, failing agreement between the Parties, would be settled by the court.

Article 8 of the Draft Code on state responsibility, 2001 lays down the same rule: 'the conduct of a person or group of persons shall be considered an act of a State under international law if the person or group of persons is, in fact, acting on the instructions of, or under the direction or control of, that State in carrying out the conduct'.

6.3 The Barcelona Traction, Light, and Power Company Limited Case (1970)

The ICJ rejected Belgium's claim by fifteen votes to one. The claim, which was brought before the court on 19 June 1962, arose out of the adjudication of bankruptcy in Spain of Barcelona Traction, a company incorporated in Canada. Its objective was to seek reparation for damage alleged by Belgium to have been sustained by Belgian nationals, shareholders in the company, as a result of acts said to be contrary to international law committed towards the company by organs of the Spanish State. The court found that Belgium lacked *jus standi* to exercise diplomatic protection of shareholders in a Canadian company with respect to measures taken against that company in Spain.

The Barcelona Traction, Light and Power Company, Limited was incorporated in 1911 in Toronto (Canada), where it had its head office. For the purpose of creating and developing an electric power production and distribution system in Catalonia (Spain), it formed a number of subsidiary companies, of which some had their registered offices in Canada and the others in Spain. In 1936, the subsidiary companies supplied the major part of Catalonia's electricity requirements. According to the Belgian Government, some years after the First World War, Barcelona Traction's share capital came to be very largely held by Belgian nationals.

In 1948, the company was declared bankrupt by Spanish court and, at about the same time, other steps were taken by Spanish authorities injuring it. Canada intervened on the Company's behalf to begin with but later withdrew. At all relevant times, 88% of the shares in the company were, Belgium claimed, owned by Belgian nationals. Belgium brought this claim in respect of the injury to its nationals who were shareholders resulting from the injury to the company. Spain objected that since the injury was to the company, not the shareholders, Belgium lacked *locus standi* to bring the claim. In the present case, it was essential to establish whether Belgium's rights were violated on account of its nationals having suffered infringement of their rights as shareholders in a company not of Belgian nationality?

The court held that the company was incorporated in Canada and had its registered office in that country. Not only did the founders of the company seek its incorporation under Canadian law but also remained under that for a period of over 50 years. It maintained in Canada its registered office, its accounts, and its share registers. Board meetings were held there for many years; it was listed in the records of the Canadian tax authorities. Thus, a close and permanent connection was established, fortified by the passage of over half a century. This connection was in no way weakened by the fact that the company engaged from the very outset in commercial activities outside Canada, for that was its declared object. Barcelona Traction's links with Canada were thus found to be manifold. So, Canada could have brought this claim on behalf of the company.

The Belgian government had also admitted the Canadian character of the company. It explicitly stated that Barcelona Traction was a company of neither Spanish nor Belgian nationality, but a Canadian company incorporated in Canada. The Belgian government even conceded that it was not concerned with the injury suffered by the Barcelona Traction itself, since that was Canada's affair. According to the court's opinion, Belgium would be entitled to bring a claim if it could show that one of its rights had been infringed and also that the acts complained of involved the breach of an international obligation arising out of a treaty or a general rule of law.

The court also held that the adoption of the theory of diplomatic protection of shareholders as such, by opening the door of competing diplomatic claims, could create an atmosphere of confusion and insecurity in international economic relations. The danger would be all the greater inasmuch as the shares of companies whose activity is international are widely scattered and frequently change hands. In the present state of law, the protection of shareholders requires that recourse be had to treaty stipulations or special agreements directly concluded between the private investor and the State in which the investment is placed. No such instrument is in force between the Parties to the present case.

Thus, the court held that the general rule on the subject does not entitle the Belgian government to put forward a claim on shareholders' behalf. In addition, Barcelona Traction Company was never reduced to a position of impotence such that it could not have approached its national State, Canada, to ask for its diplomatic protection, and that, as far as appeared to the court, there was nothing to prevent Canada from continuing to grant its diplomatic protection to Barcelona Traction if it had considered that it should do so.

7 Position of South Asian States

According to P. Sreenivasa Rao of India, who was the member of International Law Commission during the period when the code of state responsibility was drafted (he was actually the member from 1987 to 2006), the concept of international crime and the entailing responsibility of States should not be dealt with by the ILC (Rao 1997). According to him, the concept of an international crime evoked understandably mixed reactions from States and scholars, some supporting and others rejecting the same. The conviction that the present state of international law only admitted criminal responsibility of an individual is one of the reasons for rejection of this concept. The concept incorporated in ILC Draft Article 19 raised the question as to whether a crime was committed or not could not be left to the State which alleged the occurrence of such crimes. This was necessary to prevent the emergence of a anarchical system which could lead to the worst forms of intervention which occurred in international relations of the nineteenth century. But we do not yet have an agreed, structured system of determination of the crime followed by formal enforcement by the international community as a whole. In 2001, ILC Draft Article 19 was deleted from the Draft Code on state responsibility.

According to S.P. Jagota, who was also the member of International Law Commission, the articles on circumstances precluding wrongfulness are very useful (Jagota 1985). Articles 20–26 deal with such circumstances, such as consent of State (Article 20), acts in self-defence (Article 21), countermeasures in respect of an internationally wrongful act (Article 22), *force majeure* (Article 23), distress (Article 24), necessity (Article 25), and compliance with peremptory norms (Article 26). Broadly, these circumstances precluding wrongfulness of an act of a State could be divided into two types: one, where such an act was a reactive response to the wrongful act of the other State, such as in the case of countermeasures and self-defence; and secondly, where such an act was independent and had no connection with the act, wrongful or otherwise, of the affected or victim State such as in the case of consent, *force majeure* or fortuitous event, distress, and state of necessity.

According to Professor Gurdip Singh, the rule of exhaustion of local remedies (ELR) is closely attached to the principles of state responsibility (Singh 1982). According to Article 44(b) of the Draft Code of 2001, the responsibility of a State may not be invoked if the claim is one to which the rule of exhaustion of local remedies applies and any available and effective local remedy has not been exhausted. It is, therefore, evident that local remedies must be effective and genuinely available. Although there is no international yardstick for measuring the effectiveness of local remedies, guidance must be drawn from certain objective situations and jurisprudence of the European Commission of Human Rights and Human Rights Committee while determining the effectiveness of local remedies. On the issue of the burden of proof, the Human Rights Committee has regarded it as incumbent upon the respondent State to prove that local remedies are effective (i.e. they are capable of redressing the alleged wrong) just as it is incumbent upon the complainant to prove that he has exhausted the local remedies or that there were circumstances relegating him of the duty of exhaustion. The Draft Code has left the interpretation of the word 'effective' to State practice, *opinio juris* and growing jurisprudence of judicial and arbitral tribunals. However, the specification of the rule of ELR in the areas of diplomatic privileges and growing State participation in commercial ventures would lend strength to the rule and would considerably enhance its utility.

India and Pakistan's position on State responsibility can be observed in the matter of *Appeal Relating to the Jurisdiction of the ICAO Council* (*India* v. *Pakistan*). In this case, the dispute arose from the decision of the Government of India to suspend flights of its own and Pakistan's aircraft over each other's territory on 4 February 1971 by way of reaction to Pakistan's conduct on the hijacking case. Under the International Civil Aviation Convention and International Air Services Transit Agreement, both signed in Chicago in 1944, the civil aircraft of Pakistan had the right to overfly Indian territory. Hostilities interrupting over flights broke out between the two countries in August 1965, but in February 1966, they came to an agreement that there should be an immediate resumption of over flights on the same basis as before 1 August 1965. Pakistan interpreted that undertaking as meaning that over flights would be resumed on the basis of the Convention and Transit Agreement, but India maintained that those two treaties had been suspended during the hostilities and were never as such revived, and that over flights were resumed on the basis of a special regime according to which they could take place only after permission had been granted by India. Pakistan denied that any such regime ever came into existence and maintained that the treaties had never ceased to be applicable since 1966. The majority judgment of the court was rendered by Justice Sir Muhammad Zafrullah Khan, who held that the court had jurisdiction to entertain India's appeal. However, it rejected India's appeal preferred to the court against the decision of the ICAO Council assuming jurisdiction in the matter. According to the court, it is a well-settled norm that reconciliation rules must be implemented despite the fact notwithstanding that they are part of the same agreement which itself is in question and the controversy is raised with regard to its validity or effect. The reconciliation mechanism between the complainant and the respondent State is applicable to their controversy and may not allowed to put in abeyance by way of countermeasures. However, Justice Nagendra Singh delivered his dissenting opinion in this case and held that it was known to the Tribunal, and to all its members, that the overflights had been suspended. The fact of suspension was not disputed by Pakistan either.

Sri Lankan position on state responsibility is reflected in its counter-memorials filed in the matter of *Asian Agricultural Products Limited* (*AAPL*) v. *Republic of Sri Lanka* (1991). In that case, the responsibility consisted of a failure by Sri Lanka to exercise due diligence in protecting AAPL's property from attacks by Tamil Tigers. Sri Lanka wanted to exclude responsibility on the basis that Tamil Tigers had to be fought by the governmental forces as they wanted to control the area. It was argued that counter-insurgency operations of the State exclude any responsibility in case of damage to investors' property. According to the arbitral investment tribunal, however, the investors have to be provided full protection and security by the State government. The Bilateral Investment Treaty between Sri Lanka and the UK had not left the host State totally immune from any responsibility in case the foreign investor suffered losses due to the destruction of his investment which occurred during a counter-insurgency action undertaken by governmental security forces.

Professor C.F. Amerasinghe in his book 'State Responsibility For Injuries to Aliens', the capital exporting countries maintain that there is always a duty to compensate, even in case of nationalization (Amerasinghe 1967). As for expropriating States, Mexico denied this obligation in 1938. The Soviet Union took the view that there was no international obligation to compensate at all. In practice, however, nationalization decrees in many States, such as Iran, Egypt, Indonesia, and Burma expressly recognized the principle of compensation. Ceylon came nearest to conceding the obligation to compensate when it stated that 'it was at all times ready and willing to pay compensation to the oil companies, and, that in fact, provision for that purpose already existed in the Petroleum Corporation Act'.

8 Latest Debate

As indicated at the outset, the ILC articles focus on the rules by which States can invoke the responsibility of another state for breaching its international obligation. But the world has evolved considerably over the last four decades since the Commission began its deliberations. While the Commission's almost exclusive concern with states may have been appropriate at the beginning of its work, it does not reflect the international system of the twenty-first century. Three areas illustrate the significant role of individuals and non-state entities in invoking state responsibility before international dispute settlement bodies: human rights, environmental protection, and foreign investor protection. In many instances, international agreements provide for individual complaint procedures. The widespread existence of *lex specialis* contributes to the development of international law regarding the invocation of state responsibility.

Various international and regional forums recognize that individuals have standing to make claims against states for violations of human rights. Within the UN system, four international agreements give individuals or groups of individuals the right to complain about violations of the protected rights: the First Optional Protocol to the International Covenant on Civil and Political Rights, the Optional Protocol to the Convention on the Elimination of All Forms of Discrimination Against Women, the Convention Against Torture and Other Forms of Cruel and Inhuman Punishment, and the International Convention on the Elimination of All Forms of Racial Discrimination. The First Optional Protocol to the ICCPR gives individuals the right to make written representations to the UN Human Rights Committee for violations of the Covenant by those states that have accepted the Protocol. If the Committee finds the petition admissible, it receives submissions from both the individual and the targeted state and determines whether a violation has occurred. In 1999, parties to the Convention on the Elimination of Discrimination Against Women adopted an Optional Protocol (based on the ICCPR model) that give individuals or groups of individuals the right to submit written communications 'claiming to be victims' of violations of any of the rights in the Convention by states that have accepted the Protocol. The UN Committee on Economic, Social, and Cultural Rights has considered developing an optional protocol to the International Covenant on Economic, Social, and Cultural Rights, which would similarly give individuals the right to complain of a breach of the Covenant by a state party to such a protocol. The Convention Against Torture and the International Convention on the Elimination of All Forms of Racial Discrimination both create an individual complaint procedure, which states can opt into. The Committee on the Elimination of Racial Discrimination considers complaints filed by individuals or groups of persons claiming to be victims of racial discrimination by a state that is a party to the Convention and has declared that it recognizes the committee's competence to receive individual complaints.

At the regional level, the evidence is even more persuasive that individuals have become important actors in invoking state responsibility. When the International Law Commission began its work, state responsibility generally meant the substantive rules for protecting aliens, particularly in the area of foreign investment. Within the last decade or two, however, investors have increasingly resorted directly to international dispute settlement procedures for breaches. The International Centre for Settlement of Investment Disputes (ICSID) provides a mechanism for states and foreign investors to resolve their disputes voluntarily.

The International Court of Justice

Only states can bring claims against other states in the International Court of Justice for the breach of international obligations. Nonetheless, the court came close to giving effect to individual rights in the *La Grand* case and in earlier advisory jurisdiction in *Reparations for injuries suffered in the services of UN.*

The ILC's deliberations reveal that members were well aware of the possibility that entities other than states might invoke state responsibility. Some wanted to address the issue, while others did not. In the end, the ILC referred to the issue in Part Two (which addresses the content of the international responsibility of states), but not in the articles of Part Three on invoking state responsibility. The Commission's overall approach to individuals and non-state entities was to leave this matter to *lex specialis* rather than to enunciate a general rule. As a result, whether and to what extent entities other than states may invoke responsibility vary depending on the primary rule involved.

As mentioned in the ILC Report related to the task undertaken in fifty-third session (56/10), James Crawford, the last rapporteur, was certainly aware that the international community includes important actors other than states. In his excellent introduction to the articles and commentary, he notes that '[the international community includes entities in addition to States, for example, the UN, the European Communities, the International Committee of the Red Cross. Clearly there, are other persons or entities besides States towards whom obligations may exist and who may invoke responsibility for breaches of those obligations]'.

9 Conclusion

State responsibility is one of the most complex issues in the international law. The trouble of dealing with this complex issue is the difficulty to invoke state responsibility in practice. The law of state responsibility is customary international law, developed by state practice and international judgments. Even though the enforcement of public international law is rather limited because states participate on voluntary basis and reciprocal obligations, customary international law is binding on the states, as it is evidence of generally accepted state practice and *opinion juris*, accepted as law. The concept of state responsibility makes an obligation for states to act in conformity with the international agreements or customary law.

The application of the principle of state responsibility according to the Draft Rules of 2001 requires first, an act of the state which consists of either an action or an omission that is attributable to the state. As a legal entity, however, a state is not able to act by itself, its actions instead being understood as conduct of its organs and representatives which attributable to the state. The structure of the state and functions that are performed by its organs and representatives are governed solely by the internal law of that state. Therefore, the domestic law is also applicable to determine what constitutes a state organ and designation by the state of the persons empowered to exercise the authority of the state. And whereas the legal prerequisites for the international responsibility of states can be specified solely by internal law itself, the conditions under which conduct is deemed to be the conduct of the state for the purposes of state responsibility are thus independent from the different domestic laws.

In addition to the conduct of the state organs and persons or entities other empowered to exercise government authority, also the conduct of private persons or entities may be imputed to the state, provided the conduct is directed or controlled by the state. This particularly applies in cases where a person or entity is in fact acting on the instructions or under the direction or control of a state. If an injured state claims compensation for damage suffered as a result of a wrongful act of another state under the principles of state responsibility, the burden of proof lies in principle with the claimant state that has to establish in full the legal prerequisite of its claim. As per the rules of attribution discussed above, the conduct of state organs and other persons or entities empowered with public authority is attributed to the state even if the person or entity acting in official capacity has exceeded the authority or competence which was delegated by the individual instructions or different internal laws of the state. Since the internal laws of the state remain applicable as to the determination of the notion of state organs and as to assignment of public authority to other persons or entities, it would be possible for a state to avoid the attribution of a conduct by simply referring to its internal laws, rules, and regulations. Therefore, these lacunas of rules of state responsibility are required to be fulfilled.

The other obstacle in invoking state responsibility will be proving the link between activities and damage. Moreover, the activities of the states can be legal, thus no state responsibility can be attributed even if there is damage. In the light of that distinction between wrongful acts and activities not prohibited by international law, the ILC expanded its work and produced Draft Articles and Principles on State responsibility and International Liability for Injurious Consequences Arising out of Acts not Prohibited by International Law. This topic was divided into two parts: the first one deals with prevention and second covers the compensation. Draft Articles on Prevention of Trans-boundary Harm Arising out of Hazardous Activities were adopted in 2001 and Draft Principles on Allocation of Loss in the Case of

Trans-boundary Harm Arising out of Hazardous Activities in 2006. It should also be noted that the concept of state liability did not exist in the customary international law. The work of the International Law Commission reflects the progressive development of the international law. The Draft Principles on Allocation of Loss in Case of Trans-boundary Harm Arising out of Hazardous Activities suggests that the strict liability should be put on the operator or owner and demands financial funds to be established. This was the clear example where work of the International Law Commission covered the field of private international law.

When the damage has occurred, the question of state responsibility arises and it is surely too late to act. Therefore, more emphasis should be on protection and prevention as well as cooperation to avoid any kind of potential damage. It is important that the states accept responsibility to cooperate. Some of the instruments deal with prevention and cooperation such as Principles of Stockholm Declaration and Rio Declaration, two soft laws. Moreover, they have made a solid ground to encourage states to conclude multilateral and bilateral agreements in order to cooperate in the environmental matters. So this is also an important aspect of state responsibility. For example, after the Chernobyl nuclear accident, it was evident that states were reluctant to invoke state responsibility. Even though the accident covered many states, no international instrument was used and states accepted only to cooperate.

States usually do not take responsibility for the private activities if the states have fulfilled their due diligence. The lack of the state's will to assume the responsibility for trans-boundary environmental damage and practical difficulties in invoking state responsibility has led to the transposition of liability to private persons. Ultra-hazardous activities are likely to cause a risk of trans-boundary environmental damage such as regimes for nuclear damage. Strict liability is connected with activities that are considered to be dangerous. Similar is the case with the responsibility and liability regimes for marine damage, where the subsidiary funding mechanism also exists.

As we have discussed above, the legal prerequisites for bringing a claim under the principle of state responsibility can be derived from the Draft Articles on the State Responsibility, which albeit not legally binding as such, are being referred and used as *de facto* source of law even by international courts like ICJ. Therefore, it's high time that question of conventions be taken up by the General Assembly of the UN.

References

Anzilotti D (trans Gidel, 1929) Cours de droit international (Paris Pantheon-Assas/LGDJ, 1999), 517
Amerasinghe CF (1967) State responsibility for injuries to aliens. Oxford, London
ARISWA, Commentary to Art 2, para 10
Combacau J, Sur S (2009) Droit international public 526

Commentary to Draft At 2, para 2, International Law Commission Yearbook 1973, Vol. II 177. Draft art 2 as adopted on first reading was deleted on second reading, and with its accompanying commentary
Factory at Chorzow, Merit, 1928, PCIJ, series A, No 17 P 4, 29; see also Factory at Chorzow, jurisdiction, 1927, PCIJ, series A, No 9, P 4, 21
GA Resolution no. 52/156(A/49/10)
GA Resolution no. 56/83, dated December 12, 2001
GA Resolution no. A/62/61
García A (1955) Am J Int Law 49:343
Grotius H (1625) The rights of war and peace. In: Tuck R (ed) J Barbeyrac (trans), Indianapolis, liberty fund, 2005, Chap. XVII, para 1 (vol II, 884); and see the prolegomena, para 8 (vol 1, 86)
I.C.J. Reports 1949 p. 4 Judge Azavedo, in a dissenting opinion, disagreed to some extent with the court' view of the law even he went as far as to say that the circumstances gave rise to a 'presumed responsibility', p 86
Jagota SP (1985) State responsibility: circumstances precluding wrongfulness. Netherlands yearbook of international law 16:249–277
Jouanner E (1998) Emer de Vattel et l'emergencedu droit international classique, 407
Noyes Claim (1933) (U.S.A. v. Panama), 6 UN.R.I.A.A. 308
Popecu S (1966) 'Le fondement de la resposabilite juridique' Revue roumaine des science juridiques 139
Rao PC (1997) Comments on Article 19 of the draft articles on state responsibility adopted by the International Law Commission. Ind J Int Law 37:673–676
Resolution no. A/C.6/65/L.8 dated 5th November 2010
See Articles 21 ff. and Article 17 of the Universal Declaration of Human Rights
Singh G (1982) The local remedies rule and its limits in relation to state responsibility for injuries to aliens. Delhi Law Review 10, 11:118–141
Starke JG (1938) 19 British yearbook of international law
The Memorial of the British Government in the Finnish Ships Arbitration (1934), 17 B.Y.I.L. (1936) 22
The SS 'Wimbledon' (1923), PCIJ Series A, No 1, 25
UN Doc A/56/10 (2001)
Whiteman M (1937) Damages in international law (vols 1–3). U.S. Dept. of State

Author Biography

Ms Madhu Bhatti is a doctoral candidate in the Faculty of Law, University of Delhi. She has been teaching first as Guest Faculty and later as Assistant Professor in the Faculty of Law since the last decade. She obtained her LL.B. degree from Campus Law Centre, University of Delhi and practised law in the High Court of Delhi for 10 years and thereafter she joined legal academia at her alma mater Faculty of Law after getting her LL.M. degree.

Chapter 13
International Criminal Court: Baby Steps in South Asia

Anupam Jha

1 Introduction

The General Assembly of the United Nations urged the International Law Commission to elaborate a viable Statute for the creation of an international criminal court as a matter of priority. This culminated in the production of a draft Statute in 1994 (Crawford 1995). The draft Statute raised major substantive issues. In order to consider those issues, the General Assembly created an ad hoc Committee on the Establishment of an International Criminal Court, which met twice in 1995 (UN GA 50th Session 1995). After consideration of the ad hoc Committee's work, the General Assembly established the Preparatory Committee (Prep Com) on the Establishment of an International Criminal Court (GA Res 1995). The Prep Com met six times since 1996. Upon concluding its work, the Prep Com asked the General Assembly to convene a diplomatic conference for the purposes of finalizing the Statute in treaty form adoption by the international committee. A heavily bracketed draft treaty—the brackets indicating unresolved issues and details—was laid before a conference of plenipotentiaries for negotiation in July 1998 in Rome. Intense negotiations took place over there. Significant compromises were made from all sides. Ultimately, the Statute creating International Criminal Court was signed on 17 July 1998 (ILM 1998).

In addition to the Statute of the International Criminal Court, on 17 July 1998, the Diplomatic Conference also adopted a Final Act, providing for the establishment of a Preparatory Commission. The Commission was assigned, inter alia, four major tasks, namely drafting of the Rules of Procedure and Evidence, the Elements of Crime, an agreement with the United Nations on the relationship between the two organizations, and preparation of a host State agreement with the Netherlands,

A. Jha (✉)
Law Centre-II, Faculty of Law, University of Delhi,
38/12, Probyn Road, New Delhi 110007, India
e-mail: ajha@law.du.ac.in

J.L. Kaul and A. Jha (eds.), *Shifting Horizons of Public International Law*,
https://doi.org/10.1007/978-81-322-3724-2_13

which is to be the seat of the Court. The Commission finalized its work on the Rules of Procedure and Evidence and on Elements of Crime in the year of 2000. This Commission operated until the Rome Statute came into force in the year of 2002 after the deposit of sixtieth instrument of ratification, at which time the Assembly of States Parties was convened. The Assembly of States Parties adopted the Rules of Procedure and Evidence (ICC-ASP 2002) and Elements of Crime (ICC-ASP/1/3Part-B 2002) in 2002. An agreement between the ICC and the United Nations (ICC-ASP/3/Res 2004) was adopted in 2004, and the Host Agreement (ICC-BD/04-01-08 2007) was adopted in 2007. All these four instruments are now in force.

2 States Parties to the Rome Statute

At the time of voting during Rome Conference in 1998, one hundred and twenty States voted in favour of the Statute, seven voted against (USA, China, Libya, Iraq, Israel, Qatar, and Yemen) and twenty-one abstained. Despite the opposition of the United States, the Rome Statute was voted heavily in favour of its adoption. It was a remarkable diplomatic success. Now, one hundred and twenty-four (124) States have become parties to the Rome Statute. It is a major achievement because within two decades its adoption, such a large number of States have decided to join the Rome Statute system. Out of them, 33 are African States, 19 are Asia-Pacific States, 18 are from Eastern Europe, 28 are from Latin American and Caribbean States, and 25 are from Western European and other States (Assembly of States Parties 2016). Out of the 33 African States, South Africa, Nigeria, Central African Republic, Mauritius, Sierra Leone, Democratic Republic of Congo, Tanzania, Congo, and Madagascar are the prominent ones. In the Asian-Pacific region, out of the 19 ratifying States, Bangladesh, Maldives, Cambodia, Japan, Philippines, Afghanistan, South Korea, Jordan, Fiji, and Cyprus are the prominent ones.

Becoming parties to the Rome Statute entails rights and duties incumbent upon the States. Rights of States include ability to trigger the jurisdiction (Article 14, Rome Statute), participation in the election of judges (Article 36(8), Rome Statute) and prosecutors (Article 42(4), Rome Statute) of the Court, participation in the adoption of the legal texts of the Court (Article 51, Rome Statute), and participation in amendment procedure (Article 121, Rome Statute) and in the review conferences (Article 123, Rome Statute). Regarding duties, States parties are obliged to co-operate with the Court in investigation, prosecution, and sentencing matters (Articles 86–111, Rome Statute). According to the principle of complementarity laid down in Article 1 of the Rome Statute, States parties must be able to try and prosecute the persons responsible for the violation of the Statute. This ability can come only when the States parties incorporate the crimes under Rome Statute in their respective penal codes or otherwise.

3 Assembly of States Parties

The Assembly of States Parties is the management oversight and legislative body of the International Criminal Court (Assembly of States Parties 2016). It is composed of representatives of the States that have ratified and acceded to the Rome Statute. Each State Party is represented by a representative who is proposed to the Credential Committee by the head of State of government or the Minister of Foreign Affairs (Chapter IV, Rules of Procedure of the Assembly of States Parties). The Assembly of States Parties has a Bureau, consisting of a President, two Vice Presidents, and 18 members elected by the Assembly for a three-year term, taking into consideration principles of equitable geographic distribution and adequate representation of the principal legal systems of the world. Each State Party has one vote and every effort has to be made to reach decisions by consensus both in the Assembly and the Bureau (Article 112(7), Rome Statute). If consensus cannot be reached, decisions are taken by vote. The Bureau meets as often as necessary, but at least once a year. It assists the Assembly in the discharge of its responsibilities. The Assembly of States Parties decides on various items, such as the adoption of normative texts and of the budget and the election of the judges and of the Prosecutor and the Deputy Prosecutor(s).

Every effort has to be made to reach decisions by consensus in the Assembly (ICC-ASP/2/L.5). If consensus cannot be reached, decisions on matters of substance must be approved by a two-thirds majority of those present and voting provided that an absolute majority of States Parties constitutes the quorum of voting (Article 112(7), Rome Statute). Decisions on matters of procedure shall be taken by a simple majority of States Parties present and voting (Article 112(7), Rome Statute). A State Party which is in arrears in the payment of its financial contribution towards the costs of the Court shall have no vote in the Assembly and in the Bureau if the amount of its arrears equals or exceeds the amount of the contributions due from it for the preceding two full years. The Assembly may, nevertheless, permit such a State Party to vote in the Assembly and in the Bureau if it is satisfied that the failure to pay is due to conditions beyond the control of the State Party (Article 112(8), Rome Statute). If a dispute arises between two or more States as to the interpretation or application of the Rome Statute, such disputes are to be referred to the Assembly of States Parties (Article 119(2), Rome Statute). The Assembly of States Parties may attempt to settle the case or propose alternative means of settlement, including referring the case to the International Court of Justice (Article 119(2), Rome Statute). However, such a procedure can only work with States that have also accepted the jurisdiction of the International Court of Justice or that agree to its jurisdiction in a specific case.

3.1 Subject-Matter Jurisdiction of the Court

According to the Rome Statute, the International Criminal Court enjoys subject-matter jurisdiction over the crimes of genocide, crimes against humanity, war crimes, and aggression (Article 5, Rome Statute). These crimes are considered to be the most serious crimes of concern to the international community. Except the crime of aggression, all other three crimes were defined in the 1998 Rome Statute. No consensus was reached during the Rome diplomatic conference on a definition for the crime of aggression. However, since the adoption of the Rome Statute, efforts are being made by the Assembly of States Parties to define the crime of aggression. A special working group on the crime of aggression was constituted by the ssembly of States Parties in the year of 2003 for reaching an agreement on the definition of crime and the conditions for the exercise of the court's jurisdiction. After five years of its work on the topic, it came out in the year of 2009 with draft definition of aggression which was discussed by the eighth session of the Assembly of States Parties in November 2009. Ultimately, a definition of aggression was finally agreed upon in the review conference held in Kampala (the capital of Uganda) in the year of 2010. Articles 8 *bis* and 15 *ter* were added in the Rome Statute, which remain to be ratified by 30 States Parties and thereafter approved by two-thirds majority vote (Jha 2011).

Genocide has been considered to be a grave crime since the year of 1946. In that year, the General Assembly of United Nations declared genocide an international crime (GA Res. 96(1) (11 December 1946)). After two years in 1948, a convention was adopted by the General Assembly on the Prevention and Punishment of the Crime of Genocide (78 UN Treaty Series 277 (9 December 1948)). There are 147 States Parties to this convention. India, Pakistan, Sri Lanka, Bangladesh, Afghanistan, Nepal, China, and South Africa are the parties to the convention. The definition of genocide in the Rome Statute is a *verbatim* reproduction of Article II of the convention on the Prevention and Punishment of the Crime of Genocide.

Genocide means any of the following five acts committed with intent to destroy, in whole or in part, four kinds of groups, namely national, ethnical, racial, and religious group as such. Those five acts are:

1. Killing members of the group;
2. Causing serious bodily harm or mental harm to members of the group;
3. Imposing measures intended to prevent births within the group;
4. Imposing conditions on the group calculated to destroy it; and
5. Forcibly transferring children from one group to another group.

Intention to destroy a group is the essence of the crime of genocide. A special kind of intention is required to commit this crime which is called *dolus specialis* (special intent). Judicial assessment of such intention begins by first examining the existence of a genocidal plan and the commission of genocide, and then inquiring into the genocidal intent of the accused (Verdirame 2000). The next issue to be determined by the Court is to look into the quantitative dimension of the destruction of a group. The phrase used in Article 6 of the Rome Statute is 'in whole or in part'. This phrase indicates that where only a part of a group is destroyed, it must be a substantial part (Lemkin 1944).

Another requirement is that the victim must belong to any of the given four groups, namely national, ethnical, religious, and racial. The list of the four types of groups is exhaustive in nature. Political group, cultural group, and socially vulnerable groups are left out of its ambit. Thus, systematic destruction of even large number of people on political grounds does not amount to genocide under the existing definition.

The case law on genocide has evolved from Eichmann's trial in the year of 1962. Decisions of the International Criminal Tribunals for the Former Yugoslavia and the International Criminal Tribunal for Rwanda have also added a significant amount of jurisprudence on genocide in a number of cases. A survey of the decided cases by International Criminal Tribunal for the Former Yugoslavia (ICTY) and International Criminal Tribunal for Rwanda (ICTR) in Nikolic, Karadzic, Akayesu, Jelisic, Kayishema, Krstic, Ruzindana, Gacumbitsi, Blagojevic and Jokic, Milutinovic, and Seromba gives a very good understanding of the evolution of Court's jurisprudence on the issue of genocide. The International Criminal Court has also charged Sudanese President Omar al Bashir with the complicity in the commission of genocide in Darfur region.

Crime against humanity is dealt with in Article 7 of the Rome Statute. Paragraph 1 defines the crime. According to the provision, crime against humanity means any of the following eleven acts when committed as part of a widespread or systematic attack directed against any civilian population, with knowledge of the attack: (a) murder; (b) extermination; (c) enslavement; (d) deportation or forcible transfer of population; (e) imprisonment or other severe deprivation of physical liberty in violation of fundamental rules of international law; (f) torture; (g) rape, sexual slavery, enforced prostitution, forced pregnancy, or any other form of sexual violence of comparable gravity; (h) persecution against any identifiable group or collectivity on political, racial, national, ethnic, cultural, religious, gender or other grounds that are universally recognized as impermissible under international law, in connection with any act referred to in this paragraph or any crime within the jurisdiction of the Court; (i) enforced disappearance of persons; (j) the crime of apartheid; and (k) other inhumane acts of a similar character intentionally causing great suffering, or serious injury to body or to mental or physical health.

Paragraph 2 of Article 7 is explanatory paragraph. It explains several phrases and words used in para 1, such as 'attack directed against any civilian population', 'extermination', 'enslavement', 'deportation', 'torture', 'forced pregnancy', 'persecution', 'apartheid', and 'enforced disappearance of persons'. The phrase 'attack directed against any civilian population' means a course of conduct involving the multiple commissions of acts referred to in para 1 against any civilian population, pursuant to or in furtherance of a State or organizational policy to commit such attack (Article 7(2)(a), Rome Statute). 'Extermination' includes the intentional infliction of conditions of life, inter alia, the deprivation of access to food and medicine, calculated to bring about the destruction of part of a population (Article 7 (2)(b), Rome Statute). 'Enslavement' means the exercise of any or all of the powers attaching to the right of ownership over a person and includes the exercise of such power in the course of trafficking in persons, in particular women and children

(Article 7(2)(c) Rome Statute). 'Deportation or forcible transfer of population' means forced displacement of the persons concerned by expulsion or other coercive acts from the area in which they are lawfully present, without grounds permitted under international law (Article 7(2)(d), Rome Statute).

In the Charter of the IMT at Nuremberg, it was laid down that crimes against humanity could only be committed if they were associated with one of the other crimes within the jurisdiction of the Nuremberg tribunal, i.e. war crimes and crime against peace. In effect, the Allies had imposed a nexus between crimes against humanity and international armed conflict (Schabas 2001). However, the Security Council eliminated the nexus between crimes against humanity and armed conflict when it established the International Criminal Tribunal for Rwanda (Article 3, Statute of International Criminal Tribunal for the Rwanda). Such removal was also recognized by the Appeals Chamber of the International Criminal Tribunal for Former Yugoslavia in its celebrated 'Tadic' jurisdiction decision (*Prosecutor* v. *Tadic*).

The case law on crimes against humanity has evolved since the Nuremberg trial. In the Nuremberg trial, Bormann, Frank, Frick, Funk, Goring, Jodl, Kaltenbrunner, Keitel, Ley, Neurath, Ribbentrop, Rosenberg, Sauckel, Schirach, Inquart, Streitcher were convicted of crimes against humanity. However, a major thrust towards the growth of jurisprudence on crimes against humanity has been given by International Criminal Tribunal for the former Yugoslvia and the International Criminal Tribunal for Rwanda in the cases of Tadic, Jelisic, Krstic, Galic. Blaskic, Karadzic, Mladic, Akayesu, Bagilishema, Rutaganda, Musema, Kunarac, Gacumbitsi, Kajelijeli, Kambanda, Kamuhanda, and Simba among others. The International Criminal Court has also indicted Sudanese President Omar al Basheer with the charge of crimes against humanity. In the ICC, charges of crimes against humanity are levelled against civilian/military/militia commanders, Bemba, Ntaganda, Germain Katanga of Congo, Saif Gaddafi from Libya, Laurent Gbagbo from Ivory Coast, Ahmad Harun from Darfur, Al Bashir from Darfur, and Ongwen from Uganda. Bemba and Katanga have been found guilty of committing crimes against humanity.

War crimes are provided for in Article 8 of the Rome Statute. This article is the lengthiest one amongst the other subject-matter crimes. It consists of four categories of war crimes, two of them addressing international armed conflict and other two non-international armed conflicts. In the category of war crimes committed during international armed conflict, two subcategories are provided, one deals with grave breaches of the Geneva Conventions of 12 August 1949, and other deals with other serious violations of the laws and customs applicable in international armed conflict. Similarly in the category of war crimes committed during non-international armed conflict, two categories are provided, one deals with serious violations of Article 3 common to the four Geneva Conventions of 12 August 1949, and other deals with other serious violations of the laws and customs applied in non-international armed conflict.

In total, 50 acts, whether committed during international or non-international armed conflict, amount to war crimes under Article 8 of the Rome Statute. Out of the fifty, 8 acts are included in the category of grave breaches of Geneva

Conventions of 12 August 1949 during international armed conflict, 26 acts are included in other serious violations of the laws and customs of international armed conflict, 4 acts are included in the serious violations of Article 3 common to the Geneva Conventions of 12 August 1949 during non-international armed conflict, and 12 acts are included in other serious violations of the laws and customs applicable in non-international armed conflicts.

It is provided in para 1 of Article 8 that war crimes must have been committed in particular as part of a plan or policy or as part of a large-scale commission of such crimes. It must not be a stray act or an isolated act. Furthermore, existence of armed conflict, whether international or non-international, is another pre-requisite of war crime. Apart from these two basic ingredients, the next issue to be determined by the court is whether alleged act was committed during international or non-international armed conflict. If an act is committed during international armed conflict, the court has further to determine whether the conduct falls under grave breaches of Geneva Conventions of 1949 or under other serious violations of laws and customs of international armed conflict. Similarly, if an act is committed during non-international conflict, then the court has further to determine whether the conduct falls under serious violations of Article 3 common to the Geneva Conventions of 1949 or under other serious violations of the laws and customs of non-international armed conflict.

Victims of grave breaches must be protected persons under the Geneva Conventions. Subparagraph (a) of para 2 of Article 8 mentions eight acts committed against protected persons in times of international armed conflicts as war crimes, namely willful killing; torture or inhuman treatment, including biological experiments, willfully causing great suffering, or serious injury to body or health; extensive destruction and appropriation of property, not justified by military necessity and carried out unlawfully and wantonly; compelling a prisoner of war or other protected person to serve in the forces of a hostile power; wilfully depriving a prisoner of war or other protected person of the rights of fair and regular trial; unlawful deportation or transfer or unlawful confinement; and taking of hostages.

Any of the four following acts against persons not taking active part in the hostilities, including members of armed forces who have laid down their arms and those placed *hors de combat* by sickness, wounds, detention, or any other cause may amount to serious violations of Article 3 common to the four Geneva Conventions of 1949 in the case of an armed conflict not of an international character. Those acts are: (i) violence to life and person, in particular murder of all kinds, mutilation, cruel treatment, and torture; (ii) committing outrages upon personal dignity, in particular humiliating and degrading treatment; (iii) taking of hostages; (iv) the passing of sentences and the carrying out of executions without previous judgment pronounced by a regularly constituted court, affording all judicial guarantees which are generally recognized as indispensable.

Table 1 gives a comparative picture of those common eleven types of war crimes committed during international and non-international armed conflict which are neither grave breaches of the Geneva Conventions of 1949 nor serious violations of Article 3 common to those Conventions.

Table 1 Acts of war crimes committed during international and non-international armed conflicts which are neither grave breaches nor serious violations of common Article 3

	Other serious violations of laws and customs applicable to international armed conflicts	Other serious violations of laws and customs applicable to non-international armed conflicts
1	Intentionally directing attacks against the civilian population as such or against individual civilian not taking direct part in Hostilities [Article 8(2)(b)(i)]	Intentionally directing attacks against the civilian population as such or against individual civilians not taking direct part in Hostilities [Article 8(2)(e)(i)]
2	Intentionally directing attacks against personnel, installations, materials, units, or vehicles involved in a humanitarian assistance or peacekeeping mission in accordance with the charter of the United Nations, as long as they are entitled to the protection given to civilians or civilian objects under the International Law of armed conflict [Article 8(2)(b)(iii)]	Intentionally directing attacks against personnel, installations, materials, units or vehicles involved in a humanitarian assistance or peacekeeping mission in accordance with the charter of the United Nations, as long as they are entitled to the protection given to civilians or civilian objects under the International Law of armed conflict [Article 8(2)(e)(iii)]
3	Intentionally directing attacks against building dedicated to religion, education, art, science or charitable purposes, historic monuments, hospitals, and places where the sick and wounded are collected, provided they are not military objectives [Article 8(2)(b)(ix)]	Intentionally directing attacks against building dedicated to religion, education, art, science or charitable purposes, historic monuments, hospitals, and places where the sick and wounded are collected, provided they are not military objectives [Article 8(2)(e)(iv)]
4	Intentionally directing attacks against building, material, medical units and transport and personnel using the distinctive emblems of the Geneva Conventions in Conformity with International Law [Article 8(2)(b)(xxiv)]	Intentionally directing attacks against building, material, medical units and transport ad personnel using the distinctive emblems of the Geneva Conventions in Conformity with International Law [Article 8(2)(e)(ii)]
5	Pillaging a town or place, even when taken by assault [Article 8(2)(b)(xvi)]	Pillaging a town or place, even when taken by assault [Article 8(2)(e)(v)]
6	Declaring that no quarter will be given [Article 8(2)(b)(xii)]	Declaring that no quarter will be given [Article 8(2)(e)(x)]
7	Killing or wounding treacherously individuals belonging to the hostile nation or army [Article 8(2)(b)(xi)]	Killing or wounding treacherously individuals belonging to the hostile nation or army [Article 8(2)(e)(ix)]
8	Committing rape, sexual slavery, enforced prostitution, forced pregnancy, as defined in Article 7, para 2(f) enforced sterilization or any other form of sexual violence also constituting a grave breach of the Geneva Conventions [Article 8(2)(b)(xxii)]	Committing rape, sexual slavery, enforced prostitution, forced pregnancy, as defined in Article 7, para 2(f) enforced sterilization or any other form of sexual violence also constituting a serious violation of Article 3 common to the four Geneva Conventions [Article 8(2)(e)(vi)]
9	Conscripting or enlisting children under the age of fifteen years into the national armed forces or using them to participate	Conscripting or enlisting children under the age of fifteen years into the national armed forces or using them to participate actively in hostilities [Article 8(2)(e)(vii)]

(continued)

Table 1 (continued)

	Other serious violations of laws and customs applicable to international armed conflicts	Other serious violations of laws and customs applicable to non-international armed conflicts
	actively in hostilities [Article 8(2)(b)(xxvi)]	
10	Subjecting persons who are in the power of an adverse party to physical mutilation or to medical or scientific experiments of any kind which are neither justified by the medical, dental or hospital treatment of the person concerned nor carried out in his or her interest and which cause death or serious endanger the health of such person or persons [Article 8(2)(b)(x)]	Subjecting persons who are in the power of another party to the conflict to physical mutilation or to medical or scientific experiments of any kind which are neither justified by the medical, dental or hospital treatment of the person concerned nor carried out in his or her interest and which cause death or seriously endanger the health of such person or persons [Article 8(2)(e)(xi)]
11	Destroying or seizing the enemy's property unless such destruction or seizure be imperatively demanded by the necessities of war [Article 8(2)(b)(xiii)]	Destroying or seizing the property of an adversary unless such destruction or seizure be imperatively demanded by the necessities of the conflict [Article 8(2)(e)(xii)]

War crime charges have been levelled against the following military or militia commanders: Bemba of Central African Republic, Lubanga, Katanga, Ntaganda of Congo, and Ongwen of Uganda. Also, top political leaders are also charged with the commission of war crimes, such as Al Bashir and Ahmad Harun from Sudan. Civilian leaders such as Al Mahdi from Mali have also been charged with the commission of war crimes. Bemba, Lubanga, Germain Katanga have been found guilty of committing war crimes.

3.2 *Territorial, Personal, and Temporal Jurisdiction*

The general principle about the territorial jurisdiction is set out in Article 12(2)(a) of the Rome Statute. According to this provision, the ICC exercises jurisdiction over crimes committed in the territory of State Parties, regardless of the nationality of the offender. The court will also have jurisdiction over crimes committed on the territory so designated by the Security Council (Articles 12(3) and 13(b), Rome Statute). The Statute extends the concept of territory from the traditional land territory of the State to the vessels and aircraft registered in the State Party wherein the crime is committed on board (Article 12(2)(a), Rome Statute). Personal jurisdiction of the ICC can be exercised over nationals of a State Party who are accused of a crime, in accordance with Article 12(2)(b). Furthermore, the court can also prosecute nationals of non-party States that accept its jurisdiction on an ad hoc basis (UN Doc. PCNICC/2000/INF/3/Add I) or pursuant to a decision of the Security Council (In Darfur and Libya, the ICC exercised its jurisdiction due to Security Council resolution).

The temporal jurisdiction of the court is provided for in Articles 11 and 24 of the Rome Statute. The ICC cannot exercise jurisdiction over crimes committed prior to the entry into force of the Statute (Article 11(1), Rome Statute). In the case of States that become parties to the Statute subsequent to its entry into force, the court has jurisdiction over crimes committed after the entry into force of the Statute with respect to that State (Article 11(2), Rome Statute). Alternatively, the Statute declares again that no person shall be criminally responsible under the Statute for conduct prior to its entry into force (Article 24, Rome Statute).

4 Rule on Individual Criminal Responsibility

The concept of individual criminal responsibility is laid down in Articles 25, 27, and 28 of the Rome Statute. The ICC has jurisdiction over natural persons according to the provisions of the Statute (Article 25, Rome Statute). A person who commits a crime within the jurisdiction of the Court shall be individually responsible and liable for punishment in accordance with this Statute (Article 25(2), Rome Statute). Acts of abetment, conspiracy, and attempt to commit crimes punishable under the Statute are also punishable (Article 25(3), Rome Statute). Further, the Statute talks about irrelevance of official capacity. It provides that this Statute applies equally to all persons without any distinction based on official capacity. In particular, official capacity as a head of State or government, a member of a government or parliament, an elected representative or a government official does not exempt a person from criminal responsibility under this Statute, nor does it, in and of itself, constitute a ground for reduction of sentence (Article 27(1), Rome Statute). Immunities or special procedural rules which may attach to the official capacity of a person, whether under national or international law, do not bar the Court from exercising its jurisdiction over such a person (Article 27(2), Rome Statute).

Responsibility of commanders and other superiors is dealt with in Article 28 of the Statute. It provides that a military commander or person effectively acting as a military commander is criminally responsible for crimes within the jurisdiction of the Court committed by forces under his or her effective command and control, or effective authority and control as the case may be, as a result of his or her failure to exercise control properly over such forces, where: (i) that military commander or person either knew or, owing to the circumstances at the time, should have known that the forces were committing or about to commit such crimes; and (ii) that military commander or person failed to take all necessary and reasonable measures within his or her power to prevent or repress their commission or to submit the matter to the competent authorities for investigation and prosecution (Article 28, para (a), Rome Statute). With respect to superior and subordinate relationships not described in the above paragraph, a superior is criminally responsible for crimes within the jurisdiction of the Court committed by subordinates under his or her effective authority and control, as a result of his or her failure to exercise control properly over such subordinates, where: (i) the superior either knew, or consciously disregarded information which clearly indicated, that the subordinates were committing or about to commit such crimes; (ii) the crimes concerned activities that were within the effective responsibility and control of the superior; and (iii) the superior failed to take all necessary and reasonable measures within his or her power to prevent or repress their commission or to submit the matter to the competent authorities for investigation and prosecution (Article 28, para (b), Rome Statute).

5 The Concept of Complementarity

Rules regarding admissibility have been dealt with in para 10 of the Preamble, Articles 1 and 17 of the Rome Statute. Paragraph 10 of the Preamble provides that the ICC established under this Statute is complementary to national criminal jurisdictions. Article 1 reiterates this point again. The key word in both the provisions is 'complementarity'. The term complementarity in the context of Rome Statute means that the ICC and the national legal systems shall mutually complement each other and not to be hostile to each other. The ad hoc tribunals, i.e. ICTY and ICTR, did not recognize complementarity but adhered to primacy rules whereby national legal systems were subordinate to those ad hoc tribunals.

The issues of admissibility recognizing the principle of complementarity are addressed in Article 17. It States that a case is inadmissible when it is being investigated or prosecuted by a State that has jurisdiction over it, or when the case has already been investigated and the State has decided not to prosecute. In such circumstances, the court may only proceed where the State is unwilling or unable genuinely to investigate or prosecute the case (Article 17(1)(a), Rome Statute). The terms 'unwilling' and 'unable' are explained in some detail. However, an adjective 'genuinely' added to these terms provides scope for judicial interpretation.

In order to determine unwillingness in a particular case, the court has to consider whether one or more of the following three conditions are satisfied or not (Article 17(2), Rome Statute). Firstly, it shall consider whether the proceedings were or are being undertaken or the national decision was made for the purpose of shielding the person concerned from criminal responsibility for crimes within the jurisdiction of the court or not. Secondly, it shall also consider whether there has been an unjustified delay in the proceedings which in the circumstances is inconsistent with intent to bring the person concerned to justice or not. Thirdly, the court will examine whether the proceedings were not or are not conducted independently or impartially, and they were or are being conducted in a manner which, in the circumstances, is inconsistent with intent to bring the person concerned to justice. The Statute also requires the court to consider the above three issues having regard to the principles of due process recognized by international law, suggesting procedural and substantive fairness.

6 Trigger Mechanisms

The Rome Statute establishes the law on trigger mechanisms in Articles 13–15. There are three trigger mechanisms provided for in the Statute. Article 13 provides that the Court may exercise its jurisdiction with respect to a crime referred to in Article 5 in accordance with the provisions of this Statute if: (a) a situation in which one or more of such crimes appears to have been committed is referred to the Prosecutor by a State Party in accordance with Article 14; (b) a situation in which one or more of such crimes appears to have been committed is referred to the Prosecutor by the Security Council acting under Chapter VII of the Charter of the United Nations; or (c) the Prosecutor has initiated an investigation in respect of such a crime in accordance with Article 15.

Article 14 deals with referral of a situation by a State Party. It provides that a State Party may refer to the Prosecutor a situation in which one or more crimes within the jurisdiction of the Court appear to have been committed requesting the Prosecutor to investigate the situation for the purpose of determining whether one or more specific persons should be charged with the commission of such crimes. As far as possible, a referral must specify the relevant circumstances and be accompanied by such supporting documentation as is available to the State referring the situation. Thus, the State Party to the Rome Statute has *locus standi* to lodge a complaint to the Court. This mechanism has been used by three States Parties till now. Those are Congo, Central African Republic, and Uganda. These States Parties have referred their situations to the Court.

The second method to trigger the jurisdiction of the ICC is through Security Council of the United Nations. The provision regarding the reference to the Prosecutor by the Security Council has been the subject of extensive debate (Singh 1998). However, this debate was put to rest by the Statute by enabling the Security Council, acting under Chapter VII of the UN Charter, to refer a situation to the prosecutor. The capacity of the Security Council to refer a dispute to the ICC differentiates the trigger mechanism of the ICC from that of the International Court of Justice wherein Security Council has no *locus standi* to invoke the jurisdiction of the Court in contentious cases involving States. Furthermore, it is remarkable that the Statute furnishes no additional requirements with respect to Security Council referral, except to specify that the Council must be acting under Chapter VII of the Charter of the United Nations. It remains uncertain whether the Security Council must also meet the other admissibility criteria and respect the principle of complementarity. This mechanism is utilized by the Security Council in the case of referral of the situation in Darfur in Sudan.

Article 15 of the Rome Statute empowers the Prosecutor to press the trigger of the ICC and invoke its jurisdiction. It provides that the Prosecutor may initiate investigations *propriomotu* on the basis of information on crimes within the jurisdiction of the Court (Article 15(1), Rome Statute). The Prosecutor must analyze the seriousness of the information received. For this purpose, he or she may seek additional information from States, organs of the United Nations, intergovernmental or non-governmental organizations, or other reliable sources that he or she deems appropriate, and may receive written or other testimony at the seat of the Court (Article 15(2), Rome Statute). This *propriomotu* power of the Prosecutor is not absolute. It is subject to judicial control.

The Statute further provides that if the Prosecutor concludes that there is a reasonable basis to proceed with an investigation, he or she is obliged to submit to the Pre-Trial Chamber a request for authorization of an investigation, together with any supporting material collected. Victims may make representations to the Pre-Trial Chamber, in accordance with the Rules of Procedure and Evidence (Article 15(3), Rome Statute). If the Pre-Trial Chamber, upon examination of the request and the supporting material, considers that there is a reasonable basis to proceed with an investigation, and that the case appears to fall within the jurisdiction of the Court, it shall authorize the commencement of the investigation, without prejudice to subsequent determinations by the Court with regard to the jurisdiction and admissibility of a case (Article 15(4), Rome Statute). Thus, the Pre-Trial Chamber is authorized either to give or refuse to give to the Prosecutor final green signal to proceed with investigation. If the Pre-Trial Chamber refuses to authorize the investigation, the Prosecutor can make a subsequent request to the Chamber based on new facts or evidence regarding the same situation (Article 15(5), Rome Statute).

7 Position of South Asian Countries

The position of India during deliberations on Rome Statute needs to be examined here. It abstained during the voting time in the Conference (Ramanathan 2005). It did not sign the Rome Statute as the Atal Bihari Vajpayee's government had just taken over from I.K. Gujral. The new coalition government headed by National Democratic Alliance (NDA) endorsed the Non-Alignment Movement line of approach, as well as the position of Asian African Legal Consultative Committee (AALCO) 'that the ICC should be based on the principles of complementarity, State sovereignty, and non-intervention in internal affairs of States' (Sunga 2002). The Delegation of India headed by Dilip Lahiri, the then Additional Secretary (International Organizations), Ministry of External Affairs, warned that the ICC jurisdiction should be optional rather than inherent or compulsory and that it should perform a role complementary to that of domestic jurisdictions, otherwise the ICC could never become accepted as a universal institution (Lahiri 1998).

In particular, Mr. Lahiri and his teammates, such as Dr. P.S. Rao, (Joint Secretary, Legal & Treaty Division, Ministry of External Affairs) and Mr. S. Pal, Deputy Permanent Representative to the United Nations, flagged the danger of an individual Prosecutor with *propriomotu* powers as contrary to State sovereignty and stated that:

> ...[t]he success of the Court would depend in great measure on cooperation among States aimed at punishing heinous crimes of international concern...The necessary cooperation would not be promoted by allowing the Prosecutor to act on his own, on the basis of sources of information, regardless of their reliability. Such an ex-officio role for the

> Prosecutor would jeopardize the principle of complementarity which was generally accepted as the basic foundation for the establishment of the Court (United Nations Diplomatic Conference 1998).

Another objection of India was related to the fear of political interference in the ICC because of the possible use of referral power by the Security Council of the United Nations. The UN Security Council should not exercise any role in the functioning of the ICC or in any other manner on the grounds that this would accord preeminent authority to the Security Council's permanent members and violate the principle of State sovereignty and equality. The delegate also stated that:

> ...It have been argued that a role for the Council must be built into the Statute because it had set up the ad hoc tribunals for the former Yugoslavia and for Rwanda, and has therefore, established its right to do so...But what the Council seeks from the ICC through the Statute, is something else – it is the power to refer, the power to block and the power to bind non-States parties. All three are undesirable. All three were undesirable (United Nations Diplomatic Conference 1998).

On the issue of the power of Security Council to defer an investigation for a period of 12 months, the Indian delegate rallied against such powers of the Council. The granting of such powers, according to India, is a violation of the basic principles of treaty law (Reuters 1995). The law on treaties does not bind third party States without their consent. Even worse, non-States Parties could bind other non-States Parties by working through the Security Council. He stated that:

> ...If that is indeed the intention, why have we gone through this charade of a conference of Plenipotentiaries, and the agonizing over optional jurisdiction and State consent? Why wait till now for signature and ratifications if the Permanent Members of the Security Council could have got together with the like-minded and cobbled together a Statute with which the rest of the world in any case has no option but to comply if the Security Council, acting under Chapter VII, demands it. We believe, Mr. Chairman that the role for the Security Council built into the Statute of the ICC sows the seeds of its destruction (United Nations Diplomatic Conference of Plenipotentiaries 1998).

As for the definition of crimes under international law, the delegate stated his government's clear opposition to the inclusion of criminal responsibility for war crimes committed during situations of non-international armed conflict. According to S.R. Rao:

> ...There is a generally accepted definition of genocide. But as we have seen from numerous brackets, there is no such general agreement either regarding war crimes or crimes against humanity. There is also no agreement about whether or not conflicts not of an international nature could be covered under customary international law.

In December 2002, one of the spokesperson of MEA, in explaining the reasons why India had not signed the Rome Statute, pointed out, inter alia, that it blurred the distinction between customary law and treaty obligations in respect of definition of internal conflicts and crimes against humanity.

Finally, India objected to the non-inclusion of any weapons of mass destruction as a crime. That implied, said the Indian delegate that 'the use of weapons of mass destruction is not a war crime'. It also objected specifically to non-inclusion of the use of nuclear weapons during armed conflict as a crime within the competence of ICC (Sanajoba 2004). The Indian delegate stated:

> ...The third point of principle for us was that an ICC, whose Statute was being negotiated 50 years after the invention and first use of nuclear weapons should explicitly ban their use as a crime. This, however, has not happened. Expediency has prevailed. As a nuclear weapon State, we tabled a draft amendment to list nuclear weapons among those which use is banned for the purposes of the Statute. To our very great regret, this view was not accepted (United Nations Diplomatic Conference of Plenipotentiaries 1998, p. 122).

Pakistan, under the leadership of Nawaz Sharif, supported the Rome Statute and voted in favour of it during the Conference in 1998. However, it did not sign this treaty on account of several problems inherent in the Statute. In a statement issued in 2002 by Permanent Representative to the UN on the occasion of renewal of Security Council Resolution 1422, Pakistan's Ambassador Munir Akram observed:

> ...It is unfortunate that the Rome Statute did not provide for reservations by countries. This may have ensured wider adherence to the Statute. There are several provisions in the ICC Statute with respect to which Pakistan has certain concerns. These include the mechanism for the initiation of proceedings, provisional arrest, the provisions dealing with armed conflict not of an international character and the question of immunity of the heads of government or State (Akram 2013).

Members of peacekeeping forces, according to Pakistan, could also be exposed to this Court. The peacekeepers should not be exposed to any arbitrary or unilateral action by any national or international body. Pakistan wanted to reserve to itself the right to adjudicate in cases involving Pakistani peacekeepers in all peacekeeping operations and duties (Akram 2013).

Pakistan was also against the concept of aggression and internal war crimes (United Nations Diplomatic Conference of Plenipotentiaries 1998). During the Rome Conference, Pakistan's representative, ArifAyub, favoured the view that 'the jurisdiction of the Court should be limited to only the hard-core crimes, namely: (1) the crime of genocide (2) serious violations of the laws and customs of applicable in armed conflicts (emphasis added), and (3) crimes against humanity'. It is unclear whether the expression "armed conflicts" covers non-international armed conflicts. However, on 3rd November 1998, the Pakistani representative, Mr. Kanju said that "armed conflicts not of an international character fell entirely within the domestic jurisdiction of the State concerned, in which the Statute's provisions in that connection violated both the principles of the sovereignty of the States and the principle of complementarity" (Lijiang 2008).

Afghanistan deposited its instrument of accession to the Rome Statute on 10 February 2003 during the transitional administration led by Hamid Karzai. It became the 89th nation of the Assembly of States Parties to the ICC. In a statement made following the approval of Afghanistan's accession to the Rome Statute at the national level, President Hamid Karzai's spokesperson, Mr. Sayed Fazel Adkbar, said, 'We feel it is in our interest to work with the ICC...Afghanistan wants to be part of international community and engage with it...' (Afghanistan Signs Up for the International Criminal Court 2003). After such accession, the jurisdiction of

ICC over the territory of Afghanistan and its nationals extended from 1 May 2003 under the provisions of Rome Statute.

Afghanistan's accession to the Rome Statute was remarkable as the heinous acts of the members of Taliban government as well as the members of NATO forces could be examined by the ICC. As the U.S.-led coalition launched air strikes and ground operations in Afghanistan against the Taliban, suspected of harbouring Osama Bin Laden in late 2001, which continued up to 2014, allegations have been levelled against U.S. and NATO members having committed serious violations of laws of armed conflict (Bosco 2014). The ICC Prosecutor has been conducting preliminary examination of the available evidence since 2007. However, it is yet to issue a formal arrest warrant against any person.

Bangladesh was one of the 120 countries that had voted in favour of the Rome Statute in 1998. Later, it signed the Rome Statute on 16 September 1999 and ratified it on 23 March 2010. Both these acts were remarkably performed during the able leadership of Sheikh Hasina, the daughter of legendary Sheikh Mujibur Rahman. The Statute came into force with respect to Bangladesh from 1 June 2010 (Article 126(2), Rome Statute). By signing and ratifying the Statute, Bangladesh became the first South Asian country to accept the jurisdiction of ICC. During the review conference of the Rome Statute in Kampala in 2010, Mr. Shafique Ahmed, the then Minister of Law, Justice and Parliamentary Affairs observed:

> ...This conviction stems from our national experience. Bangladesh was born out of a sustained struggle for representative inclusion, democracy and rights...Our experience during the Liberation War in 1971 brought us face to face with genocide inflicted by the occupying forces. Bangladesh, therefore, is naturally committed to promoting all efforts at all levels to prevent such crimes and bring an end to impunity to crimes of genocide, crimes against humanity and war crimes.

The ratification, however, did not retroactively affect alleged war crimes committed in the 1971 War of Liberation from Pakistan, in which Bangladesh won its independence from Pakistan. Instead, Bangladesh can avail technical support from the International Criminal Court in the judicial proceedings going on in the domestic international tribunal created to try major war criminals during the War of Liberation. In the meeting with UN General Assembly President Christian Wenaweser in New York, Bangladesh Foreign Secretary Mijarul Quayes said that the ratification of the Rome Statute of ICC will provide more credibility in the trial process of war criminals (Ratification of Rome Statute to Make War Crimes Trial Credible 2010).

The smallest South Asian country, Maldives, acceded to the Rome Statute on 21 September 2011 during the Presidential tenure of Mohamed Nasheed, the democratically elected President (Welcoming Ceremony Maldives 2016). On the occasion of welcoming ceremony of Maldives to the ICC on 6 December 2011, the non-resident ambassador of Maldives to the Netherlands, Ali Hussain Didi, observed:

> Our recent transition to democracy, including agreement on a new constitution and the convening of our first ever free and fair elections, were secured on a human rights platform.

> Human rights, rule of law and justice are bedrock of the new democratic Maldives and this domestic conviction is increasingly translated to the international stage where Maldives has moved to sign eight of the nine core international human rights Convention, the Geneva Conventions, and of course, the Rome Statute (Didi 2011).

Maldives became the 118th nation to accede to this ICC system. Several Parliamentarians, led by M.P. Ahmed Mahloof lobbied for the accession. Ultimately, the People's Majlis approved the decision of National Security Committee to accede to this treaty on 14 June 2011. While speaking at a plenary meeting of the Assembly of States Parties to the ICC, the Permanent Representative of Maldives to the UN, Abdul Ghafoor Mohamed, said, 'Maldives is proud to be among the group of countries who have committed themselves to combat impunity, in respect of international law and to provide justice to those victims who have often been forgotten in the labyrinths of diplomacy (Maldives Reaffirms Its Commitment to the ICC 2011).'

Sri Lanka, under the national leadership of Sirimavo Bandaranayake, abstained from voting and decided not to sign the Rome Statute in 1998. According to Mr. John D. Saram, permanent representative of Sri Lanka to the UN and the head of the delegation at Rome Conference, it feared the ICC as it could be used to bring charges of war crimes against the country's military—if such crimes were committed by Sri Lankan soldiers in the north and the east. Asked for his comments, the then Foreign Secretary Palitha Kohona told a newspaper: 'Sri Lanka is continuing to keep the ICC Statute under review (Thalif 2008).' He pointed out that Sri Lanka, India, and a number of other countries had unsuccessfully proposed that terrorism also be brought under the jurisdiction of the Court (UN Diplomatic Conference of Plenipotentiaries 1998).

During the last stages of Civil War in Sri Lanka in 2009, about 40,000 Tamils were killed in a final offensive authorized by the then President, Mahinda Rajapaksa, who crushed the LTTE insurgency in the north and east. According to a 2015 report of UN High Commissioner for Human Rights, the Sri Lankan government led by Mahinda was involved in committing sexual- and gender-based violence, enforced disappearances, torture, and other forms of cruel, inhuman, or degrading treatment (Human Rights Council 2015). Subsequently, the Human Rights Council adopted a consensus resolution in 2015 aimed at increasing accountability and reconciliation measures in Sri Lanka. The resolution supported the Sri Lankan government's desire to prosecute alleged abuses from its 26-year long civil war using a domestic rather than an international mechanism.

Nepal's tryst with absolute monarchy came to an end in 1990, when King Birendra agreed to establish parliamentary monarchy, with the king as the head of State and the prime minister as the head of the government. A civil war ensued in Nepal in 1996 which continued till 2006, during which the Nepalese polity was in transition. As a consequence, Nepal could not decide on the issue of joining the International Criminal Court regime. However, the House of Representatives on 25 July 2006 adopted a unanimous vote of the legislators belonging to the 7 parties in Parliament a motion directing the government to ratify the Rome Statute (Johnson 2006). Under Nepalese law, this motion is compulsory for the executive headed at that time by Girija Prasad Koirala. In 2008, the King's position was made non-existent according to the interim constitution adopted during the maoist leadership of Prachanda and Nepal became a federal democratic republic. From 2008 till 2015, Nepal struggled to become stable with the help of a mutually agreeable constitution. It became possible in late 2015 when the interim constitution of 2007 was replaced with the final version (Constitution of Nepal 2015).

According to Nepal's Peace and Reconciliation Ministry, more than 16,000 people were killed during the civil war and tens of thousands disappeared. An estimated 1300 people were forcibly disappeared when the rebel groups took on the armed forces of the country (Adhikari 2014). When the Comprehensive Peace Agreement was signed in 2006, it envisioned the creation of truth and reconciliation. It took eight years long for the Nepal's leaders to formulate the laws to implement this vision, namely The Commission on Investigation into Disappeared Persons, Truth and Reconciliation Act, 2014. After the victims' intervention in Supreme Court of Nepal, the amnesty scheme created in the laws even for serious human rights violations have been declared improper (Nepal: Pillay Welcomes Supreme Court's Decision Against Amnesties For Serious Crimes 2013). Many civil rights organizations have even demanded prosecution of some leaders for the commission of war crimes (Rights Bodies Flay Ruling Parties' Deal on Nepal's Civil War Crimes 2016).

8 Major Situations Referred to the ICC

Ten (10) situations have been referred to international Criminal Court till now. Those are from Uganda, Congo, Central African Republic, Sudan, Kenya, Libya, Ivory Coast, Mali, Central African Republic II, and the latest from Georgia. In December 2003, the President of Uganda (in Africa), Yoweri Museveni, took the decision to refer the situation concerning the activities of a rebel group, Lord's Resistance Army ("LRA"), to the Prosecutor of the International Criminal Court (Nouwen and Werner 2010). According to the reports, over 85% of the LRA's forces are made up of children, used as soldiers, porters, labourers and sexual slaves, in the case of girls. As part of initiation into the rebel movement, abducted children were forced to commit inhuman acts, including ritual killing and mutilations. The members of LRA reportedly committed torture, mutilation, rape, forcible displacement, looting and destruction of civilian property. The Chief Prosecutor determined that there was a reasonable basis to open an investigation into the situation concerning the human rights abuses committed by the members of the LRA. In pursuance of Regulation 46(2) of the Regulations of the Court, the Presidency Chamber assigned the situation in Uganda to the Pre-Trial Chamber II. The judges issued its first warrant of arrest in 2005 against top members of the LRA. All suspects remained at large for a decade, until one LRA member, Dominic Ongwen, surrendered himself to the Court in January 2015.

In the Democratic Republic of Congo ("DRC"), millions of civilians died as a result of long-drawn conflict since the 1990s. According to reports by international organizations and NGOs, thousands of deaths by mass murder and summary execution took place in the DRC since 2002. Those reports alleged a pattern of rape, torture, forced displacement, and the illegal use of child soldiers. After immense domestic and international pressure, the President of DRC referred the situation to the Prosecutor of the International Criminal Court in April 2004. Pursuant to Regulation 46(2) of the Regulations of the Court, the Presidency Chamber assigned the situation in the DRC to the Pre-Trial Chamber I. Four trials are completed and one has recently opened. The first is the case of *The Prosecutor* v. *Thomas Lubanga* (ICC-01/04/06). Lubanga was held responsible in 2012, as co-perpetrator, of the commission of war crimes of enlisting and conscripting of children under the age of 15 years into FPLC (a rebel group called 'Patriotic Forces for the Liberation of Congo') and using them to participate actively in hostilities punishable under Articles 8(2)(b)(xxvi) and 8(2)(e)(vii). The second is the case of *The Prosecutor* v. *GermainKatanga ("Simba) and Mathieu Ngudjolo Chui* (ICC-01/04-01/07). On the one hand, Germain Katanga was held responsible for committing war crimes under Articles 8(2)(b)(xxvi), 8(2)(b)(i), 8(2)(b)(xiii), 8(2)(b)(xvi), 8(2)(b)(xxii), and crimes against humanity under Articles 7(1)(a), and 7(1)(g) of the Rome Statute. Chui was acquitted of these charges in 2012. The third is the case of *The Prosecutor* v. *Bosco Ntaganda* (ICC-01/04-02/06). The trial against him opened on 2 September 2015. Pre-trial chamber in *The Prosecutor* v. *Callixte Mbarushimana* (ICC-01/04-01/10), declined to confirm the charges against the accused and did not commit the case to trial. The Prosecution's appeal was also dismissed in 2011.

In the Central African Republic ("CAR"), huge human rights violations took place during armed conflicts during 1998–2003. In the course of the ongoing conflict, the then President of CAR, Ange-Felix Patasse invited the leader of a rebel group, Movement for the Liberation of Congo (MLC), of another neighbouring country, Congo, to CAR to help put down a *coup* against his government. Even then, Patasse could not be successful. His opponent, Francois Bozize, became successful in the *coup*. He became the President of the country and referred the situation of CAR to the International Criminal Court in December 2004. A case was initiated by the Prosecutor of the Court against the leader of the Congo group MLC, Jean Pierre Bemba Gombo. In *The Prosecutor* v. *Jean-Pierre Bemba Gombo* (ICC-01/05-01/08), the Court held Bemba guilty of three counts of war crimes and two counts of crimes against humanity under Articles 8 and 7 of the Rome Statute respectively. All these crimes were committed by him in the CAR in conjunction with the *coup de etat* in 2002–2003. Bemba's MLC forces are alleged to have carried out horrific crimes, including mass rapes, killings, and looting against the civilian population in the CAR. Interestingly, Bemba was also the Vice-President of Congo for some time and was elected as a senator of Congo in 2007. Another trial in the case *The Prosecutor* v. *Jean Pierre Bemba Gombo, AimeKiloloMusamba, Jean-Jacques MangendaKabongo, FideleBabalaWandu and Narcisse Arido* (ICC-01/05-01/13) also started in September 2015.

Another situation referred to the International Criminal Court is from Darfur in Sudan (in Africa). In the year of 2003 in Darfur, there was an intense armed conflict between the government backed militia group known as *janjaweed* and a coalition of three ethnic groups (Fur, Masalit, and Zaghawa) (Jha 2004). Nearly 1.5 million people were internally displaced and more than 50,000 died in the violence. The *janjaweeds* allegedly carried out systematic campaigns of rape against African women in an attempt to humiliate the women and their families and weaken tribal ethnic linkages. The government of Sudan was said to be funding the *janjaweed* militia and carrying out an ethnic cleansing campaign. On the basis of the report submitted by International Commission of Inquiry on Darfur in January 2005 to the United Nations, the United Nations Security Council referred the situation in Darfur to the Prosecutor of the International Criminal Court (SC Res. 1593 2005). This was the first Security Council referral. Three cases have been initiated by the Prosecutor of the International Criminal Court from the Darfur situation. The first case is of *The Prosecutor* v. *Ahmad Muhammad Harun* ("Ahmad Harun") *and Ali Muhammad Ali Abd-Al-Rahman* ("Ali Kushayb") (ICC-02/05-01/07). Ahmad Harun was a former Minister of State and Ali Kushayb was the leader of the *janjaweeds*. Warrants of arrest have been issued against them, but they are at large. The second case is of *The Prosecutor* v. *Omar Hassan Ahmad Al Bashir* (ICC-02/05-01/09). Al Bashir is currently the President of Sudan. Warrant of arrest has been issued against him. However, he is still at large. He has been charged with five counts of crimes against humanity and two counts of war crimes under Articles 7(1)(a), 7(1)(b), 7(1)(d), 7(1)(f), 7(1)(g), 8(2)(e)(i), 8(2)(e)(v) of the Rome Statute. The third case is that of *The Prosecutor* v. *Bahr Idriss Abu Garda* (ICC-02/05-02/09). In February 2010, Pre-Trial Chamber I decided not to confirm the charges against Abu Garda, and later rejected the Prosecutor's application to appeal the decision.

ICC investigations started in Kenya (in Africa) in the context of post-election violence in 2007–2008. On 31 March 2010, Pre-Trial Chamber II granted the Prosecutor's request to open an investigation *propriomotu* in relation to crimes against humanity within the jurisdiction of the Court between 1 June 2005 and 26 November 2009. In granting this request, the Chamber noted the gravity and scale of the violence. The Prosecutor contended that over 1000 people were killed, 900 acts of documented rape and sexual violence, displacement of over 350,000 people, and serious injury to 3500 people. In *The Prosecutor* v. W.S. *Ruto and J.A. Sang* (2016) (ICC-01/09-01/11), the Trial Chamber V(A) decided by majority that the case against Ruto (Minister of Higher Education, Science and Technology) and Joshua Sang (radio broadcaster) be terminated. Similarly in the case of *The Prosecutor* v. *U.M. Kenyatta* (2011) (ICC-01/09-02/11), the Trial Chamber V (B) withdrew the charges against the accused due to insufficient evidence. Three arrests of warrants are pending.

Although Libya (in Africa) is not a party to the Rome Statute of ICC, the UN Security Council unanimously referred the situation in Libya since 15 February 2011 to the ICC in Resolution 1970 (2011) (S/Res/1970). Under the leadership of Mohammed Gaddafi, gross and systematic human rights violation took place and peaceful demonstrators were repressed. The referral noted that the widespread and systematic attacks against the civilian population may amount to crimes against humanity and expressed concern at the plight of refugees forced to flee the violence and at the reports of shortages of medical supplies to treat the wounded. The investigation, which opened in March 2011, thus far produced one case. The arrest warrant against Muammar Abu Minyar Gaddafi (the then President) was withdrawn on 22 November 2011 due to his death. In *The Prosecutor* v. *Saif Al-Islam Gaddfi* (2011) (ICC-01/11-01/11), the arrest warrant remains pending against Saif Gaddafi (the then de facto Prime Minister) as he still remains at large.

9 Conclusion

Recognizing the need of bringing the sense of impunity amongst the perpetrators of war crimes, crimes against humanity, genocide, and aggression, the international community came together to establish International Criminal Court. Based on the Rome Statute of 1998, the Court commenced its work since the year 2002. More than a hundred States of the world have ratified this Statute. However, nations containing significant populations, such as the U.S., China, India, and Pakistan have yet not ratified it. In a short span of time, the Court has got the opportunity to decide some significant cases related to the commission of crimes against humanity, war crimes, and genocide. Through this process of decision, it has laid down a significant amount of international criminal jurisprudence on individual criminal responsibility, rules of complementarity, and subject-matter jurisdiction. The majority of situations referred to the Court are from African continent, which is widely debated by the scholars in terms of targeting the weak nations. In the ensuing debate, some States of Africa have started to withdraw from the Statute of the Court. It is a welcome sign that the office of the prosecutor of the Court is now seriously investigating some cases out of Africa. When this becomes successful, the image of Court as a neutral judicial institution may get a strong positive push. In the South Asian region, the Court is taking baby steps as it has been accepted by Bangladesh, Maldives, and Afghanistan. This is a welcome trend as the countries of South Asia have to show to the world that they are very serious when it comes to end impunity against commission of grave violation of human rights of its own citizens.

References

Address by David Johnson, Officer-in-Charge, Office of the UN High Commissioner for Human Rights in Nepal', Nepal Bar Association, Kathmandu (6 August 2006). Available at http://goo.gl/Dc1swF

Adhikari D (2014, 2 May) Seeking justice for Nepal's war crimes. AlJazeera, 2 May 2014. Available at http://goo.gl/sHgxaP

Afghanistan Signs Up for the International Criminal Court (February 10, 2003) Coalition for the international criminal court. Available at http://goo.gl/uS8tK2

Art. 12(3); and Rule 44, Rules of Procedure and Evidence (2000) UN Doc. PCNICC/2000/INF/3/Add I

Assembly of States Parties (2016) Available at http://goo.gl/xah9Ql

Assembly of States Parties. Available at http://goo.gl/XdbxNy

Bosco D (2014) The war over U.S. war crimes in Afghanistan is heating up. Foreign Policy Mag. Available at http://goo.gl/7QJrGl

Comprehensive Report of the Office of the UN High Commissioner for Human Rights on Sri Lanka, Human Rights Council, 30th Session, 28 September 2015, A/HRC/30/61. Available at http://goo.gl/ddguKl

Crawford J (1995) The ILC adopts a statute for an international criminal court. Am J Int Law 89:404

Demands made by Human Rights Watch (May 13, 2016), International commission of jurists, and amnesty international; also see, 'Rights Bodies Flay Ruling Parties' Deal on Nepal's Civil War Crimes', The Himalayan Times, Kathmandu. Available at http://goo.gl/kYaSa5

Didi HE, Ali H (2011) Non-resident ambassador of Maldives to the Netherlands, welcoming ceremony of the International Criminal Court, 6 Dec 2011. http://goo.gl/MU043l

GA Res 50/46 (December 11, 1995)

ICC-ASP/1/3 (Part II-A). Adopted on 9th September 2002

ICC-ASP/1/3 (Part II-B). Adopted on 9th September 2002

ICC-ASP/3/Res.1. Adopted on 4 October 2004

ICC-BD/04-01-08. Adopted on 7 June 2007

ILM (1998) Rome statute of the international criminal court. Int Legal Mater 37:999

Jha A (2004) Darfur crisis: acid test for international criminal law. ISIL Yearb Int Humanit Refug Law 4:143–151

Jha A (2011) First anatomy of the Rome statute during Kampala conference: a critical evaluation. XI ISIL Yearb Int Humanit Refug Law 11:161–188

Lemkin R (1944) Axis rule in occupied Europe: laws of occupation, analysis of government, proposals for redress. Carnegie Endowment for World Peace, Washington, pp 87–89

Lijiang Z (2008) Some Asian States' opposition to the concept of war-crimes in non-international armed conflicts and its legal implications. Asian Yearb Int Law 14:71–99

Maldives Reaffirms Its Commitment to the ICC as it Makes Its Debut at the 10th Assembly of States Parties to the Rome Statute (2011) Ministry of foreign affairs, government of Bangladesh. Available at http://goo.gl/5G2UCi

Nepal: Pillay Welcomes Supreme Court's Decision Against Amnesties For Serious Crimes' (January 4, 2013), Office of the High Commissioner, United Nations, Geneva. http://goo.gl/2inHAX

Nouwen Sarah MH, Werner Wouter G (2010) Doing justice to the political: the international criminal court in Uganda and Sudan. Eur J Int Law 21:941–965

Prosecutor v. *Tadic* (Case No. it-94-1-AR 72)

Ramanathan U (2005) India & the ICC. J Int Crim Justice 3:627–634

Ratification of Rome statute to make war crimes Trial credible (2010) The Daily Star, Dhaka

Report of the Ad Hoc Committee on the Establishment of an International Criminal Court (1995) UN GAOR, 50th Session, Supp No. 22, UN DocA/50/22

Reuters P (1995) Introduction to the law of treaties. Kegan Paul International, London

Sanajoba N (ed) (2004) A manual of international humanitarian laws. Regency Publications, New Delhi

SC Res. 1593 (2005) S/Res/1593 (31 March 2005). Available at https://documents-dds-ny.un.org/doc/UN (last accessed on 4 December 2017)

Schabas WA (2001) An introduction to the international criminal court. Cambridge University Press, U.K.

Singh G (1998) International criminal court: trigger mechanisms. Natl Capital Law J 3:51–59

Statement by Ambassador Munir Akram (June 12, 2013) Permanent representative of Pakistan to the United Nations, to the Security Council on the occasion of Renewal of Resolution 1422 regarding International Criminal Court. http://goo.gl/DCa1N2

Statement of 16 June 1998 to the Rome Conference of Mr. Dilip Lahiri (June 16, 1998), Head of delegation of India. http://goo.gl/xah9Ql

Sunga LS (2002) The attitude of Asian countries towards the ICC. ISIL Yearb Int Humanit Refug Law 2:18–57

Thalif D (2008) Child soldiers: Prabha, Karuna may escape through loopholes. The Sunday Times, Colombo. Available at http://goo.gl/aCk8rV

The Constitution of Nepal (2015) Available at http://goo.gl/0DBTXK

'UN Diplomatic Conference of Plenipotentiaries on the Establishment of an International Criminal Court', paragraph 52. Available at http://goo.gl/h97mi9

UN Doc. A/CONF.183/10

United Nations Diplomatic Conference of Plenipotentiaries on the Establishment of an International Criminal Court, 1998, Vol. II. Available at http://goo.gl/EF1iVM

Verdirame G (2000) The genocide definition in the jurisprudence of the ad hoc tribunals. Int Comp Law Q 49:578

Welcoming Ceremony Maldives, Statement by Vice-President of the Assembly of States Parties. Available at http://goo.gl/RH7gbr

Author Biography

Dr. Anupam Jha is Assistant Professor (Senior) at the Faculty of Law, University of Delhi. He has been engaged in teaching & research for more than 14 years. He is recipient of several prestigious fellowships and nominations, such as Raman Fellowship (U.S.A.), Commonwealth Fellowship (U.K.), UGC-TEC Nomination (Mauritius). He has also been awarded the most active participant from India by UNHCR. His current areas of teaching and research are: public international law, international environmental law, international trade law, and jurisprudence. His latest publications include the following: "The Law on Trafficking in Persons: The Quest For an Effective Model", First Published Online in ***Asian Journal of International Law (Cambridge University Press)***, 27 October 2016, ISSN No. 2044-2521 (online).

Chapter 14
Privileges and Immunities of Diplomats and Consuls: South Asian Perspective

Leena Kumari and Anupam Jha

1 Evolution of Diplomatic and Consular Immunity in South Asia

The Indian subcontinent has a long tradition of diplomacy in State and international affairs. One of the earliest texts of the subcontinent, *Manusmriti,* recognized the importance of ambassadors as it said: "The peace and its opposite (war) depends on the ambassador" (Chapter VII: 65). According to Manu, who lived tentatively during 1250 B.C. to 1000 B.C., an ambassador requires high degree of intellect. He further said that in selecting peoples for diplomatic missions, one must choose persons who are "loyal, honest, skilful, possessing good memory, fearless, and eloquent" (Chapter VII: 64). He added that a diplomat must possess sweet voice, be persuasive, industrious, having a good understanding of sciences and ability to read others' thoughts and feelings from their behaviour and appearance, etc., Buhler (1886).

In the epic *Ramayana*, the high value attached to the envoys is well documented. Lord Hanuman was sent as a diplomatic envoy by Lord Ram to persuade the demon King Ravana to return Sita whom he had abducted. The envoy was sent before the outbreak of war between Ram and Ravana. The mission failed and Ravana sentenced Hanuman to death. Ravana's youngest brother Vibhishan pleaded that the order be revoked, since "it was against all statecraft: an envoy must not be killed. He may be punished in some other way, my master" (Tulsidas 2005). In another epic *Mahabharata*, Lord Krishna acts as an ambassador of Pandavas and comes to

L. Kumari (✉)
School of Law, Guru Gobind Singh Indraprastha University,
38/12, Probyn Road, Delhi 110007, India
e-mail: jhaleenu@gmail.com

A. Jha (✉)
Law Centre-II, Faculty of Law, University of Delhi,
38/12, Probyn Road, New Delhi 110007, India
e-mail: ajha@law.du.ac.in

J.L. Kaul and A. Jha (eds.), *Shifting Horizons of Public International Law*,
https://doi.org/10.1007/978-81-322-3724-2_14

the court of Kauravas to establish peace between the two sides. He tries his best to convince Dhritarashtra and his son Duryodhana not to fight against Pandavas. However, Duryodhana decides to use violence against the envoy Krishna and to confine him. At this critical time, Dhritarashtra and Vidur strongly advise Duryodhana not to inflict any injury upon the envoy (Ganguli 2003). It means that the person of the ambassador was regarded as inviolable during the ancient times too.

The *Agni Purana* prescribed the qualities of an ambassador as a person possessing sharp intellect, soft-spoken, and affable. "Eloquence" and "soft-spoken" were regarded as the basic desirable assets for an ambassador at a time when the art of writing despatches had not so well developed (Bandyopadyaya 1920). In the classic textbook of the subcontinent, *Arthsahstra*, its author Chanakya dealt with the institution of diplomatic envoys. He explained about different types of ambassadors, their qualifications, status, duties, and immunities in detail in Chapter XVI. The envoys were divided into four categories: (a) *Duta* (ambassador Extraordinary), (b) *Nisristarth* (Charge d' Affaires), (c) *Parimitartha* (Plenipotentiaries), and (d) *Sasanhara-duta* (Diplomatic Messenger). High qualifications were needed to become an ambassador during Chanakya's times. The king usually selected the most distinguished and honoured citizens for appointment as diplomats.

It is doubtful whether permanent resident embassies were maintained by the Empire States in ancient times or not. Ad hoc diplomats, such as Megasthenes resided at the court of Chandragupta Maurya and Deimachos at that of Bindusara. It is quite likely that the Mauryas might have sent their own ambassadors at the Seleukidan court. It is not known whether the Greek ambassadors lived for a few months or whether their embassies were permanent. Heliodorus was residing at Vidisa, the capital of Malwa, as the ambassador of Antialkidas, the Greek ruler of Taxila, but it is not unlikely that he might have stayed only for a few months and for a particular mission. The embassies were received at the court of Samudragupta from the kingdom of Ceylon and at the court of Chalukya ruler Pulakesin II (c. 630) from the kingdom of Persia; but they were for specific purposes only (Altekar 2016). Harshavardhana, who ruled as the Emperor of north Indian subcontinent in the seventh century A.D., maintained diplomatic relations with China. The other kingdoms in South Asia, such as Ceylon, also appear to have maintained contacts with China through their envoys (Sen 1965). For instance, King Meghavarana of Ceylon (A.D. 352–79) had also sent emissaries to India to facilitate the visit of Buddhist pilgrims (*Id.*).

During the early medieval times, Prophet Muhammad sent emissaries abroad for religious or political purposes. According to Muslim chronicles, the Prophet is reported to have sent envoys to Byzantium, Egypt, Persia, and Ethiopia. This tradition was followed by the Sultanate ruler Alauddin Khilji, who treated the envoy of Ghazan the Great, the ruler of Persia with great honour (Niazi 1992). The Mughals had also established diplomatic relationship with the Safavid dynasty of Iran till Akbar's rule (1556–1605). Maratha ruler Shivaji used the services of his envoy Patanjali Gopinath to know the real intention of Adil Shahi ruler Afzal Khan in 1659. The envoy obtained information about Afzal Khan's real intention to kill

Shivaji on the pretext of friendship meeting (Sarkar 2010). It is interesting to know that although the art of diplomacy is as old as official intercourse between States, such a special class of officials as is now called diplomatic envoys did not exist till the second half of the seventieth century during the times of Louis XIV of France (1643–1715). Cardinal Richlieu is considered to be the originator of modern diplomacy (Nathan 1993). In India, Mysore ruler Tipu Sultan exchanged diplomatic missions with Nizam and Marathas at the same time. The diplomacy became successful and the three joined a confederacy against the British, who tried to control the whole of India (Hasan 2009). Tipu had also sent envoys to Mauritius to seek the help of France against the British rule, which resulted in many Anglo-Mysore Wars (Thompson and Garratt 1999).

During the Early British period, the East India Company used diplomacy to win over many nawabs and zamindars of India. However, those envoys could not be termed as diplomats as they were not appointed by sovereign States. The British Empire had extended its rule over the whole Indian subcontinent, including the present-day Pakistan, Bangladesh, Myanmar, parts of Nepal, and Afghanistan. It was in 1858 that an act of British Parliament transferred the power to govern from the East India Company to the British Crown. The British government established diplomatic relationship with Nepal. Lord Elgin, the Viceroy sent his envoys to Bhutanese government to seek redress for the raids made on British Territory. The envoy was treated with insult, which made Elgin to declare war against Bhutan. Although Elgin died, but his successor Sir John Lawrence defeated the Bhutanese (Sinclair 1884).

Envoys of the Burmese (Myanmarese) ruler Bodawpaya also resided in Kolkata when the British forces had defeated him and both parties signed the Treaty of Yandabo. British envoys were also present in Burma till its annexation in 1885. Afghanistan was also considered strategically important for the British Indian rule as Russian military threat was growing over there. Due to fear of a possible Russian invasion of India using Afghanistan, the British sent an envoy Alexander Burnes to Kabul in 1837 to obtain the support of Afghan ruler Dost Muhammad (Yousafzai 2013). Diplomacy, thus, played an important role in consolidating British Indian Empire in the subcontinent.

To protect the Head of other States, diplomats from legal proceedings initiated in India, the British rule in India enacted Civil Procedure Code in 1908. According to Section 86 of this Act, no foreign State can be sued in any court unless the consent of the Central government is obtained in writing by a Secretary to that government. That court may have been otherwise competent to try the suit without the consent of the Central government. The same rule applies with respect to the execution of a decree against the property of a foreign State. This section applies not only to the ruler of a foreign State, but also upon many other dignitaries. It applies further to any ambassador or envoy of a foreign State, any High Commissioner of a Commonwealth country, and any such member of the staff of the foreign State or the staff or retinue of the ambassador or Envoy of a foreign State or of the High Commissioner of a Commonwealth country as the Central government may, by general or special order, specify in this behalf.

British India's diplomatic service to handle the external affairs can be traced to a famous correspondence between the then Secretary, Planning & Development Lt General T.J. Hutton and Foreign Secretary Olaf Caroe in 1944. A separate diplomatic service to handle the external affairs of the government of India was proposed by Hutton as he thought that diplomacy required full time commitment. Not only Caroe accepted Hutton's idea, but also he recorded his comments in an exhaustive note. In that note, he dealt in detail about the scope, composition, and functions of the proposed service. In September 1946, the government of India decided to create a separate cadre called Indian Foreign Service (IFS) for India's diplomatic, consular, and commercial representation abroad.

An IFS officer begins his career abroad as a Third Secretary and is promoted to Second Secretary very soon when his service is confirmed. From Second Secretary, an IFS officer gets promotion after relevant number of years to the levels of First Secretary, Counsellor, Minister, and ambassador/High Commissioner/Permanent Representative. Ambassadors and High Commissioners are named as such because in the Commonwealth countries, only High Commissioners are appointed whereas in all other countries, ambassadors could be appointed. These IFS officers can also be posted to Indian consulates abroad. In such postings, the hierarchy (going upwards) is Vice Consul, Consul, and Consul General. The hierarchy at the Ministry of External Affairs (MEA) includes six stages: Under Secretary, Deputy Secretary, Director, Joint Secretary, Additional Secretary, and Secretary (MEA 2015).

Nepal had diplomatic relations only with four countries for a long time during Rana dynasty (1846–1951): India, France, Great Britain, and USA. After the political revolution of 1950, an independent Ministry for Foreign Affairs was established in 1951 (MOFA 2016). However, a professional batch of diplomats could be institutionalized in Nepal after the creation of Nepal Foreign Service in 2007. Currently, Nepal maintains 29 embassies (including India, Pakistan, Bangladesh, and Colombo in South Asian region) abroad. It also has 54 consulates and other representations around the world. Its capital Kathmandu hosts 26 embassies from abroad. It also hosts 35 consulates and other government's representations. Nepal has permanent missions to the United Nations in New York and in Geneva.

Sri Lankan career diplomats were recruited from Ceylon Overseas Service. The members of this service exclusively engaged in foreign affairs, as opposed to the older Ceylon Civil Service, which dealt with domestic affairs. When Sri Lanka became a republic in 1972, the name of the service was also changed to Sri Lanka Overseas Service (SLOS). The Head of this service is given the designation of Permanent Secretary of Ministry of Foreign Affairs. SLOS has three different grades: Grade I, II, and III officers. Grade III is the starting point of the SLOS. Sri Lanka has established 54 embassies/high commissions abroad (including in India, Pakistan, Nepal, Maldives, and Afghanistan).

Closer to Sri Lanka, the British had expelled the Dutch from Ceylon in 1796 and included Maldives as a British protected area. The external relations and defence of Maldives, ruled by Sultan, was influenced by the British after 1887 and onwards.

The British influence over Maldives lasted quarter to a decade from 1887 till 1965. In a national referendum in 1968, Maldives abolished the Sultanate and constituted a republic. In 1978, Abdul Gayoom replaced the authoritarian ruler Nasir and became the President. He was not only a university lecturer but also an ambassador to the United Nations. In 2012, Abdul Gayoom became the President. Maldives has established 12 resident embassies across the world, including India, Pakistan, Sri Lanka, and Bangladesh.

Bhutan's independent external affairs, since its membership of the United Nations in 1971, necessitated to evolve diplomacy to a higher level. A full-fledged Ministry of Foreign Affairs was set up in 1972. Since then, Bhutan has established diplomatic relations with 53 countries, including India, Pakistan, Bangladesh, Nepal, Maldives, Sri Lanka, and Afghanistan. Afghanistan witnessed Taliban rule and the diplomatic personnel during that time was not professional in the modern sense. After the Taliban regime, the new Afghanistan has done a lot to anglicize and to modernize the diplomatic cadre.

2 Modern Theories on Diplomatic Immunity and Codification of Law

Diplomatic immunity is justified by many theorists. Three main theories have been propounded by these theorists. These theories have helped in explaining, primarily, the need to grant immunity to the diplomats. The first theory, called "personal representative" theory, is based on the capacity of diplomat to represent the sovereign. Under traditional diplomatic practice, a diplomatic envoy personifies the sovereign she represents (Wilson 1967). The diplomatic representative's privileges are considered similar to those of the sovereign herself (*Id.*), and an insult to the ambassador is an insult to the dignity of the sovereign (Sen 1965).

Diplomatic practice prevalent today does not accept this theory for several reasons. First, this doctrine places the diplomat above the law of the host State, which cannot be acceptable to the receiving State (RS). RS asserts its supremacy over any person within its territory (Reiff 1954). Secondly, although the personal representative theory extends immunity to official acts, it offers no theoretical basis for protecting private acts. For these reasons, the representative of the sovereign theory has fallen out of use as a rationale for diplomatic immunity.

Second theory of diplomatic protection is based on exterritoriality. According to Sir E.M. Satow, the word "exterritoriality" was used by Wolff in 1749. According to him, this word is used to denote the immunities accorded to foreign sovereigns and to diplomatic agents, their families and staff, as well as to foreign residents in certain non-Christian countries by virtue of special treaty provisions (Satow 1917). Exterritoriality should not be equated with extra territoriality, which is the operation of laws upon persons, rights, or jural relations existing beyond the limits of the acting State or nation but still amenable to the operation of that State's laws

(Garner 2014). This approach adopts the legal fiction that a diplomat is always on the soil of her native country, wherever she may actually go. It is the oldest of the theories, but has received increasing criticisms in recent years. According to Biswanath Sen, "no doctrine which rests on a mere fiction can be lightly assumed to have been accepted as controlling [territorial sovereignty]…therefore, it will be best to put aside the present idea of ex-territoriality". Not only is the doctrine a mere legal fiction, but dangerous consequences could result because it "presupposes a theory of unlimited privileges and immunities which would go beyond those actually extended diplomats" (Wilson 1967).

According to Professor Brownlie, the existing legal position in truth rests on no particular theory or combination of theories, though in a very general way it is compatible with both the representative theory and the functional theory, which rests on practical necessity (Crawford 2012). More adaptable and dynamic than the other two theories, the functional necessity approach justifies immunity on the grounds that diplomats could not exercise their diplomatic functions perfectly without such privileges. To put this theory pithily, the diplomats should not be made liable to ordinary legal and political interference from the State or other individuals. Only then, they can perform their functions efficiently and would not be influenced by considerations of safety and comfort provided by the receiving state (RS).

The Vienna Convention on Diplomatic Relations, 1961 embraces the "functional necessity" theory and recognizes in its preamble that "the purpose of such privileges and immunities is not to benefit individuals but to ensure the efficient performance of the functions of diplomatic missions as representing States". It is also made clear in the Convention that the rules of customary international law would continue to govern the situations or matters not expressly regulated by it. The Convention contains 53 Articles and governs every aspect of diplomatic immunity. It lays down rules not only on accreditation of ambassadors, their hierarchy, but also on the use of flags on diplomatic vehicles, on exemption from local taxation. This Convention was adopted on 14 April 1961 by the United Nations Conference on Diplomatic Intercourse and Immunities held in the Austrian capital of Vienna. Sixty States signed this Convention, including Sri Lanka (18 April 1961) and Pakistan (29 March 1962). The Convention entered into force on 24 June 1964. Other South Asian nations, such as Afghanistan acceded to the Convention on 6 October 1965, India on 15 October 1965, Nepal acceded on 28 September 1965, Bhutan on 7 December 1972, Bangladesh succeeded to the treaty on 13 January 1978, and Maldives acceded it on 2 October 2007.

Article 1 of the Vienna Convention divides the whole staff of the foreign mission into three categories: (a) the diplomatic staff called by diplomatic rank as counsellors, diplomatic secretaries, or attaches; (b) the administrative and technical staff, such as clerical assistants and archivists; (c) the service staff, who are other employees of the mission itself, such as drivers and kitchen staff, referred to in the Convention as "in the domestic service of the mission". Two other terms are also defined in the Convention. A "diplomatic agent" is the Head of the mission or a member of the diplomatic staff of the mission (Article 1(e)); the "Head of the mission" is the person charged by the sending State (SS) with the duty of acting in that capacity (Article 1(a)).

An attempt was also made in the Vienna Convention to codify the order of precedence of diplomatic envoys. Articles 14–18 deal with these regulations. According to Article 14, Heads of mission are divided into three classes: (a) ambassadors/High Commissioners (an ambassador or a High Commissioner, usually practiced in Commonwealth countries, is a public officer possessed with significant diplomatic powers, commissioned by a government to transact the international business of his government with a foreign government) or nuncios (a papal messenger sent for general purpose or on a special mission) accredited to Heads of State, and other Heads of mission of equivalent rank; (b) envoys (a diplomat sent by a country to execute a special mission or to serve as a permanent diplomatic representative), ministers (earlier they headed not the embassies, but legations, but now a general name given to diplomatic representatives), and inter-nuncios (a papal minister of second order), accredited to Heads of State; and (c) Charge d' affaires (diplomat of inferior rank) accredited to Ministers for Foreign Affairs. Article 14 further clarifies that "except as concerns precedence and etiquette, there shall be no differentiation between Heads of mission by reason of their class'. The word "etiquette" includes ceremonial matters and matters of conduct of protocol. A diplomat's rank also determines the person to whom diplomatic credentials should be presented and the title by which the diplomat should be addressed.

The five main functions of a diplomatic mission are specified in Article 3 of the Convention: (a) representing the SS in the RS; (b) protecting in the RS the interests of the sending State and of its nationals, within the limits permitted by international law; (c) negotiating with the government of the RS; (d) ascertaining by all lawful means conditions and developments in the RS and reporting thereon to the government of the SS; and (e) promoting friendly relations between the SS and RS and developing their economic, cultural, and scientific relations. In addition, Article 41 (1) makes it incumbent upon the diplomats to respect the laws and regulations of the RS and not to interfere in the internal affairs of that State.

3 Diplomatic Privileges and Immunities

Some important principles recognized by the Convention to facilitate the operations of normal diplomatic activities are "inviolability of the premises of the diplomatic mission' and 'inviolability of the diplomatic bag". Article 22 specifically declares that the premises of the mission are inviolable. It further provides that agents of the RS are required not to enter the premises of the mission without its consent. Article 27 provides that the RS shall permit and protect free communication on behalf of the mission for all official purposes. Such official communication is inviolable and may include the use of diplomatic couriers (a person accompanying a diplomatic bag) and messages in code and in cipher, although the consent of the RS is required for a wireless transmitter.

Articles 27(3) and (4) lay down rules on the inviolability of diplomatic bags. These bags contain official correspondence and documents or articles intended exclusively for official use. It could or could not be accompanied by diplomatic courier. In addition, these bags bear visible external marks of their character. International law prohibits the diplomatic bag from opening or from detention. The packages constituting the diplomatic bag must bear visible external marks of their character and may contain only diplomatic documents or articles intended for official use. While the inviolability of the premises is accepted by the nations, there is difference of opinion on the inviolability of the diplomatic bag in view of its reported abuse (Nelson 1988). For instance, the UK contends that Article 27 does not prohibit electronic scanning of the diplomatic bag or sniffing by dogs (Hoffman 2003).

The RS is under an obligation under Article 25 to accord full facilities for the performance of the functions of the mission. Apart from prohibited zones, the RS is also under an obligation under Article 26 to ensure freedom of movement and travel in its territory unless national security demands otherwise. The RS is also under an obligation to "take all appropriate steps" to prevent any attacks on the person, freedom, or dignity of diplomatic agents.

Diplomats enjoy several personal immunities from RS's administrative, civil, and criminal legal processes. Under Article 29 of the VCDR, the person of a diplomatic agent is inviolable. The Convention has adopted the functional necessity theory to justify diplomat's personal immunities. According to Eileen Denza, this principle is the most fundamental and the oldest rule of diplomatic law (Denza 2008). In the age of growing international terrorism, diplomats, their homes, and family are targets of violent groups and oppositions. Provisions of VCDR are there to provide for the inviolability of the private residence of a diplomatic agent (Article 30(1)) and for the inviolability of his papers, correspondence, and property (Article 30(2)).

Diplomats enjoy complete immunity from the criminal jurisdiction of the host State under Article 31(1), although there is no immunity from the jurisdiction of the SS under Article 31(4). However, the host State can declare a diplomat *persona non grata* under Article 9 when serious offences are allegedly committed by her. Article 31(1) further specifies that diplomats are immune from the civil and administrative jurisdiction of the State in which they are serving except in three cases. First situation may be where the action relates to private immovable property situated within the host State (unless held for mission purposes). Second situation envisaged under the Convention is in litigation relating to succession matters in which the diplomat is involved as a private person (e.g. as an executor or heir). Finally, immunity is provided with respect to unofficial professional or commercial activity engaged in by the agent.

A diplomat cannot be obliged to give evidence as a witness under Article 31(2). Measures of execution may not be taken against such person except in the cases of private immovable property situated in the host State, succession involving diplomatic agents, or in actions relating to any professional or commercial activity exercised by the agent outside his official functions. The measures concerned can be taken without infringing the inviolability of diplomat's person or of his residence.

Under Article 36(2), diplomatic agents enjoy exemption from all dues and taxes, personal or real, regional or municipal except for indirect taxes, custom duties, and inspection. The personal baggage of a diplomat is exempt from inspection unless there are serious grounds for presuming that it contains articles not covered by the specific exemptions in Article 36(1). Inspection can only take place in the presence of the diplomat or his authorized representative.

All the above privileges are enjoyed by the members of the family of a diplomatic agent forming part of his household under Article 37, if not nationals of the RS. Members of the administrative and technical staff (and their households), if not nationals or permanent residents of the RS, may similarly benefit from all privileges and immunities, except that the Article 31(1) immunities do not extend beyond acts performed in the course of their duties. Members of the service staff, who are not nationals or permanent residents of the host State, also benefit from immunity regarding acts performed in the course of official duties.

Article 39 of the Convention describes generally that a person who is entitled to privileges and immunities shall enjoy them from the moment of appointment, lasting until the appointment has ended. The acts of such diplomat while in his official capacity will continue to be protected by immunity even after the appointment has ended.

Diplomatic immunity can also be waived. Article 32 provides that the SS may waive the immunity from diplomatic agents. Such waiver, however, must be expressed. According to Mc Clanahan, waiver of immunity has been usual, especially in criminal cases (Mc Clanahan 1989). While waiver of immunity in the face of criminal charges is not common, Professor Malcolm Shaw notes that it is routinely sought and occasionally granted (Shaw 2012).

4 Position of South Asian States on VCDR

India gave effect to the Vienna Convention on Diplomatic Relations by passing the domestic law, which is called "The Diplomatic Relations (Vienna Convention) Act, 1972". It was passed by the Indian Parliament on 29 August 1972 when Smt Indira Gandhi was the Prime Minister. Section 2 provides that the provisions set out in the Schedule to this Act of the Vienna Convention on Diplomatic Relations shall have the force of law in India. The Schedule makes it clear that Articles 1 and 32–40 of the Vienna Convention on Diplomatic Relations, 1961, are given the force of domestic law. The Central government may, from time to time, by notification in the Official Gazette, amend the Schedule in conformity with any amendments, duly made and adopted, of the provisions of the said Convention set out therein.

Section 4 of the Act gives expression to the principle of reciprocity by enabling the government of India to withdraw any privileges and immunities conferred on the diplomatic mission of a foreign State or members thereof, whenever it appears to the government that privileges and immunities accorded to Indian mission or members thereof in the territory of that State, being a party to the Vienna Convention, are less than those covered by this Act. The section empowers the government of India to take retaliatory measures on the basis of the principle of reciprocity. Further, the diplomatic agents are not entitled under Section 6 of the Act to import into Indian goods free of any duty or customs without any restrictions on their subsequent sale therein. Section 8 contains restrictions on entry into diplomatic premises.

Section 9 of the Act is of considerable procedural importance and contains a rule of evidence. It states that if in any proceedings any question arises whether or not any person is entitled to any privilege or immunity under this Act, a certificate issued by or under the authority of the Secretary to the government of India in the Ministry of External Affairs stating any fact relating to that question shall be conclusive evidence of that fact.

Following India, Pakistan also enacted The Diplomatic and Consular Privileges Act on 12 September 1972 when Zulfiqar Ali Bhutto was the Prime Minister. The only difference with the Indian Act in this case is that the Indian Act deals separately with diplomatic privileges whereas the Pakistan Act deals with both the diplomatic and consular privileges. Pakistan's Act has, therefore, two schedules attached to the Act.

Interestingly, Bangladesh has an older domestic law on diplomatic immunities than the Vienna Convention. The Diplomatic Immunities (Commonwealth Countries Representatives) Act, 1957, of Bangladesh provides immunities to the chief representative of a State as well as to the member of staff or family. Nepal passed Diplomatic Privileges and Immunities of the Foreign States and Representatives Act on 4 October 1970. Sri Lanka implemented its obligations very late during Srimavo Bhandarnayake's time. The Diplomatic Privileges Act of 1996 passed by Sri Lankan Parliament makes the Vienna Convention applicable as domestic law. Other States of the subcontinent follow the customary international law on the subject.

5 Law on Consular Relations

Functions of the "consuls" have been largely associated with the development of trade and the protection of economic interests of States. According to Professor Oppenheim, the roots of the institution of consuls go back to the second half of the Middle Ages. In the commercial towns of Italy, Spain, and France, the merchants used to appoint by election one or more of their fellow merchants as arbitrators in commercial disputes, who were called *Juges Consuls* or *Consuls Marchands* (Jennings and Watts 2008). In modern times too, the consuls are agents of a State in a foreign country and their primary duty is to protect the commercial interests of the appointing State. With the growth of international trade in twentieth century, the need for regulation of consuls was felt at the international level.

In 1949, the International Law Commission considered the inclusion of consular intercourse and immunities for codification. The Commission appointed Mr Jaroslav Zourek in 1955 as Special Rapporteur to commence the review of the matter and draft a set of provisional rules, based on *jus cogens*, national, and international law. It worked for two years from 1958 to 1960 and finally submitted draft articles to the General Assembly. The United Nations convened a Conference on Consular Relations in Vienna from 4 March to 22 April 1963 and was attended by delegates of ninety-five States. On 24 April 1963, the Conference adopted and opened for signature the Vienna Convention on Consular Relations (VCCR) and its two optional protocols. Forty-eight States signed the Convention. It came into force on 19 March 1967. At present, the Convention has 179 parties on board. In the South Asian region, Nepal acceded to the Convention on 28 September 1965, Pakistan on 14 April 1969, India on 28 November 1977, Bhutan on 28 July 1981, Maldives on 21 January 1991, and Sri Lanka on 4 May 2006. India and Pakistan have also signed Optional Protocol to the Vienna Convention on Consular Relations Concerning the Compulsory Settlement of Disputes, 1963 under which disputes arising out of the interpretation or application of VCCR shall lie within the compulsory jurisdiction of the International Court of Justice and may accordingly be brought before the court by an application made by any party to the Protocol (Article I).

According to Article 1(a) of VCCR, "consular post" means any consulate-general, consulate, vice-consulate, or consular agency. "Consular officer" under Article 1(b) means any person, including the Head of a consular post, entrusted in that capacity with the exercise of consular functions. Consular officers are of two categories, namely, career consular officers and honorary consular officers. Separate provisions apply to consular posts headed by career consular officers and by honorary consular officers. Article 9 lays down that the Heads of consular posts are divided into four classes: (a) Consuls-General (b) Consuls (c) Vice-Consuls, and (d) consular agents. Eight specific consular functions are prescribed under Article 5, which are represented by Fig. 1.

Under Article 12 of the VCCR, the Head of a consular post is admitted to the exercise of his functions by an authorization from the RS termed as an *exequatur*. A State which refused to grant an *exequatur* is not obliged to give to the SS reasons for such refusal. Paragraph 3 of this Article also provides that the Head of a consular post must receive his *exequatur* before joining his duties. Pending delivery of the *exequatur*, the Head of a consular post may be admitted on a provisional basis to the exercise of his function according to Article 13.

Under Article 28, the RS is obliged to accord full facilities for the performance of the functions of the consular post. Article 31 recognizes the principle of inviolability of the consular premises. It provides that the authorities of the RS cannot enter that part of the consular premises which is used exclusively for the purpose of the work of consular post except with the consent of the Head of the consular post. Such consent is assumed in case of fire or other disaster requiring prompt protective action. The RS is under a special duty to take all appropriate steps to protect the consular premises against any intrusion or damage and to prevent any disturbance of the peace of the consular post or impairment of its dignity. Article 32 exempts from taxation of consular premises. Article 34 ensures freedom of movement to all

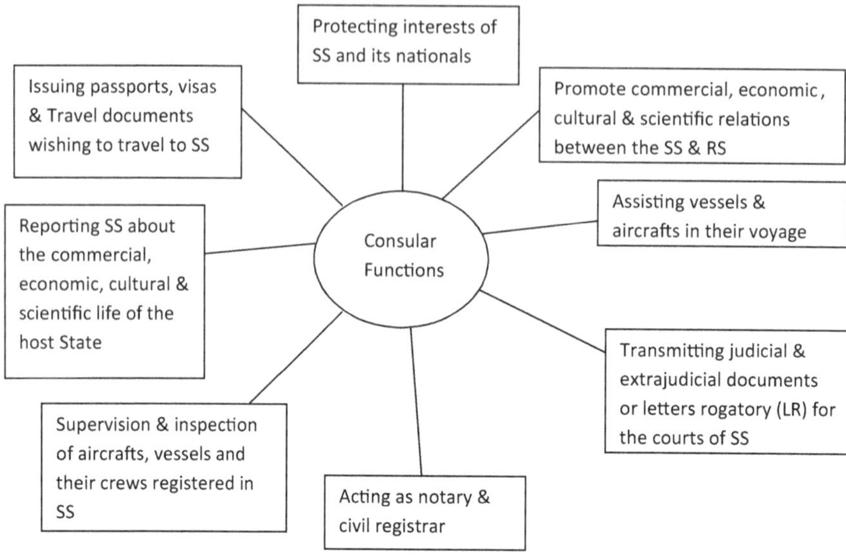

Fig. 1 Consular functions

members of the consular post. Article 35 guarantees freedom of communication of consular post for all official purposes.

In contrast with the diplomats, consuls are not completely immune from criminal jurisdiction of the RS. Article 41 lays down the rule that the consular officers are not liable to arrest or detention pending trial, except in the case of a grave crime and pursuant to a decision by the competent judicial authority. Consular officers cannot be committed to prison or be liable to any other form of restriction on their personal freedom. However, if criminal proceedings are instituted against a consular officer, he must appear before the competent authorities. He should be given respect by reason of his official position. In those circumstances in which it becomes necessary to detain a consular officer, the proceedings against him should be instituted without delay.

Regarding civil jurisdiction, Article 43 provides that the consular officers and consular employees are not amenable to the jurisdiction of the judicial or administrative authorities of the RS in respect of acts performed in the exercise of consular functions. However, the consuls could be amenable to civil jurisdiction if a dispute arises out of a contract concluded by a consular officer or a consular employee in which he did not contract as an agent of the SS or if an action is instituted by a third party for damage arising from an accident in the RS caused by a vehicle, vessel, or aircraft. In codifying the "consular functions" principle, the VCCR maintained the basic difference between consular and diplomatic immunities: "consular personnel enjoy immunity from legal process only in respect of official acts, whereas diplomatic agents have full personal inviolability and immunity from legal process". The drafters of the Convention recognized that if immunity depended on whether an act was performed in the exercise of consular functions, it was vital that courts be able to determine the functions to which immunity would apply (Kalicharan 2015). The connection of Articles 41, 43, and 5 is, therefore, vital to determine the culpability of consuls.

6 Internationally Protected Persons

The Convention on the Prevention and Punishment of Crimes Against Internationally Protected Persons, including Diplomatic Agents, was adopted by the General Assembly of the United Nations by resolution 3166 (XXVIII) on 14 December 1973. "Internationally Protected Persons" are defined in Article 1 as those persons who are either (a) a Head of State, a Head of government, or a Minister for Foreign Affairs, as well as members of his family who accompany him; or (b) any representative or official of a State or any official or other agent of an international organization of an inter-governmental character. Article 2 is the key provision of this Convention. It obligates each State Party to make punishable the intentional commission of murder, kidnapping, or other attack upon the person or liberty of an internationally protected person; violent attack upon the official premises, private accommodation or means of transport of an internationally protected person likely to endanger his person or liberty; and threats or attempts to commit, or participation as accomplices in the commission of such act.

Article 7 provides that persons alleged to have committed certain attacks against diplomatic agents and others should either be extradited or have their case submitted to the authorities for prosecution. It contains, in addition, provisions concerning cooperation, the transmission of information, and the treatment to be accorded to alleged offenders (Wood 1974). Under Article 13(1), any dispute between two or more States Parties concerning the interpretation or application of this Convention which is not settled by negotiation shall, at the request of one of them, be submitted to arbitration. If within six months from the date of the request for arbitration the parties are unable to agree on the organization of the arbitration, any one of those parties may refer the dispute to the International Court of Justice.

This Convention came into force on 20 February 1977. Currently, it has 178 State Parties, including all South Asian States. Pakistan acceded to this Convention on 29 March 1976 with a declaration that it shall not be bound by Article 13(1) of the Convention. India acceded to this Convention on 11 April 1978 with a declaration that the government does not consider itself bound by Article 13(1). Nepal also acceded to the Convention on 9 March 1990. Bhutan acceded to the Convention on 16 January 1989, Maldives on 21 August 1990, Sri Lanka on 27 February 1991, Afghanistan on 24 September 2003, and Bangladesh on 20 May 2005.

7 Cases

In this section, decided disputes pertaining to diplomatic and consular privileges, etc., by the International Court of Justice (ICJ) as well as by the national courts are discussed. The foremost dispute related to diplomatic and consular immunity decided by the ICJ in 1980 is the following:

a. *Case Concerning US Diplomatic and Consular Staff in Tehran* (USA v. Iran) (1980) Although this case is not immediately related to South Asia, but in one way, it is connected by the fact that one of the judges delivering the majority judgment in this case was from India, Justice Nagendra Singh (Govindraj 1999). Although Justice Singh did not actively participate in the writing of this judgment, except agreeing with the majority decision of imputing State responsibility on Iran (Reddy 2000), yet the judgement is a starting point for South Asian readers to connect with this case and understand it in relation to diplomatic and State immunities.

In response to a message issued by Ayatollah Komeini, several hundred Iranian students and other demonstrators took possession of the U.S. embassy on 4 November 1979 in Tehran by force. The students and others were furious over the admission of the deposed Shah of Iran into the U.S. for medical treatment. The demonstrators were not even stopped by the Iranian security forces. U.S. consulates at Tabriz and Shiraz were similarly attacked the other day. The demonstrators had seized archives and documents and continued to hold 52 U.S. nationals. Out of these 52, at least 28 persons were having the status, duly recognized by government of Iran, of "member of the diplomatic staff", at least 20 persons having the status, similarly recognized, of "member of the administrative and technical staff", and two other private persons (ICJ Reports 1980).

The U.S. approached the court for relief, *inter alia*: (a) for declaring that Iran had infringed a number of treaties, including the 1961 and 1963 Vienna Conventions on Diplomatic and Consular Relations, respectively, and (b) for declaring a call for the release of the hostages, the evacuation of the embassy and consulate, the punishment of the persons responsible, and the payment of reparation. In April 1980, while the case was pending, U.S. military forces entered Iran by air and landed in a remote desert area in the course of an attempt to rescue the hostages. The attempt was abandoned because of equipment failure. U.S. military personnel were killed in an air collision as the units withdrew. No injury was made to Iranian nationals or property.

The ICJ held that Iran was placed under the most categorical obligations under the Vienna Conventions of 1961 and 1963, as a RS, to take appropriate steps to ensure the protection of the US embassy and consulates, their staffs, their archives, their means of communication, and the freedom of movement of the members of their staff (ICJ Reports 1980). Although the militants, when they executed their attack on the embassy, had not any form of official status as recognized "agents" or organs of the Iranian State, yet Iran cannot become free of any responsibility in regard to those attacks under the contractual obligations undertaken by Iran as original signatory to Vienna Conventions of 1961 and 1963 (ICJ Reports 1980).

The court cited Articles 22(2), 24, 25, 26, 27, and 29 of the 1961 Convention as well as Articles 5, 36 of 1963 Convention and held that the Iranian government failed altogether to take any "appropriate steps" to protect the premises, staff, and archives of the U.S.' mission against attack by the militants. The government did not take any steps either to prevent this attack or to stop it before it reached its completion. The facts also show that on 5 November 1979, the Iranian government similarly failed to take appropriate steps for the protection of the U.S. consulates at Tabriz and Shiraz. In addition, they show that the failure of the Iranian government to take such steps was due to more than mere negligence or lack of appropriate means.

The court noted that the Iranian authorities were responsible for total inaction on the date of attack even when urgent and repeated requests for help were made. It gave some instances when Iranian authorities had taken positive action to protect diplomats and consulates earlier in such cases.

The court upheld the principle of the inviolability of the premises of a diplomatic mission and declared that paras 1 and 3 of Article 22 were also infringed. Secondly, they constitute continuing breaches of Article 29 which forbids any arrest or detention of a diplomatic agent and any attack on his person, freedom, or dignity. Thirdly, the Iranian authorities were found to be in continuing breach of Articles 25, 26, and 27 of 1961 Convention and of pertinent provisions of the 1963 Convention concerning facilities for the performance of functions, freedom of movement, and communications for diplomatic and consular staff. It also infringed Article 24 of the former Convention and Article 33 of the latter, which provides for the absolute inviolability of the archives and documents of diplomatic missions and consulates.

Underlining the importance of the Conventions, the court held "there is no more fundamental prerequisite for the conduct of relations between States than the inviolability of diplomatic envoys and embassies, so that throughout history nations of all creeds and cultures observed reciprocal obligations for that purpose". The institution of diplomacy, the court continued, has proved to be "an instrument essential for effective cooperation in the international community, and for enabling States, irrespective of their differing constitutional and social systems, to achieve mutual understanding and to resolve their differences by peaceful means" (ICJ Reports 1979, p. 19)

According to the court, this case was unique and of very particular gravity, because it was not only private individuals or groups of individuals that had disregarded and set at naught the inviolability of a foreign embassy, but the government of the RS itself. The court drew the attention of the entire international community to the irreparable harm that might be caused by such events. At the end, the court, by 13 votes to 2, decided that Iran had violated obligations owed by it to the U.S. under international Conventions in force between the two countries, as well as under long-established rules of general international law. By 14 votes to 1, the court decided that the form of reparation, failing agreement between the Parties, would be settled by it.

b. *Abdulaziz v. Metropolitan Dade County (1984)* In 1984, an interesting dispute arose in the U.S. The Saudi Prince Abdulaziz, his wife, his mother-in-law were residents of the Cricket Club condominium in Dade County, Florida. On 26 February 1982, representatives from Florida State Attorney's office obtained a search warrant after inquiry with the U.S. Department of State revealed that Prince Abdulaziz and his family did not have diplomatic status. The warrant was based on the affidavit of a former employee of the prince, who alleged that the prince was holding an Egyptian named Nadia against her will. The prince, who was a "special envoy" for matters concerning the government of Saudi Arabia, was given diplomatic status by the SS after the commencement of a suit against him. The 11th Federal Circuit Court held that the prince was entitled to diplomatic immunity. The court noted that under the Vienna Convention, the State Department has the broad discretion to classify diplomats. The court stated that the broadness in the language of the Vienna Convention is necessary, since it is the foreign country that actually ranks its envoys, not the State Department. The court noted that Article 14 of the Vienna Convention classifies "envoys" as Heads of Missions, and that Heads of Missions are defined in the U.S. Diplomatic Relations Act and are protected by it. The court concluded that as special envoy the prince was afforded full protection pursuant to the Act.

c. *U.S. v.* Khobragade (2014) In another interesting case pertaining to South Asia, the Southern District of New York district court reiterated the above principles laid down in *Abdulaziz* case. Dr. Devyani Khobragade, a citizen of India, served as a consular officer in the USA from 26 October 2012 to 8 January 2014, a position that cloaked her with consular immunity pursuant to the Vienna Convention on Consular Relations. According to Khobragade, she additionally obtained diplomatic immunity on 26 August 2013 by virtue of her appointment as a Special Advisor to the United Nations. On 12 December 2013, she was arrested and charged with visa fraud and making false statements to the government. The 39 years old Khobragade was strip searched, cavity searched and swabbed for DNA after her arrest in New York. She was confined with criminals before she was released under several bail conditions including a bond in the amount of $250,000 co-signed by three other people.

On 8 January 2014, she was appointed as a Counsellor to the Permanent Mission of India to the United Nations, a position that again cloaked her with full diplomatic immunity. On 9 January 2014, Khobragade was indicted on the above charges and she moved to dismiss the indictment on the basis of diplomatic immunity. She contended that diplomatic immunity due to her appointment as Special Advisor continued through 31 December 2013. The U.S. government denied that Khobragade ever had diplomatic immunity as a Special Advisor. It also asked the Indian government to waive Khobragade's diplomatic immunity "in order that the charges may be adjudicated in accordance with the laws of the U.S." The Indian government raised serious objections against the conduct of U.S. to Devyani and termed the incident as "an insult" and "an outrageous violation of standards". India retaliated by removing concrete barricades outside the consular section of the U.S. embassy in New Delhi, cancelled airport passes for U.S. diplomats and froze import requests.

After the Indian government declined to waive Khobragade's immunity, the State Department requested her immediate departure from the country. The court modified her bail conditions to permit her return to India. She left the U.S. later that evening. In its order, the court held that diplomatic immunity acquired during the pendency of proceedings destroys jurisdiction even if the suit was validly commenced before immunity applied. Referring to *Abdulaziz* case, the court held that diplomatic immunity "served as a defence to suits already commenced" (15 F. Supp. 3d 383).

d. *The Raymond Davis case* (2011) is also an interesting one in this context. Davis was a U.S. national serving as an employee of the U.S. consulate in Lahore. He killed two Pakistanis (one motorcycle rider and his pillion passenger) in Lahore on 27 January 2011. Davis was charged with murder under Section 302 of Pakistan Penal Code, 1860 (*qatl-i.amd*, which is a compoundable offence) by the local police. Davis was lodged in the jail too Shoiab (2011). The daily newspaper Guardian reported that Davis was a CIA agent (Walsh and MacAskill 2011). If he was a diplomat, this report would have been very relevant as spying by a diplomatic agent is one of the criminal offences covered by diplomatic immunity (Hassan 2011).

The U.S. actively sought the release of Davis, claiming that he had diplomatic immunity. Pakistan is already party to both the Vienna Conventions of 1961 and 1963. It had also promulgated its own Diplomatic and Consular Privileges Act, 1972. Regarding the determination of any privilege or immunity under this Act, a certificate issued by or under the authority of the federal government stating any fact relating to that question is considered conclusive evidence of that fact. In cases where the federal government chose to issue a certificate regarding any person's entitlement to any privilege or entity, the Supreme Court of Pakistan has affirmed the conclusive nature of the certificate in *Ghulam* v. *United States Agency for International Development (U.S. Aid) Mission, Islamabad*. However, the then Prime Minister of Pakistan, Yousaf Raza Gilani, chose not to issue a certificate. He left the matter to be decided by the court, but he suggested it could be resolved under Islamic/*Shariah* law if compensation was offered to the families of the victims killed in the shooting. Following the later route, the Pakistani trial court resolved the case by applying Islamic law principles (*diyat* pursuant to Section 345 of the Code of Criminal Procedure) that allowed Davis to be released after the heirs of the victims were compensated. The court observed that the legal heirs of both the victims appeared before it and recorded their separate statements, in which they unequivocally confirmed that they had received the amount of *badl-i-sulah* (mutually agreed compensation according to Shariah) as per their shares. The legal heirs compounded the offence and waived their right of *qisas* (punishment by causing similar harm to the same part of the body of the convict as the convict caused to the victim). Raymond Davis was set free by the court and was allowed to go back to his country (Hassan 2011).

e. *Jadhav Case* (India v Pakistan) (Provisional Measures) (2017): Kulbhushan Jadhav, a former naval officer, who was sentenced to death by a Pakistani military court on the charges of spying, was rescued by the International Court of Justice after India challenged the execution on the ground of the violation by Pakistan of VCCR obligations contained in Article 36. The court unanimously ordered that the government of Pakistan shall inform the court of all measures taken in implementation of its order. The court notes that the acts alleged by India, i.e. the alleged failure by Pakistan to provide the requisite consular notifications with regard to the arrest and detention of Mr. Jadhav, as well as the alleged failure to allow communication and provide access to him, appear to be capable of falling within the scope of the Convention. In view of the court, this is sufficient to establish that it has prima facie jurisdiction under Article I of the Optional Protocol. The court further observed that the right to consular notification and access between a State and its nationals, as well as the obligations of the detaining State to inform the person concerned without delay of his rights with regard to consular assistance and to allow their exercise, were recognized in Article 36, paragraph 1, of the VCCCR.

The court also examined whether there is a risk of irreparable prejudice and urgency. It considered that the mere fact that Mr Jadhav was under a death sentence and might therefore be executed was sufficient to demonstrate the existence of a risk of irreparable prejudice to the rights claimed by India.

f. *Other Instances* In many instances, diplomats and consuls abuse their official position and indulge in crimes, acts of espionage, and smuggling contraband goods. One Saudi diplomat was reported to commit rape against Nepali maids employed by him in September 2015. It was reported that the First Secretary to Saudi ambassador Majed Hassan Ashoor and his guests raped two women from Nepal at his Gurgaon residence, where he lived with his wife and three children. The local police rescued the two women from his apartment on 7 September 2015. Indian government considered expelling the diplomat if the embassy did not let him be questioned by the Gurgaon police. The Saudi embassy called the allegations false and protested the alleged police intrusion into the diplomat's house. Nepal government waited for New Delhi to take the lead. However, the diplomat first took the cover of embassy premises and later left India 6 days after he was asked by Ministry of External Affairs Chief of Protocol to cooperate with the police probe (Roy 2015).

Diplomatic immunity has also been abused by the use of diplomatic bags to smuggle illegal goods into or out of the RS. In an incident in 2013, a counsellor-level diplomat travelling from Dubai was nabbed at the Delhi airport carrying 37 kg of jewellery worth Rs. 10 crore. When asked to open his bag, he invoked diplomatic immunity. However, the bags were searched and gold was seized after the Directorate of Revenue Intelligence issued search orders. The diplomat and an Indian passenger accompanying him were detained, but not arrested. The External Affairs Ministry decided to deport the diplomat (Beniwal 2013). In another incident, Bangladesh expelled a Pakistani visa officer in February 2015 posted at the High Commission in Dhaka for allegedly running an operation to smuggle fake currency across the border to undermine India's financial system and fund terrorist groups. The officer named Mazhar Khan was arrested along with a local accomplice. However, he was released owing to his immunity. In the meantime, he was expelled by Bangladesh foreign ministry and was declared *persona non grata* (Chaudhury 2015).

In Sri Lanka too, diplomats are reported to have indulged in unwarranted acts. A Burmese ambassador to Sri Lanka, Sao Boonwaat, shot and killed his wife, Shirley, for having an alleged affair with Sri Lankan night club singer Rex de Silva in 1979. After her death, he built a funeral pyre to cremate her on the grounds of the diplomatic compound. Nearby woke up to a strong smell and the sight of a group of Buddhist monks giving the final rites. When Sri Lankan police arrived, they were not given entry inside the diplomatic premises on the ground that it was technically Burmese territory (Torsmen 2015). This led to a diplomatic dispute between the two countries, and Boonwaat was recalled to Rangoon (Hensley 2006).

In cases not of a criminal nature, it was held by the Mumbai High Court in the year 2015 that Section 86(1) of the Civil Procedure Code, 1908, provides that no foreign State may be sued in any court otherwise competent to try the suit except with the consent of the Central government certified in writing by a Secretary to that government. Subsection (2) of Section 86 provides for the manner and the circumstances in which the consent may be given by the Central government. Subsection 3 of Section 86 provides that except with the consent of Central government, certified in writing by a Secretary to that government, no decree shall be executed against the property of any foreign State. Subsection (4) of Section 86 provides that the provisions contained in Subsections (1) (2), and (3) of Section 86 shall apply to (a) any ruler of a foreign State (aa) any ambassador or envoy of a foreign State (b) any High Commissioner of a Commonwealth country; and (c) any such member of the staff of the foreign State or the staff or retinue of the ambassador or envoy of a foreign State or of the High Commissioner of a Commonwealth country as the Central government may specify in this behalf (*Viratna Vidyabanich* v. *Mohan J. Jhangiani*) (2015).

8 Conclusion

South Asia has a rich tradition of respect for diplomats and envoys of foreign States as evidenced by the available classical literature and chronicles. Long before the modern institutionalization of diplomatic privileges and immunities, this region had already imbibed such practices. As a result, the adoption of the modern law on diplomatic privileges and immunities codified in the Vienna Conventions by this whole region was very smooth. Moreover, many of these countries have passed domestic laws to implement the obligations contained in these international Conventions. Those States which have not made domestic laws for implementation follow the customary international law on the subject. The judicial wing of these States has also enforced the international commitments and domestic norms. However, these States are debating the misuse of diplomatic privileges in the recent reports of their criminal conduct. In such circumstances, the South Asian States have shown enough maturity not to prosecute them, except in the *Raymond Davis* case, which became an issue of national pride. When Devyani Khobragade was arrested in the U.S. and was strip searched, swabbed, and cavity searched like criminals, India had raised objections against such action. In cases not of a criminal nature, the discretion possessed by the executive wing of the State for the purpose of issuing certificate about the status of "diplomat" and "consuls" has also been affirmed by the judicial wing.

References

Abdulaziz v. Metropolitan dade county (741 F.2d 1328, 40 Fed. R. Serv. 2d 110)

Altekar AS (2016) State and government in ancient India. Motilal Banarsidas, Delhi

Bandyopadyaya P (1920) International law and custom in ancient India. Calcutta University Press, Calcutta

Beniwal V (2013) Return of the smuggler. The Business Standard, New Delhi

Buhler G (1886) The Laws of Manu. Clarendon Press, Oxford

Case Concerning United States Diplomatic and Consular Staff in Tehran (United States of America v Iran) (1980) ICJ Reports

Crawford J (2012) Brownlie's principles of public international law, 8th edn. Oxford University Press, Oxford

Denza E (2008) Diplomatic law: commentary on the Vienna convention on diplomatic relations, 3rd edn. Oxford University Press, U.K

Ganguli KM (2003) The Mahabharata of Vyasa (English Prose Translation). Sacred Texts, California

Garner BA (2014) Black's law dictionary, 10th edn. Thomson Reuters, Minnesota, U.S

Govindraj VC (1999) Judge Nagendra Singh of the world court: his contribution to the development of contemporary international law. Deep and Deep Publications, New Delhi

Hasan M (2009) History of Islam. Adam Publishers, New Delhi

Hassan T (2011) Diplomatic or consular immunity for criminal offenses. Va J Int Law 1:17–38

Hensley G (2006) Final approaches: a memoir. Auckland University Press, New Zealand

Hoffman J (2003) Reconstructing diplomacy. Br J Polit Int Relat 5:525–542

Jennings R, Watts A (2008) Oppenheim's international law, 9th edn. Oxford University Press, Oxford

Kalicharan ML (2015) Diplomatic immunities and privileges: critical study with special reference to contemporary international law. A Doctoral Thesis submitted to University of Mysore, India. http://goo.gl/uwvgLZ

Mc Clanahan GV (1989) Diplomatic immunity: principles, practices, problems. Hurst & Co., London

MEA (2015) Indian foreign service: a backgrounder, ministry of external affairs, Government of India. http://goo.gl/v9MvJb

MOFA (2016) History of the ministry of foreign affairs, ministry of foreign affairs, Kathmadu, Nepal. http://goo.gl/SS3lxC

Nathan JA (1993) Force, order and diplomacy in the age of Louis XIV. Va Q Rev 69: 4. http://goo.gl/hmcl2P

Nelson CM (1988) "Opening" Pandora's Box: the status of the diplomatic bag in international relations. Fordham Int Law J 12(3):494–520

Niazi GSK (1992) The life and works of Sultan Alauddin Khilji. Atlantic Publishers & Distributors, New Delhi

Reddy AS (2000) Book review of judge Nagendra Singh of the world court: his contribution to the development of contemporary international law. J Indian Law Inst 42(1):125–128

Reiff H (1954) Diplomatic and consular privileges, immunities, and practice. Ettemad Press, Tehran
Roy S (2015) Accused of rape. Indian Express, New Delhi, Saudi Diplomat gets away to Saudi Arabia
Roy Chaudhury D (2015) Bangladesh expels Pakistani diplomat for smuggling fake Indian currency funding terrorists. The Economic Times, New Delhi
Sarkar JN (2010) Shivaji and his times, 5th edn. Orient Blackswan, London
Satow EM (1917) A guide to diplomatic practice, vol 1. Cambridge University Press, New York
Sen B (1965) A diplomat's handbook of international law and practice. Martinus Nijhoff, Leiden
Shaw MN (2012) International law, 6th edn. Oxford University Press, U.K
Shoiab S (2011, 28 January) US official Raymod Davis on Lahore murder charges. BBC News, London
Sinclair D (1884) History of India. Oxford University Press, Oxford
Thompson E, Garratt GT (1999) History of british rule in India. Atlantic Publishers, New Delhi
Torsmen D (2015) 10 Cases of criminal activity by diplomats. Listverse, Belfast
Tulsidas G (2005) ShriRamacharitamanas. Tulsi Peeth Seva Nyas, Chitrakoot
U.S. v. Khobragade (2014) 15F. Supp. 3d 383, United States District Court, S.D. New York
Walsh D, MacAskill E (2011) American who sparked diplomatic crisis over Lahore shooting was CIA spy, The Guardian. http://goo.gl/4mRFQM
Wilson C (1967) Diplomatic privileges and immunities. University of Arizona Press, Tucson
Wood MC (1974) The convention on the prevention and punishment of crimes against internationally protected persons, including diplomatic agents. Int Comp Law Q 23(4):791–817
Yousafzai K (2013) Amir Dost Muhammad Khan. The great game Pashtun's history blog. http://goo.gl/kDTwFm

Author Biographies

Ms. Leena Kumari is a doctoral candidate in the University School of Law and Legal Studies, Guru Gobind Singh Indraprastha University (GGSIPU) in New Delhi. She obtained her LL.B. and LL.M. degrees from Faculty of Law, University of Delhi after which she joined academia. Before starting her doctoral research, she was teaching public international law in CPJ School of Law, New Delhi. Her areas of interest are public international law, and environmental law.

Dr. Anupam Jha is Assistant Professor (Senior) at the Faculty of Law, University of Delhi. He has been engaged in teaching & research for more than 14 years. He is recipient of several prestigious fellowships and nominations, such as Raman Fellowship (U.S.A.), Commonwealth Fellowship (U.K.), UGC-TEC Nomination (Mauritius). He has also been awarded the most active participant from India by UNHCR. His current areas of teaching and research are: public international law, international environmental law, international trade law, and jurisprudence. His latest publications include the following: "The Law on Trafficking in Persons: The Quest For an Effective Model", First Published Online in ***Asian Journal of International Law*** (***Cambridge University Press***), 27 October 2016, ISSN No. 2044-2521 (online).

Chapter 15
Changing Horizons of Modern Weaponry in South Asia: A Legal Survey

Vivek Sehrawat

1 Introduction

South Asia remains a victim of both its own internal conflicts and a wide array of external enemies employing ever-more-deadly tactics and weapons. To protect themselves from an ever-changing assortment of dangers, South Asians have been forced to evolve rapidly. This evolving sometimes occurs from clubs and arrows to swords and bullets; from bullets to canons and heavy artillery; and from simple, ordinary weapons to a very high level of technological sophistication. This sophistication can be extremely difficult to regulate or control by international overseers.

From the legal perspective, South Asia faces major challenges to control the development and use of weaponry. South Asia faces challenges from highly effective antipersonnel bullets, landmines, ballistic missiles, laser weapons, conventional weapons, explosive remnants of war (ERWs), cluster munitions, and chemical and biological weapons, to nuclear warheads. Now, the region faces a whole new level of sophistication made possible by the Internet that they and many other countries are not equipped to handle. Anonymous hackers, thousands of miles away, can carry out cyber-attacks on defense systems, waterworks, military installations, and air traffic control systems. At the same time, human pilots can direct autonomous-intelligent drones equipped with everything from cameras and audio recorders to bombs and nuclear warheads.

This chapter compares international laws of armed conflict as they relate to a plethora of evolving weaponry being built and used by South Asian militaries. It also compares these laws to the use of these weapons when co-opted or stolen by underground agents working contrary to international law standards. It discusses the

V. Sehrawat (✉)
School of Law, University of Kansas, 2720 Brittany Place Apt No. 222, Lawrence, KS 66049, USA
e-mail: viveksehrawat07@gmail.com

J.L. Kaul and A. Jha (eds.), *Shifting Horizons of Public International Law*,
https://doi.org/10.1007/978-81-322-3724-2_15

criteria set by the International Committee of the Red Cross (ICRC) for the use of weapons and subjecting weapons to legal review. This chapter also analyzes the causes and proposed rules to be applied to the different types of modernized weaponry. These rules are currently being used within the region. Analysis is given to the role of international law as it struggles to regulate an ever-changing array of combatants and weapons. Within the South Asian region, emphasis is given to India and Pakistan as amid escalating armed conflicts including an accelerated arms race between them. Lastly, it assesses the difficult task of keeping these weapons out of the hands of terrorists.

2 Historical Legal Background

Historically, the Hindu Code of Manu directs that treacherous weapons, such as barbed or poisoned arrows, are forbidden and that an enemy attempting to surrender, or the one badly wounded, should not be killed (Jayaswal 1930). Subsequently, technological advances were able to drive changes in the nature of warfare as well as lead to the changes in the laws of war. In modern times, International Humanitarian Law (IHL) governs the choice of weapons and prohibits or restricts the use of certain weapons. State practice establishes customary international humanitarian law *Rule 71* (*The use of weapons which are by nature indiscriminate is prohibited*) as a norm of customary international law applicable in both international and non-international armed conflicts (Rule 71 2016). In addition, many of the basic rules and specific prohibitions and restrictions on means and methods of warfare may be found in customary intentional law (Lawand 2006). Some weapons and weapons systems are totally prohibited. These blanket prohibitions, which may be traced to treaty or customary international laws, are applicable when the weapon in question is either indiscriminate in effect or cause unnecessary suffering.

2.1 General Principles of International Humanitarian Law

Under the watchful eyes of ICRC, the international community has been constantly trying to formulate laws to restrict the development and use of mass destruction weapons. Just as every conflict has a status, and every battlefield player has an individual status, every battlefield incident may be examined for compliance with four-core concepts of IHL. These concepts are distinction, proportionality, unnecessary suffering, and military necessity (Solis 2010). Individuals on the battlefield with weapons have a desire to survive. Therefore, it is important to consider four-core principles of IHL/LOAC when developing a weapon. This section discusses four general principles of IHL.

2.1.1 Distinction

According to Article 48 of Additional Protocol I, "In order to ensure respect for and protection of the civilian population and civilian objects, the Parties to the conflict shall at all times distinguish between the civilian population and combatants and between civilian objects and military objectives and accordingly shall direct their operations only against military objectives" (Article 48 1977). Furthermore, war is fought with weapons; Additional Protocol I prohibits the use of weapons which are "of a nature to strike military objectives and civilians or civilian objects without distinction" (Rule 71 2016). This prohibition was reaffirmed in the Statute of the International Criminal Court. It has also been included in other instruments. It is necessary to ensure that all weapons developed by the South Asian counties can fulfill this requirement of distinction: Can these weapons distinguish between civilian population and combatants?

2.1.2 Proportionality

Loss of life and damage to property *incidental* to attacks must not be excessive in relation to the concrete and direct military advantage expected to be gained. The key here is the word incidental, meaning outside of the military targets also known as "collateral damage" in news stories. This means that when considering a target, the damage to civilians and their property cannot be excessive in relation to the military advantage gained. Proportionality is not a requirement if the target is purely military. This principle brings with it an obligation to consider all options when making targeting decisions: verify the target, timing (is there a time when fewer civilians will be around?), weapons used, warnings, and evacuations for civilian populations (4 Basic Principles 2016).

Proportionality is a necessary consideration in attacks on civilians, not on combatants. Grotius writes, "one must take care of, so far as is possible, to prevent the death of innocent persons, even by accident" (Solis 2010). For example, how will an autonomous drone realize that its mission to attack a small building next to a stadium is full of football fans? It is focused on the small building not the stadium. At present, this burden is on the operators, but as drones become more autonomous, they must also become more aware of the big picture.

2.1.3 Unnecessary Suffering

The core LOAC concept of unnecessary suffering, a concept to limit unnecessary suffering to civilians and combatants, is codified in Additional Protocol I, Article 35 (2). "It is prohibited to employ weapons, projectiles and materials and methods of warfare of a nature to cause superfluous injury or unnecessary suffering" (Article 35 (2) 1977) or which are inherently indiscriminate in violation of the international law of armed conflict, provided that such weapons are subject of a comprehensive prohibition and are included in an annex to the Rome statute of the ICC (Weston et al. 1990) (147).

A weapon cannot be banned on the grounds of superfluous injury or unnecessary suffering merely because it causes a suffering, since there is no scale to measure the suffering. The effects of a certain weapon may be repulsive, but this is not, in and of itself, enough to render a weapon illegal (Solis 2010) (270). An example of this would be napalm, which was used extensively in WWII and Vietnam Conflict.

Compliance with the principle of unnecessary suffering depends upon the weapon choice and the suffering it might cause. Weapon choice is one part of satisfying this principle. However, depending upon the features of the weapons being used and how competently it carries out the missions can negate weapon choice.

2.1.4 Military Necessity

The principle of military necessity states that a combatant is justified in using measures not forbidden by international law which are indispensable for securing complete submission of an enemy at the soonest moment. Military necessity requires combat forces to engage in only those acts necessary to accomplish a legitimate military objective. Military necessity permits the killing of enemy combatants and other persons whose death is unavoidable. Also, military necessity permits destruction of civilian property if that destruction is imperatively demanded by the necessities of war. Destruction of civilian property as an end in itself is a violation of international law. There must be a reasonable connection between the destruction of property and the overcoming of enemy forces. IHL also prohibits weapon systems that cannot be directed at a specific military target (Finn and Scheding 2010) (172). It is unknown whether the weapons developed by South Asian countries are necessary for their militaries.

3 Review Mechanism Established under Treaties and Conventions

There are number of treaties and conventions under which certain weapons are prohibited because they fail to meet the standards of general principles of IHL. This section includes the kind of weapons to be reviewed and types of weapons subject to review and under what law.

3.1 What Must Be Reviewed?

The reference in international treaties to carrying out legal reviews of new weapons, means, and methods of warfare is found in Article 36 of Additional Protocol I of 1977. This rule provides that "in the study, development, acquisition or adoption of a new weapon, means or method of warfare, a High Contracting Party (describes a party to any international agreement which has both signed and ratified the treaty) is under an obligation to determine whether its employment would, in some or all circumstances, be prohibited by this Protocol or by any other rule of international law applicable to the High Contracting Party (HCP)" (Article 36 1977). "Means of warfare" are weapons and weapon systems. "Method of warfare" refers to the tactics, techniques, and procedures (TTP) by which hostilities are conducted (Schmitt 2013) (27).

Under the Article 36 of Additional Protocol I, "new" weapons are subject to review. There are two ways to determine whether a weapon is "new." First, look to the State intending to use weapon. The fact that a weapon has been in service with one State for some time before being sold to another State would not prevent the receiving State from considering the weapon as "new" for the purposes of Article 36. Second, new weapons are determined by reference to the date upon which the weapons came into service. On ratification by a State of Additional Protocol I, those weapons already in service could not be considered "new" within the terms of Article 36 (McClelland 2003). Moreover, the aim of Article 36 is to prevent the use of weapons that would violate international law in all circumstances and to impose restrictions on the use of weapons that would violate international law in some circumstances, by determining their lawfulness before they are developed, acquired, or otherwise incorporated into a State's arsenal (Lawand 2006) (4). The Declaration of St. Petersburg is the first formal agreement prohibiting the use of certain weapons in war. "The Declaration to that effect adopted in 1868, which has the force of law, confirms the customary rule according to which the use of arms, projectiles and material of a nature to cause unnecessary suffering is prohibited" (Saint Petersburg Declaration 1868). Therefore, the development of these prohibited weapons must be reviewed at an early stage so that they cannot be used during war.

3.2 Types of Weapons Subject to Review

This section will discuss the various weapons, which are subject to review under certain conventions and treaties.

3.2.1 Conventional Weapons

All conventional weapons include fragmentation weapons, antipersonnel landmines, booby traps, white phosphorus munitions, laser weapons, flamethrowers, cluster bombs, and improvised explosive devices (IEDs)—which are subject to, or are, implicated by, Certain Conventional Weapons, which seeks to define the lawful and unlawful use (Solis 2010) (577).

3.2.2 Fragmentation Weapons

Certain Convention Weapons Protocol I reads, "It is prohibited to use any weapon the primary effect of which is to injure by fragments which in the human body escape detection by X-rays." Conventional X-ray imaging cannot locate small pieces of glass, plastic, or wood lodged in human tissue, and it might violate the principle of unnecessary suffering.

The 1999 UN Secretary-General's Bulletin Section 6.2 provides: "The use of certain conventional weapons, such as [those that leave] non-detectable fragments, … is prohibited." Use of fragmentation weapons in the South Asian region is unknown. According to the United Nations Office of Disarmament Affairs, Bangladesh (september 9, 2000), India (March 1, 1984), Maldives (September 7, 2000), Pakistan (April 1, 1985), and Sri Lanka (September 24, 2004) are the parties to the Protocol I to the Convention on Prohibitions or Restrictions on the Use of Certain Conventional Weapons which may be deemed to be excessively injurious or to have indiscriminate effects (Saint Petersburg Declaration 1868). Five out of eight South Asian countries are parties to Convention. It may be inferred that most of South Asian countries are against the use of fragmentation weapons.

3.2.3 Antipersonnel Mines

An antipersonnel "mine" is a munition placed under, on, or near the ground; "primarily designed to be exploded" by pressure, proximity, or contract with a person or vehicle; and designed to injure or kill people (Solis 2010) (581–582). According to the Protocol II on Prohibitions or Restrictions on the use of Mines, Booby-Traps and other Devices, 1980, and the Convention on the Prohibition of Antipersonnel Mines (Ottawa Treaty 1997), use of antipersonnel mines is prohibited. The ICRC, along with governments, the International Campaign to Ban Landmines, and the United Nations argued for a comprehensive prohibition on use, stockpiling, production, and transfer antipersonnel mines.

In over 60 mine-affected states and areas, the legacy of the past, as well as ongoing internal conflicts, still results in thousands of casualties each year, especially in the more seriously affected states of Afghanistan and Pakistan (Antipersonnel Mines 2011). According to a report released in December 2014, Pakistan has a stockpile of six million antipersonnel landmines, the second largest in the world. Not to be left behind, India is third on the list released by the Nobel Prize winning group, the International Campaign to Ban Landmines. While Afghanistan is not comparable in its stockpile of mines, the report adds that it is one of the most heavily mined countries in the world. Afghan refugees go through complex programs before they can reenter their nation because undetonated Soviet landmines and those laid during the Taliban regime pose serious threats in the region (Rediff News 2014).

A major legal concern is that landmines clearly violate the law of armed conflict regarding the principle of distinction. A landmine cannot tell whether an enemy combatant or a member of the civilian population is triggering it. Four out of eight South Asian counties are parties to the treaty on the prohibition of antipersonnel mines that include Afghanistan (September 19, 2002), Bangladesh (September 6, 2000), Bhutan (August 18, 2005), and Maldives (September 7, 2000). India and Pakistan occupy the territory in the South Asian region not party to the antipersonnel mine treaty, along with small Island Country Sri Lanka, which is located on the Southern tip of India and Himalayan country Nepal. It may be concluded that a majority of South Asia has landmines, and these countries do not intend to prohibit the use of landmines in future.

3.2.4 Booby Traps

Booby traps are prohibited according to Rule 80 of Customary International Humanitarian Law. Article 6 of the 1980 Protocol II to the Convention on Certain Conventional Weapons provides:

1. (a) Any booby-trap in the form of an apparently harmless portable object, which is specifically designed and constructed to contain explosive material and to detonate when it is disturbed or approached, or (b) booby-traps which are in any way attached to or associated with.
2. It is prohibited in all circumstances to use any booby-trap which is designed to cause superfluous injury or unnecessary suffering (Rule 80 2016).

Hence, the legal challenge is that it may violate the law of armed conflict principle of unnecessary suffering. Moreover, it might violate the principle of military necessity because there is no point of killing a person who is merely delivering a service or distributing an item.

According to Protocol II to the Convention on Certain Conventional Weapons, "Booby-trap" means "any device or material which is designed, constructed, or adapted to kill or injure, and which functions unexpectedly when a person disturbs or approaches an apparently harmless object or performs an apparently safe act."

Pakistan's army is finally making significant gains in its campaign against Islamist militants, and some of the success can be traced back to unlikely sources: paintballs and birdcalls. Paint balls and birdcalls are the booby trap methods used to fight against the Islamic militants. Pakistan's military has built a sprawling base to train soldiers in how to defend themselves when fighting small groups of terrorists by employing booby traps. Pakistani commanders and troops say that the training conducted at the National Counterterrorism Center Pabbi helps them gain the upper hand against Islamic militants. A Pakistani spokesman said, "The terrorists don't expect us to use these tactics, so when we do, they are really badly trapped." As many as 3000 soldiers arrive each month for two dozen training scenarios (Craig 2015).

On the other hand, according to the Report on the Practice in India there is "a ban and restriction on the use of … certain booby traps" (Rule 80 2016).

According to ICRC treaties and state parties to such treaties, Bangladesh, India, Maldives, Pakistan, and Sri Lanka are the parties to the Protocol on Prohibitions or Restrictions on the Use of Mines, Booby-Traps, and Other Devices as amended on May 3, 1996 (Protocol II to the 1980 CCW Convention as amended on May 3, 1996).

3.2.5 Incendiaries

According to the Convention on Certain Conventional Weapons Protocol III on Prohibitions or Restrictions on the Use of Incendiary Weapons Geneva, October 10, 1980, "Incendiary weapon" means any weapon or munition which is primarily designed to set fire to objects or to cause burn injury to persons through the action of flame, heat, or combination thereof, produced by a chemical reaction of a substance delivered on the target. Incendiary weapons may take the form of flamethrowers, out gassers, shells, rockets, grenades, mines, bombs, and other containers of incendiary substances.

Use of these incendiaries' weapons may violate the principle of proportionality; however, they might be exempted because proportionality is not required if the target is purely military. Also, the principle of distinction regarding loose, booby-trapped ammunition makes them illegal because the booby-trapped ammunition which is designed to explode inside the weapon cannot distinguish between a weapon held by a Taliban, an American soldier, or a civilian (Chivers 2017). Most importantly, it violates the principle of unnecessary suffering.

According to ICRC treaties, Bangladesh (September6, 2000), India (March 1, 1984), Maldives (September7, 2000), Pakistan (April 1, 1985), and Sri Lanka (September24, 2004) are parties to the Protocol III on Prohibitions or Restrictions on the Use of Incendiary Weapons, Geneva, October 10, 1980.

3.2.6 Blinding Laser Weapons

Under the 1995 Protocol IV of the CCW (CCW P. IV), laser weapons are prohibited where they are specifically designed to cause permanent blindness. While CCW P. IV does not prohibit use of lasers for other purposes, precautions must be taken when using laser systems for other purposes to avoid causing permanent blindness. Also, according to Rule 86 of Customary International Humanitarian Law, the use of laser weapons is prohibited if specifically designed, as their sole combat function or as one of their combat functions, to cause permanent blindness. There are no known instances of blinding laser weapons being developed or used by any state (Solis 2010) (587). Some States believe that the use of blinding laser weapons would cause unnecessary suffering, an argument equally valid in international and non-international armed conflicts (Rule 86 2016). Bangladesh (September20, 2000), India (September2, 1999), Maldives (September 7, 2000), Pakistan (December 5, 2000), and Sri Lanka (September 24, 2004) are parties to the Protocol IV on Blinding Laser Weapons 1995 (Protocol IV to the 1980 convention). Five out of eight countries with prominent economies in the South Asian region are signatories to the treaty. This shows that these countries do not wish to use blinding leaser weapons.

3.2.7 Explosive Remnants of War

Explosive remnants of war (ERWs) are explosive munitions left behind after a conflict ends. They include unexploded artillery shells, grenades, mortars, rockets, airdropped bombs, and cluster munitions. As defined by the Landmine and Cluster Munition Monitor organization, ERWs consist of unexploded ordnance (UXO) and abandoned explosive ordnance (AXO). This definition does not include mines (Explosive remnants of war 2015). In 2003, the international community adopted a treaty to help reduce the human suffering caused by explosive remnants of war and bring rapid assistance to affected communities (Explosive Remnants of War 2011). Protocol V to the 1980 CCW Convention requires each party to an armed conflict to remove and provide assistance for the removal of these weapons and to take measures to reduce the threat to civilians. This is the first international agreement to require parties to an armed conflict to clear all unexploded munitions that threaten civilians, peacekeepers, and humanitarian workers once the fighting ceases (Houston 2006).

Every year in South Asia, large numbers of civilians are killed and injured by EWR. Pakistan has one of the world's highest levels of casualties due to landmines and ERW. The number of annual casualties identified by NGO monitoring and media reports jumped from 111 in 2002 to 636 in 2011. These casualties are mostly of them civilians, and the actual toll is higher than reported. According to the Monitor organization, in 2013, 220 casualties were identified from mines/ERW including victim-activated IEDs in the Islamic Republic of Pakistan. Among 175-recorded civilian casualties, there were at least 45 children (23 boys and eight girls) and 19 women. Pakistan (February 3, 2009) is party to the Protocol on Explosive Remnants of War (Protocol V to the 1980 CCW Convention), November 28, 2003. In the area of Afghanistan, bordering western side of Pakistan, antivehicle mines, and victim-activated IEDs pose a growing threat. Nearly one million Afghans (3% of the population) live within 500 m of landmines and ERWs, and 1578 communities remain affected in 246 districts across the country (Addressing the impact of landmines and explosive remnants of war in Pakistan 2012).

In the island nation Sri Lanka, located on the southern tip of India, two decades of armed conflict have resulted in significant landmine and ERW contamination in North and East Sri Lanka (National Mine Action Program 2015). In July 2011, the National Steering Committee of Mine Action, Sri Lanka's national mine action authority, determined that an estimated 255.22 km^2 (98.54 mi^2) of hazardous area remained in need of clearance.

According to the Monitor organization, in 2013, 23 casualties were identified from mines and other ERWs in the Republic of India, including 14 military/security personnel. Between 1999 and 2013, the Monitor identified 3,166 victim-activated mines/IEDs and ERW casualties in India (1,077 killed; 2,088 injured; 1 unknown). Nearly half of these casualties were civilians. India (May 18, 2005) is parity to the Protocol on Explosive Remnants of War (Protocol V to the 1980 CCW Convention), November 28, 2003.

In Himalayan country Nepal, according to Monitor organization, the local NGO Informal Service Sector Center of the Federal Democratic Republic of Nepal recorded 14 ERW casualties in 2013. The total number of casualties in Nepal remains unknown. In Nepal, the Monitor identified 937 mine/ERW casualties (239 killed; 698 injured) between 2003 and 2013. From 1999 to 2002, the Nepal Campaign to Ban Landmines (NCBL) reported 1326 casualties (522 killed; 804 injured).

Bangladesh is located on eastern border of India. According to the Monitor organization, in 2012, no new landmine/ERW casualties were identified in the People's Republic of Bangladesh. The last recorded casualties occurred in 2008 when there were three reported ERW casualties in two incidents. The most recently reported mine casualties were in 2001. Bangladesh (September 26, 2013) is party to the Protocol on Explosive Remnants of War (Protocol V to the 1980 CCW Convention), November 28, 2003. This research did not uncover any data about casualties caused by ERW Maldives and Bhutan.

From these statistics, it may be concluded that ERWs violate the principle of distinction because ERWs do not differentiate between civilians and combatants; subsequently, ERWs violate the principle of unnecessary suffering by causing serious injuries to human beings. Also, there is no military necessity once war is over; therefore, ERWs violate the principle of military necessity. The fact that three out of eight countries are signatories to the convention demonstrates a strong desire to discourage the use of ERWs in region. These three countries are the economically strongest in South Asia.

3.2.8 Cluster Munitions

According to the 2008 Convention on Cluster Munitions, "A cluster munition is a weapon that disperses or releases explosive sub munitions: small, unguided explosives or bomblets (each weighing less than 20 kg) that are designed to explode prior to, on or after impact. Depending on the model, the number of sub-munitions dispersed or released by a cluster munition can vary from several dozens to over 600." Cluster munitions are dropped from aircraft or fired from the ground or sea, opening up midair to release tens or hundreds of submunitions, which can saturate an area up to the size of several football fields. Anybody within the strike area of a cluster munition, military or civilian, is likely to be killed or seriously injured (Cluster munitions Coalition 2016).

Cluster munitions are notorious for the indiscriminate nature of destruction they cause and for the resulting collateral damage in war theaters where they have been used (Aroor 2008). Also, the use of cluster munitions leaves behind large numbers of dangerous unexploded ordnance. Such remnants kill and injure civilians, obstruct economic and social development, and have other severe consequences that persist for decades after use (UNDP 2010).

India is among a handful of nations that continues to stock cluster bombs, used for carpet-bombing (Sinha 2013). Jane's Information Group lists India as possessing KMG-U dispensers and BL-755, BLG Belouga, RBK-275, and RBK-500 cluster bombs. In February 2006, India bought 28 launch units for the Russian-produced 300 mm Smerch Launch Rocket System filled with dual-purpose and sensor-fused submunitions (Cluster munitions Coalition 2016). On December 9, 2010, the US government announced that it cleared the sale of 512 CBU-105 sensor-fused bombs to India by awarding a $257.7 million contract to Textron Systems Corporation, under the foreign military sales program (Choudhury 2010). Pakistan has never made a statement articulating its view on accession to the ban convention. Pakistan argues the problem with cluster munitions is not the weapon itself, but its "irresponsible use" (Munition 2014).

Afghanistan (September 8, 2011) is the only South Asian party to the Convention on Cluster Munitions. Afghanistan being the only South Asian party to the Convention on Cluster Munitions implies the presence of cluster munitions in most of the South Asian region. It can be concluded that most of South Asian countries are engaged in the stockpiling of cluster munitions with the intention to use them. Both use and stockpiling of cluster munitions lead to a violation of IHL because of indiscriminant nature of the cluster munitions.

3.2.9 Small Arms Projectiles

Small arms are widely used in conflicts in which a high proportion of casualties are civilians, and in which violence has been perpetrated in violation of international humanitarian law. Use of small arms has led to millions of deaths and injuries, the displacement of populations, suffering, and insecurity around the world. Small arms and light weapons are the weapons of choice in many contemporary conflicts, particularly in internal conflicts involving insurgent militias fighting government forces (UNGA 1999). According to the 1997 UN Panel of Governmental Experts on Small Arms, small arms are divided into three categories: light weapons, ammunition, and explosives (Arms 1997). Some small arms and light weapons fall under the St Petersburg Declaration 1868. The St Petersburg Declaration 1868 renounces the use of explosive projectiles under 400 g weight. According to The

Hague Declaration, 29 July 1899 bans certain types of bullets. Third Declaration of Hague prohibits "using bullets which expand or flatten easily in the human body" (Lawand 2006).

In South Asia, a large numbers of civilians die from small arms violence (Abeywardana and Yolanda 2006). Approximately 33,000 to 38,000 Indians die violently each year, nearly five percent of all violent deaths worldwide (Small Arm Survey 2016). Controlling illegal small arms and light weapons are some of the biggest security challenges for South Asian countries. Pakistan is among those countries in which every passing year witnesses an increase in the proliferation of small arms. The ongoing conflicts in Afghanistan and Kashmir continue to result in the proliferation of small arms. An unknown quantity of weapons, likely in the thousands, was diverted into the hands of Pakistani dealers and ended up in border arms bazaars, supplying militant sectarian groups, terrorists, drug cartels, criminals, and those seeking protection from such groups. Although the Afghan situation exacerbated the small arms problem, a "gun culture" has long existed in the northern frontier and the adjacent tribal areas (Bibi 2014).

Private firearms in Nepal are estimated to number 440,000. Roughly one-eighth (55,000) are believed to be legally registered. Most privately owned firearms are unregistered craft weapons, referred to as country-made, or "katuwas." There are estimated to be 330,000 of these. Despite a decade of warfare, private firearm ownership remains low by global standards. The rate of private firearm ownership amounts to approximately 1.7 firearms for every 100 residents (Legacies of War in the Company of Peace 2013).

The island nation of Sri Lanka is heavily affected by the proliferation of illicit small arms, which impacts community safety and security, undermines development, and is an obstacle to peace in the country (Abeywardana and Yolanda 2006). The global availability and acquisition of illegal small arms and light weapons since the end of the Cold War has allowed the Liberation Tigers of Tamil Eelam (LTTE) to develop into a formidable fighting force. LTTE is capable of becoming a conventional force equal almost in size and shape to the Sri Lankan Army deployed in the north and east of the country (Smith 2003). Sri Lanka's population today is living under the threat of circulation of illicit small arms and light weapons (SALW), many of which are still unaccounted for. The Inspector General of Police Report has a categorization on small arms usage regarding homicide, grievous hurt, abduction, attempted homicide, rape, robbery, and unnatural offenses. The types of weapons used for these crimes are shotguns, rifles, pistols, trap guns, and automatic weapons (Abhayagunawardena 2015).

The use of small arms in the South Asian region is massive, and small arms are used in day-to-day crimes causing the majority of civilian casualties. Use of small arms in conflict leads to violation of IHL because civilians must be protected under IHL. It shows that the countries in South Asian region are unable to control the use of small arms.

3.2.10 Ballistic Missiles

The Hague Code of Conduct against Ballistic Missile Proliferation (HCOC), formerly known as "The International Code of Conduct" (ICOC), was adopted at an international conference held in Hauge on the November 25–26, 2002. The HCOC, as a political initiative, aims to bolster efforts to curb ballistic missile proliferation worldwide and to further delegitimize such proliferation. The HCOC is the only multilateral code in the area of disarmament to have been adopted in recent years and is the only normative instrument to verify the spread of ballistic missiles. The Hague Code does not call for the destruction of any missiles, and it is simply an agreement between States on how they should "conduct" their trade in missiles (Hague Code of Conduct against Ballistic Missile Proliferation (HCOC) 2016).

India and Pakistan are currently jockeying for supremacy in South Asian region. India's initial success is stimulating more and more activity in Pakistan as they both try to attain or maintain capabilities based on the efficiency of their missiles and warheads. Consequently, India and Pakistan both have extensive, largely indigenous ballistic missile programs (Kayani, Ballistic missile competition in South Asia, Foreign Policy News 2015a).

The modern ballistic missile is based on a design in use since the German V-2 rocket. The Nazis used the V-2 during World War II to terrorize and kill the British. But because the warhead used conventional explosives (roughly one ton of TNT), the damage was limited (What is Ballistic missile? 2016). A ballistic missile can be launched from land, from a silo (an underground installation constructed of concrete and steel, designed to house a ballistic missile and the equipment for firing it) (Dictionary.Com), from mobile platforms on trucks or trains, from a submarine or ship, or from an airplane. After launch, a ballistic missile arches up from one point and lands at another point. Long-range ballistic missiles spend a majority of flight time in the vacuum of space where there is little or no air resistance. Long-range ballistic missiles can reach speeds up to 20 or more times the speed of sound—somewhere around 15,000 miles per hour (7 km/s)—speeds which allow ballistic missiles to go between continents. Short-range ballistic missiles have a range of 1,000 km or less, are usually capable of carrying nuclear weapons, and are preferred for regional conflicts (What is Ballistic missile? 2016).

According to the Missile Threat, A Project of the George C. Marshall and Claremont Institutes, Afghanistan has operational R-11/-17 (SS-1 Scud A/B/C/D), Short-Range Ballistic Missile and R-65 (FROG-7), and Battlefield Short-Range Ballistic Missiles. India has Agni 1 to 5 from Short-Range Ballistic Missiles to InterContinental Range Ballistic Missiles, with a range of 700–8000 km, as well as the Dhanush, Short-Range Ballistic Missiles, ranging from 250 to 350 km, the Prahaar, Short-Range Ballistic Missiles, range 150 km, Prithvi and Prithvi 3, Short-Range Ballistic Missile, ranging from 150 to 350 km, Sagarika (K-15), Sea-Launched Ballistic Missile, Single warhead 500–800 kg, range—700 km, Shaurya, Short-Range Ballistic Missile, range 700 km, and InterContinental Ballistic Missile 2500 kg, range 8000–12,000 km. Pakistan has Haft 1 to 6, Short-Range Ballistic Missile, Range—70/100 km (Haft 1/1A and 1B),

Intermediate-Range Ballistic Missile, Single warhead 700 kg, Range—2500 km, and Haft 9 (Nasr), Short-Range Ballistic Missile (Missile Threat 2016).

Deployment of ballistic missiles would pose troubling security risks given the relatively short distances between major population centers in South Asia and the brief time required for missiles to travel such distances. This factor will compress decision-making cycles for national leaders and battlefield commanders, reducing stability during times of crisis (Cohen 1996).

3.2.11 Chemical Weapons

The 1993 Convention on the Prohibition of the Development, Production, Stockpiling, and Use of Chemical Weapons and on their Destruction belongs to the category of instruments of international law that clearly prohibit weapons deemed particularly abhorrent. As soon as the First World War was over, chemical and bacteriological methods of warfare were condemned by public opinion, and their use was prohibited by the 1925 Geneva Protocol. The adoption of the Convention thus reinforces a basic principle of law relating to the conduct of hostilities whereby the right of the parties to an armed conflict to choose methods or means of warfare is not unlimited (Chemical Weapons Convention 1993).

In 1996, India ratified the CWC and in 1997 declared a stockpile of 1044 tons of sulfur mustard. Destruction was completed in 2009, making it the third State to completely destroy its chemical weapons stockpile. Statements by the Indian government after the declaration of the stockpile suggest that disarmament was partially intended to encourage Pakistani and Russian disarmament. India's chemical industry is a major sector of the Indian economy that includes trade in dual-use (an item that has both civilian and military applications) chemicals. India plays an expanding role in global nonproliferation norms by providing extensive support to the Organization for the Prohibition of Chemical Weapons and seeking greater participation in international export control regimes. In the 1992 India-Pakistan Agreement on Chemical Weapons, India and Pakistan agreed to "never under any circumstances… develop, produce, or otherwise acquire chemical weapons." It is unknown whether Pakistan has ever possessed a chemical weapons program. The country has signed and ratified the 1993 Chemical Weapons Convention and is a member in good standing of the Organization for the Prohibition of Chemical Weapons. However, the U.S. intelligence assessments from the early 1990s noted that Pakistan "has procured dual-use chemical precursors from foreign sources and hopes to achieve self-sufficiency in producing precursors." However, it is unclear to what extent, if any, Pakistan developed chemical weapons based on this capability (Chemical, India 2015). In the mid-1990s, the Afghan government accused Pakistan of supplying the Taliban militia with chemical weapons. However, this charge remains unsubstantiated (Kidwaibhai 2007).

Chemical weapons violate the principle of unnecessary suffering because they cause unbearable injuries to humans, animals, or other creatures in exposed area. The principle of distinction is violated because chemical weapons cannot distinguish between civilians and combatants. Chemical weapons are also prohibited under rule 74 of customary IHL. All South Asian countries are parties to Organization for the Prohibition of Chemical Weapons: Afghanistan (October 24, 2003), Bangladesh (April 29, 1997), Bhutan (September 17, 2005), India (April 29, 1997), Maldives (April 29, 1997), Nepal (December 18, 1997), Pakistan (November 27, 1997), and Sri Lanka (April 29, 1997).

3.2.12 Biological Weapons

Another prohibited means of warfare that has the potential to raise the specter of mass destruction are biological weapons (Beerli 2015). The Geneva Protocol banned use of asphyxiating, poisonous, or other gases, usually referred to as chemical weapons, as well as the use of bacteriological methods of warfare (Goldblat 1997).

The Convention on the Prohibition of the Development, Production, and Stockpiling of Bacteriological (Biological) and Toxin Weapons and on their Destruction entered into force on March 26, 1975 (Convention on the Prohibition of the Development, Production, and Stockpiling of Bacteriological (Biological) and Toxin Weapons and on their Destruction 1972). The use and development of biological weapons is also prohibited under the Rule 73 of customary IHL. Rule 73 of customary IHL applies to biological weapons meant to affect humans, because they violate the principle of unnecessary suffering and distinction (Rule 73 2016).

India possesses the scientific capability and infrastructure to launch an offensive biological warfare program. There is no evidence they have done so. India has defensive biological warfare capabilities and has conducted research on countering various diseases. India also has an extensive and advanced dual-use pharmaceutical industry. In October 2002, then Indian President A.P.J. Abdul Kalam asserted that India "will not make biological weapons. It is cruel to human beings…" However, India has made substantial efforts to prepare its military force for a biological attack (Biological, India 2015). India (July 15, 1974) is a party to the Convention on the Prohibition of the Development, Production, and Stockpiling of Bacteriological (Biological) and Toxin Weapons and on their Destruction 1972.

Although Pakistan has well-developed biotechnology research and development infrastructure, there is no evidence of any Pakistani program to develop, produce, or stockpile biological weapons or agents (Biological, Pakistan 2014). Pakistan (October 3, 1974) is a party to the Convention on the Prohibition of the Development, Production, and Stockpiling of Bacteriological (Biological) and Toxin Weapons and on their Destruction 1972.

All other South Asian countries do not have the capacity to develop biological weapons and show no movement in that direction. Also, except for Nepal, all the countries are parties to the Convention on the Prohibition of the Development, Production, and Stockpiling of Bacteriological (Biological) and Toxin Weapons and on their Destruction 1972. The seven of eight South Asian countries party to the Convention include Afghanistan (March 26, 1975), Bangladesh (March 13,

1985), Bhutan (June 8, 1978), Maldives (August 2, 1993), and Sri Lanka (November 18, 1986). The agreement of a majority of South Asian nations to refrain from developing or using biological weapons bodes well for establishing peace in the region.

4 Nuclear Weapons

This section discusses the effect of nuclear weapons in the region. South Asia is unique as a region in that it is almost entirely lacking meaningful nuclear arms control (Arnett 1998). The earliest agreement to limit nuclear weapons was the 1963 Nuclear Test Ban Treaty, which prohibits "any nuclear weapon test explosion… in the atmosphere; outer space; or underwater" (Treaty Banning Nuclear Weapon Tests in the Atmosphere (1963) and entered into force October 10). The Treaty represents the only binding commitment in a multilateral agreement with the goal of disarmament by the nuclear weapon States. Opened for signature in 1968, the Treaty entered into force in 1970. On May 11, 1995, the Treaty was extended indefinitely (Treaty on the Non-Proliferation of Nuclear Weapon (NPT) 2016).

Arguably, the most important nuclear weapons treaty in practice has been the Non-Proliferation Treaty of 1968 (NPT). The NPT prohibits states that already have nuclear weapons from transferring such weapons to other states and imposes a responsibility on states not already possessing weapons to refrain from acquiring them (Janis 2012). South Asia is a troubled region with growing nuclear risks of its own. Two aspects of Indian nuclear doctrine are increasingly questioned. First, New Delhi has commitment to no first use (NFU) and massive retaliation even though India has been slowly but steadily strengthening its arsenal of nuclear weapons. Second, India's nuclear doctrine "to make it relevant to challenges of current times" has heightened interest in whether Indian nuclear doctrine might indeed change (Joshi et al. 2015).

On the other hand, Pakistan, the world's fastest-growing nuclear arsenal, is unquestionably the biggest concern, reinforced by several recent developments. In April 2015, Pakistani Prime Minister Nawaz Sharif announced that he had approved a new deal to purchase eight diesel-electric submarines from China. These submarines could be equipped with nuclear missiles at an estimated cost of $5 billion. Pakistan has an arsenal of as many as 120 nuclear weapons and is expected to triple the number within a decade. An increase of that size will not help, especially since India's nuclear arsenal, estimated at about 110 weapons, is growing slowly. Pakistan is not alone in its potential to cause regional instability. China, which considers Pakistan to be a close ally and India a potential threat, is continuing to build up its nuclear arsenal. China's nuclear arsenal is now estimated to be 250 weapons. All three countries are moving ahead with plans to deploy nuclear weapons at sea in the Indian Ocean. India and Pakistan did not sign the NPT as of May 2016, increasing instability in the region. However, Bangladesh does not possess nuclear weapons and has been a state party to the NPT since 1979, giving it recognition as a non-nuclear weapon state (NNWS). It has signed and ratified the

Comprehensive Test Ban Treaty (Editorial board 2015). Similarly, Nepal, Sri Lanka, Maldives, and Bhutan are also recognized as NNWSs. Following states are parties to NPT: Afghanistan (September 24, 2003), Bangladesh (March 8, 2000), Maldives (September 7, 2000), Nepal (October 8, 1996 signature), and Sri Lanka (October 24, 1996).

India and Pakistan, two of the most prominent military powers in the South Asian region, are in a race to develop nuclear weapons. The race between India and Pakistan to develop nuclear weapons causes instability in the region and cause of concern for South Asia, as well as for rest of world.

5 Modern Technology

Technological developments have given rise to new methods and means of warfare. The South Asian region is not lagging behind in modern technological weapons such as autonomous weapon systems and drones. Also, these technologies face some legal challenges for its usage. This section will discuss the development of these modern technological weapons.

5.1 Autonomous Weapon Systems

According to the ICRC, "autonomous weapon systems" are defined as weapons that can independently select and attack targets. This means they have autonomy in the "critical functions" of acquiring, tracking, selecting, and attacking targets. (Autonomous weapons: ICRC addresses meeting of experts on lethal autonomous weapon systems (LAWS) 2014). Further, the International Committee for Robot Arms Control has stated, "given the rapid pace of development of armed tele-operated and autonomous robotic systems, we call upon the international community to commence a discussion about the pressing dangers that these systems pose to peace and international security and to civilians, who continue to suffer most in armed conflict." In particular, autonomous systems may further encourage indiscriminate and disproportionate use of force and obscure the moral and legal responsibility for war crimes (Statement 2009).

In South Asia, India and Pakistan are the only countries out of eight South Asian nations spoke about the autonomous weapons. India has consistently urged consideration of the broader proliferation aspects of lethal autonomous weapon systems on international security. At the Convention on Conventional Weapons (CCW) annual meeting in November 2014, Indian diplomat said "we would like the CCW process to emerge strengthened from these discussions" with "increased systemic controls on international armed conflicts embedded in international law in a manner that does not widen the technology gap among states." India warned against "a rush to judgment on meaningful human control" as this "would run risk of legitimizing weapons," but India does not object to discussing the term further in 2015.

Pakistan first called for a ban on fully autonomous weapons at the Human Rights Council in May 2013. At the CCW's annual meeting in November 2014, Pakistan said that use of lethal autonomous weapon systems on the battlefield would amount to "a situation of one-sided killing" depriving the combatants of the targeted state the protection offered to them by the international law of armed conflict and risking civilian lives on both sides.

Pakistan called on states currently developing such weapons to put in place an immediate moratorium on their production and use, stating the introduction of lethal autonomous weapon systems would be "illegal, unethical, inhumane and unaccountable as well as destabilizing for international peace and security with grave consequences." It called for their further development and use to be preemptively banned through the conclusion of a legally binding and dedicated CCW protocol. (Country Policy Positions 2015) (8, 9, 11, 12).

It can be summarized that there is no real support for the development of autonomous weapons without meaningful human control as well as with the present set of laws. There are no known autonomous weapon systems in the South Asian region.

5.2 *Drones or UAVs*

Unmanned aerial vehicles (UAVs), also known as drones, are aircraft either remotely controlled by "pilots" on the ground or autonomously following a pre-programmed flight path and mission. While there are dozens of different types of drones, they basically fall into two categories: first, those that are used for reconnaissance and surveillance purposes and second, those that are armed with missiles and bombs (Wright and Cole 2010). Drones have pinpoint accuracy, are lethal, increase surveillance, and are easy to deploy. These features give them a vital role in South Asia, especially in counterterrorism (New Technologies and IHL 2015). The Pakistan military has started developing its own drone fleets (Pakistan introduces fleet of locally developed drones 2013). On March 13, 2015, Pakistan took a major leap forward in achieving full-spectrum deterrence for all forms of aggression when that country's military successfully tested the *Burraq*. The *Burraq is* equipped with a laser-guided missile capable of striking with pinpoint accuracy in all types of weather. In the Quran, *Burraq* is the name of the whitehorse that took the Islamic prophet to heaven (Mirza 2015).

Pakistan's armed drone capabilities will have implications reaching beyond its borders. It is possible that Pakistan will follow some dangerous precedents set by the U.S. (Mahmood 2015). With Pakistan now sporting an armed UAV developed with Chinese assistance, India has decided to accelerate the development of its own weaponized drone fleet (Jha 2016).

Since the 1999 Kargil War, India has procured a number of Israeli military unmanned aircraft. India's current arsenal includes Israel Aerospace Industries

(IAI) Harpy and Harop unmanned combat aerial vehicles, and IAI Searcher and Heron unmanned aerial vehicles. In 2009, the Indian Air Force purchased ten Harops in $100 million contract with Israel Aerospace Industries (Parmar 2014). India's Defense Research and Development Organization (DRDO) has also developed its own domestic UAV program. The project aims to develop a domestic arsenal to replace and augment existing fleet of IAI vehicles. The following is a list of completed and pending DRDO projects:

- DRDO Lakshya: a target drone used for discreet aerial reconnaissance and target acquisition, launched by solid propellant rocket motor and sustained by a turbojet engine in flight.
- DRDO Nishant: primarily designed for intelligence gathering over enemy territory and also for reconnaissance, training, surveillance, target designation, artillery fire correction, and damage assessment. Nishant has completed its developmental phase and user trials.
- DRDO Aura: similar to Lockheed Martin RQ-170 Sentinel, a stealth drone capable of releasing missiles, bombs, and precision-guided munitions. The details of the Aura project are still classified. Aura's projected test date is set to be sometime in 2016.
- DRDO Rustom: Modeled after the American Predator UAV, Rustom is a Medium-Altitude Long-Endurance (MALE) system. Like Predator, Rustom is designed to be used for both reconnaissance and combat missions. Rustom is still in prototype stage and is expected to replace and supplement Israeli Heron model UAVs in the Indian Air Force.

Two of the medium-sized drones currently in use in Afghanistan and Pakistan are the MQ-1B Predator and MQ-9 Reaper. These strange-looking planes carry a wealth of sensors in their bulbous noses: color and black-and-white TV cameras, image intensifiers, radar, infrared imaging for low-light conditions, and lasers for targeting. They can also be armed with laser-guided missiles (Drones: What are they and how do they work? 2012).

The Indian aerial visual company Quidich is now part of a handful of organizations using the technology for aid relief in Nepal, sending drones to remote areas where they can map and assess destruction in order to speed up search-and-rescue operations. Nepal's Civil Aviation Authority banned the use of drones without permission. However, there are no known military drones in Nepal as of yet.

In Bhutan, drones were used to send antibiotics to remote villages (Ferris-Rotman 2015). In the neighbor country of Bhutan, the Bangladesh Navy, as part of its modernization plans, has started making drones for multipurpose use including air target practice and surveillance in the Bay of Bengal. Producing and using drones as air targets will significantly reduce costs, increase accuracy in air target shooting, and boost air defense systems. This is especially true in the Bay, which has become strategically important following Bangladesh winning a maritime boundary case against Myanmar in 2012. Chief of Naval Staff Vice Admiral M Farid Habib stated "we have developed our own drones and started using those as targets in the air for accurate firing" (Bangladesh Navy will acquire locally made Drone (UAV) 2014).

Similarly, Sri Lanka uses drones for surveillance purposes. According to the Human Rights Watch Report, military commanders relied heavily on photographs from UAVs. "The constant use of UAV pictures flashed to the forward commanders in up front positions were the most useful source to identify combatants with weapons, even though some of these were in civilian attire" (Adams 2011). Addressing the panel discussion on the use of remotely piloted aircraft or armed drones in counterterrorism and military operations, Sri Lanka said it was greatly concerned by the increasing use of remotely piloted aircraft or armed drones in counterterrorism operations. Use of armed drones violates the international human rights and humanitarian laws, in particular the principles of precaution, distinction, and proportionality (Sri Lanka expresses concern about increasing use of armed drones in counterterrorism 2014).

The use of drones with better technology can be extremely effective when used with strict adherence to international laws. Adherence means that drones will not be used in a way that violates the principle of distinction and proportionality.

6 Weapons Race Between India and Pakistan

According to reports, there are numerous signs of a robust weaponry race between these two neighboring countries. The test of Pakistan's ballistic missile, *Nasr,* capable of carrying a nuclear warhead, and India's ballistic missile, *Prahaar* and others, are complicated nuclear weapons race in South Asia (Jalalzai 2014). However, the advent of ballistic missiles in South Asia, with other technological advancements, has instigated a competition between India and Pakistan. This also dampened the prospects of strategic restraints (Kayani, Ballistic missile competition in South Asia, Foreign Policy News 2015b). New battle lines are being drawn for a spy drone versus spy drone face-off between India and Pakistan (Ali 2010). Hence, the establishment of an arms-control process would likely partially resolve the risk of a weapons race between these two countries.

6.1 Challenge of Keeping Weapons Out of the Reach of Terrorists

South Asia is a sophisticated part of the world when it comes to the development and use of weapons. This sophistication leads to challenges in keeping weapons out of the reach of terrorists. IHL principles and rules have entered the public domain over the past few years. This is in large part owing to debate over the relationship between armed conflict and acts of terrorism. The question that is most frequently asked is whether IHL has a role in addressing terrorism (International humanitarian law and the challenges of contemporary armed conflicts 2007). Terrorists are becoming more intelligent, and they know that states are bound by the IHL principles. Terrorists do not have to follow IHL principles in developing or using weapons. The threat of nuclear terrorism in South Asia has assumed a greater threat as India and Pakistan continue to maintain a large number of nuclear facilities (Jalalzai). As the South Asian threat matrix becomes more complex, and with concomitant progress in the nuclear field, these developments create an environment ripe for the spectacular terror attacks in New Delhi, Mumbai, Karachi, and Islamabad-Rawalpindi. As states possessing nuclear weapons, both India and Pakistan must find common objectives and mechanisms to deal with the metastasizing menace of terrorism (Burke and Khan 2014).

Subsequent to the U.S. invasion of Afghanistan in 2001, evidence surfaced that senior Pakistani nuclear scientists Sultan Bashiruddin Mahmood and Chaudhry Abdul Majeed may have helped Al-Qaeda. The evidence shows they helped develop techniques for the aerial dispersion of chemical and biological warfare agents. In the 1980s, the Soviet Union alleged that Pakistan had armed insurgents battling Soviet forces in Afghanistan with cartridges and grenades containing toxic chemicals. In the mid-1990s, the deposed Afghan government similarly accused Pakistan of supplying the Taliban militia with chemical weapons. However, neither of these claims could be independently verified (Chemical, India 2015). As tensions and violence in the region increased, states blame each other's policy choices for the scourge of terrorism that has seized the region (Burke and Khan 2014). In 2002, Pakistani police unearthed chemical laboratories belonging to the Lashkar-e-Jhangviin Karachi (a militant Islamic group with links to Al-Qaeda, in the port). Investigations revealed that the group was preparing to produce poisonous gases for possible terrorist attack. It appears that these groups and individuals were acting independently without the knowledge or support of the Pakistani government (Chemical, Pakistan 2016).

The drone issue poses another concern for South Asian countries. Drones could be modified to mount attacks with explosives or chemical weapons. This is according to a presentation by federal intelligence and security officials to their counterparts in law enforcement and people who oversee critical infrastructure. For example, authorities in the U.S., Germany, Spain, and Egypt have foiled at least six potential terrorist attack drones since 2011 (Nicas 2015). Now both India and Pakistan are developing their own drones, increasing the risk of theft by terrorists. Not lagging behind, Sri Lanka and Bangladesh are also importing drones from other countries. In the cricket enthusiast part of the world, security officials have to find ways to efficiently track drones to protect potential targets like crowded stadiums. Police can protect every side of the stadium, but not the top. There are other critical infrastructure targets, such as government buildings and prisons. A well-placed bomb could cause an enormous number of casualties. As the advancement of modern weaponry is being achieved by South Asian countries, the challenge of keeping these weapons out of the reach of terrorist is mounting at a higher rate than the development of these sophisticated weapons.

7 Conclusion

The purpose of this chapter was to compare the international laws of armed conflict as they relate to a plethora of evolving weaponry being built and used by South Asian militaries to international law standards. It has been discussed that the criteria set by the ICRC for the use of weapons and for legal review of new weapons are not fully complied in the region. In conclusion, there should be review criteria, which should have the following sources of law that could be considered for the review of a weapon.

Treaty Obligation

In conducting reviews of weapons, a state must consider provisions of all treaties to which it is a party that prohibit use of specific weapons and means of warfare or that impose limitations on ways in which specific weapons may be used.

Prohibition Under Customary International Law

As discussed with every individual weapon, there are restrictions on uses of specific weapons under customary international law. In conducting reviews of weapons, a state must also consider prohibitions or restrictions on use of specific weapons, means and methods of warfare pursuant to customary international law under the ICRC study on Customary International Humanitarian Law (Henckaerts and Doswald-Beck 2005).

Four-Core Principle of IHL/LOAC

As discussed above in the chapter, the four-core principle of LOAC must be considered in legal review of weapons. This chapter also analyzed causes and proposed rules to be applied to different types of modernized weaponry currently being used within the region and the role of international law as it struggles to regulate an ever-changing array of combatants and weapons amid escalating armed conflicts including an accelerated arms race between India and Pakistan. It is imperative that states acquire the highest standard of security best practices and learn to live as peaceful neighbors (Burke and Khan 2014).[1] Finally, it will be a challenging task to keep these weapons out of the hands of terrorists.

[1](chachcc, latesht) Accessed July 15, 2015 (revised It is imperative that both states acquire the highest standard of nuclear security best practices and learn to live as peaceful nuclear neighbors).

References

Abeywardana H, Foster Y (2006) Small arms and light weapons: challenges in Sri Lanka and options for the future. Small arms and security in South Asia

Abhayagunawardena V (2015) The need to apprehend illicit small arms, 9 February 2015. 16 May 2016 http://www.dailymirror.lk/63103/the-need-to-apprehend-illicit-small-arms

Adams B (2011) Sri Lanka: Official Report Whitewashes Military Abuses, 1 August 2011. Humans Rights Watch. 16 May 2016 http://www.hrw.org/news/2011/08/01/sri-lanka-official-report-whitewashes-military-abuses

Addressing the impact of landmines and explosive remnants of war in Pakistan (2012) November 2012. SPADO. http://www.genevacall.org/wp-content/uploads/dlm_uploads/2013/12/The-Impact-of-Landmines-and-Explosive-Remnants-of-War-in-Pakistan.pdf

Ali (2010) Can India compete with Pakistani drones? 24 May 2010. Pakistan Defense. 16 May 2016 <http://defence.pk/threads/can-india-compete-with-pakistani-drones.59012/>

Anti-personnell Mines (2011) ICRC, 15 November 2011. 16 May 2016. https://www.icrc.org/eng/war-and-law/weapons/anti-personnel-landmines/overview-anti-personnel-landmines.htm

Arms, Para (1997) 26 Definition of Small

Arnett E (1998) Nuclear weapons and arms control in South Asia after the test ban. Oxford University Press, Oxford

Aroor S (2008) 26/11 prompts India to seek cluster bombs, 13 December 2008. 16 May 2006. http://indiatoday.intoday.in/story/26-11+prompts+India+to+seek+cluster+bombs/1/23381.html

Article 35(2) (1977) Treaties, state parties and commentaries. 8 June 1977. https://www.icrc.org/applic/ihl/ihl.nsf/Article.xsp?action=openDocument&documentId=0DF4B935977689E8C12563CD0051DAE4

Article 36 (1977) Treaties, state parties and commentaries. 8 June 1977. ICRC. 15 May 2016. https://www.icrc.org/applic/ihl/ihl.nsf/Article.xsp?action=openDocument&documentId=FEB84E9C01DDC926C12563CD0051DAF7

Article 48 (1977) Treaties, state parties and commentaries. 8 June 1977. ICRC. 14 May 2016. https://www.icrc.org/ihl/4e473c7bc8854f2ec12563f60039c738/8a9e7e14c63c7f30c12563cd0051dc5c?OpenDocument

Autonomous weapons: ICRC addresses meeting of expertson Lethal Autonomous Weapons Systems (LAWS) (2014) 13 May 2014. 16 May 2016. https://www.icrc.org/eng/resources/documents/statement/2014/05-13-autonomous-weapons-statement.htm

4 Basic Principles (2016) Law of Armed Conflict. 14 May 2016. https://loacblog.com/loac-basics/4-basic-principles/

Bangladesh Navy will acquire locally made Drone (UAV) (2014) Bangladesh defence. 16 May 2016. http://www.defencebd.com/2014/05/bangladesh-navy-will-acquire-locally.html

Beerli C (2015) A century of weapons of mass destruction: enough!. 22 Apr 2015. ICRC. https://www.icrc.org/en/document/century-weapons-mass-destruction-enough-0

Bibi Z (2014) Perturbing small arms proliferation. 24 Feb 2014. Daily Times. 16 May 2016. http://www.dailytimes.com.pk/opinion/24-Feb-2014/perturbing-small-arms-proliferation

Biological, India (2015) NTI. 16 May 2016. http://www.nti.org/country-profiles/india/biological/

Biological, Pakistan (2014) NTI. 16 May 2016. http://www.nti.org/country-profiles/pakistan/biological/

Burke E, Khan FH (2014) Tackling nuclear terrorism in South Asia. 2014. Center for Complex Operations. 16 May 2016. http://cco.dodlive.mil/files/2014/09/Tackling_Nuclear_Terrorism_in_south_asia.pdf

Chemical Weapons Convention (1993) Advisory service on international humanitarian law. 7 May 2016. https://www.icrc.org/eng/assets/files/other/1993_chemical_weapons.pdf

Chemical, India (2015) NTI building a safer world. 7 May 2016. http://www.nti.org/country-profiles/india/chemical/

Chemical, Pakistan (2016) NIT. April 2016. 16 May 2016. http://www.nti.org/learn/countries/pakistan/chemical/

Chivers CJ (2017) Dirty tricks of government forces: where deception and deadliness meet inside a gun. 7 Nov 2012. 16 May 2016. http://atwar.blogs.nytimes.com/2012/11/07/dirty-tricks-of-government-forces-where-deception-and-deadliness-meet-inside-a-gun/?_r=0
Choudhury U (2010) India strikes deal with US for cluster bombs. 11 Dec 2010. DNA. http://www.dnaindia.com/india/report-india-strikes-deal-with-us-for-cluster-bombs-1479604
Cluster Munitions Coalition (2016) What is a cluster bomb? 16 May 2016. http://www.stopclustermunitions.org/en-gb/cluster-bombs/what-is-a-cluster-bomb.aspx
Cohen WS (1996) Proliferation: threat and response. Office of Secretary of Defense. 16 May 2016. http://www.dod.mil/pubs/prolif97/so_asia.html
Convention on the Prohibition of the Development, Production and Stockpiling of Bacteriological (Biological) and Toxin Weapons and on their Destruction (1972) Audiovisual library of international law. 10 Apr 1972. 7 May 2016. http://legal.un.org/avl/ha/cpdpsbbtwd/cpdpsbbtwd.html
Country Policy Positions (2015) Campaign to stop killer robots. 25 Mar 2015. 16 May 2016. http://www.stopkillerrobots.org/wp-content/uploads/2015/03/KRC_CCWexperts_Countries_25Mar2015.pdf
Craig T (2015) To fight the Taliban Pakistani military turns to unorthodox but simple tactics 14 April 2015. The Washington Post. 16 May 2016. https://www.washingtonpost.com/world/asia_pacific/to-fight-the-taliban-pakistani-military-turns-to-unorthodox-but-simple-tactics/2015/04/15/eac5b088-e1ee-11e4-ae0f-f8c46aa8c3a4_story.html
Dictionary.Com. http://dictionary.reference.com/browse/silo
Drones: What are they and how do they work? (2012) South Asia. 31 Jan 2012. BBC News. 16 May 2016. http://www.bbc.com/news/world-south-asia-10713898
Editorial board (2015) Nuclear fears in South Asia. 6 Apr 2015. The New York Times. 7 May 2016. http://www.nytimes.com/2015/04/06/opinion/nuclear-fears-in-south-asia.html?_r=0
Explosive Remnants of War (2015) June 2015. Landmine and cluster monition monitor. 16 May 2016. http://the-monitor.org/index.php/LM/The-Issues/Explosive-Remnants-of-Wa
Explosive Remnants of War (2011) ICRC. 30 Nov 2011. 16 May 2016. https://www.icrc.org/eng/war-and-law/weapons/explosive-remnants-war/overview-explosive-remnants-of-war.htm
Ferris-Rotman A (2015) How drones are helping Nepal recover from the earthquake. 7 May 2015. The World Post. 16 May 2015. http://www.huffingtonpost.com/2015/05/07/nepal-earthquake-drones_n_7232764.html
Finn A, Scheding S (2010) Developments and challenges for autonomous unmanned vehicles: a compendium. Springer, Berlin
Goldblat J (1997) The biological weapons convention. Int Rev Red Cross 318
Hague Code of Conduct against Ballistic Missile Proliferation (HCOC) (2016) NTI. 7 May 2016. http://www.nti.org/learn/treaties-and-regimes/hague-code-conduct-against-ballistic-missile-proliferation-hcoc/
Houston AG (2006) Executive series ADDP 06.4 law of armed conflict, Ist edn. Defence Publishing Services, Canberra
International humanitarian law and the challenges of contemporary armed conflicts (2007) ICRC 89.869, p 722
Henckaerts J-M, Doswald-Beck L (2005) Customary international humanitarian law. Cambridge University Press, Cambridge
Jalalzai MK (2014) Tactical nuclear weapons in South Asia. 27 Aug 2014. Daily Times. 16 May 2016. http://www.dailytimes.com.pk/opinion/27-Aug-2014/tactical-nuclear-weapons-in-south-asia
Janis MW (2012) International law, 6th edn. Wolters Kluwer Law & Buisness, New York
Jayaswal KP (1930) Manu and Yajnavalkya, a comparison and a contrast: a treatise on the basic Hindu law. Butterworth & Co., Calcutta
Jha S (2016) India's armed fleet. 25 June 2015. The Diplomat. 16 May 2016. http://thediplomat.com/2015/06/indias-armed-drone-fleet/
Joshi, M., Krepon M, White JT, Thompson J, Mason S (2015) The credibility of India's nuclear deterrent. Deterrence instability and nuclear weapons in South Asia. Stimson, Washington

Kayani SA (2015a) Ballistic missile competition in South Asia. 29 April 2015. Foreign Policy News. 16 May 2016. http://foreignpolicynews.org/2015/04/29/ballistic-missile-competition-in-south-asia/
Kayani SA (2015b) Ballistic missile competition in South Asia, Foreign Policy News. 29 April 2015. 7 May 2016. http://foreignpolicynews.org/2015/04/29/ballistic-missile-competition-in-south-asia/
Kidwaibhai (2007) Pakistan's biological and chemical weapons capabilities. July 2007. Pakistan Defense. 7 May 2016. http://defence.pk/threads/pakistans-biological-and-chemical-weapons-capabilities.6106/
Lawand K (2006) A guide to legal review of new weapons, means and methods of warfare, measure to implement article 36 of additional protocol I of 1977. ICRC, Geneva
Legacies of War in the Company of Peace (2013) Nepal armed violence assessment. Vers. Issue Brief, No. 2. 2 May 2013. http://www.smallarmssurvey.org/fileadmin/docs/G-Issue-briefs/NAVA-IB2-Legacies-of-War.pdf
Mahmood F (2015) Pakistan's indigenous armed drones: precedents and proliferation. 2 Apr 2015. South Asian Voices. 16 May 2016. http://southasianvoices.org/pakistans-indigenous-armed-drones-precedents-and-proliferation/
McClelland J (2003) The review of weapons in accordance with Article 36 of additional protocol I. ICRC 85(850):404
Mirza AM (2015) Pakistan's drones and stability instability paradox in South Asia. Foreign Policy. 16 May 2016. http://foreignpolicynews.org/2015/03/25/pakistans-drones-stability-instability-paradox-in-south-asia/
Missile Threat (2016) A project of the George C. Marshall and Claremont Institutes. 7 May 2016. http://missilethreat.com/about/
Munition, Landmine & Cluster (2014) Cluster Munition Ban Policy Pakistan. 12 Aug 2014. 16 May 2016. http://www.the-monitor.org/index.php/cp/display/region_profiles/theme/3772
National Mine Action Program (2015) Ministry of economic development Sri Lanka. 16 May 2015. http://slnmac.gov.lk/what-we-do
New Technologies and IHL (2015) ICRC. 16 May 2016. https://www.icrc.org/en/war-and-law/weapons/ihl-and-new-technologies
Nicas J (2015) Criminals, terrorists find uses for drones, raising concerns. 28 Jan 2015. Wall Street J. 16 May 2016. http://www.wsj.com/articles/criminals-terrorists-find-uses-for-drones-raising-concerns-1422494268
Pakistan introduces fleet of locally developed drones (2013) 25 Nov 2013. Dawn. 16 May 2016. https://www.dawn.com/news/1058493/pakistan-introduces-fleet-of-locally-developed-drones
Parmar T (2014) Drones in India. 4 Dec 2014. Center for the Study of Drone at Bard College. 16 May 2016. http://dronecenter.bard.edu/drones-in-india/
Rediff News (2014) Pakistan still has 6 million landmines, India third with 4 million. 5 Dec 2014. 16 May 2016. http://www.rediff.com/news/report/pix-pakistan-still-has-6-million-landmines-india-third-with-4-million/20141205.htm
Rule 71 (2016) Customary IHL. In: ICRC, 14 May 2016. https://www.icrc.org/customary-ihl/eng/docs/v1_rul_rule71
Rule 73 (2016) Customary IHL. 16 May 2016l. https://www.icrc.org/customary-ihl/eng/docs/v1_cha_chapter23_rule73
Rule 80 (2016) Customary IHL. 16 May 2016. https://www.icrc.org/customary-ihl/eng/docs/v1_rul_rule80
Rule 86 (2016) Customary IHL. ICRC. 16 May 2016. https://www.icrc.org/customary-ihl/eng/docs/v1_rul_rule86
Saint Petersburg Declaration (1868) Treaties, state parties and commentaries. 29 Nov 1868. ICRC. 15 May 2016. https://www.icrc.org/ihl/INTRO/130?OpenDocument
Schmitt MN (2013) Autonomous weapon systems and international humanitarian law: a reply to the critics. Harv Natl Secur J Featur 4(2013):10

Sinha K (2013) India continues to stock and use cluster bombs for carpet bombing. 3 June 2013. Times of India. 16 May 2016. http://timesofindia.indiatimes.com/india/India-continues-to-stock-and-use-cluster-bombs-for-carpet-bombing/articleshow/20408237.cms

Small Arm Survey (2016) India armed violence assessment. 16 May 2016. http://www.smallarmssurvey.org/focus-projects/india-armed-violence-assessment.html

Smith C (2003) In the shadow of a cease-fire: the impacts of small arms availability and misuse in Sri Lanka. Small Arm Survey

Solis GD (2010) The law of armed conflict. Cambridge University Press, New York

Sri Lanka expresses concern about increasing use of armed drones in counterterrorism (2014) 23 Sept 2014. Ministry of Defence, Sri Lanka. 16 May 2016. http://www.defence.lk/new.asp?fname=Sri_Lanka_expresses_concern_about_increasing_use_of_armed_drones_in_counterterrorism_20140923_02

Statement, Original Mission (2009) ICRAC. 16 May 2016. http://icrac.net/statements/

Treaty Banning Nuclear Weapon Tests in the Atmosphere (1963) In outer space and under water, art I (1), 14 U.S.T. 1313, T.I.A.S. No. 5433, 480 U.N.T.S. 43 (Aug 5, 1963 and 1963). Entered into force Oct 10. Moscow, 10 Oct 1963

Treaty on the Non-Proliferation of Nuclear Weapon (NPT) (2016) UNODA. 16 May 2016. https://www.un.org/disarmament/wmd/nuclear/npt/

UNDP (2010) Landmark convention on cluster munitions enters into force. 30 June 2010. The convention on cluster munitions. 16 May 2016. http://www.undp.org/content/undp/en/home/presscenter/pressreleases/2010/07/30/landmark-convention-on-cluster-munitions-enters-into-force.html

UNGA (1999) Report of the group of governmental experts on small arms. 2: UNGA

Weapons (2011) ICRC. 30 Nov 2011. 16 May 2016. https://www.icrc.org/eng/war-and-law/weapons/overview-weapons.htm

Weston BH, Falk RA, Charlesworth H, Strauss AL (1990) Supplement of the basic documents to international law and world order, 4th edn. Thomson West, Eagan

What is Ballistic missile? (2016) Missile threat. 16 May 2016. http://missilethreat.com/what-is-a-ballistic-missile/

Wright J, Cole C (2010) What are drones? Jan 2010. Drone Wars UK. 16 May 2016. http://dronewars.net/aboutdrone/

Author Biography

Mr Vivek Sehrawat is a doctoral candidate (S.J.D.) in the School of Law, University of Kansas (U.S.A.). He also serves as Teaching and Research Assistant in the same School. He obtained his LL.M. degree from University of California, Davis. He is prolific writer on the issues pertaining to public international law, especially international humanitarian law.

Kolibri 360 GmbH
Ferdinand-Jühlke-Straße 7
99095 Erfurt, Deutschland
produktsicherheit@kolibri360.de